W9-BBM-878

SCARS

of

INDEPENDENCE

America's Violent Birth

Holger Hoock

CROWN
NEW YORK

Map and illustration credits can be found on page 533.

Library of Congress Cataloging-in-Publication Data
Names: Hoock, Holger, author.
Title: Scars of independence : America's violent birth / Holger Hoock.
Description: First edition. | New York : Crown Publishing, 2017. | Includes
    bibliographical references and index.
Identifiers: LCCN 2016031348 (print) | LCCN 2016031740 (ebook) |
    ISBN 9780804137287 (hardcover) | ISBN 9780804137300 (pbk.) | ISBN
    9780804137294 (eISBN) | ISBN 9780804137294 (ebook)
Subjects: LCSH: United States—History—Revolution, 1775–1783—Social
    aspects. | United States—History—Revolution, 1775–1783—Influence.
    | Violence—United States—History—18th century. | United States—
    Civilization—1783–1865. | National characteristics, American.
Classification: LCC E209 .H657 2017 (print) | LCC E209 (ebook) | DDC
    973.3/1—dc23
LC record available at https://lccn.loc.gov/2016031348

ISBN 978-0-8041-3728-7
Ebook ISBN 978-0-8041-3729-4

PRINTED IN THE UNITED STATES OF AMERICA

Book design by Anna Thompson
Jacket design by Elena Giavaldi
Jacket art: John Trumbull (photo by Francis G. Mayer)
Author photograph: Brandy Ringer

10 9 8 7 6 5 4 3 2 1

First Edition

For Helen and Florian Frederick

CONTENTS

LIST OF MAPS

PREFACE

SCARS OF INDEPENDENCE IS A HISTORY OF VIOLENCE. IT IS the first book on the American Revolution and the Revolutionary War to adopt violence as its central analytical and narrative focus. As such, it tells the story of combatants, captives, and civilians—men and women, famous and lesser-known—who experienced violence as perpetrators, witnesses, and victims. *Scars of Independence* is also a story about stories: narratives of persecution and suffering, barbarity versus civilization, retaliation and reconciliation, that accompanied physical and psychological violence. Those who lived through these tumultuous times created such narratives to make sense of their violent struggles and foster allegiance to their respective causes.

In recovering the experience of violence in its many forms—and the physical, emotional, and intellectual responses of people living with it—we must recognize that accounts of brutality and suffering make for powerful rhetoric, not least, as the scholar Rachel Cleves points out, because the "spectacle of violence . . . both repels and attracts" us. Indeed, fierce words can be weapons in their own right. Striving for adequate ways to write about such sensitive topics, I have found inspiration in Marcus Rediker's painful, brilliant history, *The Slave Ship*, and his admonition that we not be guilty of the "violence of abstraction," of counting and thereby dehumanizing "a reality that must, for moral and political reasons, be understood concretely." As Wayne E. Lee, a specialist on the cultural history of war and violence, also reminds us, "Academic history rarely does justice to the blood, sweat, fear, and voided bowels of war's violence. On the other hand, mere stories rarely convey the complexity of the situations in which humans find themselves willing to kill or forced to die." In writing this book for a general audience as well as for fellow historians, I have sought to develop my arguments through narrative and episodic example as much as through abstract analysis. The book is based on fresh research in archives across the U.S. and U.K. and among printed sources, as well as on extensive scholarship about the American Revolution. It traces the broad chronological contours of the Revolution, but I have not attempted to offer a comprehensive survey of the Revolution, of the war, or even of violence in this period. Instead, I have chosen to focus on the key dynamics of political and military violence involving American Patriots and Loyalists, African-Americans and Native Americans, Britons and their German auxiliaries.[1]

For over two centuries, this topic has been subject to white-washing and selective remembering and forgetting. While contemporaries experienced the Revolution as frightening, messy, and divisive, its pervasive violence and terror have since yielded to romanticized notions of the nation's birth. In painting an unvarnished portrait of Revolutionary-era violence, we can shed new light on how participants understood their struggles and how survivors and subsequent generations have remembered and misremembered the conflict.

* * *

An author's final duty before sending a manuscript off to the press is also the most pleasant. I wish to acknowledge with profound gratitude the institutions and individuals that have supported this project. For enabling my research and writing, I thank the John W. Kluge Center at the Library of Congress for a Kluge Fellowship, the Library Company of Philadelphia and the Historical Society of Pennsylvania for a Barra Foundation International Research Fellowship in American History and Culture, the Massachusetts Historical Society for a Massachusetts Society of the Cincinnati Fellowship, the New York Public Library and the David Library of the American Revolution for research fellowships, the Institute for

Advanced Studies of the University of Konstanz for a Senior Visiting Fellowship, and the University of Freiburg and SFB 948 for a visiting professorship. For making my stays at those institutions both productive and enjoyable, I am especially grateful to Carolyn Brown, James N. Green, Meg McSweeney, Conrad E. Wright, Ulrich Gotter, Ronald Asch and Ralf von den Hoff, and their respective staff, as well as the other fellows in residence. I first rehearsed aspects of arguments in chapters 5, 8, and 10 in "Rape, *ius in bello*, and the British Army in the American Revolutionary War" in *Journal of Military Ethics* (2015) and "Mangled Bodies: Atrocity in the American Revolutionary War" in *Past & Present* (2016).

Numerous colleagues and friends have kindly commented on proposals, read chapters in draft, answered queries, shared ideas, and offered suggestions, including Susanne Berthold, Katherine Boo, Shelley Bookspan, John Brewer, Richard Caplan, Erica Charters, Joshua Civin, Linda Colley, Chiara Cordelli, Martin Daunton, Barbara Donagan, Tim Duggan, Philip Dwyer, Heather E. Ewing, Bill Foster, Niklas Frykman, Peter Ginna, Ulrich Gotter, Lara Heimert, Julia E. Hickey, Joanna Innes, Maya Jasanoff, Jane Kamensky, Wayne E. Lee, Elizabeth Loudon, Wm. Roger Louis, Jürgen Luh, Nino Luraghi, Peter Mandler, Holly Mayer, Michael McDonald, Rana Mitter, Bruce Nichols, Marcy Norton, Andrew O'Shaughnessy, Ed Papenfuse, Sarah Pearsall, Will Pettigrew, Todd Reeser, Daniel Richter, Rob Ruck, Hannah Smith, Stella Tillyard, Jen Waldron, and Molly Warsh. Stephen Conway and Paul Halliday generously critiqued significant portions of the book manuscript. My thinking has also benefited from the questions and comments offered by audiences at seminars and lectures, including at the Library of Congress, the Yorktown Victory Foundation, the Huntington Library, McGill University, and the Universities of Konstanz, Oxford, and Pittsburgh.

At the University of Pittsburgh, I have been fortunate to work with Marcus Rediker, Reid Andrews, and Lara Putnam as successive chairs, and to enjoy the inspiring collegiality of, among many others, Jonathan Arac, Sy Drescher, Janelle Greenberg, Diego Holstein, Patrick Manning, Pernille Røge, Bruce Venarde, and Molly Warsh, as well as scholars in the Eighteenth-Century Studies initiative. I am very grateful to my hardworking research assistants: Ashley Blakeney, Mirelle Luecke, Luke Martinez, Katie Parker, and Steve Pitt. Marcus Rediker has been a model of generous scholarly companionship. He offered constructive criticism on the entire manuscript, spurred me on when the sailing felt rough, and, throughout it all, kept faith in me and the book. I owe a special debt to my dean, N. John Cooper, for his creative and generous support, and for fostering an environment in which I could juggle departmental and other responsibilities with editing the *Journal of British Studies* while writing this book.

My agent, Susan Rabiner, has been a wonderful advocate and supportive interlocutor who believed in this project and its author from the start and found them an excellent home at Crown Publishers. It has been my great privilege to work with Amanda Cook, editor extraordinaire, whose detailed editorial letters—gems of challenging and constructive readings—coached me through revisions. Emma Berry has been an amazing associate editor, whose keen eye for detail and sharp ear for rhythm and pace improved the text immeasurably. At Crown, I am also grateful to Molly Stern, publisher, who supported this book throughout; to the editors, designers, and production managers who helped shape the manuscript into a handsome book, especially Craig Adams, David Chesanow, Jon Darga, Sally Franklin, Elena Giavaldi, Elizabeth Rendfleisch, and Anna Thompson; and to the marketing and publicity teams led by Kevin Callahan, Sarah Grimm, Rachel Rokicki, and Alaina Waagner, who are introducing the book to its readers.

The book's dedicatees have lived with it as long as they have lived with me. Helen lovingly supported my research and writing in myriad ways, let me rehearse arguments, and offered her perspective as a psychologist. The arrival halfway through this project of Florian Frederick, the American-born addition to our Anglo-German family, may have slowed down its completion a little, but he has already enriched my life immeasurably. This book is for them.

Pittsburgh, July 4, 2016

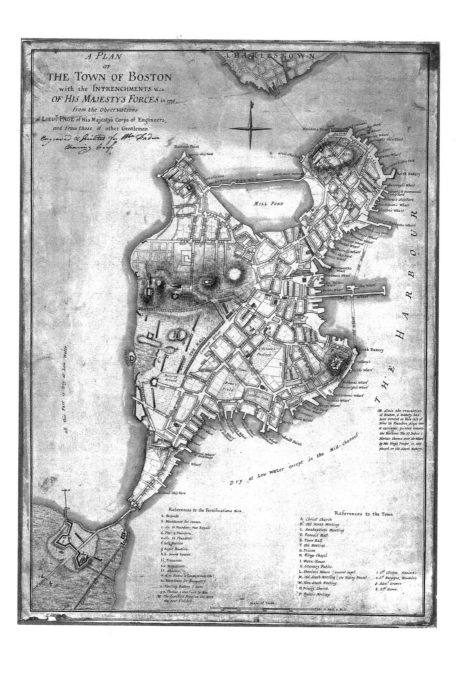

A PLAN OF THE Town of Boston with the INTRENCHMENTS &c. OF HIS MAJESTY'S FORCES in 1775, from the Observations of Lieut. PAGE of His Majesty's Corps of Engineers, and from those of other Gentlemen

A FTER NIGHTFALL ON MONDAY, MARCH 5, 1770, SMALL groups of Bostonians armed with lead-weighted clubs, cudgels, and cutlasses started accosting lone British officers and soldiers in the city's streets. Elsewhere in town, soldiers threatened and assaulted civilians. It was rumored that a missing sergeant had been murdered, while troops had beaten an oysterman bloody. By eight o'clock, angry men were confronting the redcoats outside Murray's Barracks, a sugarhouse at Draper's Alley and Brattle Street where parts of the king's army were quartered. Several dozen more had gathered in Dock Square, old Boston's commercial center by the harbor, many of them sailors wielding sticks and staves; some were breaking off the table legs from the market stalls. Windowpanes shattered under a barrage of snowballs and chunks of ice as men passed the house of an importer who had broken the boycott on British goods. The previous Friday, March 2, a long-standing dispute over scarce labor had erupted in a violent confrontation between dozens of workers and off-duty soldiers at John Gray's ropewalk south of Milk Street. There had been further scuffles on Saturday, and although no lives had yet been lost, by Monday soldiers and civilians were spoiling for a fight.[1]

Shortly after nine o'clock, bells rang out across town—Brattle Square Church led, soon Old Brick Church fell in to the west, and then Old South, too. Bells pealing at nighttime usually signaled a fire. As many more residents rushed out of their homes into the late-winter night to haul fire engines and carry bags and buckets across the ice-covered streets, armed gangs began converging on the city center. Navigating by the light of the first-quarter moon, the men joined a fast-swelling crowd in front of the Custom House at the northeast corner of King Street (today's State Street) and Royal Exchange Lane. As young Benjamin Davis soon realized, "There is no fire. It is the soldiers fighting."

Outside the Custom House, the imposing brick building that held the customs records and revenue from tariffs, a crowd of several hundred and growing were facing off against nine British soldiers. When the bells had started ringing, Captain Thomas Preston, the forty-year-old Irish captain on duty, had marched a corporal and six grenadiers of the 29th Regiment of Foot from the nearby main guardhouse through the surging mass of agitated people to support Private Hugh White, the lone British sentry at the Custom House. White had earlier struck a wigmaker's apprentice with his musket after the boy had heckled a British officer; before long, an expanding crowd was lobbing snowballs and abuse at him, making the sentry fear for his safety. He had now fallen in with the tall grenadiers to form a semicircle, their backs to the building, muskets loaded and bayonets fixed. Many men in the mob also carried weapons—from the sticks some had been wielding all evening to the knives and Highland broadswords others had slipped under their coats before heading out that night. At least three men in the crowd as well as three of the soldiers now facing them had been among those exchanging blows at the ropewalk the previous week.

The site of their renewed encounter, the Custom House, symbolized the detested imperial revenue system that Britain had saddled on its thirteen Atlantic seaboard colonies after its victory in the Seven Years' War, which had ended in 1763. Britain wanted the colonies to share in the expense of the victorious war and their future defense, not least by contributing towards the costs of a 10,000-strong British army stationed in America. For years, Massachusetts had played a leading role in opposing these new imperial policies, by means both legal and extralegal. Bostonians remonstrated against the Stamp Act, which had imposed a new tax on every piece of printed paper. After that law was repealed, they took issue with the Townshend Acts, which levied duties on imports such as glass, lead, and tea. They petitioned the imperial government and persuaded eleven colonies to adopt a non-importation ban. Crowds of men and women rioted, damaged property, and intimidated and injured customs officials as well as violators of their boycotts on British goods. Just a month earlier, a thousand-strong crowd had besieged the house of a customs informant who had reported on fellow Americans guilty of violating the imperial tax code; when he shot into the mass of people, an eleven-year-old boy was martyred.[2]

The turning point had come in 1768, when the British government sent several thousand troops to Boston to police the revenue system. For the Crown to show its military might in Boston in the manner it had previously done in Ireland or Scotland was a provocative move. In a town of 15,000 or 16,000, there now were as many imperial soldiers as there were white male residents above the age of sixteen. It did not help that among the troops were numerous Irish, and when the Afro-Caribbean drummers who served in the British regiments carried out disciplinary floggings of white soldiers on the Common, it offended Bostonians' sense of the social and racial order.[3]

British soldiers were quartered not just in barracks but in private homes and warehouses, too. The army posted sentries outside public buildings. Troops established checkpoints, questioning pedestrians and searching carriages. Drunken soldiers fueled petty crime and prostitution. Redcoats beat male residents; women faced attempted abductions and sexual assault. Soldiers who were off duty competed with maritime laborers for scarce employment, triggering violent altercations like the one that had occurred at the ropewalk. Locals routinely harassed the redcoats, hurling stones at those detested "Bloody Backs." Neither could the troops entirely prevent attacks on customs officials and their informants. Indeed, the soldiers seemed to symbolize the erosion of London's authority as much as they demonstrated imperial strength. As Benjamin Franklin had predicted at a recent House of Commons inquiry, British troops sent to America would "not find a rebellion; they may indeed make one."[4]

That early March night, John Adams, the ambitious Braintree lawyer who had moved his young family to Boston in 1768, described the sounds of rebellion near the Custom House: "[T]he people shouting, huzzaing, and making the mob whistle as they call it, which when a boy makes it in the street, is no formidable thing, but when made by a multitude, is a most hideous shriek, almost as terrible as an Indian yell." The mob taunted the redcoats: "Come on you Rascals, you Bloody Backs, you Lobster Scoundrels, Fire if ye dare, G—d Dam'n you, Fire and be damned; we know you dare not." They knew that only civil magistrates could authorize soldiers to use force to disperse an unlawfully assembled crowd. They also knew that Boston magistrates were unlikely to endorse the use of such force in the current political atmosphere. What they perhaps didn't realize was that any soldier judging his life to be in imminent danger had the right to fire in self-defense.[5]

Captain Preston, desperate to calm heated tempers, was pleading with the civilians to disperse when a shot rang out. One of the grenadiers appeared to have been hit by an object—perhaps a snowball or a piece of ice or white-barked wood that either struck him or clipped the muzzle of his musket. According to most later reports, he had slipped on the ice, some saying his musket had briefly escaped his grasp. As he got up and recovered his firearm, he discharged a shot, whether deliberately or by accident. No one seemed to have been hit. There was a brief pause while many in the crowd looked for cover. Some, though, moved towards the soldiers, and one or two apparently even sought to wrestle their muskets from them. Several Boston militia drummers started beating to arms. A man in the crowd lashed out at the soldier who had fired; in the process, the assailant hit Preston's arm hard with his club. Then the grenadiers fired a round of shots.

By the time Preston managed to stop the firing, three men lay dead in the snow, two more were dying, another half dozen were wounded. One bullet had hit the rope maker Samuel Gray, "entering his head and beating off a large portion of his skull." Through the streaming blood, one bystander ascertained a hole "as big as my hand." Crispus Attucks, a forty-seven-year-old former slave of

Native American and African heritage who was passing through Boston, was felled by two bullets to his chest, one of them "goring the right lobe of the lungs and a great part of the liver most horribly." Two bullets killed James Caldwell, a ship's mate. Apprentice Samuel Maverick, seventeen, was hit in his stomach by a bullet that had ricocheted off a wall; although a doctor was able to remove the projectile, the teenager died in the morning. Patrick Carr, a thirty-year-old Irish immigrant employee of a leather-breeches maker, was hit by a musket ball fired quite possibly by a fellow Irishman. The bullet "went through his right hip & tore away part of the backbone & greatly injured the hip bone." Carr died ten days later.[6]

Henry Prentiss had at first assumed the soldiers' guns were not loaded. But as men around him fell to the ground, he realized that he was witnessing "a scene the most Tragical, of any that ever the Eyes of Americans beheld . . . to see the blood of our fellow Citizens flowing down the gutters like water."[7]

* * *

By the spring of 1770, Americans had developed a deep sense of grievance against an empire that taxed them without their consent and sent an army in peacetime. From Rhode Island to the South, colonists intimidated customs officials and damaged property. In 1768, merchants in Boston, New York, and Philadelphia had renewed their resolve not to import British goods, soon to be joined by Virginia, Maryland, and South Carolina. Although Britain partially repealed the Townshend Acts in response to the boycott, the tax on tea, which raised the largest sums of money, remained in place. With imperial troops arriving imminently, the Boston town meeting called an extralegal convention of all the towns of Massachusetts, which promptly condemned "raising or keeping a standing army" without the people's approval. By 1770, then, Boston's neighboring towns were primed to respond to any further escalation of the brewing crisis—and whatever might happen in Boston would resonate across the colonies.[8]

As news of the fatal shootings spread through Boston that March night, the church bells rang again. Town leaders prepared to summon thousands of men who were standing by in surrounding towns to confront the redcoats. At the same time, the sound of British drums beating to arms had soldiers scrambling across the city. In their quest to reach the center, some wielded their swords to clear a path through hostile crowds; a few took punches from irate citizens. Lieutenant Governor Thomas Hutchinson, who had rushed to the scene of the shootings, eventually managed to de-escalate the situation by appealing to Bostonians from a first-floor balcony: the rule of law would prevail, a full inquiry would be held, and they should disperse peacefully. Most did as asked, but a hundred men or so stayed until the early hours while an initial inquest was conducted. By three a.m., Captain Preston was taken into custody; the following morning, the eight soldiers, too, were arrested and thrown into jail. The beacon to summon armed colonists to Boston was never lit, and no further shots were fired in anger that night.[9]

Participants and witnesses understood instantly the significance of what had occurred on King Street. Over the following weeks, both sides sought to shape the story of that evening in an effort to win the battle of public opinion, not least by publishing the depositions they solicited from local inhabitants and soldiers. Town leaders accused the British occupiers of a pattern of oppression and cruelty against innocent citizens that had climaxed in the deadliest confrontation thus far, what they quickly called the "bloody massacre." Pro-British accounts, by contrast, emphasized the premeditated nature of the incident, with armed civilians provoking soldiers into a fight that would lead to their eventual withdrawal. The morning after, the British indeed began evacuating their troops, albeit but a few miles to the Castle Island barracks. The colonial official, Andrew Oliver, recognized the ambiguity of the situation: "[I]t is difficult to determine which were the Aggressors." As Oliver was now laid low with the gout, "the Reports of killed and wounded," he reflected, "painted in my Imagination all the Horrors of a civil War."[10]

One week after the shootings, on March 12, the *Boston Gazette* published the single most influential anti-British account. Boston, the paper reported, had witnessed "a most shocking Scene, the Blood of our Fellow Citizens running like Water thro' King-Street, and the Merchants Exchange." The story was soon reprinted in other colonies, where resentment against the overbearing empire was already brewing, as well as in the British press. The article, set within thick black borders, also covered the funeral rites of the massacre's first four martyrs, attended by more than 10,000 people, and was illustrated with a woodcut showing four coffins with the initials of the slain, skulls and bones, and an hourglass and scythe.[11]

Paul Revere, The Bloody Massacre perpetrated in King Street Boston on March 5th 1770 by a party of the 29th Regt. *(Boston, 1770).*

Whereas few today will recollect the *Boston Gazette*'s prose account, most Americans and many in Britain are probably familiar with Paul Revere's iconic representation of THE BLOODY MASSACRE. The Boston silversmith and engraver adapted a composition by

Henry Pelham to produce a brilliant visual polemic that deviated in significant ways from reality. This engraving, advertised for sale only three weeks after the event, shows an unarmed crowd of exclusively white, well-dressed gentlemen (and one concerned woman in a shawl)—not the missile-hurling motley crew of waterfront boys and men, apprentices, and mechanics, including immigrants and former slaves, that had actually assembled—who face seven aggressive British soldiers arrayed like a firing squad. A sniper has discharged a gun from a window of the Custom House, now also labeled "Butchers Hall." Colonists often had their copies of the engraving hand-colored, with the red of the British uniforms matching the blood oozing from wounds in the victims' heads, chests, and stomachs.[12]

British officials delayed the trials of Captain Preston and his men until the fall, hoping that by then tempers might cool down. Supported by the Sons of Liberty, John Adams agreed to serve as attorney for the accused soldiers: everyone, he believed, deserved a fair hearing. Adams argued that the redcoats had acted in self-defense in the face of a provocative mob; at worst the soldiers were guilty of manslaughter, not murder. He alluded to the limits of troops performing urban anti-riot duty: "[S]oldiers quartered in a populous town, will always occasion two mobs, where they prevent one.—They are wretched conservators of the peace!" The jury acquitted Preston and six of the soldiers. The two men convicted of manslaughter pleaded benefit of clergy, a device that allowed for their capital sentences to be commuted; they were released after having their thumbs branded.[13]

In subsequent years, John Adams's thoughts kept returning to that violent and defining evening. The Boston Massacre had become an annually commemorated event, complete with orations, the display of relics, and guided tours of the bloodied site. On its third anniversary, in 1773, Adams recalled how much anxiety his role as defense attorney for the British soldiers had caused him. At the same time, he proudly reflected, ensuring that the defendants received a fair trial had been "one of the most gallant, generous, manly and disinterested Actions of my whole Life." He had rendered a truly patriotic service, for a death sentence would "have been as foul a Stain upon this Country as the Executions of the Quakers or Witches, anciently." In his diary Adams noted, "as the Evidence was, the Verdict was exactly right." Yet this was "no reason why the Town should not call the Action of that Night a Massacre."[14]

Adams's thoughts may have sounded contradictory, but they illuminate the reason the Boston Massacre has remained so iconic over the centuries. The shootings had been the unplanned product of the violence of imperial oppression colliding with the violence of colonial resistance. For those who lived through revolution and war, the wounds sustained by eleven men that night—wounds that foreshadowed the disfiguring and lethal injuries soon to be suffered by tens of thousands—would come to serve as a metaphor for the wounds torn open in Americans' relations with their fellow subjects on both sides of the Atlantic. For the Revolutionaries, the deaths on King Street symbolized colonial Americans' resistance in the face of wanton British cruelty. That allegation was wrong, as Adams had proven in court, but it nevertheless stuck. By 1786, when Adams was serving as the first United States ambassador to the Court of St James's, he summed up the event's complex legacy in one bold judgment: "On that night the foundation of American independence was laid."[15]

* * *

In the popular memory of the American Revolution, a quarter millennium on, the Boston Massacre is something of an anomaly: it is a violent event we acknowledge and remember. But the Revolution was also violent in ways we don't remember, and perhaps can't even imagine, because they have been downplayed—if not written out of the conventional telling altogether. Although the American Revolution has been continuously invoked since the eighteenth century in the name of all manner of causes—the Tea Party's opposition to health care reform being perhaps the most salient modern example—its inherent violence has often been minimized. The result has been the perpetuation of an overly sentimental narrative of America's originary war. Even the portrayals of George Washington's hungry, ill-clad soldiers, their feet reddening the snow at Valley Forge, nostalgically evoke martyrs rather than battle-bloodied warriors. American popular memory of this era tends to focus on great white men debating independence in Philadelphia's hallowed halls or on Mount Vernon and Monticello, "as if the war," writes the historian Edward Larkin—and, we should add, American-on-American violence—"were incidental to the Revolution."[16]

There are good reasons why Americans portray their revolution and war for independence as an uplifting, heroic tale, as the triumph of high-minded ideals in the face of imperial overreach, as a unified and unifying nation-building struggle to deliver a free and independent United States. But, in doing so, they risk neglecting its divisive and violent strands. To understand the Revolution and the war—the very birth of the nation—we must write the violence, in all its forms, back into the story. That is my aim in this book.

By "violence," I mean the use of physical force with intention to kill, or cause damage or harm to people or property. I also mean psychological violence: the use of threats, bullying tactics, and brutality to instill fear in people and influence their conduct and decisions. It was through campaigns of terror that the American Patriots enforced their revolution internally against the American Loyalists. It was through the longest war ever fought on American soil that the Patriots defended their new nation's independence from the British Empire. And it was by distinguishing acceptable from illegitimate forms of violence that the Patriots sought to fight that war in ways that matched their political ideals: by highlighting the enemy's brutishness while striving to stay within the limits permitted by the prevailing codes of war, the Revolutionaries tried to win the moral war that accompanied the war on the ground. After a decade of civil war, further violence against the Revolution's losers would complicate the transition to peacetime nation building. When at war's end Americans remained conflicted about the appropriate uses and limits of violence, it was clear that the wounds they had delivered and sustained—physically, psychologically, metaphorically—had profoundly shaped the nature, outcome, and legacies of their foundational conflict.[17]

I first became curious about Revolutionary-era violence a decade ago, as I was conducting research for my previous book, *Empires of the Imagination*. While studying examples of eighteenth-century art, I encountered a series of monuments to American Loyalists in churches and cathedrals across England. They ranged from little stone tablets in provincial churches to a substantial marble sarcophagus in Westminster Abbey, but they shared one common feature: they all told stories of American Loyalists being brutally treated—hunted, dispossessed, and, finally, driven out of the country, afraid for their lives. Evoking an era when there was "scarcely ... a village in England without some American dust in it," these memorials all spoke of the psychological and physical violence inflicted on individuals who had opposed the Revolution.[18]

Those harrowing accounts of persecution and suffering stayed with me, not least because they were hard to reconcile with the conventional narrative of a restrained, largely nonviolent revolution. Eager to uncover the stories behind the memorials, I turned to the archives and found that many of the detailed accounts the Loyalists had produced during and immediately after the war reinforced what I had seen. These reports described scenes of humiliation, bullying, torture, and even the occasional lynching. Scholars, by contrast, had given limited space to such American-on-American violence. Participants at the time referred to the American Revolution as a civil war, and writers over the past century have occasionally spoken of it in these terms. Yet the wider American public, and even many historians, still seem reluctant to embrace the notion of civil conflict as a way to describe the Revolution. Perhaps that's no surprise, if only because seeing the Revolution as America's first civil war forces us to confront the terror at its very core.[19]

Reading further in the participants' accounts, we find that American Patriots, who tended to remain silent about the violence they meted out to Loyalists, dwelled with passionate indignation on the cruelty that they themselves suffered at the hands of the barbarous British and their Loyalist, Native American, and German auxiliaries. The Patriots accused the British of indiscriminate plundering and destruction, battlefield massacres, rape, prisoner abuse, even the deportation of American captives to Asia and into slavery in Africa. They also grappled with the quandary of how to answer such abuse—for violence flowed in all directions.

Reports by British political and military leaders confirm the stories of the American Patriots' brutality towards their Loyalist neighbors. They also describe acts of cruelty against British combatants and captives by American Revolutionary forces. At the same time, they reveal the strategic and ethical dilemma that government ministers and army officers faced in orchestrating a counterinsurgency against white, Protestant, Anglophone fellow subjects—all while their own nation was deeply divided. And both American and British portrayals allow us to reconstruct at least in part the contributions and sufferings of black and Native American populations on both sides of the conflict.

The sheer scale and pervasiveness of the violence generated by the Revolution's partisan fury and by more than seven years of war is manifest in written accounts and imagery from the period. The correspondence of leaders, the diaries of individual men and women, political pamphlets, popular prints, and congressional records all vividly convey the swirl of brutality that swept up all sides. As with the Boston Massacre, these sources also show us how violence shaped the stories that participants were telling about revolution, counterrevolution, and war. Yet neither the Revolution's academic historians nor its popular chroniclers have studied this aspect of the war in a systematic way.

In this book, we will follow protagonists to battlefields and army camps; to prisons on land, underground, and offshore; onto farms and into homes. We will discover how all parties used terror: Patriots against Loyalists; British forces and their Loyalist and German auxiliaries against rebel combatants, captives, and civilians; General Washington's Continental Army against Native

Americans; white and black Southerners against one another. We will take a close look at the physical evidence of violence: the bayonet wounds in a soldier's mangled corpse; a girl's story of her rape by enemy soldiers; the emaciated, lice-ridden figures of prisoners of war; the decapitated head of a slave turned spy warning others not to join the British; columns of smoke rising over New England seaports, Southern plantations, and the vast cornfields of Iroquoia. Loyalists, women, former slaves, and rebel captives each experienced distinctive forms of violence. And all sides spun narratives of persecution and atrocity, of suffering and sacrifice, of community building and revenge, and of attempts to exercise restraint—some successful and others decidedly not.

* * *

If violence was fundamental to how American Patriots and their enemies experienced America's founding moment, why has it been moved to the margins of the story that we typically hear? First, in postwar America, the Revolution's Loyalist losers, and the violence they had endured, were systematically excluded from public discourse. As R. R. Palmer put it in his classic *The Age of the Democratic Revolution* over half a century ago, "The 'American consensus' rests in some degree on the elimination from the national consciousness . . . of a once important and relatively numerous element of dissent." A British tendency to turn a blind eye to an unprecedented defeat is also partly to blame. Britain's imperial loss occurred despite putting one in every seven or eight eligible men under arms, and recruiting large auxiliary forces in Germany to fight alongside white Loyalists as well as Native Americans and former slaves. As late as 1883, Sir John Seeley, the distinguished Cambridge historian of the British Empire, described the American Revolution as an embarrassing episode, "which we have tacitly agreed to mention as seldom as we can."[20]

Over time, even the Revolutionary-era emphasis on the blood that the Patriots shed in defense of their new republic has yielded to a strangely bloodless narrative of the war that mirrors the image of a tame and largely nonviolent Revolution. The magisterial accounts by later twentieth- and early-twenty-first-century historians such as Bernard Bailyn, Gordon Wood, and T. H. Breen that dominate American college classrooms focus on the Revolution's ideas and ideals and largely tune out the physical and psychological trauma experienced by so many participants. Meanwhile, bestselling biographies of the Founding Fathers continue to romanticize the Revolutionary era.[21]

Whether in their academic or public discourse, Americans do not generally shy away from discussing violence in their history and culture, a tendency that applies as much to the history of colonization, the frontier, and slavery up to the Revolution as it does to the violence that characterizes the modern United States at home and in its conduct overseas—from the prevalence of gun-related deaths to the controversies over preemptive military action and drone strikes. Yet Americans are curiously silent when it comes to their nation's birth. As a historian of nationalism in the early republic has demanded, "[W]e must seek to understand the tie between nationalism and violence" in the United States, especially given that few nation-states "are as renowned for their proclivity for violence."[22]

This partial blindness contrasts particularly glaringly with today's general awareness of the battlefield carnage, the ordeal of POWs, and death in the American Civil War. Indeed, acknowledging the undeniable horrors of that war, in some ways, has made the need for an immaculate conception all the more acute. "For many Americans the Revolution is their last great romance with war," writes the scholar Carol Berkin, as they imagine it as "quaint and harmless," an image that appeals in an "era of genocidal wars, terrorism, and heated debates over the meaning of patriotism." But it is precisely because we face an uncertain world of insurgencies and civil wars, stalled revolutions and failed states, that Americans should confront their own tumultuous birth. It is time to strip some of that lingering romanticism from America's foundational conflict.[23]

* * *

Writing violence back into the story of the Revolution reminds us that America's war for independence caused proportionately more human suffering than any other war in American history except the Civil War. Because to modern eyes the absolute numbers involved look comparatively small, it is easy to forget that with an estimated 6,800 to 8,000 Patriot battle deaths, 10,000 killed by disease in camps, and up to 16,000 or even 19,000 who perished in captivity, the number of Patriot soldiers killed in the Revolutionary War would be well over 3 million in terms of today's population—and significantly more than that if we consider Patriot deaths as a proportion of only the Patriot population in 1775 or 1783. More than ten times as many Americans died, per capita, in the Revolutionary War as in World War I, and nearly five times as many as in World War II. The death rate among Revolutionary-era prisoners of war was the highest in American history. In addition, at least 20,000 British and thousands more American Loyalist, Native American, German, and French lives were lost. The Revolution exacted further human sacrifice when at war's end approximately 1 in 40 Americans went into permanent exile, the equivalent of some 7.5 million today.[24]

As the Boston Massacre demonstrates, it is tempting for humans engaged in a struggle to remember the violence suffered by their own side but to neglect that endured by others. It is crucial, therefore, that we consistently look at the Revolutionary era through multiple lenses: American Patriots, American Loyalists, and the British, as well as Native American, black, and German participants. This enables us to transcend nation-centered and nationalist narratives, whether American or British, with their various myths, exaggerations, and blind spots. And it helps us avoid falling into the trap of categorizing either side as simply victims, traitors, or cruel aggressors in what Americans call the Revolutionary War and the British know as the American Rebellion or the War of American Independence. It is in this respect that—as a German-born specialist in British history who did not grow up with the national myths of either Britain or America, but who for the past two decades has researched and taught on both sides of the Atlantic—I hope to bring a fresh outlook.[25]

American casualties of British atrocities, along with the victims of General Washington's campaigns of terror in Indian country, urge us to keep multiple perspectives in mind. So do the American Loyalists. For, by the 1770s, as thousands of ordinary Americans joined the insurgency against what they saw as imperial oppression, between one-fifth and one-third of the white population continued to support Britain in sentiment, if not always in deed. Others were not yet particularly invested in either cause, or would change sides. But anyone who was not explicitly a Patriot risked being branded and persecuted as an enemy of America. As one New Yorker wrote to a London acquaintance, explaining his quandary: "I have no relish for civil Wars & there is no such thing as being a looker on." When the Anglo-American crisis escalated, Patriots targeted both their outspoken opponents and the as-yet-uncommitted—and they did so not just with moral suasion but also with threats and physical violence. There was no guillotine in Boston, New York, or Charleston, as there would be in Paris two decades later. Yet forging the new American nation entailed the forced exclusion not only of black slaves and Native Americans but also of white Euro-Americans who did not subscribe to the Revolutionary project. The Revolution's noble ideals aside, violent incidents were not the unfortunate exceptions to an orderly, restrained revolution. Rather, and especially where Loyalists were concerned, they were the norm. Both the Revolution's supporters and its opponents came to experience its inherent violence as a defining characteristic that gave meaning to their struggles.[26]

The Boston Massacre also shows us that violence cannot be separated from stories about violence. The physical reality of violence and the political, polemical, and moral uses to which it was put were inextricably intertwined. Narratives of violence, as much as ideology, helped shape allegiances and mobilize support, whether for the cause of independence or empire. Stories of persecution, suffering, and sacrifice empowered American Patriots and Loyalists—and also Britons—to make sense of the Revolution, civil war, and colonial rebellion. And it was through such stories that they each made moral claims, seeking to win the support of the American population and gain the sympathies of audiences in Britain and Europe. For this was a war of persuasion as much as strategy, manpower, and logistics. It mattered not only how each side conducted the war—materially and ethically—but what stories each could convincingly tell about its own and its opponents' conduct.[27]

A more honest rendering of the era enables us to see, then, that the American Revolution was not some glorious exception. Like other modern revolutions, and for all its transformative (and positive) effects, it required violent escalation and terror to sustain itself and combat its domestic enemies. From the victors' perspective, the prize of enjoying liberty and independence justified the fierce treatment of fellow Americans. At the same time, though, Washington, Adams, and their fellow leaders were adamant that they must fight the war against Britain in ways that matched their ideals. By following a policy of humanity, as Adams put it, vis-à-vis enemy combatants and captives, they must out-civilize the British. To be sure, reality often fell short of worthy aspirations. But at the moment of America's violent birth, the founders launched their new nation with a sense of moral purpose. If the idea of the United States is grounded not in a "common ethnicity, language, or religion" but instead in a "set of beliefs," as the historian Gordon Wood reminds us, we should include among these beliefs the conviction that a society must uphold its core values even—and especially—in times of war. Projecting the power of America's example, as much as the example of her power, was a foreign policy principle the founders embraced; it is a notion that modern leaders would do well to remember.[28]

Painting an unvarnished picture of the Revolution helps us at once recognize its defining ferocity, appreciate its lasting accomplishments, and discern its complicated legacies. Throughout the war, Americans wrestled with questions of violence and restraint against enemies foreign and domestic. The postwar United States, unlike France, Russia, and other revolutionary societies, avoided dictatorship, a military regime, and—with the partial exception of the War of 1812—more civil war. But this outcome also entailed unresolved contradictions for America's emerging empire of liberty, most painfully and violently the entrenchment and extension of slavery, and the exclusion and soon the decimation and "Removal" of Native Americans. And as the white majority population set about building a nation after a decade of civil conflict, both the Revolution's winners and its losers bore the physical and psychological scars of war, persecution, and terror—scars that were selectively acknowledged at best, and often partially covered.

Generations of Americans since have grappled with their nation's violent beginnings in a balancing act of remembering and forgetting. Repressing trauma, denying terror, and whitewashing violence have helped foster a powerful myth of American exceptionalism that fits the heroic narrative of the original war. But looking afresh at the scars of independence through the eyes of participants on all sides helps us untangle the inherent tensions between America's moral objectives and her violent tendencies. As we engage a world riven by wars, civil conflicts, and insurgencies, understanding how violence relates to nation building, and how it is represented and remembered, remains as critical as ever.[29]

Overleaf: Samuel Dunn and Robert Sayer, A Map of the
British Empire in North America *(London, 1774).*

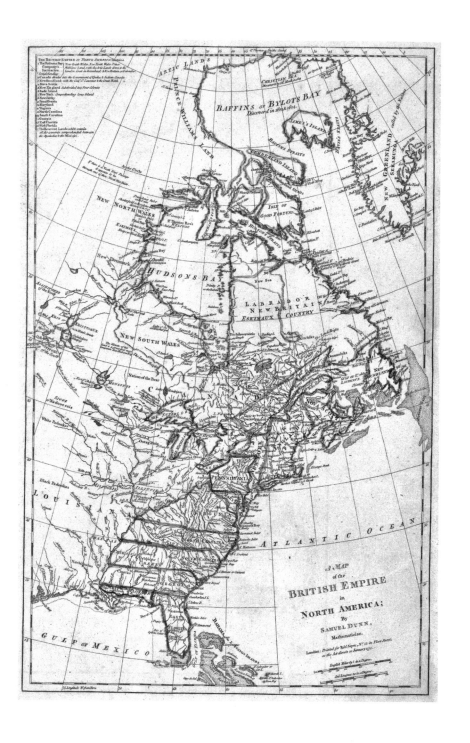

A MAP
of the
BRITISH EMPIRE
in
NORTH AMERICA;
By
SAMUEL DUNN,
Mathematician.

CHAPTER ONE

Tory Hunting

J ANUARY 25, 1774, WAS A BITTERLY COLD DAY IN BOSTON, with two feet of snow on the ground. John Malcom, a fifty-one-year-old minor customs official, was on his way home from his office near the Boston harbor, when passersby observed him suddenly cursing and physically threatening a small boy on a sled who had apparently rammed him. George R. T. Hewes, a poor shoemaker who had carried one of the Boston Massacre's mortally wounded victims to a doctor four years earlier, intervened to protect the child. Shouting and scuffles ensued. Malcom struck Hewes on the head with his cane, knocking him temporarily unconscious. Bystanders then broke up the fight, and Malcom returned home. But the crowd would not let Malcom off lightly. And even though the scene had appeared to be a private squabble, that night Bostonians made sure that their response bore the hallmarks of Revolutionary justice.[1]

Before taking on his current post, Malcom had worked for the British Empire as a sea captain and army officer fighting throughout the North American theater of the Seven Years' War. He had become notorious across the colonies after being arrested for debt and counterfeiting in 1763. A decade later, while working as a comptroller, he was suspended for malpractice and extortion. Many Bostonians knew of his checkered past and would likely remember that in 1771 Malcom had helped Governor Sir William Tryon of North Carolina murderously suppress the Regulator uprising, a revolt of backcountry farmers against colonial taxes and tax officials.

At dusk, a sizable crowd gathered outside Malcom's home at the end of Cross Street. When Sarah Malcom failed to disperse them, her husband leaned out of a window and struck one man with his sword, piercing his chest. Malcom then brandished loaded pistols, boasting that he would kill numerous opponents for the governor's bounty. As men started to bring ladders to take the house, the Malcoms barricaded themselves in a second-floor room, but the assailants soon breached a window. The irate intruders seized Malcom and, as he later declared, "by violence forced [him] out of the House and Beating him with Sticks then placed him on a sled they had Prepaird."

Some gentlemen now became concerned that matters might get out of hand. They urged restraint and appealed to official justice. But there was no stopping the frenzied crowd—1,200 people, according to the diary of a local merchant (a likely exaggeration)—in whose eyes Malcom had "behaved in the most capricious, insulting and daringly abusive manner." Anne Hulton, a recent arrival from England whose brother was a commissioner of customs in Boston, was nauseated to see Malcom undergo "cruel torture," first being "stript Stark naked, one of the severest cold nights this Winter . . . his arm dislocated in tearing off his cloaths."

Most contemporaries would have been familiar with the procedure that Malcom was about to endure. Those who needed reminding might consult the recipe recounted by another Massachusetts Loyalist: "First, strip a Person naked, then heat the Tar untill it is thin, & pour it upon the naked Flesh, or rub it over with a Tar Brush, *quantum sufficit*." That night, the crowd picked up a barrel of tar at a conveniently located wharf. "After which, sprinkle decently upon the Tar, whilst it is yet warm, as many Feathers as will stick to it." Malcom's tormentors may well have taken pillows from his own home as they began their night's work. "Then hold a lighted Candle to the Feathers, & try to set it all on Fire; if it will burn so much the better. But as the experiment is often made in cold Weather," such as prevailed that January night, "it will not then succeed—take also an Halter, & put it round the Person's Neck, & then cart him the Rounds."

After Malcom had been forced into a cart, his assailants poured

François Godefroy, John Malcom *(Paris, [1784]). In this French print, John Malcom is shown being lowered into a cart as men and women of diverse social backgrounds are looking on.*

hot tar over his head and large parts of his body. The tar burned through his skin and scalded his flesh. Next, the crowd covered him in feathers before pulling the cart on to the Town House—the seat of the governor, legislature, and courts depicted in the center of Revere's Boston Massacre image. They whipped him severely at multiple locations, and halfway between the governor's residence and the Old South Meeting House they ordered him to curse Thomas Hutchinson, now the hated royal governor of the Province of Massachusetts Bay, whose house a Stamp Act mob had virtually dismantled in 1765. Malcom refused. He was taken to the Liberty Tree, a large elm at the corner of Essex, where, again, he valiantly (or recklessly) declined to condemn the governor. He was then dragged to the municipal gallows, a rope around his neck presaging what might lie in store, and still he rebuffed them. Could they at least "put their threats in Execution Rather than Continue their Torture?" Malcom now pleaded. They bound his hands behind his back, tying him to the gallows or swinging the rope's other end across the beam, and beat him with cords and sticks. By one account, they threatened to cut his ears off. When his torturers demanded that Malcom curse the king and the governor, he defiantly damned all traitors. Finally, with the tar encasing his freezing, bruised body, Malcom could take it no more: he cursed as ordered.

Having already defiled and shamed him, Malcom's persecutors added one more insult. They made him swallow huge quantities of tea, toasting the king and other members of the royal family. Malcom gulped down the liquid until he turned pale and "filled the Bowl which he had just emptied." They beat him back to the Custom House and all the way to Copp's Hill, concluding a "Spectacle of horror & sportive cruelty," as Anne Hulton described it, that had taken as many as five hours. George R. T. Hewes, who later distanced himself from the street's brutality (he had also been unarmed the night of the Boston Massacre) had been following the procession with a blanket to shield the hypothermic Malcom. Around midnight, now back outside his family home, they finally "rolled [Malcom] out of the cart like a log." Doctors, reported Hulton, considered it "impossible this poor creature can live. They say his flesh comes off his back in Stakes."

Malcom did survive. His physical recovery would have been slow, starting with the scraping of the tar from his body. Perhaps turpentine would have been used, as with other victims of tarring and featherings, revealing his bloody skin and likely removing bits of it with the tar to expose raw flesh wounds. It would be many weeks before he would be able to leave his bed; for the rest of his life, he would bear the scars of his ordeal.

* * *

Malcom's torture, almost four years after the Boston Massacre, occurred at a moment when the town was once again at the center of colonial-imperial strife. After Britain had removed the troops from Boston and repealed most of the Townshend Acts, three

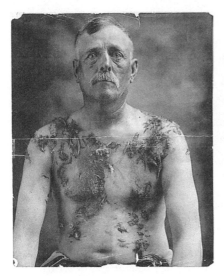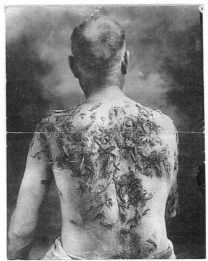

Photographs of John Meints, who was tarred and feathered in the U.S. during World War I for not supporting war bond drives, encapsulate the punishment's brutal physicality.

calmer years had ensued. But by 1773 tensions were again rising. The British government resolved to pay the salaries of the Massachusetts governor and judges from the remaining tax on tea, thus bypassing the colonial assembly. In addition, the Tea Act of that year, adopted to help the East India Company pay off its debt, gave a small number of merchants, the so-called tea consignees, a monopoly on the right to sell tea in America. Soon a coalition of Boston politicians, artisans, and merchants cut out from the trade targeted those tea consignees and their warehouses. On December 16, 1773, some one hundred men—merchants, artisans, apprentices, and local teenagers, the shoemaker Hewes among them—boarded three ships at Griffin's Wharf and threw forty-six tons of tea overboard to prevent it from being sold.[2]

The British government learned about the Boston Tea Party in late January 1774. The prime minister, Lord North, denounced the town as the "ringleader of all violence and opposition to the execution of the laws of this country." Over the following months, Parliament passed harsh legislation to punish Boston for destroying private property and resisting imperial rule. The Boston Port

Bill closed the port until full damages were paid. An amendment to the Massachusetts charter permitted the governor to appoint councillors, judges, and sheriffs. One regulation stated that any royal official or soldier accused of a capital offense could be tried in England rather than locally. Another law said that imperial troops could now be quartered in unoccupied dwellings. At the same time, the Quebec Act extended that colony's border south, protecting French Catholics' way of life but also limiting the American colonies' westward expansion.

Rather than containing the incipient American insurgency, as the British government had hoped, these Coercive Acts (or Intolerable Acts, in the rebels' words) helped unify opinion across the diverse colonies. While colonists continued tea protests from New Hampshire to Virginia, over the spring and summer of 1774 they also prepared for concerted political action. In September, fifty-six delegates sent by the legislatures of twelve of the colonies (only Georgia abstained) gathered in Philadelphia, then the largest city in North America. On average forty-five years old, most of these men were very wealthy, and several dozen of them were veteran colonial legislators. They met for seven weeks in Carpenters' Hall. The single most important achievement of this unprecedented Continental Congress was to pass the Continental Association, a non-importation, non-consumption, and non-exportation agreement boycotting British goods. The delegates hoped that by harming British manufactures, revenue, and commerce, the boycott would force Britain to repeal the legislation "calculated for enslaving these Colonies." Drawing on lessons from earlier, more fragmented economic boycotts, the Continental Congress designed the new *Continental* Association to cover all colonies, and to involve all segments of society, not just merchants. To implement this ambitious scheme, the Congress created a system of surveillance and persecution whereby Americans watched and judged the words and actions of their fellow countrymen.[3]

* * *

To enforce the boycott laid out in the Association agreement, the Continental Congress required that "a committee be chosen in every County, City, and Town" of each colony "attentively to observe the conduct of all persons touching this Association." If an individual was found to be in breach, he (and occasionally she) was to be denounced in the newspapers, so that "all foes to the rights of *British-America* may be publickly known, and universally contemned as the enemies of *American* liberty." Imagine how sinister such phrasing must have sounded to skeptics, let alone opponents of the boycott. And the Continental Congress offered little specific guidance on the workings of these committees; each was free to establish additional regulations. No one could predict how exactly this experiment in grassroots enforcement might play out.

In very little time, "committees of safety" formed in communities across the colonies—their ominous name echoing that of similar groups organized in the previous century during the English Civil War. By spring 1775, some 7,000 men served on such bodies. To the Loyalist lieutenant James Moody it seemed that the rebels "maddened almost every part of the country" with their committees, admonishing everyone to "*Join or die!*" The committees scrutinized and chastised those they suspected of violating Association rules. But anyone considered disloyal to the American cause was now at risk of being persecuted. In towns and counties across America, the committees fostered a dangerous climate that threatened psychological and physical violence to those whom the Revolutionaries derogatively called Tories and whom we now call Loyalists.[4]

According to a long-standing stereotype, Loyalists were mostly white, prosperous, Anglican elites. Yet Loyalists included not only imperial officials and large landowners but also merchants, farmers, shopkeepers, bakers, tailors, and poor craftsmen and laborers; Anglicans as well as Quakers, Methodists, French Huguenots, and Irish Roman Catholics. The historical record affords us the occasional demographic snapshot: of the one-third to one-half of the male inhabitants of Deerfield, Massachusetts, who had been identified as Loyalists, some 40 percent were merchants, tavern owners, and artisans, 30 percent farmers, and 15 percent professionals. There were Loyalists in every social echelon and geographic region. It is fair to assume that virtually every white colonial American in 1775 knew a Loyalist.[5]

Patriots regularly mocked Loyalists for their base personal and materialistic urges: the Tories, they said, lusted after office and wealth, prestige and influence. But in the same way that the motivations of the Revolutionaries were complex, Loyalists, too, acted out of both principle and pragmatism. Loyalists shared with Patriots "preoccupations with access to land, the maintenance of slavery, and regulation of colonial trade," as the historian Maya Jasanoff has put it. Until well into 1775, most in both camps professed loyalty to the British monarch. Loyalists felt a deep commitment to constitutional protections of their liberties, and many also agreed with the Patriots that specific British policies were undesirable or even unacceptable. However, unlike the Revolutionaries, who eventually sought an independent republic, the Loyalists remained devoted subjects of King George III and wished to resolve any disagreements within the existing constitutional framework. To them, separation from the mother country threatened economic dislocation and the disruption of their personal networks. Many also doubted that America could win a war against the mighty British Empire.[6]

But in addition to ideology and beliefs, Loyalists also followed their individual and group interests. Over the course of the war, many Americans would come to decisions about which army might best protect their families and their property, frequently reevaluating their options as the local military situation shifted. Minorities such as Highland Scots in North Carolina, Anglicans in New England, German immigrants in Pennsylvania, or Dutch farmers in New Jersey tended to side with what they perceived to be a more tolerant British Empire rather than throw in their lot with a potentially more oppressive American majority. Similarly, several tens of thousands of runaway slaves who joined the British, and many of America's indigenous peoples, such as five of the six

Iroquois nations, perhaps hoped that a victorious, diverse British Empire would treat them more fairly than a triumphant white America.[7]

As the lines between Patriots and Loyalists hardened, soon they cut right through communities—and indeed families. Perhaps the most famous example is that of the Franklins of Philadelphia: Benjamin, until 1774 the Empire's best friend in America but now one of its angriest and most implacable foes, and his son, William, New Jersey's last royal governor, who evolved into a passionate leader of American Loyalists. But the Revolution also divided lesser-known families, both white and of African heritage, such as the Whitecuffs. Benjamin Whitecuff was a black freeman who spied for and served with the British Army and later the Royal Navy. His father, also a freeman, was a farmer and sergeant fighting with the Patriots, as was his brother. Benjamin was twice captured and escaped the noose narrowly on both occasions; his father and brother both fell in the war.[8]

Family ties did not necessarily soften hearts. When John Adams declared that he would have hanged his own brother if he had been a Loyalist, it was easier for him to say given that, unlike others, he did not actually have a sibling on the other side of the political divide. The same was not true in the case of Gouverneur Morris, a congressional delegate from Westchester, New York, who remained in close contact with his two Loyalist sisters; his mother and most of his brothers-in-law and half brothers were also Loyalists. As a prosecutor of Loyalists, Morris nevertheless advocated public executions: terror would frighten waverers and inspire others to fight for America's cause.[9]

* * *

Committees of safety learned about suspicious individuals in various ways. Neighbors denounced neighbors, sometimes anonymously, often openly. If a committee decided to act on eyewitness accounts or hearsay, it typically interrogated a suspect, heard witnesses, and possibly intercepted the defendant's mail or searched his home for incriminating evidence. When a majority of committee members believed the charges against an individual were justified, they often pressured him to recant and apologize. If at that point a suspect was unwilling to undergo the required rituals of apology and reintegration into the community, the rebels typically shamed him publicly and asked the community to cut off all contact. One author wrote that being declared an enemy to his country was "a species of infamy . . . more dreadful to a freeman than the gallows, the rack or the stake." In a tightly knit society such as early America, these public reprimands were far more than inconsequential rhetoric: they could undermine trust between neighbors and business partners and threaten a victim's reputation and thereby his ability to obtain credit or earn a livelihood. When ostracism had such severe consequences, condemning someone to a social death in the eyes of the community was in itself a form of violence.[10]

Some committees policed their districts more proactively, asking the general population to inform on persons of doubtful loyalty in their midst, even if that meant encouraging people to settle private scores. In spring 1775, the entire committee of safety in Wilmington, North Carolina, visited each family to request that the head of household sign a paper in support of the Association or to state his motives for refusing. Few felt they could deny their signature when their neighbors were watching on their doorstep. Eleven Wilmingtonians nevertheless refused; these dissenters were effectively ostracized and called out in the *Cape-Fear Mercury,* an outlet specially founded for such purposes.[11]

The extralegal committees enforcing the Continental Association impacted Americans' lives in disruptive and sometimes violent ways. Committees imposed price controls on various goods, such as sugar and beef; checked merchants' invoices and daybooks; monitored customs houses; and inspected ships' cargoes. In multiple colonies, the very first violation of the Association occurred when ships carrying cargo banned under the new rules arrived in ports. When the *Peggy Stewart* docked at Annapolis, Maryland, and the vessel's owner paid tax under the Tea Act, enraged locals burned the ship. Several merchants and owners of vessels who were seen to import and sell boycotted goods were tarred and feathered, or were threatened with that same ordeal, up and down the eastern seaboard.[12]

Under the new consumption code, people became cautious about such seemingly innocuous gestures as offering a neighbor or a tired passerby some tea—that "pestilential herb," in the Patriots' language. Loyalist writers highlighted the hypocrisy of an increasingly tyrannical regime established in the name of freedom. As one poet put it: "Men legally punished for not breaking the law? / Tarr'd, feath'd, and carted for drinking Bohea [black tea]? / And by force and oppression compell'd to be free?" Loyalists and British officials realized quickly that the committee system created an atmosphere of suspicion, fear, and terror akin, some said, to the Spanish Inquisition.[13]

Words could get you into trouble with the Associators just as much as gestures and deeds could. Many were ensnared for phrases that someone construed as disloyal, perhaps uttered under the influence of alcohol, or, as one Loyalist put it, if they simply were "Not thinking That Words Would Be Taken notice of." Loyalists who knew they were under scrutiny, or who already had one family member under arrest, cautioned loved ones to censor their talk. In a letter intercepted by the Patriots, the Loyalist Christina Tice reassured her husband that "no rebel shall ever have the pleasure of knowing from my outward behavior my inward concerns." Less careful individuals risked being investigated if they were overheard criticizing their local committee, if they drank a royal toast or sang "God Save the King" in the wrong company, or if they expressed doubt about America's ability to stand up to Britain.[14]

Committeemen were not the only enforcers of loyalty: the Revolution was also a time of mob violence, as committees collaborated and sometimes competed with local mobs in persecuting political suspects. These mass actions were rooted in the political culture of the time. In early America, rioting crowds and mobs took a prominent role in a range of economic and political controversies. It was in this tradition that many communities in the 1770s also dealt with individuals known for, or suspected of, not supporting the American cause, as "the people's sentinels" helped enforce political loyalties.[15]

Some local committees arguably sought to limit mob excess. In early 1775, the Northampton committee in New Hampshire tried to calm tempers in the wake of severe crowd action against local Loyalists. Appealing for unity, the committee stressed that the Continental and Provincial Congresses had urged peaceful means and declared that some of the ways in which Loyalists had been treated had been "repugnant to the Dictates of Humanity and the Precepts of Religion." On occasion, committeemen were less harsh than their local community wished them to be. When the committee in Cambridge, New York, tried to restrain the local populace from whipping a Loyalist, the crowd made their committeemen walk the gauntlet between "two long Strings of Men with each a large long whip," flogging into them their expectations of stronger anti-Loyalist measures.[16]

But many committees tolerated a fair amount of vigilante action; indeed, the boundary between mob and committee was porous at best. Some committees relied quite explicitly on Liberty gangs—members of the Sons of Liberty, a militant group of artisans and laborers who had first formed in opposition to the Stamp Act a decade earlier—to extend the reach of their authority. And they knew that mobs were truly inventive in the ways they terrorized suspects and punished those they singled out as culprits. Victims were tossed into rivers and village ponds, with herrings thrown at them to eat; set upon a block of ice to cool down their mistaken loyalty; hoisted on a landlord's sign with a dead catamount (a kind of wildcat) for company; handcuffed to slaves in order to humiliate "all these cattle"; and whipped or beaten until their ribs were broken. Others had their faces marked, such as Peter Guire, who had the regal letters G.R. (for "George Rex") seared onto his forehead.[17]

That committees did condone popular violence, and in certain instances orchestrated it, had already become apparent when the Crown appointed so-called mandamus councillors in the latter

part of 1774. Massachusetts committees oversaw popular demon-
strations against these new royal officials. In many places, crowds
forced them to decline or resign their offices. One such official was
tipped off by a friend not to return home, as his enemies "thirst
for your blood." The concerted campaign of fear against royal
appointees eventually touched men like Jesse Dunbar of Bridge-
water, Massachusetts. Dunbar's crime was buying livestock from
a mandamus councillor in Marshfield. Dunbar had butchered and
skinned an ox and prepared it for sale, when rebels associated with
the Sons of Liberty struck. They seized the carcass and forced
Dunbar to climb into its open belly. Successive local mobs then
carted Dunbar for many miles; he was even repeatedly charged for
the ride. When they reached Duxbury, his tormentors wiped and
whipped Dunbar's face with ox entrails before letting him off—
bloodied, scared, and shamed.[18]

With ordinary colonists like Dunbar victimized merely for
doing business with a Crown appointee, it was clear that violence
against Loyalists was escalating. According to one Loyalist account, Dr. Abner Bebee of East Haddam, Connecticut, experienced
a vile variation of the ritual of tarring and feathering. Bebee had
complained about mob abuse of his uncle and had voiced pro-
British views when he, too, was assaulted by a mob one night.
They tarred and feathered the physician and mill owner and then
took him to a hog sty, where they rubbed dung into his eyes and
rammed it down his throat before thus exposing him to some
women. The mob attacked Bebee's house, causing his child to go
"into Distraction," destroyed his gristmill, and, finally, instructed
the community to break off all contact with Bebee. As the historian Ann Withington has put it, such public rituals of punishment
"first marked the victims as abnormal and corrupt, then rendered
them ridiculous and contemptible, and finally dramatized their
separation from the community." Patriots debased and defiled, humiliated and dehumanized, their Loyalist neighbors.[19]

Historians of the Revolutionary era typically stress that the
extralegal committees put a high value on resolving differences
within their local communities, and that they "attempted as best

as they could to avoid physical violence." Yet, even if many committees did push for renunciations and apologies, and even if they displayed a concern with at least the appearance of due process, we need to recognize that creating solidarity always relies on excluding others, often through violent means. As even those historians who emphasize the committees' restraint admit, membership was "certainly not an activity for the faint of heart." If we consider instances of abuse and violence as mere "unpleasant exceptions," we risk failing to do justice to the full range of American experiences during the Revolutionary period.[20]

Dehumanizing the enemy was an approach that the Patriots would soon also use against the British and their German auxiliaries, those "orangotangs murdering brutes," while a British officer denounced the rebels as "reptiles." And when, several months after the Continental Association, the conflict did eventually turn into skirmishing and then all-out war, the consequences for Loyalists were predictably stark.[21]

Despicable Animals

In April 1775, British redcoats seeking to confiscate rebel weapons clashed with insurgent militia at Lexington and Concord. Those violent altercations in the Massachusetts countryside would turn out to be the first battles of the American Revolutionary War. They were soon followed by Britain's Pyrrhic victory in the Battle of Bunker Hill, which took place during the siege of Boston that June. As the conflict with Britain escalated, the Revolutionaries tightened their surveillance of the internal enemy. One indicator of the heightened terror was the very language that the Revolutionaries used to describe political dissenters: non-Associators now became cursed rascals and infamous wretches, or vultures and despicable animals that needed to be exterminated. Revolutionaries defined a Tory as a "thing whose head is in England, and its body in America and its neck ought to be stretched." The Loyalists in turn referred to their rebel persecutors as "giddy headed & envenomed monsters, whose breath is sufficient to poison & blast with Ruine, not a few individuals only, but whole empires." Words are a large part of how the work of violence is done, and this was just the kind of language that might prepare Americans for a brutal war against their countrymen.[22]

News of Lexington emboldened Patriots across the colonies. As many of Samuel Curwen's neighbors were mobilizing, the sixty-year-old Salem merchant and Loyalist found that remaining in Massachusetts had become untenable. In May 1775, "unable longer to bear their undeserved reproaches and menaces hourly denounced against myself," Curwen sought asylum in Pennsylvania, where Loyalist sentiment was strongest in Philadelphia and among the merchants and farmers in the counties on the Delaware and Susquehanna. But Curwen had trouble even getting a room in a Philadelphia boardinghouse, as "so many refused as made it fearful whether, like Cain, I had not a discouraging mark upon me, or a strong feature of toryism." With Philadelphia striking him in his near panic as "wholly American," Curwen took passage to England. The following summer he congratulated a friend exiled in Antigua "on your retreat from the land of oppression and tyranny." Before long, flight, exile, and diaspora became common themes in the Loyalist story, mirroring the experiences of Patriot refugees from British-occupied areas.[23]

Also in the aftermath of Lexington and Concord, the Sons of Liberty in New York City stole five hundred muskets as well as gunpowder from City Hall. John Wetherhead, a well-to-do English-born importer in the city, felt that the Massachusetts alarm "hurried the people into violences tenfold greater than ever" as mobs seized and beat men who refused to curse the king. Wetherhead himself was later harassed until he removed his family to Long Island, narrowly escaping a mob hollering, "Damn him, Seize him, and drown him!" Farther south, the people of Dutchess County, Virginia, took justice into their own hands when a judge at the court of common pleas dared send to prison a member of a committee that had disarmed local Loyalists. Locals first rescued the prisoner and then tarred and feathered the judge. No sooner, it seemed, had the crisis with Britain turned from a political dispute into a militarized conflict than Patriots across America stepped up their persecution of unreliable neighbors. Hardest hit were those who had the capacity to act as broadcasters and multipliers of dissent.[24]

In spring 1775, a crowd in New Brunswick, New Jersey, strung an effigy of a New York printer up a tree. The printer, James Rivington, promptly illustrated the scene with a woodcut in the April 20 issue of his own newspaper, the *New-York Gazetteer.* Seeing his person hanged in effigy "merely for acting consistent with his profession as a free printer," Rivington contrasted his commitment to the liberty of the press with his enemies' "aim to establish a most cruel tyranny." The scion of a prosperous British publishing dynasty who had lost his wealth through betting and gambling, Rivington had started anew in America, founding the *New-York Gazetteer* in 1773. He initially prided himself on his evenhanded approach: "PRINTED at his OPEN and UNINFLUENCED PRESS," read the front-page title of his paper. Rivington accused the Patriots of "knocking out any Man's Brains that dares presume to speak his Mind freely upon the present Contest." But even though Rivington continued to print bipartisan materials, linking his ostensibly fair approach as a publisher with his own dual identity as an "*Englishman* by birth, . . . an *American* by choice," the *Gazetteer* was widely seen as *the* Loyalist paper. Some 3,600 copies—a very significant print run in those days—circulated in all of the Atlantic seaboard colonies, most of the West Indies, and key cities in Britain, Ireland, and even France. In April 1775, Rivington was appointed a King's Printer, emboldening Patriots to denounce him as "a most wretched, jacobitish, hireling, *incendiary*." Patriot committees as far as South Carolina ordered boycotts of Rivington's publications. Some communities searched postmen's bags to prevent the paper from reaching their towns. Elsewhere, people seen reading the paper were warned with words and blows to stop doing so.[25]

With the Patriots aggressively policing loyalties, freedom of the press was coming under increasing strain. When the *New Hampshire Gazette* refused to reveal the name of an anonymous author who had lambasted the atmosphere of fear and repression, the Revolutionary authorities shut it down. Printers elsewhere were bullied into retracting contentious statements. In other instances, Patriots seized and destroyed the entire print run of pamphlets they considered dangerous. In addition to book burnings, there were monetary rewards for the capture of certain pamphleteers. Amid such escalating levels of violence, Loyalists found it increasingly hard to make their voices heard.[26]

After Rivington's office had already been assaulted repeatedly, in November 1775 the radical New York Patriot Isaac Sears led an armed posse of some eighty mounted Sons of Liberty and volunteers from Connecticut in an attack on his print shop. They destroyed the premises and carried off Rivington's lead type. Rivington escaped unharmed and took refuge on board a British warship, prompting sarcastic calls for him to be exempted from the non-exportation agreement. Such silencing of controversial printers continued into the war years.[27]

Just as the Patriots closely watched Loyalist pamphleteers and printers like Rivington, they now also focused their attention on Anglican priests in their midst. To be sure, not all Anglicans, clergy or lay, were committed Loyalists, but among them were some of the most outspoken opponents of colonial resistance. Their pulpit offered them a powerful platform; some of the most influential Loyalist pamphleteers were also clergymen. A menace to the American cause, such counterrevolutionaries needed to be watched and, if necessary, stopped. By the summer of 1775, rebels were routinely intimidating Loyalist Anglican clergymen.

The Reverend Ebenezer Dibblee of Stamford, Connecticut, suffered "Terrors by night and Day for fear of the Violence of Lawless Mobs & ungoverned Soldiery." He survived a "bold attempt on my life being Shot at as I was going to attend a funeral. Waylaid, and not presuming to return the same way but seldom, when I went to attend the private Duties of my Cure." Dibblee's family endured the quartering of Patriot soldiers; his daughter, he bemoaned, was driven "wholly Insane" by fear. When the Reverend Richard Mansfield of two other Connecticut towns, Derby and Oxford, spoke disrespectfully of the Congress, he, like many other clerics, needed to "fly into Exile in order to escape Violence and Imprisonment, if not immediate Death." Mansfield left his thirteen children in the care of his still overwhelmingly Loyalist congregation. Because the Reverend John Beach of Newton and East Redding refused to cease praying for the king or to close his church "till the Rebels cut out his tongue," a Patriot crowd seized him mid-service and threatened to slice off the very organ that preached counterrevolution. Dragged in front of his church, Beach was told to kneel and say his last prayer. In the end, his tormentors let him off—scared, no doubt, if not physically scarred.[28]

Patriot crowds smashed the windows of Anglican churches. They stripped the interiors of houses of worship and poured bottles of rum over altars. Priests were hauled from their pulpits or had objects hurled and bullets fired at them mid-sermon. Some mobs tarred and feathered priests or marked them with the sign of the cross, using a "mop filled with excrements, in token of their loyalty to a king who designed to crucify all the good people of America." Many a cleric was eventually banished, had his property confiscated, or was imprisoned for months or even years. By 1776, several clerics had died as a result of their abuse at Patriot hands or due to the harsh conditions of their imprisonment. In addition to Anglican priests, these included the Reverend John Roberts, a dissenting minister of Charleston, South Carolina. After tarring and feathering Roberts, a rebel mob hanged him on a gibbet and subsequently burned his body on a bonfire—a punishment usually reserved for heretics and witches and, in colonial America, slaves.[29]

* * *

While printers and priests were coming under systematic scrutiny, psychological pressure, and, all too often, physical assault, Revolutionary committees were increasingly employing loyalty oaths to flush out dissenters among ordinary colonials. From mid-1775, individuals who refused to take an oath risked not just ostracism but arrest, imprisonment, property confiscation, and banishment. As with the earlier requirements, there were no doubt numerous men who took a Patriot oath as a reasonably convenient measure of self-protection—to avoid detention, escape punishment, or remain quietly on their farms. Before long, however, verbal pledges were no longer sufficient to reassure Revolutionaries preparing for all-out war. To prove his allegiance, a man now had to be ready to drill with the militia and to defend the American cause with arms. Following Patriot purges of the old colonial militias, by the fall of 1775, committees from New England to North Carolina ordered every white man capable of bearing arms to muster in armed companies and choose their officers. In Massachusetts, where the war with Britain had already demanded the first military casualties, the Provincial Congress directed local committees to disarm all unreliable men. Voluntary at first, militia service was becoming mandatory, with refusal punishable by growing fines.[30]

As the Patriots militarized, so did the Loyalists, forming counter-associations from Connecticut and Massachusetts to the Southern colonies. When Patriots began to mobilize in Westchester County, New York, in April 1775, four hundred Loyalists held a rally and some of them founded an association to defend the imperial order and their lives, liberties, and properties. As the Patriots ramped up their activities, the Loyalists matched them by forming secret military units. But elsewhere Patriot associations easily outmatched the Loyalists: that same April some 2,500 Massachusetts Patriots disarmed 300 Loyalists who had associated in Freetown to keep "the Neighbourhood in Subjection to the King's Authority."[31]

In a particularly brutal instance of Revolutionary violence, the plantation owner Thomas Brown was almost killed in the South Carolina backcountry town of New Richmond. Recently arrived from England, Brown refused to support the Patriots' Association and instead joined one of the paramilitary Loyalist counter-associations. Alas, no fellow Loyalists came to Brown's rescue when, one day in August 1775, some 130 rebels seized him at his house, struck him down with a blow from a musket butt that cracked his skull, carried him away "like a calf across a horse," tied him to a tree while still unconscious, tarred his legs, burned his feet to the point where he lost two toes, and partially scalped him. The crowd carted Brown through various locales and forced him to pledge himself to the Association, until they eventually dropped him just across the border with Georgia, a colony where Loyalists probably formed a majority.[32]

Brown survived his ordeal. He recanted his false Patriot oath and went on to found the King's Rangers, spending much of the war as a militant Loyalist leader. But groups like Brown's original Loyalist counter-association were at a fundamental disadvantage. Although the Loyalists' absolute numbers were very significant, they were unevenly spread across the colonies and regions, which made it difficult for them to form a coherent movement, a fact that was compounded by their demographic diversity. With no cross-colonial leadership to coordinate them, the Loyalists were particularly vulnerable to the Patriots' violent coercion. Indeed, by the fall of 1775, armed rebels were dismantling Loyalist counter-associations across Connecticut and New York.[33]

As Loyalist associations crumbled, Patriot committees of safety and militias refined their methods of bullying and terrorizing their domestic enemies. Janet Schaw described these developments in her diary. A Scotswoman of around forty, Schaw in 1775 visited Schawfield, the plantation of her Loyalist brother near Wilmington, North Carolina. Loyalists such as her brother faced a predicament, she wrote: "The Alternative is proposed: Agree to join us, and your persons and properties are safe; you have a shilling sterling a day; your duty is no more than once a month appearing under Arms at Wilmington." But, Schaw continued, "if you refuse, we are directly to cut up your corn, shoot your pigs, burn your houses, seize your Negroes and perhaps tar and feather yourself." On the request of the Congress and state legislatures, particularly aggressive Loyalists were now likely to be apprehended by militia units, especially in militarily sensitive areas. What had been conceived as an armed citizenry in England and then the American colonies had become a kind of Revolutionary police force that, if necessary, used violence to keep open opposition in check.[34]

Janet Schaw was largely an observer. And initially most women were somewhat insulated from Revolutionary fervor. They were not subject to loyalty oaths or to persecution, as the rebels con-

Hancock's Warehouse for Taring &
FEATHERING.

There is no evidence of women being tarred and feathered during the American Revolution, but the scene was imagined in a print, Hancock's Warehouse for Taring & Feathering, *published anonymously in London. The women here are alleged to have imported tea illegally. A woman on the left is being dunked in a barrel of tar while a second woman at center is being undressed or stuffed into a bag. A third woman, completely nude at right, is covering her private parts and averting her face in shame. The image had the power to shock an enlightened audience that used the treatment of women to gauge a society's standards of civility.*

sidered women apolitical. But before long, Patriots acknowledged that many women were in fact opinionated and politically active in their own right. After all, women sympathetic to the Revolution were taking on increasingly important roles. They were critical to enforcing the American consumer boycott and would soon begin to support the military by supplying clothing for soldiers; cooking, nursing, and washing laundry in camps; and, indeed, acting as couriers and spies. Conversely, as the conflict with Britain escalated, Revolutionary committees started to interrogate politically suspect women and administer oaths to them. Occasionally, Patriots took women hostage or put them under house arrest as a way of blackmailing their Loyalist husbands into changing their allegiance. Loyalists fleeing persecution later described how the Patriots not only confiscated their estates but also threw their wives and children out on the streets with little more than the clothes on their backs.[35]

Catacomb of Loyalty

In addition to violently expelling Loyalists from their communities, the Patriots also imprisoned opponents of the Revolution. Loyalists who survived captivity at the hands of the rebels told of the abuse they suffered en route to various jails. They were forced to march tens of miles in heavy irons, gratuitously beaten by their guards, and paraded through the streets of towns "to Make us an example to all Torries or others who should adhere to the nero of England as their fraise was." Some died as a direct or indirect consequence of such marches. Others endured months of bullying and even torture at the hands of their captors, who kept them half-starved in filthy and hot or frigid prisons where many contracted fevers, typhoid, and other diseases.[36]

In the jail at Kingston, New York, one ailing inmate described a room fourteen feet square with a little straw for the prisoners to lie on. At one end of the room, he commented sarcastically, was "one half of an Elegant Necessary House," or a lavatory. Its other half, without any partition, was being used by nine more prisoners in the adjacent room. Medical experts judged that overcrowding would result in jail fever. Anyone with "the least Spark of Humanity," they said, would make different arrangements. The Provincial Convention, which sat in the courthouse directly above the jail, permitted its members to smoke so as to counteract the "nauseous and disagreeable effluvia" rising threateningly from below. Utterly isolated from the world, the Loyalist captives were not allowed visitors other than, very occasionally, a doctor; they had only lice and fleas for company.[37]

It is true that prisoners in this period generally endured poor conditions, but the unusual number of political prisoners plus prisoners of war put extra pressure on the spaces that could be used to hold them. And even jails like that at Kingston paled in comparison to a feared underground prison in Simsbury, Connecticut, located in a converted copper mine. When Patriots arrested Colonel Abijah Willard, one of the new mandamus councillors, as a traitor, a crowd marched him several miles in the direction of that frightening place. Just imagining it was sufficient to make Willard give in to the Patriots' "outrage and violence," sign their oath, and beg forgiveness. Newspaper readers in Britain, too, caught oblique glimpses of that site where, it was said, "the loyalists are buried alive." When an Englishman visited in the early nineteenth century, he reflected on the dreaded place as an "object of terror."[38]

Detailed descriptions of the prison in the mines are not easy to come by, but from surviving fragments we can re-create a sense of what it might have been like to be incarcerated there. In 1824, the *New-York Mirror* printed a detailed account of the Revolutionary-era political trial of one Edward Huntington. Accused of being a Loyalist leader, Huntington had insisted that he was "a British subject"; as such, he demanded to be treated as a prisoner of war under the "laws of civilized warfare." With courtroom spectators crying, "Away with the traitor—to the mines with the tory," Huntington, who refused to acknowledge the court's authority, asserted: "My father was a Briton, a loyal, patriotic Briton," and although he himself had been born "in a foreign colony," Huntington insisted, "I can never forget my descent from a loyal house." Soon the accused engaged in a shouting match with his judge, who demanded that Huntington submit to his authority. "Submission!" retorted Huntington, "ha! Rebel, talkest thou of submission?" The judge placed the prisoner under military guard to protect him from the incensed crowd, only to convict Huntington for leading a Loyalist band. His sentence: to spend the rest of his life sixty to eighty feet underground in a dark, damp, claustrophobic living tomb.[39]

Arriving at Simsbury, Huntington would first have been led through the guard room and a trapdoor into a space partially

A View of the Guard-House and Simsbury-Mines, now called Newgate—
A Prison for the Confinement of Loyalists in Connecticut *(London, 1781)*.
Simsbury was a converted copper mine with a wooden cabin and later a for-
tified blockhouse for the guards sitting atop the main shaft, connecting to
unlit, airless, odious caverns that served as a makeshift prison for civilian,
political, and military prisoners. As shown in this illustration in a British
periodical, the holding area was reached by a system of trapdoors, platforms,
and ladders.

underground where, "near the foot of the stair, opened another
large trap-door covered with bars and bolts of iron, which they
called Hell." Via a six-foot ladder, Huntington reached a "large
iron grate or hatchway locked down over a shaft of about three feet
diameter sunk through the solid rock" and leading to "the bot-
tomless pit." He descended another ladder some thirty-eight feet
down to a landing, then another thirty or so feet, the darkness
increasingly enveloping him, until he reached a platform made of
boards or planks.[40]

All but the shortest inmates found they could not stand upright,
as the cavern ceilings were only about five feet high. Adding to the
disorienting experience was the fact that the holding area sloped
down eastward at an angle of 25 to 30 degrees. For the first sixty
feet or so, the space was very narrow, ranging from six to twenty

feet in width, opening up to eighty to one hundred feet farther east. The total length spanned no more than 165 feet. One wonders whether Huntington had read the articles in the Patriot papers claiming that these "subterraneous Apartments, in that gloomy Mansion" were a "suitable abode for those sons of darkness"—that is, Loyalists like him.[41]

Huntington would have been greeted not just by other British-Americans whose only crime was to remain loyal to the Empire but also by violent criminals serving sentences from one year to life for horse thievery, aggravated burglary, highway robbery, sexual assault, and accessory to murder, along with a trickle of Continental soldiers convicted by courts-martial. General Washington considered this collection of inmates "such flagrant and Attrocious villains" that he did not trust other prisons to contain them. Among Loyalist prisoners, we know that a few were sentenced to specific terms of, say, one or two years, and others, like Huntington, to life. Many no doubt assumed that they would be held for the duration of the conflict.[42]

Not all men were forced to remain deep underground in the rank caverns. Many of the felons appear to have been employed to work aboveground during the day, mostly in making nails. At dawn, armed guards led prisoners two or three at a time to their workbenches inside the structure that sat atop the mines. Chained to the benches by their feet, some were also made to wear iron collars tied via chains to beams overhead. It is unclear whether Loyalist prisoners were regularly employed as laborers as well. Edward Huntington, for one, did note that the keeper exempted him from working shifts during his early captivity. A later account suggests that at least some of the inmates considered the most dangerous were kept permanently underground and indeed chained to the rock with irons "eating into the flesh."[43]

Down below, Huntington may have found some hay or straw to lie on, barely enough padding against the hard, damp rock. Even if he managed to grab one of the basic wooden bunks along the cavern walls, he would have found that the wet hay helped the fleas thrive. An English visitor later recounted how rainwater percolated through cracks in the rock and eventually into the cavern, where the

> vapour of the damp passageways lies in large drops upon the decayed wood-work of the gloomy dungeons—moss and a saturated, flabby mould have gathered upon their sides—the water trickles along the adamantine walls—and the dingy green of the copper impregnations, imparts a most sombre aspect to the lonely caves.[44]

As the prison filled up, soon to contain several dozen and possibly a hundred prisoners at a time, the conditions in such a confined space, with very limited air circulation, no natural light, constant dampness, limited opportunities for prisoners to wash, and presumably communal tubs being used as toilets, would have provided an excellent breeding ground for diseases, including fevers, influenza, respiratory problems, dysentery, and typhoid. Sometimes prisoners managed to arrange for pots of burning charcoal to help overpower the noxious smells.

The psychological challenges of being held at Simsbury were as great as the physical hardships. When he "descended into the dark abyss," wrote Edward Huntington, any "hope seemed to have taken her everlasting flight." His mental state mirrored his dreary surroundings, as his soul appeared to be "yielding to the dark influence of despair." The dark caverns swallowed what little light "fell upon the squalid forms of the miserable wretches here incarcerated, . . . barely sufficient to show that they were men." Inmates likely suffered from nystagmus, an involuntary eye movement brought on by the constant strain of trying to see in low levels of light. The rock walls made sound waves bounce around, "imparting on the spoken word an alien metallic timbre not easily duplicated." In this "catacomb of Loyalty," wrote the Loyalist Reverend Samuel Peters, the "light of the sun and the light of the Gospel are alike shut out from the martyrs, whose resurrection state will eclipse the wonder of that of Lazarus."[45]

As if subterranean incarceration were not enough in itself,

Simsbury, like many prisons, had a special cell for the solitary confinement of particularly troublesome inmates. This was an area near the end of one of the passageways, some twenty feet square, totally dark, with bare rock on all sides and a slightly elevated rock at the center with an iron bolt to which a prisoner's leg or legs were chained. Whether in a solitary cell or not, being held against one's will, far underground, in the company of felons and military convicts, with no guarantee of ever being released, must have been a deeply frightening experience for any Loyalist. As one early historian put it, the "utter isolation of its inmates from the living world, made it to the common mind very like the 'Inferno' of Dante."[46]

Desperate prisoners plotted risky escapes. On one occasion, captives burrowed into a disused mine shaft filled with rocks and debris. When stones caved in, at least three men were buried under the rubble; it is unclear whether they ever managed to dig their way out. Another time, prisoners clandestinely cleared a former drainage tunnel. They built a fire in the hope of loosening up some larger stones that they could otherwise not move: at least one man suffocated in the smoke. Repeatedly, prisoners staged mass escape attempts by setting fire to the blockhouse sitting on top of the shaft. More than once, prisoners overpowered their guards and locked them up before fleeing; sometimes captors accepted payment to let prisoners run.[47]

The prison in the mines was temporarily closed in spring 1777 (inmates were transferred to Hartford Gaol eighteen miles away), but was re-established by 1780 with much higher security. By 1781, a lieutenant and a sergeant commanded twenty-four well-armed privates. Our English visitor concluded that "[p]risoners in this gaol are treated precisely as tigers are in a *menagerie*" and "[e]very thing that human art can do, is in this instance done, to brutify and inflame the victim." Little wonder, then, that prisoners developed a "ferocious disposition" of which their captors were rightly frightened. How many of those prisoners died there, and how many others suffered from the permanently debilitating effects of their captivity, remains unknown.[48]

* * *

Psychological torment and physical violence played a far greater role in suppressing dissent during America's first civil war than is commonly acknowledged. What is often celebrated as the Patriots' groundbreaking infrastructure of revolution—and community, district, and colonial-level committees do indeed represent a significant achievement of political mobilization—was, for Loyalists, an apparatus of oppression and terror.[49]

When an unguarded word in the wrong company, or a neighborly offer of tea, could lead to ostracism; when dissenters hazarded being hauled before committees or seized by armed guards; when search parties invaded the confines of warehouses and the privacy of bedrooms, Americans lived in a climate of distrust, self-censorship, and fearful apprehension. Countless individuals made decisions in the face of veiled or open threats, sometimes under duress or even torture, requiring them to weigh their political ideals against the desire to steer a safe course for themselves and their families, their property, and their livelihoods.

Most modern historians emphasize that the American Revolution was less violent than many other revolutions. But Loyalists on the receiving end of threats and abuse could draw no comfort from that comparison. Nor would such knowledge have lessened the anguish of those who witnessed Patriots terrorizing their neighbors, or who read in the newspapers or heard through their personal networks about the persecution or deaths of Loyalist friends and family members.

We will never be able to quantify the violence that American Loyalists endured. But as people imagined the possibility and the nature of the violence they or others might suffer, violence was as much about states of mind as it was about its physical characteristics. Even if only a minority of Loyalists directly experienced abuse, such incidents were widespread enough and sufficiently written and talked about in Revolutionary America to strike fear into the hearts of committed Loyalists, individuals suspected of being unfriendly to the American cause, and waverers practi-

cally anywhere. Their frightening unpredictability only served
to heighten the sense of permanent if often latent danger. The
Revolutionaries relied on terror—acts of violence and the threat of
violence—to crush dissent.

As the wounds inflicted on Americans in Boston's King Street,
on the Lexington Green, and at Bunker Hill reminded Patriots of
their violent break from Britain, building a new community of Patriots at home entailed purging it—with violence, if necessary—
of non-supporters. If the revolution that was started in the name of
liberty was already persecuting, beating, and torturing Loyalists
and condemning some to subterranean oblivion even well before
most Patriots seriously contemplated independence, what else did
the American insurgency have in store for its domestic enemies?
And when would the king and the Empire, in whose loyal service these British-Americans were suffering, finally come to their
rescue?

CHAPTER TWO

Britain's Dilemma

JOHN MALCOM, THE CUSTOMS OFFICIAL TARRED, FEATHERED, and beaten in Boston in January 1774, had spent two months in bedridden agony. But once he was well enough, John bid farewell to his wife, Sarah, and their five children and caught passage to England, taking with him strips of his cracked, feather-caked, putrid skin. That winter, members of the British government and Parliament would find pieces of Malcom's skin enclosed with the petitions he sent them, a grotesque proof of his loyalty. During a reception at St James's Palace in January 1775, Malcom displayed a sense of the absurd when he requested that George III appoint him the "Single Knight of the Tarr, that I was so Tarrd with for I Like the Smell of it." Such a distinction would "do Me Great Honour in North America and in a Great Measure Retaliate for all my Losses and Sufferings."[1]

At a distance of 3,000 miles, and with a lag of many weeks before colonial news reached London, ordinary Britons might have felt far removed from outbursts of colonial violence. But even well before Malcom arrived in England, graphic newspaper accounts had already been feeding the public's imagination. The London press helped readers feel Malcom's pain, allowing them to share vicariously in this episode unfolding on the other side of the Atlantic. Let "any man sitting by his own fire-side, surrounded by his family, read the treatment this unfortunate man met with," suggested one writer, "and let him conceive himself in his situation, and then let him judge what punishment is due to the miscreants at Boston, who used him so barbarously." The "atrocious deed, barbarous as it is," was sadly not uncommon in Boston, that hotbed of early colonial protest.[2]

In addition to press reports, three different prints published in London in the fall of 1774 depicted the various stages of Malcom's ordeal in Boston earlier that year. In *The Bostonians Paying the Excise-Man, or Tarring & Feathering*, a sailor, a tradesman, a man wearing ministerial clothes, and two others are compelling the tarred and feathered customs officer to imbibe tea beneath a Liberty Tree equipped with a noose. In the background, a montage of visual clues reminds the viewer how the Anglo-American conflict had evolved over the previous decade: the Stamp Act placard on the tree is reversed to indicate its repeal in 1766; men masquerading as Native Americans are dumping tea into the harbor. Carington Bowles's *A New Method of Macarony Making, as practised at Boston* suggests Malcom's imminent hanging, preceded again by the forced ingestion of tea.[3]

As 1774 turned to 1775, it was increasingly difficult for the

Philip Dawe, attr., The Bostonians Paying the Excise-Man, or Tarring & Feathering *(London, Oct. 1774).*

Carington Bowles, A New Method of Macarony Making, as practised at Boston *(London, Oct. 1774). In mid-eighteenth-century Britain, a macaroni was a fop with affected mannerisms, dress, and hairstyle.*

British to write off Malcom's case as a regrettable exception—of a minor imperial official with a long history of misconduct enraging some locals after being caught striking a boy. For by now the British leadership had credible evidence that the Americans were preparing for all-out war. And Malcom claimed to have been the very first man in America to have been tarred and feathered specifically for taking a stance against the brewing rebellion. As the crisis with the colonies escalated over subsequent months, many more stories of Revolutionary violence began to circulate in London. To those wishing to uphold British order in America, what seemed particularly disturbing about these accounts was the range of victims: not just customs officials going about the Empire's controversial business, or their local informants, but also printers, Anglican clergymen, and increasingly even ordinary British-Americans. Parliamentarians who advocated harsher measures to call the colonists to reason referred to the volatile situation in cities such as Boston, where any political dissenter was at risk of being tarred and feathered or having his house daubed, or covered with tar or excrement. Prime Minister Lord North evoked the image of Malcom enduring "greater cruelty than any that went before" when he introduced the Boston Port Bill in the House of Commons.[4]

By 1775, then, both British leaders and the informed public knew that America's Loyalists were in trouble. They suspected (as we must) that their various sources of news about the colonies—official dispatches and government intercepts, eyewitness accounts, and reports in the Anglo-American press—were not always reliable. But with cases like John Malcom's fresh in Britons' minds, the Loyalists' precarious situation soon received attention at the highest level of imperial governance. When, in August 1775, King George III finally declared the American insurgents to be in "open and avowed Rebellion," he specifically condemned their "Oppression of Our loyal Subjects." It was George's self-professed royal duty, he said, to shield Loyalists from the "Torrent of Violence" that was engulfing them.[5]

Protecting loyal Americans would need to be a critical part of any strategy to reassert Britain's dominance in America. The king and ministers trusted overly optimistic briefings from British governors and early Loyalist exiles in London, which suggested that the vast majority of Americans remained faithful to Britain and would mobilize to assist invading British soldiers to defeat the rebellious minority. British leaders were right to be concerned about the safety and well-being of loyal subjects in America. Evidence was fast accumulating that the Patriots were tightening their net of surveillance.[6]

Indeed, Britain's political class was rapidly being sensitized to new forms and degrees of political violence in the colonies. Politicians in London were already encountering "many worthy Men who have been forced to abandon their Homes in almost every part of the Continent to avoid Confinement, Confiscation of Goods & even Corporal Punishment." These frightened Loyalist exiles were eyewitnesses to the mounting Patriot violence against internal enemies. British merchants read similar stories in the letters of their concerned American trading partners. Britons of various classes met colonial Americans who had arrived voluntarily on the eve of war and now worried about Loyalist family back home. As the twenty-year-old Bostonian Mary Murray, who was visiting England, struggled to keep in touch with family members from Massachusetts to Florida, she learned of relatives who had been dispossessed or even imprisoned; an uncle had become the victim of the "violence of a[n] outrageous Mob."[7]

For those without access to such personal testimonials, British newspapers reprinted items from the American Loyalist press alongside letters to the editor that found the rebels guilty of "unheard-of-cruelties." Readers scanned litanies of abuse of imperial officials, clergymen, and ordinary Loyalists—from the poisoning of their animals to the practice of "extorting from them, by tortures of various kinds, a public recantation." Already, Southern colonies were apparently starting to execute Loyalists. In other accounts, individuals refusing to endorse the Continental Association were threatened with physical abuse, the destruction of their property, and even—although this may be apocryphal—live burial.[8]

As in Malcom's case, cartoons, too, helped their viewers in Britain imagine how the tense political atmosphere affected virtually all areas of life in the colonies. *The Patriotick Barber of New York*, published in London in February 1775, refuses to finish shaving a customer after learning of his identity: Captain John Crozer, commander of HM transport *Empress of Russia*. On the back wall, portraits of Patriot heroes, including the former British prime minister William Pitt, Earl of Chatham, are framed by a speech of Chatham's and the Articles of Association.

Prints such as *The Alternative of Williams-Burg*, a mezzotint also circulating in London in early 1775, suggested that the Revolutionaries ruled by threats and terror. It shows a Virginian Loyalist in the capitol courtyard in Williamsburg signing a document under duress, perhaps a confession and an apology, or a declaration of loyalty, issued by the Williamsburg Convention. A crowd of Liberty men menacingly wield clubs. At left, a man is being moved

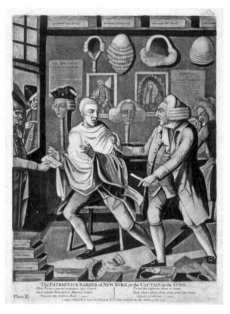

Philip Dawe, The Patriotick Barber of New York, or
the Captain in the Suds *(London, Feb. 1775).*

Philip Dawe, The Alternative of Williams-Burg *(London, Feb. 1775).*

towards a gallows—labeled "a cure for the refractory"—that towers in the background, with a bag of feathers and a barrel oozing tar dangling from it. Referencing admired British politicians, the print features the statue of Norborne Berkeley, 4th Baron Botetourt, a recent royal governor of Virginia, and, by way of the gift of the tobacco barrel, London's radical Lord Mayor, John Wilkes.[9]

Attentive readers of the newspapers learned that different regions in the American colonies specialized in different types of abuse. One technique particularly common in New York involved mobs carrying Loyalists through the streets on fence rails. In early 1775, a London newspaper gave its readers a graphic description of what such a rail riding entailed. The rebels fixed a man with his legs across the beam,

> and in that situation danced him up and down on the sharp points, till he could hold out no longer, being nearly killed with the extremity of the torture inflicted on the tenderest parts. I have seen the man; he is scarce able to move; he is a shocking spectacle; a mortification of the parts is dreaded. His wife says, if he lives, he will never be good for any thing; and she spoke it feelingly, with tears in her eyes. This most cruel of tortures, this most execrable villainy, is admired by the rebels as a grand exploit.[10]

Many a rail-riding procession involved other humiliations: victims might be stripped naked; have stones, eggs, or garbage thrown at them; or be forced to swallow large quantities of tea. The assailants eventually let most of their victims go, although sometimes only after throwing them into a river or a harbor basin. As with tarring and feathering, few who underwent these painful, traumatizing rituals of humiliation ever returned to their former communities.[11]

For a British government facing far-reaching decisions about political strategy—and soon about war—colonial governors, private citizens, and the print media were important yet imperfect sources of intelligence. In the spring of 1775, the administration therefore ordered the secret interception of all private correspondence arriving from New York and Charleston. The General Post Office employed openers, decipherers, translators, and copyists who were trained to break seals, copy large amounts of writing quickly, and forward the resealed letters to their addressees. A little-known stash of these intercepts surviving in British archives conveys the climate of suspicion and insecurity that was taking hold in the colonies. As the government learned from thus spying on its subjects, people on both sides of the Atlantic were already acutely aware of the risk that the rebels would begin intercepting correspondence as well. Some took precautionary measures, such as not signing their letters, employing personal couriers to convey the most sensitive information, or begging their correspondents to censor themselves: "P.S. For my sake pray write me nothing you would not all the World should see." By September 1775, the official in charge of coordinating intercepts realized that "the Caution in writing is excessive." But, confirming the public papers' alarming news, one man's unsigned letter was forthright about violence engulfing the colonies: "The poor proscribed Tories are hunted and worried like Beasts of Prey."[12]

Viewed from London, a picture was building up of loyal British-Americans living under mounting duress. Unless Anglo-American tensions could be defused soon, Britain would likely need to intervene militarily to protect one group of (loyal) subjects from violent treatment by another (rebellious) group. The country's leaders, therefore, faced a dilemma: they needed to crush the incipient insurgency, but in a way that would maximize the chances of reintegrating already deeply divided colonies under the imperial umbrella.

The choice to go to war, then, put the *calibration* of British violence at center stage—both in the deliberations of leaders and in the broader public debate about the Anglo-American crisis. What violent tactics could the British political leadership embrace, and to what degree? Which ways and means of war would the wider public tolerate? And when the conflict came to its end, how could harmony between two increasingly bitter and alienated groups of British-Americans be restored? Any strategy to win the war had to consider how best to win a sustainable peace as well.

War, in the words of the British military historian Sir Michael Howard, is a "highly social activity [that] involves the reciprocal use of organized force between two or more social groups, directed according to an overall plan . . . for the achievement of a political object." The force used in war is "violent, purposeful, deliberate and legitimized." By the late eighteenth century, European lawyers and officers shared certain legal, political, and ethical understandings of the limits of that force. These "codes of war" distinguish between legitimate and illegitimate methods of waging war, proscribing excessive violence, or cruelty, against enemy combatants, captives, and civilians. Hence, for instance, the requirement to grant quarter to a surrendering enemy, and the conventions governing the treatment of enemy prisoners.[13]

How the British viewed the Anglo-American conflict, what kinds and levels of violence they felt justified in using against the enemy, and what codes of war they recognized depended to a significant extent on how they answered one particular question: Who exactly were the Americans? American identity was a complex matter, with constitutional, cultural, economic, ideological, and emotional dimensions. Until the middle of the eighteenth century, the British saw American colonists as fellow Britons, who were "of the same language, the same religion, the same manners and customs [and who] spring from the same nation, intermixed by relation and consanguinity." The colonists, too, thought of themselves primarily as British subjects living as "Americans"—by the late eighteenth century a common term—or as colonial residents in the North American part of the Empire. They felt tied to Britain through the Crown and a shared heritage of political rights that they traced back to the Magna Carta, English common law, and the achievements of England's seventeenth-century revolutions. These bonds were reinforced by a flourishing trade and, at an elite level, by Anglicized cultures of gentility and consumption, epitomized by the ritual of tea drinking and the ceramic and silver paraphernalia that graced drawing rooms from Bath to Boston.[14]

At the same time, many in Britain increasingly noticed differences. As a frontier people, the colonials seemed less polished, less well educated, less widely traveled. The transportation of convicts from the British Isles, large-scale immigration from other countries, and the presence of a quarter of a million African slaves had diluted the colonists' Britishness. In the wake of its global triumphs in the Seven Years' War, Britain asserted a more exclusive patriotism. The English, pronounced one high-ranking official, considered the British-Americans, "though H.M.'s subjects, as foreigners." Americans could now be seen, writes the historian Stephen Conway, "less as distant parts of the same nation and more as another set of people to be ruled." Such condescension helped the British imagine separation and support a hard-line approach towards colonial insurgency, although it also fed conflicting sentiments. Whether they emphasized similarity or difference, however, both groups recognized the American Revolution as a civil war within the British Empire—rebellious colonials until 1776; Loyalists and the British until 1783.[15]

Given that it touched on such sensitive matters of identity, it is hardly surprising that the American crisis constituted one of the most divisive issues Britain had encountered in the eighteenth century. During 1775 alone, well over 40,000 individuals signed addresses to the king and petitions to Parliament either for or against the use of force in America. Moreover, nearly half of the counties and boroughs that sent such petitions submitted documents at once for *and* against subduing the rebellion. Partisan newspapers amplified these divisions. Non-Anglican Protestants, as well as shopkeepers and artisans in towns and cities, tended to sympathize with the American rebels and, like the Protestant Irish, opposed going to war. But most of the Anglican clergy, as well as attorneys, customs and excise officers, and other professionals and gentlemen living in cities, favored the use of force, as did a majority of Scots and inhabitants of northern English counties.[16]

The American crisis divided even the British Army. Most of the officers ordered to serve in America did eventually obey, among them several critics of coercion. When faced with tough choices, loyalty to the Crown seemed to prevail over personal political preferences, at least among the largely aristocratic officer corps. But several officers in the king's service felt that they could no longer reconcile their duties as commissioned officers and as British citizens. They included aristocratic scions, career soldiers, and political reformers. Proportionately, twice as many officers resigned their commissions near the start of the American Revolutionary War than had done in the Seven Years' War.[17]

One officer's decision to step down whipped up particularly high waves. The Earl of Effingham, an ambitious career officer from a military family, resigned the moment his regiment was ordered to America in April 1775. Emphasizing his fierce allegiance to the king and the immense personal sacrifice he was making, Effingham explained that his conscience forbade him from bearing arms "against my fellow subjects in America." When his duties as soldier and citizen conflicted, the latter must always trump the former, until they could be reconciled again in a war against Britain's "real enemies" (meaning her historic Gallic foe). Effingham felt Britain's strategic-moral dilemma on an intensely personal level; he resolved it by refusing to get embroiled in an imperial civil war. As Effingham's decision became known across the British Atlantic world, it instantly made him an icon of American Patriots, who named armed boats after him. He also won the adulation of British war critics, who thanked Effingham in very public ways for courageously taking a principled stance as an Englishman by refusing to "imbrue his hands in the blood of his fellow-subjects."[18]

Against this background of deepening divisions, an inner circle of policy makers in London confronted critical decisions. At one end of the spectrum, hard-liners advocated the use of extreme punitive force to crush the colonial insurgency, in line with the ways that Britain (or other European powers, for that matter) had responded to earlier rebellions. At the opposite end stood leaders who proposed conciliation, not war, or who suggested that minimal force be deployed to pressure the colonists to negotiate a settlement. Members of this latter group were motivated by both political expediency and humanitarianism, suggesting that only if the army showed consideration towards civilians could the support of the Loyalists be permanently secured and any deluded rebels be won back.[19]

The stakes for the British Empire were extremely high. King George III was concerned for the dignity of his crown and took seriously his royal duty to protect loyal subjects who were under duress overseas. He also shared with other British leaders a commitment to the principle of parliamentary sovereignty. There was, furthermore, Britain's international standing and wealth to consider. The monarch and many of his ministers worried that the loss of America would not only deal a devastating blow in its own right but might also loosen the country's grip on Ireland and the British West Indies. Finally, once leaders began to plan military actions, Britain's reputation as a humane and civilized empire would come under scrutiny. For if the British wanted to maintain their legitimacy in the eyes of Europe, would they not need to demonstrate their continued commitment to moderation and civility, even—or especially—in war?[20]

The Dye Is Now Cast

George III had ascended the British throne in 1760 at the age of twenty-three. After a rocky first decade characterized by constant changes of government, by the eve of the American Revolution George had grown into a seasoned politician. Serious-minded, with a powerful sense of royal duty, the king possessed a strong work ethic and a clear Christian moral compass. As ruler, George took a close interest in foreign policy and military affairs. He would keep tabs on the planning and conduct of the American war. In the early stages of the escalating crisis, George III had exerted a moderating influence on some of his ministers' more extreme proposals. But after insurgents had destroyed private property in the Boston Tea Party in 1773, the king embraced a more punitive approach.[21]

And yet no one perhaps felt the growing rift between the mother country and the colonies more intensely, and on a more personal level, than George. It was a political commonplace that the king was the father of his subjects, British and colonial. He was in charge of their welfare; as his children, they owed him love and obedience. Pre-Revolutionary America, well into the early 1770s, in fact displayed a heightened emphasis on royalist ritual and symbolism, as shown, for example, in celebrations of the monarch's birthday. Against this background, rebellious colonials appeared to the king like spoiled, ungrateful children. The Revolutionaries in turn charged that their king did not allow them to grow and flourish: to them, the benevolent father was turning into a cruel, tyrannical figure.[22]

Benjamin West, George III *(1779). The Pennsylvania-born Benjamin West, a founding member (and later president) of the Royal Academy of Arts, maintained good professional and personal relations with his royal patron throughout the American Revolution. Halfway through the war, and probably for the Audience Chamber at Hampton Court Palace, West portrayed the monarch as a military commander wearing a uniform and the star and sash of the Order of the Garter. The crown, orb, and scepter are placed on a table at left. In the far background is a military encampment by the seashore; the* Royal George *is firing a salute.*

For George III, the idea of the nation as a family with him at the head was more than a political metaphor. As the king's most psychologically astute modern biographer, Stella Tillyard, describes it:

> A loving and tender father to young children and to his siblings as long as they remained dutiful and loyal, George had never . . . developed any means of negotiating and compromising with those in his family . . . who wanted to live in different ways than the ones he thought the best for them. Towards his American subjects he behaved in exactly the same way. As his children, and like his children, they must be brought to acknowledge their duty to their father and their king. If honour would not bring them back to their motherland, then force must do so instead.

The American crisis escalated just as the king's younger brothers rebelled against his authority as head of the royal family. So, "when the American men and women who were a part of his family repudiated his fatherly love and protection," concludes Tillyard, "it almost broke him." At the same time, George's sense of obligation towards his faithful Loyalist children became perhaps even more pronounced.[23]

Serving the king as first minister was one of the country's most experienced politicians, Frederick North, known as Lord North, who had been in the role since 1770. Six years older than the monarch, North enjoyed the king's trust and friendship. While North was clear about the need to uphold the principle of parliamentary sovereignty, he was much less certain about how best to achieve that objective. Generous observers saw North, a moderate by temperament, as seeking to balance firmness with compromise while also defending his parliamentary majority. Opponents, though, portrayed him as dithering at best and, at worst, lacking principles and a coherent plan. An effective, witty, and frequent orator—he gave several hundred parliamentary speeches in his first four years as prime minister—and adept at managing the House of

Commons, North would be the first to admit that he was not well suited as a wartime leader.[24]

Even as his prime minister was still grasping at the last conciliatory straws, the king forged ahead with his coercive mission: "The dye is now cast," George told North in September 1774, "the Colonies must either submit or triumph. I do not wish to come to severer measures, but we must not retreat." By late January 1775, the king's government, having received intelligence that the American rebels were arming themselves and preparing to attack Boston, sent new orders to Lieutenant General Thomas Gage, the British commander in chief in North America, who had also replaced Hutchinson as governor of the Province of Massachusetts Bay. Gage was now to receive significant reinforcements and arrest the leaders of the Provincial Congress of Massachusetts if it convened again. He was authorized to use military force as necessary to quash the rebellion in that commonwealth, and in neighboring Connecticut and Rhode Island. But by now Gage's own subordinates felt that their commander—who was married to a well-connected woman from New Jersey—was unsuited to the task of ending the rebellion. In February—around the same time that the government's lawyers ruled that the Provincial Congress of Massachusetts was guilty of treason—George III personally selected several officers to support Gage in America. These officers were also Members of Parliament, and as such held their own political views on how the Empire should deal with rebellious colonies.[25]

George III's choice for General Gage's number two, General William Howe, soon to be the new British commander in chief in America, embodied the equivocation of British leadership. Howe was the third son of the 2nd Viscount Howe, an Irish peer and colonial governor, and his wife, Charlotte, whose (illegitimate) royal blood blended with her husband's aristocratic pedigree to give their offspring a privileged start in life. But what the historian David Hackett Fischer has written of William's elder brother, Richard, whom we shall soon encounter as Britain's new top naval commander in

The Hon. Sir Willm. Howe Kt. of the Bath, Commander in Chief of all his Majesty's Forces in America *[1780].*

America, is equally true of William: his "opportunities came by privilege, but his achievements were won by merit." Both brothers grew up to be tall, athletic, and of a swarthy complexion; both were known to be taciturn. Both forged stellar military careers, serving with valor and distinction in the Seven Years' War and gaining experience at the tactical cutting edge of imperial warfare in North America and the Caribbean. Richard rose to become the navy's youngest admiral and acquired a reputation as a humanitarian who cared for the welfare of his crew and as an innovator in the design of boats and weapons as well as in command and control. William developed light infantry tactics that were uniquely valuable in North American terrain. Like Richard a reformer, William was invested in improving training and discipline.[26]

Richard and William's oldest brother, George Augustus, the 3rd Viscount Howe, had been killed in the Seven Years' War, falling at Ticonderoga in 1758. When the Massachusetts assembly commis-

sioned a monument to commemorate him, Richard, now the 4th
Viscount, oversaw its erection in Westminster Abbey. Over subsequent decades, Richard and William would honor their brother's
memory by retaining their affection for the colonies, especially
the people of Massachusetts. In 1757 and 1758, respectively, the
Howes entered Parliament, where their stance on America was
deeply ambivalent. They strongly supported Parliament's absolute sovereignty and Britain's imperial mission. At the same time,
they opposed the Coercive Acts, the punitive legislation passed in
response to the Boston Tea Party that ultimately prompted the
Continental Association. Instead, they favored conciliatory measures towards the colonies. Right up to William's appointment as
the army's second-in-command in America, Richard facilitated secret talks with Benjamin Franklin in London. But when all signs
pointed to war in the winter of 1774–75, the brothers were poised
once more to serve their king. In the late summer of 1774, William
(now Major General Howe) had put several companies of light
infantry through intensive training exercises on Salisbury Plain.
When a special demonstration was arranged for George III, the
impressive display no doubt recommended Howe to his monarch.[27]

Like Howe, the second major general George III chose in early
1775 also approached his mission with mixed feelings. John Burgoyne had first entered Parliament in 1761 (just after the Howes)
and subsequently opposed the repeal of the Stamp Act and supported the Declaratory Act and the Coercive Acts. By the early
1770s, Burgoyne's approach mirrored George III's, seeing in America "a child who had been ruined by the misplaced indulgence,
'lenity and tenderness' of Britain." Still, Burgoyne's preference
until well into 1775 continued to be a negotiated settlement.[28]

But Burgoyne was also a tremendously ambitious man. Of
military stock, he, like the Howes, had made a reputation for
himself in the Seven Years' War. In 1772, the year that Burgoyne
(like William Howe) was promoted to major general, George III
elevated Burgoyne's regiment to a royal unit, the Queen's Light
Dragoons—a rare distinction. When the government approached
Burgoyne about a subordinate command in America, Burgoyne

Sir Joshua Reynolds, General John Burgoyne *(circa 1766). Contemporaries often lampooned Burgoyne, the tall, handsome officer-politician-playwright who openly indulged his love of gambling, drink, and women. Portrayed here in the uniform of the 16th Light Dragoons at the height of his early career, Burgoyne is today best remembered for surrendering a British army at Saratoga in 1777.*

hesitated at first but was swayed when he was told that the king had personally selected him.

Before leaving for America, Burgoyne did something that no other senior commander had dared: he used his dual role as an army officer and a Member of Parliament to justify Britain's American mission in the House of Commons. Burgoyne reassured Parliament and the wider public that they need not worry that British commanders in America "might be influenced either by inflammatory speeches in favor of violence or by advocates for humiliating concessions." He would combine "bravery and compassion." Yes, the army "would inevitably be made the instrument of correction," but it was his view that it should not indulge in "the sudden and impetuous impulse of passion and revenge." If force must be used, how to justify it and how to calibrate it was of paramount importance. Ultimately, however, "[w]hile we remember that we are contending against brothers and fellow subjects, we must also remember that we are contending in this crisis for the fate of the British Empire." And a civil war, unlike a foreign war, ought to concern the entire nation, not just its leaders. After hinting at the deepening divisions over the American issue, Burgoyne cautioned that a commander in chief in America would require "a genius of the first class, together with uncommon resolution," but also "a firm reliance upon support at home."[29]

Perhaps William Howe ought to have explained himself in Parliament as John Burgoyne did. Howe had previously promised his Nottingham constituents that he would never serve in a war against the American colonials. Within a week of Howe's appointment, Samuel Kirk, a Nottingham grocer, told Howe that the general's decision had let him down: "The most plausible excuse that is made among us, is, that the King sent for you and what could you do?" Howe indeed pleaded patriotic duty, but the grocer was not alone. An anonymous author warned in prominently placed harangues that the Howe family honor was at stake. Should the British be defeated, and Howe "fall ingloriously in the devastation of those fields which your brother so nobly exerted himself in protection of," the "name of Howe will never be mentioned in America without a sigh." Worse still, if instead Howe were to "deluge the continent of America in blood," then he would suffer in the afterlife for his crimes against nature and humanity.[30]

When even the second-in-command was publicly chastised for accepting his king's commission to serve in America, and when some naval and military officers risked their careers over the American issue, the political fault lines were clearly deepening. What British partisans could agree on across the aisle was that the emerging conflict seemed "unnatural": to loyal supporters of the Crown's aggressive stance, it felt like an unnatural rebellion, while advocates of peaceful conciliation saw it as an unnatural civil war. Indeed, as one historian has put it, this was the "first time in modern history that a literate public sustained a major, widespread critique of their government's use of military force as a tool of public policy." The issue's divisiveness further exacerbated the dilemma that America posed for Britain's decision makers. The tough counterinsurgency tactics favored by the king and some of his advisors were unlikely to guarantee unity at home—and domestic discord could, in turn, affect the war overseas.[31]

The Butchery of a Civil War

During the spring of 1775, British leaders and the wider public became aware of reports that the American insurgents had not only started to engage the British Army, but that in doing so they had apparently violated the codes of civilized warfare. It was at the end of May that the British first learned that skirmishes between redcoats and American rebels had taken place in Lexington and Concord, outside Boston, on April 19. As would eventually become known, seventy-three British soldiers and forty-nine colonial militiamen had been killed and several hundred men wounded.[32]

Just as in the aftermath of the Boston Massacre five years earlier, a fierce rhetorical battle would accompany this violent event and those that followed. In the wake of Lexington and Concord, the American rebels circulated colorful allegations of British atrocities against American militia and civilians. Given the traction that the earliest, unverified reports of such atrocities gained in parts of the British press (the *Stamford Mercury* even alleged a massacre), the rebels could claim a polemical and political success. London's Constitutional Society advertised a subscription to benefit the widows, orphans, and aged parents "of our BELOVED American Fellow Subjects, who, FAITHFUL to the character of Englishmen, preferring Death to Slavery, were, for that reason only, inhuman[e]ly murdered by the KING's Troops," a phrasing that led to the war's only libel conviction in Britain.[33]

As the conflict's first major battle for public opinion was being waged, the British government under Prime Minister North's still-reluctant leadership accelerated preparations for full-scale war. In early July 1775, the Admiralty sent new orders to the British squadron in America. The navy was instructed to work with the army to crush the rebellion by protecting Loyalists and their property. British warships were to retaliate against towns that were obviously in rebellion against the Crown and its servants. And the navy was authorized to destroy rebel merchantmen and naval vessels. Rebel sailors were to be impressed (i.e., forcibly enrolled) in the Royal Navy and supplies commandeered as required. By the fall, the first American coastal towns would stand in flames.[34]

But even before the Admiralty's orders reached British commanders, news of Britain's Pyrrhic victory at Boston's Bunker Hill (June 17) arrived in London. It was July 25, and Parliament was in recess. Cabinet members rushed from the countryside to meet in the capital. Stunned ministers read in General Howe's dispatches that the loss of so many officers at Bunker Hill had filled him with horror. With hindsight it would become clear that more than one-eighth of all British officers killed in the entire war had indeed died at Bunker Hill or as a result of injuries received that day. Although rumors of poisoned musket balls remained unproven, it appeared that the Americans had charged some of their muskets with old nails and other pieces of iron and directed them at the legs of their British opponents in order to maim them. General Sir Henry Clinton observed that a "few more such victories would soon put an end to British domination in America." Another British officer judged: "The Rubicon is now passed & matters are become very serious indeed."[35]

When some two hundred survivors of Bunker Hill disembarked on England's south coast at the end of the summer, Britons at home caught their first glimpse of the reality of war against the American insurgents. Newspapers covered the veterans' arrival, "some without legs, and others without arms; and their cloaths hanging on them like a loose morning gown, so much are they fallen away by sickness and want of proper nourishment," all stepping off a vessel wrapped in an unbearable stench from their wounds, making for "a most shocking spectacle." According to the morale-boosting gloss of some papers, those wounded heroes were all said to be hoping defiantly "for the use again of their limbs, to employ them against the Americans, whom they call a set of villains, and the most inhuman of enemies."[36]

In the eyes of British hard-liners, the tales of atrocity that emerged from Lexington and Bunker Hill reinforced long-standing prejudices against the colonial military. British officers and troops felt that American insurgents were fighting with unfair, ungentlemanly tactics—firing from behind walls and hedges, aiming at sentries and officers, using sham surrenders—that amounted to an "unmanly and infamous kind of War, which no civilized nation will allow. An uncommon Spirit of Murder & Cruelty seems to actuate them in all their Proceedings." In short, Britons did not consider colonial soldiers part of what the historian Stephen Conway has called "military Europe," that fraternity of European standing armies sharing similar ranks, weapons, tactics, and dress—and a commitment to the codes of war. It was now not only their treatment of American Loyalists that put the rebels beyond the pale: it was also their use of illegitimate violence against the redcoats. At the same time, the Revolutionaries demonized the British for the allegedly barbarous conduct of "King George's plundering, murdering army."[37]

With the positions staked out, and mutual allegations aired in public, intercepted correspondence showed that private citizens on both sides of the Atlantic already had apocalyptic visions of the "Sea of Blood" that would result from such an unnatural civil war. If the British government continued "to breathe Vengeance, Fire & Sword ag:st the Colonies," not just America, but the British Empire, too, would suffer the horrific consequences. Yet after Lexington and Bunker Hill, one American correspondent after another also stressed something else—namely, the unifying impact that British aggression seemed to have from New England to South Carolina. The "[v]oice from one Extreme of British America to the other is," asserted one New Yorker, "[w]e have nothing to depend on but our united Virtue, & a vigorous Opposition—The Time is come, the Sword must determine whether we are to enjoy Liberty, or Slavery."[38]

Royal governors and early Loyalist exiles were continuing to feed the administration in London reports of Americans' overwhelming loyalty. But the government's own secret intercepts painted a very different picture of the colonial reality. Ministers thus informed General Gage that, if Boston were to be abandoned, the king insisted "care must be taken that the Officers and friends of government be not left exposed to the rage and insult of rebels who set no bounds to their barbarity." That fall of 1775, British leaders further escalated the conflict by issuing a proclamation authorizing an entirely different kind of war, one that permitted levels of violence considered unacceptable in conventional armed conflicts between European nations.[39]

Open and Avowed Rebellion

What American insurgents justified as lawful resistance to imperial tyranny their sovereign saw as treachery. As early as the Boston Tea Party in late 1773, some British politicians had called for heads to roll. One peer of the realm suggested: "Hang, draw, and quarter fifty of them." On August 23, 1775, after George III refused to receive the Olive Branch Petition that the Continental Congress had sent him in July in a last-ditch effort to avert war, the Privy Council issued a proclamation "for suppressing rebellion and sedition." It declared that the Americans were now in "an open and avowed rebellion by . . . traitorously preparing, ordering, and levying war against us." When the American insurgents learned that the king had refused to receive their loyal petition and instead declared them rebels, the more radically minded became committed to the goal of cutting ties with the Empire.[40]

Moderates still continued to appeal to the British people. Three days after agreeing to petition the king, the Continental Congress had also addressed the inhabitants of Great Britain on behalf of "your American brethren." Laying out their constitutional and economic grievances and their fears of enslavement by a cruel, tyrannical regime, the colonials pleaded with their British fellow subjects. Did not their common ancestry, their traditions of political liberty, and the blood they had shed in the Empire's previous wars bind them together? And was there not a risk that "[s]oldiers who have sheathed their swords in the bowels of their American brethren" would next turn them on their fellow citizens at home? Exactly one year later, Congress would recite these futile appeals to the British people when justifying America's leap into independence.[41]

The implications of the king's official declaration were stark, for rebellious combatants and captives stood outside the conventions that governed Britain's wars with foreign enemies. Rebels could be tried in courts and, if convicted, executed for treason. It was that convention that General Gage, anticipating the king's proclamation, referred to when he told the newly appointed American commander in chief, General George Washington, that any enemy captives the British were holding were, by law, not prisoners of war but rebels, and as such "destined to the cord."[42]

For Britons, the most pertinent example of insurgency in living memory was the 1745 rebellion of the Jacobites, supporters of the exiled Stuart dynasty that had been ousted from the thrones of England and Scotland in the late seventeenth century. After that so-called '45, the British Army had arrested thousands of Jacobites as criminals, brought several hundred of them to trial, and hanged or beheaded between 80 and 120 as traitors; some were drawn and quartered. Similar numbers perished in prisons and on prison ships. To George II's army, Highland Jacobites were not only rebels but also savages. This stereotype justified a war *in terrorem*, intended to inspire fear in the enemy. The customary codes of war were suspended and unrestrained violence was unleashed: the systematic destruction of houses, farms, and livestock; a grain embargo aimed at starving the rebels; bounties for the heads of Highland clan chiefs; sexual assault on women and girls.[43]

Several British leaders who were involved in the escalating American crisis in the 1770s had helped suppress those Jacobites thirty years earlier. These included Generals Thomas Gage and Charles Grey, as well as Lord George Germain, soon to be Britain's new secretary of state for America. Scots, who had experienced the Crown's response to rebellion firsthand, were disproportionately represented in the British Army, including among officers serving in North America during the Revolution. Could the brutal suppression of the '45 and its quasi-genocidal aftermath be a strategic model to follow in North America? The answer depended in part on whether the objective was peace through conciliation or pacification through terror and devastation. Americans were not Highlanders. They were culturally much more similar, motivated by ideas very different from those of the Jacobites, and better armed, too. Some British hard-line officers serving in America nonetheless demanded that Britain shed any "false humanity towards these wretches." They wanted to restore British "dominion of the country by laying it waste, and almost extirpating the present rebellious race." Even conciliators such as Lord North eventually insisted that any rebellion be put down, as the British Crown had done over the centuries in Scotland and Ireland: civil wars "were no novelties in this country. Were not the Irish our fellow-subjects in 1690? Were not the Scotch so in 1715, and 1745? And did any person ever assign it as a reason that those rebellions should not be crushed, because the rebels were our fellow-subjects?"[44]

By the fall of 1775, George III was moving inexorably towards quashing the insurgency. In late October, he laid out his toughened stance in a defining speech to Parliament. The king analyzed the situation in America, where the insurgents "now openly avow their Revolt, Hostility, and Rebellion." They were raising an army, levying taxes, and usurping "Legislative, Executive, and Judicial Powers." In response, the monarch offered a clear sense of mission: he would restore the colonies to obedience and rescue his loyal American subjects from the rebels' violent oppression. He had already increased his armed forces by land and by sea. And his aides were in the process of negotiating troop conventions with foreign powers. By the 1770s, Britain enjoyed a long-standing tradition of hiring foreign troops as auxiliaries to help fight its wars overseas and to crush rebellions closer to home. This was necessary if only because the British constitution did not allow the monarch to keep a large standing army in peacetime. In order to mobilize large forces quickly at the start of a war, he therefore needed to look beyond Britain's shores. In 1775, the British Army could only muster some 36,000 men, including 8,000 in North America; by war's end, there would be 100,000. George III's envoys had held secret negotiations with German representatives as early as the winter of

1774–75, proving that the Crown was seriously exploring the use of military force well before Lexington.[45]

But at the same time that he was beginning to put the country on a war footing, George III now reassured Parliament, he would combine military action against the rebels with magnanimity. Their royal father would receive any repentant colonials with "tenderness and mercy." Opposition politicians nonetheless responded with outrage: "as Englishmen, as Christians, [and] as Men of common Humanity," they objected to "the Prosecution of a cruel Civil War, so little supported by Justice." Despite such vocal dissent, the government carried the day with a handsome majority in support of the king's address.[46]

Two weeks after delivering his aggressive speech to Parliament, in early November 1775 George III masterminded a significant cabinet reshuffle to complete the shift to a more hard-line administration. Most importantly, the monarch elevated Lord George Germain, known already for his tough stance against the American insurgents, to the pivotal position of secretary of state for the American department. It is not surprising that, when George III sought to replace the conciliatory Earl of Dartmouth, he tapped a man who even before Lexington had publicly urged "Roman severity" in suppressing insurrection. Germain now held the single most important cabinet position with responsibility for directing a major British war. It was a remarkable comeback for a man who, born as Lord George Sackville, the third son of the 1st Duke of Dorset, had seen a glittering military career crash under humiliating circumstances fifteen years earlier.[47]

Germain was a man whose "integrity commanded esteem, his abilities praise; but to attract the heart was not one of those abilities"—and that was an admirer speaking. At first, he had done his military ancestors proud. After stints at Westminster School and Trinity College Dublin, and following some administrative experience in Ireland, he had joined the army in 1737. Wounded in the War of Austrian Succession, he had gained firsthand experience with the brutal suppression of domestic insurrection during the Jacobite rebellion. When clansmen raided his baggage train

Johann Jacobé (after George Romney), Lord George Germain, one of his Majesty's Principal Secretaries of State *(London, 1780). Six feet tall and highly intelligent, the British secretary for the American colonies, Lord George Germain, conveyed command and dignity. Like his monarch, Germain believed in answering rebellion with a rigorous counterinsurgency.*

in the aftermath of the Battle of Culloden in 1746, he allowed his men to take revenge at the next settlement: the women were raped in front of their husbands, fathers, and sons. Germain then had the men shot and bayoneted in sight of the already traumatized women. Despite such brutality, Germain's career continued to flourish. A decade later, he served with distinction in the opening campaigns of the Seven Years' War alongside the Howe brothers; by 1757, already a lieutenant general and colonel of the Queen's Bays, Germain seemed on track to become the army's next commander in chief.[48]

Yet in 1759, Britain's year of global triumph against France in theaters from North America to India, Germain suffered a devastating setback. Accused of disobeying a superior officer in the Battle of Minden, in northern Germany, Germain requested a court-martial to clear his name. But as a result of the trial he was dismissed dishonorably, declared unfit to serve the king in any military capacity, and had his name struck from the list of privy councillors at George II's personal request. Humiliated as a gentleman-officer, he doggedly rebuilt a career in public life. Within a few years of George III's accession in 1760, Germain returned to court. Before long, he assumed minor executive positions and was restored to the Privy Council. In Parliament, he carved out a profile as a staunch advocate of firm measures against the troublesome colonies, and by 1774 it was obvious that Germain's approach was close to that of his monarch. After being elevated to secretary of state, a position he would hold until 1782, the veteran of the brutal anti-Jacobite campaign insisted that the American rebellion must be put down decisively. A "sentimental manner of making war" against armed rebels would "not have the desired Effect."[49]

By the time Germain was admitted to the innermost circles of government, mutually reinforcing forms of aggression and violence—imperial oppression, colonial resistance, anti-Loyalist terror, the first Anglo-American military clashes, and the king's declaration of open rebellion—had propelled all sides dangerously close to a full-scale war. Over subsequent years, Germain's travails would embody Britain's deeper strategic and ethical dilemma concerning the forms and levels of violence to deploy against colonial rebels. Halfway through the war, he would help orchestrate a dramatic escalation of the conflict. But even before Germain entered the cabinet in the fall of 1775, the Royal Navy had begun to give Americans a taste of Roman severity.

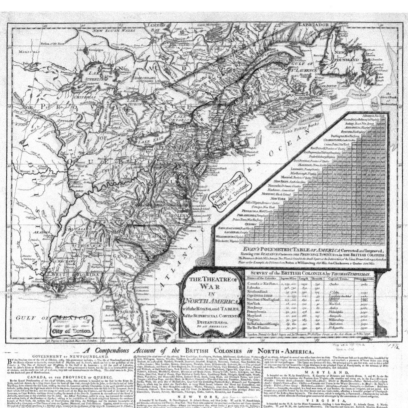

THE THEATRE OF WAR IN NORTH AMERICA, with the ROADS and TABLES of the SUPERFICIAL CONTENTS, DISTANCES, &c. BY AN AMERICAN.

A Compendious Account of the BRITISH COLONIES in NORTH-AMERICA.

Printed for R. SAYER, and J. BENNETT, Map, Chart, and Print Sellers, No. 53, Fleet-Street, London. Price Three Shillings.

CHAPTER THREE

Rubicon

O N OCTOBER 6, 1775, FORTY-ONE-YEAR-OLD CAPTAIN Henry Mowat sailed out of the Boston harbor aboard the armed ship *Canceaux*. Mowat was commanding a mini-squadron of Royal Navy vessels—his own ship, carrying eight guns; the *Halifax*, a schooner with six guns; and two armed transports ferrying some one hundred soldiers. Their mission: to discipline and punish nine coastal towns in Massachusetts, New Hampshire, and Maine by shelling the settlements and destroying vessels in their harbors. Those seaports were hotbeds of colonial resistance and sheltered rebel privateers. It had taken three months for the Admiralty's harsh instructions to reach Vice Admiral Samuel Graves, the commander of Britain's American squadron. His new orders empowered Graves to warn coastal towns to cease immediately any violent actions against Loyalists and British officials. If they failed to comply, Graves was to "proceed, by the most vigorous efforts, against the said Town, as in open Rebellion against the King."[1]

Graves had long wanted to chastise the seaports he knew were home to the American privateers insulting his ships. As tensions escalated, Graves had witnessed "the King's people killed and made prisoners, lighthouses destroyed, commerce interrupted, and the preparations for war daily making in the different towns." It was high time that he neutralize expendable seaports across New England. But dispatching Mowat to execute the Admiralty orders would likely carry a steep human cost—and significant political and moral consequences.[2]

When he was advised that his initial target, Cape Ann, Massachusetts, could not be bombarded effectively, Mowat instead took course for Falmouth (modern Portland, Maine). A successful lumber-trade port with a population of some 2,000, Falmouth had a deep and broad harbor that would allow his ships to shell the two- and three-story wooden buildings along the hillside at close range. The town also had a history of militant rebelliousness dating back to the mid-1760s, when the locals had burned stamped papers, attacked customs officials, and boycotted East India tea. Rebels there had even briefly held Mowat captive in spring 1775. For Mowat, strategic advantage and an opportunity for personal revenge coincided perfectly at Falmouth.

Mowat anchored offshore in the afternoon of October 16 and sent his ranking officer to address the population gathered in the local meetinghouse. Since the inhabitants had "been guilty of the most unpardonable Rebellion," the proclamation read, the king's ships would now "execute a just Punishment." Mowat would grant the locals a brief moratorium to evacuate before the bombardment commenced. As the warning sank in, a "frightful consternation ran through the assembly, every heart was seized with terror, every countenance changed color, and a profound silence ensued for several moments." Residents had only partially evacuated the town when at 9:40 the next morning the Royal Navy demonstrated what havoc even two small ships could wreak.[3]

"Never was there a fairer autumnal day," recollected one witness; "the sky was cloudless; the wind gentle; the atmosphere invigorating." Into this idyllic New England scene, "a shower of cannon-balls, carcasses, bombs, live shells, grape-shot, and even bullets from small-arms, was raining down upon the compact part of the town." Our onlooker experienced the bombardment as sublime, a terrible spectacle that would have been fascinating "but for the wanton destruction the missiles immediately wrought. They crashed through the warehouses, they plowed up the streets, they cut off the limbs of the trees, they sank the shipping, they set fire to the dwellings." To witnesses, these inanimate agents of destruction seemed diabolical as they "screamed and hissed, they whirled

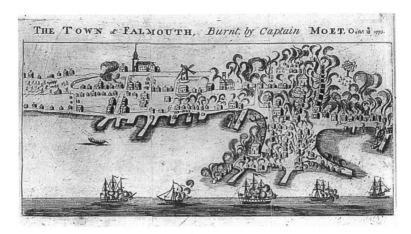

John Norman, The Town of Falmouth, Burnt by Captain Moet, Octbr. 18th 1775 *(Boston, 1782). In a punitive mission in fall 1775, the Royal Navy destroyed large parts of modern Portland, Maine. This fairly crude but effective engraving was published as the frontispiece to an early history of the war when America had all but won the conflict. A bird's-eye view of the bombardment, it remembers Britain's early warfare of desolation that fueled the ire of war critics on both sides of the Atlantic.*

and danced, they shrieked and sung, like so many demons rejoicing over the havoc they were making." Evacuees who were still in the town found that the oxen pulling the carts with their belongings were so "terrified by the smoak and report of the guns" that they "ran with precipitation over the rocks, dashing every thing in pieces, and scattering large quantities of goods about the streets." Seeing that buildings towards the southern part of the town failed to catch fire, Mowat sent landing parties to set alight wharfs and storehouses. The flames kept spreading, fanned by the early afternoon breeze. A Mrs. Barton, whose husband had enlisted with the Continental Army, was home alone with their young son, when "the hot shot and shells began to fall near, and several of the neighboring buildings were on fire." Gathering just a few pieces of clothing, she and the boy evacuated a mile away, braving what must have felt like an endless obstacle course; several times, bombs with still-smoking fuses fell near her.[4]

Even as the attack was under way, Patriot militias from nearby Brunswick and Scarborough were slipping into Falmouth. Envious of the town's commercial wealth, and frustrated by its mixed politics, the militias looted the property of suspected Loyalists. And although Graves had reassured the Admiralty that he had ordered Mowat to "protect the persons and property" of Loyalists, British shells did not discriminate between Patriot and Loyalist targets.[5]

During nine hours of pandemonium, more than 3,000 projectiles hit Falmouth, one every eleven seconds. Eleven ships were destroyed; Mowat captured an additional four in the harbor. The day after, the log of the attacking ship *Canceaux* noted that fires continued to burn in the town. When it was all over, roughly three-quarters of the buildings lay in ashes—including the Episcopal church, the new courthouse, the old meetinghouse, the distillery, most wharves, almost every store—and some 160 families would begin the winter without shelter.[6]

Rumors flew of similar squadrons setting a course for towns up and down the New England coast. Benjamin Franklin considered safeguarding his writings and accounts and suggested that his daughter evacuate her family even from faraway Philadelphia. But before the Royal Navy could destroy any more towns, Britain's escalation of violence produced an immediate backlash, both in America and at home. The American Patriot press denounced Mowat as a monster. Falmouth bolstered the case for independence a full nine months before that notion became a reality. "The savage and brutal barbarity of our enemies in burning Falmouth," wrote the *New-England Chronicle* as early as October 19, proved that Britain was "fully determined with fire and sword, to butcher and destroy, beggar and enslave the whole American people. Therefore we expect soon to break off all kinds of connection with Britain, and form into a Grand Republic of the American Colonies." News of the highly localized attack spread fast and far. John Adams, then at the Congress in Philadelphia, received numerous letters whose authors interpreted the destruction of Falmouth as a declaration of war, or at least as a clear indication of the malicious intent of the *"British barbarians."*[7]

One man who took a special interest in the events at Falmouth was General George Washington. Just four months earlier, the

Continental Congress had elected the delegate from Virginia as commander in chief of all American forces. Washington, who always claimed he had not sought the appointment, was a natural choice: few colonial men possessed his military experience or his reputation for skill and courage in the field. A key political reason for his selection was that a Southerner was needed to "nationalize" America's struggle, given New England's disproportionate influence in the early days of the rebellion. Washington's character and his personal values were crucial, too: contemporaries described him as temperate, earnest, and prudent, with a commanding and dignified presence. Washington embodied what John Adams called the "great, manly, warlike virtues." "There is not a king in

Charles Willson Peale, George Washington *(1776). John Hancock, the president of the Continental Congress, commissioned this portrait of Washington as commander in chief. One of the most politically engaged artists of his generation, in 1776 Peale enrolled in the Pennsylvania militia; the following year he was at the Battle of Princeton. During the Revolution, Peale served on thirty committees, as agent for confiscated Loyalist estates in Philadelphia, and as a representative in the state legislature. When Martha Washington asked Peale to paint her a miniature of her husband, he modeled it on this portrait.*

Europe," said Dr. Benjamin Rush, a future signatory to the Declaration of Independence, "that would not look like a valet de chamber by his side."[8]

Congress had instructed Washington to "regulate your conduct in every respect by the rules and discipline of war." When he was now briefed about Falmouth at the Cambridge headquarters of his Continental Army, Washington condemned the "Outrage exceeding in Barbarity & Cruelty every hostile Act practised among civilized Nations." And if other public and private correspondence is any indication, the attack appears to have helped steel the rebels' resolve. It injected new urgency into their struggle and infused it with political and indeed spiritual meaning: "[T]he unheard of cruelties of the enemy have so effectually united us," wrote one man, "that I believe there are not four persons now in [P]ortsmouth who do not justify the measures pursuing in opposition to the Tyranny of Great Britain." Imperial violence, far from terrifying rebellious colonials into submission, seemed instead to fan the flames of insurrection.[9]

The government's outspoken critics in Britain understood as much. One of the most prescient was Edmund Burke, MP, whose towering intellect and soaring rhetoric made for many a memorable hour in the House of Commons. In a famous speech advocating reconciliation with the colonies that he had given in March 1775, the Irish-born Burke explained why any policy of coercion must necessarily fail in America—in part because the colonists were descendants of freedom-loving Protestant Englishmen and in part due to their sheer distance from central government. But all of Burke's cogent reasoning could not slow the momentum. By the fall, Burke turned his attention to the dangers of what was then called desolation warfare—punitive raids against vulnerable military targets, civilians, and property that were designed to shock the enemy into compliance. To hard-liners, desolation warfare was a necessary answer to rebellion. But Burke doubted the rationale of such an approach: at best, "the *predatory*, or war by distress" might irritate one's opponents, but it could never entice them to accept the aggressor's rule over them. Burke was adamant that the strategy would only strengthen the resolve of the colonists and prolong the conflict.[10]

What Burke and his fellow MPs could not yet know was that the war of desolation was already well under way across the Atlantic. Once news of the bombardment broke, responses both at home and overseas vindicated Burke's analysis. Skeptical newspapers in Britain warned that the "coercive and sanguinary Measures pursued against the Americans . . . will produce nothing but the bitter Fruit of Ruin, Misery, and Devastation." Writing under the nom de guerre "Nauticus," one author accused Lord Sandwich, First Lord of the Admiralty, of frivolously ordering the horrendous burning of Falmouth. "[S]porting with the Miseries of Mankind," he had waited for the onset of winter, so that the displaced "aged Parent and the helpless Child were to be exposed to the Severity of the Frosts." The burning of Falmouth became a cause célèbre for American Patriots and for British conciliators. The foreign secretary of Britain's archenemy, France, rather like Edmund Burke, was more farsighted than many British leaders when he characterized the events at Falmouth as an "absurd as well as barbaric procedure on the part of an enlightened and civilized nation." Falmouth seemed, indeed, a British public relations disaster of the first order.[11]

After the naval shelling, many of the king's loyal subjects left Falmouth for Britain, Halifax, or Boston, although they would be forced to relocate once again when the British withdrew from that town the following spring. Not long after Falmouth, Admiral Graves was replaced amid allegations of corruption and incompetence. He remained adamant, though, that—since leniency towards those ungrateful rebels had only encouraged "farther Violences"—they must "be severely dealt with." And already another imperial commander was preparing to lay waste to the largest city in the largest American colony. Only this time the British compounded, in the rebels' eyes, their criminal escalation of violence by arming runaway slaves. The British initiative, and the cunning American response, would change the trajectory of the conflict: it proved a turning point in public opinion that helped solidify the Patriots' resolve.[12]

Flaming Arguments

On the eve of the Revolution, Norfolk, Virginia, was a flourishing coastal town of some 6,000 inhabitants. A key hub in the transatlantic trade network, it also served as a regional shipbuilding center. Many of Norfolk's Scottish-born tobacco merchants enjoyed close links with native Virginia merchants and planters. When the Continental Association was introduced in 1774, however, most of its documented local violators were Scots, who in due course became avowed Loyalists; most native Virginians complied with the insurgents' new regime.[13]

Like other British leaders during the American crisis, Virginia's governor, John Murray, 4th Earl of Dunmore, had previous experience with rebellion: his father had supported the doomed Jacobite rising of 1745, taking his young son with him on campaign. It had only been through John's uncle's connections at George II's court that his father's sentence was commuted from death to lifelong house arrest.[14]

On April 20, 1775, as British troops to the north regrouped after Lexington and Concord, Dunmore ordered marines to remove the gunpowder from Virginia's public magazine in Williamsburg. White slaveholders were particularly anxious about the threat of slave revolts at the time, and seeing their defensive capabilities eroded made them feel vulnerable. As the conflict with local rebels escalated, Dunmore feared for his life and he evacuated his family to Scotland. By June, he had fled his impressive palace, installing himself at a makeshift military headquarters on board a flotilla off Norfolk just before rebels pillaged his official residence.[15]

In October, Dunmore's raiding parties seized rebel weapons in Norfolk and Princess Anne Counties. Patriot leaders now openly discussed their options: Should they fortify Norfolk against British aggression, or should they demolish it to deny the British access to a Loyalist stronghold, with its valuable garrison and trading base?

Sir Joshua Reynolds, John Murray, 4th Earl of Dunmore *(1765). Dunmore's family was deeply implicated in the British Empire's history of rebellion and counterinsurgency, from the Scottish Highlands to the Virginia tidewater. In this painting by the preeminent portrait painter Sir Joshua Reynolds, Dunmore—sporting a tartan jacket and kilt—is striding into the wind, leaving behind a tree trunk symbolizing perhaps the devastated Highlands of his youth. In his future lay the governorships of New York and Virginia, a war against the Shawnee in a campaign to open up the western lands, and the emancipation of rebel slaves to buttress the Crown's cause in Revolutionary America.*

Adapting the Roman senator Cato's dictum, Thomas Jefferson recommended the latter course: "Delenda est Norfolk"—Norfolk must be destroyed! Some members of the local committee of safety agreed, as did the top military commanders for the region, the Virginian colonel William Woodford and his senior colleague, Colonel Robert Howe, the commander of the 2nd North Carolina Regiment of the Continental Army. But Revolutionary Virginia's civilian leaders kept procrastinating over Norfolk's fate. Meanwhile, many of the town's inhabitants from across the political spectrum began to seek refuge in surrounding areas.[16]

Since the spring, rumors had been circulating that the British government was considering arming slaves or inciting insurrection. Slaves repeatedly petitioned General Gage in Boston for their freedom in return for military service. General Burgoyne suggested to George III that Native Americans in the North could help move arms to Southern slaves. And Secretary Germain received a proposal that Lord Dunmore raise "the bravest & most ingenious of the Black Slaves, whom he may find all over the Bay of Chesapeak," for unlike "African[s] born black in the West Indies, . . . the meanest of Mankind," those born in Virginia or Maryland were "full of Intelligence & Courage." In South Carolina, the jittery white ruling elite ordered Thomas Jeremiah, a free black fisherman and pilot, hanged and burned for allegedly intending to help the British. A slave known as George was executed for preaching that "the Young King" would "set the Negroes Free." To South Carolina governor Lord William Campbell, their executions amounted to judicial murder committed by "a set of barbarians who are worse than the most cruel savages any history has described." Meanwhile, plantation owners in the Carolinas and Virginia strengthened their slave patrols to control the movement of slaves beyond the plantations.[17]

Dunmore initially rebuffed runaway slaves seeking his protection. But since he had previously raised the possibility of emancipating slaves, Southern slaveholders remained suspicious of his intentions. Meanwhile, William Henry Lyttelton, an ex-governor, successively, of South Carolina and Jamaica, had proposed in the British House of Commons that the Crown should actively encourage slave insurrections. A majority opposed his ideas as "horrid and wicked," but it must have unnerved Southern plantation owners to learn that over a quarter of the House of Commons did in fact side with Lyttelton. For slaves, their masters' anxiety translated into terror. Among the first slaves who risked running away to Dunmore in 1775 was a fifteen-year-old girl, caught before she reached the governor's base; her punishment consisted of eighty lashes with the whip, "followed by hot embers poured on her lacerated back," her treatment clearly intended to intimidate others who might be considering escape.[18]

Many enslaved people, including Thomas Jeremiah and George, seemed to believe that the purpose of a British invasion of the Southern colonies would be to liberate the region's slaves. But even though the British never tired of highlighting the hypocrisy of rebels talking the language of liberty while owning slaves, for the British, arming slaves was ultimately a question of military manpower. Enlisting sufficient troops, especially at the start of wars, was a recurring challenge for Britain's formidable war-waging machine. Indeed, from his vantage point as commander in chief watching developments from the heart of insurgent New England, General Gage had no doubt that Britain now needed to recruit soldiers wherever it could find them. In addition to arming black men, Gage urged hiring auxiliary troops in Europe. He also suggested shipping spare weapons to equip the American Loyalists, a strategy that over the course of the war would become increasingly important.[19]

* * *

By November 1775, Dunmore had been without instructions from London for several months. Sensing he could wait no longer, he issued an emancipation proclamation, promising to set "all indented Servants, Negroes, or others, (appertaining to Rebels,) free, that are able and willing to bear Arms, they joining His Majesty's Troops." The British Empire had occasionally armed black slaves, especially in the Caribbean, and sometimes granted freedom to particularly meritorious black soldiers. Dunmore's decree went further, promising an entire group of slaves freedom in exchange for their military service. While the proclamation applied only to male slaves of Patriot owners who were fit to serve, in practice Dunmore armed the slaves of some Loyalists, too; he also sheltered black women, children, and elderly men.[20]

Dunmore's dramatic action was motivated more by military strategy than by humanitarian concerns. Though largely intended to boost manpower, emancipation was also, in the words of one historian, "conceived, perhaps unwisely, as an instrument of intimidation." It did confirm slaveholding Patriots' worst fears. "Hell itself could not have vomited anything more black than this design of emancipating our slaves," commented one observer in Philadelphia to a friend overseas. At the same time, Patriots, in both their public utterances and their private musings, noted that Dunmore's proclamation had a mobilizing and unifying effect. It reaffirmed rebels in their stance and turned, or so at least they hoped, neutrals and even Loyalists against the governor, king, and Empire. As one scholar of African-American history has written, "Dunmore's proclamation probably did more than any other British measure to spur uncommitted Americans into the camp of rebellion."[21]

By early December, some eight hundred male slaves, traveling primarily by canoe or boat from the Chesapeake and tidewater Virginia—as well as from the Carolinas, Georgia, and Maryland, and as far as New York—had eluded the Patriots' redoubled patrols and defied their threats of punitive hard labor in lead mines, retribution against family members, or even death. And then there were the women and children arriving with the male escapees. Slaves "flock to him in abundance," panicking Patriots whispered, arriving in "boatloads" at that "monster," "Our Devil Dunmore." Unrecorded scores more tried but failed to reach Dunmore's waterborne safe haven. Dunmore organized some three hundred black men in the so-called Ethiopian Regiment; their uniform was to display the motto "Liberty to Slaves." Others worked as pilots, diggers, foragers, or spies, and their wives as laundresses, cooks, nurses, or servants to officers. Patriots meanwhile seized and auctioned off the majority of Dunmore's own slaves, whom the governor had left behind at his residence.[22]

Having thrown down the gauntlet of slave emancipation, Dunmore raised the royal banner in Norfolk. He demanded that each white man swear an oath of allegiance to the Crown and wear a red strip of cloth as a badge of loyalty. No sooner were Dunmore and the Loyalists back in charge in Norfolk than Patriot militia routed a force of some six hundred British regulars, Loyalists, and ex-slaves at Great Bridge, the southern land approach to the town, on December 9. Dunmore's beaten men retreated to his floating base; the Virginia Patriot troops retook Norfolk. Among the wounded soldiers they captured were two former slaves, James Anderson, his "Bones shattered and flesh much torn" in his forearm, and Caesar, who had been hit "in the Thigh, by a Ball, and 5 shot—one lodged." Any armed slaves who asked pardon from the Patriots were jailed, appraised for their value as property, and shipped off to a life of bondage in the West Indies or Honduras.[23]

By year's end, Norfolk's political fault lines were drawn. During the preceding months, as the area kept changing hands, threats and arrests by both sides had driven an ever-deeper wedge through the community. Most Scottish merchants now evacuated their families and movable goods to Dunmore's provisional headquarters, which had grown to one hundred vessels, thus leaving their houses and estates exposed to the rebels' designs. With Dunmore were perhaps 1,000 white local residents, between 1,000 and 1,500 runaway slaves, some 140 British military personnel, and a motley crew of European, Caribbean, and African sailors and civilians. The rebels imposed a cordon to control the flow of people and goods in and out of Norfolk.[24]

To provision his floating town, Dunmore oversaw land raids and the capture of enemy vessels. When Loyalists on his ships asked permission to go ashore to fetch fresh food and water, the Patriots laid down unacceptable conditions: women and children would have to remain in town; men would be arrested and tried. With local Patriots regularly taking potshots at Dunmore's flotilla, his men became resentful and restless. "I hope," wrote one unidentified "gentleman" aboard Dunmore's flagship on Christmas Day, "the time will soon arrive, when these rebellious Savages will be severely punished for their crimes." The 2,000 or so Loyalists of that region, he added with concern, "they treat with the greatest cruelty." He speculated that the British warships were on the brink of destroying the town.[25]

On New Year's Day 1776, Patriot troops openly defied British warnings by parading in the Norfolk streets in full view of the fleet. Dunmore's officers could take no more. Around 3:15 in the afternoon, the British ships opened fire on the town from more than one hundred cannons—not without first giving notice, Dunmore stressed later, so that women and children could be evacuated. Meanwhile, Dunmore sent landing parties to set fire to wharfs and buildings near the waterfront in order to deny cover to American riflemen who had been harassing the vessels. Fires spread rapidly among the mostly wooden houses. One British officer writing from offshore relished the devastation: "It is glorious to see the blaze of the town and shipping. I exult in the carnage of these rebels."[26]

Many aboard the British ships might not have been aware that during their bombardment Patriot troops slipped into Norfolk, where they plundered warehouses, looted private homes, and burned numerous structures. Thomas Newton saw his two elegant mansions, nine tenements, ten warehouses, and one shop go up in flames. The Patriot colonel Robert Howe seemed to let the marauders roam freely. And even when he received reports that Patriot properties, such as Newton's, were being destroyed alongside those of Loyalists, he chose not to intervene.

When it was all over, Colonel Howe sent a report to the president of the Virginia Convention. He had seen "women and children running through a crowd of shot to get out of the town, some of them with children at their breasts; a few have, I fear, been killed." But despite such a heavy barrage, "we have not one man killed, and but a few wounded." What Howe failed to reveal was that most of the physical destruction of Norfolk had in fact been caused not by British cannons but instead by those Patriot troops who had looted and burned houses under the cover of what turned out to be an only moderately effective bombardment from sea. Afterward, Howe and Woodford concealed the Patriot troops' actions and their own complicity. "The wind," they told their civilian superiors, "favoured their [the Britons'] design, and we believe the flames will become general."[27]

Accepting the Patriots' challenge in the realm of polemics, Dunmore issued his own version of events from his shipboard printing press. Using meteorological arguments, just as the Patriots had done, Dunmore blamed most of the destruction on the rebels:

> As the wind was moderate, and from the shore, it was judged with certainty that the destruction would end with that part of the town next the water, which the King's ships meant only should be fired; but the Rebels cruelly and unnecessarily completed the destruction of the whole town, by setting fire to the houses in the streets back, which were before safe from the flames.[28]

Perplexed by the conflicting reports, the committee of safety conducted an inquiry. Alas, no depositions have ever been found— the man in charge of the investigation was none other than Colonel Howe. What we do know is that after the initial bombardment by Dunmore's ships, the Convention ordered the evacuation of the remaining population of Norfolk. It then secretly authorized the destruction of what was left of the town, as well as the demolition of nearby Portsmouth, should military commanders consider such action advisable. In early February, Howe did indeed raze Norfolk's remaining 416 structures: "We have removed from Norfolk, thank God for that! It is entirely destroyed; thank God for that also."[29]

Meanwhile, as Dunmore departed for New York City, he abandoned some 1,000 dead or dying African-Americans ravaged by smallpox and other epidemics, leaving stretches of the Virginia coast "full of Dead Bodies, chiefly negroes." Patriots also accused him of having sent infected black men ashore as a cynical farewell gesture.[30]

In 1777, Virginia legislators would revisit the unresolved issue of which side had caused precisely what amount of destruction. An investigatory committee painstakingly gathered depositions and professional valuations of destroyed properties. The official report concluded that "very few of the houses were destroyed by the enemy"; indeed, most houses that *were* set on fire could have been saved. Instead, the Patriot soldiers "most wantonly set fire to the greater part of the houses within the town, where the enemy never attempted to approach, and where it would have been impossible for them to have penetrated." In total, American troops devastated some 863 structures worth over £110,000. The British destroyed 54 buildings and personal property valued at barely over £5,000. In other words, the British were responsible for less than 6 percent of destroyed buildings and 4.3 percent of the value of total losses. The Revolutionaries suppressed this inconvenient report for the duration of the war; it was in fact first published in 1836. The Patriots thus not only achieved their initial objective of denying the British a valuable coastal base while punishing the local Loyalists; they also managed to lay the blame entirely at the feet of the British.[31]

In early 1776, Patriots saw that Norfolk's burning could be used to rally public opinion behind the American cause—and they seized the opportunity. It did not hurt that it followed hard on the heels of Falmouth's destruction. Samuel Adams felt that the attack did more to help people make up their minds to support the Revolution than "a long Train of Reasoning." For John Hancock, the president of the Continental Congress, the attack confirmed that Britain was opting for brutality, with evidence of "inhumanity so contrary to the rules of war and so long exploded by all civilized nations." The rebels were fast occupying the moral high ground: they claimed European-style codes of war as their ethical baseline while accusing the British of violating those codes. At the same time, they played the registers of psychological and propaganda warfare with a virtuosic flourish. The recipient of Hancock's letter, George Washington, hoped that Falmouth's and Norfolk's destruction, and similar threats to other towns, would "unite the whole Country . . . against a Nation which seems to be lost to every sense of Virtue, and those feelings which distinguish a Civilized People from the most barbarous Savages. A few more of such flaming Arguments" would encourage Americans to embrace independence. Violence, especially when spun appropriately, had a powerful unifying effect.[32]

In Britain, those who favored crushing the rebellion took heart that their army and navy would "strike such a terror, into these deluded people." By contrast, those opposed to escalating the conflict seized on Norfolk to lament the prospect of all-out civil war in the

Empire, "attended with circumstances of cruelty, civil rage, and devastation hitherto unprecedented in the annals of mankind." Making war, emphasized the Duke of Richmond, a prominent opposition peer, "in a manner which would shock the most barbarous nations, by firing their towns, and turning the wretched inhabitants to perish in cold, want, and nakedness," harmed not just Britain's enemies: it hurt her loyal subjects, too.[33]

At Norfolk, then, Dunmore's decision to escalate the conflict had provided cover for the Patriots to intensify their violent suppression of Loyalist dissent, sacrificing one of America's flourishing port cities in the process. America's new leaders, including Adams and Washington, may initially have been unaware of the real agents of destruction. But Howe and Woodford, who successfully hushed up the Patriot troops' part, could not have hoped for a greater triumph in their war of words. The British dilemma had been thrown into sharp relief. Had the "fire and sword" approach—which had come to haunt the British after Falmouth, and which at Norfolk had given the rebels the perfect excuse for their own tactical unleashing of violence—already discredited itself completely? Or could a persistent application of maximum force still break the back of the rebellion before it gathered irreversible momentum?[34]

* * *

During the spring of 1776, a vast armada assembled off Britain's coast, poised to launch the largest-scale overseas invasion in European history. Among the tens of thousands of soldiers were not only Britons but large contingents of Germans. For, true to George III's recent promises, in early 1776 the Crown had signed the first treaties for auxiliary troops with the rulers of Hessen-Kassel, Hessen-Hanau, and Brunswick. Over the course of the war, Britain contracted 36,000 German soldiers. Partly because Hessen-Kassel provided more than half of those troops, German auxiliaries were generally referred to as "the Hessians." What made the Hessians not just a formidable military force but a potential weapon of terror was precisely what disqualified them in the eyes of conciliators. In America as in Britain, the Hessians were widely considered to be fierce fighters, reared in despotic lands, with no interest in the conflict or true allegiance to Britain. "Foreigners were to slaughter our oppressed Fellow-subjects in America," complained one British critic, when Englishmen were "too noble, too generous, too brave, too humane, to cut the Throats of Englishmen." But despite some vocal domestic opposition, the British government's policy of hiring foreign troops received the customarily strong parliamentary backing, setting in motion the deployment of thousands of Hessians to the colonies. By the second half of the war, such troops would make up one-third of all British-led forces in North America. Their conduct would remain a bone of contention on both sides of the Atlantic.[35]

While the formidable British fleet was making ready that spring, bad news kept arriving at the Continental Congress in Philadelphia. Well into 1775, the Revolutionaries had been trying to convince Britain to change political course; for the vast majority of Americans, reconciliation remained preferable to all-out war. Their dispute had been with Parliament and the king's ministers. As yet, American insurgents were still pledging allegiance to the Crown. But the tide of Anglo-American relations was turning fast. After the king had proclaimed them to be in rebellion, he had ordered all American ports closed, beginning in March 1776. The Royal Navy was authorized to seize any American ships, as well as their crew and cargo, as if they belonged to avowed enemies. Evidence of Britain's aggression kept amassing: after Lord Dunmore had armed Southern slaves and destroyed Norfolk, the British had defeated an American assault on a stronghold at Quebec led by Benedict Arnold. In May, delegates at the Congress found out that Britain was hiring Hessians, one of the most shocking pieces of evidence yet that their king was abandoning them. John Hancock concluded that "the British Nation have proceeded to the last Extremity." New Hampshire's delegate, Josiah Bartlett, was preparing himself for "a severe trial this summer, with Britons, Hessians, Hanoverians, Indians, Negroes, and every other butcher the gracious King of Britain can hire against us."[36]

At the same time as the British were escalating the war by shelling coastal towns and mobilizing non-Anglo forces, imperial authority was collapsing throughout the colonies. Patriot committees and militias stepped into the breach, shoring up the defensive posture of their regions. They oversaw the production of saltpeter and bought up gunpowder, lead, ammunition, and arms. They banned the export of items required to put the colonies on a war footing. They blocked waterways against the threat of a British raid or invasion. In the South particularly, they mounted slave patrols and disarmed black men. By June, Congress was busy drafting a treason law and discussing foreign alliances. After America's internal civil war had been simmering for several years, her declaring independence would trigger a civil war in the British Empire.[37]

Repeated Injuries and Usurpations

As an elderly man, Dr. Jacob Dunham would remember that he had been about nine years old when the Declaration of Independence arrived in his New Jersey hometown of New Brunswick. It was most likely July 9 or 10, 1776. Dunham's father, Colonel Azariah Dunham, was an active Patriot—a member of the colony's committee of safety, the county committee of correspondence, and the local committee of inspection and observation. The county and town committees resolved that the Declaration should be read in Albany Street in front of the White Hall tavern. A Colonel John Neilson was chosen as the reader. Aware of how divided the community was politically, New Brunswick's Patriots left little to chance. The two committees charged their members with assembling "the staunch friends of independence, so as to overawe any disaffected Tories" and to counteract any design to interrupt the ceremony. As the younger Dunham recalled, those Loyalists were not large in number but included "men of wealth and influence, and were very active." All in all, "[t]here was great excitement in the town over the news, most of the people rejoicing that we were free and independent, but a few looking very sour over it." It is striking that Dunham remembered just how contested the local political scene was, and that the Patriots felt the need to orches-

Hamilton, The Manner in which the American Colonies Declared themselves Independant [*sic*] of the King of England, throughout the different
Provinces, on July 4, 1776 *[1783]. In this engraving, illustrating a history of
England published at the end of the war, a horseman is reading the Declaration of Independence surrounded by a dense group of listeners. On the wall
at the left, a notice is being posted, reading "America Independent. 1776."*

trate a positive reception of the declaration. At the birth of the
American republic, its viability was far from assured.[38]

In New Brunswick and in dozens of communities across Britain's rebellious colonies that July, sizable crowds gathered in public
squares, in front of courthouses, and in churches or town halls.
There were civic processions and military parades; bells rang,
and preparations were afoot for fireworks, bonfires, and illumi-
nations. Colonel Neilson and his fellow readers in other localities

announced that the congressional document their audiences were about to hear was titled the "unanimous Declaration of the thirteen united States of America." Neilson read the preamble, containing the premise of all that was to come: if one people separated from another, it ought to state its reasons for doing so. The second paragraph contains the famous enunciation of self-evident truths: "that all men are created equal, that they are endowed by their Creator with certain unalienable Rights, that among these are Life, Liberty and the pursuit of Happiness."[39]

The Declaration's central and longest section was much discussed at the time but is barely remembered by most Americans today. Yet it is this section—an extensive catalogue of King George III's political crimes—that helps us understand how, in Patriot eyes, it was British violence that justified both independence and the harsh means by which it would be achieved. To introduce this catalogue of grievances, the Declaration asserts that "[t]he history of the present King of Great Britain is a history of repeated injuries and usurpations, all having in direct object the establishment of an absolute Tyranny over these States." There follows a litany of accusations, starting with twelve counts of the king unduly meddling in colonial affairs by vetoing colonial laws, discouraging immigration, interfering with judicial freedom, opposing resistance to parliamentary authority, and introducing a standing army. In addition, the king had given his assent to parliamentary legislation harming the colonies: trade was cut off; trials were being relocated "beyond the Seas"; the "free System of English Laws" was being abolished "in a neighboring Province" (Quebec); and so on.[40]

The recitation of grievances climaxed in a section on the king's aggressively violent acts against the colonies: "He has plundered our seas, ravaged our Coasts, burnt our towns, and destroyed the lives of our people," the Revolutionaries charged. And he was mobilizing all manner of unacceptable, non-Anglo fighting forces:

He is at this time transporting large Armies of foreign Mercenaries to compleat the works of death, desolation and tyranny, already begun with circumstances of Cruelty & perfidy scarcely paralleled in the most barbarous ages, and totally unworthy the Head of a civilized nation.

. . .

He has excited domestic insurrections amongst us, and has endeavoured to bring on the inhabitants of our frontiers, the merciless Indian Savages, whose known rule of warfare, is an undistinguished destruction of all ages, sexes and conditions.

By now, the crowds listening in America's town squares could be in little doubt as to who was to blame for imperial oppression: "He has," "he has," "he has"—refused, forbidden, obstructed, abdicated, excited, indeed plundered, ravaged, burned, and destroyed.

With his aggressive, unethical conduct, Congress was saying, the king had removed his colonial children "out of his Protection." George III had "effectively placed the colonies 'beyond the line' of civilized practice in warfare" by introducing illegitimate forms of violence. By using this kind of language, the Declaration's authors were also speaking to a wider international audience. When the king continually refused to listen to their petitions for redress, the Patriots' final accusation now concluded, it had become clear that such a "Prince whose character is thus marked by every act which may define a Tyrant, is unfit to be the ruler of a free people."[41]

After these hard-hitting accusations, a penultimate paragraph reminded Americans of their fruitless pleas to the British people. One last time they invoked the historical and affective bonds that were supposed to bind the Anglo community. When their attempts to seek redress failed, the colonials had been left with no choice but to announce their separation. The final section of the Declaration delivers that farewell, declaring "that these United Colonies are, and of Right ought to be FREE AND INDEPEN-DENT STATES; that they are Absolved from all Allegiance to the British Crown"; and that they would henceforth enjoy the rights of all legally sovereign states in the community of nations, including the ability to forge commercial alliances, wage war, and declare peace.[42]

The Declaration circulated in printed form as well. A broadside version was available as early as July 5; newspapers started printing it on the sixth. By the nineteenth it had been reprinted in seven colonies, and by the end of the month it had appeared in more than thirty papers. But it was public readings, like the one that Dunham still remembered nearly six decades later, that evoked the most powerful and immediate responses.[43]

Across the colonies, American citizens moved to concretize the separation from the former mother country by destroying the visible symbols of monarchy. Crowds removed the royal coats of arms from courthouses, churches, and other public buildings. They tore down images of the king from coffeehouses and taverns. In Dover, Delaware, the president of the committee of safety threw a portrait of George III on a fire: "[T]hus we destroy even the shadow of that King who refused to reign over a free people." In Huntington, Long Island, an effigy of the king, "with its face black like Dunmore's Virginia regiment, its head adorned with a wooden crown stuck full of feathers like . . . Savages," and its cloak "lined with gunpowder," was hanged, exploded, and burned. In Lower Manhattan, New Yorkers and Continental soldiers toppled the equestrian statue of George III on the Bowling Green, at the foot of Broadway. They "drove a musket Bullet part of the way" through the statue's head before carrying it off in a nighttime procession to the tune of the Rogue's March, typically the musical accompaniment for community punishments such as a tarring and feathering. After Patriots and Loyalists had struggled to take custody of parts of the statue, the Patriots transported large chunks of it to Connecticut, where female volunteers converted them into 42,088 bullets of "melted majesty," ready to be fired at the king's troops. Where until recently Americans had been celebrating royal birthdays with parades, toasts, and fireworks, they now expended gunpowder, alcohol, and violent communal energies on rituals renouncing America's last king—all while George III's forces were on the verge of launching an invasion.[44]

A Hesitant Invasion

In March and April 1776, George Washington had moved the bulk of his Continental Army from Boston to New York. The city was the geostrategic key to America and widely expected to be the main target of a British attack: if they held New York City, the British would control one end of the Hudson; with their northern army coming from Canada holding the other, they would be able to sever New England from the remaining colonies. Over recent months, Washington's soldiers, civilian laborers, and slaves had erected forts, redoubts, and barricades across parts of Manhattan Island and Long Island. As Continental forces cracked down harshly on suspected Loyalists and waverers, thousands of New Yorkers fled the city; the prewar population of 25,000 dropped to just 5,000 in September 1776.[45]

On June 29, General Sir William Howe's invasion armada—110 ships carrying 9,000 troops—had first been spotted off New York. To one rebel lookout it seemed like a "wood of pine trees trimmed," and, indeed, as if "all of London was afloat." By July 2, the British were landing on Staten Island. In an exquisite piece of dramatic timing, it was the very same day that the Continental Congress in Philadelphia had voted to dissolve the connection with the mother country. Over the following weeks, as word of the Declaration of Independence spread across the colonies, Howe staged his massive force in preparation for the invasion of New York.[46]

The fall campaign of 1776 perfectly reflects Britain's ongoing strategic and moral dilemma. Howe planned to seize New York City, capture the Hudson corridor, occupy Rhode Island, and sweep all of New Jersey. He would offer amnesty to any moderate colonials swearing allegiance to the king. The historian David Hackett Fischer judges it a plausible and humane plan that combined a show of force with conciliatory gestures, all with a view to restoring imperial harmony. But what Howe didn't know was that his brother Richard, the admiral, was en route from England with a different mission for them both: not only were they to lead the war against the rebels, but they were also to act as a two-man peace commission charged with brokering a negotiated settlement.[47]

Richard Howe, who had been appointed commander in chief of naval forces in America in January 1776, had apparently made his acceptance of the war mission contingent on his also being named the head of Lord North's peace commission. Eventually the Howe brothers became the sole commissioners, as North insisted, but Lord Germain limited their remit: they could grant pardons but could not make any substantive concessions to the rebels; surrender was a nonnegotiable prerequisite of any negotiations. But any British diplomatic initiative was running out of time: when Admiral Howe finally departed for America, the Congress in Philadelphia had already begun moving towards independence.[48]

Admiral Howe's military orders were to pursue an aggressive war by supporting the army led by his brother William and blockading the North American coast to cut off the rebels' war supplies. The admiral's fleet arrived off New York on July 12: 10 large warships and 20 frigates leading some 150 ships manned by roughly 10,000 sailors and transporting 11,000 troops. They would join William Howe's 9,000-man army on Staten Island, where one officer acknowledged that local Loyalists had already suffered much. Now, finally, their protectors had arrived.[49]

And more were on the way. The first German troops contracted by the Crown soon landed in America. After an unusually long Atlantic crossing, the Hessians were exhausted, with many suffering from scurvy and contagious fevers. To speed their recovery, Howe gave them excellent campsites on Staten Island, where the Germans appreciated the "beautiful forests composed mostly of a kind of fir-tree, the odor of which can be inhaled at a distance of two miles from land." Over the following weeks, British and German troops kept arriving, bringing the total number of troops to some 32,000—the largest invasion force seen in the eighteenth century. More than 400 British ships of varying sizes were controlling the waters around New York—and whoever commanded the waterways would eventually hold the city. But instead of launching the offensive as soon as all his assets were in place, William Howe allowed his brother Richard to persuade him to prioritize conciliation. This two-pronged and hesitant approach characterized the remainder of the 1776 campaign. Arguably, it would cost Britain thirteen colonies.[50]

Admiral Howe's initial attempts to negotiate with Washington foundered on diplomatic protocol and the sheer incompatibility of their positions. The American commander refused to accept letters addressed first to George Washington, Esq., and then to George Washington, Esq., etc., etc.—he was *General* Washington, his staff insisted. Quite apart from the fact that the British only had a pardon to offer, when "[t]hose who have committed no fault want no pardon," Washington made it clear that he was, in any case, not authorized to negotiate. Their peace overtures overtaken by the momentum of American independence, the Howe brothers now pivoted to their military mission.[51]

The plan for the opening moves of the campaign had been designed by General Henry Clinton. As the third of the major generals appointed by George III in February 1775, Clinton was subordinate to both Howe and Burgoyne. He had just returned from a disastrous Southern mission to Charleston, South Carolina: British forces had had to abort a naval bombardment, amphibious landings, and a ground assault in the face of unfavorable topography, poor coordination among the army and navy, and an unexpectedly vigorous rebel defense. His ego bruised, Clinton sought redemption in the North. As a man and as an officer, Clinton was very different from his colleagues. He had grown up in America, mostly on Manhattan, as the son of Admiral George Clinton, the governor of New York. After joining the army at age fifteen and training in France, Clinton served in Germany during the Seven Years' War. Even though he had grown into an experienced officer, Clinton had never held an independent command. Unlike Howe and Burgoyne, he lacked self-confidence. The biographer of British wartime leaders Andrew O'Shaughnessy summarizes Clinton's faults: "He sulked and brooded. He was jealous and tempestuous. He quarreled with colleagues." But by the end of the American war, Clinton would be the longest-serving British commander in the entire conflict.[52]

Like his fellow commanders, Clinton preferred a peaceful set-

Engraved for Murray's History of the American War.

GENERAL CLINTON.

Printed for T. Robson, Newcastle upon Tyne.

This portrait of General Sir Henry Clinton adorned a wartime publication, the Reverend James Murray's An impartial history of the war in America; from its first commencement, to the present time *(Newcastle upon Tyne, 1782).*

tlement to war. Unlike the Howe brothers, though, Clinton had not opposed the British policies that had led to armed conflict. Upon arriving in Boston to assume his command in May 1775, he had advocated a harsh approach. At the same time, a memorandum of a conversation dated February 1776 suggests that Clinton approached the situation in the colonies with nuance: "I did not doubt but that this Country might be conquered, but did much [doubt] whether it was worth while to [have] it when conquered." Clinton therefore concluded that "to gain the hearts & subdue the minds of America was in my opinion worth while." But Clinton also had clear views on the military strategy most likely to lead to a British victory: in the absence of a political center of gravity—an established seat of American power—Britain must crush the Continental Army in order to force the colonials to seek a settlement. This contrasted sharply with Howe's more cautious approach of using the minimum force necessary to demonstrate British superiority and thus compel the Americans to negotiate.[53]

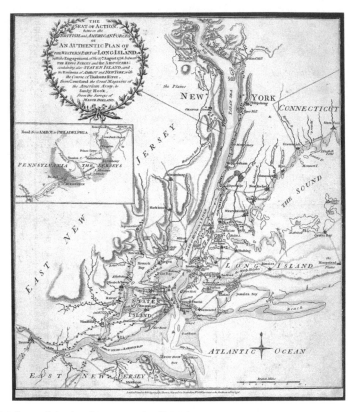

The Seat of Action between the British and American Forces; or An Authentic Plan of the Western Part of Long Island, with the Engagement of the 27th August, 1776 *(London, 1776). In anticipation of the British attack, Washington posted guards along the major roads through the Brooklyn Heights but left the Jamaica Pass exposed.*

Nevertheless, by mid-August, Clinton had managed to persuade Howe to adopt his proposal to envelop the American forces on Long Island. Having learned their lessons at Bunker Hill, the invaders now prepared for what they feared war against the insurgents entailed: officers removed the insignia from their uniforms lest enemy snipers identify them too easily. On August 22, as New York recovered from a severe thunderstorm that had killed three American soldiers in their tent, Howe landed 15,000 troops without opposition on Long Island. Misled by repeated intelligence failures, Washington had posted only 9,000 soldiers there, leaving the rest in Manhattan. Some 130 miles long and 20 miles across at its widest points, Long Island was sparsely populated with farming communities. Rich as it was in foodstuffs, and with a substantial neutral and Loyalist population ensuring good intelligence for the British, it was an excellent staging area for Howe's invasion army.[54]

Over the next few days, Howe reinforced his contingent to a total of some 20,000 men. On August 27, Clinton's plan delivered perhaps the greatest British triumph of the entire war. Clinton himself led the encirclement of Washington's left wing, bringing some 10,000 troops virtually undetected through the undefended Jamaica Pass. Meanwhile, Hessian artillery and infantry with bayonets under General Leopold Philip von Heister attacked General John Sullivan's forces south of Brooklyn Heights; when Sullivan realized that Clinton was about to trap him, he ordered a retreat to the heights. To the southwest, General Lord Stirling held off British forces under General James Grant until he, too, was about to be encircled and ordered a retreat; the British did capture Stirling. Many of the cornered American units experienced what Michael Graham, an eighteen-year-old volunteer with the Pennsylvania Flying Camp, described as a panicked rout, a scene of "confusion and horror," with "artillery flying with the chains over the horses' backs, our men running in almost every direction, and run which way they would, they were almost sure to meet the British or Hessians." Although Graham survived, he was one of the luckier ones, escaping through swampy areas that claimed the lives of many a less fortunate comrade.[55]

The Americans pointed to the Hessians, in particular, as aggressive, immoral fighters. As they anticipated the Hessians' arrival, it was suggested that Washington post 500 to 1,000 Patriots painted like Native Americans at German landing places in order to terrify the reputedly brutal enemy. Howe had in turn strategically used Americans' fears of the ruthless Hessians by stationing them across from Washington's camp at Amboy Ferry. According to later reports, during the action on August 27, Continental troops that could no longer resist sought to surrender to any forces other than Hessians, fearing that the latter were least likely to grant them quarter. One American soldier alleged that the Hessians "behaved with great Inhumanity" and "knocked on the Head of Men that were lying wounded on the Field of Battle." There were even unconfirmed allegations of Hessians spitting enemy soldiers to trees with their bayonets and throwing hundreds of enemy corpses into a mass grave.[56]

One German officer, in a passage written in code in a letter home, admitted to atrocities against prisoners. When a regimental patrol brought some prisoners to camp, he detailed, "[m]any high ranking individuals at this time shed their ideas of being heroes. The prisoners who knelt and sought to surrender were beaten." In addition, German soldiers did bayonet a number of Americans after they had given themselves up, although in at least a few cases this appears to have been in response to sham surrenders by Patriots who promptly resumed firing on the approaching Hessians.[57]

It may not have been the Hessians' inherently aggressive disposition that led to all of these atrocities. A British officer in Fraser's Highlanders summarized proudly that "[t]he Hessians and our brave Highlanders gave no quarter, and it was a fine sight to see with what alacrity they dispatched the Rebels with their bayonets after we had surrounded them so that they could not resist." But then he revealed a psychological ploy to encourage the Germans' ferocity: "We took care to tell the Hessians that the rebels had resolved to give no quarters—to them in particular—which made them fight desperately, and put all to death that fell into their hands." Yet, he rationalized, "all stratagems are lawful in war, especially against such vile enemies to their King and country." Hessian deserters later confirmed that Britons had sought to indoctrinate them; they had even told their German auxiliaries that the rebels cannibalized soldiers they took captive. British and German troops also accused each other of battlefield abuses, with one German officer reporting that the "English gave little quarter to the enemy and encouraged our men to do the same thing." In fact, there is little definitive evidence that the Hessians fought more brutally in that battle, or violated the codes of war more egregiously, than did British units. By and large, atrocities appear to have been the exception rather than the rule. But when rumors, exaggerations, or even false reports resonated with Hessians' sinister reputation, they could instill real fear and fan a desire for revenge.[58]

* * *

According to the best estimates, the Americans suffered between 300 and 500 casualties on Long Island; nearly 1,100 men were taken captive, including three generals. The redcoats, irate at American snipers, instantly destroyed the rifles of those they captured. British-German casualties totaled roughly 370, among them members of Dunmore's Ethiopian Regiment. Displaying the characteristic optimism of British officers in the aftermath of the battle, Lord Percy wrote home that the Americans "will never again stand before us in the Field. Every Thing seems to be over with Them & I flatter myself now that this Campaign will put a total End to the War."[59]

Long Islanders' responses to their British invaders varied. One field officer felt "[t]he inhabitants received us with the greatest joy, seeing well the difference between anarchy and a mild regular government." On the other hand, a Loyalist reported British atrocities against men and sexual abuse of women, without distinction between friend and foe. The would-be liberators also revealed themselves to be indiscriminate plunderers. In a letter to his father, the former British prime minister the Earl of Bute, Colonel Charles Stuart commented on the situation he had experienced on Long Island, where crews of British transport ships had started robbing the locals even as the battle was still raging. As Stuart saw it,

> Those poor unhappy wretches who had remained in their habitation through necessity or loyalty were immediately judged by the soldiers to [be] Rebels, neither their cloathing or property spared, but in the most inhuman and barbarous manner torn from them ... Thus we went on persuading to enmity those

minds already undecided, and inducing our very Friends to fly to the opposite party for protection.[60]

Whatever the impact of the invasion on local civilians, Clinton's plan was a tremendous strategic success: the American forces had been routed. But when Clinton urged Howe to press on and eliminate the Continental Army by landing the British troops north of Manhattan and preventing Washington from retreating across the King's Bridge, Howe held back, apparently torn between his two roles as destroyer and peacemaker.[61]

The Americans seized their unexpected chance. During the night of August 29 and the morning of the thirtieth, undetected by the British, Washington evacuated some 9,500 men, with almost all their weapons and baggage, across the East River to Manhattan. A fierce nor'easter earlier in the evening had moved southwest by midnight; by morning, dense fog helped cover the retreat. Some of the Marblehead fishermen manning the rowing boats made five or even ten round trips with muffled oars. Washington was reportedly among the last to leave Brooklyn. His officers were astonished at Howe's failure to pursue their badly beaten army after their rout on Long Island. General Putnam had only two possible explanations: "General Howe is either our friend or no general." General Clinton, the mastermind of Britain's earlier triumph, was clear also that "[c]omplete success would most likely have been the consequence of an immediate attack."[62]

It is one of the great counterfactuals of the American Revolution that this was probably Britain's best chance to end the war victoriously. Had Howe seized the momentum he had created on Long Island, pursued the Continental Army when their morale was low, trapped Washington in Manhattan, and delivered a decisive blow, it is quite likely that the insurgents would have had no option but to surrender and negotiate a settlement. Crushing the Continental Army, conjectures the historian Joseph Ellis, "would have generated traumatic shock waves that in turn would have destroyed the will of the American people to continue the war." But instead of seeking the definitive strike that Clinton proposed,

Howe pursued a more cautious strategy for the remainder of the campaign, informed in part by his concern to avoid large-scale casualties that would be hard to replace: between mid-September and mid-November, he gradually dislodged the Americans from their positions in New York, with partial victories at Kip's Bay, at White Plains, and at Fort Washington, where he captured 2,600 American soldiers and more than 200 officers. By late fall, the British had driven the Continental Army from Long Island, Manhattan, and eastern New Jersey, the latter a crucial foraging area for the British Army that winter. In order to gain an ice-free harbor—New York's more enclosed waters froze seasonally—they had also seized parts of Rhode Island. The British established their headquarters in New York City, where they would stay for the duration of the war.[63]

General Howe was later accused of allowing his pro-American sympathies to cloud his strategic thinking. But the Howe brothers' real mistake was to assume that a British victory over the poorly prepared colonials was virtually inevitable even if maximum force was not applied. They also overestimated the strength of active Loyalism, relying on a counterinsurgency with overwhelming homegrown support that, in fact, never quite materialized.[64]

The Battle for American Loyalties

In July 1776, the final thread that had been tying the colonies formally to the Empire was cut. For the Patriots, there was now no turning back. As a newly sovereign state, the United Colonies—from September styled officially the United States—as well as the thirteen constituent states demanded undivided loyalty from those living in their territory. Across America, everyone, at least in principle, now had to decide whether to be a British subject and leave or remain as a citizen of America. Neutrality was no longer an option—not in theory, and not in practice, either: "Sir, we have passed the Rubicon," John Jay told Beverley Robinson, a prominent landowner in the Hudson Valley who was still bent on neutrality, early the following year, "and it is now necessary every man Take his part." For the Revolutionaries, allegiance was volitional: all individuals were given a period of grace to pledge their loyalty to the British Crown or to the United States. Given a generous six weeks to make up his mind and sign an oath, Robinson eventually evacuated his family behind British lines.[65]

After they had declared their independence, the Patriots put their policing of political loyalties on a stronger legal footing. First, the Congress and then the states passed treason laws and confiscation and banishment acts. Preparing in June 1776 for the eventuality of independence, Congress had already defined treason as levying war against the United Colonies, adhering to the king of Great Britain, or giving the enemy aid or comfort. Recruiting for the enemy and joining them—even acting as a local guide— became capital offenses. John Adams, who denounced the Loyalists as "an ignorant, cowardly pack of scoundrels," was buoyant, judging that the treason laws would "make whigs by the thousands . . . A treason law is in politics like the article for shooting upon the spot a soldier who shall turn his back. It turns a man's cowardice and timidity into heroism, because it places greater danger behind his back than before his face." Eight states banished named Loyalists and threatened to execute them in the event that they ever returned. Over the course of the war, several states would execute convicted Loyalist traitors.[66]

In addition to treason laws, the states enacted test laws, which required citizens to swear loyalty towards their states of residence. In most areas, the relative harshness of anti-Loyalist laws depended on how strong pro-British sentiment was perceived to be and which side had the upper hand militarily. In New Hampshire, where active Loyalism was fairly marginal and where the war had a limited direct impact, oaths of allegiance were only required from state servants, officers, and lawyers, starting in late 1777. By contrast, residents of the strongly Loyalist Westchester County in New York were at much greater risk of being declared open enemies. Under the direction of New York's Committee for Inquiring into Detecting and Defeating all Conspiracies, and supported by a sizable militia, local committees would go on to try some 1,000 individuals by 1779. During that same period, Loyalist refugees swelled British-controlled New York City's population to 33,000.[67]

The repercussions for those who did not comply with the test laws were typically harsher than the punishments for those who had refused previous loyalty oaths. They were now regularly banned from voting and barred from holding office, practicing their professions, and trading. Nowhere could they serve on juries, acquire property, inherit land, or even travel at will. Confiscation of property affected tens of thousands of Loyalists during the war, allowing the states to accrue assets and condemn traitors to a social death without engaging in widespread executions. Some refugee populations were repeatedly dispossessed and displaced, like the Connecticut Loyalist exiles who retreated to Long Island, only to be targeted there by Patriot raiding parties across the sound.[68]

In this messy period of transition, as prosecutions under the new laws intensified, committees and mobs across the colonies continued to spread terror among Loyalists and waverers alike. In today's Darien, Connecticut, an "American guard" arrested Walter Bates, the fifteen- or sixteen-year-old son of an Anglican Loyalist family. The Patriots suspected Walter of knowing the whereabouts of fugitive armed Loyalists, including his own brother, who were thought to be hiding out in the neighborhood. His interrogators, Walter later recounted, "threatened [him] with sundry deaths," including by drowning, unless he confessed. At night, an armed mob took Walter to a local salt marsh, stripped him naked, and tied him by his feet and hands to a tree. He despaired that over as little as a two-hour period, the mosquitoes would draw "every drop of blood . . . from my body."[69]

After they had softened him up, two of the committee members then presented Walter with a choice: either he could confess and be released, or he would be handed back to the mob, which might well kill him. When he refused, Walter was told he would receive a punishment of one hundred lashes. If the whipping did not kill him outright, Walter was reassured, he would be hanged. After an initial twenty lashes had been administered, Walter was returned to the guardhouse, to be further "insulted and abused by all." His tormentors had apparently reconsidered the lash count, but Walter's ordeal was far from over.

The following day the committee discussed various means of extracting a confession by torture. As Walter told it, "[T]he most terrifying was that of confining me to a log on the carriage in the Saw mill and let the saw cut me in two." After the agonies he had already been through, Walter had every reason to assume the Patriots meant business. But then his fate turned again. Reprieved from meeting his end as a human log, Walter was brought before a man he referred to as Judge Davenport. Marveling that he had never seen anyone withstand greater suffering without exposing his comrades, Davenport eventually ordered Walter released. Like many persecuted Loyalists, he lay low in the woods and mountains until the "frenzy might be somewhat abated." His sacrifice was not in vain: Walter's brother managed to evade the Patriot search parties and went on to fight with General Charles Cornwallis at Yorktown.

As the Tory hunting intensified across the states, women and entire families increasingly felt the impact, too. In most states, confiscation laws mandated that family members abandoned by male Loyalist refugees be left with some clothing, furniture, and provisions when their estates were seized. In Massachusetts, a wife's customary right to a third of her husband's property remained protected. In South Carolina, by contrast, even wives who did not share their husband's Loyalist sentiments were considered guilty by association unless proven otherwise. Being displaced from their homes and seeing their belongings taken from them carried a tremendous psychological cost for the women and families affected. Rachel Noble, the widow of an active Loyalist in New Jersey, recorded the harassment she suffered at the hands of her neighbors in Ramapo. Narrowly escaping arrest by local authorities, she fled "with an infant at her Breast on foot and unprotected and suffered everything which can be felt from Terror, Inclemency of Weather [and] want of Food." Noble left three more children at the mercy of the Patriots, who stripped them of their clothes and pillaged and destroyed their home. After an odyssey of escape and imprisonment, Rachel was eventually reunited with her children in New York; in 1780, all departed for England.[70]

Women who actively assisted the British by aiding prisoners, ferrying goods across the lines, or gathering intelligence knew they were risking particularly severe treatment if found out. The New Yorker Lorenda Holmes "was stripped by an angry band of committeemen and dragged 'to the Drawing Room Window . . . exposing her to many Thousands of People Naked.'" On that occasion, Holmes, who apparently had been smuggling letters in her underwear from a British warship to Long Island, escaped with "shame and horror of the Mind." Not only did Holmes continue to carry secret mail, but she also guided Loyalist refugees to safety in a British camp. When the latter activities were discovered, an American soldier came to her house to execute a more physically painful form of punishment. Making Holmes remove her shoe, her tormentor took "a shovel of Wood Coals from the fire and by mere force held [my] right foot upon the Coals until he had burnt it in a most shocking manner." As he did so, her assailant admonished her that "he would learn [i.e., teach] her to carry off Loyalists to the British Army." Patriots may have felt that she got off lightly for treason, but Holmes no doubt had the consequences of her loyalty seared into her mind as much as into the sole of her foot.[71]

Like Lorenda Holmes, other American Loyalists, too, experienced Revolutionary terror at the hands of Continental soldiers, not just their civilian neighbors. In May 1777, a North Carolina unit under General Francis Nash moving through Richmond, Virginia, was followed by a shoemaker shouting, "Hurray for King George!" When he had had enough, Nash ordered his men to take the shoemaker to the James River: "The soldiers tied a rope around his middle, and seesawed him backwards and forwards until we had him nearly drowned, but every time he got his head above water he would cry for King George." The general next ordered a tarring and feathering, but the shoemaker "still would hurrah for King George." Drummed out of town, and told not to return at the threat of being shot, the shoemaker never yielded to his tormentors.[72]

Over the months and years following independence, Patriots would continue the purgation of American communities by prosecuting, physically harming, and imprisoning their Loyalist neighbors. Thirty thousand Loyalists ultimately fled their homes for the British garrison cities of New York, Charleston, and Savannah—a share of the colonial population that corresponds to some 3.8 million Americans today. By 1781, New York had recovered its prewar population of some 25,000 citizens, not including the fluctuating numbers of armed services personnel. Ten thousand Loyalists left America altogether during the war; 19,000 enlisted in Loyalist corps to fight alongside the British Army; thousands more volunteered as partisan fighters. Off the battlefield, too, Loyalists died for their political beliefs and actions, killed by mobs or at the hands of marauding bands, hanged by order of councils of safety or assemblies in various states, or executed following court-martial. But in a civil war, violence flows both ways, and for the next six years Loyalist soldiers as well as prison guards would commit both legitimate and illegitimate violence. "We are cast into a strange friendless world," bemoaned a correspondent of Continental Congress president John Hancock, "where Nation against Nation, Family against Family, and Man against Man are embattled and opposed to each other, tearing every Enjoyment, every Property, and even Life itself from the Possessor."[73]

Even while the leaders of the new United States were clamping down on internal dissent, General Sir William Howe was already launching his own loyalty offensive. At the end of November, as his army was advancing steadily to clear the Continentals from New York, Howe issued his fourth proclamation that year. It offered a pardon to all rebels who would submit within sixty days. When Howe tested the allegiance of Suffolk County by asking for two hundred wagons to move his army's baggage, the local population helped him exceed his target. To London, the Howe brothers reported that reassuring numbers of rebels were coming into British lines. Already, there were some 1,900 on Long Island and 3,000 in New Jersey in the first week alone, some 15 percent of all free male adults. But Secretary Germain warned that granting insurgents amnesty risked alienating the long-suffering Loyalists. He instructed Howe to proclaim publicly that all those rebels who failed to submit within sixty days, and anyone not meriting a royal pardon, were to receive their due punishment. As the British leadership remained divided on the strategies of violence and restraint, Germain needed to see the stick being waved alongside the dangling carrot. There must be no doubt that death always remained a possibility for a rebel.[74]

* * *

The American Patriots had scored some early rhetorical victories with their opening salvos over Lexington and Concord and in the aftermath of the British bombardments of port cities, enhanced by the cover-up at Norfolk. They had centered their declaration of independence on George III's illegitimate violence that helped legitimate their break from the mother country. After Howe had failed to trap Washington in New York, the war looked set to move into another campaign season. If the American Revolutionaries wanted to seize and retain the moral high ground, they would need to continue to discredit the British as barbarous. At the same time, they must set a positive example, a virtuous counterpoint to their enemy's alleged viciousness. It was a mission that Washington stood ready to embrace. But it remained to be seen how well his moral leadership would hold up under the pressures of command, and amid the contingencies and hardships of war.

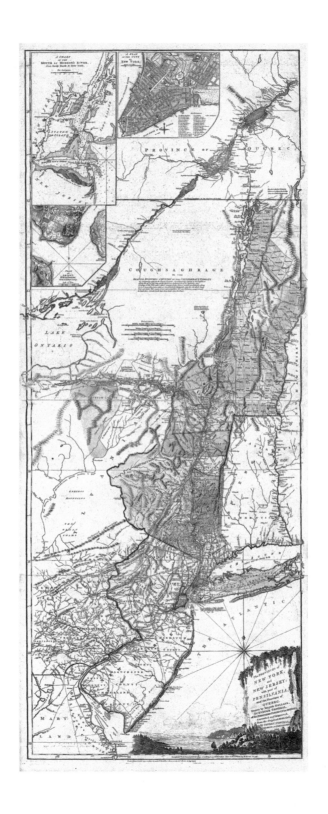

CHAPTER FOUR

Plundering Protectors

N EARLY EVERY DAY NOW IT WAS THE SAME DEPRESSING routine. Among the voluminous papers that required his attention, General George Washington found the verdicts of courts-martial awaiting his approval. He read about yet another instance of his own troops callously plundering the local population—and not just the Loyalists but Patriots and the uncommitted, too. With grim determination, he sanctioned immediate punishment. Sometimes violence could be curbed only by violence.

Just the previous week, on September 6, 1776, Washington had issued orders warning his army that he was "resolved to put a stop to plundering," whether of horses, or furniture, or merchandise of any kind. Any soldiers caught plundering, or found to be colluding with plunderers, would be brought before a court-martial and "broke with Infamy: For let it ever be remembered, that no plundering Army was ever a successful one." It was now over a week since the nearly disastrous Battle of Long Island, when his troops had survived, barely, their first major encounter with the British Army. As his forces regrouped on Manhattan, Washington had to make some key tactical and strategic decisions: Should he abandon New York or defend it as long as possible? If he quit the city, should he burn it to deny the invaders a viable base? When and where would the British confront him next? And how could he persuade his men to reenlist when their term expired at year's end? These were fundamental questions that could make or break the fall and winter campaign—and yet Washington was also concerned his troops' behavior vis-à-vis civilians might threaten the entire enterprise.[1]

Washington understood that plundering—a form of military violence against civilian property—undermined republican, Revolutionary ideals. He also knew that the line between the plundering of property and physical violence to civilian owners could be perilously thin, and that both types of transgression threatened to erode force discipline. And he appreciated that in order to win the war on the moral front, with both American and international audiences watching, he must out-civilize the enemy. This meant, for instance, granting quarter to surrendering enemy forces and treating prisoners of war according to established conventions. But first and foremost he must prevent his own troops from hurting the very people they were serving to protect. British and German soldiers had been plundering civilians from the start of the New York campaign. And as the imperial invaders continued to pillage their way through America, the Patriots' cause benefited: here was an opportunity to indict British abuse as proof that America's cause was legitimate, her Revolutionary insurgency necessary. But when Washington's own troops harmed American civilians, they eroded trust in the new nation's army, and with it the Revolutionaries' chances in the contest for American hearts and minds. As such, Washington believed, plundering had to be curtailed—even if that meant using extreme violence against his own men. If words did not sway wayward soldiers, the whip just might.[2]

The Adjutant's Daughter

September 12, 1776, promised to be another hot late-summer day. That morning, Washington's troops knew what they were in for. A court-martial had found their comrade Daniel Donovel guilty of "plundering the House lately occupied by Lord Stirling," the brave officer who had held out long enough during the recent Battle of Long Island to allow the main American force to retreat to safety. Perhaps Donovel's spoils were discovered during a search of his knapsack or tent—or had a jealous comrade given him up? There appear to be no eyewitness reports of this particular flogging, but contemporary accounts of similar scenes allow us to reconstruct how it might have looked and felt.[3]

Donovel would likely have been stripped of his coat and shirt and tied to a tree or a post, known in the army as the "adjutant's daughter" because the regimental adjutant supervised the administration of punishments ordered by courts-martial. Mustering on the Grand Parade to witness the punishment they called "putting on a new shirt," the troops would have formed a hollow square around the post or, alternatively, parallel lines with the post at the head of the regiment. The public, demonstrative administration of military justice they were about to observe was designed to instill terror. Like all soldiers in the Continental Army, they would have signed a copy of the Articles of War, which included regulations for the protection of civilians. With the chaplain warning them against repeating the culprit's crime, the company drummers would have readied themselves to execute the punishment, probably taking off their jackets for maximum freedom of movement and strength. One former British drummer, who later campaigned for the abolition of military flogging, experienced this preliminary "practice of stripping" as "so unnatural, inhuman, and butcher-like" that he "often felt most acutely [his] own degradation in being compelled to perform it." One final time the first drummer might have checked his instrument of terror, the cat-o'-nine-tails. It consisted of nine thongs, or tails, of whipcord. Three hard knots were tied into each cord so as to maximize the damage and pain it inflicted when it lacerated human skin.

With the troops lined up and Donovel bound to the post, the drummer would have separated the cords, perhaps swung the cat over his head as they did in the navy, and brought it down hard on Donovel's naked back. With each lash the drummer's whip would have drawn more blood, and after a few stripes he would have had to wipe the cords free of Donovel's blood and tissue. The unit drum major's job was to see to it that each of the thirty-nine lashes—the convention of forty less one derived from Mosaic law—was "well laid on"; the rotation among drummers ensured that each strike landed with maximum strength. Involuntary onlookers would have remembered their own painful experiences at the post. Some would now be flinching with each stroke of the whip; we know from other descriptions that some fainted. Such public displays of military discipline were routinely performed in front of a culprit's own companies; the men who shared Donovel's tent may have found the torturous display particularly hard to witness. Herman Melville's novel *White-Jacket*, which contains a powerful scene of a naval flogging, imagines that others among such crowds, "either from constitutional hard-heartedness or the multiplied searings of habit," would already "have been made proof against the sense of degradation, pity, and shame."

Although Donovel would probably have been given a lead bullet to chew on, the physical pain was likely overwhelming. As Alexander Somerville, one of the few soldiers who ever wrote about his experience of being flogged, recalled, "I felt an astounding sensation between the shoulders, under my neck, which went to my toe nails in one direction, my finger nails in another, and stung me to the heart, as if a knife had gone through my body." By the time that two dozen lashes had torn his flesh, Donovel's lacerated back would have "resemble[d] roasted meat burnt nearly black before scorching fire; yet still the lashes fall." Lash by lash, each hitting "as though the talons of a hawk were tearing the flesh off their bones," as one British victim wrote, the army's violence ensured that the culprit's crime, punishment, and shame would be permanently inscribed on his flesh.

When they had finished with him, Donovel's shoulders and back would have been grazed and rent, bruised and blistered, skin flaying off his back, and pieces of it torn off his bound wrists, too. As Melville writes, "stripped like a slave; scourged worse than a hound," the publicly whipped man might feel the indignity and insult as much as the physical pain that would be with him for days or weeks, especially if this was his first whipping: "while his back bleeds" at the post, he "bleeds agonized drops of shame from his soul!" The drummers would have cleaned the cat of Donovel's flesh to prepare for the next flogging later that day, or the next. Perhaps one of them would have been wondering whether his comrades saw him lay on the lashes all too well and might beat into him a lesson better to calibrate his future floggings. Their witnessing duty done, the troops were dismissed, retreating to the relative safety of Harlem Heights.

The brutality of the punishment reflected the seriousness of the crime. Few civilians would have attended the floggings of any of their plunderers. But having their homes plundered by one or several armies was a common and scary experience for Americans during the war. Most Patriots, unsurprisingly, laid the blame on the British, the Hessians, and the Loyalists. General Howe, whom Thomas Paine denounced as "the chief of plunderers," had also promised the Hessians "plunder and destruction" for their service.[4]

Contemporaries often compared the impact of plundering enemy troops on a community to that of a natural disaster. Wherever the British Army marched, it was said, they left landscapes in their wake that resembled areas hit by tornadoes, earthquakes, or the plague. On June 27, 1777, the Patriot colonel Israel Shreve arrived at Westfield, nine miles west of Elizabethtown, New Jersey, just hours after a 13,000-strong British army had left the area. Bivouacked near the town, the redcoats had taken 2,365 fence rails to keep their fires going. In a looting spree fueled by cider, gin, port, rum, and whiskey, soldiers had entered over ninety houses, plundering 11,000 items. The soldiers had taken hundreds of pieces of clothing—not just men's breeches and coats but also women's apparel and children's items. They pillaged miles of linen, lace, ribbon, and wool, as well as hundreds of items of bedding. They took 342 fowl, 665 sheep, and 106 hogs, as well as 28 beehives; carted away 11 tables, 18 chairs, and 26 mirrors; and stole 19 axes, a dozen hammers, and even a plough. It would take several pages to list the miscellaneous objects that were stolen, ranging from 105 pounds of candles to three barrels of soap. In the immediate aftermath, Shreve observed the "shocking havock" the British had left: "I saw many famalys who Declared they had Not one mouthful to Eat, [nor any] bed or beding Left, or [a] Stich of Wearing Apparel to put on, only what they happened to have on, and would not afoard Crying Children a mouthful of Bread Or

Water Dureing their stay." The community would claim a very sizable £8,700 worth of damages.[5]

At the same time, the British and Loyalists capitalized on any evidence of the rebels plundering American civilians. "The Ravages of the Rebel Army in and about the Jersies," proclaimed the British-Loyalist *New-York Gazette*, "are shocking to Humanity." The rebels, it was said, targeted not only Loyalists and their property, but all farmers, to the point where agriculture had virtually ground to a halt and famine threatened.[6]

It is perhaps not surprising that plundering was widespread throughout the war. An army, Frederick the Great of Prussia had written on the eve of the American Revolution, is a body whose foundation is the stomach. Yet most early modern armies experienced perpetual supply problems. As mobile armies often had to live off the land, continual foraging and impressment were essential for their survival. Foraging was defined as the taking of livestock, grain, and other foodstuffs by soldiers under the supervision of officers, with or without immediate payment or receipt or promissory notes for future compensation. Impressment was a forced sale of foodstuffs, often with insufficient compensation for the involuntary sellers. By the eighteenth century, uncontrolled pillaging and looting were supposedly on the wane. Still, the line between organized foraging and regular impressment on the one hand and unlicensed and arbitrary plundering on the other was thin.[7]

American historians like David Hackett Fischer distinguish between different kinds and degrees of plundering in the Revolutionary War. American troops committed mostly "petty theft and careless destruction," writes Fischer; the British and their German auxiliaries were guilty of worse crimes. But the distinctions are perhaps not so clear-cut. Although precise assessments are hard to come by, the historical record affords us the occasional snapshot. After 1781, citizens of New Jersey could claim compensation for losses suffered since 1776 at the hands not only of British forces but also of the Continental Army and Patriot militias. British soldiers did seem to seize items much more indiscriminately: in addition to foraging for grain, crops, and livestock, they routinely took household goods and personal effects—for their own use or for sale on the black market outside army camps and in occupied cities.

Claims against Washington's own troops were on average significantly lower than those against the British Army, covering mostly items of forage and men's clothing. At the same time, claims against the Continental Army were more frequent. Continental soldiers seized oysters from oyster beds, plucked apples in orchards, uprooted turnips and cabbages, dug out potatoes, and stole corn and watermelons from the fields. Chicken, geese, turkeys, hogs, sheep, cattle, oxen, and horses were snatched at night or driven from pastures in the broad light of day. Continentals routinely turned horses and cattle loose in grain fields or meadows. Soldiers stole salt, beef, cheese, flour and sugar, tea and coffee, cider, rum, and wine from shops and cellars, both for immediate consumption and for sale or exchange with other articles. Officers occasionally abetted such for-profit plundering or even took their cut. In short, inhabitants living near American armies felt their plundering presence as much as the enemy's.[8]

As in other war zones, it is the ordinariness of much of this plundering that is striking. But plundering troops didn't just pose a risk to homes and goods. Whenever soldiers approached a homestead or farm to plunder, physical violence always threatened, especially if citizens tried to defend their property against often inebriated soldiers. In one such instance, a British foraging party entering the Frazer residence in Chester County, Pennsylvania, found only Mary Worrall Frazer, the wife of the Patriot major Persifor Frazer, and one female slave. In the nick of time, Mary had sent her four children, a servant, and two other slaves into hiding. The soldiers were getting drunk from the liquor they found while searching her house, when, "just as one of the men was going to strike me," Mary later recorded, their commanding officer restored a degree of order. But the invaders continued to remove Mary's possessions; when they left, she had insufficient supplies to feed her family.[9]

Whether physical violence was latent or threatened, as in Mary Frazer's case, or overt—as it was for one Andrew Miller on Long

Island, whom whaleboaters from Connecticut struck so severely with the breech of a musket that he suffered facial fractures and was left for dead—plundering brought the war right to people's farms and into their homes. It stripped them of their belongings and destroyed their sense of safety. Plundering also challenged American citizens' identity, rooted as it was in the sanctity of property—a notion (inherited from England) in defense of which the Revolutionary War was in part being fought. As a form of wartime violence, then, plundering was a serious material, political, and ethical problem.[10]

Precisely because plundering posed such an acute challenge for military-civilian relations, as well as for internal army discipline, army commanders on all sides meted out harsh punishment. Donovel, the culprit that September morning, as well as the men whipping him and the Continental troops ordered to witness his flogging, were well accustomed to the daily violence that ruled army life. Armies depend on the strict regulation of individuals, including the physical disciplining of their bodies. Officers in eighteenth-century armies routinely beat, caned, and clubbed soldiers in camps, in barracks, and on parade for even the smallest infractions, and sometimes just because they could. In addition to floggings for offenses trivial or severe, other painful forms of corporal punishment included riding the wooden horse (a wooden sawhorse structure, with weights or muskets attached to the offender's legs) and running the gauntlet, when an officer might hold a sword's tip to the culprit's chest so as to slow down his progress through the beating ranks. American soldiers locked up in the whirligig, a cage that was turned at great speed, were said to go mad. Defenders of military flogging highlighted that it was prompt, cheap, and efficient; rarely did it deprive the army of a valuable fighting man. There is no clear evidence, though, that flogging actually reduced the incidence of military crimes.[11]

To put military justice in context, we should remember that Anglo-American criminal law at that time imposed corporal punishment, including whippings, very regularly on civilians, both men and women, for crimes against persons as well as against property. And while it is true that the eighteenth century saw a transition away from exemplary punishment to modern penal codes, there were two very major exceptions: military discipline and slavery. The terror of the whip ruled on slave ships and colonial plantations. And while abolitionists were then starting to brandish the accusing image of the slave's lash-scarred back, humanitarian reforms of military discipline still lay in the distant future. Those defending military flogging—including the new republic's slaveholding commander in chief—remained adamant that it was indispensable for army discipline.[12]

We cannot be certain that Washington personally witnessed the corporal punishment of any of his soldiers. But even as a young colonel he had issued strict orders against plundering on marches and around campsites. Washington had studied select classical war writings, including Julius Caesar's *Commentaries on the Gallic War* (in translation, always painfully aware of his lack of formal education), and modern military texts, some lent to him by older British officers like Lieutenant General Thomas Gage, who would later become his enemy. Practical army manuals such as the widely read Humphrey Bland's *Treatise of Military Discipline* (Washington purchased his copy in the 1750s) suggested that destroying the countryside or laying it under contributions—that is, exacting goods, money, and labor—"only serve[d] to render the poor Inhabitants more miserable . . . without contributing anything to the service."[13]

A scholar of military justice in the Continental Army, Harry M. Ward, notes that Washington "seems never to have been concerned . . . with the terrible suffering endured by soldiers being punished." And Washington left no one in any doubt that he was a strict disciplinarian. An army, as he had proclaimed on New Year's Day in 1776, "without Order, Regularity & Discipline" was "no better than a Commission'd Mob." Even during his late teenage years, as Washington had been perfecting his skills as a surveyor, he was, writes the historian Richard N. Smith, "stamping order on chaos by fixing his name on previously uncharted territory." By his twenties, Washington was learning British-style rigor when fighting alongside the redcoats on the frontier during the Seven Years' War. "I have a Gallows near 40 feet high erected," he boasted, "and I am determined . . . to hang two or three on it, as an example to others."[14]

When Washington had taken charge of the Continental Army at Cambridge in the summer of 1775, he found the Massachusetts provincials in a sorry state, barely fit to fight the mighty British Empire—indeed, "an exceeding dirty & nasty people," as he put it privately. Officers were using their civilian skills to shave their men or mend their shoes while allowing themselves to be addressed by their first names, which risked undermining the strict hierarchy of ranks. As on the frontier two decades earlier, discipline and order were, yet again, Washington's first priority. He remembered the lessons from Bland's military treatise and recommended officers in his new army read the book.[15]

Paradoxically, it seemed, the army defending the ideals of liberty would need to embrace authoritarian principles in order to survive. The Continental Army embodied the Revolution, and the relationship between the American people and the army was critical to the Revolution's success. But just like other professional armies, the new republic's fighting force needed to be "an absolute Tyranny," as Washington's top military justice official, William Tudor, put it, where "every Man who carries Arms, from the General Officer to the private Centinel, must be content to be a temporary Slave." America's struggle for freedom required them to win the moral war against the British invaders, and that necessitated the frequent use of the whip.[16]

And yet, Washington realized that the floggings were not working. Even if laid on with the appropriate severity to lacerate the backs of plundering miscreants like Donovel, 39 lashes were simply not enough. This punishment paled in comparison with the draconian lash counts for British soldiers convicted of the same offenses, and for whom 400, 600, 800, even 1,000 lashes or more, were not at all uncommon: not for nothing did Americans call British soldiers bloody backs. In part, the severity of British court-martial sentences for plunderers reflected the concern with protecting private property that the officer class shared with the country's ruling elites more broadly. Even women who violated the sanctity of property were subject to harsh corporal punishment. Perhaps refugees or spies from Boston had told the story of Winifred McCowan, who was convicted of having stolen the town bull and having it killed. McCowan was sentenced "to be tied to a Carts Tail, and thereto receive 100 lashes on her bare back, in different portions in the most publick parts of the town and Camp," the indecent exposure of her flesh compounding the humiliation. During the British occupation of Philadelphia, a mariner was to be sentenced to 1,000 lashes for stealing a black inhabitant's cow. The invading army had already hanged some of its own men for plundering stores and private houses.[17]

Compared with the justice meted out by the British military—his model of discipline and now his formidable enemy—the maximum punishment at Washington's disposal was no credible deterrent for a hungry soldier, a private eager for adventure or profit, or an enlisted man who simply took what he considered his. For Washington knew that his troops, much like British soldiers, had a contractual understanding of what the army owed them in return for their service. When pay was in arrears or supplies were short, when they saw embezzlement was ripe or perceived that their officers and civilian authorities were treating them poorly, soldiers were more easily prepared to supplement their provisions by irregular means. "The devil would now and then tell us," wrote Private Daniel Barber, that "it was no harm to pull a few potatoes and cabbages, and pluck, once in a while, an ear of corn, when we stood in need." Some drew the line at pumpkins and potatoes, others at poultry or pigs, and still others only at the robbing of homes. By the time resources became very scarce during the first difficult winter at Valley Forge, even officers admitted to feeling the urge: "I am ashamed to say it," confessed the army surgeon Dr. Albigence Waldo, "but I am tempted to steal Fowls if I could find them, or even a whole Hog, for I feel as if I could eat one." Washington, then, faced a formidable task balancing his soldiers' immediate needs with the ideals of the American cause.[18]

Consider for a moment the food requirements of the Continental Army. Washington estimated that 15,000 men consumed 20 million pounds of meat and 100,000 barrels of flour annually. Until the evacuation of Manhattan in fall 1776, the American forces were reasonably well provisioned with pork and beef, bread, rice, and cornmeal, as well as fresh produce. But for the remainder of the war, supplies of meat, flour, and bread fluctuated widely; vegetables were often scarce, with the most severe shortages experienced in winter camps at Valley Forge and Morristown in 1778 and 1779. (Prices in Pennsylvania rose by 700 percent during 1779.) In February 1778, soldiers had only three ounces of meat and three pounds of bread each to last them for an entire week. Washington acknowledged a paradox: "With respect to Food, considering we are in such an extensive and abundant Country, no Army was ever worse supplied than ours."[19]

The new American state was ill-equipped to feed its defenders. Yet Washington had to balance his army's urgent need for provisions with the equally important priority of maintaining good army-civilian relations. Thus, when he was forced to obtain food directly from the citizenry, Washington paid if he could, or at least issued bills of credit in compliance with civilian oversight rules imposed by Congress and the states. Commissary agents, accompanied by armed guards, would buy foodstuffs in the countryside and forward them via supply depots to the army.[20]

However, this system was often hampered. Inadequate roads and waterways created transport problems, which were compounded by insufficient wagons, horses, and oxen, as well as a shortage of skilled workers, such as teamsters, hostlers, and blacksmiths. Lack of salt limited the ability to preserve meat. American farmers and merchants, irrespective of their political loyalties, often ferried their livestock and produce across considerable distances to sell them to the British, who tended to pay better. Embezzlement and theft were widespread in the army, as goods were sold to inhabitants in exchange for liquor and other desired articles. Some quartermasters and commissary generals of the stores, whose pay was low, turned to profiteering, although it appears the Continental Army may have prosecuted fraud more rigorously than the British did. When other methods yielded insufficient supplies, Washington had no choice but to resort to foraging and, from the winter of 1777–78 onward, to impressment.[21]

Washington's army competed with the British for limited resources, especially of fresh foods, hay, oats, horses, and wagons. From 1775 to 1781, the British Army experienced more or less continuous and occasionally acute food shortages. In order to feed between 60,000 and 90,000 troops each year, it had to source the vast majority of its supplies from Britain. The quantities passing through the commissary general's office from spring 1777 to autumn 1781 included nearly 80 million pounds of bread, flour, and rice; 11 million pounds of salt beef and over 38 million pounds of salt pork; 3 million pounds of fresh meat; nearly 4 million pounds of butter; some 427,000 bushels of peas; 177,000 gallons of molasses; 134,000 gallons of vinegar; and 2.8 million gallons of rum.[22]

The British military even tried to ship fresh foodstuffs across the Atlantic. It encouraged the development of methods to avoid the bruising of onions and potatoes in transit. Casks with spring-loaded pressure relief valves allowed sauerkraut to complete the fermentation process belowdecks. Those managing to deliver animals alive received premiums. But the high incidence of livestock fatalities en route, inadequate preservation techniques, and mistakes in warehousing—not to mention the ravenous rats—curbed the transatlantic delivery of edible foods. Often the quality of rations was so poor that hungry soldiers refused to eat the "mouldy bread, weevily biscuit, rancid butter, sour flour, wormeaten pease, [and] maggoty beef." As one observer remarked, "[O]ur army moulders away amazingly: many die by the sword, many by sickness" caused by foul provisions. In the end, therefore, the British Army had to rely very heavily on local (American) supplies of fresh meat and greens, flour, grain, and rice, as well as forage of hay and oats.[23]

But procuring fresh food in America posed considerable challenges for the invaders. James Murray, a veteran Scots officer, wrote a letter home in June 1776—even before the main troop contingents arrived—complaining of his meager rations. Officers, Murray lamented, were allotted no more than the soldiers, "nor have I tasted 4 morsels of fresh provisions for 4 months. Broiled salt porc for breakfast, boiled salt porc for dinner, cold salt porc for supper." With the move of army headquarters to New York and the occupation or domination of large parts of New Jersey and Rhode Island in late 1776, provisioning the army from America temporarily became easier for the British. For Washington, it would mean he had to find supplies elsewhere, or claw them from the invaders' greedy hands.[24]

Indeed, the opposing armies' immense appetite for food and fuel led to regular foraging wars between them—"fighting for our daily bread," as one British officer called it. British foraging parties scoured the countryside near their base camps for fresh provisions, horses, hay, and fuel. Seeking to deny them supplies, Americans harassed the foragers. The latter therefore required large covering parties of 500 to more than 2,000 men, making foraging extremely expensive. It also was dangerous. By the end of the 1776–77 winter, Howe's army had been reduced to half its size, with most of the casualties due to skirmishes and minor raids, often in the context of such foraging expeditions.[25]

Given that their supply situation was frequently dire, British and American troops were all too easily tempted to supplement their rations and clothing by plundering civilians. Both sides thus risked alienating populations whose support they needed in order to win the war. For Washington, it was the very values underlying the American cause that were at stake—not to mention his army's credibility in defending that cause.

The Terror of Example

Since Washington was forced, all too often, to resort to foraging and impressment, it was imperative that he control his troops' conduct towards civilians. To that end, he put practical measures in place to curtail the soldiers' opportunities for misbehavior. Washington set up posts near mansions along army routes in order to prevent straggling soldiers from peeling off. He ordered guards and patrols around campsites to be enhanced. Commanders limited the numbers of passes from camp and the distance enlisted men could travel even if they did have a pass. Roll calls were ordered two or three times per day, often unannounced, while officers checked soldiers' tents and knapsacks for illegally obtained goods. Soldiers were banned from leaving camp after the nightly roll call and from taking weapons out of camp. A barrage of orders warned against pilfering and burning houses and barns; damaging mowing grounds, gardens, and orchards; and burning rails, fences, shrubs, and trees as firewood. Washington's appeals that the troops treat civilians with decency were sometimes posted in public places and published in the papers in an attempt to reassure the wider population.[26]

Even though such preventive measures were necessary, they were not sufficient. If Washington and his officers were to stem the spread of plundering that threatened to corrode army discipline and undermine civilian trust, and if they wished to assert America's moral superiority over the invading forces, courts-martial needed to be able to impose much tougher sentences than thirty-nine lashes. Throughout the summer of 1776, the Congress had been revising the Articles of War, with Thomas Jefferson and especially John Adams taking leading roles on the Committee on Spies. As far as Washington was concerned, they could not finish their work soon enough.

One week after Donovel's flogging, Washington took the unusual step of shaming his army by comparing it unfavorably with that of the British. The king's forces, Washington wrote in orders that were read out at every army post, were "exceeding careful to restrain every kind of abuse of private Property." By contrast, "the abandoned and profligate part of our own Army, countenanced by a few officers, who are lost to every Sense of Honor and Virtue, as well as their Country's Good, are by Rapine and Plunder, spreading Ruin and Terror wherever they go." When soldiers caused destruction and inspired fear instead of upholding notions of republican virtue, honor, and patriotism, the Revolutionary cause suffered. Washington reiterated his previous orders that he would "punish without exception, every person who shall be found guilty of this most abominable practice, which if continued, must prove the destruction of any Army on earth."[27]

With no updates from the politicians in Philadelphia, and in the face of incessant civilian complaints, Washington and his staff were feeling increasingly desperate for alternative measures. By September 25, a sleepless Washington—"[F]rom the hours allotted to Sleep, I will borrow a few moments"—wrote a very long letter to John Hancock, the president of the Congress. The general urged his civilian superiors once more to allow for harsher discipline to curb the alarming spread of plundering. His soldiers were using any excuse to steal from civilians. They threatened to commit arson to make inhabitants flee their houses and then rob them with impunity; afterward, they often did burn homes to conceal their actions. Washington reassured Hancock that he had tried his utmost, including instituting summary corporal punishment, "to stop this horrid practice, but under the present lust after plunder, and want of Laws to punish Offenders, I might almost as well attempt to remove Mount Atlas."[28]

To underscore his frustration with the lenient punishments for plunderers, that same day Washington forwarded to the Congress the records of one recent court-martial that had particularly outraged him. Ensign Matthew Macumber, of Taunton, Massachusetts, had been caught red-handed by Brigade Major Daniel Box as Macumber was leading twenty of his men in plundering a house just outside American lines. Box had demanded that Macumber put down his loot or return it to its rightful owners. Instead, Macumber ordered his men to prepare to fire on Box. The latter beat a tactical retreat, later to return with a larger party to disarm and arrest Macumber, who was brought before a court-martial. At the trial, presided over by the delightfully named Colonel Comfort Sage, Box testified that he found Macumber's troop "loaded with plunder, such as House furniture, table Linen and Kitchen Utensils, China & Delph Ware." Box's men supported his story, adding women's clothing to the items of plunder and confirming that the offenders would have fired on them had they tried to seize the stolen goods. Two of Macumber's men testified in their superior's defense, saying that he had ordered them specifically not to plunder. The court acquitted Macumber of plundering and robbery, requiring only that he ask Box's pardon and be reprimanded for insubordination and threatening a superior officer.

In disbelief, Washington refused to confirm the verdict and, as was his privilege as commander in chief, asked the court to reconsider, tersely annotating the copy of the trial minutes that he forwarded to the Congress: "[T]he Men who were to Share the Plunder, became the evidence for the Prisoner." At the retrial, another officer corroborated that he, too, had challenged Macumber, from whose overflowing knapsack some wax toys were protruding, while his men were carrying off chairs, kettles, and other items; their pistols cocked, the men were ready to fire on Box. The court now ordered Macumber cashiered, or dismissed in disgrace. Washington saw to it that the revised verdict was implemented immediately.[29]

Macumber may have narrowly escaped a much harsher sentence. For, as yet unknown to Washington, on September 20, Congress had finally passed revised Articles of War. Drafted largely by John Adams and modeled on the British articles, these tightened the regulations for protecting civilians from the plundering and destruction of their property. The death sentence could now be imposed for a total of sixteen offenses ranging from mutiny, sedition, and desertion to plundering. The maximum corporal punishment was raised from thirty-nine lashes to one hundred, a significant increase, if still massively lower than the average lash sentence in the British Army.[30]

Repeatedly during the war, Washington requested that Congress either permit a maximum lash count of five hundred or remove any cap at all. A broader spectrum of corporal punishments, his thinking went, would also help reduce excessive and arbitrary beatings of soldiers by their officers, who often resorted to such spontaneous punishment instead of going to the trouble of a court-martial and its limited set of sanctions. Congress, however, rejected Washington's urgent recommendation. Washington would

144 | Scars of Independence

mostly adhere to the hundred-lash limit, although occasionally he also approved up to five hundred. Lacking the legal option of much more severe lash sentences, he periodically authorized the execution of plunderers, both as a result of courts-martial and even in the form of summary executions without trial. But, in the fall of 1776, Washington was still relying mostly on the whip rather than the rope as he sought to rein in his plundering troops. The extent to which he was successful would shape the battle for American popular support.[31]

The Politics of Plunder

By mid-November 1776, as the British were completing their sweep of New York, the imperial high command had already decided to extend its reach. A major British army led by the thirty-seven-year-old aristocrat and career officer Major General Charles Cornwallis would drive the American forces out of eastern New Jersey, making it the third colony (after New York and Rhode Island) restored to British rule and, crucially, turning it into a supply base for the army. Washington learned of this objective and moved his forces into New Jersey in anticipation of a British invasion, which Cornwallis launched on November 18 with some 10,000 men. Cornwallis's army moved relatively slowly—it daily consumed seventeen tons of food; it needed to stop early each day to collect wood for fuel and to bake bread; the 1,000 horses drawing the massive baggage train required hay and water. But liberated Loyalists were flocking to the British standard: more than one-tenth of New Jersey households swore an oath of allegiance once Howe promised to pardon them. The strategy of regaining territory and loyal subjects for the Crown appeared to be working.[32]

In order to maintain popular American support, however, British commanders knew that their troops needed to be seen as liberators, not conquerors. If they were students of history, they might remember that excessive plundering during the previous century's English Civil War had alienated civilian populations there. General Howe opposed plundering with more or less explicit reference to the ongoing battle for American sympathies. Charles Stedman, who served under Howe as a British Army commissary, later nonetheless confirmed that the British Army in New Jersey had indulged in the politically indiscriminate "business (we say business, for it was a perfect trade) of plunder. . . . The friend and the foe, from the hand of rapine, shared alike." Until now, the people of the Jerseys had generally been sympathetic to Britain, many enlisting to fight for the Empire. Yet, when they realized that they enjoyed little or no protection, that the British frequently seized their property, and that, in many instances, "their families were insulted, stripped of their beds, with other furniture—nay, even of their very wearing apparel," more than a few switched sides. Perhaps the American army would at least compensate them for losses. Another officer reflected on the effect of British troops tearing clothing and property from locals: "[W]e went on persuading to enmity those minds already undecided, and inducing our very Friends to fly to the opposite party for protection."[33]

As Lexington, Falmouth, and Norfolk had shown, the application of violence that could be portrayed as excessive consistently backfired on the British. After those early public relations disasters, any evidence or rumors that the British were continuing their war of depredation aided the Revolutionaries in their polemical and moral war. Some suggested that, in the face of widespread American plundering, the British could have ended the rebellion quickly. But "unfortunately the indiscriminate Plunder of the British Army" neutralized any potential political and moral advantage. With both armies causing destruction, the population kept changing sides according to the fluctuating fortunes and the more or less destructive behavior of the opposing armies.[34]

Meanwhile, Washington's army was at real risk of simply "melting away," to use David Hackett Fischer's phrase, as the terms of soldiers' enlistments expired. When they moved through Princeton and Trenton by the start of December, barely 2,500 men were left. But supplying even that rump with blankets, clothes, and shoes increasingly posed a problem, and "the ground was literally marked with the blood of the soldiers' feet." Still, Washington did not waver from his principles—even if that meant protecting the treacherous Loyalists from Continental plunderers.[35]

Washington looked at the politics of plunder with great moral clarity. While many Continental soldiers considered Loyalist property fair game, their commander in chief insisted they not indulge in politically motivated looting. The prosecution of internal enemies should instead be left to civilian authorities. For Washington, discipline and principle trumped any disdain that his troops or officers might feel towards the Loyalists. In limited circumstances, Washington did sometimes permit his soldiers to appropriate Loyalist assets. He did not condone, however, when soldiers turned carefully delimited appropriation orders "into a mere plundering scheme" against anyone they chose to label as Tories.[36]

The extent to which Washington's consistent disciplinarian efforts succeeded in curtailing plundering is impossible to ascertain, as it is asking for a counterfactual: How much more devastating to civilians—and damaging to the American cause—might plundering have been without Washington's strict approach? What perhaps mattered more was the unambiguous message he sent to his army, to the civilian population, and to the enemy in his attempt to project a positive image of America's armed forces. Washington tackled the formidable challenge of plundering with all the tools of command, communication, and chastisement at his disposal. The steady stream of agonizing orders issuing forth from headquarters testify to his continuous frustration.[37]

* * *

Since starting their retreat from New York City, Washington's troops had marched some one hundred miles. By the time General Cornwallis reached the Delaware River, Washington had moved his troops to the Pennsylvania side, avoiding a direct confrontation. As Anglo-German forces entered Trenton, New Jersey, on December 8, General William Howe—much to the vexation of his subordinates—ordered the army to move to winter quarters.

If the American troops had not starved by spring, Howe would resume the pursuit. But Washington, whom the Congress on December 12 vested with "full power to order and direct all things relative ... to the operation of the war" for six months, had a surprise in store for the invaders. His next move wouldn't just expel the enemy from much of New Jersey and deprive them of that crucial granary; it would also gain Washington a vital foothold for congressional investigators to collect evidence of enemy plundering as well as some of the war's more abhorrent developments: atrocities on the battlefield and the rape of American women. If Britain's success depended on winning American popular support, their troops' abusive behavior already threatened to undermine the Empire's mission.[38]

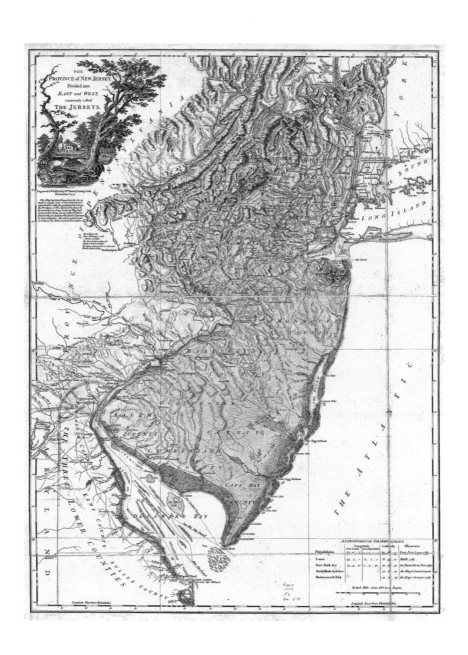

THE
PROVINCE of NEW JERSEY,
Divided into
EAST and WEST,
commonly called
THE JERSEYS.

CHAPTER FIVE

Violated Bodies

O N MAY 31, 1777, A CONTINENTAL ARMY PATROL OF TEN
men under Lieutenant William Martin was ambushed
by a British-Hessian unit, fifteen strong, between Rari-
tan Landing and Bound Brook, New Jersey. When two German
soldiers were gravely wounded, their comrades became so enraged
that "they hacked to death the Rebel officer and 6 men on the
spot," observed Colonel Count Carl von Donop, the commander of
German forces in New Jersey, whose unenviable task it had been
to hold a series of exposed towns along the Delaware River the
previous winter.[1]

General Washington had Lieutenant Martin's body recovered
the day after his slaying and taken to his headquarters at Bound
Brook. He then ordered the mangled corpse to be washed and put
on display as evidence of the enemy's brutality. Washington's close
aide Alexander Hamilton shared his observations with the New
York congressman John Jay. As Hamilton reported from the scene,
Martin had become the victim of "a most barbarous butchery." He
had sustained

> not a single bullet wound, but was hacked to pieces with the
> sword. He had several cuts in his head, each of which was suf-
> ficient to dispatch him, besides a number of more inconsider-
> able scars about his body and hands. It is evident, that the most
> wanton and unnecessary cruelty must have been given him
> when utterly out of a condition to resist. This may be relied on
> as a fact.

Within days, Patriot newspapers gave details of how Martin, despite asking for quarter, had been "butchered with the greatest cruelty; seventeen wounds were plain to be seen, most of which, it is said, were sufficient singly to be mortal." In private diary entries such as those of the Reverend Dr. Henry Melchior Muhlenberg, Martin's injuries became—though most likely not witnessed firsthand—torturous mutilation: "[H]is eyes were knocked out, his nose was cut off, and finally, he was killed by the stabs of seventeen men and his body was left lying in the field." The seventeen wounds had turned into an image of seventeen enemy soldiers thrusting cold steel into the American's unresisting body.[2]

On the day following the camp equivalent of a lying in state, Washington had a military party escort Martin's corpse in a cloth-covered box to the nearby British headquarters of General Cornwallis. Sentries refused to let the cargo pass their perimeter. They did, however, examine Washington's cover letter in which he protested "that spirit of wanton cruelty, that has in several instances influenced the conduct of your soldiery." Martin had thus been "unnecessarily murdered with the most aggravated circumstances of barbarity." He, Washington, had therefore decided to deliver Martin's "mangled body, to your lines, as an undeniable testimony of the fact, should it be doubted, and as the best appeal to your humanity for the justice of our complaint." One British officer took a single look at the makeshift casket and retorted "that *he was no coroner*," a dismissive comment that gestured towards the Americans' standard of evaluation—namely, an expert assessment of bodily evidence in judging a breach of the codes of war—while simultaneously rejecting it. In his official response to Washington, Cornwallis denied that Martin had ever asked for quarter. Instead, it was the nature of his killing by the sabers of multiple opponents that had resulted in the mutilation that Washington was wrongly producing as proof of an atrocity. "When a man is kill'd in that manner," Cornwallis concluded, "his body must of course be mangled."[3]

When Washington delivered Martin's body in such a theatrical fashion, he chose an unusually emphatic way of producing evidence of British wrongdoing. But that spring—as reports kept coming in that the British routinely offended against the codes of war—the American Revolutionaries, and especially the Continental Congress and Continental Army, were also experimenting much more widely with investigative and forensic methods. They thus hoped to turn bodies mangled in small-scale military defeats into moral and polemical assets in their war for popular American support—and even to attract British and international sympathies.

* * *

The night of December 25, 1776, as a snowstorm was "changing to sleet" that cut "like a knife," Washington executed the now-legendary surprise nighttime crossing of the icy Delaware River with some 2,400 of his troops. "Soldiers keep by your officers for Gods Sake keep by your officers," the commander in chief had told his men "in a deep & Solemn voice." Shoeless soldiers

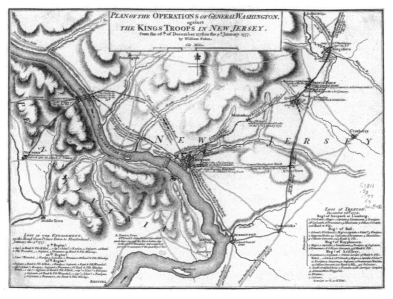

William Faden, Plan of the Operations of General Washington against the Kings Troops in New Jersey from the 26th of December 1776 to the 3rd of January 1777 *(London, 1777)*.

had "tied old rags around their feet; others [were] barefoot" as they were rowed across by those Marblehead fishermen who had previously manned the boats on Washington's retreat from Long Island.

Around eight a.m., Washington's troops surprised some 1,500 Hessians at Trenton, a small town on the Delaware. Many of Trenton's one hundred houses lay deserted by their residents; Hessian troops and Loyalist refugees from the surrounding countryside shared a large stone barracks dating from the Seven Years' War. As one Hessian noted, "We have not slept one night in peace since we came to this place." In the prevailing conditions of snow, rain, and wind, the Continentals had difficulty firing their muskets. They did much of their fighting—street-to-street, house-to-house—with musket butts, bayonets (short in supply), swords, and their bare hands. When it was over, after little more than an hour, one hundred Hessians were dead or wounded, and more than nine hundred had been taken prisoner. Eight Americans were injured

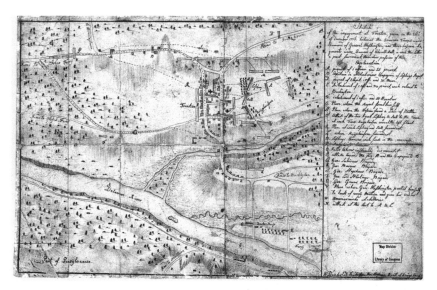

Andreas Wiederholdt, Sketch of the engagement at Trenton, given on the 26th of December 1776 betwixt the American troops under command of General Washington, and three Hessian regiments under command of Colonell Rall, in which the latter a part surrendert themselves prisoner of war *[1776]*.

and four dead. Washington withdrew and soon began preparing a second raid.[4]

On January 2, General Cornwallis arrived at Trenton with some 5,500 British troops. He had already posted 1,200 men in Princeton, including light dragoons under Lieutenant Colonel Charles Mawhood. Washington, who had by then recrossed the Delaware once again, overnight withdrew his army from their position southeast of Trenton. He sent General Hugh Mercer with 350 infantry to block the approach to Princeton two miles to the southwest, by the Stony Creek Bridge. The next day, January 3, Mawhood clashed with Mercer in a nearby orchard. After firing one volley at fifty yards' distance, Mawhood ordered a bayonet charge that broke up the opposing force. Mercer's horse was shot from under him; surrounded by multiple British soldiers, he was mortally wounded. But the Americans prevailed in the Battle of Princeton, with 23 killed and 20 wounded; 28 Britons were killed, 58 wounded, and 187 missing or captured. As witnesses later recounted, the frozen ground of the battlefield ensured that "all the blood which was shed remained on the surface, which added to the horror of this scene of carnage." The area was strewn with the bodies of British and American soldiers; the next day, some were buried in a joint mass grave. From Trenton to Princeton, the British had lost some 2,000 men to the Americans' 200.[5]

It would take until mid-February 1777 for news of Washington's victories to reach London. With the prime minister recovering from a riding accident, the hard-liner Lord Germain led the cabinet's response: Howe was to act "with less lenity." Six major warships and 6,000 additional troops were to be sent to America. Loyalists and Native Americans should harass the western frontier from New York to Virginia. And British armies were to go on the offensive in Canada and New England and capture Philadelphia.[6]

In the aftermath of Washington's unexpected victories at Trenton and Princeton, the British Army withdrew from all of New Jersey except for Amboy and their winter camp at New Brunswick. Patriots reestablished civilian and military control throughout much of the state. As part of that effort they hanged two Loyalists; at least thirty more chose to enlist in order to avoid that fate. New Jersey's Loyalists, writes one historian, "fought on but never established an effective regional base to support a revival of royal political authority." Reports of Trenton and Princeton boosted Patriot morale: "A few days ago they had given up the cause for lost," noted Nicholas Creswell, a British traveler then in Virginia. "Their late successes have turned the scale and now they are all liberty mad again. Their Recruiting parties could not get a man . . . no longer since than last week, and now the men are coming in by companies."[7]

After the Hessians' humiliation at Trenton, Donop had instructed his men to take no prisoners. It was these orders that may have led to Lieutenant Martin's brutal killing later that spring. And indeed, throughout the winter campaign, rumors persisted that the British were breaking the codes of war on the battlefield. In mid-January, Congress took the unprecedented step of appointing an investigatory committee charged with looking into those allegations. The nation's representatives, many of whom had legal training, made it their business to expose possible war crimes. In the midst of battle, no one had the time to observe, let alone verify, such transgressions, and so it had to be done in the aftermath. Sorting facts from rumor, hearsay, supposition, and fabrication would test the skill and judgment of the congressional investigators. But telling a plausible, well-evidenced story of enemy atrocities against America's combatants, as well as her captives and civilians, would prove to be a crucial new weapon in the imperial civil war—and a critical tool, too, in the project of forging the new American nation.[8]

* * *

The official chair of the investigatory committee was Samuel Chase of Maryland. Its effective leader, however, was the Reverend John Witherspoon, the fifty-five-year-old Presbyterian cleric and president of the College of New Jersey (later Princeton University).

Witherspoon was among those Patriot leaders whose effigy—along with Washington's—vitriolic Loyalists had burned one night after a thunderstorm on Staten Island in July 1776. Later, as British-Hessian forces went on plundering sprees in the areas around Hopewell and Maidenhead, Witherspoon and his family fled Princeton ahead of the approaching enemy. Now Witherspoon returned to his hometown, in whose vicinity many of the alleged transgressions had occurred, to establish a makeshift headquarters.[9]

Dr. Benjamin Rush, a cosigner of the Declaration of Independence, an advisor to Washington, and a surgeon on the New Jersey campaign, painted a picture of Princeton in early January 1777. It was "a deserted village" that appeared as if it "had been desolated with the plague and an earthquake as well as with the calamities of war," its church and college lying in ruins, the inhabitants plundered. The Witherspoon residence, writes a historian of the campaign, was "a shambles, its valuable furnishings taken off or ruined, his library of rare books ransacked, while the contents of Nassau Hall [the oldest college building]—books, scientific apparatus, and a 'celebrated orrery,' a planetarium reputed to be the best in the world—had disappeared." In January 1777, a Sergeant Young serving in a Philadelphia infantry company noted the effect of the enemy's plundering: "I cold not help taking Notice of the Devastation and Destruckion done By those Sons of Blood and Murder." In Trenton, "the houses are tore in a Shoking Monar and all the Valoubel Goods taking off."[10]

Witherspoon and his colleagues opened their investigation by talking and listening to the locals. They "found it to be the general opinion of the people in the neighbourhood of Princeton and Trenton, that the enemy, the day before the Battle of Princeton, had determined to give no quarter." The testimony of inhabitants who might have overheard enemy officers and soldiers, or who might have helped care for the wounded and dying, pointed to transgressions such as the killing of wounded and defenseless soldiers. Hearsay was supported by physical evidence in the form of bodies: "Officers wounded and disabled, some of them of the first rank, were barbarously mangled or put to death." Where this enemy was concerned, the committee was finding, not even gentlemen officers appeared to be protected by the codes of war.[11]

The investigators next pored over British order books captured in battle or discarded by fleeing enemy units. One such document, discovered at Trenton, revealed the British commander in chief's instructions that all inhabitants found in arms without an officer present were to be "immediately taken & hung up." The order probably referred to militia, irregular troops, and illegal combatants, not regular soldiers. But Thomas Paine also cited this very order book in the second of his famous *Crisis* essays as proof of the enemy's barbarity. Paine indicted the British Empire for inflicting bodily suffering across Britain's global domains. The Empire had committed "national sins" that demanded "national punishment," Paine charged. "The blood of India is not yet repaid, nor the wretchedness of Africa yet requitted," Paine continued, shaming the imperial conscience. "Of late she has enlarged her list of national cruelties by her butcherly destruction of the Caribbs of St. Vincents," referring to the suppression of a revolt in the West Indies just a few years earlier. With these accusations of Britain's worldwide brutality ringing fresh in his audience's ears, Paine then extended the argument to America. The invaders' recent New Jersey campaign was intended "to kill, conquer, plunder, pardon, and enslave: and the ravages of your army through the Jersies have been marked with as much barbarism as if you had openly professed yourself the prince of ruffians."[12]

In its search for plausible evidence of war crimes, the committee also interrogated enemy prisoners (or perhaps some captives provided information freely). Chairman Chase wrote to Washington that he had learned that some British soldiers taken captive at Princeton had reported a major's orders, "to stand 'till they were cut to pieces and to take no Prisoners." Washington, however, was still unable to confirm this conclusively.[13]

Persisting with their quest for hard evidence, the committee documented in some detail a story that involved two clerics, one the victim, the other a witness. After the Battle of Trenton, the

Reverend George Duffield made a deposition to a justice of the peace. Duffield's testimony was based in part on local hearsay, albeit from people "on whose veracity," he reassured the legal official, "I could well depend." The subject of Duffield's story was a fellow clergyman, the Reverend John Rosbrugh, a sixty-three-year-old Scots Presbyterian chaplain from Allen Township, Pennsylvania, and the father of five young children. A few weeks before, Rosbrugh had rallied members of his congregation and led them to join Washington's army. On December 27, as he was about to cross the Delaware to New Jersey, Rosbrugh jotted down a brief note to his wife while mounted on his horse. He wanted her to be prepared that "[t]his may be the last letter ye shall receive from your husband."[14]

On January 2, Rosbrugh had been refreshing himself in a Trenton tavern when he heard fighting outside. He exited the tavern and was running away from a party of Hessians when they overtook him on the bank of a creek. Rosbrugh surrendered, "imploring mercy, and begging his life," but one Hessian allegedly struck him on his head with a sword or cutlass, cutting through his wig and into his skull. He also stabbed Rosbrugh several times with his bayonet, calling him a "damn'd rebel minister." Enemy officers were said to have "highly applauded the perpetrator for what he had done. That after he was thus massacred, he was stripped naked, and in that condition left lying in the open field." (Other accounts have the assailants rob and strip the minister first and then kill him while he is kneeling, naked, and praying for mercy.) Duffield, who saw his fellow minister's corpse, "observed that besides the strokes that had been given him on the head with some edged weapon, he had been stabbed with a bayonet in the back of the neck, and between his ribs on the right side, which last appeared remarkably deep and"—now perhaps stretching medical credulity—"from which, even then, there issued a large quantity of blood." Locals later buried the minister's mangled body.[15]

Testimony such as Duffield's relied on a mixture of hearsay and personal observation. The committee was eager to obtain additional first-person accounts. In one particularly moving document, Lieutenant Bartholomew Yates of the 1st Virginia Regiment gave an affidavit on his deathbed, testifying to the manner in which he had sustained his fatal wounds at Princeton in early January. Yates recounted the sequence of events as a British soldier approached, swearing and raising his musket, when Yates "begged for Quarters," but the enemy soldier "loaded his Musquet deliberately and Shot him thro' the Breast, and afterwards Stabed him in thirteen Places with his Bayonet. Some time after this the Same or another Soldier came up to him, who perceiving Some Signs of Life in him, [beat Yates] with the Club of his Musquet." (Note the anatomical detail, including the precise counting, also seen in Martin's case, of the number of wounds, even when the testimony was taken by a legal and not a medical professional, as it was in other instances.) Washington wrote about Yates's case to Governor William Livingston of New Jersey, asserting that he had been begging for quarter but instead was "butchered by a British soldier."[16]

American reports grouped Yates's fate with that of General Hugh Mercer. As a young surgeon's mate with the rebel army at Culloden, Mercer had gone into hiding after the Jacobites' defeat and eventually escaped to America, where he practiced as a frontier physician. After serving in the Seven Years' War, Mercer became a physician in Fredericksburg, Virginia, and a member of the same Masonic lodge as his friend George Washington. At the outbreak of the Revolutionary War, for the second time in his life, Mercer went to war with rebels against the Hanoverian monarchy. Promoted to brigadier general, Mercer accompanied Washington on his retreat through New Jersey.

On January 3, after Mawhood's regiment had broken Mercer's brigade with a bayonet rush in that orchard two miles from Princeton, the redcoats repeatedly "skewered or bludgeoned the handful of abandoned wounded." Mercer, his horse shot from under him, found himself split up from his men and surrounded by a British detachment. When he refused to surrender, they clubbed and bayoneted him repeatedly. As the congressional committee learned,

Jonathan Trumbull, The Death of General Hugh Mercer *(1786).*

when Mercer lay dying in a farmhouse near the battlefield, he predicted that his fatal wound was not the injuries to his head or stomach about which Dr. Rush expressed concern; it was, instead, a small wound underneath his right arm that resembled the bayonet wounds under the right sword arms of the Highlanders cut down at Culloden.[17]

Of course, Mercer's case differed from Yates's in one key respect: the British had not denied quarter to Mercer—Mercer had refused to request it. In terms of the prevailing codes of war, Mercer was thus legitimately killed "in the heat of action" rather than murdered "in cold blood." However, that didn't diminish the incident's propaganda value. Mercer's corpse was subsequently displayed at a Philadelphia coffeehouse, a carefully choreographed spectacle of death, like Martin's, designed to incite Patriot indignation. In the early days of 1777, the story of Mercer's cruel treatment in the act of surrendering quickly gained notoriety, boosting the political and spiritual significance their struggle held for the Patriots. Mercer was buried as a martyr-hero who had died for his adopted country: "It was the Nation mourning for her first Child," explained an orator on the occasion of Mercer's reinterment in 1840.[18]

* * *

After the committee finished piecing together the scraps of hearsay, eyewitness testimony, and physical evidence and summarized its findings, the Continental Congress formally accepted its report on April 18, 1777. It was immediately serialized in the *Pennsylvania Evening Post.* Newspapers across the states quickly reprinted it, complete with the evidence the committee had assembled. The New York Council of Safety urged Congress to issue the entire report as a pamphlet to maximize its distribution and impact. Indeed, it argued, copies should also be sent to Europe and the West Indies to "furnish the advocates of humanity and the rights of mankind with a proper idea of the spirit with which the King of Britain wages and conducts this wicked war against us." That summer, the Congress ordered 4,000 English and 2,000 German copies of the report to be published, the latter to persuade the heavily German populations of states such as Pennsylvania of Britain's moral inferiority and the righteous urgency of America's cause. No copy has so far surfaced, but the substance of the report did circulate in America and Europe by means of the printed press and word of mouth. By 1778, leading British opposition politicians were spotlighting the investigation to remind the political class of their nation's tarnished image: the congressional report outlining "the barbarities exercised by his Majesty's officers, and those under them in America," had been serialized in the pro-American *Gazette de Leyde*, one of continental Europe's leading political newspapers. Yet, because it was so full of "odious and revolting facts," the editor would not publish the material in its entirety, his pro-American stance notwithstanding.[19]

It is worth remembering that this was a period in which most people would have found it difficult to obtain even mainstream war news. Thomas Paine—who served as secretary to General Daniel Roberdeau on Long Island in August 1776, as General Nathanael Greene's aide-de-camp at Fort Lee, and then with Washington during the retreat through New Jersey—came as close as anyone to reporting from the campaign. But otherwise the main sources of information about the progress of the war were the accounts General Washington sent to Congress and other senior officers to their respective state governments, which were regularly excerpted or reprinted.[20]

And while wartime shortages of printers, paper, and ink—combined with poor roads and the vagaries of the weather and the dangers of traversing shifting war zones—affected the production and distribution of news media, it was through print media, and newspapers in particular, that people everywhere received updates about the war. In so doing, they gained a sense that they were involved in a national rather than just a local effort. Newspapers, explains one historian, "united the colonies in a way that was beyond the ability of the jerry-built wartime government."[21]

Leaders on both sides recognized the power of print media. When Washington petitioned the Congress for a small traveling press and an "ingenious man to . . . be employed wholly in writing for it," he stressed that he wished to counter any "falsehood and misrepresentation" spread by the enemy. Apparently, Washington's request was never approved. But it was the combination of America's first quasi-national institutions on the one hand—the Continental Congress and the Continental Army—and the press on the other that allowed the Patriots to rally support for the war. A congressionally authored investigative report, drawing on intelligence obtained from the army's high command as well as from local eyewitnesses, could touch on otherwise elusive aspects of the war with unrivaled authority.[22]

In today's age of international courts, war crimes tribunals, and truth and reconciliation commissions, we perhaps take the systematic investigation of irregularities in armed conflicts for granted. But in 1777, a fact-finding mission conducted under the auspices of the Congress was truly new. No comparable effort was undertaken by any British body, military or political. The American report carried significant political and moral weight with audiences both at home and abroad. And some of the revelations were explosive: British soldiers posed a danger not just to America's soldiers on the battlefield but also to women in their own homes.

Recounting Rape

Even before the congressional committee started its work in January 1777, private individuals and Revolutionary committees operating in the borderland between Pennsylvania and New Jersey had started to investigate reports of rape. In mid-December 1776, as Washington's army was facing Howe's across the Delaware, a broadside printed in Bucks County detailed sexual abuse in New Jersey: "The progress of the British and Hessian troops through New Jersey has been attended with such scenes of desolation and outrage, as would disgrace the most barbarous nations." Three women, including a girl as young as fifteen, had been abused by British soldiers and even an officer, continued the broadside, which newspapers in various states soon reprinted. Sixteen other women had tried to evade their assailants by hiding in the woods but had been discovered, forcibly taken to a British army camp, and, it was implied, raped. Major General Nathanael Greene, too, was at that time speaking of hundreds of women being raped in New Jersey—the number unprovable, and probably inflated, but one that speaks to the very real concern about sexual abuse by enemy soldiers.[23]

The Pennsylvania Council of Safety urged America's men to mobilize not only to defend their liberties, and "to secure your property from being plundered," but also "to protect the innocence of your wives and children." Even British newspapers acknowledged that American recruitment drives were succeeding in part because of British atrocities, including "many authentic cases of rapes" as published in the American press.[24]

Other voices, too, both publicly and in private, characterized British soldiers and even their officers as voracious sexual predators. They targeted girls and women, whether single, married, or pregnant, from teenagers to septuagenarians, with no apparent sense of shame or decency. The high proportion of references to girls and teenagers being raped does not correspond to verifiable data, but it served to highlight the particularly heinous conduct of the imperial invaders. Since early modern notions of male honor depended heavily on the reputation of a man's wife and his exclusive control over her, the sexual abuse and humiliation of women was also directed at men, and even more so during wartime. It was in this context that commentators highlighted instances in which British soldiers raped American women in front of their fathers and husbands.[25]

As British and German soldiers were allegedly assaulting American women across the Northern theater, farther south an anonymous contributor to the *Virginia Gazette* demanded that "the depositions of parents and husbands who saw their wives and daughters ravished, be published throughout the world." Washington ought to parade all prisoners before the victims' relatives; any offenders identified in the lineup ought to be "first castrated, and then hanged."[26]

The metaphorical image of Britain "raping" its American colonies had been circulating since before the war. *The able Doctor*, a print first published in the *London Magazine* in May 1774 and copied by Paul Revere for the *Royal American Magazine* that June, shows the sexual endangerment of America at the hands of lascivious British government ministers.[27]

The able Doctor, or, America Swallowing the Bitter Draught
(*London, May 1774*).

Lord Mansfield is holding down the bare-breasted, prostrate, helpless America. Lord Sandwich, restraining her legs, has lifted up the sheet that covers her torso and seems to be peeping at her genitals. Prime Minister Lord North, his left knee pointing at America's groin, forces tea down her throat. At right stands an overbearing soldier, his sword inscribed "Military Law." A second female allegory, representing Britannia or Liberty, averts her face in shame. America is being abused on a visual axis between a paper inscribed "Boston petition" and a scene that anticipates "Boston cannonaded"—the Massachusetts capital serving, once more, as a site of violent confrontation. The threat of military attack is conveyed through implied sexual violence.

In this period, both in literary works and in everyday language, sexual pursuit was framed in aggressive terms, not least by way of analogy with military strategy. When men talked about "thrusting" or "giving a flourish," they imagined sex as a battle in which a woman was to be conquered and subdued. If sexual conquest, in the words of one historian, had become "an acceptable way of validating masculinity, of demonstrating dominance and superiority over women," and if armies offered soldiers a conception of masculinity that validated aggression, war likely accentuated such patterns of thinking and conduct among soldiers.[28]

One problem with using rape as a metaphor, as in *The able Doctor*, is that it erases the individual traumatic experience of the assaulted woman. Indeed, the very ways in which Revolutionary Americans deployed rape as a political tool to discredit the British Empire have tended to obscure the actual practices of wartime rape. Reading public narratives of rape from the period, we find they highlight the injured reputation of dishonored fathers and husbands. And they emphasize the symbolic violation of the body politic. To gain a fuller understanding of this aspect of the war, we need to write the abused women (and their abusers) back into the story.[29]

For, once the war with Britain was fully under way, rape was no longer just a metaphor for imperial oppression and abuse. Rape became an extraordinarily effective political tool for the Patriots precisely because enemy soldiers posed an actual, concrete threat to real American women. And Patriot men were adamant that this abuse of women constituted a war crime.

* * *

Rape, an ancient English felony punishable by death, was defined in the eighteenth-century British Atlantic world as the unlawful "carnal knowledge of a woman forcibly and against her will." Under the prevailing laws of war, as the leading author on international law, Emer de Vattel, clarified, invading and occupying armies had certain rights over women as enemies. Yet, as long as women offered no active resistance to invading troops, soldiers had "no right to maltreat their persons, or use any violence against them," just as with "children, feeble old men, and sick persons." Vattel considered it "so plain a maxim of justice and humanity, that at present every nation, in the least degree civilised, acquiesces in it." Acknowledging that there was often a difference between officers and soldiers, Vattel was quick to add: "If sometimes the furious and ungovernable soldier carries his brutality so far as to violate female chastity . . . the officers lament those excesses; they exert their utmost efforts to put a stop to them; and a prudent and humane general even punishes them whenever he can." Vattel's formulation acknowledges that a degree of abuse might be virtually inevitable in war and that it might easily go unpunished. In other words, in the ideal of enlightened warfare, the officer codes of honor and civility imposed restraint and discipline. But the reality of war was messier and more brutal. Soldiers might have considered sexual assault on the enemy's women as an extension of war, indeed integral to armed conflict, not altogether different from plundering private property; it is telling that the word "ravish" was used for both offenses.[30]

As is the case in most wars, and in most societies, the incidence of rape in the Revolutionary War is impossible to quantify. It is almost certain that many more such atrocities were committed than were reported. Washington, Livingston, and Witherspoon and his colleagues on the congressional committee recognized that rape would be "more difficult to prove than any of the rest [including battlefield atrocities], as the person abused, as well as the Relations are generally reluctant against bringing matters of this kind into public Notice." Still fewer soldiers who committed sexual assaults were ever tried, let alone punished. Circumstances often imposed silence on rape victims intimidated by threats, lacking witnesses to corroborate their stories, or fearing the additional humiliation and social consequences of discussing their sexual integrity in public. Even British soldiers referenced the hidden incidence of rape committed by their comrades. On the very cold Christmas Eve of 1776, in Newport, Rhode Island, John Peebles recorded in his diary: "A man condemned to suffer death for a Rape, but pardon'd at the intercession of the injured party; the second instance; tho there have been other shocking abuses of that nature that have not come to public notice."[31]

George Washington, in his general orders for the new year, 1777, contrasted American soldiers with their enemies: "[I]t is expected that humanity and tenderness to women and children will distinguish brave Americans, contending for liberty, from mercenary ravagers, whether British or Hessians." As he had done with plundering and battlefield atrocities, America's commander in chief was framing his version of the war while he was fighting it. And it was Washington who helped the congressional investigation reach a breakthrough in early March 1777. The general recovered an internal army memorandum on rape from when his troops had been on the Pennsylvania side of the Delaware. It was subsequently mislaid and has not been identified by modern scholars. But Washington now passed on hints about specific locals who might have information about rape cases. These references eventually allowed the Hunterdon County, New Jersey, justice of the peace, Jared Saxton, to depose six rape victims. Their harrowing testimony, contained in the appendix of the congressional report, would soon reach a wide audience on both sides of the Atlantic.[32]

In late March 1777, Abigail Palmer, a thirteen-year-old girl from Hunterdon County, told her story to Jared Saxton (the published versions concealed her identity). The previous December, several British soldiers had come to the house of Abigail's grandfather, Edmund Palmer, who farmed near Pennington, New Jersey. The men had taken control of the premises and raped Abigail for "three Days successively" as more soldiers kept coming and going. They also assaulted Edmund Palmer's married and pregnant daughter, Mary Phillips, as well as Elizabeth and Sarah Cain, fifteen and eighteen years of age, who happened to be visiting the Palmer family. On one occasion, several soldiers seized Abigail and Elizabeth, "pull'd them both into a Room together," and—ignoring their screams and Abigail's father's attempt to shield them—"Ravishd them both." The soldiers threatened to poison them. They said they would run a bayonet through their hearts or "blow their brains out." On the third day, the two girls were eventually dragged to a British army camp, about a thousand yards away, where "they was both Treated by some others of the Soldiers in the same Cruel manner," remembered Elizabeth. Only after further assaults did an officer put a stop to the girls' abuse and arrange for them to return to their families.[33]

There is no indication that the British soldiers had picked the Palmer house for any specific political or military rationale. Instead, soldiers roaming the environs of camp, possibly looking for vulnerable women, came upon the girls and women at that house. They then abused them systematically. Like Abigail, Mary, Elizabeth, and Sarah, most American women who were raped by British soldiers had no opportunity to formally charge their assailants: it was only in the court of American and international public opinion that their attackers—and the character of the British Army—were called to account. Local experiences were talked and written about as a nationally relevant morality tale: What happened to the women of New Jersey in the winter of 1776–77 could happen to American women anywhere near a British army. The fact that we know about their abuse at all, let alone in such detail, is due to the persistence of Patriot leaders in seeking to convey the full picture of British atrocities. It also is due to the courage that some of the victims mustered to tell their story.[34]

As we have seen, physical evidence—indeed, the precise nature of wounds—took center stage in American investigations of battlefield atrocities. By contrast, neither in American inquiries and propagandistic publications, nor in those cases where the British held a court-martial of a soldier accused of rape, does physical evidence appear to have played a major role in sexual assault cases. In British and colonial American civilian courts, third-party women who had examined unmarried and supposedly sexually inactive rape victims typically testified to bruises, cuts, and other signs of resistance, as well as to indications of recent sexual intercourse. But depositions before American authorities were of married or widowed women who were assumed to know about their own bodies.[35]

In certain conflicts, rape serves as a weapon of war, and in rebellions and civil wars, rape can take on distinctive political connotations. In the aftermath of the 1745 Jacobite rebellion, as recounted above, British soldiers physically and sexually assaulted girls and women in the Scottish Highlands. Their commanding officers mostly remained oblivious or silent, or considered attacking wives an effective way of making their husbands change allegiance. Some English regiments deliberately used rape as a reprisal for earlier defeats.[36]

Even though the British Army did not officially endorse rape during the American war, tolerance for sexual abuse remained high across divisions of rank and class. Even forces quartered in their own communities raised anxieties about sexual assault. And with major armies in America employing thousands of (mostly American) female army followers—prostitutes as well as sutlers and cooks, washerwomen and seamstresses, nurses and servants—it was well known that women and girls traveling with the army faced a very high risk of sexual violence. Rape, in other words, was endemic within the British Army.[37]

Francis, Lord Rawdon, the Anglo-Irish adjutant to General Sir Henry Clinton and a future governor-general of India, expressed regret that women in New York were not as compliant as those at Charleston (where he had accompanied Clinton earlier that year):

The fair nymphs of this isle are in wonderful tribulation, as the fresh meat our men have got here has made them as riotous as satyrs. A girl cannot step into the bushes to pluck a rose without running the most imminent risk of being ravished, and they are so little accustomed to these vigorous methods that they don't bear them with the proper resignation, and of consequence we have most entertaining courts-martial every day. To the southward they behave much better in these cases.[38]

Public commentators back home in Britain echoed officers in the field like Rawdon. London's *Morning Chronicle* printed an article that considered a multiple rape scenario in New Jersey as "a most fortunate stroke for the Yankees in mending the breed." The very fact that it could be considered humorous to justify rape as a way of improving the gene pool illustrates attitudes towards sexual assault in eighteenth-century society. Rape was widely accepted as a by-product of war.[39]

According to Rawdon, the British Army did prosecute soldiers on charges of rape. There is very little documentation of what triggered these prosecutions, but we know that in a few cases an assault happened to come to the attention of an officer who, instead of looking the other way, had the alleged offender arrested and brought before a military court. Some women, after being raped, by happenstance identified their attackers in a public setting. Still others courageously visited the headquarters of the occupying forces to demand an identification and trial. An American woman wishing to see a British soldier prosecuted during the war faced even greater challenges than a woman reporting a rape in peacetime, starting with the very question of where and how to bring charges. On the other hand, women claiming rape by enemy soldiers were more likely to be believed by their own communities.[40]

In fall 1776, the widow Elizabeth Johnstone gave evidence to a British military court at Newtown, Long Island. She alleged that two British soldiers had raped her at her home. John Dunn and John Lusty had entered her house, held her down, and—threatening to kill her—took turns raping her in front of her four-year-old daughter, who lay on the same bed and who at one stage was nursed to stop her crying. Johnstone testified that each man raped her twice in a quarter hour. In response to specific questions by members of the court-martial intended to prove the guilt of the accused, Johnstone confirmed that she had cried out and that both men had penetrated her and ejaculated. Two British officers, Donald McIntire, surgeon to the 43rd Regiment, and Kevin Terrence, who happened to be nearby, shortly after encountered the visibly distressed Johnstone and apprehended the alleged offenders, who appeared to be "very much in liquor." When challenged, the soldiers deflected the accusations; trying to undermine Johnstone's credibility, they referred to her as "a yankee whore, or a yankee bitch, and it was no great matter or words to that purpose." A promptly held court-martial, however, found Dunn and Lusty guilty of rape; they were both sentenced to be executed by hanging. The punishment of other soldiers found guilty ranged from corporal punishment to demotion and dismissal; some were acquitted.[41]

One of the New Jersey victims who, alongside the Palmer and Cain women, gave evidence to the congressional investigation in March 1777 was Rebekkah Christopher. She testified to her gang rape by enemy officers and the attempted rape of her ten-year-old daughter. At one point, as Christopher told Jared Saxton, JP, one British officer accused her of harboring rebels. Such allegations were repeatedly mentioned in the testimony of rape victims during the war. British soldiers invading households may have used an ostensible search for rebels as a pretense to force their entry or talk themselves in. On the other hand, women like Rebekkah Christopher may have felt that claiming that the British had been searching for rebels might enhance their credibility when they testified before Patriot investigators. Like battlefield atrocities but in an even more immediate, intimate way, sexual assault on American women brought the war closer to home—and demonstrated that an imperial power whose soldiers committed such abuse could never again be trusted to rule America.[42]

By bringing court cases against men accused of rape, British officers sought to uphold military discipline, albeit less consistently than in the context of other crimes, such as plundering. Prosecuting rape also allowed individual officers to appear honorable and enlightened in the face of misogyny and abuse among fellow officers and troops. In addition, there was perhaps an implicit acknowledgment that proscribing and prosecuting rape was in the army's self-interest, as it might help defuse tense military-civilian relations. This applied equally to the area surrounding the main garrison city, New York, and to temporarily occupied places like Philadelphia. Yet individual British officers possessed considerable discretion—from how they supervised their troops around campsites, on marches, and during raids to whether or not they prosecuted soldiers accused of sexual abuse. The choices these officers made clearly affected an assaulted woman's chances of obtaining justice. This very inconsistency in British responses to rape also provided the American Patriots with rhetorical ammunition.

* * *

But as always with America's first civil war, the story is more complicated than simple Anglo-American enmity. Just as Washington's soldiers and Patriot militias plundered Americans, as we saw in the previous chapter, some American soldiers were guilty of raping American women. The Loyalist press very occasionally accused Continental soldiers of sexual abuse, and there are some hints at soldiers being whipped for rape; recorded detail, however, is very sparse. Since other types of atrocity stories were published on rather slim evidence, the relative scarcity of references to rape by Patriot soldiers in Loyalist newspapers and petitions *might* suggest that soldiers in the Continental Army and Patriot militias only rarely engaged in sexual violence. If this was indeed the case, it may have been due to greater officer oversight. The fact that many men served more temporarily than their British counterparts—or, in the case of militia, closer to home—may have played a role, too. Continental troops, in contrast with the invading British forces, were perhaps also conscious of needing to coexist with their Loyalist opponents once the war was over.[43]

Loyalist units, on the other hand, were more frequently the subject of rape allegations, with several court-martial cases even resulting in death sentences. When Loyalist soldiers assaulted American women, one of the motives might have been revenge for earlier ordeals suffered at the hands of Patriot persecutors. In December 1776, Nathanael Greene had warned his young wife, Catherine, of the Loyalists as "the cursedest rascals amongst us, the most wicked, villainous, and oppressive." He was referring to their role in aiding and abetting the British, as they "lead the relentless foreigners to the houses of their neighbors and strip the poor women and children of everything they have to eat or wear; and after plundering them in this sort, the brutes often ravish the mothers and daughters, and compel the fathers and sons to behold their brutality; many have fallen sacrifices in this way." The rape of America, by Britons *and* their Loyalist auxiliaries, could be taken as a manifestation of illegitimate imperial power.[44]

* * *

When the Continental Congress and the Continental Army—the new country's earliest quasi-national agencies—reported on the enemy's barbarous activities, they pursued moral truth and justice while also hoping to rally Americans to the Patriot cause. Just as attacks on Boston had attracted subscriptions and offers of armed support from beyond Massachusetts, and just as the flaming arguments of Falmouth and Norfolk had inspired fear and stiffened resolve among insurgents—and perhaps moved some would-be neutrals to the Patriot side—the unprecedented congressional report of 1777 transcended the specific sites of its investigation. At a time when the colonies were relatively poorly connected, a widely cited congressional report highlighting the perspective of the commander in chief had the potential to shape perceptions of the war. Addressed to the "country in general," and serialized and excerpted in papers across the colonies and even in Europe, it could help the wronged American nation cohere around a common experience of danger and fear.

Witherspoon's committee had relied on a small number of cases, sometimes with less-than-clear-cut evidence, but it succeeded in telling a plausible and coherent story about the British Army's cruelty. Across the colonies, the congressional report and similar official publications resonated with, and amplified, the experiences of individual readers. Many of them had already been, or over the course of the war would become, witnesses if not victims of British atrocities in their own cities and towns. The circumstances of each incident varied. But their retelling over time, in pamphlets and poems and from pulpits and in taverns across the land, revealed a common rather than a regionally diverse American culture and accentuated shared experiences. Who, then, could hear of the enemy's "wickedness and brutality," asked a poet in the *Independent Chronicle*, "and not with patriot zeal, / Nobly step forth, to guard their wives and children! / And sheath a dagger in the villain's heart / Who'd rob us of our peace, our all, our honour!" Such Patriot pens stirred the emotions of wronged republican citizens. In the emerging United States, the print media, and newspapers in particular, were key to forging a political consciousness and a sense of national community and belonging. In this effort, allegations of war crimes provided powerful narrative content.

While they were not above concocting stories of war crimes when it suited them (as with General Mercer), the Patriots also invented novel ways of documenting battlefield atrocities to bolster a credible narrative of victimhood and help them legitimize a rebellion and civil war. Inspired by their enlightened epoch's empirical turn in legalistic thinking and scientific approaches, and drawing on their members' journalistic savvy, the Revolutionary authorities deployed mangled and raped bodies to help them build a unified nation and win sympathies abroad.

The congressional experiment of 1777 was an original approach to exposing war crimes rooted in legal argument and forensic evidence. By witnessing and constructing a victims' narrative of bodily harm, political and military authorities thus sought to legitimate their war. The war of wounds fed the war of words in the battle for support both domestically and overseas. It is reasonable to assume that the Patriots had a particular interest in documenting enemy abuse in order to make up for the legitimacy deficit with which they, as insurgents, had entered the conflict in the eyes of the international community. Establishing the clear differences between themselves and their British enemies and their auxiliaries was key to this effort.

* * *

In the context of a 1779 parliamentary inquiry into the command of the Howe brothers, the exiled Loyalist spokesman Joseph Galloway published a pamphlet. Galloway had helped the British run Philadelphia during their occupation of that city in 1777–78; when the British Army left, so did Galloway, first to New York and then to London. In addition to detailing cases of rape (and of plundering) by British soldiers, Galloway now highlighted the Patriots' acumen in capitalizing on British abuse for their own political gain. His perceptive take on the war of wounds and the war of words serves as a fitting epilogue to this chapter: "If the British General was indolent and neglectful in putting a stop to these cruelties," Galloway criticized Howe, "the Rebel Commander and the new States were not so in converting them to their own benefit. Every possible advantage was made of these enormities." The American Patriots took affidavits of every offensive British deed and published them in the newspapers, continued Galloway,

> to irritate and enrage the people against his Majesty and the British nation. The British soldiers were represented as a race of men more inhuman than savages. By these means, the minds of many were turned against the British Government, and many in desperation joined the rebel army. The force of the rebels was

increased, the British weakened, and the humanity and glory of Britons received a disgraceful tarnish, which time can never efface.[45]

By the time Galloway published his comments, it had become clear that not only Patriot combatants and civilians but thousands of American captives, too, were the victims of widespread British mistreatment. Once again, creative Patriots knew how to use the stories of malnourished, diseased, lice-ridden, beaten prisoners for their own benefit.

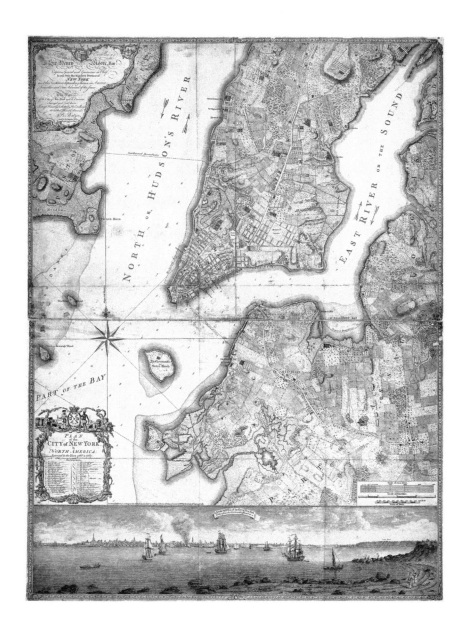

CHAPTER SIX

Slaughterhouses

T HE GEORGE WASHINGTON OF AMERICAN LEGEND IS THE
humanitarian who, in a young lady's widely published
acrostic, "Intent on virtue, and her cause so fair, / Now
treats his captive with a parent's care!" From the very start of the
conflict, Washington had been adamant that his army's conduct
towards prisoners of war align with European customs. The honor
of the American nation, as well as Washington's own obligations
as a gentleman officer and wartime leader, was at stake. It was,
after all, for a place among the world's civilized nations that America was vying. For leaders like Washington, treating prisoners of
war adequately was a genuine moral concern that also made sound
strategic sense.[1]

Washington had a personal history to reckon with. In his very
first combat mission, on the Ohio frontier in 1754, he had failed to
prevent his Native American allies from committing the gruesome
ritualistic murder of a French envoy, Joseph Coulon de Villiers,
Sieur de Jumonville, and then massacring other French soldiers
after they had surrendered to him. Washington had covered up
the disaster as best he could. His official report glossed over the
extreme violence, making it sound as if all French casualties had
been sustained during an honest fight. But when he had to surrender Fort Necessity to the French later that year, Washington—
unable to read French—signed terms of capitulation that held
him responsible for Jumonville's "assassination."[2]

When the British and American Loyalists resurrected the murder charges two decades later, we can only imagine how it must
have nettled Washington, who guarded his honor and reputation

as jealously as any gentleman officer in the British Empire. He appreciated that he must go out of his way to observe—and, crucially, to be seen observing—the codes of civilized warfare. Washington knew that defending "the sacred Cause of my Country, of Liberty" required him and his army to embrace Enlightenment ideals and what John Adams called a "policy of humanity."[3]

Washington had absorbed the codes of war pertaining to the capture, treatment, and exchange of prisoners of war, as far as conflicts among European powers were concerned, when fighting alongside British officers in the Seven Years' War. These codes of war allowed an army to imprison any enemy soldier or officer in order to prevent him from taking up arms or as a ransom for peace terms. Captors, however, had no right over the life of a surrendered soldier: prisoners of war were not to be killed unless they made a new attempt to fight or had committed a crime warranting death. Both sides had a vested interest in the preservation, and ultimately the exchange, of expensively trained captive soldiers.[4]

In the eighteenth century, conventions of war dictated that captive soldiers were to be fed, housed, and cared for like one's own armed forces, although they were to receive clothing and payment from their own state or army (and not their captors). Enlisting prisoners of war in one's own military was forbidden. During most eighteenth-century conflicts among Western European powers, ransoms and, increasingly, agreements between belligerent powers, so-called cartels, regulated the imprisonment, provisioning, and exchange of captives. Although a state was bound to procure its own prisoners' release—a promise that was crucial to recruitment—commanders might delay exchanges in order to temporarily impose a greater economic burden on their opponents or deny them fighting strength. At war's end, ransom or compensation would settle mutual claims. Unlike soldiers, captured officers were commonly released back home or allowed to move freely within a specified territory, on their honor and parole—from the French for "spoken word"—to abide by certain restrictions.[5]

These principles of prisoner treatment were not easy to uphold under the conditions of war. Unequal numbers of captives, inadequate record keeping, and the sheer scale of transcontinental warfare in the eighteenth century meant that exchanges were complex to organize. There was, therefore, a broad trend away from large-scale exchanges and towards holding prisoners for longer periods of time in the captors' homeland. In the American Revolutionary War, unique politico-legal circumstances further complicated matters: the British refused to designate captured rebel combatants as prisoners of war, since that would mean recognizing the United States as a sovereign state. In doing so, they rendered large-scale exchanges characteristic of wars between European nations impossible, which meant that both sides faced the challenge of keeping unusually large populations of captives. Throughout much of the war, British officers sought to arrange partial, ad hoc exchanges on the honor of the local commander and without formally invoking the king's name, so as not to compromise the government's position.

Whereas Washington was bent on a pragmatic humanitarianism and hence willing to participate in exchanges in order to alleviate prisoner suffering, Congress wanted to use the issue of prisoners to force Britain to recognize the United States. It also wished to avoid returning too many British soldiers. It was keen not to pay for large exchanges if accounts could not be settled. And it preferred to conceal the short terms of enlistment of American soldiers. Throughout the war, American and British leaders blamed each other for the repeated collapse of exchange negotiations. The numbers of prisoners exchanged through ad hoc arrangements, though probably totaling several thousand over the war as a whole, proved too small to relieve in a meaningful way the pressure on detention sites in most places at most times.[6]

Some British officers in America demanded that "rebel" captives be treated as such, and not like prisoners from legitimate, conventional European armies. At least keeping them indefinitely, suggested the Irish-born Captain Frederick Mackenzie, "and in a state of uncertainty with respect to their fate, would certainly strike great terror into their army." He worried that the failure to implement capital punishment—"Not one rebel has suffered death, except in Action"—only encouraged the insurgency. Nevertheless, even Mackenzie later insisted that it was "right to treat our Enemies as if they might one day become our friends. Humanity is the characteristic of the British troops, and I should be sorry they should run the risque of forfeiting what redounds so much to their honor, by one act of even necessary severity." Mackenzie advocated strategic humanitarianism in order for Britain to create the right climate for postwar reconciliation. In practice, the British could hardly treat American captives as traitors without any rights. This was, first, because officials in charge of recruiting German troops had asked the British government not to complicate their task by repeating the situation of the anti-Jacobite campaign of 1745: prisoners then could not be exchanged, a predicament the German negotiators were now well aware of. And once the Americans had captured significant numbers of British troops, Britain had to treat American captives as de facto prisoners of war in order to protect their own from retaliation.[7]

* * *

Washington set the tone early on in the Anglo-American debate about prisoners. Just weeks after taking charge of his new army at Cambridge in 1775, he complained to General Gage that "the Officers engaged in the Cause of Liberty and their Country, who by the Fortune of War have fallen into your Hands, have been thrown indiscriminately into a common Gaol appropriated for Felons—That no Consideration has been had for those of the most respectable Rank, when languishing with Wounds and Sickness. That some have been even amputated in this unworthy Situation." Washington demanded that politics be set aside; instead, he asserted, "[o]bligations arising from the Rights of Humanity, & Claims of Rank, are universally binding and extensive, except in Case of Retaliation." With this caveat, Washington invoked another principle in the laws of war, thus putting Gage on notice that in the future his treatment of Anglo-German captives would mirror the treatment of American prisoners in British hands.[8]

Gage replied that, to "the Glory of Civilized Nations, humanity and War have been compatible; and Compassion to the subdued, is become almost a general system." The British, he reassured Washington, "ever preeminent in Mercy, have outgone common examples, and overlooked the Criminal in the Captive. Upon these principles your Prisoners, whose Lives by the Laws of the Land are destined to the Cord, have hitherto been treated with care and kindness, and more comfortably lodged than the King's Troops in the Hospitals." It was Britain's natural humanitarian impulse, Gage was saying, not her obligations under the laws of war, that had ensured the good treatment of rebel prisoners. If he indeed had ignored distinctions of rank, it was only because "I Acknowledge no Rank that is not derived from the King." Retaliation worked for Gage as well, he reassured Washington, especially since he also had the American Loyalists to consider:

My intelligence from your Army would justify severe recrimination. I understand there are of the King's faithfull Subjects, taken sometime since by the Rebels, labouring like Negro Slaves, to gain their daily Subsistence, or reduced to the Wretched Alternative, to perish by famine, or take Arms against their King and Country. Those who have made the Treatment of the Prisoners in my hands, or of your other Friends in Boston, a pretence for such Measures, found Barbarity upon falsehood.[9]

But Washington was not going to be intimidated by imperious saber-rattling. He lectured Gage that he had deliberately avoided political questions, such as whether "British, or American Mercy, Fortitude, & Patience are most preeminent," or "whether our virtuous Citizens whom the Hand of Tyranny has forced into Arms" deserved to be hanged as rebels. As far as the Loyalists were concerned, however, Washington had made inquiries and reported that "[n]ot only your Officers, and Soldiers have been treated with a Tenderness due to Fellow Citizens, & Brethren; but even those execrable Parricides, whose Counsels & Aid have deluged their Country with Blood, have been protected from the Fury of a justly enraged People." Congress duly published the Washington-Gage correspondence for propagandistic effect. By this time, not only in America but in Britain, too, Washington was becoming widely recognized as an honorable gentleman officer who sought to uphold high ethical standards.[10]

Even as allegations of British maltreatment of American captives soured relations, and perhaps especially then, Washington continued to cling to these standards: he would always try to "render the situation of all prisoners in my hands as comfortable as I can, and nothing will induce me to depart from this rule, not a contrary line of conduct to those in your possession. Captivity of itself is sufficiently grievous, and it is cruel to add to its distresses." Noble ideals, captured in soaring rhetoric, found their real test in the actual treatment of prisoners under the strains and stresses of a grueling war. As Patriot soldiers learned throughout the conflict, being a rebel prisoner in British hands was a precarious and often violent experience.[11]

Capture to Burial

American soldiers surrendering to British and Hessian forces lived in fear of what awaited them. Many had heard stories of mistreatment and even death at the hands of the enemy. In early 1777, a Patriot newspaper published an ironic fictional account of General Sir William Howe's release of all captive American privates at New York: "Half he sent to the world of spirits for want of food: the others he hath sent to warn their countrymen of the danger of falling into his hands, and to convince them by ocular demonstration, that it is infinitely better to be slain in battle, than to be taken prisoner by British brutes, whose tender mercies are cruelties." American Patriots often portrayed the British treatment of prisoners as intentionally brutal: they appeared to abuse American captives as the result of "cool reflection, and a preconceived system," opined the anonymous author of a very widely circulated essay. As a naturally cruel people, the British murdered American captives "by inches" to punish them for rebelling.[12]

During the war's first full campaign in the fall and winter of 1776, one American burial detail on Harlem Heights had encountered a dozen dead Americans who had had their heads split open, allegedly after surrendering to Hessian units. Continental soldiers who survived the act of surrender were commonly robbed of watches, money, rings, shoe and knee buckles, and any other valuables they might be carrying. They were also regularly deprived of parts of their clothing, such as their shoes or coats, a serious matter in the harsh winter months. Even when the terms of capitulation guaranteed that a particular set of prisoners could keep their belongings, items were sometimes still taken from them. Captive officers later reported capriciously varying treatment: some had been shown respect at the moment of capture, others were ridiculed.[13]

In the early hours and days of captivity, prisoners routinely endured verbal harassment. Not infrequently, they also suffered beatings and other physical assaults. Even where the captors' officers did not officially condone violence, they did not necessarily prevent it. The Hessian army chaplain Philip Waldeck admitted after the surrender of Fort Washington that, against strict orders,

> the prisoners received a number of blows. Especially comical, I watched the treatment handed out by a Hessian grenadier. One of the rebels being led through looked around proudly . . . The grenadier grabbed him on the ears with both hands . . . Another tied him up with his scarf. Two others hit him on the sides of his head. A third gave him a kick in the rump so that he flew through three ranks . . . The poor guy never knew what hit him, nor why he had been hit.

Other Hessians reportedly subjected a Pennsylvania rifleman to a mock hanging on a tree three times; they also used a prisoner for target practice. British soldiers were said to stage sham executions, carting off captives seated on coffins with nooses around their necks, all the while crying terms of abuse: "rebels," "scoundrels," "murderers." Whether true, half-true, or purely fabricated, such stories had the power to instill fear in American soldiers. They shaped their expectations of the enemy and sometimes their conduct at the point of surrendering.[14]

Most captives were initially held in some sort of makeshift prison near their place of capture: a warehouse, jail, or private house or barn. Such accommodations were crowded and unsanitary; adequate bedding and clothing were usually lacking. Captured in the New York area, Samuel Young was confined in a stable with five hundred men, who had food thrown to them "as if to so many hogs, a quantity of old biscuit, broken, and in crumbs, mostly moulded, and some of it crawling with maggots, which they were obliged to scramble for . . . the next day they had a little pork given to each of them, which they were obliged to eat raw."[15]

Prisoners detained in temporary accommodations on private estates eventually had to be moved. A lucky few were exchanged locally to reduce the immediate demands on food, fuel, and clothing. Most, however, were transferred to the main British prison system in New York City. This brought further hardship, as columns of marching captives regularly suffered verbal and physical abuse both from their captors and from local inhabitants. Of the ten-mile-long trek from Harlem Heights to New York City, one Connecticut soldier recalled that he and his fellow captives were "marched through the British and Hessian army where we were insulted, kicked, beaten with the butt of their guns. Some of us were smashed down with poles on our heads and robbed of blankets." John Adlum recalled that crowds of Loyalists, Hessian army followers, and "soldiers' trulls" along the route and in New York City pelted the captives with abuse—calling them "damn'd rebels" who "ought to or would be hanged"—and sometimes pelted them with stones, too.[16]

Transport by ship was in many ways worse. Major Abraham Leggett, a veteran of the New York campaign, was captured when Fort Montgomery on the Hudson fell. Together with three hundred officers and men, Leggett was shipped to New York on the small transport *Mertell*, under conditions so crowded "that Several was near suffocated." The only water offered was too foul even for the desperately thirsty to drink. Leggett's captors were so worried about an insurrection that they placed four-pounders, a type of small cannon, on the deck facing the hold, "with a threat if we made the least noize they would Fire Down amongst us." Transfer by sea also carried its own special risks. The commanding officer of one British prisoner transport from the Turks Islands, southeast of the Bahamas, to Rhode Island shared with his Revolutionary captive, George Ballerman, his standing orders in case of a fire on board: Let the prisoners burn belowdecks, and shoot to kill anyone jumping overboard.[17]

Unsurprisingly, the conditions and treatment of captives varied, sometimes even at the same site. Ebenezer Fletcher commented that in a British field hospital near the place of his capture in the state of New York, some of his captors were "very kind; while others were very spiteful and malicious." Occasionally, British officers appeared to invest in a form of strategic magnanimity. General Sir Guy Carleton's considerate treatment of American prisoners captured in Canada in 1776 was designed to let "all moderate Men in the Colonies [understand] the way to mercy is not yet shut against them." Some American officers later acknowledged that they had received good treatment overall. There was even the rare American Loyalist, typically vilified as the most spiteful of opponents, whom captive Patriots praised for his humanitarianism. However, overwhelmingly, the wartime testimony of American Patriots suggests not only that captives routinely suffered inhumane conditions but that they believed they did so as a result of premeditated and gratuitous British cruelty. Such understandings of abuse and violence shaped captives' responses, helping explain, for instance, their steadfast resistance to British attempts to recruit them into their armed forces.[18]

The customary rations for prisoners of war in the eighteenth century were two-thirds of the weekly rations of a regular soldier on duty. In the British Army, that amounted to seven pounds each of bread and beef, four ounces of butter or cheese, eight ounces of oatmeal, three pints of peas, and a few ounces of rice if available, for a total of just under 2,500 calories per day. Prisoners should therefore have received around 1,600 daily calories. Even if they did, a sedentary prisoner weighing 160 pounds would lose 1 pound per week. But the same problems that beset the provisioning of British troops also dogged British prison sites. The challenges of acquiring, storing, shipping, preserving, and distributing rations meant that prisoners rarely received the official allocations.[19]

The quality of the foodstuffs they did receive was often dismally poor. A Lieutenant Catlin from Connecticut alleged that he was not given anything to eat for the first two days of his captivity, a common complaint that in other testimony extended to three, four, or even five days. Catlin then had to survive on "scraps of spoiled pork, wormy bread, and brackish water." After a demanding march to New York City, John Adlum received but meager quantities of "broken biscuit," which "appeared to me to have been the refuse and the bottoms of the casks out of which the army or navy had been supplied, they had yellow and green streaks of mould in them." Captives sometimes were reduced to eating old shoes, bones, and even garbage that their cruel captors sold to them. They turned to grass, wood, and bricks as food; some scraped the bran from the hogs' troughs and boiled it on the fire; one account even has men gnawing on the flesh of their own limbs.

Many captives also lacked adequate clothing and bedding, and the official allocations were rarely sufficient. Prisoners might obtain supplementary clothing through paroled officers and sometimes from local citizens; there was also a prison market for the clothes of deceased inmates and those who had been granted freedom through exchange. Even after Congress assumed responsibility for providing clothing directly to American captives in British hands, problems persisted. In a vicious circle of deprivation and degradation, a prisoner who somehow managed to buy a decent item of clothing, such as a warm coat, often had to trade it for a piece of bread to survive the day.[20]

Conditions in the prisons—foul air heavy with the stench of ill and decaying bodies, putrid water, the men "overrun with lice from head to foot," sometimes having to lie down "upon the excrements of the prisoners"—inevitably bred disease. In theory, wounded and sick captives were supposed to receive care as British soldiers did in field, army, and prison hospitals. In practice, though, medical inspections in military prisons were at best infrequent. Infected patients were not isolated. Inoculation or other preventive measures—by then increasingly common in the British armed forces—were hardly ever implemented. The hospitals that did exist for the treatment of captives were often as crowded as the prisons themselves, and not necessarily any healthier. One young Connecticut militiaman wrote to his father that, despite being ill, he "would not go to the Hospital, for all manner of diseases prevail there."[21]

New York City, the primary British garrison throughout the war, housed the imperial army's main prison system. American and other captives were kept in the Provost (in the Old Jail), "Liberty House" on Broadway, old sugar refineries, and at least half a dozen churches as well as the Quaker Meeting House, the City Hall on Nassau and Wall Streets, and, briefly, King's College (today's Columbia University).[22]

Particularly rough conditions prevailed at the Provost, a municipal jail with twelve cells and three basement dungeons that

The Provost, built in 1759, housed prisoners of war during the Seven Years' War, and American military and civilian prisoners during the Revolution.

had been turned into a prison for high-ranking American officers and "state prisoners"—civilians charged with helping the rebellion. A dozen officers were crowded into each room. They received limited and meager rations, such as raw salt beef and what one inmate described as "a little Damaged sea bread—as soon as the bread fell on the floor it Took legs and Ran in all Directions—so full of life—the flower was Very Filthy—more like Hog sty than anything else." The secret prison diary of John Fell, a notorious Tory hunter whom Loyalists had snatched from his New Jersey bed and delivered to the Provost, records the agonies of captivity. The temperatures fluctuated wildly depending on the weather outside. Men were arbitrarily confined in isolation in the dungeons below. There were "[h]orrid scenes of whipping." The entry for November 16, 1777: "Jail exceedingly disagreeable—many miserable and shocking objects [i.e., prisoners] nearly starved with cold and hunger—miserable prospect before us."[23]

The site was run by the notorious provost marshal, Captain William Cunningham. The son of a British dragoon, Cunningham had arrived in New York City in 1774. After a violent and humiliating altercation with the Sons of Liberty in the spring of 1775, when he had publicly avowed his loyalty to King George, Cunningham fled to the protection of the British Army at Boston. General Gage appointed Cunningham provost marshal in charge of rebel prisoners as well as of military discipline and executions. Before long, he was transferred to oversee prisoner administration in British-occupied New York and then Philadelphia. Contemporaries ascribed his brutality towards rebel prisoners directly to his earlier violent treatment, which "he never forgot or forgave."[24]

Following complaints by George Washington about Cunningham's abusive regime in Philadelphia, Howe simply had him transferred back to New York. In the city of prisons, stories abounded of Cunningham's cruel behavior. He took sadistic pleasure in kicking over the bowls of soup that charitable townsfolk left outside cells. He ran his sword through the shoulder of one prisoner who dared ask for a pen and paper to write to his family. He threatened prisoners with hanging. There were even allegations that Cunningham tortured captives with searing irons. With such a provost marshal embodying the worst of the imperial oppressors, the reports and rumors surrounding Cunningham seeped into the Patriot consciousness, underscoring the deeper meaning of their struggle for independence.

Almost every church in New York City that was not Church of England was soon commandeered as a prison, as if the British were taking revenge for the Patriots' earlier desecration of Anglican churches across the colonies. Seven or eight hundred men were crammed into the Old North Dutch Church on William Street without adequate food, clothing, bedding, or heating fuel. One man reported that for ten days he and fellow prisoners lived only on green apples and water from old pork barrels. A Pennsylvanian named Thomas Boyd, captured at Fort Washington, endured three days without food, followed by several more on scant provisions. The bread was "wormy and tasted bitter, and seemed of a poisonous rather than of a nourishing quality." Only those graced with an "iron constitution," like Boyd, stood a chance of surviving.[25]

Other captives were locked up in massive sugar refineries, called sugarhouses, where the conditions were at least as bad as in the churches. The sugarhouses were overcrowded, dirty, stiflingly hot in the summer, and unbearably frigid in the winter, as some lacked windowpanes, allowing the snow to blow right in. Widespread malnutrition and rampant illness quickly weakened prisoners.[26]

In such an atmosphere of fear, abuse, and suffering, wild rumors flourished. In 1777, a mysterious "French doctor" was accused of murdering American captives in New York with poisonous powders, although one prisoner, Andrew Sherburne, pointedly remarked: "No—there was no such mercy there. Nothing was employed which could blunt the susceptibility to anguish, or which, by hastening death, could rob its agonies of a single pang." In 1781, the seaman Willis Wilson claimed that the British deliberately infected with smallpox some one hundred prisoners at the provost in Portsmouth, Virginia, by purposefully bringing them into contact with contagious black men. This was not the first time

Van Cortlandt's Sugar House.

that charges of biological warfare had been leveled at the British. General Thomas Gage had been among those British officers who had sanctioned the deliberate infection of Native Americans with smallpox during the siege of Fort Pitt on the Pennsylvania frontier in 1763. In 1775, Washington had taken allegations of a British germ plot in and around Boston seriously enough to warn local authorities and the Continental Congress, describing the spread of smallpox in the besieged town as "a weapon of Defence, they Are useing against us." Rumors of germ warfare resurfaced, as we have seen, around Dunmore's black troops in Virginia in 1775 and again in the shape of a Loyalist plot in New Hampshire in 1777. In the Portsmouth case, at least, these fears remained unsubstantiated: prisoners most likely caught the disease from fellow inmates who had been infected before they were imprisoned. Black men who had been inoculated were not kept in strict quarantine due to an acute labor shortage, and they were deployed as nurses even while they were still infectious. But the veracity of specific allegations did not necessarily determine their impact on an audience already primed to be receptive to stories of the enemy's callousness.[27]

Prisoners weren't only concerned about threats to their physical well-being, however. American officers in particular felt uncomfortable when their captors ignored the hierarchies of rank and even race, keeping "all Crouded promiscuously togeather without Distinction or Respect, to person office or Colour," locking up American officers alongside "Indians, Mullattoes, Negroes, &c." John Barrett objected to being held in a sugarhouse with "common Soldiers, Sailors & even Negroes [who] were all treated alike both as to Provisions & other Matters & indiscriminate Insolence & Cruelty." White American prisoners in Philadelphia wrote of their outrage not only that they were held alongside black captives, but that the British even refused to punish a black man who had struck a white officer. When their social standing was undermined, Americans could protest as vociferously as any officer of the Crown.[28]

Congress in 1777 identified one other highly sensitive issue—namely, the surprising and nearly complete absence of charitable support from private American citizens in the surrounding population. Such neglect "was never known to happen in any similar case in a Christian country," admitted an embarrassed committee. The exceptional local who did act charitably risked suffering repercussions. In spring 1778, for instance, Patriot officials sent five barrels of flour to "a poor Woman [who] had saved the Lives of a number of our Prisoners by exerting herself in serving them far beyond her Abilities, and [who] was now in a suffering Condition for want of Provision." And when a New York tavern keeper took leftovers to prisoners in the sugarhouse on Crown Street, he sometimes observed British guards taunting starving prisoners with pieces of meat: "[T]he commonest Acts of Humanity was at that time Considered as a Crime of the deepest Dye."[29]

* * *

Common soldiers typically had to endure the insalubrious conditions of their captivity until the end of the war, unless they belonged to the minority who were exchanged—or died first. By contrast, most captive American officers were eventually granted parole, in line with the customary practice in European wars at that time. A paroled officer might enjoy freedom of movement within a delineated area of enemy territory, or be allowed to return within his army's lines, or even be permitted to go home. If the latter, he gave his word of honor not to take up arms again until he was formally exchanged for a British counterpart. Most officers captured in the New York campaign at the start of the war were paroled and moved to areas just outside New York City. Assigned to local families in pairs or three men per house, each man paid for his room and board and hoped to be reimbursed by Congress. Some men spent more than half of the war living under these circumstances. Major Abraham Leggett, for instance, was released from the Provost on parole on November 1, 1777; he was finally exchanged four years later, when he rejoined the Revolutionary army and saw further action in New Jersey and Long Island. Other paroled officers had the run of the occupied city. The conventions of gentlemanly warfare trumped concerns for secrecy and safety, although American officers paroled in New York City had to promise not to jeopardize the British war effort. An officer violating the conditions of his parole risked having his privileges revoked and being put into close confinement.[30]

Officers on parole often received medical attention, sometimes including inoculation against smallpox; as far as we can tell, most seemed to stay in reasonably good health. Surviving diaries show that officers enjoyed a leisurely life, with the freedom to read, swim, go on fishing expeditions, and attend local races; many formed relationships with local women, and some later married them. Others had their wives and families visit or live with them. When, occasionally, paroled officers complained about their uncomfortable conditions, they admitted that a poor diet of salt beef and pork was especially hard on those brought up "in the Lap of Luxury." American officers visiting their paroled colleagues sometimes thought that their conditions were, if anything, too comfortable. Of 235 paroled officers in the country villages of Long Island in February 1778, one high-ranking American official noted privately: "Was sorry to find many of the officers had been very extravagant in their Clothes, getting Laces &c."[31]

When confronted with the miserable conditions their men experienced in the city's prisons, some of their paroled officers delivered what supplementary supplies they could; others would visit their starving troops and then return to dine on beefsteak and roast pig. After one of his dinners at a local home, Lieutenant Jabez Fitch took some soup to the prisoners in the Old Church. The following day he visited again and described how the sick prisoners were in a "very Pityfull Cituation"; later he saw three prisoners buried in one grave. One paroled prisoner, Ethan Allen, found on his visits

> several of the prisoners in the agonies of death, in consequence of very hunger, and other[s] speechless and very near death, biting pieces of chips . . . Hollow groans saluted my ears, and despair seemed to be imprinted on every of their countenances. The filth . . . was almost beyond description. The floors were covered with excrements. I have carefully sought to direct my steps to avoid it, but could not. . . . I have seen . . . seven dead at the same time, lying among the excrements of their bodies.

Allen soon discontinued his visits, as it "was too much for me to bear as a spectator."[32]

Inadequate burial was the final indignity of captivity. "Twenty or thirty die every day," wrote one released prisoner. "They lie in heaps unburied." The corpses of American soldiers were mistreated by both Loyalists and the British, remembered another: "I have seen whole gangs of tories making derision, and exulting over the dead." In New York City, frozen corpses were dragged out from the churches and sugarhouses every morning, "thrown into wagons like logs, carted away, and then pitched into a large hole or trench to be covered up like dead animals. In a brief time, the naked bodies would be exposed because of the weather conditions." Other bodies were said to have simply been thrown on the ground outdoors, where they were "[e]xpos'd to the unnatural

Devouring of Swine & other greedy Animals" before being buried, mostly naked, in shallow mass graves, where their remains might again be defiled by swine or feral animals. There even were stories of men being buried alive. Whether such tales were true or apocryphal, they certainly added to captivity's horrors.[33]

Worrying Myself off My Legs

By April 1777, as evidence of abuse and very high death rates among American captives was accumulating, Congress indicted the British for maltreating American prisoners, concluding, perhaps surprisingly, that the rank and file among the enemy were, if anything, more sympathetic towards their prisoners' plight than their officers were, and—echoing comments in prisoners' narratives—the Hessians more than the British. As Washington protested again, his obstinate counterpart, General Howe, replied with increasingly absurd denials of responsibility. All prisoners had received "sufficient and wholesome food" and medical attention in "the most airy Buildings" or the largest transports, "the very healthiest Places of Reception, that could possibly be provided for them." How so many could have died so fast, "I cannot determine." With Howe shrugging his shoulders, Washington dismissed any hopes for a cartel. Sarcastically he added, "[H]owever successful, ingenious miscolourings may be in some instances, to perplex the Understanding in matters of Speculation, Yet, it is difficult to persuade Mankind to doubt the Evidence of their Senses, & the reality of those facts for which they can appeal to them." Airy buildings might not be beneficial in wintertime, and the provisions could not have been adequate in quantity or quality, given the captives' appearance and testimony. Washington's British prisoners, by contrast, "were not stinted to a scanty pittance" but received the same rations as American soldiers in the field. Howe's refusal to allow an American procuring agent to provision their captives, along with the lack of a formalized agreement, required the two commanders to rely on each other's generosity: he, Washington, had exercised that generosity, but he had been wrong to expect Howe to reciprocate.[34]

It was not until spring 1777 that Congress appointed officials with responsibility for prisoners of war. Elias Boudinot now served as commissary general of prisoners. Lewis Pintard, a forty-five-year-old East India merchant from New York, became the resident agent to prisoners in New York. Deputies were also appointed in other states and at specific prison sites. In addition to caring for enemy captives in American hands, these officials were to provide American captives of the British with money, food, clothing, and other items. The Board of War instructed the new commissary to clamp down on malpractice by local committees, which were variously "unneccesarily rigorous" or "culpably lax" in their care of enemy prisoners. The tall, handsome, religious Boudinot, a well-to-do lawyer from Elizabethtown, New Jersey, confessed to his wife that by accepting his appointment he had allowed himself to be drawn into "the boisterous noisy, fatiguing unnatural and disrelishing state of War and slaughter."[35]

As Boudinot built up his staff and made initial inquiries, his work was being severely impeded. Howe would at first not admit Pintard to New York City, and later allowed him to visit only in an unofficial capacity lest his mission be construed as British recognition of American independence. Congress had also resolved that each state appoint a commissary of prisoners to negotiate the release of its captives. Boudinot and Washington urged that control be centralized, but those states that negotiated directly with the British, including New York, Connecticut, New Jersey, and Massachusetts, rarely cooperated as fully as Boudinot would have liked.[36]

Boudinot's efforts were further hampered by a lack of resources, so that from the summer of 1777 onward he paid very large sums from his private funds and borrowed from friends. In the winter of 1777–78, for instance, Pintard thus issued 796 pairs of shoes, 1,310 stockings, 787 coats, 1,253 shirts, 549 vests, 376 pairs of trousers, 184 hats, 616 blankets, and 8 mattresses to American officers and soldiers held captive in New York City. In the first half of 1778, Boudinot sent 857 barrels of flour to British-occupied Philadelphia to raise cash, as well as 117 head of cattle and 4 hogs to provide American captives with fresh meat.[37]

It was only in February 1778 that Boudinot was permitted to visit American captives in New York City, where the more accommodating General Clinton was now in charge. Boudinot found the two hospitals with their 211 prisoners "in tollerable good Order, neat and clean and the Sick much better taken care off than I expected." Even in the sugarhouse that he visited, 191 captives had sufficient clothing and blankets to see them through the winter. However, those prisoners told Boudinot that their conditions had only improved over the previous couple of months, possibly as a result of the British defeat at Saratoga, where an army of nearly 6,000 went into American captivity. As for the conditions at the Provost, Boudinot wrote, "I was greatly distressed, with the wretched Situation of so many of the human Species." After his first visit, Boudinot received an anonymous note describing the corrupt and brutal prison regime. On a return visit to the Provost, Boudinot found American officers and soldiers as well as some political prisoners in a "wretched Situation." They shared that William Cunningham had killed two prisoners with the jail key. He beat officers and sent them to the dungeon for weeks at a time for the most trivial of "offenses," visiting them periodically only to administer more sadistic beatings. However, as Boudinot concluded with remarkable frankness, the captives also included "a sett of sad Villains, who rob each other of their Cloaths and Blanketts, and many of them sell their own Shoes, Blanketts, and even Shirts for Rum." When Boudinot confronted the city commandant, General James Robertson, he obfuscated, like Howe before him, and denied any wrongdoing.[38]

Boudinot eventually borrowed some $30,000 to purchase clothing and blankets for 300 officers and 1,100 men and to ensure that they would receive daily supplemental rations of bread and beef for fifteen months. He also oversaw some limited prisoner exchanges. But the constant stress had taken its toll. After a year of "worrying myself off my Legs," and perilously close to bankruptcy, Boudinot resigned in April 1778. He threatened to declare himself insolvent, and a letter from his successor was recited in the congressional chamber, warning that the closure of Boudinot's accounts had prompted an alarming rise in the mortality rate of American prisoners. Congress eventually voted the very significant sum of £20,000 to compensate, at least partially, their former commissary general. Boudinot's frustrating experiences with inadequate resources and poor coordination between Continental and state authorities had highlighted the limits of the nascent American state. But despite those constraints, the fledgling state and the nation's leaders by and large committed the resources required to treat their own prisoners comparatively well.[39]

A Sordid Set of Creatures in Human Figure

The fact that British and German prisoners of war fared better overall than American rebel captives was due to practical circumstances as much as principle. Washington and the Congress were committed to honor the laws of war, and Revolutionary leaders sometimes modeled magnanimity. When a prisoner was known to have been kind to American captives, as was the case with one Francis Dorrel, the Board of War ordered he be put on parole and duly exchanged, "for we wish to embrace every opportunity of shewing kindness to such of our enemies as have given proofs of their humanity to the Americans." But American captors were greatly helped in their mission by the simple fact that they operated on home ground, with much more space to house prisoners, which meant fewer large, overcrowded facilities where epidemic diseases could wreak havoc. Shorter supply lines and lower costs facilitated supporting prisoners. In addition, larger numbers of British prisoners of war were able to escape, as prisoner marches and detention sites were less closely guarded than British garrison cities or prison ships.[40]

Nevertheless, for the individual British or German prisoners of war, captivity in American hands was often a harrowing experience. Like American prisoners, they experienced inadequate accommodations and shortages of provisions and clothing immediately after capture, and endured exhausting and occasionally fatal marches to permanent detention sites. Moreover, the gentlemen officers' sense of honor was challenged when they were held in close confinement or alongside their men or common felons.[41]

The British Army was quick to complain when they felt that Americans violated the codes of war. At one point, the United States proposed that the British send supplies to their captive soldiers in American hands, the standard European practice. To the British, though, this amounted to violence by logistical stratagem. Howe protested that the American proposal would mean starvation for many Anglo-German prisoners who simply were too widely dispersed, sometimes hundreds of miles from the nearest British lines. When the United States agreed instead to have their own commissaries provision prisoners of war, and demanded that the British pay in coin within thirty days, they thus exacted a costly arrangement; this helped the Americans both to fund the needs of their own captives held in New York and to redress a national shortage of coins.[42]

One way to alleviate the hardships of German (and some British) prisoners was the semi-privatization of the prison regime. Such an effort apparently started up spontaneously in the partially German-speaking Lancaster area of Pennsylvania in the winter of 1775. By the summer of 1777, when an additional 1,000 prisoners were stretching accommodation and provisions to the limits, both Pennsylvania authorities and private citizens routinely hired German prisoners of war at Lancaster as laborers. Most worked as farmhands or helped in craftsmen's shops. Some German sergeants and ensigns became temporary servants in farmers' homes in exchange for food and cider. Significant numbers worked in their skilled trades, especially as weavers, tailors, and shoemakers, as well as smiths, carpenters, joiners, and masons. Some made clothing and even shot and shells for militias and the Continental Army. At one stage, the Board of War set up an entire shoe factory with prisoner-laborers. One soldier, originally from Berlin and conversant in both German and French, advertised himself as a schoolmaster and secretary to German immigrants. A Hessian military band captured at Trenton famously played for the

Congress at the celebratory dinner on the first anniversary of the signing of the Declaration of Independence, and at Revolutionary feasts subsequently.[43]

Most employers took on just one or two prisoners at a time, although furnaces, ironworks, and mills demanded larger numbers. Civilian employers usually made a deposit with the authorities to ensure the prisoners' return. As part of the contract, they provided the prisoner-laborers with meals and housing and paid them wages. Men who worked near the barracks had to return twice daily for roll call; those who worked farther afield reported twice weekly. Such arrangements had obvious appeal for the captives, who gained respite from crowded quarters plagued by vermin and disease, and for their captors, as small prisoner-laborer detachments were easier to control and required fewer guards than larger groups of enemy soldiers. What had begun as a pragmatic exercise thus yielded a humanitarian dividend. Still, conditions were far from universally rosy. And, ironically, the group of enemy prisoners promised the best conditions ended up enduring some of the worst.[44]

* * *

In March 1777, the British government appointed General John Burgoyne as commander of the northern army. His mission that fall called for two other British armies to converge with his combined British-Loyalist and Canadian–Native American force to capture the strategically vital Hudson Valley. As he moved south from Quebec towards Saratoga, New York, Burgoyne took the fortresses at Crown Point and Ticonderoga. But supply shortages and an unexpectedly strong Patriot resistance slowed his progress along the Hudson. The additional British armies he had been counting on never arrived, largely due to inadequate communication and coordination. By October, Burgoyne's hungry troops faced American forces outnumbering them four to one. The surrender of a field army at Saratoga—close to 6,000 British and German troops—marked the first major British defeat of the war.

It triggered vicious attacks on Lord Germain by the opposition in Parliament and hastened the conclusion of a formal Franco-American alliance.[45]

For our purposes, it is the aftermath of Saratoga that is illuminating, especially the unexpectedly epic journey of the so-called Convention Army. The fate of those 5,700 to 5,900 British, German, and Canadian troops surrendered by Burgoyne helps us understand how—humanitarian principles notwithstanding—limited resources, the pressures of war, and human frailty could produce punishing conditions for captives.[46]

The liberal terms of surrender agreed upon between the American and British commanders under the Convention of Saratoga provided for Britain's Canadian and Loyalist auxiliary troops to go to Canada, and for all others to be taken to Boston and then shipped to Europe. No baggage was to be searched. The men were to have the same provisions as soldiers in the American army, not the two-thirds ration that prisoners of war usually received. However, when the British Crown refused to ratify the Convention in order to avoid acknowledging the Congress—and hence American independence—Congress likewise refused to honor the agreement. American leaders had by then realized that releasing thousands of soldiers to fight elsewhere in the Empire meant that Britain would be able to replace them in America.

Unable to leave for Europe, more than 5,000 "conventioners" were forced upon American states ill prepared to cope with these additional captives (plus their minders) on top of existing prisoners, their own populations, and American forces. As a result, substantial numbers of British and German prisoners suffered from intermittent if sometimes severe food shortages, lack of firewood, inadequate winter shelter, and disease, as well as physical violence at the hands of their overstretched guards.

The Convention Army's ordeal started with a march from Saratoga to Cambridge, Massachusetts—some twelve miles a day through mountainous terrain in the rain- and snowstorms of late October and November. At least two men froze to death; a dozen more died en route from disease, exhaustion, and hypothermia. Hannah Winthrop witnessed the exhausted survivors march into Cambridge: "I never had the least idea that the creation produced such a sordid set of creatures in human figure—poor, dirty, emaciated men." Winthrop commented on the large number of women accompanying the captive army, also "barefoot, clothed in dirty rags. Such effluvia filled the air while they were passing, that had they not been smoking all the time, I should have been apprehensive of being contaminated."[47]

In Cambridge, the troops, along with the women and children who arrived with them, were held in poorly built barracks on Winter Hill and Prospect Hill, the snow drifting through the holes that served as windows. Each room, thirteen by thirteen feet at most, accommodated three or four officers, or alternatively sixteen to twenty soldiers. Lieutenant Jacob Heerwagen wrote to his parents in Hanau, Hesse, that initially he and his fellow captives had to lie on the bare ground in the poorly heated cabins, although eventually they built themselves makeshift beds. As the British Army considered the Convention violated, they refused to send clothing and blankets even though winter was fast approaching. Hessian sources suggest that the American captors took adequate care of the sick. But by the spring of 1778, foodstuffs were so scarce that Congress requested Pennsylvania as well as states farther south to send victuals to Boston, where the local population was now petitioning to have the prisoners removed. By then, Congress had suspended the Convention entirely.[48]

Yet the conventioners' odyssey continued. Those German prisoners who had remained at Cambridge, along with British captives who had been moved to Rutland, were later marched in six columns to Charlottesville, Virginia. Trekking hundreds of miles, through snow that sometimes reached their knees, the men regularly had to sleep in the open: "[O]ne night upon the green Mountains," remembered Corporal George Fox of the 7th Foot, "there was snow upon us ½ yd deep." British officials protested the dispersal of the Convention prisoners across more than two dozen settlements in multiple states, where they were "so secreted as to be lost, which may properly be deemed a positive Slavery."[49]

Arriving at Charlottesville, the British ensign Thomas Anburey experienced the encampment, larger than any city in the state, as truly horrific. The barracks lacked doors, windows, and roofs, and were filled high with snow. The men and even their officers had to complete their own quarters. They built themselves huts, dug wells, and constructed toilets, in addition to erecting a hospital, church, and even coffee rooms; they laid out vegetable gardens and a graveyard. Major General Friedrich Adolf Riedesel, the Brunswick officer who had commanded all German and Native American forces at Saratoga, described conditions in Virginia as even worse than they had been in Boston, where he had alleged that the Americans were swapping good prisoner provisions for codfish and "still poorer articles." The men adjusted with difficulty to the new diet: "Animal food and maize were chiefly used; vegatables were scarcely known." Since quarters and food were in short supply, officers were eventually given a parole area one hundred miles in radius. Some, such as Riedesel and his entire family, enjoyed Thomas Jefferson's hospitality and musical company at Monticello and surrounding estates.[50]

By the time Congress classified the conventioners as standard prisoners of war in 1781, they had marched to far-flung locations such as Winchester, Virginia; Fort Frederick, Maryland; and various towns in Pennsylvania. Meanwhile, the Patriots' limited resources hampered their ability to guard captives, facilitating escape. In the first year in Massachusetts alone, more than 1,000 British and some 330 German soldiers fled during marches and at various stops; only some 3,000 prisoners made the journey to Maryland in late 1780. It has been estimated that about half the British deserters made for British enclaves and eventually rejoined their army. Many others would blend into the local population and stay in America permanently. By the time the remaining prisoners were released in 1782, the group had shrunk to just 470.[51]

* * *

The conventioners' odyssey is a sobering reminder of how much prisoners might suffer when resources were limited, even without any official policy of abuse or systematic neglect. Anglo-German prisoner populations enjoyed significantly better overall conditions than did Americans, but these were as much the result of greater space, fewer logistical challenges, and prisoner-labor schemes as they were proof of the higher humanitarian standards of their captors.

As for Britain's treatment of American prisoners, it is unlikely that any eighteenth-century state could have provided adequate conditions for such a large number in such small areas of a very partially occupied land, thousands of miles from the captors' main supply bases. The failure of both powers to negotiate large-scale exchanges compounded this structural problem. Then, too, the patchwork of responsibilities shared between British military and civilian authorities, and the limitations of the fledgling American state, kept both countries from implementing even the basic quality of prisoner treatment they had agreed upon. Wherever large numbers of captives were crowded in substandard conditions, disease was endemic and squalor, discomfort, and suffering inevitable. Neglect and a lack of compassion on the part of captors, human frailty among desperate prisoners, and the absence of charitable support from the surrounding American population further reduced a captive's chances of surviving, let alone staying healthy.[52]

The British surrender of a field army at Saratoga in late 1777, which led to the conventioners' travails, also had geostrategic implications. As early as the summer of independence, the rebellious colonies had begun wooing Britain's European archenemy, France. At first, the French court had provided only secret support, using a shell company run by the inventor and author of *The Marriage of Figaro*, Pierre-Augustin Caron de Beaumarchais, to supply the United States with cannons, muskets, explosives, tents, and uniforms. On behalf of Congress, Benjamin Franklin subsequently negotiated a preferential trade agreement with France and nudged the foreign secretary, Charles Gravier, Comte de Vergennes, to commit further loans and war matériel to the American cause. In the fall and winter of 1777–78, the French government completed the war preparations it considered a precondition for an official alliance with the United States. By December 1777, news of the first major American military success—the capture of Burgoyne's army—accelerated the move towards French intervention in the war.[53]

On February 6, 1778, representatives of the French monarchy and the American republic signed in secrecy (or so they thought) the treaties of commerce and of alliance. The two countries granted each other most-favored-nation status in trade and guaranteed each other's possessions in North America forever. Most importantly, France promised to support America's war until independence was secured. America would, in return, give France free rein in the West Indies, the lucrative sugar islands perennially subject to Anglo-French rivalry. Franklin had turned France's desire to use the Anglo-American conflict to humiliate Britain into an advantage. But what Franklin perhaps did not foresee was how this realignment might affect Britain's conduct of the war, including her treatment of American captives.

At the same time as he was negotiating treaties with France, Franklin was using his diplomatic perch to help alleviate the suffering of American prisoners held across the English Channel and draw attention to the appalling conditions under which American captives were kept in Britain's Asian and African empire. But one of the war's greatest humanitarian disasters in fact played itself out much closer to home. For if the prisons in New York were the slaughterhouses of America's soldiers, as Congress once put it, British prison ships anchored offshore and holding thousands of seamen were far, far worse.[54]

Overleaf: Carington Bowles, Bowles's New and Accurate Map of the World, or Terrestrial Globe *(London, [1780]).*

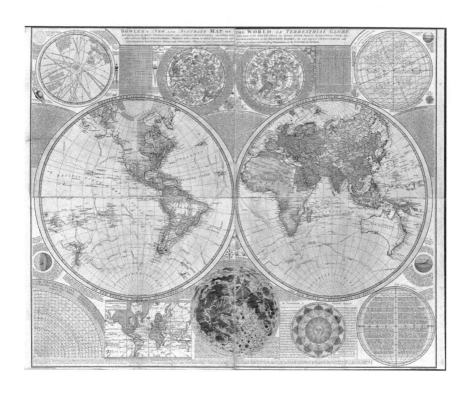

BOWLES'S *New and Accurate* MAP of *the* WORLD *or* TERRESTRIAL GLOBE.

Chapter Seven

Black Holes

I N AN ESSAY THAT CIRCULATED WIDELY IN THE TRANSATLANTIC press in early 1777, an anonymous author signing as "Miserecors" described the shipboard transfer of captured American soldiers to prisons in New York. "[T]hrust down into the hold," Miserecors wrote, "they were nearly suffocated for want of air." Their treatment was not only "more murderous, more blood-thirsty" than Americans had ever experienced at the hands of the Indian savages, but this "murder ... by inches" was so heinous that even "the famous instance of Calcutta is not to be compared with this."[1]

Evoking the same comparison, "Humanitas" had earlier described the arrival of the first American maritime prisoners in England in similar tones. The condition of American captives was "truly shocking and ... barbarous and miserable." On one ship moored in the Thames, twenty-five men were "inhumanly shut close down, like wild beasts, in a small stinking apartment, in the hold ... without a breath of air, in this sultry season, but what they receive from a small grating overhead." With such openings just two inches square, the sun beating down, and "putrid streams issuing from the hold ... so hot and offensive that one cannot, without the utmost danger, breathe over it," the writer concluded, "the resemblance that this barbarity bears to the memorable Black Hole at Calcutta ... strikes every eye to the sight."[2]

Eighteenth-century Britons, and many literate Americans, too, required no explanation of the "famous instance of Calcutta" in 1756, when soldiers of Siraj ud-Daula, the Nawab of Bengal, had imprisoned some 150 Europeans overnight in an eighteen-by-fourteen-foot cell in the city's Fort William. The only two airholes were barricaded with iron bars. By the following morning some fifty captives had died from heat, dehydration, and lack of oxygen. Many had been trampled to death by panicking fellow captives. As one survivor later testified in the House of Commons, some had perished quickly, "others grew mad, and having lost their Senses, died in a high Delirium." Publicized in the print media and commemorated in a monument to the victims of "Tyrannic Violence," the incident epitomized the cruelty of the colonized.[3]

Throughout the American Revolutionary War, British and American writers of both fiction and nonfiction routinely evoked the Black Hole of Calcutta as a setting for tales of horror and a metaphor for individuals' unimaginable sufferings in captivity. War critics on both sides appropriated the myth for their own purposes. Donning the humanitarian mantle, writers such as Miserecors and Humanitas, and soon American officials and captives, too, used the image of Britain's earlier humiliation at the hands of inhumane colonials in India to accuse the rulers of the British Empire of having descended to the level of savage barbarity.[4]

The story of the Black Hole of Calcutta was scary and unsettling in part because the truth about that dark night in Bengal was very difficult to ascertain. The discrepancy between rumored and actual casualty figures; disagreement over whether the deaths were intentional or accidental; the absence of any visual depictions—in other words, the very *unknown* of the black hole—allowed contemporaries to conjure the worst. America, of course, had its own black holes during its first civil war. Contemporaries imagined the most horrific of them as floating dungeons, at once reminiscent of the Simsbury mines and of slave ships.

This Floating Pandemonium

However dismal and brutal the conditions in New York or Philadelphia, American Patriot captives endured far worse on the prison ships anchored just off New York City. These "shifting 'black holes' " held the majority of American prisoners throughout the war—initially soldiers captured in the Battle of Long Island and elsewhere in the New York campaign, as well as political prisoners, and soon large numbers of seamen, too. The first prison ships were former cattle transports and other store ships located in New York's Gravesend Bay, then moved to the Hudson and East Rivers and, in 1778, to Wallabout Bay, along the northwest shore of Brooklyn. Over the course of the war, Britain used some two dozen vessels as floating prisons in New York, most of them former warships; sloops; depot, hospital, and fire ships; and transports, plus another half a dozen in Charleston and one in Saint Lucia. To American captives the ships symbolized British cruelty at its extreme. One seaman, who was seventeen at the time of his imprisonment, recalled that the "very idea of being incarcerated in this floating Pandemonium filled us with horror."[5]

As he was being rowed towards his place of confinement, a new captive would have noticed the nauseating smell pouring out of the few air ports on the side of a ship, "a strong current of foul vapor" common also on slave ships. Captain John Van Dyke remembered that when he boarded one of the prison ships, "her stench was so great, and my breathing this putrid air—I thought it would kill me." Of his first night one seaman recollected "dismal sounds meeting my ears from every direction; a nauseous and putrid atmosphere filling my lungs at every breath; and a stifled and suffocating heat, which almost deprived me of sense, and even of life." Ichabod Perry from Fairfield, Connecticut, then a seventeen-year-old private, later told his children about the utter darkness of his first night aboard another prison ship, when a third of the prisoners "suffocated from want of space." Others called to mind the

> continual noises during the night. The groans of the sick and the
> dying; the curses poured out by the weary and exhausted upon
> our inhuman keepers; the restlessness caused by the suffocat-
> ing heat and the confined and poisoned air; mingled with the
> wild and incoherent ravings of delirium, were the sounds, which,
> every night, were raised around us, in all directions.

The smells onboard became so overpowering that men sent ashore on burial duty would bring back clods of soil and patches of turf for those shipbound to smell, the earth "being passed . . . from hand to hand, and its smell inhaled, as if it had been a fragrant rose." The experience of captivity also diminished individuals' sensory perception, more so even than in the Simsbury mines, as some lost their voice and others their hearing. An unknown number of captives became mentally unstable, as happened to the man, recalled by one Thomas Andros, who stalked through the ship at night carrying a knife.[6]

Prison hulks, as such ships were known, had been in use in Britain throughout much of the eighteenth century. They housed Jacobite rebels after 1745, French prisoners of war during the Seven Years' War, and British civilians when terrestrial prisons became overcrowded. Even into the Victorian era, Charles Dickens's *Great Expectations* featured those terrifying black prison ships moored on the Thames. Although conditions on these ships were dire—a recent scholar catalogues poor rations, hard labor, widespread disease, and a mortality rate of one-third—the prison ships on which Britain held Americans captive were worse.[7]

As was the case for prisoners on land, food was a constant worry. Even if the official rations were issued, which they were often not, they were frequently of poor quality. Malnutrition and dangerous weight loss were common. The steward of each six-man mess prepared food in a common copper boiling vat that held half freshwater and half salt water for peas and oatmeal and for meat, respectively. As the teenage seaman Ebenezer Fox remembered, in addition to the typically wormy bread,

[a]s for the pork, we were cheated out of it more than half the time, and when it was obtained one would have judged from its . . . exhibiting the consistence and appearance of variegated soap, that it was the flesh of the porpoise or sea hog, and had been the inhabitant of the ocean, rather than a sty. . . . The provisions were generally damaged, and from the imperfect manner in which they were cooked were about as indigestible as grape shot. The flour and oatmeal was often sour, and when the suet was mixed with the flour it might be nosed half the length of the

ship. The first view of the beef would excite an idea of veneration
for its antiquity ... [I]ts color was a dark mahogany, and its solid-
ity would have set the keenest edge of a broad axe at defiance to
cut across the grain ... It was so completely saturated with salt
that after having been boiled in water taken from the sea, it was
found to be considerably freshened by the process.

The salt water used for boiling the meat corroded the copper boiler
in which oats and peas were also prepared. The freshwater brought
by tankers from New York was often foul on arrival, giving rise to
the suspicion of a deliberate ploy, as water could in theory have
been fetched from much closer Long Island. Junior and privateer
officers enjoyed the privilege of admission to the gun room, where
they prepared their food in freshwater on little fires in the galley.
Yet everyone's diet lacked fresh produce, and scurvy was predictably widespread: "Among the emaciated crowd of living skeletons
who had remained on board for any length of time, the cook was
the only person who appeared to have much flesh on his bones."[8]

One of the most notorious ships of the Revolutionary era (and
one of the best documented) was the *Jersey*, a decommissioned,
64-gun British ship of the line, on whom a crew of 450 had served in
the Mediterranean since the 1730s. By the time she started service
as a prison ship no later than 1779, now anchored with massive chain
cables in the channel between the mudflats some one hundred yards
off the Long Island shore, the British apparently considered her capable of holding up to 1,000 prisoners. Her skeleton crew consisted of
the captain, two mates, a dozen seamen, two or three dozen marines
sheltered by an awning aft on the quarterdeck, and some thirty
soldiers. The hulk of the *Jersey* became infamous as a dirty, disease-
ridden, deadly place. Visual depictions helped feed the Patriot imagination, as did Philip Freneau's epic poem *The British Prison-Ship*.
Freneau accused the "ungenerous Britons" of conspiring "to murder
whom you can't subdue," and evoked "The dreadful secrets of these
prison caves, / Half sunk, half floating on *my Hudson*'s waves."
Even well after the war, terrifying tales from the *Jersey* still found
a wide audience. The posthumous narrative of Thomas Dring, a

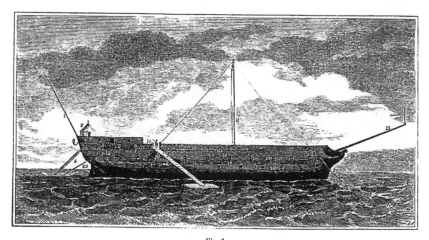

Fig. 1.
THE JERSEY PRISON SHIP,
AS MOORED AT THE WALLABOUT NEAR LONG ISLAND, IN THE YEAR 1782.

Jersey prison ship, moored in Wallabout Bay, New York. There are no known contemporary depictions of the *Jersey*. This illustration accompanies the 1829 edition of Thomas Dring's Recollections of the Jersey prison-ship.

master's mate from Newport, Rhode Island, who had been a captive on the *Jersey* for two months, portrayed "unspeakable sufferings."[9]

The *Jersey* featured two tiers of ports fore and aft, air ports, and large hatchways, which should have allowed for a relatively free circulation of air. However, the gun ports and portholes had been sealed with timber and replaced with two rows of twenty-inch-square glazed air ports secured with iron bars. No lamps or candles were allowed belowdecks, where the only light came through the lattice of the hatchway grill or the air ports. Much like on a slave ship, a ten-foot-high barricade extending several feet beyond the sides of the ship near the aft hatch was manned by armed sentries who would rake the hatchway or deck with gunfire in the event of an insurrection:

> *At evry hatch a group of centries stands,*
> *Cull'd from the Scottish or the English bands;*
> *As tigers fierce for human blood they thirst,*
> *Rejoice in slaughter, as in slaughter nursed.*[10]

David Sproat, the British commissary general of naval prisoners from 1779, was said to run a brutal regime on the *Jersey*, much like William Cunningham onshore. A Scottish-born Loyalist merchant in Philadelphia whose house Patriots had ransacked before converting it into an army hospital, the commissary seemed out for revenge. While Sproat was in charge, on the first two days after their arrival, new prisoners could not get or prepare any food. The commissaries also frequently reduced rations or substituted poor ones to make a profit for themselves. Forced to seize any opportunity to augment their meals, captives took on work, such as water detail or the hoisting of provisions. Those who had held on to some money were allowed to buy supplementary foods from outside sources, such as merchants or the entrepreneurial women who rowed up along the side of the hulk, but these were unreliable channels.[11]

The lack of clothing, too, could spell serious illness if not death. There was no regular British policy for issuing garments and bedding. The American commissary general and his New York agent could procure some items, which did make a difference, but were rarely enough. Some captives were lucky to keep what they had on when captured; others depended on donations by a few caring locals onshore. Men with previous experience of captivity wore their clothes in layers and hid their money and other belongings in linings or boots. Several prison hulks were uncaulked, so that in winter snow blew through the seams—although at least that allowed prisoners to quench their thirst.

Onboard hygiene was appalling, disease rampant. The captives, who spent most of their time belowdecks, had hardly any facilities for washing, and the odors of their own excrement and urine were pervasive. In such conditions, infection spread easily. The salt water for cooking meat was usually procured from the same spot where the waste tubs were emptied over the ship's side. Vermin crept up on sleeping prisoners at night. Scurvy and dysentery were common. So were yellow fever, pneumonia, typhoid, influenza, and that feared mass killer of civilian and military populations, smallpox. As one British medical official warned, it was almost impossible to eradicate contagious diseases, such as smallpox, once they had taken hold on a prison ship, which endangered the lives not just of prisoners but of their guards, too.[12]

Smallpox is transmitted through airborne droplets. Crowded conditions in towns, army camps, and prisons are thus ideal breeding grounds for the disease, which can be carried in the clothing and bedding of those infected. After an incubation period of ten to twelve days, as the historian of medicine Erica Charters describes, "sufferers experience back, muscle, and head pains, high fever, and the characteristic rash." The rash can cause "septic skin infections and massive hemorrhages of the skin, lungs, and other organs." Survivors might suffer permanent "blindness, skin infections, infertility, and a horrifically ravaged appearance." Smallpox cannot be cured, but those who survive the disease are immune to future infection.[13]

Smallpox was endemic in eighteenth-century British towns, and since most British Army recruits came from urban population centers, many recruits had survived smallpox in childhood and thus entered the army already immune. But the disease was far less widespread in America, and, as a consequence, rates of immunity among Continental recruits were low. American soldiers, including Loyalists among British forces, therefore remained at greater risk of epidemic outbreaks compared to the British.

The Continental Army began inoculating thousands of soldiers against smallpox in 1777. Some American prisoners also inoculated themselves. Inoculation had been practiced much earlier in parts of Africa and Asia, but was only introduced to Europe in the early eighteenth century and in America a generation later. The procedure, in the words of the author of *Pox Americana: The Great Smallpox Epidemic of 1775–82*, Elizabeth A. Fenn, was "both frightening and fascinating." As John Adams had experienced during a smallpox outbreak in Boston in 1764, it "consisted of deliberately implanting live *Variola* in an incision, usually on the patient's hand or arm." Thomas Dring on the *Jersey* used a pin to infect himself, taking the disease from a patient whose smallpox had advanced to the right stage. Dring experienced a mild form of the disease and recovered; other captives followed his example.[14]

Most sick prisoners appear to have received no attention from British doctors. Since the Americans' own surgeons were typically on parole, they were usually not available, either. When on occasion an American doctor was permitted to board a ship to care for the ill, he was quickly overwhelmed; one doctor who attempted to do so at Charleston in 1780 said that in his professional judgment only death could improve the sickly conditions caused by human miasma and putrid fevers ravaging overcrowded ships. The prisoner George Ballerman testified that the sick were only allowed to go to a hospital when they were already so weak that they often did not survive the transfer. On the rare occasions when a full-scale disinfection of a ship was attempted, many weakened prisoners died of exposure during their temporary evacuation, especially if the weather turned severe.[15]

The psychological impact of being held captive on these moored ships was as stark as the physical suffering: "[T]he prisoners had lost almost every feeling of humanity for each other; . . . self-preservation appeared to be their only wish." Monotony and the sheer uncertainty of their fate weighed on captives. William Slade of New Canaan, when he was transferred from the North Dutch Church to the *Grosvenor*, found men sinking into a state of unresponsive stupor:

> Sunday, 8th. This day we were almost discouraged, but considered that would not do. Cast off such thoughts. We drawd our bread and eat with sadness . . . Spent the day reading and in meditation, hoping for good news.

> Wednesday, 11th. Still in hopes.

> Friday, 13th. We now see nothing but the mercy of God to intercede for us. Sorrowful times, all faces look pale, discouraged, discouraged.

> Saturday, 14th. Times look dark. Death prevails among us . . . At night suffer with cold and hunger.

Sunday, 15th. Paleness attends all faces, the melancholyst day I ever saw.

Tuesday, 17th. We are treated worse than cattle and hogs.

Wednesday, 18th. Hunger prevails. Sorrow comes on.

Friday, 20th. Prisoners hang their heads and look pale. No comfort. All sorrow.

Sunday, 22nd. Last night nothing but grones all night of sick and dying. Men amazeing to behold. Such hardness, sickness prevails fast. Deaths multiple . . . All faces sad.

Monday, 23rd. One dies almost every day.

Friday, 27th. Three men of our battalion died last night.[16]

This sketch has long been thought to depict American prisoners on board a British prison ship. It has been attributed to Jonathan Trumbull, whose grand scenes of the Revolutionary War adorn the Rotunda of the U.S. Capitol. More recently, it has been suggested that the apathetic figures with gaunt features and ragged clothing might instead represent inmates of a mental asylum—the uncertainty perhaps a telling commentary on the perceived conditions of American captives.

* * *

Death was one way captivity could end for American prisoners. The other three were exchange, escape, or enlistment with the enemy. As we have seen, the codes of war prevalent among Europe's armies forbade recruiting prisoners into one's own forces. This, however, did not stop British officers from attempting to do so. Congress alleged that the British commonly deprived new captives of food for three, four, even five days, then tempted them with enlistment to save their lives. George Ballerman would testify in 1780 that when British recruiting officers on New York prison ships found that American officers had told their men not to enlist, the American officers were removed to the Provost; when the recruiting officers still failed to enlist American soldiers, they deprived the captives of water. Despite the effort, British recruitment among American prisoners, which disproportionately attracted British-born colonists, does not appear to have been particularly successful.[17]

Instead, many prisoners attempted to escape. Christopher Hawkins slipped through an open gunport on the *Jersey* after only three days of captivity and swam for two hours until—evading Hessian sentries—he reached the relative safety of Long Island. James Forten, a fifteen-year-old African-American from Philadelphia, and described as tall, literate, and a determined Patriot, first chose captivity on the *Jersey* over being sent to England. He later forsook a chance of escaping by ceding his place in a "chest of old clothes" lowered down the side to his thirteen-year-old, white "companion in suffering," Daniel Brewton. Forten was eventually exchanged and lived to become a wealthy Philadelphia citizen and prominent abolitionist.[18]

Joseph Bartlett's memoranda tell of his captivity among hundreds of prisoners on the *Scorpion* on the North River. Every morning, fifteen men were found dead, including many "that was not sick at all only from weakness & Stagnated air." When petitions for improvements remained unanswered, an escape bid resulted in casualties on both sides: "[T]he Capt. of the P. Ship was a savage fellow & they all much exasperated to see some of the guard lay dead & many Missing & wounded they pointed their Muskets down the Ships hatchways and fired for half an hour the Ships hold was all of a blaze we cryed out for quarters." The carnage, which left a dozen men dead and two dozen wounded, was stopped only when a senior naval officer boarded the ship and reprimanded its captain. None of the wounded, Bartlett reports, were seen to until the following day, by which point several had bled to death.[19]

Many of those who did not escape or enlist, and who were not exchanged, died on the prison ships—altogether more than half the captives. Precise mortality rates and the total number of deaths are impossible to establish for any of the war's prisoner populations. But even the fragmentary if fairly consistent evidence that historians have been able to gather is dramatic: the death rate on the New York prison ships was rarely if ever below 50 percent and may have been as high as 70 percent during the hot summers. Mortality rates in the city's prisons were lower but perhaps not by very much. By the end of 1776, at least half of the captives taken at Long Island and two-thirds of those captured at Fort Washington had died of starvation, disease, and untended wounds—a total of some 2,000 to 2,500 in just a few months. Of 69 men captured from one company in December 1776, just 16 were still alive the following May, half of whom were too weak to walk. Thomas Dring estimated that there were an average of 5 deaths per day on the *Jersey* prison ship, more on some days. Among his own crew, the mortality rate was well over 40 percent, mostly from disease. By comparison, during World War II, 11 percent of American POWs died in prison camps (although in Japanese camps much higher proportions did not survive), and 38 percent during the Korean War, the highest rate by far since the Revolutionary War.[20]

Adding the very substantial number of deaths of prisoners in the Southern theater to what we know about New York and Philadelphia, and not even including the unknown number of deaths among captives held in other locations—Detroit, a St. Lawrence River island, the disease-ridden West Indies, India, and possibly Senegambia—between 16,500 and 19,000 American prisoners are

Robert Smirke, Cruelty Presiding over the Prison Ship (Cruelty holding the Register of Death). *An early-nineteenth-century British vision of the deadly horrors of "the black Prison Ship's expanding womb Impested thousands, quick and dead, entomb."*

estimated to have died in British captivity during the war. Given that between 6,800 and 8,000 American Patriots were killed in action and that some 10,000 more died of their wounds or of disease in camp, it is safe to assume that roughly half of all the Patriots under arms who died in the Revolutionary War died in British prisons and on prison ships.[21]

Burying the dead from the prison ships was a daily ritual. Each morning, a working party on the *Jersey* carried the bodies to the upper deck, where they were laid on the gratings. If they could find any, the captives were allowed to sew blankets around the corpses before strapping them onto boards. Onshore, the sailors would dig a trench in the sand wide enough to receive the day's bodies; they were permitted no ceremony and were only allowed to shovel a slight cover of sand over the corpses. All around them was evidence of previous burials. A teenage farmworker, who lived near where the shallow mass graves were being dug, remembered: "The atmosphere seemed to be charged with foul air from the prison ships and with the effluvia of dead bodies washed out of their graves by the tides. . . . The bodies of the dead lay exposed along the beach, drying and bleaching in the sun, and whitening the shores."[22]

Death or Liberty

Charles Herbert joined the privateering brig *Dolton* at Newburyport, Massachusetts, in November 1776, just shy of his nineteenth birthday. After only six weeks at sea, however, Herbert and his comrades were captured by the British 64-gun HMS *Reasonable*. The *Dolton*'s crew was transferred to Plymouth on England's southern coast, crowded in the *Reasonable*'s cable tier, the area where cables and spare rigging were stowed and where they "almost suffocated with heat." Over the course of the war, perhaps some 3,000 American captives—sailors of the Continental Navy, American merchantmen, and rebel privateersmen like Herbert— made a similar passage to be imprisoned in Britain. Unless the capturing vessel was already en route to the British Isles, American maritime prisoners were often held for a few weeks or months at temporary sites such as disused sugarhouses in Halifax where prisoners were described as being kept like "Herrings salted in Casks."[23]

Just like the conditions at these sites, the transatlantic passages that ensued were extremely trying. Typically, the capturing vessels were already crowded, and resources were scarce. Prisoners were confined to the holds, sometimes "under five decks," as one American lieutenant described it, "and consequently under at least *thirty feet of water*—in a dungeon the area of which was twelve feet by twenty, and its height *three feet*—without light, and almost without air—where they were necessarily compelled to remain always in a bent or a recumbent posture." In this marine version of Simsbury, the victuals were generally of limited quantity and poor quality. The little water they had was "thick with animacules" and had to be drunk "through closed teeth." Captains used threats of hanging and condoned the theft of clothes to encourage defections.[24]

When Charles Herbert's prisoner transport arrived off the English coast, he and his fellow captives underwent several more transfers between ships. Herbert spent nineteen days on the cable tier of the *Bellisle*, where planks and boards laid over the cable chains provided a bare modicum of comfort. A few days in an over-crowded area between the decks of HMS *Torbay* exposed Herbert's crew to the wintry conditions: "[W]e begin to grow very sickly." Herbert described the visit of local British sailors' wives who came to inspect the Americans, their ignorant reactions encapsulating the confusing nature of Anglo-American relations: "Are they white? Can they talk? . . . Why, they look like our people and they talk English."[25]

Herbert and the other men from the *Dolton*'s crew were moved on to HMS *Burford*, where the sleeping arrangements were finally more comfortable. They were now also allowed to walk on deck in groups of twenty. But their lengthy oceanic passage and subsequent confinement had taken a toll. By mid-April, Herbert and several other men from the *Burford* were transferred to the Royal Hospital at Plymouth; they had contracted smallpox, and for the next few weeks it was unclear whether Herbert would live.

While Herbert was convalescing in Plymouth, politicians in London were about to introduce a fundamental change to his status. Earlier that year, around the same time that the Continental Congress started investigating British prisoner abuse in America, the British Parliament revisited the legal standing of American captives. Prime Minister Lord North's government had increasingly found itself in a practical and legal dilemma. General Washington demanded that Britain acknowledge the United States as "an independent State, at least so far as respects prisoners of war." Otherwise, he warned, the treatment of British captives might reflect exactly that of Americans by the British. After Howe had failed to deliver a knockout blow in New York, and Washington had triumphed at Trenton and Princeton, the British government was preparing for another campaign season. It could not grant

American captives prisoner-of-war status, since that would acknowledge American independence. But neither could it keep rising numbers of captives that had been moved to Britain on prison ships offshore or, by bringing them ashore, risk them applying for writs of *habeas corpus*, a legal action through which civil prisoners *as Englishmen* could claim the right to be released on bail while awaiting trial.[26]

In February 1777, Lord George Germain, the government's chief hard-liner, introduced a bill to suspend *habeas corpus* for American captives. Eventually known as North's Act and renewed every year through 1783, the law allowed American captives to be confined "like other prisoners of war." At the same time, however, it kept them in the legal category of rebels and traitors, as agents of a rebellion "traitorously levied . . . in certain of his majesty's colonies and plantations in America." Specifically, the law permitted the imprisonment "without bail or mainprise" of those taken up for high treason or piracy in America or on the high seas on the order of "any magistrate of competent authority." It applied only to those "as shall have been out of the realm" when committing their alleged offense. Herein lay the law's chief and, for its opponents, most dangerous innovation: it distinguished subjects by the location of their arrest. In essence, the 1777 act redrew the zones of law within the British Empire. It ended the subjecthood of certain individuals in colonial British America and on the high seas. At a time when the British were still confused about Americans' identity, Anglo-American difference had now been legally codified in one crucial respect.[27]

Even in Britain, opponents of the law denounced the measure as cruel and unconstitutional, a dangerous assault on English liberties that was "shocking to humanity." The lawyer John Dunning, MP, mocked the measure. Traditionally, only necessity in the case of domestic rebellion or the threat of invasion had justified suspensions: "Are we afraid that the people of America will pass the Atlantic on a bridge, and come over and conquer us?" The premise of British (and American) critics of the measure was that *habeas corpus* represented a fundamental right of the king's subjects, wherever on the globe they might be. The opposition leader, Charles James Fox, called the law "nothing less than robbing America of her franchises ... and, in fine, of spreading arbitrary dominion over all the territories belonging to the British crown."[28]

One of the most devastating critiques of the suspension law came from the same man who had previously warned of the inherently violent nature of revolution and of the disastrous consequences of a war of desolation. Edmund Burke decried illegitimate or ill-advised violence wherever and whenever he saw it. In his *Letter to the Sheriffs of Bristol*, a publication that was widely excerpted in the American press, Burke acknowledged that all were "heartily agreed in our detestation of a civil war ... we feel exactly the same emotions of grief and shame on all its miserable consequences," including any "legislative regulations which subvert the liberties of our brethren, or which undermine our own." The government's argument from necessity, however, was both dangerous and flawed: "All the ancient, honest juridical principles, and institutions of England, are so many clogs to check and retard the headlong course of violence and oppression." Above all, Burke opposed the distinction that the law made between subjects: "Liberty, if I understand it at all, is a *general* principle, and the clear right of all the subjects within the realm, or of none. Partial freedom seems to me a most invidious mode of slavery. But, unfortunately, it is the kind of slavery the most easily committed in times of civil discord." If there was to be any suspension of *habeas corpus*, it had to apply to all. All subjects on both sides of the Atlantic must live under the same regime of both liberty and security. In Burke's analysis, then, the prime minister's new law undermined time-honored English constitutional checks on oppression and violence.[29]

Before long, news of the ripples that North's Act had caused at home reached the other side of the Atlantic. General Sir Henry Clinton's mailbag contained letters that described the legislation as an example of how the "spirit of the Nation [was] fully against America," although American newspapers had been assiduous in covering the controversy the measure had sparked in Britain. In the eyes of George Washington, who denounced the suspension as "arbitrary imprisonment [that] has received the sanction of British laws," it was yet another wrong that Britain inflicted upon North Americans. Those directly affected referred to North's Act as "the execrable act of parliament." Being denied *habeas corpus* became a badge of honor that steeled Revolutionary resolve.[30]

* * *

Before falling ill, Charles Herbert had read in a newspaper of the Act of Parliament that found him and his fellow captives "guilty of high treason." After his pox had spread, accompanied by high fever, vomiting, and severe headaches for several weeks—"[M]y flesh feels as if I was raked up in a bed of embers"—Herbert gradually recovered under good medical care and full rations; he was finally released in early June. Six of his comrades had succumbed to the smallpox, including one who "in a most shocking manner" had had to be "jammed" into a coffin six inches too short. Shortly thereafter, Herbert and several other captives were brought up before a board of Admiralty judges. In response to questions, they confirmed that they were Americans and had been sailing with a congressional commission. As Herbert told the judges, "[W]e were out to fight the enemies of the thirteen United States." When the magistrates were reassured of a prisoner's identity as an American rebel, and they had established that a captive was not a British deserter, they pronounced that he was committed to prison "for Rebellion, Piracy, and High Treason on his Britannic Majesty's High Seas, there to lay during His Majesty's pleasure, until he pardons or otherwise disposes of you."[31]

After their committal hearing, captives like Herbert were issued with warrants charging them with treason and escorted under guard to one of a dozen or more facilities. By far the largest of these were Forton Prison in Portsmouth and Mill Prison in Plymouth, both holdovers from the Seven Years' War. Run by the Commissioners for Sick and Wounded Seamen (also known as the Sick and Hurt Board), a small committee that reported to the Lords Commissioners of the Admiralty, they held a total of about 2,500 American captives over the course of the war.[32]

Herbert was transferred to the Mill Prison, a purpose-built facility located on an exposed tidal headland between Plymouth and Plymouth Dock, or Devonport, and surrounded by fourteen- to twenty-foot-high double stone walls topped with broken glass. Forton Prison, which stood across Portsmouth Harbor in Alverstoke, Hampshire, bordered on a lake, farms, meadows, and woodlands. It did not boast as much security and was enclosed only with an eight-foot-high picket fence. Prison guards were recruited from the local militia, companies of invalids, and regional army garrisons; at first, eleven and ten sentinels, respectively, were on guard duty at Mill and Forton; by the following summer, that number had risen to two officers and sixty men at Forton, and at Mill to forty-five armed men inside and outside the perimeter. Smaller numbers of prisoners were also kept at Kinsale in Ireland, in the Scottish capital of Edinburgh, in Pembroke in Wales, and in Liverpool, Shrewsbury, Bristol, Weymouth, and Falmouth.[33]

Examining the treatment of rebel captives held in Britain helps us put the experiences of American captives kept in America in proper perspective, illuminating the extent to which resource limitations and logistical difficulties—rather than policies of cruelty or some deep flaw of national character—were responsible for the suffering that prisoners endured. All in all, conditions at Forton and Mill Prisons were significantly better than at British prison sites in America. Although some captives, like John Haskins, described Mill as a "shocking place," others compared exchanging prison ships for these new sites with "coming out of hell and going into paradise." To be sure, American prisoners in England, too, suffered at least intermittently from lack of clothing; poor meat, bread, or water; overcrowding; bad health; and abusive guards. However, the only ways in which the American captives were officially treated differently from legitimate prisoners of war, such as the French captives who soon arrived, were that they received only two-thirds of the full naval ration, that their clothing was provided by the British government and not their own, and that they could be put in irons as a disciplinary measure.[34]

Regulations allowed the prisoners' delegates to observe the weighing and preparation of foodstuffs, to verify that provisions corresponded with the officially agreed-upon diet. That victualing scheme prescribed, per week, seven quarts of beer, seven pounds of bread, four and a half pounds of beef, four ounces of butter and six of cheese, two pints of peas, and, according to some sources, salt as well. In addition, most mornings, prisoners with surplus money could buy fruit and other refreshments at the private market that had sprung up at the prison gates; they could also pay an agent or the keeper to procure such items for them, much like civilian prisoners at the time. Some keepers took an interest in ensuring their charges received their proper rations, but others were suspected of shorting them and pocketing the difference. Indeed, captives' journals and diaries describe guards and staff as petty, corrupt, and inhumane, often arbitrarily so. Samuel Cutler considered William Cowdry (or Coudray), the supervisor at the Mill, "as great a tyrant as any in England, [who] uses us with the greatest severity." Cowdry was accused of watering down the beer, short-weighing rations, and giving prisoners' food to the pigs, as well as condoning brutalities. In the summer of 1777, starving captives were reported to be eating grass and the snails in the yard, or sucking on old bones; others rooted in the yard rubbish for cabbage stumps that one prisoner felt hogs in America would scarcely eat. But then, by Christmas of that year, they had more pudding than they could eat, as well as bread donated by visitors and outside benefactors.[35]

The navy's medical authorities were also in charge of the captives, meaning that American maritime prisoners benefited from a regime of naval hygiene, medical expertise, and hospital organization of which captives on the prison ships in America could only have dreamed. There were tubs, water, and soap for prisoners to wash themselves as well as their linen and clothes. "In general," Herbert observed, "we are tolerably clean." The captives were given tools to sweep the prison; other hygienic measures included the spreading of oil of tar, to which "powerful antiseptic virtues" were ascribed. Regular fresh-air exercise was mandated, and in December 1777 the Admiralty invested £98 to build a covered walkway at Forton to allow the captives to exercise even in inclement weather. Staff regularly fumigated the prisons with charcoal and sulfur; when infections were diagnosed, clothing and bedding was burned and contagious prisoners were quarantined. During a smallpox outbreak at Forton, the surgeon inoculated those who wished to undergo the procedure. Comparatively low death rates confirm that Americans in English prisons were being held under much better conditions than their counterparts in America. At the Mill, 52 of 1,101 Americans are reported to have died from 1777 to 1782. From June 1777 to November 1782, 69 deaths are recorded to have occurred among the roughly 1,200 American prisoners at Forton. At less than 5 percent and less than 6 percent, respectively, these mortality rates were less than one-tenth of those that likely occurred on New York prison ships.[36]

Prison discipline was often capricious. The Admiralty's instructions did not permit guards to beat prisoners, but captives could end up in solitary confinement for serious offenses such as disobeying orders or attempting to escape. Yet others suffered the same fate for merely selling their clothes, complaining about bad meat, burning a candle after curfew, or not answering to their names. Captives thrown into the "Black Hole" for up to forty days had to survive alone, on the bare ground, on half rations. So harsh was this punishment that a private British lawyer warned the keeper at Forton in December 1777 that he would have him indicted for murder if any prisoner were to die in the confining hold. The Admiralty recommended that coroners' inquests be conducted as demanded by the attorney—even though there was no precedent for this with regard to wartime prisoners—in order to prevent the expense of possible prosecutions.[37]

There is impressionistic evidence that American prisoners of British ancestry and especially those of African heritage were singled out for physically violent treatment. African captives also seem to have been handed the hardest and sometimes lethal tasks, such as nursing smallpox patients. Discriminated against on account of their origin and supposedly fickle loyalties, and on racial grounds, respectively, both these groups of prisoners suffered disproportionately.[38]

American captives also ran their own disciplinary regime, not least to counter British recruitment drives. In both Forton and Mill Prisons, large numbers of American captives signed an anti-defection agreement with harsh penalties: "[W]e are fully determined to stand loyal to our Congress, our country, our wives, children and friends, and never to petition to enter on board any of His Britannic Majesty's ships or vessels, or into any of his services whatsoever." Fellow captives harassed, threatened, and physically abused those among them who toyed with the idea, which, along with patriotic fervor—or perhaps an appreciation of the very tough conditions on the king's ships—meant few opted to enlist. Allegations of physical force or whippings to make captives sign up, as the U.S. commissioners in Paris alleged in a letter to Prime Minister North in December 1777, have not been verified. In 1780, however, Americans claimed more credibly that the British used psychological harassment to encourage recruitment. American prisoners at Forton informed Benjamin Franklin that their captors had the bodies of dead fellow captives carried through the prison en route to the burial grounds: "[T]heir Corpse is brought through the Midst of us sometimes nine or ten of a day quite Contrary to all Humanity."[39]

* * *

We rightly think of captivity as an experience of violence and suffering. But during the Revolutionary War, one could also find evidence of compassion in the captors' broader society. Civilian Britons had been sensitized to the plight of rebel prisoners early on when writers like Miserecors and Humanitas reminded them of the Black Hole of Calcutta. By 1777, North's Act served as a further rallying point for British humanitarians and those critical of the war. In addition to violence by law, the sight or reports of suffering American captives on English soil moved sympathetic Britons to send them donations. Others put money in the charity boxes that prisoners had constructed and left at the prison gates. The newspapers printed thank-you notes from prisoners who promised to inform their fellow Americans that there were "gentlemen in England whose breasts are open to the feelings of humanity."[40]

By late 1777, news of the severe punishments meted out to recaptured escapees, and the arrogant response of British officials to American pleas for improved conditions, helped prompt more systematic relief efforts. An "Englishman" writing in the *Public Advertiser* pointed out that the magnanimous treatment of British prisoners in America, in the face of "the wanton Cruelty which has marked the Progress of our Arms," demanded a reciprocal "Display of that Humanity which has ever distinguished the British Empire." Prominent City of London merchants led a fund-raising drive, to which opposition MPs and peers—including the Earl of Shelburne, later the home secretary who would negotiate the exchange of prisoners at the end of the war—were early and substantial contributors. Humanitarianism could make good politics: by donating to enemy soldiers, the government's critics highlighted the calamities of an unnatural civil war. But the subscription attracted donors from a wide social spectrum. A "Mr. Robert Goodwin, out of gratitude for the very generous and kind manner in which he was treated when a prisoner among the Americans," donated £50. More humble individuals contributed what they could: "A laboring Man, said his Name was Lawson desired to give his Mite to the poor Sufferers, being all he could spare": five shillings. The subscription raised the very sizable sum of £4,647 in the first two months. Similar if smaller subscription schemes operated in other cities. As a result, between early 1778 and mid-1779, common sailors received one shilling and two pennies per week, and officers double that.[41]

* * *

One other source of hope for American captives held on England's southern coast came in the person of the diplomat negotiating the Franco-American alliance, Benjamin Franklin. As one of three American commissioners in Paris, Franklin involved himself heavily in the welfare of American prisoners. Without orders or congressional permission, Franklin committed substantial time, energy, and private money, not to mention scarce embassy funds, to tend to the prisoners' needs.[42]

From late 1777 onward, Franklin helped organize a humanitarian relief program for Americans at Mill and Forton Prisons. On the one hand, his response was deeply pragmatic: to reduce desertion rates and avoid jeopardizing naval recruitment in America, the United States needed to assure seamen they would receive minimal standards in captivity. On the other hand, Franklin and his main British political contact, the MP and war critic David Hartley, a fellow scientist, agreed that prisoner relief could be a step towards Anglo-American reconciliation: "Some considerable Act of Kindness in England towards our People," wrote Franklin, "would take off the Reproach of Inhumanity, in that Respect from the Nation," as distinct from the British Army in America. Hartley, too, believed in "[a]cts of national kindness and generosity," and wanted to "civilize even the laws of war where the case will admit." Franklin immediately made £300 in public funds available for distribution. He dispatched as an American envoy John Thornton to inspect the prisons; distribute tea, tobacco, and money; and make arrangements for supplementary food rations. By the spring of 1778, local priests helped allocate weekly cash allowances among American prisoners.[43]

Franklin never achieved his primary objective, which was to orchestrate a general exchange of American for British prisoners. After protracted negotiations, and only after the Franco-American alliance of 1778 made detention facilities available in France for captured British prisoners, a total of perhaps some three hundred American prisoners were exchanged. When a general prisoner exchange scheme collapsed in the spring of 1780, Franklin shifted his efforts towards helping American captives escape. A network of local sympathizers and American expatriates in Portsmouth, Plymouth, and London assisted fugitives with immediate needs, including shelter, clothing, and money. They then facilitated transport to the Continent, where Franklin set up a network of agents in French and Dutch ports.[44]

Most captives at one time or another probably considered escaping. "Mining for elopement," some dug tunnels under the fences and perimeter walls. Others climbed the pickets, scaled the walls, or broke out of a privy. By pretending they were grievously ill, some men had themselves transferred from Forton Prison to a lower-security hospital nearby and then tried their luck there. Officers with access to money bribed the guards (the going tariff appeared to be half a guinea); others masqueraded as clerics or even as British officers. None of the recorded escape attempts involved physical violence by prisoners, which probably reflects a risk-benefit calculus: prisoners were guarded by armed sentries, and violent breakouts would likely result in more severe treatment of recaptured escapees and those they left behind. The majority of escapees appear to have been recaptured, and recapture carried serious risk: from forty days' confinement on half rations in the black hole to being placed at the bottom of the exchange list. Still, a number of captives tried their luck repeatedly; one man was recaptured fifteen times after absconding from Forton. Those escapees who made it to the coast signed on with British merchantmen, privateers, or warships. Others crossed the Channel as paying or clandestine passengers, or stole vessels, often to join American privateers in France.[45]

Just after Christmas 1778, Charles Herbert escaped from the Mill as part of a mass breakout. Herbert himself was recaptured the next day, and over the following week 87 of the 109 escapees were returned to the prison. But 11 men managed to make their way to a port in Devon, where they joined the armed lugger *Dolphin*. When they were far enough out in the Atlantic, the escapees took over the *Dolphin* by force, making the officers evacuate the ship and row themselves to a nearby English vessel, and set course for Martinique. In an ironic twist that points to the identity muddle created by the civil war in the British Empire, the escaped Americans were arrested by the French authorities upon arrival: they had mistaken them for Englishmen. Herbert was eventually exchanged alongside ninety-six other captives in February 1779. Shipped initially to France, he reentered the service of the United States; by August 1780, Herbert was back in his native Newburyport. Herbert and his fellow captives had moved exclusively within the Atlantic—the U.S., Canada, Britain, the West Indies. But other rebel prisoners were by then already experiencing the truly global scale of Britain's empire at war.[46]

Beyond

A few years after the war, Americans would read about the trials of a young sailor whose capture in 1777 sent him halfway around the world. John Blatchford, aged fourteen, and described as being of medium height, with broad shoulders, dark eyes, and curly black hair, had joined the U.S. frigate *Hancock* as a cabin boy. His ship was captured after just six weeks by HMS *Rainbow*. From the time he was taken to a makeshift detention facility in Halifax to his eventual return home six years later, Blatchford's story was one of repeated escape and recapture as he crisscrossed the world's oceans from Nova Scotia to Antigua to Nova Scotia to England, and on to Saint Helena, Batavia, Sumatra, then to Brazil and back to Saint Helena, on to England again, and via Antigua to New York, before returning once more to Europe and, finally, home to Massachusetts. When he was first taken to England, Blatchford escaped imprisonment under North's Act on account of his youth and was sent back to North America to await a prisoner exchange. By mistake, however, he was instead put on a ship bound for the East Indies.

From early on in the war, American officials alleged that the British government was plotting to send American captives via Gibraltar to stations in British India. And indeed there appears to have been a plan to offset the East India Company's recruitment problems in the wake of the British Army's mobilization for war in America. Dispatches from London to various East India

Company stations called for a dozen ships to take on up to a hundred captives each at Gibraltar. The scheme—another instance of captives deployed as servile labor, like German prisoners in North America—seems to have been scrapped for practical reasons; it remains unclear precisely how many captives were sent to India. What we do know is that the conditions that would have awaited them there were often dire.[47]

In summer 1780, John Blatchford arrived alongside some eighty other American rebel captives on Sumatra. Most of the prisoners were now drafted into the East India Company army for a term of five years. For many of them, this amounted to a death sentence, given the disease-ridden climate. But Blatchford and a few others proved (deliberately) rebellious and were transferred to a pepper plantation, where their servile labor in the fields benefited the Company. As other Americans were dying from the heat and inadequate food, Blatchford attempted to escape, but his plan was foiled, resulting in eight hundred debilitating lashes for the teenager (and in the execution of his older collaborator). In a second escape bid, Blatchford braved hazardous conditions to trek several hundred miles across the island. While his companion on that journey died, Blatchford somehow made it back via Batavia, Brazil, Saint Helena (where he served in the British garrison), and Antigua, then on to a French vessel bound for the United States, when he was again captured by the British, this time to be imprisoned on the *Jersey* in New York. After just one week, though, he was transferred as a French sailor to be exchanged in France. He subsequently traveled from the French port of Saint-Malo to Lorient, and, finally, via Lisbon, made his way home to Massachusetts.

In his quest for survival, Blatchford had sailed and worked in various capacities under six flags—American, British, Dutch, Spanish, Portuguese, and French—a global odyssey that he may well have embellished in the telling after the war. What he did not fail to foreground, alongside the colorful details about his repeated injuries and close encounters with tigers, was the "most barbarous treatment" he had received by the British. The preface to the 1865 edition of the narrative still offered it "as a record of malignant spite and savage brutality on the part of the British" while reassuring the readers of its veracity not least by pointing out the author's scars as "proof." As Blatchford's captors had removed him so far beyond the sphere of the knowable, his tall tale would have rung plausible enough for Americans who were hard to surprise about the lengths to which Britain would go in punishing rebels.[48]

Perhaps the most astonishing and serious allegation Americans leveled at the British was that they transported American captives to slavery in Africa. While the full details may be impossible to establish, the evidence suggests that the charges were grounded in a degree of truth. In 1777, the American commissioners in Paris repeatedly accused Britain of sending "American Prisoners of War to Africa . . . remote from all Probability of Exchange, and where they can scarce hope ever to hear from their Families, even if the Unwholesomeness of the Climate does not put a speedy End to their Lives." It was an approach to "treating Captives that you can justify by no Precedent or Custom, except that of the black Savages of Guinea." Indeed, as they put it in one letter to the British prime minister that was excerpted in the London press: "Numbers are now groaning in bondage in Africa . . . to which they were compelled by menaces of an immediate ignominious death; as contrary to every rule of war among civilized nations, as to every dictate of humanity." By 1778, the commissioners had received "authentic Information, that numbers of such Prisoners, some of them Fathers of Families in America, having been sent to Africa, are now in the Fort of Senegal, condemned, in that unwholesome Climate, to the hardest labour, and most inhuman Treatment." Unless the men were returned and exchanged, "retaliation will be the inevitable consequence in Europe as well as in America."[49]

Then, in May 1779, the American mariner John Paul Jones alerted Benjamin Franklin in Paris about sixteen Americans who had petitioned to serve under him. They had been made prisoners by the British at Quebec in January 1777, Jones reported, and were now among the prisoners the French had taken when they seized the British garrison at Senegal in January 1779; the terms of surrender apparently obligated them to repatriate all prisoners to England. The petitioners, signing as "your Well Wis[h]ers," stated that "some" had been captured at Quebec, and "there is 2 or 3 Seamen With us and the rest is Willing to Due the Best they Can." By the time Franklin intervened on behalf of the petitioners, he characterized them as having "been sent as slaves to Africa."[50]

Enslavement in the literal sense seems unlikely here, but it is conceivable that the sixteen men captured by the French at the British garrison at Senegal and wishing to serve under Jones were indeed American prisoners who had ended up performing coerced labor at the fort. The British had been trying to expand their Crown colony in Senegambia since the mid-eighteenth century, but their attempts had been frustrated by deadly diseases that were said to have killed at least one of every two men sent there between 1755 and 1776. To stem the drain, in 1769 George III had directed that British "[c]onvicts should be pardoned upon Condition of serving in Africa." This was part of a broader trend to commute sentences in exchange for service in the most deadly imperial outposts, from the Caribbean to the East Indies. One British deserter during the American Revolutionary War received a gallows pardon and had his sentence commuted to life service in Senegal. These were postings, then, writes the historian Emma Christopher, that were "used as a threat to scare the disobedient, recalcitrant or unruly soldier, and the sentence no criminal wanted to serve."[51]

If American prisoners were indeed sent to serve alongside the lowest of British felons and deserters in one of the least hospitable places in the Empire—and Jones's report suggests that this was not simply a propaganda ploy on Franklin's part—then, once again, Britain appeared to have deviated from the most basic codes of civilized war. Assuming that some of those sixteen men had been transported from Quebec to Senegal, and perhaps others from different places in North America, they could have been the surviving portion of a larger initial contingent of coerced laborers. The fact that no one would have known for certain where the men had been sent—cut off from their loved ones, from correspondence, and from any possibility of exchange—meant that, from the perspective of their commanders and comrades, their families and friends, they had disappeared into a black hole. And who was to say how many more Americans had been taken to Senegal, or to destinations equally dangerous and deadly, without anyone ever hearing from them again?

By 1780, Britain was no longer just shipping rebel captives to far-flung imperial outposts: the American Revolutionary War had become a truly global conflict fought on multiple continents and oceans. This was due to the dramatic geopolitical shift signaled by the alliance that the United States had concluded with France in 1778, and the subsequent entries of France, Spain, and the United Provinces (the Netherlands) in the war. But the implications of the Franco-American alliance went beyond altered geostrategic circumstances. When the new American republic tied itself to Britain's traditional archenemy, it changed the tectonics of Anglo-American politics and the dynamics of war. In ways perhaps unexpected by its diplomatic architects, the alliance with France set the stage for the further escalation of violence in America.

Overleaf: Louis Denis, Carte du theatre de la guerre presente
en Amerique *(Paris, 1779).*

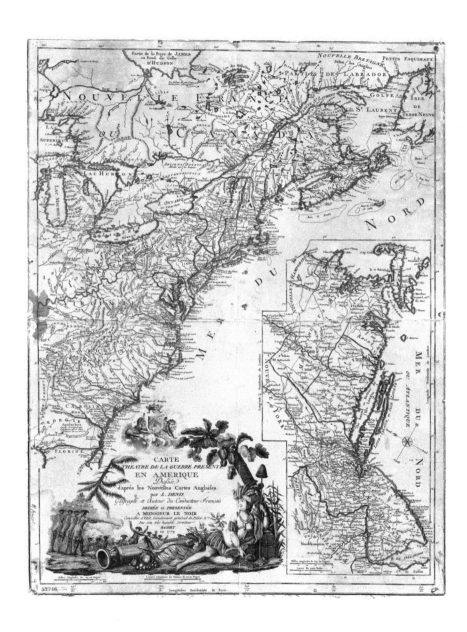

CHAPTER EIGHT

Skiver Them!

O N FEBRUARY 20, 1778, THE BRITISH GOVERNMENT DIS-
patched the warship *Andromeda* with draft copies of
Prime Minister Lord North's conciliatory bills. Fresh
off the press and not yet even passed by Parliament, this legislation promised to end British taxation of the American colonies;
Americans would always be given preference for colonial offices;
the bills even held out the possibility of colonial representation
in Parliament. As soon as a livid George III and his government
had learned (via their spy in the American embassy in Paris) of
the as-yet-unannounced Franco-American alliance, Prime Minister Lord North had redoubled his legislative efforts to engineer
a credible counteroffer. But already the London papers put their
finger on the deeper political and emotional implications of the
Franco-American alliance: "Are rebels, and traitors our brethren,
and fellow-subjects?" asked the *Morning Chronicle*. "Are they not
now aliens, and enemies . . . joined with Frenchmen, and Papists?"[1]

The *Andromeda* raced the French frigate *Sensible,* bearing
Simeon Deane, the brother of Benjamin Franklin's diplomatic
colleague Silas Deane, along with copies of the Franco-American
treaty signed earlier that month. The *Sensible* arrived first, on
April 13, but because the frigate had had to circumvent British
warships, she put in far north, at Falmouth, the town in modern
Maine that the Royal Navy had shelled at the start of the war.
Deane then set out overland for York, a small, mostly German-
speaking town four days from Philadelphia, where the Congress
was sitting because the British were still occupying the capital.
On April 14, the *Andromeda* reached New York, where Governor

Sir William Tryon, as he remained in imperial eyes, immediately published the conciliatory bills and forwarded copies to American authorities.

Within just eight days of the *Andromeda*'s landing in New York, Congress unanimously rejected Britain's conciliatory proposals. The majority of delegates saw them as a ruse to manipulate the emotions of Americans and sow divisions among them. The *sine qua non* for any negotiations, Congress insisted, remained that Britain either recognize America's independence or withdraw all armed forces unconditionally. It was a daring gamble, given the state that Washington's army was in after the trying winter at Valley Forge, where hundreds of soldiers had died of disease, malnutrition, and the sheer cold, and the fact that the British were still occupying America's largest city. No one in America knew that in mid-March the French ambassador had informed the British government that France had officially recognized the United States and that shortly thereafter Britain had declared war on France. While they put up a united public front, some U.S. legislators were privately discussing the possibility of seeking reconciliation with Britain.[2]

Then, on May 2, just as Congress had adjourned for the weekend, Simeon Deane arrived in York, "express from France," to present the president of the Congress, South Carolina's Henry Laurens, with signed copies of the February treaties. Laurens immediately reconvened Congress to consider the treaties all weekend; they were ratified unanimously on Monday, May 4. At Valley Forge, General Washington ordered fireworks and thirteen-gun salutes as 12,000 republican soldiers cheered, "Long live the King of France!" and each man received a gill of rum (a measure equal to four fluid ounces). On Tuesday, Congress sent six separate copies of the signed treaties on six different ships back to France to maximize the chance that at least one would make it. When the alliance was announced to the people of the United States the next day, Congress urged them to "treat the subjects of France as those of a magnanimous and generous Ally" in their "war with a powerful and cruel enemy." Frenchmen were now, strikingly, "their

Daniel Berger, 1. General Washington. 2. General Gates. 3. Dr. Franklin.
4. Präsid Laurens. 5. Paul Jones. *(1784).*

brethren," a term previously reserved for Americans' fellow subjects in Britain.[3]

Congress immediately followed up its announcement with a
much more elaborate and emotionally powerful "Address to the
People of the United States," to be read out by the clergymen of
all denominations after services in communities across the thirteen states. As they had done at many a critical juncture since
the signing of the Declaration of Independence, the Congress yet
again focused Americans' minds on Britain's systematic cruelty:
"The course of their armies is marked by rapine and devastation
[and] the wanton conflagration of defenceless towns. Their victories have been followed by the cool murder of men, no longer
able to resist." Urging steadfast commitment to America's cause,
the Congress held out the prospect of liberty and independence
in perpetuity, warning that any negotiated settlement with Britain would ultimately lead to "the most humiliating slavery." With
the French alliance secured—a French battle fleet would soon be

sailing for New York—Congress rallied Americans back to arms: "Arise then! To your tents, and gird you for the battle! It is time to turn the headlong current of vengeance upon the head of the destroyer."[4]

[Britannia toe] Amer[eye]ca *(London, May 1778). Political satire in the form of a rebus was a popular genre in the eighteenth century. The two letters refer to America's alliance with France and the British peace commission.*

Translation: "Britannia to America. My dear daughter, I cannot behold without great pain your headstrong backwardness to return to your duty in not opposing all the good I long intended for your sole happiness, and being told that you have given your hand to a base and two-faced Frenchman, I have sent you over five wise men, the greatest of all my children, to put you to rights and hope you will listen to them and mind what they say to you. They have instructions to give you those things you formerly required. So be a good girl, discharge your soldiers and ships of war, and do not rebel against your mother. Rely upon me and do not trust to what that French rascal shall tell you.... N.B. Let not hate take too much hold of your heart. I am your friend & mother."

[America toe] her [miss]taken [moth]er *(London, May 1778)*.

  Translation: "America to her mistaken mother. You silly old woman, that you have sent a dove to us is very plain, to draw our attention from our real interests, but we are determined to abide by our own ways of thinking. Your five children you have sent to us shall be treated as visitors and safely sent home again.... If you are wise, follow your own advice you gave to me. Take home your ships [and] soldiers. Guard well your own trifling and leave me to my self, as I am at age to know my own interests without your foolish advice, and know that I shall always regard you and my brothers as relations but not as friends. I am your greatly injured Daughter Amerik."

On June 4, George III's fortieth birthday, and a full month after the Congress had ratified the French alliance, a British peace commission finally arrived in America with Parliament's official offerings. Laurens was unimpressed with the didactic seal on the package that contained the official British acts: a mother embracing her returning offspring. He responded bluntly that America would enter negotiations only if and when the king was sincere about offering terms appropriate to "the honor of independent nations."[5]

Not easily deterred, the commissioners still hoped to persuade American leaders that theirs was a generous offer. They especially trusted in the additional concessions that the king had authorized them to make in person: Britain would no longer keep standing armies in America, provided the colonies maintained a self-defense force of their own. And no Americans would be sent to Britain to stand trial for treason. But the Congress did not budge; Britain's envoys failed to secure a single meeting with American officials.[6]

No one in America could yet know it, but Britain and France had already begun fighting naval battles off the Brittany coast. The conflict that started in America had now expanded into a worldwide war. The British would have to juggle the demands of safeguarding the homeland against invasion, attacking French interests in the Caribbean, and protecting British outposts from the Mediterranean to West Africa and India. There were signs that Spain might enter the war as well. The Virginian Richard Henry Lee predicted confidently (and wrongly): "Great Britain has its choice now of madness, or meanness. She will not war with the house of Bourbon and N. America at the same time." Briefly in the spring the king and the prime minister had in fact considered pulling all troops out of America, but that drastic option was rejected: British leaders continued to feel a duty to protect the Loyalists, and they still thought the war was winnable. The Empire instead rebalanced its forces between North America, other overseas theaters of war, and the homeland. In the process, Britain Americanized the war in North America, giving greater weight to Loyalist forces, especially in the South. With the stakes rising, Britain's emissaries in America, separated from London by many weeks of postal time, needed to seize the initiative, even if it meant operating without formal instructions from the capital.[7]

After a frustrating summer spent lobbying individual congressional delegates to little effect, and driven by "a deep sense of the insults they have received," the commissioners adopted a more pugnacious stance. They would appeal over the heads of congressmen directly to the state assemblies and to the people of America. At the beginning of October, the commissioners, who now included Howe's successor as commander in chief, General Sir Henry Clinton, published a "Manifesto and Proclamation" to all Americans. Their Congress, they argued, emboldened by the American victory at Saratoga and the unnatural alliance with a Catholic power, had rebuffed the generous British Empire. America had one final chance. All Americans willing to return to the imperial fold would be granted amnesty. Appealing to common Anglo-American values and interests, and recapitulating for the benefit of "our fellow-subjects the blessings which we are empowered to offer," the commissioners again promised the colonists everything they had previously demanded, short of independence. Thus far, they said, British benevolence in a conflict among fellow subjects had prohibited any extreme measures. But after the carrot came the proverbial stick. Should Americans *not* accept this gracious imperial gesture, "the whole contest is changed." If America persisted with a course "not only of estranging herself from us, but of mortgaging herself and her resources to our enemies," the commissioners threatened, "the question is, how far Great-Britain, may, by every means in her power, destroy or render useless a connection contrived for her ruin."[8]

British officers in the field did not unanimously support the unlimited warfare that this new proclamation seemed to imply. But while some still viewed unrestrained violence as counterproductive, others applauded moves towards a more aggressive counterinsurgency—such as the raids recently led by Major General Charles Grey. Grey's troops had overrun and burned most of New Bedford and Fairhaven, Massachusetts, before moving on to Martha's Vineyard, where they seized 10,000 sheep and 300 oxen: two weeks' worth of meat for the entire British garrison in New York. Grey then set his sights on New Jersey, and the horrific news of what transpired there reached Americans at almost precisely the same time as the British commissioners' manifesto.

No-Flint Grey

At one in the morning on September 28, 1778, near present-day River Vale, New Jersey, General Charles Grey gave his several hundred redcoats the order to march. The 2nd Battalion of Light Infantry, the 2nd Regiment of Grenadiers, the 33rd and 64th Regiments, and several dozen dragoons would close in on their intended target—an elite light cavalry unit of the Continental Army—around three a.m., the ideal time for a surprise attack. The enemy's guards would be struggling to stay alert, while their soldiers would be slow to waken. It would make for an easy rout.[9]

General Grey was reacting to a rare opportunity. His forces were part of a much larger mission to forage, observe enemy movements, and support an expedition to Egg Harbor, New Jersey. The previous day, Grey had learned that a unit of General Washington's Continental Army was nearby, most likely intending to intercept Grey. The Continentals were now encamped for the night near a bridge over the Hackensack River, about a mile and a half southwest of Old Tappan. As a battle-hardened veteran officer, Grey grasped that, in one short night's work, he could eliminate an elect American fighting force. And he would go about it his way, as he had done before, and with devastating effectiveness.

Grey was well aware of the vexed debate among political leaders and the public back home about when to follow the conventional rules of war. Even British officers in America argued vehemently about how Britain should fight the war with her American fellow subjects. Grey belonged to those who had earned their spurs in imperial counterinsurgency thirty years earlier, during the slaughter of the Scottish Highlanders. Why treat those "damn'd American rebels," as he and his fellow officers routinely referred to them, any differently?

Previous experience had taught Grey that night attacks were risky. They were perhaps best fought with bayonets to maintain silence and the element of surprise. Fighting with bayonets also reduced the risk of friendly fire when visibility was poor and battlefield awareness limited. Preparing soldiers for night battle, Grey's options were either to forbid soldiers to prime their muskets or to order them to put in the priming charges and close the firing pans but remove the flints. If necessary, soldiers could then prime or reinsert the flints, opening fire as a last resort. But that night the general took no chances: he ordered both the charges and the flints taken out.

That Grey's men were willing to follow him into a night operation relying solely on their bayonets spoke well of his reputation as a leader. It may also reflect the men's expertise in the art of such surprise attacks. Some had perfected their skills during a highly controversial affair the previous year when they overran a large Continental Army encampment and inflicted very heavy casualties on their stunned enemy. The Battle of Paoli in Pennsylvania had resulted in a much higher ratio of killed to wounded than was the norm for encounters in the Northern theater at that time. Grey's men had probably not been instructed to deny quarter. But a congressional investigation found afterward that it was extremely likely that American soldiers had been attacked, wounded further, and killed even after some had given up resisting. How else to explain the fact that a number of soldiers suffered a dozen or more wounds? Or that some Americans had apparently chosen to burn to death in their booths—structures built of brush, leaves, cornstalks, straw, and fence rails—when the British set them alight? Some commentators at the time, and some historians today, would argue that the codes of war for granting quarter did not apply to nighttime attacks. It was now a year since Paoli, but the mere mention of that night still had the power to terrify Patriot soldiers.[10]

The attack at Paoli had earned the general the nickname "No-Flint Grey," and it was as No-Flint Grey that he now went into battle. Grey's redcoats used a socket bayonet. First invented by the famous French military engineer Vauban in the late seventeenth century, it attached to the musket via a collar that slipped around the barrel. Its triangular, pointed blade had a flat side towards the muzzle of the musket, and two outer fluted sides some fifteen inches long. With the full force of a soldier's body behind it, a bayonet could cause terrible damage to tissue, arteries, and bones. The challenge was that the closer the soldier got to the enemy, the more psychologically difficult it became to kill him. The British military worked hard to teach its soldiers how to overcome that reluctance, explaining to new recruits that "in the hands of men who can be cool and considerate amidst scenes of confusion and horror," the bayonet is, by far, "more safe to those who use it, as well as more destructive to those against whom it is used, than powder and ball."[11]

That might have been true, but it was still difficult to get a man to thrust that bayonet into an enemy's body at close quarters. Bayonet drill then, and to this day, exploits aggression. It might have helped that, from as far back as Lexington and Concord, the rebels' fighting methods had been portrayed as an insult to any professional soldier serving His Britannic Majesty. Firing from hidden emplacements, making feigned requests for quarter, picking off sentries, pickets, messengers, even officers, with snipers—these were all tactics more worthy of frontier savages than the soldiers of civilized nations. A British spy characterized Washington's troops not as the self-described "respectable body of Yeomanry, fighting pro aris et focis; but a contemptible band of vagrants, deserters and thieves."[12]

Grey was also keenly attuned to psychological advantage: American troops had an intense horror of bayonet attacks. This seemed to be in part because they were much less accustomed to bayonet combat than European armies of the time. The bayonet, the embodiment of British martial professionalism, was to Continental soldiers what the tomahawk and scalping knife were to many redcoats—a weapon of terror.[13]

First, Grey and his soldiers had to get within striking range. As usual on such missions, Grey was meticulous in his preparations. He had timed his approach for the dead of night to maximize the surprise effect. For another two hours, as they closed in on the Americans, the operation would proceed silently. Grey's men needed to move undetected through largely unknown terrain, a task that depended on local intelligence and guides. Luckily, there were strong pockets of Loyalists in the region. These were men who bore a deep grudge. For several years, they had been suffering persecution, dispossession, and worse at the hands of their Patriot neighbors. They wanted revenge, and tonight, hopefully, they would get it. At least a dozen local Loyalists assisted Grey's column—men like Wiert C. Banta, a nearly illiterate carpenter in his mid-thirties, whose Revolutionary neighbors in Hackensack had picked him up as "a dangerous Tory" at the start of the war. For that supposed crime, he had languished for ten months in an Albany jail. When he escaped, he lost no time in offering his services as a spy and guide for Loyalist and British forces. It was Banta's Loyalist clique who ensured that Grey's troops found a safe and speedy passage along paths where they were unlikely to be spotted.[14]

By three a.m., Grey was within one mile of Old Tappan. Intelligence suggested that the American officers were quartered in two or three houses along Rivervale Road. Six troops of dragoons were thought to be sleeping in half a dozen nearby barns. Grey detached several companies of light infantry to encircle the enemy. The Loyalist guides led Major Turner Staubenzie's six companies along narrow pathways and lanes to the rear of the American positions from the west. Six more companies under Major John Maitland completed the encirclement; their orders were to prevent any guards or patrols they might come across from warning the encampment and to cut off their target from any American forces in the region that might try to come to their rescue.

The American privates keeping watch on a bridge near their leaders' makeshift headquarters were huddled in their coats and took turns complaining to their superiors about the bitter frost. In the moonless night, preoccupied with their own discomfort, they never saw their attackers coming. Grey himself led a small group of soldiers towards the house where the top American officers were sleeping. Methodically, and mostly silently, they dispatched several guardsmen with their bayonets.

Grey next had to ensure that the American officers wouldn't be able to communicate with the troops in the barns. On his signal, Staubenzie's troops attacked the American headquarters in the house of Cornelius Haring. Inside, Colonel George Baylor and his regimental major, the military intelligence agent Major Alexander Clough, heard a commotion, realized that something was wrong, and found a few seconds to react. With nowhere else to go, they tried to conceal themselves by climbing up the large Dutch chimney. Why, Baylor must have been wondering with a sense of foreboding, had his guards not sounded the alarm?

The redcoats entered the house. Apparently the Continentals did not know that just a year before, local Patriots had arrested Haring as a disaffected person. Perhaps the owners now let Grey's men in; perhaps they forced their entry. Searching the property, they soon detected the two American officers hiding in the chimney. Ferociously jabbing upward with their bayonets, they wounded Major Clough, who had climbed after his colonel. Baylor tried to hold on but was easy prey. Three powerful stabs to his thigh and groin dropped him. Someone slashed a broadsword across his hands. As he lay on the floor in excruciating pain, he spotted his adjutant, Cornet Robert Morrow, in a corner with seven stab wounds to his body; he was also "excessively bruised in his Head," explaining the awful sound of musket butts against a skull that Baylor had heard moments earlier. Clough was already mortally wounded.

Whether they were aware of it or not, Grey's men had just bagged a significant prize. Baylor, the twenty-six-year-old scion of a leading Virginia family, was a protégé of George Washington. He had served as the general's first aide-de-camp. After distinguishing himself at the Battle of Trenton in January 1777, and bearing the captured Hessian standard to Congress, Baylor became the commander of a regiment newly raised and paid for by Virginia, the proud 3rd Continental Light Dragoons. Now that regiment was in grave danger.

In another house nearby, one of the overpowered officers demanded to know which corps had attacked them. Told it was the British Light Infantry, he despaired: "Then we shall all be cut off." Grey's orders were holding. The enemy's commanders were disabled, any communication with their men severed. Now it was time to see to the rebel troops in the barns.[15]

* * *

The 104 men sleeping in the barns were the mounted troops of Baylor's regiment, also known as Lady Washington's Horse. Most were Virginians, among them the sons of some of the colony's finest families; all were between the ages of eighteen and twenty-six. They were proud to be serving under Washington's favorite. Recently, the general had even attached part of his elite household guard to the regiment with his own nephew, Captain George Lewis, as their lieutenant. Their routine duties had consisted of carrying out scouting missions, pursuing scattered enemy troops after a battle, and conducting the occasional raid. For the past four days their assignment had been to assist the Bergen County militia in a cattle drive to get local herds out of reach of British raiding parties known to be in the area.

As they did every night, the soldiers had posted guards along the perimeter of their camp, although their level of preparedness would later come under scrutiny: the area was known to be infested with Loyalists, but the 3rd seems not to have investigated properly. William Bassett, then twenty-four, testified half a century later that, in their experience, "the Inhabitants of the place pretended to be very friendly to the cause of the Americans, and some of them made parties for the American soldiers and furnished large quantities of spirits of the choicest kind for the troops—and the American soldiers supposing themselves safe and in the hands of these friends became merry to excess." As they bedded down near their unsaddled horses, many were inebriated. Indications were that soon, perhaps even the following day, they would attack the invaders, who like locusts were foraging their way through the American countryside.[16]

The sleeping dragoons woke suddenly to the sound of screams. Trying to get their bearings in near-total darkness, some attempted to reach their pistols or sabers; others sought to hide farther back in the barn. Bassett failed in his attempt to wake two men sleeping under the same cover with him. They remained in a blissful sleep, "insensible through drinking." Those sober enough to respond had no way of telling the size or nature of the assault force that was about to overrun them, although they soon realized that their guards must have been taken out. Whoever had done that was likely approaching with silent weapons. Did they think of Paoli, or flash back to the Battle of Long Island two years earlier, when it was said that Continental riflemen had been "spitted to the trees with bayonets" by their attackers?[17]

A crescendo of men screaming and boots stomping yanked them back into the present. Southward Cullency and his comrades from Baylor's 1st Troop decided resistance was futile. They stumbled out of their barn into the frosty night to surrender honorably. But instead of granting them quarter, the British soldiers instantly set upon the dragoons. In a matter of seconds, Cullency sustained twelve stab wounds to his chest, stomach, and back. The redcoats left him lying on the ground, probably assuming he was dead. Cullency could hear the command "[T]ake no prisoners" ring through the air and the crack of musket butts trying to shatter skulls.

The dragoons of 2nd Troop, who had been sleeping in a neighboring barn, were awakened by the confused cries of 1st Troop. They realized that they, too, were surrounded, but apparently had no idea what had happened to their comrades. Expecting to be "treated as prisoners of war," they demanded quarter. Thomas Benson observed that his comrades were instead greeted with insults and stabs, and so "did not ask quarter for himself, believing it in vain." No sooner had Benson stepped out of the barn than he found himself cornered by numerous redcoats, who stabbed him a dozen times in the back, shoulders, arms, and hip. During the confusion that ensued, Benson somehow still managed to heave his badly mangled body over a fence in the yard.

Back inside the barn, Julian King and George Willis (or Wyllis) observed that, on their own initiative, the British soldiers were now sending for orders from one of their officers, passing along the question to Captain Ball: "What [were] they . . . to do with the Prisoners?" Were they really supposed to coldly kill a defenseless enemy who was asking for mercy, appealing, in their own language, to their shared ancestors and to the same God? Maybe they were hoping they could just leave them there and move on, or take them into custody. But after an anxious few minutes of waiting, the order came: "[K]ill every one of them."[18]

The British started to bayonet their defenseless victims, crushing bones and leaving gashing wounds in the men's stomachs, chests, backs, and limbs. Withdrawing the blade, as much as plunging it in, tore muscles, arteries, and organs. When the British moved out, Julian King had sixteen wounds, including eleven in his breast, side, and belly; George Willis had sustained between nine and twelve wounds, some in his back. At first, it seemed that Thomas Talley would escape this wave of the bloody assault; he was taken prisoner. British soldiers had moved him outside and stripped him of his breeches, when his captors received orders to kill him, too. They took Talley back inside the barn and lethally jabbed him half a dozen times.

* * *

In those barns that the British had not yet reached, men startled from their sleep were frantically trying to make sense of what was going on in the surrounding darkness. Sergeant James Sudduth of 5th Troop was torn from his slumber by bellowing of "kill them kill them," then the cries of men begging for quarter. Sudduth peeked out of the barn door to see the outlines of soldiers emerge from the structure nearest his own, "unarmed and with intent to surrender themselves prisoners of war." The British offered quarter. But next, Sudduth witnessed how "the Enemy bayonetted them, & five of them were killed after they came out of the barn." After a British officer had ordered "his Men to put all to Death," he asked, "if they had finished all?"

Different British officers seemed to be giving somewhat different instructions, heightening the unpredictability and confusion. One American overheard a Captain Ball inquire how many of the enemy had been killed thus far. When learning the tally, he ordered "all the rest to be knock'd on the head." His men now "muttered about it, and asked why they had not been made to kill them all at once." Perhaps this killing of unarmed enemies was beginning to take a physical and mental toll on some of them. As the British men vacillated between aggression and restraint, the situation became even more terrifying for the Americans trying to survive that night. It also seemed to entangle their British assailants more explicitly in the dilemmas of war than they might have been accustomed to as ordinary soldiers. Still, orders were orders. The redcoats returned to the gruesome business of finishing off the wounded. Lying on the ground, some men turned their heads when they saw the blow coming; the musket butt cracked their skulls.

The British were now half an hour into the assault, and for another thirty-five minutes or so they would continue to bayonet and club their way through the grisly scene. Having watched their comrades being killed in the act of surrender, the dragoons' only hope was to try to escape into the darkness. Some pretended to be dead and crawled off when they thought no one was looking, diving into a dense thicket nearby. Badly injured, Corporal Henry Rhore of 3rd Troop took the reverse course; he managed to crawl back into a barn, presumably hoping to wait out the onslaught; he would die there of his wounds the next day.

Samuel Houston Jr. assessed his situation. Realizing that his best chance to survive was to make a dash through a gauntlet of British bayonets, he endured thirteen jabs to jump a fence and swim away in a stream. William Bassett had asked for quarter but was told, "God damn your Rebbel soul we will give you quarter." He eyed a fence when he was briefly left unguarded, but a British soldier closed in and plunged a bayonet into his back. Almost fainting from the deep wound near his spine, Bassett clawed his way to safety. He must have wondered whether his two drunken comrades back in the barn were being put to the bayonet, still curled up in their sleeping positions. More than half a century later, at age seventy-nine, Bassett could still feel the emotional scars, for "the horrors of that night will never be effaced from his memory."[19]

Mangled Bodies, Moral Victory

In the waking morning's stillness, British soldiers walked around with candles to examine the dead and wounded. Coolly robbing them of any valuables and even their clothes, they left the men half-naked in the autumnal air. Joseph Carrol, a man belonging to 6th Troop, had gotten dressed quickly as the British attacked. He had tried to escape with a horse but was surrounded. Begging for mercy, he was stabbed repeatedly in his breast and both arms to shouts of "there is no quarter for you" and "run him through." Carrol was now pretending to be dead, even as British soldiers examined him close-up by the light of a candle and stripped his badly injured body down to his shirt.

John Robert Shaw, a seventeen-year-old British soldier, arrived at the scene just before dawn. His regiment had been stationed three miles off when "the cruel carnage" first began. As they approached, Shaw later recalled, "the shrieks and screams of the hapless victims whom our savage fellow soldiers were butchering, were sufficient to have melted into compassion the heart of a Turk or a Tartar.—Tongue cannot tell nor pen unfold the horrors of that dismal night." The teenager, who spoke of "a most inhuman massacre," with 250 killed or wounded, some "having their arms cut off, and others with their bowels hanging out crying for mercy," had absorbed through common parlance the original meaning, in old French, of the word "massacre"—a butcher's chopping block. Shaw, for one, knew that there was a price to pay: "Let Britain boast no more of her honour, her science and civilization, but with shame hide her head in the dust; her fame is gone; Tappan will witness against her."[20]

Rumors and reports of the massacre spread fast. By ten a.m. on September 28, local inhabitants had carried the news to the Continental general Charles Stewart, who was the first to inform George Washington at his headquarters in Fredericksburg, New York, northeast across the Hudson from Baylor's devastated corps. All through the night and into the early morning, a captain, a sergeant, and a dozen soldiers who had escaped the massacre made their way to the Paramus camp of Colonel Otho Williams. By eleven a.m., Williams had heard and seen enough: "I am exceeding sorry to be the Author of bad News," Williams wrote in a letter to Washington, "but lest a more imperfect account shod reach Head Quarters, I think it my Duty to acquaint your Excellency of the misfortune sustain'd by Coll Baylors Corps."

Private Samuel Brooking had run four miles to Paramus with a bayonet stuck through his arm, which he had wrenched from the firelock, hearing British soldiers in pursuit yell, "skiver him!" That phrase, "skiver him" ("skewer him"), was repeated in the testimony of several survivors. Throughout the day, as rumors and vague reports traversed the New Jersey–New York borderland, additional letters were dispatched to Washington. By eight p.m., Major General Israel Putnam informed his commander in chief from Highlands, New York, that a sergeant of Baylor's regiment had brought him intelligence of the assault. "It is probable he may exagerate a little," especially in claiming that only he and two officers got away, "but I believe they have met with a verry severe blow."[21]

Casualty figures were still vague, but the Patriot view as to the nature of the assault was forged early on. By the following week, regional newspapers were printing accounts of the "horrible murders," most likely based on local hearsay and snippets picked up from survivors. All the evidence suggested that British officers had ordered their men to "give no quarter to the rebels" so that "a considerable part of the regiment unavoidably fell sacrifice to those cruel and merciless men. Several of our soldiers were murdered after they had surrendered." Soon, Patriot newspapers were ready to claim with reference to intelligence from headquarters that all noncommissioned officers and privates had been "in the most barbarous and unheard of manner murder'd in cold blood."[22]

For George Washington, the blow was personal. Just two days before the assault, he had received Baylor's most recent update from the vicinity of Tappan; now his protégé was presumed dead, Lady Washington's Horse decimated. It would be another two weeks before Baylor had sufficiently recovered from his wounds (both American and British papers had declared him dead) to dispatch a letter to Washington about the "horrid Massacree." By the thirtieth, Washington was referring to an event that "appears to have been attended with every circumstance of barbarity." Four days later, Washington followed up with more specific casualty figures and his own assessment, still somewhat cautious, as to the nature of the assault: "I should estimate the loss at about fifty men and seventy horses. Major Clough is dead of his wounds. This affair seems to have been attended with every circumstance of cruelty." Congress later had extracts of Washington's letter published in the press.[23]

* * *

As tales of an unprecedented massacre began to spread— along with British threats of unbounded war—the pressure mounted for an immediate inquest into what precisely had transpired at Old Tappan. As we have seen, Congress had already accumulated considerable experience in holding inquiries into Britain's illegitimate use of violence and, by doing so, helped turn some of America's lost battles, the trauma of her raped women, and her captives' sufferings into moral assets for the Revolutionary cause. Now the families of Baylor's recruits were demanding answers: Had their sons been captured, wounded, or killed, and under what circumstances? The "disagreeable suspense of all parents" had to be ended, and soon.[24]

On October 6, Congress empowered William Livingston, the governor of New Jersey, to conduct an investigation into whether Baylor's men had been "Bayonetted in cold blood." Livingston understood from his previous experience with documenting war crimes that gathering reliable information wasn't enough: it needed to be disseminated fast and for the greatest impact. He would eventually take eight depositions from survivors himself, in Princeton and Morristown. He also quickly reached out to army officers in the region, asking Lord Stirling as theater commander to coordinate the inquiry. Stirling—who had already given his

views to Washington the previous week, saying that never had
there been a "more determined Barbarous Massacre"—in turn
recruited an expert in both human anatomy and the immortal
soul, the army surgeon and chaplain Dr. David Griffith, to help
him ascertain the truth about the allegations of the "many Acts of
Cruelty [at] the horrid Scene."[25]

Griffith was a thirty-six-year-old New Yorker by birth who had
received his medical training in Britain and been ordained in the
Episcopal Church there. He was also a man who enjoyed Washington's confidence; their acquaintance went back several years.
The day after the attack, Griffith had obtained a British pass to
care for the American wounded at Tappan. To that extent, at least,
the British were playing by the conventional rules of war. General
Cornwallis even upheld a polite custom among civilized enemy
officers when he sent tea, sugar, wine, and lemons to the convales-
cent Colonel Baylor.[26]

The British had left those prisoners who had been too wounded
to march at the Reformed Church in nearby Tappan, New York,
which became a makeshift prison and hospital. (Two years later,
the British spy Major John André would be tried in the same
place.) While seeing to their immediate medical needs, Griffith
must have quietly made note, soldier by soldier, of the nature and
number of their wounds. He talked to Baylor and with inhabitants of the area. He must also have seen some of the badly mutilated bodies of the dead. These soldiers had been butchered: some
bore marks of ten, twelve, even sixteen bayonet wounds. So when
Livingston and Stirling enlisted Griffith for the official congressional inquiry in mid-October, the doctor had probably already
amassed considerable evidence. Methodical even in his anger, he
interviewed a dozen or so survivors coherent enough to testify. By
October 20, Griffith sent his report to Stirling, who forwarded it to
Congress the next day.

When they combined all the testimony they had heard with
the physical evidence they had seen, Griffith and Livingston concluded that there was overwhelming proof that British soldiers had
outright refused to give quarter. They had, moreover, killed Amer-

icans even after assuring them of protection. In some cases, after requesting clarifying orders, they were commanded to bayonet and club to death any soldiers that they had already disarmed and disabled, even though these soldiers begged for mercy. Griffith's summary, read out in Congress, confirmed that the nation's political leadership were "not misinformed respecting the Savage Cruelty attending the surprize of Colonel Baylors Regiment."[27]

The evidence indicated strongly that British officers must have planned the atrocities. The fact that "the Charges were drawn from their Firelocks & the Flints taken out that the Men might be constrained to use their Bayonets only" offered further proof of the British approach. Grey's subordinate officers, including Captain Ball, were listed as the "Principal Agents" of the bloody business, for it was their companies that were "at the Places where the greatest Cruelties were exercised." The British officers had counted on their men's violent anger once they were let loose on the Americans, and "none, of the British Officers, entered the quarters of our Troops on this occasion, that no Stop might be put to the Rage and Barbarity of their Bloodhounds." But one officer at least, Captain Sir James Baird, was afterward observed to "swagger through the streets" with a "bloodstained bayonet hanging from his back."

In the wake of Griffith's thorough report, more precise casualty figures became available. Sixty-five minutes of frenzied killing and cold-blooded murder had left some thirty-five men dead or critically injured, of whom eleven had been killed outright. Four others would soon succumb to their injuries. Thirteen wounded had been left behind. Thirty-three were taken as prisoners to New York, including eight wounded. Most of the remainder had somehow managed to conceal themselves or escape under the cover of night. Including officers, the total casualty count stood at around seventy. In contrast, just one Briton was killed, apparently when some dragoons got off several pistol shots.

Given that some forty Americans had escaped, and that others were left wounded or taken prisoner, Griffith judged that, "[n]otwithstanding the Cruelty of the [British] Orders, it does not appear that they effected their Purpose so fully as they intended, or might have been expected." The investigators singled out the sole British light infantry captain who had intervened with "feelings of remorse, & ventured to disobey his Orders" by giving quarter to Baylor's entire 4th Troop: the magnanimous exception proved the merciless nature of the assault. Unfortunately "[f]or the Honour of Humanity," that captain's name remained unknown.

A week after Stirling, Livingston, and Griffith had forwarded their materials to Congress, their report, complete with survivors' depositions, was already printed in full in the *Pennsylvania Packet*. The massacre at Old Tappan became a pivotal document in the Patriot atrocity narrative. Newspapers from New Hampshire to South Carolina used it to show that the Empire had descended to the rank of a barbarous nation. The *Virginia Gazette* excoriated the British "savages" who had "put to the sword, & butchered in the most cruel & rascally manner" their gallant Continental officers and troops. Grey in particular earned himself the enduring hatred and contempt of Americans. One American officer even hoped that, should he ever be captured, Grey would be "burnt alive, in a manner agreeable to the Indian custom."[28]

* * *

As the sun rose over Old Tappan on that crisp, cool morning, September 28, General Grey had already left the site. We do not know whether he observed close-up the results of the assault he had just orchestrated. Although he must have learned of the controversy raging over the event—not just among the rebels but, to an extent, within British ranks as well—he never publicly responded. His biographer surmises that, given Grey's "awareness of the psychological factor in warfare, he probably dismissed the Americans' pratings as exercises in propaganda and those on his own side as uninformed opinion-mongering." He must have felt content in the knowledge of the laudatory reports that traveled up the British chain of command, from Cornwallis near Tappan via Clinton in New York, reaching Germain six to eight weeks later. His superiors praised Grey for having "conducted his march with so much

Order & so silently" that he "entirely surprised" the dragoons, "and very few escaped being either killed or taken." Thanks to his superb leadership and the "usual spirit and alacrity" of the British troops, they had lost only one soldier. Pro-government papers in Britain would widely print these official narratives; no reference was made to the contested nature of the nighttime attack.[29]

British newspaper readers were also treated to a widely published article that was even more flattering though full of errors and even more overtly partisan. Claiming to be based on the personal recounting of the assault by "an officer present in the Affair," it, too, celebrated Grey's effective and efficient action. Praising the quality of the American dragoons—"very well appointed Cavalry

In 1967, archaeologists sponsored by the Bergen County Historical Society followed leads from local oral tradition and undertook an excavation near Tappan. There they found the skeletons of six soldiers buried in three abandoned leather-tanning vats, some apparently half-naked, others lying near pieces of shorts, breeches, a waistcoat, and coat buttons. The skull of one dragoon (at center) shows a clearly outlined roughly oval fracture on the left side where a portion was punched into the cranial cavity. He suffered a similar fracture of the same size, but of lesser intensity, on the reverse side. Most likely, the soldier was first bayoneted and then, while he lay on the ground with his head turned, battered and likely killed with the butt of a musket. The dragoons' remains were reinterred in 1972. The area, saved from suburban development, continues to serve as a county historical site as well as the final resting place for Baylor's Dragoons.

with extreme good Horses and neat accoutrements"—the paper gloated: "[O]ur troops dashed upon them with their bayonets to such effect, that only three of that corps escaped." For this writer, the encounter at Old Tappan represented an unmitigated success.[30]

Such triumphalism sat uneasily with only a small minority of British officers, and those who did express remorse did so only in their private correspondence: "As they were in their beds and fired not a shot in opposition," wrote the officer Charles Stuart to his father, the former British prime minister Lord Bute, the "credit that might have been due to the Corps that effected the surprise is entirely buried in the barbarity of their behaviour." Lieutenant Colonel Stephen Kemble, who had been close to the former commander in chief, Sir William Howe, also felt moral qualms. He admitted to gratuitous violence on the part of the British: "[T]he 2d. Battalion Light Infantry were thought to be active and Bloody on this Service, and it's acknowledged on all hands they might have spared some who made no resistance, the whole being completely surprised and all their Officers in bed." These Britons, at least, understood all too well that their army's perceived or actual cruelty was their enemy's best recruiting agent.[31]

* * *

With hindsight, we know that the events of September 28, 1778, were unusual. Grey's massacres—whether the more ambiguous proceedings at Paoli or the more egregious atrocities at Old Tappan—had not been ordered by HQ, although Grey's superiors later condoned his actions. Nor would they turn out to be typical of a new approach to the war on Britain's part. The actors on both sides, however, could not have known that at the time. Indeed, to American Patriots in 1778 it must have felt as if the British and their auxiliaries were rapidly escalating the levels of brutality. In March, British-Loyalist forces had killed several dozen unresisting New Jersey militia as well as nonfighting men sleeping in a private house at Hancock's Bridge, New Jersey. At Crooked Billet in Pennsylvania that May, they had bayoneted some of General

John Lacey's militia after they had surrendered; they even burned wounded men in piles of buckwheat straw. And even while the Baylor investigation was under way, the Patriots alleged that another massacre had occurred not far from Old Tappan. As part of the Egg Harbor expedition, Captain Patrick Ferguson, a thirty-four-year-old Scottish officer today best known for his invention of a breech-loading rifle, led 250 men in a raid on Brigadier General Count Pulaski's sleeping legion, killing some fifty and taking only five or six prisoners. In Ferguson's widely published report to General Clinton, the Scotsman offered a dual excuse: during a "night attack, little quarter could, of course, be given"; besides, a Patriot deserter had (falsely) informed Ferguson that Pulaski had ordered his men not to give any quarter; hence, the same orders applied "against a man capable of using an order so unworthy of a gentleman and a soldier." Like Howe earlier, Ferguson gestured towards recognition of the rules that ought to govern war even while, in the Patriots' understanding, he was breaking them. Within two years, Ferguson would find a spectacularly violent end in a controversial battle in the South.[32]

In their print media, the Patriots presented such atrocities as part of a broader pattern of British excessive violence. As they tended to their wounded warriors and buried their dead, they were also skillfully developing the forensic practices that would help justify their war—rendering mutilated American bodies with vivid anatomical detail and emotionally powerful rhetoric. British massacres thus became highly effective assets in the Patriots' moral war: they helped them win the battle for the support of the American population while shaming Britain in the eyes of the world.

The *Virginia Gazette*, a newspaper from Baylor's Dragoons' home state, sarcastically juxtaposed the British peace commission with the intelligence received of the Baylor Massacre, where men were "butchered ... by the British peace-seeking savages. O ye knight-errant Commissioners, ye sordid fallen patriots, ye shallow hearted politicians, get you home to Old England, & sing lullabies to the conscience of your bloody-minded King." The commissioners had better tell their superiors that the severance of virtuous America from the evil British Empire was now irreversible: "the brightest diadem" had been broken, most definitively, from the British Crown.[33]

* * *

In response to the British peace commissioners' manifesto of early October, and under the cumulative impact of this wave of escalating brutality—Hancock's Bridge, Crooked Billet, Old Tappan, Little Egg Harbor—the American Congress issued its own counter-manifesto on October 30. It came hard on the heels of their Baylor Massacre report, although Congress had been working on it intermittently since January. The closely argued single-side broadsheet, intended to alert the civilized world to the imperial outrage and to deter Britain from making good on its commissioners' threats, hammered away at by now familiar themes. Any future illegitimate violence, Congress vowed, would be met with retaliation. Congress also subsidized the publication of 1,300 copies of a book-length pamphlet authored by its delegate Gouverneur Morris. In *Observations on the American Revolution*, Morris argued that Britain had finally shown its hand: since it could not conquer America, it would try to destroy it. Echoing Congress, Morris threatened attacks on the British homeland, raising the specter of unbounded war.[34]

Dagger of France

When word of the manifesto that the British commissioners had issued without consulting London first reached the other side of the Atlantic in the winter of 1778, it triggered a political uproar. Opposition leaders in the House of Commons cautioned that it offended against British traditions of "humanity and generous courage" and violated Christian principles. It also risked undermining force discipline and threatened "to expose his Majesty's innocent subjects . . . to cruel and ruinous retaliations." Even former British commanders in America, such as Generals Howe and Burgoyne, counseled against cruel measures. And Edmund Burke, once again raising his voice as the conscience of the House, argued that the manifesto forewarned of nothing less than Britain abandoning its customary "lenity" and "humanity" as dictated by the laws of war. Instead, it held out the specter of inexcusable "extremes of war, and the desolation of a country." In the House of Lords, one agitated earl exhorted the bench of bishops that, should they support such "unchristian-like measures," they would be "up to their very necks in the blood of America."[35]

Government spokesmen in both houses defended the proclamation as an appropriate, morally and legally justifiable response to the circumstances in which the country now found itself. France, bent on commercial and maritime empire at Britain's cost, needed to be stopped, by means consonant with the laws of wars. But the Earl of Shelburne, who as prime minister in 1783 would conclude peace with the victorious United States, denounced the "rapine, plunder, and wanton destruction" threatened by the proclamation. Other peers appealed to Britain's sense of national pride: an international public was watching and would be disgusted by how their country conducted the war.[36]

The tension in the House of Commons was palpable when the administration's chief spokesman, Lord George Germain, finally rose to his feet. A series of impassioned indictments had put the government on the defensive, and the pressure on Germain was intense. He had been blindsided by the manifesto that he, as the responsible cabinet minister, now needed to defend. But if he played his cards right, perhaps he could turn the predicament into an opportunity to unite the country behind the vigorous prosecution of a war for which enthusiasm had been waning ever since Saratoga.

First, however, Germain had to calm the nerves of the House, assuaging his critics' worst fears while defending the manifesto from censure. For the man many still ridiculed as the once court-martialed coward of Minden, it would be a make-or-break moment. Germain's brief speech reads as an object lesson in political weaseling and psychological manipulation. Neither the king nor any Briton promoted "wanton cruelty," he said. The government would never order a British army to commit barbarities, nor would (or should) any British army ever obey such orders. What the proclamation truly meant was that "the Americans, by their alliance, were become French," Germain told the Commons, "and should in future be treated as Frenchmen."[37]

With just a few sentences, Germain had changed the terms of the debate. Previously redeemable rebels had now been lost irrevocably to the greater British family. It was an astounding argument, which, he knew, was also flawed. For, strictly speaking, the French (as other Europeans) were legitimate opponents falling under the protection of the laws of war, which colonial rebels as a matter of law did not. But Germain acknowledged the psychological and emotional power that Americans' standing as fellow subjects had held in the minds of many of his colleagues and his countrymen. It had allowed the conciliators among politicians and in the army to keep the upper hand in the debate over harsher counterinsurgency measures. That imagined bond had to be cut, just as the American Patriots had done by declaring their independence two years before.

By identifying the rebellious Americans no longer as King George III's wayward children but as allies of Britain's historical enemy France—indeed, *as Frenchmen*—Germain had made it virtually impossible for anyone to speak up for America. Any member who did so now risked sounding unpatriotic. After all, as Lord Lyttelton helpfully put it, America had become "the dagger of France," and "the instrument of the assassination of her parent!" Germain's rhetorical sleight of hand was designed to prepare the nation to turn a page in the conflict; to suspend, if not sever, all emotional ties with America; and to brace itself for a new, unlimited kind of war.[38]

No one seemed to rise to contradict Germain in the House of Commons chamber, although a long "protest" against the commissioners' manifesto—signed by over twenty peers, including prominent opposition figures—was entered in the parliamentary record. The dissidents invoked the laws of nature and of nations as well as Christian principles, which forbade extreme warfare for mere expediency. The opposition felt obligated to hold the line that a civilized empire, even and especially when at war, must not cross. But once both Houses of Parliament had rejected the motions to censure the manifesto, it was clear that the British commissioners in America had created a new (rhetorical) reality.[39]

In Paris, John Adams envisaged the consequences with a sense of foreboding: "Burn the sea coast and massacre upon the Frontiers, is now the Cry." Britain's objectives, both Adams and Franklin asserted, were now "entirely changed. Heretofore their Massacres and Conflagrations were to divide Us, and reclaim us to Great Britain. Now despareing of that End, and perceiving that we shall be fait[h]ful to our Treaties, their Principle is by destroying us, to make us useless to France." In London, a large majority of the Robin Hood debating society affirmed the proposition that "an extreme rigorous war of short duration [was] more humane on the whole, than a lenient long one." Ever since the Franco-American alliance had become known in February, Britain had been in response mode. But following the commissioners' desperate act of rhetorical aggression, embraced retroactively by Germain, the Empire now seemed to pivot to a more forceful counterinsurgency.[40]

* * *

Within weeks of the Baylor Massacre, the "British peace-seeking savages" were initiating their Southern campaign; before the year was out, they had captured Savannah, Georgia, and, barely six months later, Charleston, South Carolina. Most histories of the second half of the war look primarily to that Southern theater. But it was in the North that both the British and the Continental Armies launched virtually simultaneous campaigns of terror in the summer of 1779. John Adams's predictions of burning coastlines and "massacre upon the Frontiers" would indeed come to pass. As far as frontier violence was concerned, however, Americans were about to become the aggressors as much as the victims.

Overleaf: John Lodge, A New and Correct Map of North America: in which the Places of the Principal Engagements during the Present War are accurately inserted *(London, 1780).*

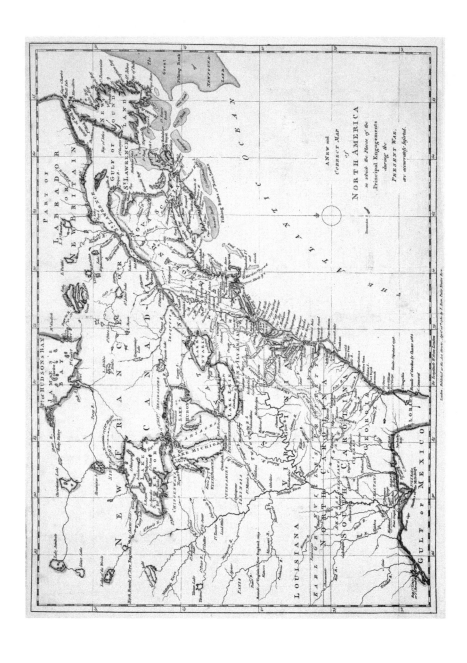

A NEW and
CORRECT MAP
of
NORTH AMERICA
in which the Places of the
Principal Engagements
during the
PRESENT WAR,
are accurately inserted.

CHAPTER NINE

Town-Destroyer

O N JULY 5, 1779, COMMUNITIES OF PATRIOTS ACROSS THE United States were celebrating the third anniversary of their independence (July 4 had been a Sunday). That night, General John Sullivan presided over a dinner at Wyoming, a town on the Pennsylvania frontier. The company toasted "General Washington and the army" alongside the king and queen of their new ally, France. Sullivan, a second-generation Irish immigrant and country lawyer from New Hampshire, had represented his colony in the first Continental Congress before taking up arms for America. "Broadshouldered and barrel-chested," with "black, curly hair and black, piercing eyes," Sullivan was a heavy drinker prone to annoying his fellow officers and civilian superiors alike. But after being captured in the Battle of Long Island and subsequently exchanged as a prisoner, he had performed well at Trenton and Princeton. Sullivan was now at the helm of the Continental Army's most ambitious mission in the 1779 season: a campaign of terror against the Iroquois Confederation.[1]

Adam Hubley, a junior officer serving under Sullivan, described the setting as picturesque. Wyoming was situated in an "elegant & delightful" location on the east side of the eastern branch of the Susquehanna River, in an "extensive valley" that Hubley portrayed as "a mere Garden, of an excellent rich Soil, abounding with large Timber," framed by chains of mountains. The town itself consisted of about seventy log cabins, along with several large bake- and smokehouses, which kept the hundred-strong garrison in the local fort supplied. The inhabitants presented a pitiful contrast to their idyllic natural surroundings. Two-thirds of them were widows and orphans, "who by the vile hands of the savages have been most cruelly deprived" of husbands, parents, and friends, and "robb'd and plundered of all their furniture and Cloathing."[2]

Many of Sullivan's officers and soldiers had spent the previous days touring a gruesome battlefield, where skeletal parts and rotting corpses, scattered over a two-mile area, evoked the unspeakable atrocities they had heard so much about. The rank and file roamed on their own, while officers had local tour guides pointing out skulls, "[s]calped and inhumanly mangled with the Hatchet," or "shockingly gashed and bruised." These remains offered irrefutable proof "that the poor creatures must have suffered amazingly." The tourists were also shown the site of a mass grave with more than seventy bodies. Nathan Davis, then seventeen years old, later remembered, "Here and there lay a human skeleton bleaching in the woods or in the open field, with the marks of the tomahawk upon it." In one place, recorded another soldier, "seven or eight other persons were found nearly consumed, they having been burned to death." At a spot where the grass now grew differently, fourteen men had evidently been made to sit in a circle before being tomahawked one by one. The pilgrims-in-arms called it "a place of skulls," an American "Golgotha."[3]

Exactly one year earlier, warriors from the Iroquois Confederation under the Mohawk leader Thayendanegea, a fluent English-speaker also known as Joseph Brant, had alongside Colonel John Butler's Loyalist Rangers attacked settlements in the Wyoming Valley—a region that for two decades had been the scene of violent conflict among Pennsylvania and Connecticut settlers and between those whites and Delaware Indians. On July 3, 1778, Butler and his mostly Seneca warriors killed between 220 and 300 Patriot militia and Continentals in battle or in the act of taking flight. While Butler sanctioned the burning of 1,000 homes and multiple forts, he managed to protect surrendering survivors among militia as well as civilians. But the Patriots cried massacre. They exaggerated the number of dead to four hundred and embellished lurid stories of atrocity.[4]

Now, as Sullivan's western army rested at Wyoming, and as

eighty officers celebrated the anniversary of America's independence, they hoisted two skulls to dramatize one more toast: "Civilization or death to all American Savages." Later that month, Sullivan's army would collect the bones of two supposed Wyoming martyrs who had, it was said, been tomahawked, scalped, and speared by savage warriors and even a war woman. As they were reinterred in a Masonic-cum-military ceremony, it mattered little that, in fact, Captain Davis and Lieutenant Jones had been killed while out hunting several months before the battle. The veracity of specific allegations counted less than their emotional power. To the Continental soldiers, the bones and skulls that they handled on the eve of their campaign corroborated the fearsome stories of Indian massacres and helped justify their own mission. After all, experience had shown that excessive violence was the only language the savages seemed to understand.[5]

In 1775, as historians of early America remind us, "[m]ost of North America was still Indian country." But for generations, land-hungry settlers pushing west had been confronting North America's indigenous peoples in murderous contests over land and ways of life. To be sure, settlers and Indians did engage in trade and cultural exchange; they struck diplomatic and military alliances—indeed, the British Crown relied upon Native Americans in its imperial wars with France; and white colonists and Indians sometimes intermarried. But fragile accommodation never eliminated violence. For decades before the Revolution, colonials had also waged wars of desolation against Indian settlements, destroying crops and killing noncombatants, including women and children. As one Revolutionary military leader on the western frontier put it bluntly, whites' objective against Indians was "to excel them in barbarity."[6]

Indeed, on the frontier, endemic conflict was characterized by particularly brutal ways of war. Native Americans deliberately used relatively small forces to create maximum panic. They attacked noncombatants and practiced scalping and torture. They mutilated dead bodies and then displayed them to scare the enemy. By the mid-eighteenth century, responses to such tactics of terror were framed in what the historian Peter Silver has called the "anti-Indian sublime," blood-soaked language and imagery conveying seemingly unlimited cruelty. This idiom in turn legitimated violence against Native Americans as colonials—and from mid-century the British, too—increasingly employed the techniques of Indian war, including scalping. If the British manifesto of 1778 was unprecedented for its threats of unrestrained violence among white Anglo-American forces, it was perhaps less shocking to Americans on the frontier who had long since become habituated to unlimited warfare.

The historian Wayne E. Lee has shown that frontier violence spiraled out of control in part due to largely incompatible European and Native American cultures of war. For Indians, so-called mourning war was a way of restoring a depleted population, whereby captives replaced, in literal and symbolic terms, their dead, and helped alleviate the grief of those who mourned such loss. Indians, unlike whites, did not rape women, but they did torture prisoners. Meanwhile, Europeans killed more combatants outright but their laws of war demanded that a surrendering enemy be granted quarter. With such disparate systems of force and restraint, the other side's violence always seemed less legitimate, more deserving of retribution.[7]

By 1775, Britain's failure to protect American colonials against Indian aggression had contributed to the rebels' insurrection. Patriots cited fear of Indian war to justify a preventive invasion of Canada and listed British incitement of the "merciless Indian Savages" when indicting George III in the Declaration of Independence. That summer and early fall, troops from Virginia and the Carolinas brought total war to the Cherokee homeland, burning crops, destroying entire villages, and killing defenseless Indians, including women and children. Across Indian country, the American Revolution exacerbated existing conflicts and introduced new fault lines. In the North, most Indian nations were unable to preserve their initial neutrality. After 1776, they came under growing pressure to align themselves either with the British or with the American Patriots. The Abenaki of northern New

England split over the decision. By 1777, civil war had erupted among the Iroquois Confederation, known also as the Six Nations. Many Oneida joined the rebels. But the vast majority of the remaining five nations—the Cayuga, Mohawk, Onondaga, Seneca, and Tuscarora—were pushed by trade needs and distrust of land-hungry American rebels into an alliance with the British. The American Revolutionary War was shaping up to be, in the historian Carroll Smith-Rosenberg's words, "perhaps the most brutal of all European–Native American wars" in the eighteenth century.[8]

In Britain, deploying Native Americans against rebellious white former fellow subjects was highly contentious, even more so than the arming of enslaved or freed African-Americans. Since Indian ways of war were widely seen as barbaric, public opposition in Britain to the use of Native American warriors against the colonials was extensive. Only a small minority of hard-liners advocated sending Native Americans into war against rebellious British-Americans. One of them was William Markham, Archbishop of York, the second-highest Anglican prelate, whose strident support of Indian alliances was satirized in the print *The Allies*, issued in London in 1780.[9]

Over the course of the war, both sides forged alliances with Native American warriors and both sides employed Indian war techniques. Both sides predictably cried foul over the other's alleged barbarian conduct. But once again the American Patriots proved to be the superior polemicists. They equated stereotypical Indian savagery with British and American Loyalist barbarity, to the point where prints and broadsides routinely depicted the latter in the acts of scalping and cannibalizing Patriots. Such stories were so effective in part because they drew on actual events. The year 1778 saw not only the Wyoming Massacre but also a particularly brutal frontier encounter at Cherry Valley in eastern New York, where more civilians than soldiers were killed, including women and children. Secretary Germain coolly pronounced Cherry Valley a "Success."[10]

Indians later explained that they had been angered by being falsely accused of atrocities at Wyoming and by the fact that

John Almon [publ.], The Allies—Par nobile Fratrum *(London, 1780).*
Archbishop Markham is seen bringing scalping knives, tomahawks, and
crucifixes to George III, who feasts on the remains of an infant alongside
an Indian chief. The Bible is turned upside down underneath George III's
shredded standard, "Defender of the Faith." A child's body parts are strewn
across the ground as a dog vomits.

American Patriots who had surrendered there returned to fight despite promising they would stay out of the conflict. But neither this reasoning nor the many attacks on Indian settlements by frontier rangers and militias could dent the traction that the composite image of Indian-British-Loyalist barbarism was gaining among Patriots. By 1779, Benjamin Franklin and the Marquis de Lafayette were developing a series of prints to "illustrate British Cruelties" for American schoolbooks. They prominently included scenes of "Savages killing and scalping the Frontier Farmers and their Families" and of British officers presiding over Native Americans cannibalizing their white American captives.[11]

It was against the backdrop of this long-standing fear and hatred that in February 1779 the Congress yielded to pressure from frontier states to launch a punitive mission into Indian country. In response to pleas from New York and Pennsylvania to counter Indian "depredations on the [western] frontiers," Congress instructed Washington "to take effectual measures for the protection of the inhabitants, and chastisements of the savages." On the frontier, the American Revolution would meet violence with unlimited violence.[12]

Total Ruin

The campaign against Iroquoia would be one of the largest and most complex Continental Army operations of the entire war. Led by General John Sullivan, along with Brigadier General James Clinton, the brother of Governor George Clinton, it involved well over one-third of the army and was funded by Congress to the tune of nearly £33,000. Washington directly supervised the planning and preparation.[13]

Washington laid out the Continental Army's objective in the campaign against the Six Nations as nothing less than "the total destruction and devastation of their settlements and the capture of as many prisoners of every age and sex as possible. It will be essential to ruin their crops now in the ground and prevent their planting more." There were to be no peace overtures until "the total ruin of their settlements is effected." He continued, "Our future security will be in their inability to injure us the distance to which they are driven and in the terror with which the severity of the chastisement they receive will inspire [them]." Washington was well aware that the Indians' supply situation was already precarious. Crop failures in the previous two years meant that this year's harvest was vital to stave off a famine. By destroying the 1779 crop at a point when it was too late to plant a new one, Washington was ordering an extreme version of the "feed fight," for decades the default strategy of European Americans against Native Americans. Today we would consider this a form of genocide. In the eighteenth century, the most commonly used term was probably "extirpation." Towards the end of the Sullivan campaign, one American soldier wrote that their objective was "to extirpate those Hell-Hounds from off the face of the earth." Major Jeremiah Fogg, echoing that earlier toast with skulls, also recommended "either to civilize, or totally extirpate the race."[14]

Much to Washington's frustration, Sullivan repeatedly delayed his army's march from Wyoming, asking for more and more men and matériel. His excessive caution would cost him the elements of speed and surprise, for the expedition that left Wyoming at the end of July, writes Sullivan's biographer, was "no light expeditionary force trying to move swiftly through Indian country; it was a fully equipped army starting upon an invasion of alien land." In early August, Sullivan and Clinton finally led some 4,000 Continentals virtually unopposed deep into Seneca and Cayuga country. With 1,200 packhorses and 800 head of cattle, this army stretched out over two miles, and up to six in narrower terrain. Over the coming weeks they would need to clear roads through unsurveyed territory, ford waist-deep rivers, and traverse extensive swamps. When encountering Native Americans, their instructions were to

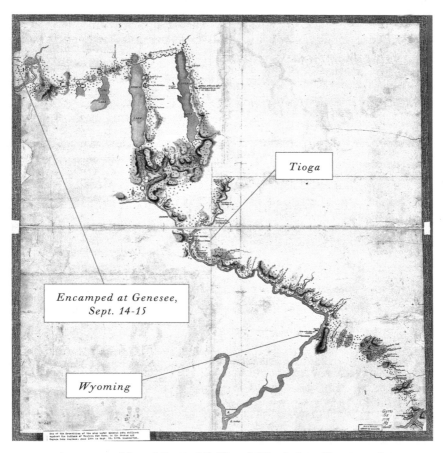

Anonymous, Map of General Sullivan's March from Easton to the Senaca & Cayuga Countries *[1779]*.

"rush on with the war whoop and fixed bayonet. Nothing will disconcert and terrify the Indians more than this."[15]

In practice, they only fought one battle, defeating a much smaller Indian-Loyalist force at Newton on August 29. Continental casualties during the entire campaign were very low: some forty men died of various causes, including accidents and diseases; sixteen were killed in Indian attacks. Their day-to-day experience was not one of battles or skirmishes. Instead, they would march to the next Indian town or to the vicinity of a variety of settlements. As the vast, slow-moving army announced itself from afar, the Native Americans evacuated. By the time the troops arrived, the towns were empty, although the Continentals sometimes found their fires still burning, corn roasting, and kettles boiling. They would make camp and gorge themselves on the local produce that healthily supplemented their rations before setting about the hard labor of destruction.[16]

The numerous journals that survive from the campaign abound with references to this daily grind; they also reveal glimpses of soldiers' amazement at the quality of the housing, the expansive, fertile lands, and the sheer extent and excellence of the Indians' crop cultivation. In early September, thirty-five-year-old Lieutenant Obadiah Gore marveled at Canandaigua, a "Chosen Spot," very "pleasantly situated," its twenty-three mostly framed "Buildings good and eligant Corn & Vegitables in great plenty." For Lieutenant Gore, this campaign was personal: his family had helped pioneer the Wyoming settlement. After three of his brothers and two brothers-in-law had died and two more brothers were injured at Wyoming, Gore had had himself transferred to service in the Wyoming Valley. Once he had admired the Indians' civilizational accomplishments, he helped burn Canandaigua to the ground.[17]

* * *

The initial design for the summer campaign had been for three separate armies under Sullivan, Clinton, and Colonel David Brodhead to move through New York and converge near Tioga. Brodhead ultimately failed to meet up with Sullivan and Clinton. Instead, his six hundred to seven hundred Continentals, militia, and some friendly Delaware marched up the Allegheny River in late summer, destroying sixteen towns along with crops and foodstuffs. They killed an unknown number of Native Americans and left Seneca and Lenape threatened by starvation in the upcoming winter. When they returned to Pittsburgh after a thirty-three-day, two-hundred-mile march, they carried plunder worth $30,000. In related but independent campaigns in spring 1779, Colonel Evan Shelby had already burned nearly a dozen Indian towns and 20,000 bushels of corn in Chickamauga Cherokee country. And Colonel Goose van Schaick's troops destroyed houses, corn, and other food supplies belonging to the Onondaga, and killed and captured men, women, and children.[18]

Throughout the campaign, Continental commanders issued warnings to their troops not to plunder army stores or fellow soldiers, and especially the local white population. As one orderly book put it, with no sense of hypocrisy: "Humanity dictates to every soldr. that he should not add to their distresses being already made miserable by a savage Enemy."[19]

In less than two months, Sullivan's army destroyed at least forty-one Indian towns, with between 450 and 700 houses, most of them multifamily dwellings some twenty-five feet wide and up to sixty or eighty feet in length. This tally does not include any outlying hamlets that soldiers burned without explicit orders. Virtually the entire Iroquoia housing stock was destroyed that summer. Before burning homes, soldiers often looted them, taking everything they could, from blankets, clothing, and animal skins to household goods, money, and even pieces of furniture. They found signs of intensive European trade and gift diplomacy, such as stoneware and ceramics, as well as traditional craft objects. Indian women often tried to hide valuables and foodstuffs, but the soldiers just as often discovered them. As homes were torched, any remaining household goods went up in flames with them. At Big Tree, Nathan Davis helped burn the Grand Council House, its "gable ends painted red with vermillion," plus over one hundred houses, cabins, and wigwams, many of the structures filled with corn. "The sight of so many buildings on fire, the massy clouds of black smoke, and the curling pillars of flame bursting through them," Davis noted, "formed an awful and sublime spectacle."[20]

The Continentals took the Indians' horses, cows, and pigs. They targeted food stores, the next year's seed stock, and farm produce. What the army did not consume on the spot or save for future consumption they destroyed, waging war on copious quantities of beans, potatoes, and onions, pumpkins, squashes, and cucumbers, as well as the watermelon that had first been cultivated there in the seventeenth century. When on occasion the soldiers were overwhelmed by the size of the task, they threw vegetables into nearby rivers rather than burning them in piles.

Corn had been at the heart of Iroquoian civilization for centuries, a crucial staple that was closely interwoven with their origin myths and spiritual life. And it was Iroquoia's cornfields that now proved the hardest to destroy. The Continentals were stunned by the sheer scale of Indian corn cultivation, the size of individual fields, the height of stalks measuring twelve, fifteen, and even eighteen feet, with cobs as long as sixteen inches. Large parts of the army, sometimes the entire force, would routinely stop for one or several days to cut down the stalks or burn them. At the westernmost point of the expedition, in mid-September, the whole army, "with the greatest Chearfulness," reported Moses Sproule, spent a day burning two hundred acres of corn at Little Beard's Town. The following day they burned even larger amounts of "corn, beans, potatoes, and other vegetables, which were in quantity immense," wrote Adam Hubley, "and in goodness unequaled by any I ever yet saw." Sullivan estimated that in total his force destroyed 160,000 bushels of corn, or some 5,600 tons. Moses van Campen, one of Sullivan's quartermasters, summarized the extent of the destruction: "The country which, a month previous, appeared like a beautiful and flourishing garden, now presented to the eye little else than a dreary waste, or a smoking heap of ruins." When some Seneca returned to their once thriving villages, they found "there was not a mouthful of any kind of sustenance left, not even enough to keep a child one day from perishing with hunger."[21]

The one element of ruination that triggered some recorded protest and even passive resistance among Continentals was the girdling of fruit trees—that is, the removal of a strip of bark from the circumference of tree trunks that caused the trees to die. In discussing the limits of destructive warfare, international lawyers of the day, such as Emer de Vattel, often drew a line at girdling, as well as the uprooting of vines, because this ruined a country for the long term. Indeed, some of Sullivan's own officers considered it a "degradation of the army to be employed in destroying apple and peach trees, when the very Indians in their excursions spared them, and wished the general to retract his orders for it." Sullivan is reported to have responded that the "Indians shall see, that there is malice enough in our hearts to destroy everything that contributes toward their support." Some of his subordinates nevertheless turned a blind eye to orchards while they continued to burn cornfields with abandon, anticipating, perhaps, their future wants as they imagined supplanting the Native Americans in the region. Still, many thousands of peach, pear, and apple trees were damaged beyond recovery that summer. It was not until 1838 that a U.S. general first openly criticized Sullivan's "war of extermination waged against the very orchards."[22]

* * *

Even as they fled their villages, Native Americans found ways to terrorize their attackers. Late in the Sullivan campaign, a group of Native Americans killed members of a Continental patrol under Lieutenant Thomas Boyd. Before Boyd and his sergeant, Michael Parker, died, the Indians tortured them. They continued their mutilation posthumously, leaving their mangled, barely recognizable corpses in plain view to scare the invaders. Lieutenant Erkuries Beatty described the bodies, which could be identified by some distinctive physical features:

They was both stripped naked and their heads Cut off, and the flesh of Lt. Boyds head was intirely taken of and his eyes punched out. the other mans hed was not there. they was stabed, I supose, in 40 Diferent places in the Body with a spear and great gashes cut in their flesh with knifes, and Lt. Boyds Privates was nearly cut of & hanging down [his penis and scrotum had been skinned], his finger and Toe nails was bruised of, and the Dogs had eat part of their Shoulders away likewise a knife was Sticking in Lt. Boyds body.

Other diarists tried to reconstruct what had happened to the tortured officers. Lieutenant Hubley thought that the "most cruel & barbarous" torture and massacre must have started with "plucking their nales from hand & feet then Spearing, cutting & whipping them and mangling their Bodys, then cutting off the flesh from their shoulders by pieces, tomahawking & severing their heads from their Bodys and leaving them a prey to their Dogs."[23]

Whereas most American reports assumed that the torture had occurred prior to death, Bucktooth, an Indian warrior who had witnessed the killings, claimed that the Americans had been stripped and made to run the gauntlet and beaten to death; only then had their limbs, faces, torsos, and genitals been mutilated. Either way, the beheading, skinning, and purposeful display of body parts were well-established Native American practices. Some Indian peoples believed that beheading their victim meant that his soul, thought to reside in the head, would fail to gain admission to the land of eternal prosperity; to them, beheading was a way, as Jill Lepore has put it, "of winning the war forever." The army buried the dismembered bodies with military honors. At a dinner on September 24, officers toasted the patriotic memory of Lieutenant Boyd and his troops, "who were horribly massacred by the inhuman savages, or,"—note the climax—"by their more barbarous and detestable allies, the British and Tories."[24]

While participants commented widely on Boyd's and Parker's mangled bodies, they were conspicuously silent about instances of white brutality against Indians. Bringing home scalps from anti-Indian campaigns was by then considered standard. Pennsylvania paid $1,000 for each Native American scalp. Several American diarists also record that Continentals skinned the legs of two dead Native Americans "from their hips down for boot legs: one pair for the Major and the other for myself," in one officer's calm prose. On another occasion, Continental soldiers burned to death an old woman and a crippled boy who could not be taken as hostages, even though their commander had ordered them to be left unharmed.[25]

Native Americans narrated further instances that are not recorded in any of the white men's diaries. An Onondaga chief told the story of troops, apparently on Van Schaick's campaign, invading his town: "[T]hey put to death all the women and Children, excepting some of the Young Women, whom they carried away for the use of their Soldiers & were afterwards put to death in a more shameful manner." As Sullivan's co-commander, General James Clinton, reminded his troops, the Native Americans "never violate the chastity of any women." Anthropologists tell us that Indians in eastern North America indeed did not rape or otherwise assault female captives, probably because warriors as part of their ritual observances refrained from sex, and also because the adoption of captives, a common practice in Indian war, would mean that rape amounted to incest. When white men raped Indian women, their crimes must have been particularly traumatizing to their victims as well as their communities.[26]

It is impossible to know how many other examples of cruelty against Native Americans remained unrecorded. What the campaign journals do note is the desecration of Indian graves, an abusive practice that white settlers had been indulging in ever since the Pilgrims landed in the early 1600s. At Tioga in August 1779, Continentals discovered some one hundred Indian burial mounds, four to six feet high. Soldiers rifled through them for grave goods that were buried alongside the bodies to take home as mementos. One man recorded that they "found a good many laughable relics, as a pipe, Tomahawk & Beads &c." Soldiers also looted and destroyed false-face masks, which had spiritual and medicinal significance. Some officers made careful sketches of warriors' tombs before joining in the looting: Barbara Alice Mann distinguishes between officers who justified mound digging and grave robbing as a form of early archaeology, and the rank and file, who casually desecrated graves (sometimes scalping freshly buried Indians) and plundered grave goods for pleasure or profit. It was as if the Continentals, deprived of the chance to face Native American warriors in battle, assaulted the Indians' civilization and mutilated their dead bodies instead. Contemporary accounts, whether by officers or soldiers, betray little sense of the violation of the Indians' spiritual integrity, let alone any shame or remorse.[27]

American Empire

By the time Sullivan's army was on its retreat from Iroquoia—he had turned around just forty miles from Niagara, "with considerable regret," albeit prudently, given the advancing season—more than 5,000 Native Americans, or over one-third of the targeted population, had taken refuge at the British garrison and trading post of Niagara. The garrison could not cope with such large numbers of starving exiles, whose influx exacerbated a medical crisis at a station that already housed a range of Native Americans and Loyalists who had fled there previously, along with British soldiers and enemy captives. The previous winter, the fort had supplied more than 7,000 Native Americans with food and clothing. With several thousand new refugees squeezing already scant resources in the fall of 1779, a rumor spread that the British poisoned flour with gunpowder to reduce the number of hungry Indian mouths. Whether this particular allegation is true or not, many Native Americans did die of malnourishment, exhaustion, dysentery, and hypothermia. The British at one point tried to make the refugees hunt for their food, but the harshest winter on record dumped five feet of snow on western New York; the spring snowmelt would reveal hundreds of deer and other animals that had frozen to death. The thaw also unveiled entire Indian families who had perished in dugouts near the fort. At least 1,000 Iroquois did not survive the destruction of their homelands, shelter, and food supplies.[28]

On September 30, Sullivan informed Congress that the destruction of Iroquois towns, houses, and resources was virtually complete. His report was published by numerous newspapers, among them the triumphant *Virginia Gazette*, which wrote that Sullivan had "taught [the Indians] by severe experience, the power of the American empire." Congress, for its part, thanked Sullivan for chastising those who had "perfidiously waged an unprovoked and cruel war against these United States."[29]

One Loyalist paper reprinted Sullivan's reckoning before mocking—with no more empathy for Britain's Indian allies than their assailants had shown them—"[h]is description of the elegant palaces, blooming orchards, and extensive corn-fields, which he pretends to have found and destroyed in a wilderness where nothing but wigwams and small cultivated patches ever appeared." Newspaper readers in Britain had had the occasional glimpse of the campaign since Sullivan had been preparing at Wyoming. By Christmas, they read exultant American reports that "[t]he whole country of the Senecas, and other tribes of the six nations, have been over-run and destroyed, and they compelled to fly to Niagara for security," while Brodhead's expedition had destroyed another ten towns and five hundred acres of corn.[30]

The historian Page Smith memorably called Sullivan's campaign "the most ruthless application of a scorched-earth policy in American history," matched only by Sherman's March to the Sea in 1864. But insofar as it was intended to terrorize the Indians into abandoning their frontier raids, Sullivan's campaign had little effect. As early as the spring of 1780, Native Americans, in league once again with white Loyalist rangers, resumed their raiding with renewed vigor. By the fall, Indians had ravaged frontier settlements west of Schenectady. According to various estimates, they ruined between 150,000 and 600,000 bushels of wheat, quantities comparable to—or indeed significantly exceeding—Sullivan's tally of corn destruction. In total, dozens of war parties on the New York–Pennsylvania frontier killed at least 142 settlers, captured 160 individuals alongside several hundred horses and head of beef cattle, and destroyed multiple forts and hundreds of houses and

farm buildings. The Seneca also razed the towns of those Onei-
das who had supported Sullivan the previous summer; as a result,
some switched allegiances to the British. Sullivan's army had taken
captive only four Native Americans—all of them women—on the
entire campaign, leaving Washington without leverage to forge
a peace. The scorched-earth policy had also diminished the food
available to Patriot frontier militias, who could no longer raid the
fertile fields of Iroquoia. Above all, Washington and Sullivan's
genocidal campaign had failed in its essential goal of breaking
the will of the Iroquois. As Major Jeremiah Fogg concluded, "The
nests are destroyed, but the birds are still on the wing."[31]

* * *

Rare was the Continental soldier or officer who expressed any doubt
about his mission in Indian country. Dictating his memories of the
campaign many years later, Nathan Davis considered the moral
dilemma of destroying the Native Americans' crops and housing.
It did not, Davis reminisced, "entirely escape our reflection what
must have been the inevitable consequence resulting from the destruction of all the sustenance of a multitude of natives." Yet Davis
considered the campaign a necessary response to Indian aggression: "[W]hen we reflected on the inhuman barbarities they had
inflicted on our own people, the scalps that we had seen hanging
around their wigwams, from the aged parent of grey hairs, down
to the resistless infant at the breast," he wrote, invoking age-old
atrocity motifs, "we could not but feel justified in the act, whilst
we lamented the dreadful necessity that impelled us to it."[32]

Another officer was more ambivalent, writing to his fiancée,
"I really feel guilty as I applied the torch to huts that were Homes
of Content until we ravagers came spreading desolation everywhere ... Our mission here is ostensibly to destroy but may it not
transpire that we pillagers are carelessly sowing the seeds of Empire?" Territorial dominion and empire were indeed never far from
the western army's minds. Although the campaign was ostensibly
waged to destroy Iroquoia and strike fear in its inhabitants, the

"land-grabbing agenda of [Sullivan's] expedition was an open secret," as Barbara Alice Mann reminds us. Surveyors were attached to the army to project order onto the wilderness and facilitate a future division of the spoils of war. (Washington himself had, of course, started out as a surveyor and had received thousands of acres of Native American land for his services as a frontier commander in the 1750s.) Officers on Sullivan's campaign habitually appraised the quality of the land, vegetation, and water, and the aesthetic value of their surroundings. Even the army chaplain Israel Evans rhapsodized on "this addition of immense wealth and extensive territory to the United States."[33]

Veterans of the campaign returned both during and after the war to claim land. In the summer of 1783, Washington undertook a seven-hundred-mile prospecting tour of the New York frontier, appraising the land and waterways and purchasing with Governor Clinton 6,000 "amazingly cheap" acres at Oriskany. Under the peace settlement later that year, the U.S. would obtain the so-called right of preemption over the entire Iroquois or Haudenosaunee homeland, superseding any European rights to negotiate with the Indians. Within another fifteen years or so, Native Americans, whether they had sided with the British or the Americans in the Revolutionary War, had surrendered almost all lands in what is now New York State. Sullivan's campaign is a perfect example of what Carroll Smith-Rosenberg has described as the Patriots' Janus face: "[W]hen facing east, European American patriots proclaimed themselves as anti-imperialists dedicated to the defense of Independence and liberty. But, when they faced west, they . . . assumed the role of imperialists staking claims to a vast empire and its subject peoples." A decade afterward, the Seneca chief Garganwahgah, or Cornplanter, remembered that the mere mention of George Washington's Indian name still struck terror among his nation, where "our women look behind them and turn pale, and our children cling close to the neck of their mothers." They called him "Town-destroyer."[34]

* * *

The mission ordered by "Town-destroyer" left behind spoils of violent destruction. In April 1782, the Geneva-born artist, antiquary, and naturalist Pierre Eugène du Simitière opened what he called the American Museum at his house near Fourth and Arch Streets in Philadelphia—the first public museum in North America. A lifelong collector, Du Simitière gathered objects ranging from manuscripts, books, and drawings to dried herbs, fossils, insects, jars with fish and small mammals pickled in spirits, and items documenting cultures from various parts of the globe. Early in the Revolution, Du Simitière had petitioned Congress to finance his projected "Memoirs and Observations on the Origin and Present State of North America." But although a committee recommended appointing him "Historiographer to the Congress of the United States," nothing came of the plans. Trying to make ends meet, the collector thus opened his museum, where alongside a broadside of the Declaration of Independence, a printed copy of the Franco-American treaty of alliance, and shelves of Revolutionary-era pamphlets, he displayed extensive Indian collections. In addition to maps, papers, and notes on Native American history and languages, visitors could expect "Ornamental Dresses," weapons, and "Utensils." During the Revolutionary War, Du Simitière collected at least 110 such artifacts, many of them trophies of the Continental Army's campaigns against Native Americans: bows and arrowheads, hatchets and a spear, pipes, porcupine quills, a headdress, and a tobacco pouch made of skin.[35]

After the 1779 campaign against Iroquoia, Du Simitière specifically requested donations of Native American objects and human remains from General Brodhead and Governor Clinton. That November, he received what he described as "a vizor or mask of wood representing a ghastly human face, the color of an Indian with a mouth painted red the eyes of yellow copper with a round hole in the middle to peep thro' the forehead covered with a piece of bear skin by way of a cap." The false-face mask, Du Simitière noted, had been "found with several more to the number of about 40 in an Indian town called *Chemung* which was burnt by the Cont:l army under Gen Sullivan in his expedition last Summer into the

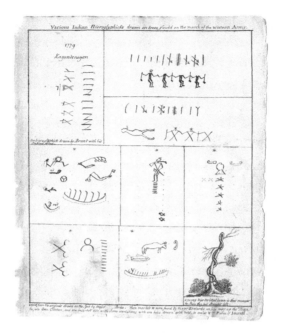

Pierre Eugène du Simitière, "Various Indian Hieroglyphicks drawn on trees, found on the march of the western Army." The collector, artist, and naturalist Du Simitière copied this undated ink sketch from originals made during the 1779 campaign. Heavily in debt, and always a semi-outsider in America, Du Simitière died of starvation in 1784; he was forty-seven.

country of the Six nations." John Devetter, of the 4th Pennsylvania Regiment, had apparently taken the mask after watching or participating in an Indian dance, and subsequently donated it to Du Simitière. The collection quite possibly also included the scalp donated by the Supreme Executive Council of Pennsylvania in 1782 of an Indian killed near the Ohio River.[36]

After Du Simitière's death in 1784, the Library Company of Philadelphia bought many of his manuscripts and printed items, but to this day the fate of his Native American objects remains unclear. One tradition has it that the painter Charles Willson Peale acquired parts of the collection. In 1790, Peale's museum in Philadelphia displayed a "DRESSED skin of the leg and thigh of an Indian, killed in the march of General Sullivan into the Western country during the late war." Donated by a member of the Pennsylvania Supreme Executive Council, this may well have been one of the leggings referenced by soldiers on that campaign.[37]

By collecting and displaying the human remains and objects of Native Americans, white men—first on campaign, then in the genteel, safe settings of museums—represented Indians as the inferior subjects of America's aggressive colonialism. As the Patriots' anti-Indian rhetoric surrounding violence helped forge a national consciousness, Indians were deliberately excluded from such nation-building efforts. When Du Simitière's Indian objects vanished without a trace, their disappearance presaged the fate of Native American civilizations in an era of relentless settler expansion and forced cessions of land.[38]

* * *

Historians of the Revolutionary War typically give short shrift to the year 1779. With no major battles taking place, the war was supposedly in limbo. That, however, was emphatically not the sense of populations targeted by campaigns of terror that summer. On the frontier, Revolutionary violence enforced an unequivocally expansionist, racially charged agenda; in Iroquoia, the effects of Revolutionary warfare would be felt for decades. By the end of 1779, the weight of military action in North America had shifted south. After the British and Americans had issued threats and counterthreats in the battle of the manifestos, it remained to be seen whether they were in fact prepared to wage unlimited war against one another. As Britain Americanized the conflict by relying more on armed white Loyalists and on black fighters and laborers, Southerners—Patriot and Loyalist, white and black— became embroiled in a particularly brutal civil war. And, as on the western frontier, in the South—where black slaves constituted between 40 and 60 percent of the population—the war was inextricably linked to the violence of racism.

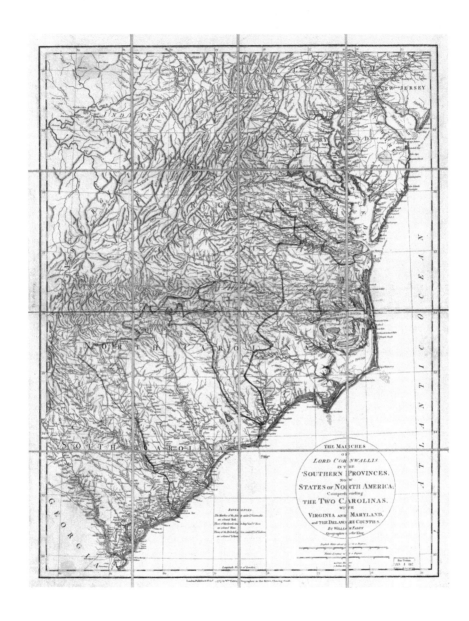

THE MARCHES
OF
LORD CORNWALLIS
IN THE
SOUTHERN PROVINCES,
NOW
STATES OF NORTH AMERICA:
Comprehending
THE TWO CAROLINAS.
WITH
VIRGINIA AND MARYLAND,
AND THE DELAWARE COUNTIES.
BY WILLIAM FADEN
Geographer to the King.

CHAPTER TEN

Americanizing the War

A CANNONBALL CRASHED THROUGH THE ROOF OF THE STA-ble that sheltered David George; his wife, Phyllis; and their children, Jesse, David, and Ginny. British troops had taken Savannah, Georgia, in January 1779, and American forces and their French allies were now laying siege to the city. Under the relentless bombardment of their mortars and fifty cannons, David's temporary place of refuge was turning into yet another site of danger in his turbulent life.[1]

Born into slavery in Virginia around 1740, David had as a child and teenager carried water, carded cotton, and worked his master's tobacco and cornfields. The whip ruled life on the plantation. David remembered seeing his eldest sister flogged till her back seemed "as though it would rot." When one of his brothers ran away, they hunted him down with hounds and strung him up by his hands. After they had laid on five hundred lashes, they rubbed salt water into his wounds and sent him straight back to the fields. David, too, had been whipped, "many a time on my naked skin, and sometimes till the blood has run down over my waistband." When he heard his mother, the master's cook, beg for mercy as she was flogged, and when he then witnessed her dying from the constant abuse, he couldn't take it any longer. In his twentieth year, David ran away, pursued by his master's son over hundreds of miles, escaping only to be enslaved again, first by Creek Indians, and then by the Natchez, who in 1770 sold him on as a servant to an Indian agent at Silver Bluff, Georgia.

There, David married a half-black, half-Indian woman named Phyllis, and the couple had the first of what would eventually be ten children. When he was exposed to Baptist teaching, David found his calling: he learned to read, and on the eve of the Revolution became a charismatic preacher to a flock of eight, soon to number thirty. He had, in effect, founded the first exclusively black Baptist church in America. As the British approached the area in 1779, David's "Antiloyalist" master fled. David led his family and fifty or more of his fellow slaves towards Savannah.

David George and his family were among thousands of slaves from Georgia, the Carolinas, and Virginia who responded to a proclamation that the British commander in chief General Sir Henry Clinton had issued in June 1779. Clinton decreed that slaves owned by rebels who fled to British lines must not be claimed as property or sold. He also promised any blacks deserting the rebel standard that they would be free to follow "any Occupation" within British lines. Unlike Dunmore's proclamation, Clinton's did not require the former slaves of rebels to fight for the Crown to earn their freedom. But, Clinton warned, "any NEGROES taken in Arms or upon any military Duty, shall be purchased for a stated price" and sold, with the proceeds benefiting the officers and soldiers who had captured them.[2]

Like Dunmore's before, Clinton's emancipation decree was not a moral measure but a strategic one designed to stoke white fear, decimate the rebel South's labor force, and strengthen the British Army's support infrastructure. By employing blacks as pioneers—felling trees, clearing roads, building fortifications—as well as smiths, carpenters, and armorers, Clinton could thus release white soldiers for armed duty. In the Georgia capital, David and his family were surrounded by other black men, women, and children, both free and enslaved. Numerous black laborers, nurses, and laundresses worked for the occupiers, and a total of 620 black recruits helped defend the city under siege. General Prevost would later praise their resolve: "They certainly did wonders in the working way and in fighting they really shewed no bad countenance." One of those armed black men was Scipio Handley. A fishmonger in Charleston, South Carolina, Scipio had escaped execution at the hands of Patriots in 1775 after he had been sentenced to death for carrying messages for the governor. He then served in the Royal Navy before making grapeshot in the Savannah armory. When carrying ammunition to a redoubt, Scipio was shot in the leg; the gangrenous wound nearly cost him a limb, and soon he was evacuated alongside injured British soldiers. Handley and his peers faced other blacks among their assailants. These were men like Shaddrack Battles with the 10th Virginia Regiment, who had previously fought at Brandywine, Monmouth, Germantown, and Stony Point, as well as free blacks from Saint-Domingue who served with America's French allies.[3]

After their narrow escape in the stable, David George evacuated his family to nearby Yamacraw, where they all hid under the floor of an empty house. But George had contracted smallpox and he sent his family away for their own protection. Left without medical care or food—a dog had devoured most of the little Indian corn David had left—he managed to recover thanks to some rice donated by passersby. By the time he was reunited with his family in Savannah, the siege had been lifted: black guides had led British reinforcements to the city just in time. The retreating allies counted their eight hundred killed and wounded to Britain's several dozen. David and his family remained in Savannah, where he kept a butcher's stall and Phyllis washed laundry for British officers. His military pass affirmed that David was, for now, "a free Negro" and "a good subject to King George."[4]

* * *

Mobilizing greater numbers of blacks, such as for the defense of Savannah, was part of a new British strategy that had been triggered by dramatic changes in the war's international contexts. After France had entered the fight as an ally of the United States in 1778, Spain—even though it did not yet recognize American independence—declared war on Britain the following year, hoping to recapture former possessions like the Floridas, Jamaica, Gibraltar, and Minorca. What had started as a war in North America had expanded into a worldwide conflict. By 1779, British naval and military forces were confronting the Bourbon powers in Central America and the Caribbean, West Africa and India, as well as in Europe, where the Spanish were blockading Gibraltar and the French were preparing to invade the British Isles. From London's perspective, the war against the thirteen rebellious American colonies was no longer the most important theater in Britain's newly global struggle.[5]

In early 1778, the British government had briefly considered ending the war in North America altogether; a sense of duty towards the Loyalists weighed heavily in the decision to carry on. But it was clear that Britain would need to adjust its American strategy to fit its new geostrategic circumstances. The government thus executed a pivot to the Southern colonies that it had been contemplating since the winter of 1777–78. Holding the American South was still seen as vital to supplying Britain's Caribbean sugar islands, the economic powerhouse of the Empire. But with regular British troops increasingly required to fight the Empire's wars globally—by 1779, several regiments had already been redeployed from North America to the Caribbean, with others recalled to the British Isles—Britain would now need to rely on homegrown support. And the South held two large reservoirs of manpower to tap: white Loyalists, and blacks. Both of these groups would be key to the process of Americanizing the war. But their mobilization would also significantly alter the dynamics of the conflict.[6]

Much of the South, and especially the backcountry regions of North and South Carolina, had been in the grip of violence for almost two decades. Frontier militia conducted scorched-earth raids against the Cherokees. Western settlers clashed with eastern elites in North Carolina in the Regulator Wars. Rival ethnic and religious groups and families carried their feuds with them as they migrated. Such social and political friction played out against the constant backdrop of slavery—of white oppression and of slave resistance. The British invasion intensified these preexisting tensions in the South, such that it became "a society struggling to contain the savagery of war, sometimes succeeding and sometimes failing," as the historian Wayne E. Lee puts it.[7]

By recruiting Southern blacks for both support and fighting roles, Clinton aimed to use whites' fear of ferocious slave unrest for tactical advantage. But blacks were not just pawns in the conflict among Anglo-American whites: they were also independent actors in their own right. And for many, Clinton's proclamation presented an opportunity. Only a minority of the half a million blacks living in Revolutionary America in 1775 actively supported either side, with perhaps 20,000 fighting for or against the British during the war. But, as the historian Douglas Egerton reminds us, "several hundred thousand slaves tried to use the chaos of war to their own advantage." In myriad acts of resistance, African-Americans took on the struggle to assert their own interests and identity in the turmoil that was the Revolutionary War. Whether they decided to run from their masters—either to join the British or to liberate themselves and slip away into the countryside—or whether they stayed on the plantations, blacks in the South continued to face the violence of racial discrimination and of war, and, in many cases, displacement and disease, too. For them the Revolution brought both unfathomable dangers and new possibilities.[8]

Americanizing the war also entailed a greater role for armed white Loyalists, both in semiregular, so-called provincial regiments in the British Army, which were typically led by British commanders, and in local Loyalist militias. In the South, as elsewhere, Americans chose sides—or tried to remain neutral—based on ideological and pragmatic considerations. There were Loyalist concentrations among Scottish merchants from the Chesapeake south to Georgia, Scottish Highland clansmen in the Cape Fear Valley in North Carolina, and small farmers across the Southern backcountry. In 1778, the United States' alliance with France boosted the Loyalist camp, as collaborating with an absolutist, Catholic power went one step too far for some previously passive Loyalists and hitherto uncommitted individuals. One British officer argued that—unlike using German auxiliary troops, which alienated the American population—recruiting American Loyalists promised to end the "bloody Rebellion" sooner. For Loyalists were "bound by every tie which can affect the human heart, to extenuate the ravages and depredations of war." But after years of civil strife, that was probably as optimistic, if not naïve, an assessment as British officers' evaluation of the strength of Loyalist support generally. In fact, by enabling more Loyalists to act on the powerful motivation of revenge after years of rebel persecution, the British were more likely to fan the flames of civil war.[9]

Indeed, Britain's new approach particularly encouraged the expansion of irregular warfare—the kind of war, in the words of one historian, between "small flexible units which were local in their concerns and objectives, which were dedicated to partisan activity and to making the countryside uninhabitable to the enemy, and which resorted to fear and intimidation to hold the civilian population in line." With both regular armies and irregular forces turning the South into the most active theater of war in North America, it was this conflict between militias and other nonregular troops that would dominate the experience of the Southern war for not only many soldiers but civilians, too.[10]

Some commanders still worried that unlimited violence might make it difficult to reconcile Americans with one another after the war. But by 1779, attitudes among the officer class as a whole had shifted: a majority of British officers serving in America now advocated a war of depredation and destruction. They felt that temporarily escalating the levels and forms of violence was a necessary and justified means towards the ultimate pacification of the rebellious colonies. To the Revolutionaries, Britain's new strategy confirmed that the peace commissioners' manifesto had not just been an empty threat: their former imperial masters seemed indeed to be moving towards ever more unlimited ways of war.[11]

* * *

After the Franco-American siege of Savannah was lifted, General Clinton left New York at the close of 1779 to lead the invasion of South Carolina. Clinton's 10,000-odd troops landed 30 miles south of Charleston, a city of 12,000 inhabitants, half of them slaves. While David George and his family stayed in Savannah until near the end of the war, other former slaves in the city moved north with British Army units, including a corps of 186 black pioneers and the 170 women and children traveling with them. In May 1780, General Benjamin Lincoln surrendered Charleston along with the single largest contingent of American troops lost in the entire war, at least 4,500 soldiers. As at Savannah, blacks had served on both sides: among Charleston's defenders had been hundreds of blacks who, in the words of one historian, "risked their lives, sometimes under British fire, to preserve the capital of their masters."[12]

One of the black men who had joined Clinton's Southern campaign was Harry Washington, George Washington's former slave. Born in the Gambia River region of Africa, Harry had worked at Mount Vernon for a decade before running away to Lord Dunmore, with whom he had moved on to New York. It was as a corporal in the Black Pioneers, a corps originally formed in New York from remnants of Dunmore's Ethiopian Regiment, that Harry entered Charleston alongside the Royal Artillery. In the city, the Black Pioneers swelled to more than two hundred men, receiving decent clothing and the same rations and pay as white soldiers. With the Prince of Wales's American Regiment came Samuel Burke, who later claimed he was a freeborn black man from Charleston and had worked as a servant to Governor Browne of the Bahamas; he helped Browne recruit men for his Loyalist regiment in New York before returning to his hometown.[13]

And then there was Boston King, whose story exemplifies the wider perils that war held for blacks. A skilled carpenter who had run away from a particularly brutal master to find work in British-occupied Charleston, King became the personal servant of a Loyalist captain. When King almost died in Charleston, it was not of a war injury, although the conflict was at least indirectly to blame. Blacks like King who fled to British lines suffered disproportionately from camp diseases. Typhus, typhoid, dysentery, and smallpox affected both whites and blacks, of course, but overworked and undernourished ex-slaves were hit particularly hard. They were also the last to receive help and were often considered expendable when resources were scarce. In 1780, an especially severe outbreak of smallpox struck Charleston. King was quarantined: "[A]ll the Blacks affected with that disease, were ordered to be carried a mile from the camp," he remembered later, "lest the soldiers should be infected, and disabled from marching." Left without any medical care, "[w]e lay sometimes a whole day without any thing to eat or drink." King probably owed his life to a kind British soldier who brought him supplies. When the British paroled 1,200 to 2,000 Patriot militiamen they had captured in Charleston, those men spread smallpox throughout the South Carolina countryside, as did British forces when establishing a chain of garrisons from Augusta to Rocky Mount and to Georgetown. And still, thousands more slaves kept surging towards the British Army.[14]

Historians have estimated that during the war up to 80,000 or even 100,000 out of half a million black slaves living across America may have fled slavery for at least temporary freedom (although the most conservative estimates have the total at just 20,000, including 12,000 from the South). In 1782, between 5,000 and perhaps as many as 10,000 slaves escaped from South Carolina during the British evacuation. To be sure, even after Clinton had issued his proclamation, tens of thousands of slaves did *not* leave the plantations, deciding instead to remain with their families and not risk the dangers of flight. They knew that if they were caught, they could be severely beaten and whipped or even killed. Those slaves who stayed behind on rebel plantations witnessed British soldiers lay hands on their overseers and masters, previously the untouchable tyrants of their worlds. At Silk Hope in April 1780, "in full view of the plantation slaves, a passing British patrol 'bound the overseer . . . & whipped him most unmercifully.'" At the same time, the British Army was known to send detachments to Loyalist plantations where the slaves were rebelling, sometimes executing a slave to make an example. The king's army also claimed thousands of captured slaves as property. It used them as laborers on deserted plantations and in the army's quartermaster department, with the commissaries, in hospitals, as servants to officers, and as guides, scouts, and spies. Others were sold so that provisions could be bought from the proceeds. There is even evidence that British officers participated in an illicit slave trade.[15]

Blacks were also used as a psychological cudgel. The British-Loyalist raiding parties out to plunder estates and seize slaves routinely included black men—a clear affront to the racial order upheld by Southern whites, and a conscious effort to use blacks to terrify white rebels into submission. Eliza Wilkinson, who lived in the South Carolina Sea Islands during the British invasion, recalled one "day of terror" in spring 1780 when British troops with "several armed negroes" stormed into her house with "pistols in their hands" and "making as if they'd hew us to pieces with their swords." The invaders, demanding to see "these women rebels," plundered Wilkinson's chests and clothes, stripped her shoes of their buckles, snatched her sister's earrings, and, threatening to shoot her, ripped another woman's wedding ring from her finger. With the black-and-blue imprint of one of the earlier intruders' hands marking the attacks on Wilkinson's arm, her household went on to suffer further raids, putting them so on edge that they "could neither eat, drink, nor sleep in peace."[16]

Elsewhere, it was slave refugees trailing the paths of regular British troops who spread fear. Such semi-independent groups of blacks attacked Patriot and Loyalist plantations alike. Even the former royal governor of South Carolina, William Bull, saw his plantation, Ashley Hall, "plundered and greatly damaged by the irregular and great swarm of Negroes that followed" the British Army. The Hessian officer Johann von Ewald marveled at the spectacle of escaped slaves who raided plantations alongside British foraging parties, only to appear from their forays dressed in their former masters' and mistresses' clothes: "A completely naked Negro wore a pair of silk breeches, another a finely colored coat, a third a silk vest without sleeves, a fourth an elegant shirt, a fifth a fine churchman's hat, and a sixth a wig. All the rest of the body was bare!" As one historian has put it, "A stronger image of social revolution could hardly have existed in the South than a band of black foragers swooping down on a small farm and stripping it of foodstuffs and livestock"—and, we should add, the family's personal items and their slaves.[17]

Congress, too, tried to mobilize more black soldiers and laborers by authorizing the formation of black regiments in the South. One delegate from New Hampshire hoped that such regiments would lay the foundation for full-scale emancipation and spread "the Blessings of freedom to all the Human Race in America." Most colonies had stopped importing slaves in 1774; in 1780, Pennsylvania passed a law gradually phasing out slavery in the state. Over the course of the war, some 9,000 black men did serve with Revolutionary forces—as laborers and servants, spies and soldiers. But when Congress left the final decision on large-scale recruitment of blacks in the South to the state legislatures, the project was doomed. The South Carolina House of Representatives, dominated by slave-owning planters who feared the loss of property, labor, and control, resoundingly rejected the idea. However, this did not stop Revolutionary forces raiding Loyalist plantations in the South from seizing slaves, including some 130 from Lieutenant Governor John Graham's plantation outside Savannah; there is some evidence that the British Army tried to counter such raids by arming the slaves on deserted Loyalist plantations.[18]

Whether they went off to join the fight or remained on their plantations, blacks in America were becoming embroiled in new forms of violence—as both perpetrators and victims. But it was still unclear whether Britain's strategy would cause white rebels' resistance to crumble or merely stiffen their resolve.

Beasts of Prey

By June 1780, with Charleston secure, Clinton returned to New York City, which he feared was under threat from a combined attack by the French navy and the Continental Army. Six French ships of the line and 5,500 French troops would arrive in early July, helping boost recruitment to the Continental Army in Pennsylvania and New Jersey, and giving momentum to allied planning. Clinton left General Cornwallis in charge in the South and dispatched a supporting force under Major General Alexander Leslie to Virginia to cut off rebel supplies. The corpulent, aristocratic Cornwallis was a career officer who had opposed both the Stamp Act and the Declaratory Act before the war but then volunteered to serve in America. After playing a prominent role in several campaigns in the North, Cornwallis had returned home in 1779, advising the government that the "subjugation of America was 'impracticable.' " But when his king asked him, Cornwallis nonetheless returned to America, now as second-in-command to Clinton, with a dormant commission to replace him if he resigned or died; he joined Clinton at the siege of Charleston in February 1780.[19]

At home, the British government had weathered a political storm over the winter of 1779–80, when high taxation, a credit crisis, and concern over the use of public funds fueled demands for political reform that threatened to topple the ministry. The capture of Charleston in May 1780 was a much needed tonic to an administration under duress. But by then wide swaths of the American lower South presented a scary scene—a virtually permanent little war of raiding and plundering between Patriot and Loyalist militias, prisoner abuse, even outright murder. In addition, armed gangs unaffiliated with any real military units operated in the semi-lawless wasteland between the lines. To put the levels of violence into perspective, it is worth recalling that South Carolina in 1780 and 1781 saw nearly one-fifth of all battlefield deaths of the *entire* American war, and nearly one-third of all battlefield wounded. Strikingly, the majority of these casualties resulted from American-on-American violence.[20]

One British officer who operated at the center of this partisan war was Colonel Banastre Tarleton. As commander of the British Legion—a semi-independent, highly mobile force of American Loyalist cavalry and light infantry, typically between four hundred and six hundred strong—Tarleton became one of a set of younger, ruthless British leaders of Loyalist forces in the South who would have a disproportionate impact on the ways the war was fought and perceived. The son of a prominent Liverpool slave trader and sugar merchant with extensive West Indian plantation holdings, Tarleton was educated at University College, Oxford, and the Middle

Temple, London, where he spent as much time playing cricket and tennis, boxing, riding, and gambling as he did studying. His early inheritance largely frittered away, Tarleton purchased a commission in the 1st Dragoon Guards in April 1775: he was twenty, and war in America presented an opportunity. Tarleton fought across New Jersey, Pennsylvania, and New York. In July 1779, when skirmishing in Westchester County, New York, Tarleton outlined his method for subduing his opponents: "I proposed to the militia terms, that if they would not fire shots from buildings, I would not burn [those buildings]. They interpreted my mild proposal wrong, imputing it to fear. They persisted in firing till the torch stopped their progress, after which no shot was fired."[21]

Once he had moved south, Tarleton also relied on mixed-race raiding parties to scare white masters and undermine the plantation economy: "Upon the approach of any detachment of the King's troops, all negroes, men, women, and children," wrote Tarleton, "thought themselves absolved from all respect to their American masters, and entirely released from servitude. Influenced by this idea, they quitted the plantations and followed the army." In the words of John Cruden—the British commissioner for sequestered estates who oversaw 5,000 slaves growing supplies for the British Army on four hundred rebel plantations—seizing slaves from rebels was a method that struck "at the root of all property" and promised to "bring the most violent to their senses." Since, in the South, men were "great in proportion to the number of their Slaves," Cruden argued, undermining their wealth and status would be the best means of finally pacifying the rebels. African-Americans were soon deeply implicated in whites' partisan war in the South. One "Gibson, a coloured man and his party of tories," were known to murder white rebels. Conversely, Moses Knight (or Moses McIntosh), an African man brought up by General Alexander McIntosh in South Carolina, spent his military service from 1779 to 1782 "chiefly in pursuit of Tories." Where blacks helped whites hunt Loyalists or Revolutionaries, the levels of feared and actual violence were bound to rise.[22]

Tarleton, and those among his fellow officers who also led Loy-

This engraving of Tarleton, derived from Sir Joshua Reynolds's grand oil portrait that was about to be shown at the 1782 annual exhibition at London's Royal Academy of Arts, accompanied a highly laudatory article about the officer in the Westminster Magazine *that spring.*

alist units, were favored by the new British commander in the South, General Cornwallis. Once Charleston was secured, Cornwallis ordered Tarleton to conduct a sweep through South Carolina's interior. With some 270 Loyalist legionnaires, Tarleton rode 105 miles in just over two days to catch up with Colonel Abraham Buford's Continental force at the northern South Carolina border. Tarleton demanded Buford's surrender, warning that, should he decline, "the blood be upon your head." The Continentals held their fire until Tarleton's cavalry was within just ten yards; the British crashed through the rebel line. As Buford's troops first sought to surrender, Tarleton's horse was shot from under him. Both sides quickly recommenced firing. The "rage of the British soldiers," as one American participant wrote decades later, "excited by the continued fire of the Americans, while a negotiation was offered by flag, impelled them to acts of vengeance that knew no limits." A rebel doctor added that "for fifteen minutes after every man was prostrate [the British] went over the ground plunging their bayonets into every one that exhibited any signs of life, and in some instances, where several had fallen one over the other, these monsters were seen to throw off on the point of the bayonet the uppermost, to come at those beneath."[23]

There is debate about whether Tarleton had explicitly condoned or even ordered the atrocities. What is clear is that a veritable slaughter took place. Out of approximately 420 Continentals, 113 were killed and 150 wounded; the casualty rate among Tarleton's smaller British force was perhaps one-tenth of that. The disproportionate American losses were largely due to cavalry breaking infantry lines, enhanced by battlefield confusion and a desire on the part of British and Loyalist soldiers to avenge Tarleton. Nonetheless, even Charles Stedman, a British officer and early historian of the war, who commended the British Army for their "activity and ardor on this occasion," conceded that "the virtue of humanity was totally forgot." While the encounter was perhaps not the mass atrocity of historical legend, Patriots quickly dubbed it Buford's Massacre. Their new battle cry, "Tarleton's quarter," helped them explain, if not justify, future atrocities as revenge.[24]

Tarleton became notorious for allowing loose discipline among his troops. A few snapshots suffice to convey the general picture. The British Legion robbed, physically assaulted, and raped several women at a plantation near Moncks Corner, twenty miles outside Charleston. When Tarleton failed to capture or kill Francis Marion, a Patriot guerrilla leader notorious, wrote Cornwallis, for "the terror of his threats and the cruelty of his punishments," the legion marked its retreating path by the columns of smoke rising over thirty plantations. Tarleton had a woman named Mary Carey Richardson flogged for not revealing Marion's whereabouts and allegedly exhumed the body of her late husband, the Patriot general Richard Richardson, in front of his widow and children. People said Tarleton's Loyalist corps "exercised more acts of cruelty than

any one in the British Army." The colonel was building his reputation as "Bloody Tarleton" and "the Butcher"—the latter a moniker
he shares in British military history with George III's uncle, the
Duke of Cumberland, who had earned his in the Scottish Highlands in 1746. Here was not just another Charles Grey in charge
of British regular troops, horrific though the Baylor Massacre had
been. The Southern war had enabled a different type of aggressive,
less rule-bound commander to emerge—and, by leading American Loyalists against their own neighbors, to lastingly alienate
local populations. Seeing or experiencing these violent excesses reinforced Americans' understanding of their Revolutionary struggle as a violent confrontation with a degenerate, oppressive empire
that must be defeated at almost any cost.[25]

* * *

Just after Buford's Massacre, and just before he returned to New
York in early June 1780, Clinton toughened the British policy towards armed white rebels. All militiamen on parole were now required to swear an oath of allegiance to the king: by forcing them
to take an explicit stance, the Crown was essentially nullifying
their paroles. If a rebel militiaman was captured and found to have
previously served with the British, he was to be executed. There
was no doubt in Cornwallis's mind that "in a civil war there is no
admitting of neutral characters, & . . . those who are not clearly
with us" must be disarmed. As rebels fled to North Carolina and
Virginia, many took their slaves with them. Others who previously
had been inactive or outwardly neutral were driven into the rebels'
arms. After Cornwallis scored a critical victory against General
Horatio Gates's larger force at Camden in August—the Continentals and North Carolina militia suffered some 250 killed; another
800 men were wounded and taken captive—he put these policies
into action, ordering the execution of several rebel fighters.[26]

Some of Cornwallis's subordinate officers, such as Major James
Wemyss of the 63rd Foot, made it their primary mission to destroy

plantations across middle and up-country South Carolina. That September, Wemyss's men burned dozens of houses and plantations in his quest to terrorize the rebels into submission. When one rebel's wife refused to give away her husband's whereabouts, Wemyss's men locked her and her children inside their house and set it on fire. The family eventually escaped, but Wemyss's men incinerated their pigs and chickens. Stories circulated of another British officer who trusted his men would rather overcome scruples against murder than forfeit alcohol: every soldier who took prisoners would lose his rum ration for two months. Such conduct by the British Army, combined with Clinton forcing Americans to take sides, spurred rebel resistance in South Carolina.[27]

So did the conduct of Loyalist militia—and the war of American militias in the South was particularly fierce. Militias, whether Patriot or Loyalist, were more prone to committing excessive violence than regular armies. With a background in frontier conflict and Native American warfare, they specialized in nighttime and dawn attacks, hit-and-run raids, and feed fights. Operating with limited central oversight, their officers rotated frequently, and their composite nature eroded their sense of community, leading to less hierarchical control or peer restraint.[28]

After the British had captured Charleston in May 1780, Cornwallis appointed Captain Patrick Ferguson as British inspector of militia for Georgia and the Carolinas. A path quite different from Tarleton's had brought Ferguson to the American South. The son of a minor Scots aristocrat, Ferguson had joined the British Army at age fourteen and purchased a commission in the 70th Foot in 1768. While Tarleton was enjoying himself in Oxford and London, Ferguson helped suppress a major rebellion of the Carib population in Tobago, where his brother was the governor. After his right arm was permanently injured at Brandywine in 1777, the rebels began calling Ferguson the "one-armed devil." As the British officer newly in charge of Southern militias, Ferguson worked over the summer of 1780 to form some 4,000 Loyalists into seven battalions and led them in multiple controversial actions.[29]

On October 1, Ferguson issued a proclamation meant to rally locals in northern South Carolina to the British cause:

> Unless you wish to be eat up by an inundation of barbarians, who have begun by murdering an unarmed son before the aged father, and afterwards lopped off his arms, and who by their shocking cruelties and irregularities, give the best proof of their cowardice and want of discipline; I say, if you wish to be pin-ioned, robbed, and murdered, and see your wives and daughters, in four days, abused by the dregs of mankind—in short, if you wish or deserve to live and bear the name of men, grasp your arms in a moment and run to camp. The Backwater men have crossed the mountains . . . If you choose to be degraded [one vari-ant has "pissed upon"] forever and ever by a set of mongrels, say so at once and let your women turn their backs upon you, and look out for real men to protect them.

Patriots had indeed recently attacked some unarmed Loyalists, "butchering two young men" and maiming two elderly men. But Ferguson's militias had also left a sad trail across the western Carolinas—of burnt homes, slaughtered cattle, and traitors dan-gling from trees. The proclamation hardly swelled his Loyalist ranks.[30]

Ferguson and his force of some 1,100 men were now out of con-tact with the main British army under Cornwallis. On October 7, Ferguson made a stand on Kings Mountain, South Carolina, where his 900 Loyalists (200 men were away foraging) were about to face some 1,700 Patriot riflemen. Both forces had been marching for weeks. The Loyalists had been moving for two days without provi-sions. Many of the Patriots—hunters, farmers, and artisans from the valleys around the headwaters of the Nolichucky and Watauga Rivers—had endured up to thirty-six hours without sleep, with minimal food. Among the Virginia Patriot militia were at least four free blacks, including the former slave Ishmael Titus, who had been freed for substituting for his master's son and had later reenlisted, as well as one slave. Ferguson was to be the single British participant in the war's largest and most consequential all-American battle.

On Kings Mountain, Ferguson chose a nearly bald-topped plateau at the northeastern end as his fighting ground. This forced a European linear formation on the defendants while allowing the attackers to maximize the impact of their Indian-style fighting. The assailing forces divided into four main columns to encircle the mountain. To tell friend from foe, the Patriots wore pieces of paper in their hats and the Loyalists pine sprigs. The seventeen-year-old Patriot James P. Collins participated in the assault: "We were soon in motion, every man throwing four or five balls in his mouth to prevent thirst, also to be in readiness to reload quick. The shot of the enemy soon began to pass over us like hail." Collins and his fellow soldiers, fighting from tree to tree, "soon attempted to climb the hill, but were fiercely charged upon and forced to fall back to our first position." Eventually the Patriots forced their enemy into an ever-smaller killing zone in the northeast corner, where Ferguson's men were constrained by their own wagons, tents, and formations. When Loyalists initially attempted to surrender, Ferguson cut down their white flags. As he charged on a white stallion, several sharpshooters took him down, one large-caliber round hitting his face, others drilling through his limbs and puncturing his torso. For several more minutes, the frightened horse paraded Ferguson's body, caught in the stirrup.[31]

Abraham De Peyster, next in command, soon sent a flag of truce, "but as the [Patriots] resumed firing, afterwards ours renewed under the supposition that they would not give quarter. And a dreadful havoc took place." With Loyalists trying to surrender, Patriot officers eventually had to knock down the loaded rifles of their own men with their swords to stop the slaughter. In the melee, most soldiers had barely known their own unit's role, less still grasped the overall battle situation. Yet an element of vindictive retaliation was also at play. For even after Loyalists surrendered themselves as prisoners, some Patriots, "who had heard that at Buford's defeat the British had refused quarter to many who had asked it," continued firing.[32]

The night after the battle presented a grim scene: "The groans of the wounded and dying on the mountain were truly affecting— begging pitteously for a little water; but in the hurry, confusion, and exhaustion of the Whigs, these cries, when emenating from the Tories, were little heeded." One injured Loyalist beseeched his Patriot brother-in-law to help him but was coldly turned away. Attending to perhaps two hundred wounded men, a single doctor worked throughout the night, dressing gunshot wounds with rags and amputating limbs with a field surgeon's crude tools. The following day the Patriot James Collins witnessed local Loyalist wives and children finding their "husbands, fathers, and brothers, [lying] dead in heaps, while others lay wounded or dying." The Goforth family had three Loyalist and two Patriot sons; four of them fell on Kings Mountain. The Brandon family, likewise, had six members on the mountain; the Loyalist father would be killed, while four Patriots lived, as did Josiah Brandon, who fought on the Loyalist side that day but would switch to the Patriot militia soon after.[33]

The victors inspected Ferguson's bullet-riddled body for evidence of their marksmanship. They then stripped it for souvenirs and, according to local tradition, urinated on it. Later, though, the Patriots allowed the Loyalists to wrap up the corpse in a cowhide and bury it. Both sides hastily buried their other dead, covering them so thinly with logs, tree bark, and a few rocks that the bodies soon fell prey to scavenging animals. Roaming wolves attracted to the corpses made it too dangerous for locals to venture out at night. Half of the region's dogs had to be put down when they went "mad." People even refused to eat their fat hogs, as they had "gathered in to the place, to devour the flesh of men."[34]

The following day began the march north. With almost as many prisoners as guards, Patriot leaders became concerned about their captives' safety. Colonel William Campbell ordered all officers "to restrain the disorderly manner of slaughtering and disturbing the prisoners." But on October 14, Patriot leaders held what one Loyalist dismissed as a mock trial of men whom their rebel enemies accused of murder, arson, or robbery. Colonel Ambrose

Mills was charged with inciting the Cherokees to make war on the South Carolina frontier. Of some thirty-six Loyalists tried and up to thirty condemned to death, the Patriots hastily hanged nine on a tree before reprieving the others and moving on, lest British forces surprise them. Colonel Mills's wife had said farewell to her husband just before his execution; she and her young child were now seen sitting through the rainy night alongside the colonel's corpse. Together with an old farmhand, the widow of a Loyalist who had just been killed on the mountain cut down the last bodies and buried them in a shallow trench.[35]

British officers complained less about the battle itself than about the murders committed afterward. General Cornwallis remonstrated that "the cruelty exercised on the prisoners taken under Major Ferguson is shocking to humanity; and the hanging of poor old Colonel Mills, who was always a fair and open enemy to your cause, was an act of the most savage barbarity" that would not go unanswered. But by then Washington and his subordinate commanders routinely highlighted Britain's "Violations of the Laws of Nations" and humanitarian outrages across the Southern theater; Cornwallis's protest over the Kings Mountain murders apparently received no official American response.[36]

At Kings Mountain, the Loyalists had suffered their worst debacle of the entire war. Within 65 minutes, 157 Loyalists had been killed and 163 wounded too heavily to be moved; more than 600 men were taken prisoner. The Patriots counted only 29 killed and 62 wounded. The battle cost the British one-third of their effective force in that theater. Cornwallis had to reverse his advance into North Carolina, where he had hoped to mobilize the Loyalists, and instead took his army to spend the winter at Winnsboro, South Carolina. The British force under Major General Leslie that had been destroying rebel supplies in Virginia was ordered to join Cornwallis. Among Revolutionaries, meanwhile, morale rallied. Partisan leaders such as Francis Marion and Thomas Sumter stepped up their guerrilla fight, while Loyalists felt discouraged from further aiding the British. As one British officer saw it, the brutal defeat "put an end to the disposition of arming for us, renewed the spirits and encreased the number of the rebels." And yet, despite this setback for Britain's Americanization strategy, the civil war in the South for now continued virtually unabated.[37]

* * *

Washington's new man in the South was General Nathanael Greene. In the fall of 1780, after losing two armies at Charleston and then at Camden, the Continental commander in chief had put Greene in charge of a third Southern army. The stocky, handsome Quaker from Rhode Island was a gifted strategist whom Washington had long valued as a potential successor, should something happen to him. Greene used the breathing space provided by the Patriot victory at Kings Mountain to reorganize his forces. He found "nothing but murders and devastations in every quarter" as Patriots and Loyalists "pursue[d] each other with as much relentless fury as beasts of prey." Both sides seemed bent on mutual annihilation, worried Greene, and unless "those private massacres" ended, "this Country will be depopulated . . . as neither Whig nor Tory can live." Writing to his wife, Catherine, from camp at Little River, a frustrated Greene exclaimed: "My dear you can have no Idea of the horrors of the Southern war. Murders are as frequent here as petty disputes are to the Northward."[38]

As both Patriots and Loyalists recognized the war in the South as particularly violent, predictably, each side blamed the other. Among the most notorious rebels was Colonel Benjamin "Bull Dog" Cleveland, who terrorized Loyalists in the Yadkin country. When Ferguson's proclamation just before Kings Mountain mentioned the rebels "murdering an unarmed son before the aged father, and afterwards lopped off his arms," he was referring to an infamous incident involving the "Bull Dog." In another instance, Cleveland's men broke out two Loyalists from a prison, stood one of them "on a log, put the noose around his neck, threw the end of the rope over a tree limb, fastened it, and kicked the log out from under him." Cleveland then gave the second Loyalist a choice: he, too, would be hanged, unless he cut off his own ears. The man grabbed a knife, sliced off his ears, and was let go.[39]

Loyalists gave as brutally as they got. One of the Loyalist partisans guilty of excessive violence was Thomas Brown, the South Carolina victim of Patriot torture who lost several toes to his tormentors in 1775. Brown later oversaw the hanging of one, two, or even three dozen rebel captives near Augusta, and the beheading of four more by Native Americans. William "Bloody Bill" Cunningham, another Southern Loyalist partisan leader, became infamous for murdering sick rebels he dragged from their beds. And one historian narrates the horrific moment when a Loyalist band, passing the house of a Patriot, "found his pregnant wife. They stabbed her with bayonets, cut open her breasts, and in her own blood wrote on the wall, 'thou shalt never give birth to a rebel.'"[40]

Such sadistic American-on-American cruelty naturally affected the individuals perpetrating, witnessing, and suffering from it. Some men seemed to become accustomed to the "savage fury" of civil war. In his old age, Moses Hall reflected on how the experience of atrocity had hardened him. In February 1781, Hall, twenty-one years old, served with Henry Lee's Continental dragoons. A Loyalist group moving through North Carolina under Dr. John Pyle approached the dragoons, mistaking their green uniforms for Tarleton's Loyalists. When the truth was discovered, a brief but intense fight broke out at extremely close quarters between two long columns of opponents. Some ninety to one hundred Loyalists were killed; the remainder fled. Apparently no Patriots died. The event became known as Pyle's Massacre.[41]

In his recollections, Hall zoomed in on the murders of six Loyalist prisoners in the aftermath of the fighting. Initially, Hall had reacted with shock and criticism to that "scene which made a lasting impression on my mind. I was invited by some of my comrades to go and see some of the prisoners. We went to where six were standing together." Suddenly someone shouted, "Remember Buford"—Tarleton's slaughter of Colonel Buford's troops at the Waxhaws—

and the prisoners were immediately hewed to pieces with broadswords. At first I bore the scene without any emotion, but upon a moment's reflection, I felt such horror as I never did before nor have since, and, returning to my quarters and throwing myself upon my blanket, I contemplated the cruelties of war until overcome and unmanned by a distressing gloom from which I was not relieved until commencing our march next morning before day by moonlight.

But then Hall made a gruesome discovery near a camp recently abandoned by Tarleton: "Being on the left of the road as we marched along, I discovered lying upon the ground something with appearance of a man. Upon approaching him, he proved to be a youth about sixteen who, having come out to view the British through curiosity, for fear he might give information to our troops, they had run him through with a bayonet and left him for dead. Though able to speak, he was mortally wounded." Experiencing the teen's senseless murder, rather than reinforcing Hall's earlier doubts about Americans killing each other, desensitized him to his own side's brutality. "The sight of this unoffending boy, butchered rather than be encumbered . . . on the march," Hall concluded, "relieved me of my distressful feelings for the slaughter of the Tories, and I desired nothing so much as the opportunity of participating in their destruction." For Hall—who first had felt "unmanned" by his exposure to atrocity—to deal with war's brutalities, he had to turn off sensibility (a notion that peculiarly defined manliness in this period) and recover a form of masculinity that saw him inure himself to violence and thrive on vengefulness.[42]

This hunger for retribution among American partisans eroded Britain's ability to pacify the Southern states. As Greene's Continentals and irregular rebel troops swept through the lower South, he largely avoided pitched battles with the British Army in favor of a strategy of attrition. Gradually, Greene was thus able to expel the British from most areas except for a strip between Charleston and Savannah. When the enemies did clash in larger battles, the Revolutionaries acquitted themselves well. In the Battle of Cowpens in early 1781, a combined force of Continentals, state troops, and Patriot militias under Daniel Morgan dealt a heavy blow to British regulars and Loyalists commanded by Tarleton: casualties amounted to one-sixth of Cornwallis's army. The victorious Morgan proudly reported to General Greene that, despite Tarleton's "most cruel Warfare, not one man was killed[,] wounded or even insulted after he surrendered." Alas, after the British had ignored many previous "Lessons of Humanity," Morgan feared "they are incorrigible." British Pyrrhic victories like the one they clinched in the Battle of Guilford Courthouse in March 1781, where the Crown sustained vastly greater casualties than the defeated Revolutionaries, further depleted the British Southern army. Throughout this period, the rebels' war of attrition against British supply lines and posts was also continuing to take its toll. British officers were finding it increasingly difficult to persuade local couriers to transmit messages to Cornwallis, as the rebels were said to be murdering any Loyalists they captured. Indeed, "fear or intimidation" drove previously loyal subjects towards the insurgents.[43]

Harry's Head

Even though their strategy of Americanizing the war appeared to be backfiring on the British, the Empire's prospects in America were not entirely bleak. There were signs that not only the American people but their French allies, too, were tiring of the war, while "widespread disaffection" coursed through the half-starved Continental Army "over wage arrears and poor conditions" after the exceptionally harsh winter of 1779–80, when New York City's waterways were frozen for five weeks, and the Delaware at Philadelphia for nearly eleven. And although control of the South Carolina countryside was gradually slipping away from Cornwallis—he found Loyalist support to be "more passive" than he had anticipated—during the spring and summer of 1781 he launched a concerted attempt to cut off rebel supplies at their source, in Virginia. In the historian Andrew O'Shaughnessy's assessment, Cornwallis's broader aim was "to occupy Virginia sufficiently to overturn the government and establish a loyalist militia to police the population."[44]

After the destruction at Norfolk at the start of the conflict, the largest and most populous state had avoided the war until Britain pivoted south. At that point, Virginia repeatedly became the target of British-Loyalist assaults. In mid-1779, coastal raiders destroyed huge amounts of tobacco, salted pork, and naval stores, as well as more than one hundred naval and merchant vessels, and seized 1,500 slaves and several thousand horses and head of cattle. In late 1780, General Greene saw his supply lines seriously disrupted when the traitorous former Patriot general Benedict Arnold led a 1,600-strong raiding force into Virginia. Loyalists, white and black, risked severe repercussions if the rebels caught up with them. After Shadrack Furman, a free black man, provided Arnold's troops with quarters and supplies, rebels burned Furman's house and crops and tortured him to extract intelligence; his Loyalism left Furman blinded and crippled, his back scarred.[45]

Throughout early 1781, British soldiers and Loyalist privateers were pursuing scorched-earth tactics along Virginia's rivers and coastline. They burned warehouses, magazines, shipyards, and naval and merchant vessels, as well as private property. As Johann von Ewald commented, "Terrible things happened . . . churches and holy places were plundered." Compounding injury and insult, all along the way British troops seized scores of slaves, while thousands more streamed towards the army of their own accord. George Washington and Thomas Jefferson numbered among the many planters whose slaves defected during this time. Nathaniel Lyttleton Savage tabulated damage and very substantial losses totaling £583 that he suffered at the hands of the British Army that spring. Alongside 10,000 fence rails burned, horses and livestock taken, tobacco and grain destroyed, and various goods plundered, including a library of "100 volumes of the best authors," Savage's single most expensive item was "one Valuable Y.g Negro Fellow taken by the Army."[46]

In May, Cornwallis moved his army across the Roanoke, joined up with Arnold at Petersburg, and conducted raids up and down the York and James Rivers, seizing horses in order to rebuild an effective cavalry. Slaves were now defecting all along the Potomac and Rappahannock. By June, Cornwallis was marching from Richmond via Williamsburg and Jamestown to the small tobacco port of Yorktown. Josiah Atkins, a Connecticut soldier with the American forces chasing the British, observed the toll the war continued to take on the British Army's black followers: "I have marched by 18 or 20 Negroes that lay dead by the way-side, putrifying with the small pox . . . These poor creatures, having no care taken of them, many crawl'd into the bushes about & died, where they lie infecting the air around with intolerable stench & great danger."[47]

The Revolutionary authorities were now struggling to recruit war-weary Virginians for army and militia service. Some Patriot men of serving age fielded free and enslaved blacks as substitutes. Yet despite significant incentives in terms of land, cash, and slaves, Virginians widely and often violently evaded the draft, even during the British invasion of their state—or perhaps especially when their local area was affected. As the historian Gary B. Nash explains, plantation owners prioritized securing their human property over fighting for independence. They either moved with their slaves out of the path of the approaching British or swore an oath of loyalty to the king, as long as they could hold on to their chattel; as Nash writes, "The idea of independence had its limits."[48]

General Clinton, holding out in New York, still expected a Franco-American attack on the city. When he realized that the real threat was instead to Cornwallis's army in Virginia, Clinton desperately tried to lure Washington back north. He ordered his forces to lash out at the Connecticut coast: New London was burned and Fort Griswold stormed in late September, giving rise to allegations that the garrison was massacred. In response, congressional committees recommended that the U.S. retaliate: reducing English coastal towns "to ashes," executing British prisoners, and having any soldiers captured in the act of burning an American town "immediately consigned to the flames." Alas, Washington did not allow himself to be distracted but continued his army's four-hundred-mile march south.[49]

Cornwallis learned only in early September that the French and American armies were approaching his position at Yorktown; it was not until the twenty-third that he became aware of the size of the French fleet. Still, he felt assured that Clinton's reinforcements would reach him by October 5. But by then a French fleet had forced the Royal Navy to leave its Chesapeake station. An allied army of 16,000 troops and naval forces now had Cornwallis fully surrounded. It was precisely the scenario that British commanders had feared ever since France had entered the war more than three years earlier: combined French naval and American land forces cutting off a major British army in a coastal outpost. The British had extricated themselves from somewhat similar traps twice before: at Newport, Rhode Island, in 1778, and again at Savannah in 1779. But at Yorktown, Cornwallis's besieged troops—heavily outnumbered after the steady force depletion over recent months, separated from reinforcements, their supply lines severed—were reduced to slaughtering their artillery and baggage horses, whose bloated carcasses were soon seen floating in the York River.[50]

Smallpox, too, began infesting the British camp. To prevent the further spread of the disease and preserve scarce resources, Cornwallis expelled his black soldiers, laborers, and laundresses. One Patriot officer saw "numbers in that condition starving and helpless, begging us as we passed them for God's sake to kill them, as they were in great pain and misery." Other Patriots cried biological warfare, believing that the British were deliberately spreading smallpox among enemy forces and civilians. Such accusations had a ring of plausibility to them. In 1777, the British officer Robert Donkin had suggested in a treatise on military science: "Dip arrows in matter of smallpox, and twang them at the American rebels, in order to inoculate them; This would sooner disband these stubborn, ignorant, enthusiastic savages, than any other compulsive measures. Such is their dread and fear of that disorder." Donkin's book was published to raise funds for the widows and children of "valiant soldiers inhumanly and wantonly butchered" when "peaceably marching to and from Concord the 19th April, 1775." In all but two of the known copies of the treatise, the footnote on page 190 that contains the proposal of germ warfare has since been excised.[51]

Donkin's suggestion was never implemented, but when, in July 1781, Major General Leslie wrote to Cornwallis at Portsmouth, Virginia, that "[a]bove 700 Negroes are come down the River in the Small Pox. I shall distribute them about the Rebell Plantations," he did as promised. And when Cornwallis expelled infected blacks from Yorktown three months later, many Patriots assumed something similar was afoot.[52]

It soon became clear that the decision stemmed from desperation as much as strategy. On October 17, 1781, after twenty days of siege, including nine days of constant artillery fire from more than one hundred enemy cannons, with his defenses crumbling, ammunitions running very low, and hundreds of his men killed

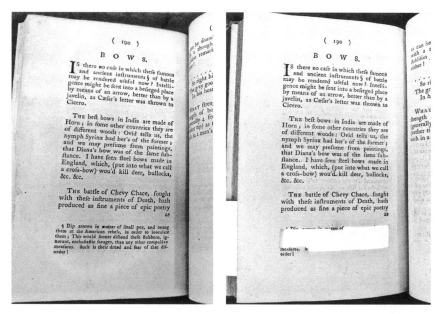

Robert Donkin, Military Collections and Remarks *(New York, 1777), with the footnote at page 190 preserved in one copy and neatly cut out in another, retaining the ornament and catchword "BOWS" on the reverse.*

already, Cornwallis asked for a parley; two days later his forces surrendered. It was four years to the week since the British defeat at Saratoga—and two days before Clinton's promised reinforcements set sail from New York.

As had become typical, blacks were among the hardest hit at Yorktown. One local lawyer, St. George Tucker, noted in his diary: "An immense number of Negroes have died in the most miserable manner." It is estimated that of 4,000 to 5,000 black recruits with Cornwallis at Portsmouth and Yorktown, perhaps 2,000 survived smallpox, typhus, and injuries. Around half of those were reenslaved, some captured by soldiers turned bounty hunters hired by their former masters. Jefferson retrieved five or six of his slaves; Washington recovered two young black women but not a dozen other slaves who had run away from Mount Vernon. They were among the hundreds who managed to slip away and make new lives for themselves as free blacks in the North, building communities where they would continue to pursue their own political interests. But not even patriotic service was enough to guarantee freedom. Among the slaves who had served with the Continentals at Yorktown was James Armistead, a black spy who had carried vital intelligence from the British camp to the Americans. He had not been promised his freedom when he enlisted, nor was he offered it afterward. It was only in 1786 that the Marquis de Lafayette, Armistead's former commanding officer, persuaded the Virginia legislature to free him.[53]

The terms of capitulation at Yorktown granted Cornwallis's dispatches and any officers he selected free passage to New York on HMS *Bonetta*. Although Washington suspected runaway slaves were hiding on the ship, he honored his word and let it depart unexamined. And, indeed, on board were men like Thomas Johnson, a free black man who had served as a guide to Tarleton from Charleston to Yorktown. Washington's officers had specifically asked that Johnson be handed over: they saw him as thoroughly tainted by his work with Tarleton. But as the historian Christopher L. Brown notes, while the British "liberated to win a war, not to promote emancipation," the protection they offered to at least "some black loyalists in the aftermath of the Revolutionary War represented a partial attempt to honor obligations." Had the British not smuggled Johnson, his wife, Margaret, and their children out on the *Bonetta*, he would almost certainly have been executed. Instead, he and his family went via Nova Scotia to England, where they are last recorded in London, receiving payments from the Committee for the Relief of the Black Poor in 1787.[54]

Some white Loyalists sold their slaves or freed them, sometimes in exchange for payment by the slaves themselves, before going into exile; others brought them along. In total, some 15,000 blacks left America as slaves when the British evacuated their last American footholds at the end of the war, plus some 9,000 as free Loyalists. Peter Anderson, formerly of Dunmore's Ethiopian Regiment, who had been captured and expected to be executed but managed to flee to the British, and who had subsequently been at Savannah and Charleston, went to England, leaving behind his wife and children. Samuel Burke was already in London, selling paper flowers, after he had been evacuated with an injury in 1780; with him was his wife, a free black woman named Hannah. The George family, Boston King, and Harry Washington were first evacuated, at British cost, to Nova Scotia, where David George founded the first Baptist church; they later helped settle the free black colony of Sierra Leone, where streets were named after Tarleton and Howe.[55]

Tarleton may have been remembered well in Sierra Leone, and he went on to brandish his war injuries when running for the British Parliament, but he had long lost his honor in America. While American and French officers dined other British officers, as was customary among the gentlemanly fraternity of European armies, Tarleton was snubbed. It was Tarleton who, in a ceremony separate from the British surrender to Continental officers, had surrendered British forces to the French army. The French granted him protection against the assassination he feared, but not without Jean-Baptiste-Donatien de Vimeur, Comte de Rochambeau, snarling, "Colonel Tarleton has no merit as an officer—only that bravery every Grenadier has—but is a butcher and a barbarian."

As officers of the rebellious American colonies joined with their French allies in European-style civility, Tarleton's brutish conduct had put him beyond the pale.[56]

* * *

When some 7,000 British and German soldiers marched into captivity at Yorktown in fall 1781, major combat activities between the British and Continental Armies largely ended. Recognizing the limitations of finance and manpower, its parliamentary majorities eroding, and finally beginning to realize that they had been consistently overestimating the extent of Loyalist support, the British government would not send any new troops to North America. Instead, they adopted a primarily defensive posture to hold their current possessions: New York City with more than 15,000 troops and, in the South, Charleston, Savannah, Penobscot, and St. Augustine with a total of some 10,000 rank-and-file effectives; they also continued to control their positions in Canada and frontier forts on the Great Lakes. Washington pushed for joint U.S.-French attacks on the British strongholds at New York and Charleston, but France— refocusing on her broader geostrategic interests, especially in the Caribbean and also in India—demurred.[57]

Britain's global war was continuing apace. In 1781, British forces defeated three Mysore armies in India. After declaring war on the Dutch Republic in December 1780, in 1781, Britain seized all Dutch trading posts in India and captured Dutch stations at Padang and on Sumatra. The following year British forces took Dutch trading posts in West Africa and a base in Ceylon (Sri Lanka), but elsewhere suffered setbacks against France and Spain. So when the Royal Navy triumphed over the French in the Battle of the Saintes in April 1782, that victory not only protected Britain's Caribbean jewel, Jamaica, it gave national morale a much-needed boost.[58]

Even as Parliament voted for peace and a new government under the 2nd Marquess of Rockingham replaced Lord North's in March 1782, British naval and land forces were thus continuing to defend imperial interests on several continents and oceans. In the American colonies, as Britain still called them, the conflict would sputter on for well over a year after Yorktown. In the South in particular, where animosities between neighbors ran deep, the civil war of irregular troops and privateers continued to simmer. From late 1781, Major General Alexander Leslie, who had recently used smallpox-infected blacks to spread the contagion, established black cavalry units that were called the Black Dragoons. Specializing in foraging, capturing deserters, and protecting confiscated rebel estates, they also fought skirmishes and some battles. Whatever mission they were carrying out, the British counted on the fact that the Black Dragoons would be sowing fear among their white rebel targets—especially since some units were, atypically, led by black officers. As one British official reported to Germain, rebel officers were avowing their "abhorrence of the indiscriminate outrages committed by our Black Dragoons, to which," he admitted, "their savage nature prompts them much more when furnished with Arms."[59]

As Leslie's Black Dragoons struck fear into the hearts of white Southerners, rebel guerrilla leaders like Francis Marion and his band of white and black men continued to terrorize escaped slaves. When a black man known as Harry, previously enslaved to a Charleston Loyalist but now spying for high-ranking British officers, set out one day to gather intelligence on rebel partisans, Marion's men captured and killed him. The rebels beheaded Harry and mounted his head on a stake near the Greenland swamp—the gruesome way marker a deterrent for escaped slaves daring, still, to support the Crown.[60]

* * *

British strategists plotting and executing the Southern pivot proved unable to control to their advantage the effects of the violence they unleashed with their two-pronged Americanization of the war. The brutal excesses of Tarleton's British Legion, as well as those committed by militias and other irregular forces, alienated a war-weary population while reminding them of the purpose of their continued struggle. Loyalist support proved difficult to maintain beyond areas under the immediate protection of the British Army; anticipating their neighbors' future wrath dampened Loyalists' ardor. The war in the South confirmed the very point of having codes of war: "[A] war in which the violence of the means undermines the political ends is counter-productive." Loyalists' vindictiveness corroded Britain's ability to pacify and engineer reconciliation in the South.[61]

As for relying on Southern blacks, historians agree that, in the final analysis, Clinton's emancipation proclamation was counter-productive, too. Even though many rebel slave owners chose to swear a loyalty oath in order to hold on to their chattel, such measures were expedient and largely temporary; on balance, Britain's strategic emancipation of rebel slaves did not so much demoralize white rebels or scare them into submission as bolster their will to resist. And although the British Army did rattle the Southern labor regime, it ultimately protected the plantation economy and helped it prevent slave uprisings.[62]

For blacks striving to obtain their individual freedom and resist the system of slavery, the war yielded new possibilities but also new perils. Slaves exposed to the dangers of war on plantations, as well as those current and former slaves fighting on both sides of the conflict, experienced the mutually reinforcing violence of racial oppression and war. For thousands, that combination proved lethal. Britain's use of more white Loyalists and blacks, then, did not achieve its intended aims, but it did make the partisan and racially charged war in the South particularly vicious. And if peace came too late for former slaves like Harry, parts of the Northern theater, too, experienced the reverberations of war until well after the surrender of a British army at Yorktown.

Overleaf: A New and accurate Map of New Jersey, from
the best Authorities *[London, 1780].*

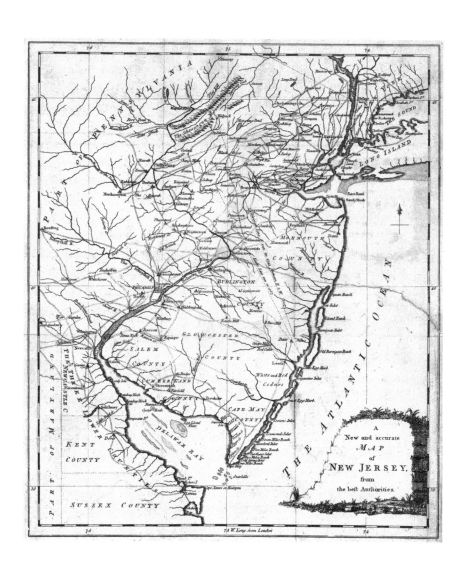

A
New and accurate
MAP
of
NEW JERSEY,
from
the best Authorities.

CHAPTER ELEVEN

Man for Man

A T FOUR O'CLOCK IN THE AFTERNOON, THE DEAD PATRIOT'S
neighbors cut him down from the makeshift gallows
made of fence rails. In his coat pocket they found his will,
dictated that morning as he stood on the now-overturned flour
barrel, the noose already girdling his neck. Fastened to his chest
was a placard penned by his Loyalist executioners:

We the Refugees having with Grief Long held the Cruel Murders
Of our Brethren and Finding Nothing but such Measures Daily
Carrying into Execution
We therefore Determine not to Suffer without taking Vengeance
For numerous Cruelties and thus begin and have made use of
Captn
Huddy as the First Object to present to your Views, and Further
Determine to Hang Man for Man as Long as a Refugee is left
Existing.

UP GOES HUDDY

FOR

PHILIP WHITE.

A local tailor would later describe watching from across the bay
as a party of armed men landed with a prisoner and improvised
the gibbet. Their leader shook hands with the captive standing on
the barrel; then a "negroe" kicked it from under his feet. One of the
first press reports on the hanging would attribute the outrage to a
"mixed Company of Negroes, Tories and Englishmen," as unholy a
trinity of modern barbarians as American Patriots could imagine.[1]

Joshua Huddy's execution at Highlands Beach, New Jersey, on April 12, 1782, and the events it unleashed are an emblem of the bitter American civil war that continued to embroil Americans in violence around British-held New York well after Cornwallis had surrendered his army at Yorktown. Over subsequent months, the case would trigger legal proceedings, preoccupy congressional committees and the Anglo-American press, and elicit international interventions. It would also test the moral compass of leaders on both sides of the conflict. As Generals George Washington and Sir Henry Clinton (and his successor, Sir Guy Carleton) struggled to uphold the laws of war under intense political pressure, each man sought to square the demands of his own conscience and honor with the imperative of his nation's standing in the world.[2]

The deliberate execution of a captive Patriot by organized armed Loyalists was an exception in the Northern war. But it gained the notoriety it did because of what it seemed to suggest about the conduct of the war at this late stage. Formal exploratory talks between British and American peace negotiators only started in Paris the very day of Huddy's execution—six months after Yorktown. It would be another half year before preliminary terms were reached, and several more months before the Crown ordered a cessation of hostilities in America. Meanwhile, seven long years of civil conflict had inspired in many Americans an enduring desire for revenge. And indeed, at heart, this multilayered episode—a lynching, a legal case, a congressional cliffhanger, a family drama, an international affair—revolved around the *lex talionis*: the law of retaliation grounded in ancient ideas of retributive justice that by the eighteenth century was part of the codes of war. All parties to the war were of the view that the *lex talionis*—the idea that retaliatory violence in response to breaches of the codes of war was a legitimate means of deterring the further use of illegitimate force—was a necessary element of regulating warfare, as long as the retaliation matched the offense in kind and degree. Yet all sides equally recognized that in practice the *lex talionis* risked further escalating the levels of violence in a zone of war. This was especially the case when irregular forces were involved.

The Loyalists' alleged murder of a Patriot in retaliation for the death of one their own might also have ramifications for how Americans would treat one another once their civil war ended. And since the Huddy affair unfolded against the never-too-distant backdrop of the Anglo-American peace talks in Paris, both sides worried that it might impact their delicate diplomatic negotiations, too: when the execution of one man, the Patriot Joshua Huddy, prompted responses from the leaders of three countries, clearly much was at stake both for the individuals and for the nations concerned.[3]

In those parts of New York, New Jersey, and Connecticut that surrounded British-held New York City, the partisan conflict between armed Patriots and Loyalists had continued since 1776, virtually impervious to the ebb and flow of the wider Anglo-American war; the surrender at Yorktown affected these local civil wars as little as it contained the guerrilla warfare in the South. By 1781, the Crown had expanded armed Loyalist involvement in the Northern theater. Small bands of armed Patriots and Loyalists were soon engaging in guerrilla warfare across much of New Jersey—a "dirty little war," as the military historian John Shy has characterized it, of raids, break-ins, plundering, kidnappings, and arrests. Among the areas of New Jersey most fiercely affected was Monmouth County, whose coastline stretched from Sandy Hook south to Little Egg Harbor. On the eve of the war, it had an estimated population of some 10,000 whites and 1,400 black slaves; racial tensions were mounting. Throughout much of the conflict, Loyalist refugees launched raids into the county from bases in British-held New York and the Sandy Hook peninsula, while Patriots harassed Loyalists who had stayed behind. Since 1778, Monmouth County had also been the target of the guerrilla operations of a former slave of African descent, Titus Cornelius. In 1775, Titus, then twenty-two years old and described as "not very black, near 6 foot high," had run away from his Quaker master in Shrewsbury. Titus served in Lord Dunmore's Ethiopian Regiment in Virginia and survived the smallpox epidemic that killed at least 1,000 blacks. He next resurfaced in mid-1778 in New Jersey—now

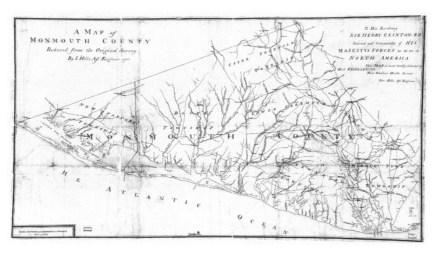

Benjamin Morgan and Anthony Dennis, A Map of Monmouth County *[1781].*

known by the honorific title Colonel Tye—and fought valiantly in the Battle of Monmouth.[4]

Over the following year, Colonel Tye led runaway black slaves and white Loyalists in plundering raids, often targeted at the former slaves' ex-masters. In response, in 1780, Monmouth County Patriots chartered the Association for Retaliation. Their professed motive was self-preservation in the face of the Loyalist threat, which they argued justified retaliatory violence. They took as their motto the biblical injunction "An eye for an eye, & a tooth for a tooth." Following each incident of Loyalist violence that took place in the county, the association would select an appropriate target to retaliate against. The Retaliators repeatedly requested that the New Jersey assembly legalize them. State authorities refused to do so, distancing themselves from what they considered illegal, terroristic methods—but neither did they try to rein them in.[5]

By late 1780, Loyalist refugees in New York chartered the Associated Loyalists to counter the Association for Retaliation. Frustrated with Britain's failure to protect Loyalists from vengeful Patriot violence, this group wanted to disturb rebel trade, harass coastal areas, and launch hit-and-run raids to grab prominent Patriots and profitable plunder. Presiding over the board of directors of the Associated Loyalists was none other than William Franklin, Benjamin's estranged, staunchly Loyalist son. Franklin's biographer describes him as "vain, ambitious and authoritarian. He could be unbending, vindictive, and a little paranoid. But he was also intelligent, industrious, and charming." Formerly the royal governor of New Jersey (1762–76), Franklin had spent more than two years as one of the rebels' most prominent prisoners until he was exchanged in the fall of 1778. By 1780, he was operating from New York City, where he became one of the most forthright advocates of Loyalist raids into American-held territory in Connecticut, Rhode Island, and New Jersey, against the more restrained course recommended by General Clinton. Supported by Secretary Germain in London, Franklin's side largely prevailed, and as the Associated Loyalists were launching their first raids, predictably, levels of violence in New Jersey's dirty little war escalated further.[6]

* * *

When General Cornwallis surrendered his army to the Franco-American forces at Yorktown in October 1781, he agreed to a concession that must have made armed Loyalists throughout America feel both humiliated and frightened. For Article X of the treaty of capitulation distinguished between British troops, who were to be considered as prisoners of war, and Loyalist soldiers, whom the American Patriots might regard as treasonous citizens, to be punished under civil procedures. Loyalists, wrote William Franklin to Germain, were distressed to see that they were considered "in no better Light than as Runaway Slaves restored to their former Masters." It was one thing for Patriot forces to treat individual Loyalists as rebels to their usurped government. But for the British Crown to expose the Loyalists in this manner seemed to them ungrateful at best, and criminally negligent at worst. The Associated Loyalists of New York feared that they might be abandoned next. Franklin sought reassurances from Clinton that any future treaties of capitulation would put Loyalists on the same footing as British captives. Clinton agreed, but he rejected Franklin's related request to threaten retaliation against Patriot prisoners for any mistreatment that Loyalist captives might experience. Despite surrendering the largest British army in the entire war, Cornwallis returned to Britain to find his reputation largely intact. But he faced one major criticism: he had failed to obtain a provision in the articles of surrender that would have guaranteed the safety of the Loyalists.[7]

Justice

Not long after local citizens buried Huddy, several hundred Monmouth County residents petitioned General Washington to demand revenge for Huddy's "horrid and most unparalleled Murder." These citizens were outraged that the Refugees—that is, the board of directors of the Associated Loyalists—had singled out a captive Patriot guerrilla leader, Joshua Huddy, to be executed under a new policy of retribution, "Man for Man," for the alleged murder of a Loyalist, Philip White. According to depositions enclosed with the Patriot petition, White had been offered quarter but had nonetheless attempted to escape six days after Huddy's arrest; his killing, while perhaps regrettable, was thus in line with the laws of war. (For their part, Loyalists insisted White's killer had acted out of personal vengeance: White had once led a Loyalist raid on his killer's house, murdering and maiming members of his family.)[8]

To these Patriots, the revenge killing of Huddy, which had occurred without legal proceedings, was "barbarous in the Extreme," and they held General Clinton ultimately responsible for that barbarity. The laws of nature and of nations suggested that only retaliation could deter such acts in the future, these Patriots held, citing the congressional manifesto of October 1778 with its evocation of the *lex talionis*.

Washington referred to the Monmouth petition twice—first in recommending a course of retaliation to Congress, and again when he demanded justice from his British counterpart, Clinton, for "the most wanton, unprecedented, & inhuman Murder that ever disgraced the arms of a civilized People." No sooner had Washington given Britain the benefit of the doubt—suggesting that the British might still be considered a civilized people, to whom such outrage should be repugnant—than he threatened Clinton: "To save the innocent, I demand the guilty." Should the British not hand over Captain Richard Lippincott, the man generally suspected of having overseen Huddy's execution, or others responsible for Huddy's death, he would seek justice for the murdered Patriot by other means.[9]

Clinton must have known that he was dealing with a highly sensitive matter; he had already put the case before an army board of inquiry to advise him on the appropriate course of action. While reassuring Washington that he agreed that Huddy's murderer must face justice, Clinton took exception with the American's tone and the implications of his accusations: "The Mildness of the British Government does not admit of Acts of Cruelty or persecuting Violence." As he had "never yet stained my Hands with innocent Blood," he asked Washington to trust him that he had not authorized any cruel acts potentially carried out under his command.[10]

Clinton considered Washington's threat to retaliate against a random British-Loyalist target both morally reprehensible and counterproductive. "To Sacrifice Innocence under the Notion of preventing Guilt, in Place of suppressing," Clinton warned, "would be adopting Barbarity and raising it to the greatest height." Rather than escalating the spiral of violence, both sides ought to commit themselves to preventing future illegal killings. Mutual charges of barbarity were by then, of course, well rehearsed. But here was an unusually tricky situation: the *lex talionis*, meant to help regulate violence, had itself become the object of contention. Either side might easily emerge from the ethical tangle looking more cruelly vindictive.[11]

While Clinton refused to hand over Captain Lippincott to the Americans, he did have him court-martialed for Huddy's murder. The court-martial would become a forum for Loyalists and the Crown to air their views on the regional civil war and the law of retaliation that increasingly seemed to govern it. The proceedings were set to begin in early May but were delayed by jurisdictional wrangling. When General Sir Guy Carleton arrived in New York City to take over from Clinton as commander in chief, he ordered a review of the proper jurisdiction. Carleton's primary mission was to implement the new British government's agenda of ending the war: the Huddy-Lippincott case could not have hit his desk at a worse time. Meanwhile, the affair was beginning to be widely publicized in the American press, with numerous papers carrying the story of the placard pinned to Huddy's corpse as well as extracts from the Monmouth citizens' petition and the commanders' correspondence. For a brief moment there was some speculation that the British might yet deliver Lippincott to satisfy Washington's demand after all.[12]

Preoccupied with the *lex talionis* and what it might mean in practice at this late stage of the war, both commanders in chief explained themselves to William Livingston, the governor whose state was being ravaged by civil war. Washington recognized the implications of reciprocity: since he demanded that the British hand over a suspected war criminal, he would need to do the same in return if ever an American soldier violated the laws of war. For Carleton, it didn't much matter whether feelings of private or public revenge had caused the recent escalation. He wished to focus instead on ending the cycle of violence and retaliation that threatened to bring dishonor to all.[13]

* * *

General Carleton eventually instructed the court-martial to convene in mid-June. Captain Richard Lippincott was charged with the premeditated murder of Joshua Huddy, "a Prisoner of War to the Associated Loyalists, by hanging or causing him to be hanged by the Neck until he was dead." The undisputed facts were few: The board of the Associated Loyalists had handed over custody of Huddy to Lippincott on April 9. Lippincott subsequently removed Huddy from the New York Provost and transferred him to the British guard ship *Britannia*; on April 12, Lippincott was present at Huddy's execution. For the prosecution, the army's deputy judge advocate, Stephen Payne Adye, the author of the standard British work on courts-martial, argued that the board had released Huddy and two other prisoners to Lippincott for the purpose of exchanging them for Loyalist prisoners. Lippincott instead planned from the beginning to use Huddy to retaliate for assumed Patriot atrocities against Loyalists. He was driven by malice, operated without orders from the board, and was clearly in command of the execution: witnesses testified that he had asked for a rope, shook hands with the prisoner, and did not seek to prevent the killing. Lippincott, in other words, was guilty of Huddy's murder.[14]

The accused conducted his own defense, although he had prepared with legal counsel. Lippincott opened with a Loyalist's lament of great personal sacrifice and loss. In front of a court-martial of fourteen officers, including eight senior Loyalists, he described a wave of Patriot murders crying out for Loyalist retribution to stem the tide of unrestrained violence. Captured Loyalists, including friends of his, had not been treated as prisoners of war under the laws of war but had instead been "tried by *Rebels* as *Rebels* to their usurped forms of Government, while others have been executed in cold blood" without even the pretense of any legal process. Loyalist pleas for British protection against such outrages had been unsuccessful. Some retaliatory killings of rebels, however, had helped temper the treatment of the Loyalists. The *lex talionis*, in other words, was working. Huddy's execution had not been motivated by private feelings of revenge but followed instead a public policy of proportionate retaliation. Having previously executed several Monmouth County Loyalists, Huddy was an appropriate target for such retribution.[15]

Lippincott's legal case rested on circumstantial evidence suggesting that he had followed verbal orders from the board authorizing him to execute Huddy. Acting under the reasonable assumption that such orders were lawful, and that he was bound to obey superior officers led by Franklin, he had proceeded to carry out the execution. In support of his argument, Lippincott produced the record of a conversation held with the provost marshal, William Cunningham. Cunningham had taken notes according to which Lippincott claimed to have acted with Franklin's approval; he also had shared with Franklin the "label that was intended to be fixed on Huddy's breast." In court, Lippincott paraded witnesses who testified that they had heard Franklin say—or had heard it said that Franklin said—that Huddy must be hanged lest the Loyalists all be hanged.[16]

Since no written orders existed, and no other party could confirm the verbal orders, and as Lippincott could not—and Franklin would not—testify under oath, the court faced a serious problem of evidence. There also was the issue of the mystery paper— apparently a version of the Huddy placard or label—that Lippincott claimed to have shown to board members, but which no trial witness had admitted seeing. Bookending his opening Loyalist apologia, Lippincott reminded the court in his closing statement that "several of my Friends and Neighbours and vast numbers of my countrymen, united in one Common cause, by all the Ties of Affection, and Interest, have fallen a Sacrifice to Rebel Barbarity." In a transparent rhetorical move, Lippincott, the much-suffering Loyalist, thus turned the Patriots' charge of cruelty against them.[17]

Retaliation

On May 3, 1782, the same day that Lippincott's court-martial had opened in New York, Washington initiated contingency planning in case the British Army failed to deliver justice for Huddy. He ordered the commander of the prisoner camp at Lancaster, Pennsylvania, General Moses Hazen, to select a British captain to be hanged in retaliation for Huddy's murder. Washington specified that he required a so-called unconditional prisoner—that is, one who had been captured on the battlefield and was not under the protection of any terms of capitulation, such as those agreed to at Yorktown, that would prevent his execution. When it became clear that Hazen was unable to identify such a person, Washington ordered a conditional prisoner to be chosen instead. On May 27, Hazen assembled thirteen British captains who had surrendered with Cornwallis's army at Yorktown. These men felt their rights under the laws of war were being violated and refused to draw their own lots, forcing the Patriots to draw for them. Two hats were produced with two sets of papers: one with the thirteen names, one with twelve blank notes plus a thirteenth that said "unfortunate." Several reports refer to Hazen calling a small boy from the street to draw the lots.

The dreaded piece of paper didn't turn up until only two names were left. The unlucky man was Charles Asgill. Hazen's conscience seemed troubled when he described the loser of this lottery as "Charles Asgill of the Guards a young gentleman of Seventeen [he had in fact just turned 20]; a most amiable character, an extensive fortune and great interest in the British Court and Army." Asgill wrote personally to Washington to protest the violation of Article XIV of the Yorktown capitulation that protected him from reprisals, a treaty "in which the Honor & Faith of Nations are the Pledges."[18]

Asgill, the son of a former Lord Mayor of London and heir to a baronetcy, had entered the army in 1778, at age sixteen, as an

John Fielding (publ.), Captain Asgill *(London, 1786).*

ensign in the 1st Foot Guards. Deployed to America as a lieutenant in 1781, he was almost immediately captured with the British Army at Yorktown. No sooner had Washington overseen Asgill's selection than he questioned its legal and moral implications. Washington confessed that the choice of the young officer "has distressed me exceedingly." He added, "I am deeply affected with the unhappy Fate to which Capt. Asgill is subjected." Even as duty required him to prepare for the possibility of retaliation under the laws of war, Washington continued to hope that Asgill's life could somehow be saved. "Humanity dictates a tear for the unfortunate offering," he wrote. But, he continued, British leaders could protect Asgill by ensuring that "the Manes of the Murdered Capt. Huddy will be appeased." In the meantime, Washington wanted Asgill, who had been transferred to an army encampment near Morristown, to be treated there "with every tender Attention and politeness" that the situation permitted.[19]

With Lippincott's court-martial still in process, the Patriot press published a special issue of Thomas Paine's *Crisis* series. In the form of a letter addressed to Carleton, Paine denounced Huddy's murder as "contrary to the practice of all nations but savages"—although, come to think of it, he wrote, even the Native Americans had some "formality in their punishments." Stringing up a prisoner for sheer diversion was worse than anything even the most savage Indians practiced. The case demonstrated that British generals had, once and for all, forfeited their right to talk of "British honor, British generosity, and British clemency"; there was now indeed "not a meaner or more barbarous enemy, than the present British one." To execute a protected prisoner for sport was "an original in the history of civilized barbarians, and is truly British." Unless he handed over Lippincott, Carleton personally would become "the executioner of Asgill, as if you had put the rope on his neck." The broader moral lesson was that the British needed to put the militantly wicked Loyalist genie back into the bottle. Paine chastised Britain for employing American Loyalists in the role of hunting beasts. Carleton's predecessors had trained them "like hounds to the scent of blood, and cherished in every species of dissolute barbarity." Carleton's duty was now clear: "[G]ive up the murderer, and save your officer, as the first outset of a necessary reformation."[20]

On June 22, the military court rendered its verdict. While it condemned Huddy's execution as an illegal act, it exculpated Lippincott, finding that his conduct could not be proven malicious. We will never know for certain whether or not the board gave Lippincott explicit verbal orders to execute Huddy. But William Franklin's conduct as the board's president points towards his culpability. Franklin's first response after the hanging had been to justify the execution in a letter to Clinton. The killing was hardly surprising, he argued; indeed, it was a just act of self-preservation, especially since the British were not willing or able to adequately protect the Loyalists from Patriot vengeance. Franklin followed up by reminding Clinton of the murders of well-situated Loyalists by Patriots, including Joshua Huddy's own hanging of one or several men from families of good standing over the preceding years.[21]

After Lippincott's acquittal, however, Franklin sought to distance himself from the affair. In August, he sent a lengthy letter to Clinton's successor, Carleton, asserting that he had not issued written or verbal orders for any executions when Lippincott came before the board, nor had he ever claimed the authority to do so, even though he had made clear that, in his judgment, only retaliation could curb rebel violence and stop murders. As far as Lippincott's mysterious piece of paper was concerned, Franklin had read only the first line or two before a senior colleague stopped him and he immediately handed it on. Franklin admitted that the opening phrases made him suspect it contained a threat of retaliation and that he should probably have read it through, but the fact that he did not do so was confirmed by the affidavits of additional board members. Thus feebly declining to take any responsibility, Franklin sailed into exile in England. With Lippincott acquitted and Franklin beyond reach, those seeking justice for Huddy would have to look elsewhere.[22]

* * *

The British public did not learn of Huddy's execution until June. The London paper the *Public Advertiser* reprinted parts of a month-old letter from New York, sent to "put the public upon their guard against listening to the insinuation that a Mr. Huddy, who was executed by the loyalists, did not suffer according to the rules of war." The letter was a harshly worded pro-Loyalist gloss on Washington's letter to Clinton demanding justice for Huddy's murder. Washington's missive was designed to allow the "abettors of treason, both here and in England" to construe a legitimate retaliatory measure such as Huddy's execution as "a savage murder." Once all sides had been heard, the rebel leader's epistle surely would appear as "atrocious and unjustifiable," and the Loyalists' enemies would no longer be able to "murder their reputations." By mid-July, British newspapers had carried the story of Huddy's execution, had reprinted the correspondence between the board and Clinton as well as between Washington and Clinton, and were covering the developments leading up to Lippincott's indictment and Asgill's selection for potential retaliation.[23]

British readers thus were aware that British and American commanders had committed themselves in lofty language to preventing and punishing any breaches of the laws of war, indeed to exercising "tenderness & humanity," as Washington put it. They also saw that each side asserted its own reading of the laws of war and how they ought to be applied in particular circumstances. Loyalists and those speaking for them insisted that Britain was to hold the enemy to their promises of humane conduct; a failure to seek redress for cruelties must be considered "*impolitic, inhuman, and criminal.*" Commentators wrestled with the law of retaliation and what it meant in the American war. "Grotius," an anonymous writer adopting as his pseudonym the name of the leading early modern European jurist, argued that the moment for retribution had long passed. Now that American independence was a fait accompli, it would be "highly impolitic and improper for us to enter into the horrid course." Britain could "no longer retaliate without having it returned with tenfold vengeance." This would leave commanders in a terrible dilemma: they would be responsible for protecting Loyalists serving with the British Army while knowing that Washington could theoretically execute any armed Loyalists he captured.[24]

What the British reading public may not have appreciated was how concerned their government was that the affairs might jeopardize their peace efforts. Just after taking office as prime minister at the start of July 1782—the Marquess of Rockingham had died suddenly, just months into his premiership—the Earl of Shelburne wrote a letter marked "secret" to General Carleton in America, expressing his hope that "the unfortunate execution of the American officer in New Jersey will not provide an obstacle in the way of accommodation." Those anxious to conclude a war that had cost much blood and treasure were acutely aware that specific experiences and perceptions of violence continued to impact how participants understood the conflict.[25]

For several weeks in August and September—by which time Paine's *Crisis* essay had also circulated in British papers—contradictory accounts of the case, referencing various sources in America and received via ports in Ireland and the Netherlands, appeared in the press. One set of reports said that Lippincott had been handed over to the Americans for execution back in mid-June. Other versions had Lippincott still awaiting his court-martial verdict. According to one newspaper, he had been convicted of murder and the trial transcript had been sent to the king. Next, rumors began spreading of Lippincott's acquittal. Asgill therefore remained in danger, but at least one newspaper trusted that Washington's "humane heart" would not allow the young officer to come to any harm, while another writer hoped that Congress would intervene rather than risk the "detestation of all mankind," including that of their French allies. In France itself, this writer observed, "the first question asked of all vessels that arrived from any port in North America, was always an inquiry into the fate of this young man." Then, in late September, the *London Evening Post* reprinted a letter from the American foreign secretary, Robert R. Livingston, to a gentleman in the Dutch town of Leyden. Livingston's letter suggested that this time Congress did mean business: Asgill might well have to pay for Huddy's execution. After numerous occasions when Congress had threatened to retaliate for English barbarity, but had ultimately allowed their "humanity to prevail over their resolutions," Huddy's murder had finally tilted the balance. Asgill's execution would be a necessary means of containing the illegitimate violence of "the most savage nation on earth."[26]

Lippincott's acquittal had further lowered the sword of Damocles that had been dangling over Asgill's head since May. Transmitting the court-martial records to Washington in late August (a two-month delay), Carleton reassured his counterpart that he had ordered further inquiries into Huddy's murder. Already, the board had ceded the power to confine and exchange prisoners of war to the commander in chief. Carleton offered a realistic appraisal of the cycle of violence and counterviolence in New Jersey's civil war: the "same Spirit of Revenge has mutually animated the People of New Jersey and the Refugees under our Command, equally criminal and deserving of Punishment in all, as they lead to Evils and Misfortunes of the blackest and most pernicious Sort." He advocated joint efforts to contain excessive violence. At the same time, he lectured Washington on his flawed reading of the laws of war: threatening retaliation without giving the British a chance to respond, and arresting a protected prisoner of war while the court-martial had yet to rule, was inappropriate.[27]

For Washington, though, Carleton's conciliatory language offered the opening he had been looking for. He might now be able to save Asgill's life without compromising the nation's honor, and his own. Given Carleton's concessions, executing Asgill at this stage would risk tarnishing America's hard-won reputation for civility, respect for the laws of war, and proportionate violence. After all, Carleton had demonstrated a desire to deliver justice "by disavowing the act—by declaring that it is held in abhorrence—by not even sanctioning the motives which appear to have influenced Lippencot to become the executioner of Huddy—and by giving the strongest assurances that further inquisition shall be made."

Washington urgently requested Congress's input on this "great national concern" that to him seemed too significant to be left to him alone to decide. At the same time, he flatly rejected Carleton's accusation that he lacked "humanity, in selecting a Victim from among the British Officers so early as I did." Washington continued to feel fully entitled to execute an enemy officer immediately and inform his British counterpart after the fact.[28]

Once Congress learned of the court-martial proceedings at the end of August, it took its time to respond. Asgill, meanwhile, was placed on temporary parole and permitted to take rides in the countryside around Morristown. Elias Boudinot, the former commissioner of prisoners and a delegate for New Jersey, later remembered that, during that summer and early fall, feelings were running high in Congress, where a large majority still favored Asgill's execution. Freeing the officer might be interpreted as a sign of weakness. Only a minority, Boudinot among them, thought that Carleton's promise of conducting a more humane war, and of investigating the murder further, ought to make Congress reverse course.[29]

As Congress was pondering, if not procrastinating, James Duane of New York, a key ally of Boudinot's, wrote a lengthy epistle to Washington. Duane explained that he considered retaliatory acts in response to illegitimate violence, intended to "stop the wanton Effusion of human blood, or repress the Extremes of War," as justified even if innocent individuals were killed as a result. But in light of recent British concessions, their promises to conduct the remainder of the war with restraint, and their general war-weariness, executing Asgill now could no longer be defended. Duane recognized that some insisted that Huddy's murder still demanded justice; others were concerned that America's "national Glory" might suffer were Asgill simply to be freed. But, for Duane, America's moral standing trumped all other considerations: she must conclude the war as she had conducted it throughout—namely, "with the Humanity, which a benevolent Religion, civilized manners, and true military Honour inspire."

It was an approach "worthy of the Patrons of Liberty" that would secure "this Infant Republic a distinguished Rank among refined and civilized Nations" as well as invite divine endorsement.[30]

A majority on the committees reviewing the court-martial records still saw no reason to desist. On their recommendation, however, Congress directed Washington to delay Asgill's execution to give Britain one final chance to surrender Lippincott. It was now late October. After several days of debate, the minority conceded that it had lost the argument and asked only that Congress defer a final vote on such a grave matter by one more night. The next morning, October 29, just as Congress was about to resolve Asgill's fate, an express courier delivered a letter from George Washington with two enclosures from Europe. These missives, in Washington's words, constituted "a very pathetic & affectionate Interposition in Favor of the Life of Capt Asgill." The letters struck Congress like "an electrical shock," wrote Boudinot. Foul play was suspected. "The President [of Congress] was interrogated, the cover of the letters was called for, the general's signature was examined." By the time the delegates had verified the materials' authenticity, the mood in Congress had irrevocably changed.[31]

Sentimental Patriotism

When Lady Theresa Asgill, Captain Asgill's mother, first heard of her son's predicament, she had apparently pleaded with King George III to intercede. The British monarch had indeed ordered that Lippincott be handed over to the Americans, as his crime had "dishonored the English nation." If this was true, then either the royal order was lost in transit or commanders in America had ignored it. Lady Asgill next turned to America's ally, and Britain's archenemy, France, in the person of the foreign secretary, the Comte de Vergennes. Lady Asgill set out her case: "My Son (an only Son) and dear as he is brave, amiable as deserving to be so, only nineteen, a prisoner under articles of capitulation of York-Town, is now confined in America, an Object of retaliation! Shall an innocent suffer for the guilty?" Linking from the start the personal and the public—the dear, only son who had been mistreated under the laws of war—and echoing Washington's initial demand, "To save the innocent, I demand the guilty," Lady Asgill asked Vergennes to picture her family's anguish: "Represent to yourself, Sir, the situation of a family under these circumstances, surrounded as I am by Objects of distress, distracted with fear and grief; no words can express my feelings or paint the Scene." Her husband was so critically ill that the news was kept from him lest it kill him; her "daughter [was] seized with a fever and delirium, raving about her brother." Would Vergennes please let his "own feelings . . . plead for my inexpressible misery" and ask Washington to release her brave, virtuous, honorable son? The minister's intervention would resound like "a voice from Heaven," and his humanity would "drop a tear on the fault and dissolve it."

Lady Asgill's letter, drenched in the language of sentimentalism, "with its emphasis on emotional truth, candor and naturalness," that had been in vogue in England since the 1760s and was increasingly taking hold in France, made a deep impression on Vergennes—so much so that he took the case to King Louis XVI and Queen Marie Antoinette. Encouraged by their majesties, Vergennes composed a letter to George Washington, stressing that he was writing "not in quality of Minister of a King, the friend and Ally of the United States (tho' with the knowledge & consent of his Majesty)" but instead "as a Man of sensibility and as a tender father who feels all the force of Paternal Love" interceding on behalf of "a Mother and a family in Tears." Vergennes predicted that Washington, like him, would not read Lady Asgill's letter "without being extremely affected; it had that effect upon the King and upon the Queen to whom I communicated it.—The goodness of their Majesties Hearts induces them to desire that the inquietudes of an unfortunate Mother may be calmed and her tenderness reassured." Switching back and forth between his private and public personas, Vergennes went on to justify his intercession on additional grounds. First, Lady Asgill was appealing to the humanity of an enemy nation when her own had failed her. Second, French military support at Yorktown had helped deliver Asgill into American captivity in the first place, so France ought to have some say over his fate. In other words, both moral sentiment and national obligation clamored for Asgill's release.[32]

Once Congress had digested the trio of letters—Lady Asgill's alone, said Boudinot, was "enough to move the heart of a Savage"—it soon became clear that it would need to order Captain Asgill's release. The case returned to committee, with a vote by the full body scheduled for November 7. In the meantime, Boudinot had been elected the new president of Congress. But one question remained unanswered: Should the resolution cite the French intervention in order to preserve America's national honor in no longer demanding retribution, or would it then appear that Congress was kowtowing to the French monarchy? Should they instead cite Carleton's recent concessions to explain their restraint? In the end, Congress did not give any specific reasons for Asgill's release. Hearing of the news in Paris, John Adams—one of the peace negotiators—felt "so exquisite a relief to my feelings that I have not much cared what interposition it was owing to. It would have been a horrid damp to the joys of peace if we had received a disagreeable account of him." The congressional resolution did clarify that Continental Army commanders could henceforth demand satisfaction for any excessive violence occurring contrary to the laws of war and, failing that, exact retaliation. Congress also instructed Washington to insist that Carleton deliver on his mid-August promise to continue the Huddy investigations. With Lippincott acquitted and Franklin in London, however, Carleton soon informed Washington that his army's legal authorities had no one else to prosecute. In keeping with his mission of managing the transition from war to peace, Carleton repeated his request that the belligerent powers cooperate on preventing further such atrocities.[33]

* * *

When Washington informed Asgill of his release in a widely publicized letter in mid-November, he reassured the young Englishman that he had never acted with "sanguinary motives." It had simply been his duty to seek justice and to prevent further illegal violence: "[T]hat this important end is likely to be answered without the effusion of the Blood of an innocent person is not a greater relief to you than it is to [me]." On November 30, Anglo-American negotiators signed a preliminary peace treaty in Paris. As news of Asgill's reprieve had then not yet reached Europe, diplomats may have feared that the case might still impact their efforts to agree to a definitive treaty.[34]

In the United States, Lady Asgill's motherly passions inspired responses well beyond her son's release. On New Year's Eve 1782, an anonymous writer in the *Pennsylvania Packet* linked the lady's letter with the miseries of many American mothers whose sons perished under horrible conditions on British prison ships:

> [W]hat must be the feelings of the many hundreds of . . . tender American mothers, whose sons in the early bloom of youth have perished in that sink of misery, the prison ship at New York, where they endured scorching heat in summer, pinching cold in winter, naked and hungry, tormented, with vermin, and every species of human filth, parched with burning fevers and deliriums, until finally relieved by the cold hand of death.

On the day of the last judgment, the writer concluded, those dead American captives would rise as witnesses against the British, who continued to treat prisoners with such cruelty.[35]

A more widely publicized letter by "An American" appeared at the turn of the year. Empathizing with Lady Asgill's motherly relief, the author highlighted that "many mothers, wives, and sisters on this side of the Atlantic" had experienced similar "horrors of distress." The Southern states in particular were "filled with widows, orphans, and bereft mothers, made so by British executions." The author discussed the specific case of Colonel Isaac Hayne, who had been condemned to death because he had once enlisted with the British but had then been captured when fighting for the Americans. The ladies of Charleston petitioned for Hayne's life with "melting arguments." Hayne's sister-in-law, accompanied by his four motherless children, begged British commanders on her knees to spare him—alas, to no avail. A once brave and humane nation now coldheartedly executed those they could not conquer. By contrast, America's rulers had yielded to Lady Asgill's pleas to the extent that many felt that "national honor and character" had been "sacrificed to the finer feelings of humanity." But, as Congress had proven, American Patriots could and ought to be men of both honor and sensibility.[36]

Washington remained troubled by the affair well after his retirement from the army. In 1785 and 1786, he learned of rumors circulating in London that he had presided over the cruel treatment of Asgill during his captivity. Such stories—which had no basis in fact—had first been told when Asgill had returned to Britain in late 1782. London papers had then described Asgill as "in pretty good health, considering what he has suffered in his confinement. His legs are still swelled with the chains with which he was loaded." He had also been beaten up by his guard, and "he had the satisfaction to see out of his window, a gallows 80 feet high, with this inscription on it,—*For the execution of Capt. ASGILL.*"[37]

When those allegations resurfaced, Washington oversaw the publication of documents in his possession to show that the episode had posed a genuine ethical dilemma for him. He wanted to explain and justify his actions in light of enemy aggression and in the context of the prevailing laws of war. Perhaps most importantly, he wished to deny the gallows story and other allegations of cruelty, and to demonstrate that, throughout, he had been concerned that his captive, a young gentleman of "humor and sentiment," be treated with "tenderness & every civility."[38]

After the war, Captain Asgill and his family made a pilgrimage to the court of Versailles to thank the French king and queen in person. The Asgills were reaffirming the bonds of civility and sensibility that cut across traditional national enmities between European empires. And while London society was still considering rumors of Washington's cruelty, in Paris the Asgill affair became a literary fashion, with the publication of a sentimental novel as well as poems and plays focusing on Washington's ethical dilemma of how to balance justice for Huddy and for Asgill. Although Washington lacked the French to read Jean-Louis Le Barbier's five-act play, *Asgill*, the retired general and lifelong theater enthusiast thanked the author personally for his dramatic efforts.[39]

* * *

The Huddy episode blurred the boundaries between private sentiment and public affairs. Leaders on both sides faced difficult ethical choices as they judged how to apply the *lex talionis* in the context of internecine warfare among irregular forces. For Alexander Hamilton, Washington's longtime aide, both America's "national character" and Washington's humanitarian reputation had been at stake. While Lippincott's court-martial was still in process, Hamilton had argued that retaliation against the innocent Captain Asgill was no longer justifiable, especially once the British had made concessions. Giving in to the temptations of revenge would offend against "the genius of the age" and make America surrender the moral high ground for a "state of barbarism"—at the very moment when her envoys were negotiating with Europe's leading powers in Paris. It would reverse the hard-won moral superiority the young nation had gained through years of fighting—and of careful rhetoric meant to set America apart from her imperial oppressors. When the Anglo-American peace talks resulted first in a preliminary and then in a final treaty, Hamilton once again sharply critiqued shortsighted, vengeful approaches—only this time the young Patriot war hero defended the Revolution's American losers.[40]

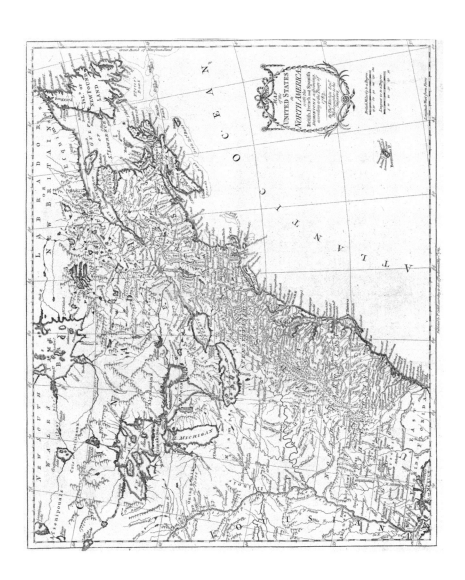

CHAPTER TWELVE

Returning Losers

I T MUST HAVE BEEN ONE OF THE MOST EMOTIONAL AND NERVE-racking journeys of Ward Chipman's young life. Not that it was his first dangerous trip. Seven years earlier, in spring 1776, the then twenty-two-year-old Harvard-educated lawyer, known to his family and friends as "Chip," had fled from the countryside to Boston and then evacuated that town with the British. Given his position as a clerk-solicitor in the Custom House and a signatory to a loyal address to General Gage—along with his public association with prominent Loyalists like his mentor, Massachusetts attorney general Jonathan Sewell—Chipman's decision had surprised no one. He left after transferring what limited property he possessed to his mother and five siblings lest the rebels confiscate it.[1]

After a frustrating year in exile in London, Chipman had returned to New York City to serve the occupying British Army as deputy muster master general. Soon he was also practicing as a private lawyer. By 1782, his annual income amounted to a sizable £500. But when news broke, in spring 1783, that the United States had concluded a preliminary peace treaty with Great Britain in Paris the previous November, his future—and that of hundreds of thousands of Loyalists in America—seemed precarious.

British and American envoys in Paris had been in peace talks since April 1782, and the treatment of Loyalists was the first issue they considered. It was also the last item they resolved. Even after American independence had been conceded, fishery rights agreed upon, and territorial disputes and boundary questions settled— the United States was granted a land area totaling 900,000 square miles, compared to the thirteen colonies' 384,000—the status of the Loyalists remained a sticking point. So did the question of compensation for property and income they had lost due to persecution and war. Among America's negotiators, Benjamin Franklin was the most passionate opponent of generous measures for the Loyalists. Franklin—who never forgave his own son, William, for his Loyalism—demanded that any compensation be tied to reparation payments to the United States for wartime damage caused by British-Loyalist forces, citing the burning of towns such as Falmouth and Norfolk, and the butchering of men, women, and children by British-allied Indians. Franklin's co-negotiator, the New York lawyer John Jay, had sustained ties with Loyalist family and friends during the war. Yet Jay now also warned that Americans would rather fight for another half century than "subscribe to such evidence of their own iniquity" as allowing "provision for such cutthroats."[2]

In the end, the preliminary articles of peace, signed in Paris on November 30, 1782, called for Congress to "earnestly recommend" that the states restore confiscated estates and properties belonging to "real British subjects"—referring to individuals to whose loyalty American states made no claim, such as former governors Dunmore and Tryon—and those residing in districts then held by the British who had not borne arms against the United States. Other wartime exiles would be allowed to return for twelve months to try to recover property. While states were free to comply with these recommendations at their own discretion, the treaty required them to grant a general amnesty, forbade further persecutions and confiscations of property, and demanded that ongoing prosecution cases be closed. Americans, the treaty decreed, should move peacefully beyond their wartime divisions.[3]

In London, Lord North, the former prime minister, and his circle stridently condemned the government's handling of the Loyalist question. Richard Wilbraham Bootle, an independent Member of Parliament, also considered the treatment of Loyalists "scandalous" and "disgraceful": these were "men, so cruelly abandoned to the malice of their enemies. . . . They had fought for us, and ran every hazard to assist our cause, and when it most behoved us to afford them protection, we deserted them." In April 1783, the treaty, and related accords with France and Spain, helped topple the government of the new prime minister, the Earl of Shelburne, the former war critic who had headed the administration since July 1782. Concessions of land, from Florida and Tobago to Senegal and territories in India, were in part to blame, but the perceived betrayal of the American Loyalists—not least the nonbinding treaty provisions—clearly played a role.[4]

Graphic satirists had a field day when the government apparently disowned Britain's loyal American subjects. Engravings depicted British visions of Indians—literally and figuratively; that is, American Patriots imagined as Indians—slaughtering, tomahawking, scalping, and hanging Loyalists.

In one print, entitled *Shelb—ns sacrifice*, Britannia is attacking a smiling Shelburne with a spear; an English butcher is weeping at the sight of Native Americans assaulting well-heeled Loyalists. In another, *The Savages Let Loose*, Indians are hanging and threatening to tomahawk and scalp Loyalists.

Shelb—ns sacrifice / invented by Cruelty; engraved by Dishonor: Or the recommended Loyalists, a faithful representation of a Tragedy shortly to be performed on the Continent of America *(London, Feb. 1783).*

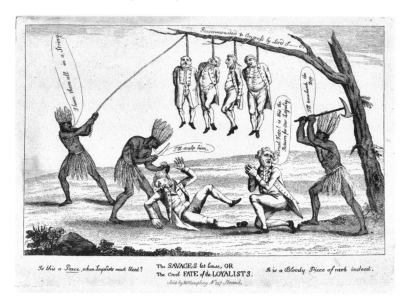

The Savages Let Loose, or The Cruel Fate of the Loyalists
(London, Mar. 1783).

When they learned of the preliminary treaty, Loyalists felt they had been betrayed. But as Abigail Adams, writing to her husband, John, the third U.S. negotiator in Paris, rightly predicted, even America's relatively weak concessions "raised the old spirit against the Tories to such a height that it would be at the risk of their lives should they venture here." The potential return of thousands of Loyalists from temporary exile—seeking restoration of property and even running for public office—incited deep anxiety among their Patriot neighbors. Zabdiel Adams, John's cousin, felt the British had at least "virtually acknowledged their faults" and it was therefore "our duty to forgive, if not forget." The Loyalists, by contrast, could not be forgiven, much less integrated in the new nation. A decade of brutal civil war had habituated Americans to violent conflict resolution and generated a thirst for vengeance that no treaty could quickly assuage.[5]

If the 60,000 or so white Loyalists who went into permanent exile after the war faced uncertain futures, the several hundred thousand who wished to stay in their home communities or return there had to brace themselves for what might lie in store. They knew that animosity towards Loyalists ran deep and that their former neighbors would be unlikely to receive them with open arms. Soon the returnees—and those who had remained in their communities during the war—found out that they would need to deal with legal discrimination, renewed persecution by crowds and committees, and possibly violent expulsion. Even so, a mixture of economic pragmatism, the strength of family and neighborly ties, and genuine tolerance ultimately led many communities to reintegrate, if not embrace, their Loyalist members.

Ward Chipman initially seemed unperturbed by news of the peace treaty. He planned to hunker down in New York and continue practicing the law. But soon the victorious Patriots banned Loyalists from the New York bar. Chipman, like tens of thousands of Loyalists, now weighed his options: Should he stay in America, either in New York or his native Massachusetts, or should he start a new life in exile, perhaps in Britain, or its remaining colonies? Chipman's friend Thomas Aston Coffin, a fellow Harvard graduate and Loyalist, had spent much of *his* war aiding the British in New York and Philadelphia, most recently as a secretary to Carleton. Two of Tom's brothers fought with the British Army. His father lived out the war on Long Island, while his mother and sisters stayed behind in Massachusetts, trying to protect the family property from confiscation. The Coffins had been keeping in touch by correspondence, but Tom had not seen his mother and sisters since 1776. By year's end, Coffin, like Chipman, had to decide where to go when the British evacuated New York.[6]

That spring, the last forty or so American prisoners were released from the prison ship *Jersey* in New York City, along with the final two prisoners from the Provost (both civilians held on charges of treason). Among the *Jersey* survivors was William Russell, a Boston schoolteacher who had been present at the Tea Party, saw his home plundered by Anglo-Loyalist forces, served thirty months in the Patriot militia, and was eventually captured on a privateering ship. After nearly three years at the Mill Prison in England, Russell had been among more than 1,000 American captives the British released during the 1782 peace negotiations. But as the war was not formally over yet when William arrived in Boston in August 1782, he joined another privateer—only to be captured again and imprisoned on the dreaded *Jersey*, the "awfulest place I ever saw." Weakened by the tuberculosis he had contracted on the *Jersey*, Russell would die in Cambridge at age thirty-five, less than a year after his final release.[7]

While former Patriot captives were returning to their families—some, like William Russell, only to become delayed casualties of war—the signs were also pointing towards further violence between America's Patriots and Loyalists. In April 1783, as Americans learned that their envoys in Paris had signed an armistice, town meetings in Boston resolved to give returning Loyalists a warning of just six hours to leave voluntarily before being deported. Communities across the state followed Boston's lead, putting on notice those "declared Traitors to their Country." Marblehead, Massachusetts, Chipman's hometown, resolved to prevent the return of Loyalists lest their readmission spark renewed civil war and conflict with Britain. The Roxbury committee opposed the return of "Absentees, Conspirators, Refugees, and Tories" who threatened to become a Trojan Horse for the "Crafty Machinations of Britons." Some Patriots were even using the language of extirpation that had previously been reserved for Native Americans: the Loyalists were "villains, scoundrels, double hearted knaves" who should be "Extirpated from the Face of the Earth."[8]

As Chip must have known, when belligerent committees issued threats, and when Boston newspapers warned Loyalists of the gallows awaiting them on Copp's Hill, they weren't just scaremongering. Accounts of verbal and physical abuse of Loyalists were circulating widely, both by word of mouth and through the press. A Mr. Triest returning to Townshend, Massachusetts, was promptly picked up and fitted "with a handspike [a wooden rod with an iron tip] under his crotch, and a halter around his neck." His assailants strung Triest up on the masthead of a sloop overnight. When they took him down after sixteen hours, they put him in irons and deported him and his family by boat. Under duress, Triest signed a paper promising not to come back, on pain of death. Throughout that spring and early summer, Loyalists returning to the state to recover debts or property as the peace treaty permitted were arrested and subsequently imprisoned or deported. As Patriots revived their committees of inspection and observation to prepare for the Loyalist influx, they exercised long-standing grudges. They also distinguished between degrees of Loyalist culpability. Particularly severe violence awaited anyone who had actively aided the British.[9]

This was especially the case for former Loyalist soldiers like Cavalier Jouet. That spring, Jouet came home to New Jersey to explore the possibility of recovering confiscated property and resettling his family there. He chose to enter via the Woodbridge area, where he had been a prisoner on parole for three years during the war and where the locals had treated him with civility. But now, Jouet reported, "I received the most outrageous insults and narrowly escaped the most shameful and degrading abuse." Some of the same men who had previously been courteous now wielded sticks and whips. Once peace had rendered void all paroles, Jouet had no right to be in their town, and they were "determined to give (as they insultingly called it) a Continental Jacket" to this American traitor. The local citizens, with the support of their magistrates, had formed an association to expel by whipping any would-be returnee. A justice, no less, escalated matters further, shouting: "Hang him up, hang him up!"[10]

With the help of a local clergyman and a man who claimed that Jouet's son had once helped him when he was a captive himself, Jouet eventually escaped and reached the safety of British lines. Personal motives, of gratitude or honor, could determine the fate of returning Loyalists such as Jouet as much as abstract political principles and community sentiment. Others connected to the British Army were less fortunate when they returned to the Woodbridge area, and this perhaps gave rise to the dictum of Peter Oliver, formerly the chief justice of Massachusetts's highest court, that in New Jersey "they naturalize [returnees] by tarring and feathering."[11]

To the north, Prosper Brown, who had served on a British

privateer, went home when the war was over to claim property in his native New London, Connecticut. Brown was promptly seized by a "licentious and bloodthirsty mob and hung up by the neck with his hands tied onboard a vessel laying alongside the wharf." They subsequently took him down, stripped him, flogged him with a cat-o'-nine-tails, and tarred and feathered him before again hanging him up the yardarm, this time naked, "exposed to the shame and huzzas of the most diabolic crew that ever existed on earth." Finally released, though not without first being robbed of the money he carried, Brown was shipped back to New York with the injunction never to return on pain of death. He begged Carleton to evacuate his family of four to Nova Scotia.[12]

All around Chipman and Coffin, thousands of Loyalists— soldiers and families, white and black—were now preparing to depart New York City on Carleton's amassing fleet. But many others still held out hope that they might be able to stay or return to their home communities, despite the escalation of anti-Loyalist sentiment. In their precarious situation, some Loyalists preemptively collated evidence in self-defense, such as the three widows who had former Patriot prisoners testify in writing to their relief efforts during the war. A Dr. Richard Bayley claimed to have cared well for wounded prisoners and published statements of survivors and Patriot officials to that effect, although others accused the doctor of cruelty. Bayley and his young daughter Elizabeth, later to be canonized as the first American-born saint, did manage to stay in America.[13]

In May, Carleton, who was "much affected by the dishonorable Terms" regarding the Loyalists, alerted the British government to the renewed terror they were facing: "Almost all of those who have attempted to return to their homes have been exceedingly ill treated, many beaten, robbed of their money and clothing, and sent back." Such stories, and the fear, confusion, and distress they reflected, would probably have come to the attention of Chipman, and even more likely of Coffin, who served on Carleton's staff. As they considered their own options, the two friends surely sensed the real danger to Loyalists across America. That month, Chipman informed a London contact that he would go into exile "unless there is a great change in the temper and conduct of the Americans who are at present very violent and threaten proscription & exile to every man who has adhered to the King's cause." Carleton meanwhile was delaying the evacuation of New York: he agreed with Lord North that the king's sense of duty and Britain's honor demanded that every American Loyalist who wished to elude the "violent . . . associations" and the "barbarous menaces" of committees be found a space on his ships.[14]

While the diplomats continued to negotiate a final treaty in Paris, Patriots in America ramped up their anti-Loyalist agitation—and not just in the areas of New York and New Jersey and the South where regional civil wars had wreaked the most havoc but throughout the country. Patriots held public gatherings in ten states. Legislatures and executives enacted discriminatory policies from New England to the lower South. With Revolutionary committees back in operation, militias scouring the countryside, and courts ready to issue indictments, the Revolution's victors were prepared to once again use their apparatus of oppression and terror against their domestic enemies.[15]

By September 1783, Ward Chipman seemed to have given up any hope of staying in what felt like a country yet again succumbing to mob rule. He decided to settle permanently in Nova Scotia. First, though, he wanted to undertake a farewell journey to see his family, from whom he had been separated for nearly a decade. Thomas Coffin would accompany him. The diary Chipman kept of their travels—from New York via Connecticut to Boston and his native Marblehead, Massachusetts, then back via Rhode Island—makes palpable his anxiety. Given how strained the atmosphere in the war-torn country had become, neither he nor his Loyalist companion could predict how vengeful Patriots might receive them.

Final Journeys

On September 21, Chipman and Coffin left New York in an open carriage, their pistols loaded. Within a day, they were crossing Westchester County, where bands of robbers controlled a landscape altogether "barren, poor, and desolate, not a house with a whole window, many without any at all." Earlier that year, in this very area, the elderly Loyalist grandee Oliver DeLancey had been beaten "in a most violent manner." Now a gang under Israel Honeywell had once again gone Tory hunting. Isaac Foshay, formerly of Philipsburg, had left his farm in the care of his son William, who sided with the Patriots; Isaac fled to the British lines. After peace terms had been agreed upon, Isaac had returned to his farm; but Israel Honeywell, ostensibly in his capacity as "commissioner," approached the area with thirty to forty armed men, intent on seizing the elder Foshay "dead or alive." He ordered William to drive his father, who was too ill to walk or ride, to Morrisania, "shaking his sword over s.:d W.:ms head to make him drive faster telling him to drive his Corpse to Nova-Scotia." Isaac, whom William dragged along on a wooden sled, started spitting blood and died within days. Such cruel expulsions, which made the Patriot son complicit in his Loyalist father's final ordeal, laid bare the deep rifts in the community after years of civil war.[16]

Had they turned to the northwest, Chip and Coffin would have encountered pillars on the roads leading into Albany County carrying this sinister inscription:

> Ye Enemies to American Independence, take
> heed to the following:
> Turks, Pagans, Jews, 'tis a true story,
> May enter here before a tory;
> The many crimes by them committed,
> Prevents their being here admitted.[17]

Instead, they proceeded into Connecticut, where a chance encounter with General Benjamin Lincoln, the American secretary of war, at Horseneck (West Greenwich), provided the travelers with a brief respite from their worry. Over a shared bottle of Madeira, Lincoln showed himself "very affable & polite" as he chatted with Coffin about old Boston friends. Earlier in the year, Lincoln had expressed concern about the intimidating editorials in the Boston press, which he feared would drive Loyalists into exile to the demographic and economic detriment of the U.S.—arguments that foreshadowed those made by conciliatory Patriots later on. Chipman and Coffin passed through Stamford, still badly damaged from British raids, where several returning Loyalists alleged to have fought for the king had recently been assailed by an armed party and beaten with split hoop poles. Yet it was also in that area that they witnessed the joyful reunion of the Lloyd brothers: the Patriot merchant John; Henry the Loyalist, who had fled in 1776; and the Loyalist doctor, James, who had spent the war in Boston.

At Springfield Ferry, where the American Supreme Court was then sitting, Chipman "felt for the first time an uneasiness lest we should be known. There was a great concourse of people & had they found us out, we should probably have been insulted. Tom tho't one man walk'd round him in a suspicious manner. I conceited I saw Violence and resentment the characteristic of them all." Apprehensive they might get into trouble, the friends decided to leave early, though "coolly to all appearance."

As they approached Boston, Chip became increasingly nervous. Even harmless occurrences rattled him. When they eventually arrived, Chipman learned that the rebels had confiscated his mentor Sewall's house. Feelings were welling up inside him of "[p]ity, resentment, indignation, grief . . . But as I pass'd the house, I felt the influence of other sensations, the effect of which will not suddenly be lost." He was now truly afraid, for in the fall of 1774 he had helped defend the Sewall residence against a violent Revolutionary mob. Cautiously, Coffin and Chipman slipped through the back door into an old acquaintance's tavern "& skulked into the little back Room, with all the circumspection & conscious Guilt of the vilest miscreants." After dusk, they ventured out on a clandestine tour of old college haunts, ending the night in *"hush'd* conversation" with a friend over a bottle of wine. Daylight brought reassuringly civil encounters about town. When Chipman finally saw his sister, Nancy, it was a moment "worth a world," followed by an affectionate reunion with his mother in Marblehead.

Friends urged Chip to return permanently to Massachusetts

and rebuild his life there. Throughout the thirteen states, many Loyalists did indeed reactivate prewar friendships and draw on family connections to facilitate their return. While revolution and war had split many families, elsewhere the ties of kinship and friendship had held fast, even in the environs of the main British garrison city, New York. After 1783, these networks enabled Loyalists to recover confiscated property, collect evidence in hope of future compensation, and obtain pardons as well as residency and citizenship rights. But while some Loyalists rejoined their families and recovered property, albeit often with substantial taxes affixed, others were discouraged by what they learned. Many were actively prevented from returning even for brief visits, the guarantees in the peace treaty notwithstanding. (As late as August 1784, a Boston mob would tar and feather one returnee.) Despite his friends' pleas, Ward Chipman's mind was made up; he and Coffin departed with heavy hearts for New York City, to go from there into exile abroad.

Chipman and Coffin had never taken up arms for the British. Their former communities harbored no specific grievances against them. They weren't even planning a permanent return. And yet, even these two comparatively inoffensive men feared for their safety on a brief visit home, indicating just how volatile and dangerous the immediate postwar period must have felt for Loyalists across America. As Chipman and Coffin prepared for exile, reports of the terror of physical and mental abuse that Patriots were once again unleashing against Loyalists kept coming in from across the states. Threats of physical violence against returnees persisted right up to, and indeed beyond, the departure of the last evacuees: "a bitter and *neck-breaking* hurricane," wrote one New York paper, would visit any Loyalists who failed to go into exile. Coffin and Chipman held out until the final evacuation in November 1783. Chip first sailed via Halifax to England; he later settled in Nova Scotia to practice law and help create New Brunswick. On November 25, 1783, Coffin sailed at General Carleton's side out of the New York harbor en route to England.[18]

* * *

In January 1784, Congress ratified the final peace treaty, which had changed little from the preliminary version; the implementation of key provisions concerning the Loyalists would be left to the states' discretion. Ignoring the congressional recommendation that they comply fully with the treaty, many states still refused to modify their anti-Loyalist programs. A total of nine states either enforced existing confiscation laws or passed new ones in contravention of the peace accord. New Jersey, Virginia, Maryland, and North Carolina had each enacted discriminatory citizenship laws before January 1784 and now failed to rescind them. Massachusetts enacted a new banishment law in March: all aliens—defined as those who had joined the British military or had left between October 1774 (when Congress had passed the Continental Association) and 1780—would be expelled, their estates forfeited to the state, yet another violation of the peace treaty. An amnesty clause introduced in June triggered popular protests and warnings of the feuding horrors that might ensue. In Virginia, as late as 1786, legislation prohibited Loyalists from voting or holding public office.[19]

In the South especially, the wounds of war still felt very raw. South Carolina had at first ordered returning Loyalists to leave immediately. Members of the Marine Anti-Britannic Society, formed by the commander of the state's navy, Commodore Alexander Gillon, agitated against returnees and picked street fights. A poet who was attacked pointed to the enduring split in local (and national) society: "Who can brook a Rebel's frown?—or bear his children's stare / When in the streets they point, and lisp, 'A Tory?'" Auctions of confiscated Loyalist property continued in the interior. Even as the South Carolina state legislature gradually removed restrictions on individual Loyalists, citizens continued to intimidate their traitorous neighbors—hanging them in effigy, threatening their families, ordering them to leave the state. Elsewhere, Patriots staged frequent nighttime raids on private homes, menacing residents with swords while ransacking their property.[20]

For some men, the journey home proved fatal. During the war, Matthew Love had participated in Loyalist raids in the Ninety-Six district of South Carolina. When he returned to the area in 1784, locals recognized him and charged him with murdering wounded Patriot combatants and prisoners during the war. Gruesome details surfaced of how Love had walked around after a skirmish in 1781 stabbing wounded and dead opponents with his sword, among them his former neighbors. But the judge presiding over his trial, Aedanus Burke, had annulled the charges, arguing that under the peace treaty Love enjoyed immunity from prosecution. Love was released. The local citizenry, however, was less forgiving: they hanged him from a tree.[21]

Whether a place was more or less conciliatory towards Loyalists, and whether an individual Loyalist received a hostile or friendly welcome, depended on a whole host of factors. Political leaders at state and local levels set the tone either for exclusion or integration. Areas with smaller proportions of wartime Loyalists who had maintained social and economic ties with Patriot neighbors and family, and who were perceived to pose a relatively low threat, were reintegrated more easily than communities where divisions had run deeper, especially if they had also experienced British occupation, high levels of military violence, or both. As we have seen in the case of Matthew Love, communities took into account the wartime record of individual returnees. Memories of vocal, and especially of violent, Loyalism, as well as personal grudges, inspired the strongest desire for revenge.

Some towns took a pragmatic approach to furthering their postwar economic recovery by embracing Loyalists who offered skills and services that were in local demand. But then, economic self-interest could also work against harmonious integration, especially if locals saw a particular would-be returnee as a potential rival in trade or wanted to keep a prewar creditor at bay. With so many factors in play, and states failing to comply fully with the peace treaty's push for reconciliation, Loyalists across the United States experienced the immediate postwar period as a time of renewed uncertainty and unpredictability.

Reconciliation

Judge Burke, who tried to save Love, was an outspoken advocate of reconciliation. Publishing under a pseudonym, Burke argued that anti-Loyalist measures must be revoked and discriminatory legislation struck from the record. An act of general amnesty ought to be passed, just as after the English Civil War of the previous century. Even though the British had been guilty of cruel and violent oppression in America, and even though South Carolina alone had suffered the deaths of 3,000 white men, the loss of 20,000 slaves, and considerable damage to property, he argued, Americans must move beyond their wartime differences. If the survivors of the much more violent English Civil War had been capable of healing rifts, then surely it was time now for Americans of all political persuasions to "shake hands as brethren, whose fate it is to live together." Reconciliation would "stand as a more lasting monument of our national wisdom, justice and magnanimity, than statues of brass or marble."[22]

Judge Burke was not alone. Concerned about preserving the Revolution's ideals and maintaining America's international reputation as an honorable, treaty-abiding nation, an increasingly vocal group of individuals, General Washington prominently among them, began pushing for reconciliation. After winning the moral war, they believed, America also had to win the peace by conducting itself in accordance with international law and enlightened ethical standards—even, or especially, when it came to the Loyalists. If dead Patriot heroes could comment, said Israel Evans, formerly a chaplain in Sullivan's army in Iroquoia, "they would ardently pray you to forgive your and their enemies, rather than to indulge any ignoble passion of resentment and revenge, which any ways be injurious to the credit and reputation of the confederated States." One of the key figures of the postwar era, Washington's former close aide Alexander Hamilton, took a strong stance on reintegrating the Loyalists. Hamilton—who had also argued against retaliation in the Huddy-Asgill affair—had returned to New York towards the end of the war, studied law in Albany, and quickly gained admission to the bar. Short and slight, elegant and charming, the twenty-nine-year-old Hamilton was a rising lawyer in a city seeking to negotiate the transition from war to peace.[23]

A decade earlier, on the eve of the war, Hamilton, then a precocious student at King's College (today's Columbia University), had witnessed an incensed crowd march on the house of the college president, whom they suspected of leading a Loyalist network. They apparently intended to tar and feather him. Hamilton held off the mob so their target could escape over a fence. With popular violence continuing to grow, Hamilton cautioned that in politically turbulent times, when "the passions of men are worked up to an uncommon pitch there is great danger of fatal extremes."[24]

As Loyalists in New York and elsewhere were once again being tarred and feathered, Hamilton took up his pen. Writing under the apt pseudonym "Phocion"—the Athenian soldier who served a great general and later advocated conciliation with former foes— Hamilton warned of the diplomatic, political, economic, and moral costs of persecuting the Loyalists. In the face of violence and legal discrimination, he urged tolerance. Hamilton insisted that the rights of Loyalists be safeguarded: this was the best way to preserve liberty and stability in the new nation. Embittered Americans, he observed, allowed their thirst for "revenge, cruelty, persecution, and perfidy" to drive arbitrary expulsions and disfranchisement without trial by jury. Instead, law, order, and justice must prevail over "the little vindictive selfish mean passions of a few." In addition, as the "world has its eye upon America," the new republic needed to "justify the revolution by its fruits"—even, and especially, by integrating its former internal enemies.[25]

The future U.S. Treasury secretary also feared the drain of capital if Loyalists left en masse, and worried it would create obstacles to revitalizing Anglo-American trade: "Our state will feel for twenty years at least, the effects of the popular phrenzy." Besides, if America failed to honor its obligations under the peace treaty, might not Britain do the same? Indeed, a decade later, during the negotiations over the so-called Jay Treaty with the U.S. that was designed to regulate trade, avert a future war, and resolve issues outstanding since 1783, the British government cited U.S.

land seizures from Loyalists to justify why it had been maintaining military outposts in the U.S.-Canadian borderlands in breach of the 1783 accord.

New Yorkers hotly debated the relative merits of revenge and reconciliation in the immediate postwar era. The state legislature had passed a Confiscation Act in 1779 and the so-called Citation Act in 1782, which deprived Loyalists of their property and impeded British creditors' chances to collect Patriot debts. In 1782 and 1783, as Loyalist and Patriot refugees encountered each other in large numbers for the first time in years in New York City, Patriots who had fled the British occupation demanded back rent and compensation for damage and theft. Robert R. Livingston, the chancellor (highest judicial officer) of New York, shared Hamilton's concerns about the exodus of Loyalists and its impact on the city and state. He attributed the "violent spirit of persecution" in some Patriots to "a blind spirit of revenge & resentment," but "in more it is the most sordid interest. One wishes to possess the house of some wretched Tory, another fears him as a rivale in his trade or commerce, & a fourth wishes to get rid of his debts by shaking of his creditor or to reduce the price of Living by depopulating the town." In peace, as in war, Americans pursued private feuds under the thin veil of a patriotic cloak. Hamilton's frustration with the situation is apparent in a letter he wrote to Gouverneur Morris in February 1784. New Yorkers were focusing their energies on the wrong projects, Hamilton complained: instead of improving "our polity and commerce, we are labouring to contrive methods to mortify and punish the tories and to explain away treaties."[26]

In a test case that has since become famous in U.S. legal history, in 1784, Hamilton defended a rich Loyalist against the Patriot widow Elizabeth Rutgers. In 1776, Rutgers had fled New York, abandoning her family's alehouse and brewery. By 1778, British merchants refitted the derelict brewery at a cost of £700; from 1780, they paid rent to the British Army. A fire in 1783 caused £4,000 worth of damage. At war's end, Rutgers returned to New York City to sue one of the British merchants for £8,000 in back rent under New York's new Trespass Act, which allowed Patriots to seek compensation from individuals who had occupied or damaged their property behind enemy lines. The Patriots had returned with a vengeance to the Loyalists' former stronghold, and they left no one in any doubt about who was in charge.[27]

Hamilton argued that the wartime owners had restored the derelict property and acted properly under British martial law. He articulated what was to become the nationalist theory of federalism: international treaties and national laws were higher authorities to which all statutory and state laws had to conform; if the two conflicted, international and national law trumped state law. New York's Trespass Act contravened the peace treaty, which prohibited punitive suits. Laying out an early version of the doctrine of judicial review, Hamilton argued that the court therefore needed to strike it down. In a split verdict, the judge granted Rutgers back rent, but only for the period up to 1780. In doing so, although he did not strike down the law, he implicitly validated Hamilton's argument. Throughout the 1780s, Hamilton's law practice flourished as he defended dozens of Loyalists under the Confiscation, Citation, and Trespass Acts. The radical Patriot press vilified him as a Tory, and rumors circulated of assassination plots. But when in 1787 the New York legislature repealed the Trespass Act, assemblyman Alexander Hamilton had the satisfaction of cosponsoring the bill. Practicing what he preached, Hamilton would soon appoint the former Loyalist Tench Coxe of Pennsylvania as his assistant secretary at the Treasury.[28]

* * *

As American communities transitioned from a decade of civil war, they each needed to reconcile competing demands—from wartime grievances in need of resolution, to yearnings for peace and reconciliation, to economic self-interest. New Haven, Connecticut, is a case in point. In the summer of 1779, Major General Sir William Tryon, formerly the royal governor of New York, had launched strikes against several Connecticut coastal towns in an (unsuccessful) attempt to draw Washington's army out of its defensive position in the Highlands. Tryon's British, Hessian, and Loyalist troops raided New Haven, then America's sixth-largest town. The British considered western Connecticut a Loyalist stronghold, and a fair share of New Haven's population, including some prominent and prosperous citizens as well as Yale College students and graduates, did not support the Revolution. Now Patriots, Loyalists, and uncommitted locals alike were forced to decide whether to take a stand, collaborate, or flee. Amid frantic looting, sexual assaults on women, and the gratuitous killing of some unarmed men, political loyalties and personal ties alike were being tested. Elizur Goodrich, a Yale senior in one of the local companies that had tried to delay the British assault, was wounded in his leg. As he looked for medical assistance, a British soldier bayoneted him. Elizur managed to escape to the house of Abiather Camp, who, though a Loyalist, was friends with the younger man's father. Camp tended to Elizur's bayonet wound and sheltered him from further assault. (He'd survive to become a congressman and Yale professor of law.) The Loyalist aunt of a local Patriot officer braved enemy troop visits unharmed. One man who had been unable to flee because of his wife's illness pretended to be a friend to King George and thus successfully protected his property from looting. But a Mr. Kennedy, also a well-known Loyalist, who was said to have rejoiced at the arrival of the British, was robbed of his silver shoe buckles. When he protested this unexpected treatment, he was stabbed to death.[29]

Once the invaders had moved out, the physical damage at New Haven was valued at some £25,000. However, a large proportion of claims concerned the personal property of residents rather than their homes or public structures. And at least half of those losses were the result of neighbor-on-neighbor looting: Loyalists had pilfered under the cover of the British invasion; Patriots had looted and burned deserted homes, including many owned by fellow Patriots who had fled. For months afterward, citizens offered rewards for the return of goods, "[p]lundered by some of the militia" or, as they would delicately phrase it, "[l]ost . . . immediately after the enemy left this town."[30]

After the raids, the citizens of New Haven asked themselves whom they could still trust in their community. Not only had neighbors brazenly stolen from neighbors, but a substantial number of men appeared to have remained in town during the raid without offering resistance. Later that summer, the town meeting launched a fraternization inquiry. Three dozen men gave satisfactory reasons for choosing not to flee or defend the town. Twenty men had made forgivable errors of judgment in staying behind rather than intending to "put themselves under the protection of the Enemies of the united States of America." However, at least five men failed to give adequate reasons for their conduct during the raid. And a final dozen or so had stayed in New Haven during the raid but had either been captured by the British or had since relocated. Indeed, entire Loyalist families had left town with the British invaders, such as the wealthy Yale alumnus Joshua Chandler (whom the Patriots had previously imprisoned as a Loyalist), his wife, and their seven children, chief among them two sons who had guided the invaders to New Haven. Unlike the military commanders who had covered up the destruction of Norfolk earlier in the war, the citizens of New Haven confronted the messiness of civil war head-on while it was still raging all around them.[31]

In a move fairly typical of communities immediately after the war, the New Haven town meeting in 1783 voted against the return of any "Miscreants who have deserted their country's cause, and joined the enemies of this and the United States of America, during the late contest." But as early as 1784, elections produced mixed results: the mayor, two aldermen, and five members of the Common Council were Patriots; two aldermen and eight councillors were Loyalists; five councillors were "Flexibles but in heart Whigs," meaning Patriots. With the local Loyalists' political rehabilitation well under way, Ezra Stiles, president of Yale, suspected "an Endeavor silently to bring Tories into an Equality & Supremacy among the Whigs."[32]

A month after those city elections, on March 8, 1784, the citizens of New Haven formed a committee to "[c]onsider the Propriety and Expediency of admitting as inhabitants of this Town persons who in the Course of the Late war adhered to the cause of Great Britain against the united States." The actual work had evidently already been done, for the committee produced a detailed report that same day. They stressed states' rights and emphasized that under Connecticut law it was for individual towns to decide who could live there. A "Spirit of real peace and philanthropy towards our [Loyalist] Countrymen" had guided the definitive peace treaty and the congressional recommendation that states enforce it. Since the "National Question" on which Loyalists and Patriots had differed had been settled "authoritatively in favor of the United States," the committee recommended that New Haven admit as inhabitants any Loyalists judged to be "of fair character" and who would be "good and usefull members of Society, and faithfull citizens of this State." But there were clear limits to forgiveness: anyone who had "committed unauthorized and lawless plundering or Murder," and anyone who had "waged war against these United States, contrary to the laws and Usuages of Civilized Nations," would not obtain residency or citizens' rights.[33]

Evoking the same language of virtuous warfare that Congress, the army leadership, and wartime propagandists had employed throughout the conflict, the committee continued its high-minded rhetoric: "In our opinion no nation, however distinguished for prowess in arms and success in war, can be truly great, unless it is also distinguished for Justice and Magnanimity. None can properly claim to be just who violate their most solemn treaties, or to be magnanimous who persecute a conquered and submitting enemy." A desire for revenge, however understandable in light of recent sufferings, must be laid aside for a more measured approach. Given the importance of the city's port and of commerce to New Haven's prosperity, welcoming Loyalists back was also economically prudent. A disgruntled President Stiles recorded in his diary: "This day Town-Meeting voted to readmit the Tories."[34]

Even with the Loyalists' reintegration proceeding apace, local preachers ensured that Patriots also kept fresh the memory of their wartime sufferings. On Independence Day in 1787, David Daggett vividly remembered Tryon's raids:

> There the unrelenting foe, with more than hellish malice, assaulted a venerable, a respectable old man, plunged a poignant dagger in his body, and left him languishing, and languishing he died!—Here one of your neighbours was in a moment struck dead!—and yonder you saw one, whom you had long known, weltering in his blood, till his agonizing struggles had stretched him a breathless corps!—Such scenes we have beheld, and such have been realized in many other towns.[35]

Remembering the Patriots' sacrifice was compatible, then, with reconciliation. Indeed, the former was a necessary part of the latter, as the Revolution's winners reminded their former opponents that they owed their reintegration to the magnanimity of their victorious, morally superior neighbors. In the wake of a violent nation-building conflict, the Loyalists' suffering, by contrast, would not be recalled in the future story of America's founding.

＊ ＊ ＊

The economic argument put forward by proponents of reintegration in New Haven was also a catalyst for treaty compliance elsewhere, from New Jersey to South Carolina. Communities realized that their war-torn economies would benefit from the return of skilled and specialized professionals as well as consumers, regardless of their wartime loyalties. On the initiative of merchants, the New Jersey state assembly established Perth Amboy and Trenton as free ports, exempt from customs duties, and passed liberal citizenship legislation in the hope of attracting Loyalist refugees and merchants. Alas, only two dozen or so Loyalist merchants made the move before federal regulations prohibited free ports after 1789. At a local level, individuals who could provide a community with particular services—whether as merchants, shopkeepers, doctors, or lawyers—on the whole seemed able to reintegrate more easily.

But then, Dr. Samuel Stearns, a Loyalist physician from Paxton, Pennsylvania, who returned there in the fall of 1784, was arrested and imprisoned for nearly three years. Not every professional was welcomed home with open arms.[36]

Those leaders of the early United States who, like Hamilton, favored a policy of reconciliation and reintegration worked with the states to repeal discriminatory laws that undermined the peace accord. New Hampshire, Connecticut, New Jersey, the Carolinas, and Georgia permitted many Loyalists to return over the course of the 1780s. Their confiscated property was restored and they earned citizenship rights. Eventually even Benjamin Franklin, who in Paris had most strongly opposed any concessions to the Loyalists, supported their reintegration as president of the Supreme Executive Council (or quasi governor) of Pennsylvania, where a 1786 citizenship law allowed individuals who had refused to take Patriot oaths during the Revolution to become citizens upon swearing a loyalty oath. However, Franklin's newfound magnanimity did not extend to his son. En route back from France to America in the summer of 1785, Benjamin had met with William for a few days in Southampton, England. The father used their first encounter in years to force his son to sell him his American landholdings in settlement of debts owed. In 1788, Benjamin effectively disinherited William for the "part he acted against me in the late War."[37]

If the Franklins were never reconciled, remnants of official anti-Loyalist policies survived in many states at least until the turn of the new century. So did unofficial persecution. Throughout the 1780s and '90s, there were "feverish witch hunts for traitors who allegedly sought to reverse the verdict of the war," as Hamilton's biographer Ron Chernow has put it. Until the early nineteenth century, anti-Loyalist sentiment also remained a useful tactical weapon in elections. Yet, despite such undercurrents of animosity, the founding generation did gradually integrate their new nation.[38]

Among the returnees experiencing harmonious homecomings were now-forgotten Loyalists like Mary Robie, who in July 1784 moved back to Ward Chipman's native Marblehead, Massachusetts:

"We are hardly a minute alone," Mary reported happily, "continually some old acquaintance is calling to congratulate us." Her family's former debtors selectively paid off loans. Mary encouraged her husband, Thomas, to return, too, and open a retail store, considering that the wartime discord was already "buried in total oblivion[;] we hear every day of people who wish to return, but of none that object to it," as locals were "both gentle & simple." By 1787, Mary was running her own dry goods store; Thomas is documented as a resident by 1791.[39]

In Poughkeepsie, a community in rural New York where wartime allegiances had been divided, but also unstable and malleable, at least twenty-seven Loyalists had had their property confiscated. Twenty more had spent some part of the war in prison; another dozen or so went into exile in Canada. In May 1783, Poughkeepsie's inhabitants formed committees, as one man described the tense situation, to "prevent the plunderers, and Murderers (which now daringly attempt to Schelter themselves among the no less *rascially* Cru who have hitherto been distinguishd as peaceable Tories) from Working them selves into the company of the Worthy Citizens." One particularly notorious Loyalist received death threats to discourage him from returning to practice law. But eventually the community integrated the majority of those among their families and neighbors who had previously offered vocal opposition to, or less than consistent support for, the Revolution— although, crucially, all but one of these were politically ostracized and never again able to obtain even the most lowly local offices.[40]

Elsewhere, those perceived to have been only moderately offensive Loyalists were reintegrated fairly comprehensively within a decade or so of the war's conclusion. Roeloff Josiah Eltinge, a shopkeeper in the small town of New Paltz in the rural Hudson Valley, had been tried by a Revolutionary committee in 1776 for refusing to accept Continental currency at his family's general store. Following two years in various prisons, Eltinge declined a final chance to take a Patriot oath of allegiance in 1778 and was banished to the British lines in New York City. In May 1784, Eltinge, along with two dozen other cast-out New York Loyalists, was permitted to return home. Eltinge—who had never taken up arms for the British, and whose property had not been confiscated—resumed his business in New Paltz; by the 1790s, he was sufficiently rehabilitated to serve in elected local office. By then, New York had repealed the 1784 act that had barred from voting and holding office any men who had served with the British, outfitted a ship, left the state, or otherwise joined the enemy; in 1792, the state finally lifted the banishment of all New York Loyalists.[41]

Even some of the more prominent Loyalists succeeded in being gradually reintegrated, and eventually assumed public responsibilities. Andrew Bell, a Loyalist landowner and lawyer from Perth Amboy in New Jersey, served during the Revolution as confidential secretary to Sir Henry Clinton and Sir Guy Carleton. Andrew also saw military action, including in the Battle of Monmouth in 1778. The following year Andrew's sister Cornelia married New Jersey's attorney general William Paterson. Cornelia's father objected to her marriage to a leading Patriot, but Paterson and Andrew Bell both promised to tolerate Cornelia's connections; Paterson even facilitated the siblings' illegal wartime correspondence. At the same time, as one of the state's key legal officers responsible for prosecuting Loyalists, Paterson indicted Andrew Bell in absentia and started the process by which the property he had inherited from his father would be confiscated. Neither Andrew nor Cornelia seemed to waver in their opposing political convictions, but neither did they attempt to convert each other. One of Cornelia's most prized possessions was a miniature portrait her brother sent her of himself: holding and wearing the intimate representation connected Cornelia closely to Andrew, at the same time as it reminded her sorely of their separation.[42]

When peace came, Andrew pondered his options. Should he stay in America, where his prospects were "but small," or should he go into exile and hope for British compensation for his loyal service? He weighed economic self-interest against the emotional cost of "leaving my dear relations and friends." In July 1783, the siblings were finally reunited after seven years: the three days were "the most valued of my whole life," reflected Andrew, grateful that his brother-in-law had permitted the meeting. In Andrew's last known letter to Cornelia, he later asked her to solicit her husband's help in obtaining documentation to support his claim for British compensation; Paterson did indeed assist with valuations. But a few weeks later, Cornelia died after giving birth to a son; she was twenty-eight. In spring 1784, her widower, William—who would go on to represent New Jersey at the Constitutional Conventions and serve the state as senator and governor—encouraged Andrew to return to his native New Jersey and meet his deceased sister's children. Bell did indeed resettle in Perth Amboy, where he became a successful merchant. His integration proceeded apace, so that from 1806 until his death in 1842 he even served as surveyor general for the East Jersey proprietors.

Other Loyalists reactivated their prewar connections with men who had since risen to leadership positions in the United States. The New York Loyalist lawyer Peter Van Schaack had been a classmate, at King's College, of later Founding Fathers such as John Jay, Gouverneur Morris, and Robert R. Livingston. After 1774, Van Schaack first helped administer the Continental Association but opposed independence—as, initially, did his friend John Jay. When he refused to swear an oath of allegiance in 1778, Van Schaack went into exile in England. In 1782, he sought reconciliation with Jay, then serving as a U.S. diplomat in Europe. (Jay's own family, it's worth remembering, included Loyalists.) Jay explained to Van Schaack that, "as an independent American, I considered all who were not for us, and you among the rest, as against us: yet be assured that John Jay did not cease to be a friend to Peter Van Schaack." By the time the two men were reunited in London in October 1783, Van Schaack had become convinced that the British political system was corrupt; finally, he, too, embraced American independence. When Van Schaack returned to New York City in 1785, Jay awaited him at the pier; their rekindled friendship would endure for another four decades. With both his citizenship rights and his previously revoked law license restored, Van Schaack soon practiced the law again. Although Van Schaack did not hold political office—unlike some prominent ex-Loyalists who rose to state or even national positions, such as Tench Coxe—he advised New York officials on the state's evolving judicial system; he also taught dozens of aspiring lawyers at his home, even after going blind in 1792. As the country celebrated half a century of independence in 1826, Van Schaack received a doctorate in law from Columbia College.[43]

And yet, as both the Revolution's winners and, increasingly, its losers helped build the postwar United States, scars continued to mark the deep divisions that so recently had rent American society.

During his journey from New York to Massachusetts, Ward Chipman had noted the toll the war had taken on America's cultural institutions, from Harvard College to the library of a synagogue in Newport, Rhode Island. Chipman also bemoaned deforested landscapes and lamented the ruins of Fairfield, Connecticut, which "must have been a very beautiful Town before it was burnt." These traces of the war remained visible decades after it had ended. In New York City, the Wallabout Bay beaches kept revealing the skeletons of American prisoners as they washed out of their shallow graves, initially with "fragments of flesh not quite consumed."[1]

Eight years later, in 1791, when he toured the Southern states, President George Washington remembered the Revolutionary War dead on the battlefields at Camden and Augusta. At Savannah, he noted that changes to the landscape, such as the "cutting away of the woods," were already beginning to obscure the lines of defense and attack during the Franco-American siege a mere twelve years earlier. As white settlers and Native Americans began moving back into frontier regions ravaged by war, they rebuilt log houses and tended to fruit trees growing from stumps. Yet, at the same time, travelers in the South Carolina backcountry passed "trees, their limbs cropped and torn by the balls, on their messages of death," and found the "unburied bones of men and horses" strewn across silent battlefields. Children playing in the streets of New York kept picking up the skeletal parts of sugarhouse prisoners until the construction boom of the 1840s, when locals had pieces of wood from the old sites of suffering carved into walking sticks before the buildings disappeared. In that same decade, the "mouldering relics" of Lieutenant Boyd, whom Native Americans had tortured and killed during Sullivan's campaign, were exhumed in the Genesee Valley and reburied in Rochester.[2]

Even after the devastation wrought by the Civil War, traces of the century-old war continued to surface. Americans learned that General Hugh Mercer's "blood still stains the floor of the room in which he died." And in a building implicated in the 1778 Baylor Massacre, "some of the posts and beams still retained the bloody evidence of British inhumanity." (Colonel Baylor himself had died in 1784, aged thirty-two, from complications of the injuries he had received during the British assault.) When workers at the start of the twentieth century dug up the timbered remains of the prison ship *Jersey* from underneath fourteen feet of silt, fund-raisers turned them into poignant mementos in their campaign for a national monument to the prisoner-martyrs.[3]

* * *

Individuals and communities on all sides bore the scars of revolution and war. In peace, the Patriots continued to tell themselves the stories that had carried them through the conflict. In 1793, Elias Boudinot, formerly commissioner for prisoners and president of the Congress, rhapsodized that those "who have mingled their blood together, as it were in one rich stream . . . must surely be more than brethren—it is a union cemented by blood." Violence and the experience of violence were central to the project of nation building. The memory of blood shed at the hands of the cruel British helped the victors identify as Americans.[4]

Within just decades of the Revolution, the former rivals were again at war. In the War of 1812, the United Kingdom sought to contain a rising rival power and limit the United States' growth in trade, maritime prowess, and continental expansion; for the United States, the conflict was a war for national self-determination, "sovereignty over its citizens, and the right to be treated as an equal by European nations." At one level, writes the historian Alan Taylor, the struggle was another "civil war between competing visions of America: one still loyal to the empire and the other defined by its republican revolution against that empire." Memories of American Revolutionary violence were never far from the minds of those participating in the renewed conflict. The House of Assembly of British Upper Canada, where many Loyalists had settled after 1783, condemned the Americans as "a people whose lands are manured with the blood of our friends and kinsmen, who drove our wives and children from their houses into the woods, or threw them into dungeons." For their part, American writers invoked the Baylor Massacre to inspire renewed militant patriotism. Others drew a direct line from the Loyalists during the Revolution to "our internal enemies now." And as brothers, once again, confronted each other in battle, one former Loyalist commented after realizing he had killed his Patriot sibling: "served him right for fighting with the rebels, when the rest of his family fought for King George."[5]

While forging an identity around the excessive violence they had endured at the hands of the British, Americans scrubbed their own Revolutionary War record, which they celebrated as "untarnished with a single blood-speck of inhumanity." In 1815, one orator felt confident that "[o]ther revolutions have been conducted with sanguinary violence; ours with a spirit of dignified moderation, worthy of the cause, and characteristic of the nation. The patriots of the revolution were as humane as they were brave." Already the whitewashing was well under way.[6]

By this time, Americans had started paying attention to their aging veterans. With independence secured, a nation born in violence celebrated the sacrifices of its suffering soldiers. As they applied for federal pensions, Continental veterans proudly displayed their physical scars. The aptly named Noel Battles listed successive injuries bravely borne: at Brandywine, he had received "only a flesh wound" in the arm; a musket ball hitting his knee at Germantown "kept him lame only for a few days"; and when a "sharp stick [ran] through the fleshy part of his arm" as he was negotiating the abatis at Stony Point, he had it removed in but a few moments. Other men described wounds that had left them permanently impaired, with muscles never fully healed after a bayonet stab, or strenuous work causing pain and shortness of breath. During their depositions, some veterans literally bared the scars that gunshot or bayonet wounds had permanently inscribed on their bodies.[7]

Public commemorations of the war, too, highlighted the physical consequences of British cruelty. It is no coincidence that the first Revolutionary War monuments were those at Lexington, Massachusetts (1799); Paoli, Pennsylvania (1817); and Fort Griswold at Groton, Connecticut (1826–30)—all firmly fixed in the Patriot imagination as sites of British barbarity. The monuments imprint in stone the sacrifice of a particular type of Revolutionary martyr. In 1825, at an event honoring Patriot heroes of the alleged massacre at Fort Griswold in 1781, one survivor wore the vest in which he had been run through from side to side; it was also "perforated by a musket-ball." Reviving the Revolutionary era's creative focus on documenting wounds, newspapers pointed out that the "numerous scars on these venerable men were striking memorials of the severity of the conflict and too plainly depicted the brutal character of the enemy." At the cornerstone ceremony at Groton, a crowd of 8,000 applauded "the small remnant of mutilated and grey Survivors of the Massacre."[8]

More quietly, and a decade later, one "old man, bent down by age and infirmities, was almost daily seen with a small paper which he occasionally handed to some of the passengers" on the Brooklyn ferry. In asking for charity, his note told how he "had lost a leg and received thirteen bayonet wounds" when defending Fort Griswold.[9]

* * *

While Patriots displayed their old scars as cause for national pride, Loyalists had little choice but to hide their trauma. The dominant national narrative of Patriot martyrdom branded the Loyalists as un-patriotic, un-American dissenters. They were effectively eliminated from public discourse, and a mantle of collective amnesia fell over the violence that Patriots had inflicted on their neighbors.

We find little trace in the American historical consciousness of the threats, physical abuse, and imprisonment endured by thousands. The Patriots controlled the story of Revolution, war, and peace—in monuments and histories, in Revolutionary parades and Fourth of July speeches. While the Patriots wore the scars of their own war wounds openly, the Loyalists did not nurture a melancholy folklore of loss like the Jacobites after the 1745 rebellion or American Southerners after the Civil War. The few Loyalists who sought to spread their version of events found no American publishers. The price for the losers' reintegration in America was to keep their own scars hidden.[10]

Only in Britain could Loyalists reveal their scarred backs and seared foreheads. It was here that they dared share their stories of persecution, torture, and loss. And it was here, in their place of refuge, that exiled Loyalists built monuments such as the memorial in Westminster Abbey to the prominent South Carolinian Loyalist William Wragg, who in 1777 had been banished—"compell'd to leave his distrest family and ample fortune," as the inscription tells the visitor to Britain's coronation church. Sailing for England via Holland, Wragg was shipwrecked and drowned just twelve hours off the Dutch coast; his slave Tom Skene saved Wragg's infant son by supporting him on a piece of wreckage until they were both washed ashore—a scene vividly illustrated on the monument's frontal relief.[11]

Britons could also follow the story of John Malcom, whose stinking skin flaps eventually earned him a respectable annuity and a commission as an ensign in a company of invalids at Plymouth. When the government suspended wartime pension payments to Loyalists in 1782, officials took pity on Malcom "for the uncommon ill treatment which he sufferd being the first Man who was tarrd & feathered & escaping narrowly with his Life." As "he appears to us to be in some degree insane," they even topped up his pay. Malcom died in the winter of 1788; not once had he returned to his wife, Sarah, and their children in America.[12]

In 1783, Parliament had established a commission to evaluate Loyalists' claims for property and income lost due to their allegiance to Britain. The commission examined the accounts of more than 3,200 people, including nearly 500 women. In front of commissioners, and in reams of written statements accompanied by certificates from British officers and witness testimony, Loyalists exposed their battered bodies and traumatized psyches to plead for imperial support. John Bevins, who had served with a North Carolinian volunteer force, "because of his sufferings has almost lost hearing, and fears intellect has been weakened." Robert Palmer, a British colonial official and landowner in North Carolina, had left his son behind to administer the family property, but, facing constant Patriot threats, the younger Palmer had taken to the bottle and become mentally ill. Papers concerning Beaufort Smith, a former naval officer from Port Royal, South Carolina, explained that he had died from "oppression and grief having been stript of all his property and Employments." Others blamed Patriot terror for men suffering memory lapses or committing suicide, and for women miscarrying, bearing deaf and dumb children, or dying of a broken heart. A total of 2,291 Loyalists eventually received compensation for property, and 588 a pension. In this unprecedented paternalistic effort to subsidize refugee subjects from abroad, the British state ultimately paid out more than £3 million, a sum equivalent to roughly 15 percent of government spending on the armed forces in 1782.[13]

The Empire's paternalism didn't just embrace white Loyalists. At the end of the war, Britain had honored its obligations towards several thousand of the surviving blacks who had supported its cause, evacuating some 3,000 free blacks to New Brunswick and Nova Scotia, and more than 5,000 to England. William Pitt, the British prime minister from 1784, explained afterward to John Adams that the Empire had protected black Loyalists "in obedience to the dictates of the higher law of humanity." As the historian Christopher L. Brown concludes, "[T]he British government had learned that displays of benevolence toward liberated Africans could help sanctify the pursuit of national interest" by accruing moral capital after defeat in war.[14]

To be sure, in Loyalist petitions, black people feature most commonly as items of lost property catalogued by their former masters. But among the Loyalist claimants were also forty-seven black men. Even humble white Loyalists faced difficulties proving their record of wartime service with limited connections and resources, and often limited literacy, too. For black Loyalists, racial prejudice added to these obstacles. Only one black man—Scipio Handley, the former Charleston fishmonger who had been shot in the leg during the siege of Savannah—ultimately received property compensation, worth £20. Peter Anderson, who had survived the travails of Dunmore's campaign, and later Savannah and Charleston, and then Yorktown, too, ended up in London, aged thirty-nine, unable to find work: "I am realy starving about the Streets Having Nobody to give me a morsel of bread." With Lord Dunmore's personal intervention, Anderson obtained £10, making him one of twenty blacks to receive small sums of money. And Shadrack Furman, who had been crippled and blinded for his loyal service in Virginia, could be heard fiddling in London's alleys until he was awarded an annual pension of £18 for life.[15]

While the war offered at least some African-American soldiers the opportunity for a different life, for Native Americans the Revolutionary War was but another chapter in their painful history since colonization. Native American communities had barely any time to heal from their wartime wounds before renewed violence engulfed them. Whether they had supported or opposed the United States, Native Americans would lament the Revolution as a time, in Colin G. Calloway's apt litany, of "[b]urned villages and crops, murdered chiefs, divided councils and civil wars, migrations, towns and forts choked with refugees, economic disruption, breaking of ancient traditions, losses in battle and to disease and hunger, betrayal to their enemies." The peace treaty of 1783 made no mention of Indians. But with the treaty, Britain had agreed to cede the forts on the Great Lakes, including Niagara and Oswego, to the United States, thus abandoning most of the Six Nations in U.S. territory. By 1783, some 3,500 of the Iroquois refugees who had survived Sullivan's campaign of terror and the subsequent winter were settled at Loyal Village, eight miles south of Niagara, as well as at Buffalo Creek and near Lake Erie. The threat of Indian violence against British interests in the borderland was partly responsible for the British holding on to the forts for another decade. (London justified this treaty breach by pointing out that the U.S. illegally prevented British merchants and Loyalists from reclaiming debts and property.)[16]

Britain did relocate a group of Mohawks to Grand River farther west and built a school and church for these wartime allies. Such protection was short-lived, however, as American settlers increasingly threatened Indian settlements. With the Jay Treaty of 1794, Britain finally fulfilled its obligations under the 1783 accord and abandoned the Great Lakes forts, and with them the borderland Indians. As the Treaty of Greenville the following year ceded Indian lands to the U.S. in what today is the state of Ohio, President Washington's secretary of war, Henry Knox, admitted: "[O]ur modes of population have been more destructive to the Indian natives than the conduct of the conquerors of Mexico and Peru." As late as 1796, one eight-year-old Cherokee boy was found screaming uncontrollably when a white man visited his family: the boy's relatives had shared tales of their wartime suffering.

As the expanding American empire of liberty asserted its territorial claims and embraced its white racial identity, old wounds in Indian country reopened. Iroquoia would face more violence, dispossession, and ethnic cleansing until, by the mid-nineteenth century, the Iroquois in New York were reduced to a few disparate reservations. Native Americans elsewhere in the United States formed new confederacies with former enemies as they braced themselves for further encroachments on their lands or migrated, as did the Ohio Valley Indians who moved to more sparsely settled areas west and south. But by the 1820s the large-scale "Removal" of Indians west of the Mississippi was well under way.[17]

* * *

On both sides of the Atlantic, the Revolution prompted a moral reckoning of sorts. For the British Empire, the loss of America was a catalyst for broader reforms. Historians largely agree that the defeat "caused much introspective reflection, leading to a campaign for moral regeneration," in Stephen Conway's words, and a shift towards a "humane, civilized, and regulated despotism" in an empire that was moving decisively east and towards majority nonwhite populations. Having held its own against France and Spain on multiple fronts, in the definitive peace of fall 1783 the British Empire not only retained most of its Caribbean possessions but strengthened its position in India by adding the Dutch base at Negapatam—a portent of a massive expansion in Asia. At the same time, defeat in a war in which both former fellow subjects and British skeptics had critiqued the country for abandoning humanitarian standards focused the attention of the political class and the wider public on the big moral questions facing their empire: slavery and abolition, and corrupt exploitation and crimes against humanity in British India.[18]

The man sent to restore a sense of imperial probity in India in 1786—as governor-general of Bengal and commander in chief of British forces in India—was none other than General Cornwallis, who had emerged from the American war with his reputation largely intact. Indeed, Cornwallis became something of an "imperial troubleshooter," next dispatched to Dublin during the 1798 Irish uprising. While Germain, Grey, and Ferguson had drawn on their previous experiences suppressing rebellious populations to advocate Roman severity and oversee controversial military encounters in America, Cornwallis condemned both sides in the Irish conflict for their bloodthirsty approach to the religious civil war. After defeating a French invasion attempt and helping end the uprising, Cornwallis advocated a general amnesty, though not without executing some of the rebellion's leaders, as he had done previously in the American South. By then, the total wars of the French Revolutionary period had spurred a pacifist movement in Britain, for which the antiwar petitions and the critique of specific ways and means of war during the American Revolutionary War had helped pave the way.[19]

The British Empire's abolition of the slave trade in 1807, and of slavery itself in 1834—milestones that built on the moral reckoning following the American war—contrasted sharply with slavery's entrenchment and expansion in the United States. Although thousands of blacks had fought on the Patriot side, the United States failed to resolve the contradiction between a war waged in the name of liberty and the enslavement of Africans and their descendants in America. As the number of slaves in the country grew, tripling from 1775 to 1825, Southern women petitioning the authorities to forgive their banished Loyalist husbands emphasized that their menfolk had helped return stolen slaves to their owners during the British occupation. Hoping that their contributions to preserving "white supremacy," writes Cynthia Kierner, might "compensate for their political errors," these women invested in a vision of the United States as a slaveholding society that in 1787 was enshrined in the Constitution.[20]

The United States did draw some moral and practical lessons from its experience of wartime violence. The sufferings of combatants and captives on all sides—and of American civilians, too— had laid bare the fiction of civilized warfare. But the war had also demonstrated the value of appealing and adhering to humanitarian standards while relentlessly highlighting their violation by the enemy. Indeed, Britain's defeat was due not just to issues of manpower, the logistics of a war fought 3,000 miles across an ocean, imperial overstretch in a global conflict conducted without allies, and the inability to occupy and pacify half a continent with more than two million people. For even American setbacks during the war ultimately promoted American victory as the Revolutionaries used innovative forensic and polemical strategies to turn ruined towns, plundered farms, and the violated bodies of women and men into moral assets for the Revolutionary cause. An effective narrative of victimhood helped the Revolutionaries legitimate their rebellion, stir national sentiment, and rally support—even and especially when they suffered defeats. By contrast, the British were hampered both by divisions over what forms and degrees of violence to deploy, and by an unwillingness or inability to match the Americans in the war of rhetoric.

Returning American prisoners reminded their communities of one of the war's greatest tragedies: the captivity of tens of thousands that resulted in as many as half of all military deaths on the Patriot side and that exposed the severely limited capacities of the fledgling American state. After the war, the memory of those martyred on ships like the *Jersey* and others feared dead in Asia and Africa prompted the United States to begin thinking creatively about international law. When the United States signed a treaty of amity and commerce with Prussia in 1785, the document included an unprecedented clause setting guidelines for the treatment of prisoners of war in a future conflict. These regulations mandated minimum standards for food, accommodation, and fresh-air exercise, and guaranteed the belligerent powers access to prisoners in enemy hands. They banned the use of dungeons and prison ships, and outlawed transporting captives to Asia or Africa. Frederick the Great of Prussia and the United States were teaching "a good Lesson to Mankind," a satisfied John Adams proclaimed. Jefferson boasted that they were "humanizing by degrees" the law of nations. America continued to out-Europeanize her former imperial parent. At the moment of her violent birth, the United States led with the power of moral example—at least on the international stage.[21]

Remembering, Forgetting, Re-remembering

Until well into the nineteenth century, Americans kept memories of excessive British violence and Loyalist treachery alive. Anti-British sentiment was easily roused to score political points, whatever the issue: the British Empire's influence on American politics or commerce, its leadership in the fight against slavery, or opposition to U.S. territorial expansion. Democratic-Republican Jeffersonians favoring France brandished the bones of Revolutionary prisoners in their struggle with pro-British Federalists in New York. In turn, Federalists—prompted by frightful visions of the violence of the French Revolution and its American sympathizers, as well as by disturbances on the Pennsylvania frontier over the excise tax—threatened violence against the government's domestic opponents.[22]

The memory of the American Revolution could still serve to unify. But just as the war itself was not the uncomplicated nation-building effort of historical myth, the memory of the Revolution also had the potential to divide communities—along lines of class, race, and increasingly region. During the Civil War, evoking Revolutionary martyrs helped rally patriotic support in both the North and the South. When a Unionist monument in memory of the 1778 massacre of Patriots at Crooked Billet, Pennsylvania, was unveiled in 1861, the keynote speaker denounced the Loyalists: their treachery was outdone only by the current secessionists. The monument's inscription, too, explicitly linked the founding with the Union's acute crisis: "The Patriots of 1776 achieved our independence, their successors established it in 1812. We are now struggling for its perpetuation in 1861. *The Union must and shall be preserved.*" It was also during the Civil War that the German-American jurist Francis Lieber codified—and President Abraham Lincoln officially promulgated—the law of war; the Lieber Code prohibited torture and specified protections for prisoners and civilians.[23]

Only in the decades before World War I did historians and public intellectuals on both sides of the Atlantic finally transcend their narrow partisan perspectives on the Revolution. Moses Coit Tyler, a Yale graduate who later went on to hold the first U.S. chair in American history, had helped lay the groundwork in the 1860s when he spent three years lecturing in England. There he began a lifelong mission "to interpret American civilization to the British and vice versa." Crucially, Tyler acknowledged that the Loyalists were patriotic Americans with deeply held beliefs of their own. Tyler's new reading of Revolutionary history resonated in an era of Anglo-American rapprochement around the turn of the century, when East Coast elites sponsored a plethora of Anglophile organizations such as the Mayflower Society, the Daughters of the British Empire in the USA, the English-Speaking Union of the United States, and the Anglo-American Society. Foreign policy think tanks established in the wake of World War I, such as the Council on Foreign Relations and the Woodrow Wilson Foundation, would help to maintain these transatlantic ties.[24]

In 1914, there were even plans to celebrate a century of peace since the Treaty of Ghent that had ended the War of 1812 by erecting a statue of Queen Victoria in Washington, D.C., and one of George Washington in London. The outbreak of war, ironically, suspended the project, and Victoria's statue never arrived in the U.S. But a replica of Jean-Antoine Houdon's Washington statue was eventually placed outside the National Gallery at Trafalgar Square, resting on a patch of Virginian soil lest the Revolutionary general step on British ground. It was also in this period that more than one hundred American heiresses married into the British aristocracy. As historians, too, helped nurture a Special Relationship between the United Kingdom and the United States, they minimized the legacy of violence between kindred Anglo-Saxon peoples, adopting a pragmatic position that gradually gained traction in American public opinion.[25]

When the United States entered the world war in April 1917, any reference to Revolutionary-era British violence became politically toxic, as the Anglo-American alliance was key to defeating the German Empire. One man who suffered draconian consequences for ignoring that shift was the costume company owner turned film producer Robert Goldstein, a U.S. citizen of German-Jewish ancestry, who had just completed a Revolutionary War drama, *The Spirit of '76*. Ahead of the film's poorly timed May 1917 premiere in heavily Irish- and German-American Chicago, the chief of the city's police censorship board, Major Metallus Lucullus Cicero Funkhouser, demanded that Goldstein delete several scenes lest they arouse antagonism between the United States and the United Kingdom. Goldstein temporarily excised those scenes to satisfy the censors, but he reinserted them for the movie's public screenings in Los Angeles that fall. A district attorney then had the 12,000-foot film seized and Goldstein was arrested.[26]

In *U.S. v. "The Spirit of '76"*(!), Goldstein was tried under President Woodrow Wilson's Espionage Act. The jury was shown the offending scenes—apparently four seconds in a two-and-a-half-hour film—in slow motion: British soldiers bayoneting a baby, shooting unarmed women, and abusing teenage girls. Goldstein was found guilty of inciting mutiny though not of conspiracy to commit treason. The judge ruled that the film's purpose was to "incite hatred of England and England's soldiers." At a time when Anglo-American cooperation was essential, the film had the potential to deter Americans "from giving that full measure of sympathy . . . and sacrifice which is due to Great Britain [during] this great catastrophe." Goldstein's defense, that the soldiers in the contested scenes were in fact Hessians, fell predictably flat. He was sentenced to ten years in prison and a $5,000 fine; his film was destroyed and a few stills are all that remain.

When the *Times* of London in 1918 reported Goldstein's conviction under the headline "Cinema as German Agent. Slander of British Soldiers," it misrepresented—unwittingly, perhaps—the movie as "depicting British soldiers in the Irish rebellion [of 1798] bayoneting babies, and in general committing the outrages which the Germans committed in Belgium." That same year, Winston Churchill, himself the product of one of those transatlantic unions of British titles with American money, and then serving as the U.K. minister for munitions, invoked the American Revolutionary tradition and the importance of conducting wars steered by a moral compass: "We are bound by the principles for which we are fighting. Whatever the extent of our victory the German people will be protected by these principles. The Declaration of Independence, and all that it implies, must cover them." But, as Goldstein experienced, the protectors of the American Revolution's promise were by then enforcing a highly selective memory.[27]

After the war, President Wilson commuted Robert Goldstein's sentence to three years, but the producer never quite revived his career. The last trace of Goldstein appears to be a letter he sent from Nazi Berlin in 1935, begging the Academy of Motion Pictures for $9 so he might renew his passport. The plea seems to have remained unanswered.[28]

If British violence in the Revolutionary War was increasingly marginalized in American public memory, so, too, was the notion of America's first civil war. Witness the scene on Kings Mountain on October 7, 1930, the 150th anniversary of the battle. That day,

President Herbert Hoover became the first sitting commander in chief ever to visit a Revolutionary War site in the South. "This is a place of inspiring memories," Hoover told a crowd estimated at between 30,000 and 75,000:

> Here less than a thousand men, inspired by the urge of freedom, defeated a superior force entrenched in this strategic position. [In fact, the relative force size had been the reverse.] This small band of patriots turned back a dangerous invasion well designed to separate and dismember the united colonies. It was a little army and a little battle, but it was of mighty portent. History has done scant justice to its significance, which rightly should place it beside Lexington and Bunker Hill, Trenton, and York-town, as one of the crucial engagements in our long struggle for independence.

In his address, broadcast on the wireless, Hoover reassured Americans pummeled by the Great Depression that "[t]here need be no fear for the future of a Republic that seeks inspiration from the spirit of the men who fought at the Battle of Kings Mountain."

What the president failed to mention was that it was Americans who had been fighting Americans on the mountain. Nor was any reference made to battlefield irregularities or post-battle executions. Indeed, immediately after Hoover's address, and in the presence of a high-ranking representative from the British embassy, a memorial was dedicated to the British captain Patrick Ferguson. Once vilified, his body desecrated prior to burial, Ferguson was now heralded as "[a] Soldier of Military Distinction and Honor" and remembered by "the citizens of the United States of America in token of their appreciation of the bonds of friendship and peace between them and the citizens of the British Empire."[29]

On Kings Mountain in 1930, then, the scars of violent internal and international conflict seemed to be all but erased. By the end of that decade, with another world war on the horizon, historical fiction about the American Revolution by authors such as Robert Graves cast as the villains not British redcoats but savage Indians and brutish Hessians—and, still, the occasional Loyalist—or acknowledged that all sides committed atrocities, while stressing the unpopularity of the Revolutionary War in Britain. World War II also spurred a deepening interest in American history among British scholars who appreciated the traditions of democracy and liberty grounded in the spirit of '76. As Harry Cranbrook Allen, who held the oldest established chair for American history in the United Kingdom, put it: "In a fearful sense, Hitler made Americanists of us all."[30]

The broad trend continued with the Cold War, when so-called consensus historians offered new, counterprogressive interpretations of America's past that focused on unifying experiences. To consensus historians, the American Revolution was a "conservative and traditionalist response to recent provocations by England—indeed, hardly a revolution at all," and certainly very different from other modern revolutions, like those in France and Russia. This American Revolution was a restrained struggle over ideals, in which any acts of violence were carefully controlled by elites; the ordeals participants had suffered were largely written out of the story. Professional misremembering suited and entrenched the political moment.[31]

The violence of the Revolution briefly resurfaced as a topic of conversation in the 1960s and '70s as the nation prepared for the bicentennial celebrations in the midst of social and racial upheaval. Martin Luther King Jr. invoked the Boston Tea Party as "a massive act of civil disobedience." President Lyndon Johnson compared Selma to Lexington, only to use the announcement of his bicentennial commission to promote U.S. intervention in Southeast Asia in the name of America's global democratic mission. After President Richard Nixon's inauguration, African-American leaders such as Jesse Jackson urged blacks to boycott the celebrations, while an antiwar activist founded the Peoples Bicentennial Commission (PBC) to protest what they lambasted as the state's and corporate America's "Love It or Leave It Political Program," offer alternative commemorations, and claim a Revolutionary legacy for the New Left.

After the killing by the Ohio National Guard of four students at Kent State during a protest against the invasion of Cambodia, the antiwar movement seized the bicentennial spotlight. Agitated by Vietnam and the draft, they looked to the Revolutionaries' argument against standing armies and displayed posters of Revere's two-hundred-year-old Boston Massacre print. With protests spreading to Concord and to Bunker Hill, the Vietnam Veterans Against the War consciously evoked the Revolutionary traditions of citizen-soldiers and of popular dissent. As reenactors dumped tea in Boston Harbor at the bicentennial of the Tea Party in 1973, activists tarred and feathered an effigy of President Richard Nixon and burned it amid calls for his impeachment. For one urgent moment, Americans were conjuring up their heritage of violent protest as well as their founding era's struggle with the legitimate and illegitimate uses of military force.

With racial injustice baked into the very founding, and America's role in the world under intense scrutiny, the crisis over the commemorations continued right through 1976. That March, a Senate committee chaired by a Southern segregationist held hearings into "[t]he Attempt to Steal the Bicentennial" by the PBC. When a white teenager sought to impale a black man with an American flag at the Boston anti-busing riots the following month, a Pulitzer Prize–winning photograph of the scene captured the deep chasms in American society that no surge of state-programmed parades and fireworks could suture. With the Bicentennial thus mired in protests from the left and reactionary responses from the right, most professional historians stood aside with disdain, failing, in Jill Lepore's conclusion, to "offer an answer, a story, to a country that needed one." It was not until the Tea Party movement of the early twenty-first century that such large numbers of Americans would again get "so agitated about early American history"—and by then, a few historians, such as Lepore, had reclaimed an older tradition of professional historians writing thoughtfully and for broader audiences about the relationships between the past and the present.[32]

* * *

When I was first developing the ideas in this book as a Kluge Fellow at the Library of Congress in the fall of 2009, Tea Party activists, who equated rejecting health care reform with the 1773 Boston harbor protest, routinely greeted me on my way to Capitol Hill. I had recently moved from the United Kingdom, where I had spent the previous decade researching and teaching British history while frequently crossing the Atlantic to lecture, research, and visit friends. The Library's invitation would now afford me the privilege of researching my new book in the heart of the nation's capital, amid the hopeful atmosphere at the dawn of the first African-American presidency—and the noisy reminders of the strong currents of resentment it unleashed.

On entry to the United States to take up my fellowship, the immigration official probed the foundations of my scholar's visa: Why would a German specialist in British history write a book about the American Revolution? We discussed how this was a subject of fundamental importance in both British and American (and indeed world) history. And once he shared that his cousin was a Revolutionary reenactor, testing questions turned into a leisurely conversation about how an outsider—someone not brought up on the myths of either country—might approach the American Revolution. Rather than telling the story of the *Revolutionary War* just from Patriot perspectives, or narrating the history of the *American Rebellion* primarily on British terms, I explained, I wanted to shed light on aspects of this shared Anglo-American history that risked falling in the cracks between national—and nationalist—interpretations: to explode those myths that had been perpetuated by both sides.[33]

In the years since I had last been on extended fellowship in the U.S. in 2001—including on the East Coast during 9/11 and its aftermath—an American exceptionalism of a stridently imperialist and anti-internationalist flavor had been driving a neoconservative agenda of aggressively spreading the benefits of American freedom and democracy. Echoes of Revolutionary-era violence reverberated in warnings of the corrosive effect that America's nationalist approach was having on her influence in the world.

Against the backdrop of the Second Gulf War, "extraordinary rendition," and enhanced interrogation of "unlawful combatants," critics both within and outside the U.S. Congress were holding up George Washington's insistence on the humane treatment of prisoners of war to remind the nation of its core values. Arguments over the international role of the United States seemed to reflect, however obliquely, both the Revolution's horrors and its hopeful legacies.[34]

As they engaged global terrorism, Americans appeared to be clinging to a romanticized image of their original war—at least if the continued success of founders' biographies, and campaign narratives privileging Patriot perspectives, are anything to go by. But, as I have suggested in this book, we should be mindful of the messy and intrinsically violent nature of America's Revolution and first civil war. The violent story of the nation's not-so-immaculate conception reads as a cautionary tale for the American empire, with its persistent impulse to intervene in other countries' revolutions and civil conflicts, and its quest for nation building in little-understood regions. Seeing the contradictions of America's founding more clearly, and being alert to the complexities and potential pitfalls of pursuing moral objectives by violent means, advises an approach to global leadership less missionary and aggressive, more restrained, finely calibrated, and generously spirited.[35]

At a moment when Americans are beginning to face many painful truths about their society perhaps more directly than they have for some time, they might be ready to reappraise their nation's beginnings, too. If Americans let go of their last great romance with war, the whitewashing and strategic forgetting of Revolutionary-era violence may yield to a candid reckoning and honest remembering—one that allows both for proud, grateful celebration and for frank reflection on the ambiguities and the contradictory legacies of the nation's violent birth.

ABBREVIATIONS

Add MS   BL, Additional Manuscripts
ADM   TNA, Admiralty
AH   Alexander Hamilton
AHR   *American Historical Review*
Am. Arch.   Peter Force, *American archives: consisting of a collection*
                of authentick records, state papers, debates, and letters
                and other notices of publick affairs, the whole forming
                a documentary history of the origin and progress of the
                North American colonies; of the causes and accomplish-
                ment of the American revolution; and of the Constitution
                of government for the United States, to the final ratifica-
                tion thereof, 9 vols. (Washington, D.C., 1837–53)
AO   TNA, Audit Office
Bancroft   Bancroft Collection, NYPL
BF   Benjamin Franklin
BHQP   British Headquarters (Sir Guy Carleton) Papers, NYPL
BL   British Library, London
CC   Continental Congress
Clinton Papers WLCL, Sir Henry Clinton Papers
CO   TNA, Colonial Office
CSHS   Commissioners for Sick and Hurt Seamen (Sick and
                Hurt Board)
DAR   K. G. Davies, ed., *Documents of the American Revolu-*
                tion, 1770–1783 (Colonial Office Series), 21 vols. (Shan-
                non, 1972–81)
Dartmouth MSS   Staffordshire Record Office, Dartmouth MSS, D(W)
                1778
DLAR   David Library of the American Revolution, Washing-
                ton Crossing, PA
EHR   *English Historical Review*
Evans   Early American Imprints, Series I, 1639–1800
Germain Papers WLCL, George Germain Papers

GG	George Germain
GW	George Washington
HC	Henry Clinton
HEH	Huntington Library, San Marino, CA
HL	Henry Laurens
HMC	Historical Manuscript Commission, U.K.
HSP	Historical Society of Pennsylvania
IOR	BL, India Office Records
JA	John Adams
JCC	Worthington Chauncey Ford et al., eds., *Journals of the Continental Congress, 1774–1789*, 34 vols. (Washington, D.C., 1904–37)
JSAHR	*Journal of the Society for Army Historical Research*
LCP	Library Company of Philadelphia, PA
LDC	Paul Hubert Smith, Gerard W. Gawalt, Rosemary Fry Plakas, and Eugene R. Sheridan, eds., *Letters of Delegates to Congress, 1774–1789*, 26 vols. (Washington, D.C., 1976–2000)
LOC	Library of Congress, Washington, D.C.
Mackenzie Papers	WLCL, Frederick Mackenzie Papers
MHS	Massachusetts Historical Society, Boston
NARA	National Archives and Record Administration, Washington, D.C.
NDAR	William Clark Bell, ed., *Naval Documents of the American Revolution*, 11 vols. (Washington, D.C., 1964–2005)
NEQ	*New England Quarterly*
NG	Nathanael Greene
NMM	National Maritime Museum, Greenwich, U.K.
NYCD	John Romeyn Brodhead, *Documents relative to the colonial history of the State of New York*, 15 vols. (Albany, NY, 1853–87)
NYPL	New York Public Library, New York City, NY
OED	*Oxford English Dictionary*: http://www.oed.com
PAH	Harold Coffin Syrett and Jacob Ernest Cooke, eds., *The Papers of Alexander Hamilton*, 27 vols. (New York, 1961–87)
Parl. Hist.	William Cobbett and T. C. Hansard, *Cobbett's Parliamentary history of England. From the Norman conquest, in 1066. To the year, 1803*, 36 vols. (London, 1806–20)
PBF	Leonard W. Labaree and Whitfield J. Bell, eds., *The Papers of Benjamin Franklin*, 41 vols. to date (New Haven, CT, 1959–)

PGW	Theodore J. Crackel et al., *The Papers of George Washington Digital Edition* (Charlottesville, VA, 2007–), http://rotunda.upress.virginia.edu/founders/GEWN .html
PGW/EA	Theodore J. Crackel et al., *The Papers of George Washington Digital Edition* (Charlottesville, VA, 2007–), Early Access, http://rotunda.upress.virginia .edu/founders/FOEA.html
PHL	Philip M. Hamer et al., eds., *The Papers of Henry Laurens*, 16 vols. (Columbia, SC, 1968–2003)
PJA	Robert J. Taylor, Mary-Jo Kline, Gregg L. Lint, et al., eds., *Papers of John Adams*, 17 vols. to date (Cambridge, MA, 1977–)
PMHB	*Pennsylvania Magazine of History and Biography*
PNG	Dennis M. Conrad, Robert E. McCarthy, E. Carp, and Richard K. Showman, eds., *The Papers of General Nathanael Greene*, 13 vols. (Chapel Hill, NC, 1976–2005)
PTJ	Julian P. Boyd et al., eds., *The Papers of Thomas Jefferson*, 41 vols. to date (Princeton, 1950–)
PWL	Carl E. Prince, Dennis P. Ryan, Pamela B. Schafler, and Donald W. White, eds., *The Papers of William Livingston*, 5 vols. (Trenton, NJ, 1979–88)
RDC	United States Department of State, *The Revolutionary Diplomatic Correspondence of the United States*, 6 vols. (Washington, D.C., 1889)
SP	TNA, State Papers
TJ	Thomas Jefferson
TNA	The National Archives, Kew, U.K.
WH	William Howe
WJA	Charles Francis Adams, ed., *The Works of John Adams, Second President of the United States: With a Life of the Author*, 10 vols. (Boston, 1850–56)
WL	William Livingston
WLCL	William L. Clements Library, University of Michigan, Ann Arbor, MI
WMQ	*William and Mary Quarterly*
WO	TNA, War Office

NOTES

N OTE ON SOURCES: THE ORIGINAL SPELLING HAS BEEN RE-
tained throughout; [*sic*] has not been used.

    The bibliography of archival and printed primary
sources as well as scholarly literature cited in the notes can be
accessed at: http://www.holgerhoock.com/scars-of-independence
-bibliography.pdf.

Preface

1. Rachel Hope Cleves, *The Reign of Terror in America: Visions of Violence
   from Anti-Jacobitism to Antislavery* (Cambridge, 2009), 13, 15 (quotation); Marcus Rediker, *The Slave Ship: A Human History* (New York,
   2007), 12, with reference to novelist Barry Unsworth; Wayne E. Lee,
   Barbarians and Brothers: Anglo-American Warfare, 1500–1865 (New
   York, 2011), 11.

Introduction

1. My depiction of the Boston Massacre and its background, unless otherwise noted, is based on Richard Archer, *As If an Enemy's Country:
   The British Occupation of Boston and the Origins of Revolution* (Oxford,
   2010); Dirk Hoerder, *Crowd Action in Revolutionary Massachusetts,
   1765–1780* (New York, 1977), 219–41; Russell Bourne, *Cradle of Violence: How Boston's Waterfront Mobs Ignited the American Revolution*
   (Hoboken, NJ, 2006), 145–68; Neil Longley York, *The Boston Massacre: A History with Documents* (New York, 2010); John W. Shy, *Toward
   Lexington: The Role of the British Army in the Coming of the American
   Revolution* (Princeton, 1965), 306–19; John Ferling, *John Adams: A Life*
   (New York, 2010), 65–6; idem, *Independence: The Struggle to Set Amer-
   ica Free* (New York, 2011), 26–34; Hiller B. Zobel, *The Boston Massacre*
   (New York, 1970), with the quotation from Davis at 191. Zobel is best

read alongside Pauline Maier, "Revolutionary Violence and the Relevance of History," *Journal of Interdisciplinary History* 2:1 (1971), and Jesse Lemisch, "Radical Plot in Boston (1770): A Study in the Use of Evidence," *Harvard Law Review* 84:2 (1970).

2. For a brief overview of longer- and short-term contexts and causes of the Revolution, see Stephen Conway, *A Short History of the American Revolutionary War* (London, 2013), ch. 1. For concise introductions to the colonial protests of 1764–70, see also Laurel Thatcher Ulrich, "Political Protest and the World of Goods," and Craig B. Yiruch, "The Imperial Crisis," in *Oxford Handbook of the American Revolution*, ed. Edward G. Gray and Jane Kamensky (Oxford, 2013); Archer, *As If an Enemy's Country*, chs. 1–5. For the nature and chronology of pre-Revolutionary violence, see Bourne, *Cradle of Violence*, 148–52; Hoerder, *Crowd Action*, 219–23; Paul A. Gilje, *The Road to Mobocracy: Popular Disorder in New York City, 1763–1834* (Chapel Hill, NC, 1987); David C. Rapoport, "Before the Bombs There Were the Mobs: American Experience with Terror," *Terrorism and Political Violence* 20:2 (2008); Joseph S. Tiedemann, "A Tumultuous People: The Rage for Liberty and the Ambivalence of Violence in the Middle Colonies in the Years Preceding the American Revolution," *Pennsylvania History* 77:4 (2010).

3. O. M. Dickerson, comp., *Boston under Military Rule (1768–1769) As Revealed in a Journal of the Times* (New York, 1970); Archer, *As If an Enemy's Country*, 126–35, and the points on Irish and Afro-Caribbean soldiers at 106, 117. For a standing army as a provocation in light of seventeenth- and eighteenth-century British and North American history, see Patrick Griffin, *America's Revolution* (New York, 2012), 88. For the British government underestimating the impact of revenue reforms and a standing army, see Nancy L. Rhoden, "The American Revolution I: The Paradox of Atlantic Integration," in *British North America in the Seventeenth and Eighteenth Centuries, Companion Series to the Oxford History of the British Empire*, ed. Stephen Foster (Oxford, 2013), 275.

4. York, *Boston Massacre*, 21–5 (Franklin quotation 21).

5. Adams is quoted in Zobel, *Boston Massacre*, 290. "Come on you Rascals": *New-York Gazette*, Apr. 2, 1770, "Extract of a Letter from Boston, Mar. 19, 1770." For this and the following paragraph, see esp. Archer, *As If an Enemy's Country*, 190–93.

6. All quotations from the *Boston Gazette*, Mar. 12, 1770, except the bystander, John Hickling, quoted in Zobel, *Boston Massacre*, 199.

7. Prentiss is quoted in Benjamin L. Carp, *Defiance of the Patriots: The Boston Tea Party & the Making of America* (New Haven, 2010), 42.

8. Ulrich, "Political Protest"; Yiruch, "Imperial Crisis" (quotation 91).

9. Archer, *As If an Enemy's Country*, 202; Zobel, *Boston Massacre*, 205; Bourne, *Cradle of Violence*, 163; *A fair account of the late unhappy dis-*

turbance at Boston in New England (London, 1770), 9, 19; Jill Lepore, *Book of Ages: The Life and Opinions of Jane Franklin* (New York, 2013), 155.

10. For the published depositions collected to support the Boston and British versions of events, respectively, see *A short narrative of the horrid massacre in Boston* (Boston, 1770), sent to London by Samuel Adams, with Revere's image as frontispiece, and *A fair account*. For the depositions of twenty-two British soldiers and civilians secretly recorded by a friendly magistrate working for Hutchinson, see CO5/88, XC1580. See also York, *Boston Massacre*, 129–57. Andrew Oliver to Benjamin Lynde, Mar. 6–7, 1770, MHS Collections Online, at http://www.masshist.org /database/2714?ft=Boston%20Massacre&from=/features/massacre /initial&noalt=1&pid=34.

11. All dates in 1770: *Boston Gazette*, Mar. 12. Also in *Connecticut Journal* (supplement), Mar. 16; *New Hampshire Gazette*, Mar. 16; *Providence Gazette*, Mar. 10–17; *Pennsylvania Gazette*, Mar. 22; *Georgia Gazette*, Apr. 11. British: *Lloyd's Evening Post*, Apr. 20–23; *St James's Chronicle*, Apr. 21–24; *Dublin Mercury*, Apr. 28–May 1. For neutral and pro-British accounts, see *Boston Chronicle*, Mar. 8; *New-York Journal*, Mar. 15; *New-York Gazette*, Apr. 2.

12. For Revere, see York, *Boston Massacre*, 32; Jill Lepore, *The Whites of Their Eyes: The Tea Party's Revolution and the Battle over American History* (Princeton, 2010), 63. For the Revolutionary role of the motley crew, see Peter Linebaugh and Marcus Rediker, *The Many-Headed Hydra: Sailors, Slaves, Commoners, and the Hidden History of the Revolutionary Atlantic* (Boston, 2000), ch. 7. It was not until William C. Nell published *The Colored Patriots of the American Revolution* (Boston, 1855) that Crispus Attucks was depicted as black.

13. For the trials, see *The trial of William Wemms . . . held at Boston* (Boston, 1770); [William Wemms], *The trial of the British soldiers* (Boston, 1807); "Adams' Argument for the Defense, December 3–4, 1770," Founders Online, at http://founders.archives.gov/documents/Adams/05-03-02 -0001-0004-0016. On anti-riot duty carried out by soldiers lacking non-lethal weaponry, see Bruce Lenman, *Britain's Colonial Wars, 1688–1783* (New York, 2001), 199–200.

14. JA, Diary, Mar. 5, 1773, at http://www.masshist.org/digitaladams /archive/browse/diaries_by_date.php.

15. JA to Matthew Robinson, Mar. 2, 1786, *WJA*, viii: 383–5.

16. The quotation from Edward Larkin, "American Revolutionary War Writing," in *The Cambridge Companion to War Writing*, ed. Kate McLoughlin (Cambridge, 2009), 126. For the distortion of the collective American memory of the Revolution and war, see Michael A. McDonnell, ed., *Remembering the Revolution: Memory, History, and*

Nation Making from Independence to the Civil War (Amherst, MA, 2013), 5, 20–21, 35 n. 7, and passim. See also Griffin, *America's Revolution*, 155. For the American right's antihistorical appropriation of the founding, see Lepore, *Whites of Their Eyes*. Although scholars have more recently studied aspects of Revolutionary violence—Amerindian warfare; partisan and guerrilla fighting in the Southern backcountry and on the New York frontier; the fate of prisoners in New York City—such specialist literature remains too fragmented to convey fully the nature and significance of violence and of its politicization, and it has yet to transform the Revolution's popular narrative. See annotations to subsequent chapters for detailed references to the important work of Wayne E. Lee, Edwin Burrows, Sarah Purcell, John P. Resch, et al.

17. Notions of violence are products of their time. By ascertaining how protagonists on all sides defined the limits of legitimate violence, and by probing how they invoked and contested these limits, we can attempt to evaluate allegations of excessive violence and war crimes. At the same time, rumors, exaggerations, and unproven claims of violence in the historical sources can provide useful insights into the mindset of historical actors, their fears, moral dilemmas, and polemical strategies. The *Oxford English Dictionary* defines "violence" as the "deliberate exercise of physical force against a person, property, etc." In a legal context, violence refers also to "the unlawful exercise of physical force, intimidation by the exhibition of such force." See "violence, n.," and "terror, n.," *OED*, at http://www.oed.com. "Terror" was a word regularly used by all sides to refer to extreme fear in the face of physical and psychological violence, or the threat thereof, and the use of fear to intimidate people. See, e.g., Robert Beverley Letterbook, LOC; Dartmouth to WH, Sept. 5, 1775, BHQP 31; GW to Continental Congress Camp Committee [Jan. 29, 1778]. Unless noted otherwise, Washington's correspondence and military orders are cited from *PGW*. On American ambivalence regarding the laws of war, see John Fabian Witt, *Lincoln's Code: The Laws of War in American History* (New York, 2012), 15, 48.

18. Holger Hoock, *Empires of the Imagination: Politics, War and the Arts in the British World, 1750–1850* (London, 2010), 75–81 (quotation 75).

19. Historians have been more comfortable recognizing a string of local civil wars in New Jersey, New York, or the Southern backcountry. As David Armitage has pointed out, we tend to consider civil war and revolution as antithetical: "Civil wars are destructive; revolutions are progressive . . . Civil wars mark the collapse of the human spirit; revolutions, its unfolding and self-realisation." David Armitage, "Civil War and Revolution," *Agora* 44:2 (2009): 20. For a working definition of civil war, with reference to Stathis Kalyvas, see ibid., 19: "organized

collective violence within a single polity which leads to a division of sovereignty and consequently a struggle for authority." On the dynamics of revolution and counterrevolution, see Jerry Bannister and Liam Riordan, "Loyalism and the British Atlantic, 1660–1840," in *The Loyal Atlantic: Remaking the British Atlantic in the Revolutionary Era*, ed. Jerry Bannister and Liam Riordan (Toronto, 2012), 5. For the marginalization of the Loyalists, see Maya Jasanoff, *Liberty's Exiles: American Loyalists in the Revolutionary World* (New York, 2011).

20. R. R. Palmer, *The Age of the Democratic Revolution: A Political History of Europe and America, 1760–1800*, vol. I, *The Challenge* (Princeton, 1959), 190. For British mobilization, see Stephen Conway, *The British Isles and the War of American Independence* (New York, 2000), ch. 1. Seeley is quoted in Eliga H. Gould, *The Persistence of Empire: British Political Culture in the Age of the American Revolution* (Chapel Hill, NC, 2000), xvi.

21. Bernard Bailyn, *The Ideological Origins of the American Revolution* (Cambridge, MA, 1967); Gordon S. Wood, *The Radicalism of the American Revolution* (New York, 1992); see also, more recently, T. H. Breen, *American Insurgents, American Patriots: The Revolution of the People* (New York, 2010). For the history of Founders Chic, see Francis D. Cogliano, "Founders Chic," *History* 90:299 (2005).

22. "we must seek": Carroll Smith-Rosenberg, *This Violent Empire: The Birth of an American National Identity* (Chapel Hill, NC, 2010), 1–2. On violence in American history and culture, see, highly selectively, Richard Maxwell Brown, *Strain of Violence: Historical Studies of American Violence and Vigilantism* (New York, 1975), with references to America's violent birth at 5, 7; Richard Hofstadter and Michael Wallace, eds., *American Violence: A Documentary History* (New York, 1970); Michael A. Bellesiles, ed., *Lethal Imagination: Violence and Brutality in American History* (New York, 1999); Christopher Waldrep and Michael A. Bellesiles, eds., *Documenting American Violence: A Sourcebook* (Oxford, 2006); Richard Slotkin, *Regeneration through Violence: The Mythology of the American Frontier, 1600–1860* (Middletown, CT, 1973); Peter Rhoads Silver, *Our Savage Neighbors: How Indian War Transformed Early America* (New York, 2008); Mark A. Neely, "Was the Civil War a Total War?," *Civil War History* 50:4 (2004); idem, *Civil War and the Limits of Destruction* (Cambridge, MA, 2007); John Tirman, *The Deaths of Others: The Fate of Civilians in America's Wars* (Oxford, 2011).

23. Drew Gilpin Faust, *This Republic of Suffering: Death and the American Civil War* (New York, 2008), has movingly deromanticized notions of the Civil War. For the Civil War and cultures of death, see also Mark S.

Schantz, *Awaiting the Heavenly Country: The Civil War and America's Culture of Death* (Ithaca, NY, 2008). Carol Berkin, *Revolutionary Mothers: Women in the Struggle for America's Independence* (New York, 2005), ix.

24. 1.25 percent of Americans died on the Patriot side, compared to 0.12 percent and 0.28 percent of Americans in World War I and World War II, respectively, and 1.6 percent in the Civil War. If we assume that some 200,000 Patriots bore arms during the conflict, more than 17 percent of those soldiers were killed, compared to 13 percent of Union troop losses in the Civil War. My estimates follow Howard Henry Peckham, *The Toll of Independence: Engagements & Battle Casualties of the American Revolution* (Chicago, 1974); Edwin G. Burrows, *Forgotten Patriots: The Untold Story of American Prisoners during the Revolutionary War* (New York, 2008), 204; John Shy, *A People Numerous and Armed: Reflections on the Military Struggle for American Independence* (New York, 1976), 249–50; Allan Kulikoff, "The War in the Countryside," in *Oxford Handbook of the American Revolution*, ed. Gray and Kamensky, 218; Michael A. McDonnell, "War and Nationhood: Founding Myth and Historical Realities," in *Remembering the Revolution*, ed. McDonnell et al., 21, 29. For British casualties, see Nick Bunker, *An Empire on the Edge: How Britain Came to Fight America* (New York, 2014), 382–3 n. 7.

25. On comparative and transnational approaches, see Maya Jasanoff, "The Other Side of Revolution: Loyalists in the British Empire," *WMQ* 65:2 (2008). Matthew H. Spring, *With Zeal and with Bayonets Only: The British Army on Campaign in North America, 1775–1783* (Norman, OK, 2008), xiii, highlights that campaign narratives for popular audiences privilege Patriot over Loyalist, British, and German sources.

26. Even at the most conservative estimate of 20 percent—those who signed a document, did business with the army, took up arms, or went behind British lines or into exile—some 400,000 people opposed the Revolution. John Adams referred to an estimated one-third of the people in the colonies actively opposed to the Revolution; on another occasion, he referenced "one third . . . averse to the revolution," an "opposite third" for it, and a "middle third" who were waverers. JA to Thomas McKean, Aug. 31, 1813, *WJA*, x: 62–3; JA to James Lloyd, Jan. 1815, ibid., 108–14. The classic estimate of 20 percent Loyalists is Paul H. Smith's in "The American Loyalists: Notes on Their Organization and Numerical Strength," *WMQ* 25:2 (1968). On the difficulties of determining numbers, see Jasanoff, "Revolutionary Exiles: The American Loyalist and French Émigré Diasporas," in *The Age of Revolutions in Global Context, c. 1760–1840*, ed. David Armitage and Sanjay Subrahmanyam (Basingstoke, 2010), and *Liberty's Exiles*. See also Jack P. Greene and J. R. Pole, eds., *A Companion to the American Revolution* (Malden, MA,

2000), 234; Shy, *People Numerous and Armed*, 236. For degrees of loyalism, see Robert M. Calhoon et al., "Author's Note," in *Tory Insurgents: The Loyalist Perception and Other Essays*, ed. idem (Columbia, SC, 2008), 11. Many British-Americans tried to sit on the fence as long as possible: Leonard W. Labaree, *Conservatism in Early American History* (New York, 1948), 158; Henry J. Young, "Treatment of the Loyalists in Pennsylvania" (PhD diss., Johns Hopkins University, 1955), 76; Sung Bok Kim, "The Limits of Politicization in the American Revolution: The Experience of Westchester County, New York," *JAH* 80:3 (1993). On the disaffected, see Michael A. McDonnell, "Resistance to the American Revolution," in *Companion to the American Revolution*, ed. Greene and Pole. "I have no relish": J. Seagrove to Jn. Blackburn Esq., New York, July 2, 1775, Dartmouth MSS, II/1348 [copy].

27. On the violence, and the rhetorical and emotional power of descriptions of violence, see, e.g., Cleves, *Reign of Terror*, 12–15. Older histories of the Revolution—such as Philip Davidson, *Propaganda and the American Revolution 1763–1783* (Chapel Hill, NC, 1941), Allen Bowman, *The Morale of the American Revolutionary Army* (Washington, D.C., 1943), and Carl Berger, *Broadsides & Bayonets: The Propaganda War of the American Revolution*, rev. ed. (San Rafael, CA, 1976)—speak of "propaganda," the systematic, misleading dissemination of information. I prefer to consider instead the polemical war, whereby "polemical" means "relating to dispute or controversy; contentious, disputatious, combative," or, borrowing the terminology of Jill Lepore, *The Name of War: King Philip's War and the Origins of American Identity* (New York, 1998), the war of words. See "polemical, adj.," *OED*, at http://www.oed.com.

28. Cf. Brown, *Strain of Violence*, 42; Peter Thompson, "Social Death and Slavery: The Logic of Political Association and the Logic of Chattel Slavery in Revolutionary America," in *Between Sovereignty and Anarchy: The Politics of Violence in the American Revolutionary Era*, ed. Patrick Griffin et al. (Charlottesville, VA, 2015). Adams: JA to Abigail Adams, Feb. 17, 1777, at http://www.masshist.org/digitaladams/archive/doc ?id=L17770217ja. "common ethnicity": Gordon S. Wood, *Revolutionary Characters: What Made the Founders Different* (New York, 2006), 4. As the idea for this book was first taking shape, Presidents Clinton and Obama were reminding Americans of the importance of conducting foreign policy by the power of example. See William J. Clinton, Speech at Democratic National Convention, Aug. 27, 2008, at http://www.nytimes .com/2008/08/27/us/politics/27text-clinton.html?pagewanted=all. Barack H. Obama, Inaugural Address, Jan. 20, 2009, at https://www .whitehouse.gov/blog/2009/01/21/president-barack-obamas-inaugural -address.

29. On exceptionalist ideology, see William Huntting Howell, "'Starving

Memory': Antinarrating the American Revolution," in *Remembering the Revolution*, ed. McDonnell et al., 94; Godfrey Hodgson, *The Myth of American Exceptionalism* (New Haven, 2009); Donald E. Pease, *The New American Exceptionalism* (Minneapolis, 2009).

Chapter One

1. My rendering of Malcom's story is based on Benjamin H. Irvin, "Tar, Feathers, and the Enemies of American Liberties, 1768–1776," *NEQ* 76:2 (2003), and Frank W. C. Hersey, "Tar and Feathers: The Adventures of Captain John Malcolm," *Colonial Society of Massachusetts Publications* 34 (1941) with the quotations in this section, unless otherwise referenced, at 446, 444, 447, 452, 445. See ibid., 435, for Malcom and the Regulator uprising, for which see also Steven Wilf, "Placing Blame: Criminal Law and Constitutional Narratives in Revolutionary Boston," *Crime, History & Societies* 4:1 (2000). See also AO12/105/41; 13/75/41–5; Nathaniel Philbrick, *Bunker Hill: A City, a Siege, a Revolution* (New York, 2013), 14–22; James Barton Hunt, "The Crowd and the American Revolution: A Study of Urban Political Violence in Boston and Philadelphia, 1763–1776" (PhD diss., University of Washington, 1973), 381–3. Merchant's diary: Anne Rowe Cunningham, ed., *Letters and Diary of John Rowe* (New York, 1969), Jan. 25, 1774. For Hewes, and a reading in terms of class differences, see Alfred F. Young, *The Shoemaker and the Tea Party: Memory and the American Revolution* (Boston, 1999), ch. 7. For newspapers, all in 1774, see *Boston Gazette*, Jan. 31, Feb. 4 and 20; *Massachusetts Gazette*, Jan. 27, Feb. 3; *Boston Evening Post*, Jan. 31, Feb. 14, Apr. 4; *Massachusetts Spy*, Jan. 27, Feb. 17; *New-York Journal*, February 17. Hulton is quoted from Ann Hulton, *Letters of a Loyalist Lady, Being the Letters of Anne Hulton* (Cambridge, MA, 1927), 71. For the recipe, see Douglass Adair and John A. Schutz, eds., *Peter Oliver's Origin & Progress of the American Rebellion. A Tory View* (Stanford, 1961), 94. For tarring and feathering as a "ritual articulation of waterfront justice" against British officials and customs informers, see Benjamin L. Carp, *Rebels Rising: Cities and the American Revolution* (Oxford, 2007), 53–5 (quotation 54).

2. For this and the next paragraph, see Yirush, "Imperial Crisis," 94–6; Carp, *Defiance of the Patriots*, 1–3, 191–4 (North is quoted at 191: "ringleader").

3. Carp, *Defiance of the Patriots*, 199; Michael A. McDonnell, "The Struggle Within: Colonial Politics on the Eve of Independence," *Oxford Handbook of the American Revolution*, ed. Gray and Kamensky, 106, but see also 108 on how "radical action masked deep divisions" in many places. For the First Continental Congress and the profile of

the delegates, see Jack N. Rakove, *Revolutionaries: A New History of the Invention of America* (Boston, 2010), 31, 53–63; Richard R. Beeman, *Our Lives, Our Fortunes, and Our Sacred Honor: The Forging of American Independence, 1774–1776* (New York, 2013), 57–61, 173. My reading of the Continental Association and the committee system relies on published committee records cited in this chapter and on T. H. Breen, *The Marketplace of Revolution: How Consumer Politics Shaped American Independence* (Oxford, 2004), 325–9, and *American Insurgents*, chs. 6, 7. See also Benjamin H. Irvin, *Clothed in Robes of Sovereignty: The Continental Congress and the People Out of Doors* (Oxford, 2011), 28–51; Jack N. Rakove, *The Beginnings of National Politics: An Interpretive History of the Continental Congress* (New York, 1979), 50; Catherine S. Crary, *The Price of Loyalty: Tory Writings from the Revolutionary Era* (New York, 1973), 28; Robert Stansbury Lambert, *South Carolina Loyalists in the American Revolution* (Columbia, SC, 1987), 23; Jerrilyn Greene Marston, *King and Congress: The Transfer of Political Legitimacy, 1774–1776* (Princeton, 1987), 103, 111; Beeman, *Our Lives*, 120–21. Quotations from the Association in this section are from *JCC*, i: 79.

4. Virginia had 1,100 committeemen across 33 counties and 3 towns by the end of 1774; 900 committeemen served in the much less populous Maryland, where 11 of 16 counties featured committees by 1775. Sizes varied from an average of some 20 men per committee in Virginia to 50 or 60 in New York City and 100 in Maryland. See Green and Pole, eds., *Companion to the American Revolution*, 219; Kevin Phillips, *1775: A Good Year for Revolution* (New York, 2012), 261–2; Hermann Wellenreuther, *Von Chaos und Krieg zu Ordnung und Frieden: Der Amerikanischen Revolution erster Teil, 1775–1783* (Berlin, 2006), 27, 43, and 32–3 for quotations from local and provincial resolutions; Breen, *American Insurgents*, 200–201, 170, 185. James Moody, *Lieut. James Moody's narrative of his exertions and sufferings*, 2nd ed. (London, 1783), 5.

5. For the demographics of Loyalism I have drawn on Jasanoff, *Liberty's Exiles*, 8. See also Crary, *Price of Loyalty*, 3–4; Kevin Phillips, *The Cousins' War: Religion, Politics, and the Triumph of Anglo-America* (New York, 1999), 168–232; William H. Nelson, *The American Tory* (Oxford, 1961), 61, 86, and passim; N. E. H. Hall, Peter C. Hoffer, and Stephen L. Allen, "Choosing Sides: A Quantitative Study of the Personality Determinants of Loyalist and Revolutionary Political Affiliation in New York," *JAH* 65:2 (1978); Kenneth Schuyler Lynn, *A Divided People* (Westport, CT, 1977). Deerfield: Bruce G. Merritt, "Loyalism and Social Conflict in Revolutionary Deerfield, Massachusetts," *JAH* 57:2 (1970), 282; Larry R. Gerlach, ed., *New Jersey in the American Revolution, 1763–1783: A Documentary History* (Trenton, NJ, 1975), 242.

For the social diversity of New York Loyalism, see Jasanoff, *Liberty's Exiles*, 33; Crary, *Price of Loyalty*, 138–40; Ruma Chopra, *Unnatural Rebellion: Loyalists in New York City during the Revolution* (Charlottesville, VA, 2011), 65–7.

6. Materialistic reading: *Pennsylvania Evening Post*, June 1, 1776. See Nancy L. Rhoden, "Patriots, Villains, and the Quest for Liberty: How American Film Has Depicted the American Revolution," *Canadian Review of American Studies* 37:2 (2007), for the persistence of this interpretation. On loyalist ideology, see Robert M. Calhoon, *The Loyalist Perception and Other Essays* (Columbia, SC, 1989); Bernard Bailyn, *The Ordeal of Thomas Hutchinson* (Cambridge, MA, 1974); John E. Ferling, *The Loyalist Mind: Joseph Galloway and the American Revoution* (University Park, PA, 1977); Janice Potter-MacKinnon, *The Liberty We Seek: Loyalist Ideology in Colonial New York and Massachusetts* (Cambridge, MA, 1983); Chopra, *Unnatural Rebellion*; Anne Y. Zimmer, *Jonathan Boucher; Loyalist in Exile* (Detroit, 1978); Jasanoff, *Liberty's Exiles* (quotation 24). See also Edward Larkin, "Loyalism," in *Oxford Handbook of the American Revolution*, ed. Gray and Kamensky, 294–5. Loyalist historiography lacks a modern synthesis. For orientation in the literature, see the classic Bailyn, *Ordeal* (and the critique in Bannister and Riordan, "Loyalism and the British Atlantic"); Calhoon, *Loyalist Perception*, with bibliographical essay at 216–27, to be read alongside Calhoon et al., *Tory Insurgents*, with bibliographical essay at 375–85; Joseph S. Tiedemann, Eugene R. Fingerhut, and Robert W. Venables, eds., *The Other Loyalists: Ordinary People, Royalism, and the Revolution in the Middle Colonies, 1763–1787* (Albany, NY, 2009); Wallace Brown, *The King's Friends: The Composition and Motives of the American Loyalist Claimants* (Providence, RI, 1965). Philip Gould, *Writing the Rebellion: Loyalists and the Literature of Politics in British America* (Oxford, 2013), stresses the ambivalence of Loyalist identities, and Loyalists' sense of loss and displacement. For the Loyalist experience in North American, Atlantic, and global contexts, see Judith L. Van Buskirk, *Generous Enemies: Patriots and Loyalists in Revolutionary New York* (Philadelphia, 2002); Andrew Jackson O'Shaughnessy, *An Empire Divided: The American Revolution and the British Caribbean* (Philadelphia, 2000); Jasanoff, *Liberty's Exiles*; Alan Taylor, *The Divided Ground: Indians, Settlers, and the Northern Borderland of the American Revolution* (New York, 2006); idem, *The Civil War of 1812: American Citizens, British Subjects, Irish Rebels, & Indian Allies* (New York, 2010); Bannister and Riordan, eds., *Loyal Atlantic*.

7. Joseph S. Tiedemann and Eugene R. Fingerhut, "Introduction," in *Other Loyalists*, ed. Tiedemann, Fingerhut, and Venables, 10, and in

the same collection, David J. Fowler, " 'Loyalty Is Now Bleeding in New Jersey': Motivations and Mentalities of the Disaffected," 65. Studies of Revolutionary allegiance in many areas suggest that preexisting political, social, and economic divisions helped shape choices. For studies of Loyalism in local context, see, e.g., Chopra, *Unnatural Rebellion*; Adele Hast, *Loyalism in Revolutionary Virginia: The Norfolk Area and the Eastern Shore* (Ann Arbor, MI, 1982); Philip Papas, *That Ever Loyal Island: Staten Island and the American Revolution* (New York, 2007); Christopher J. M. Sparshott, "The Popular Politics of Loyalism during the American Revolution, 1774–1790" (PhD diss., Northwestern University, 2007); Philip Ranlet, *The New York Loyalists* (Knoxville, TN, 1986). For analyses in terms of individual and collective psychology, see Lynn, *Divided People*; George Athan Billias, "The First Un-Americans: The Loyalists in American Historiography," in *Perspectives in Early American History*, ed. George Athan Billias and Alden T. Vaughan (New York, 1973), 303–4; Hull, Hoffer, and Allen, "Choosing Sides"; Ronald Hoffman, *A Spirit of Dissention: Economics, Politics, and the Revolution in Maryland* (Baltimore, 1973). For black loyalists, see James W. St. G. Walker, *Black Loyalists: The Search for a Promised Land in Nova Scotia and Sierra Leone, 1783–1870* (London, 1976); Mary Beth Norton, "The Fate of Some Black Loyalists of the American Revolution," *Journal of Negro History* 58:4 (1973); Robin W. Winks, *The Blacks in Canada; a History* (New Haven, CT, 1971); Cassandra Pybus, *Epic Journeys of Freedom: Runaway Slaves of the American Revolution and Their Global Quest for Liberty* (Boston, 2006); Simon Schama, *Rough Crossings: Britain, the Slaves, and the American Revolution* (New York, 2006).

8. For an analysis of mixed, unstable, and malleable loyalties in one rural New York community, see Jonathan Clark, "The Problem of Allegiance in Revolutionary Poughkeepsie," in *Saints and Revolutionaries: Essays on Early American History*, ed. David D. Hall, John M. Murrin, and Thad W. Tate (New York, 1984). For the Franklins, see Sheila L. Skemp, *William Franklin: A Son of a Patriot, Servant of a King* (New York, 1990); eadem, *Benjamin and William Franklin: Father and Son, Patriot and Loyalist* (Boston, 1994); Sarah C. Chambers and Lisa Norling, "Choosing to Be a Subject: Loyalist Women in the Revolutionary Atlantic World," *Journal of Women's History* 20:1 (2008): 44–5. Whitecuffs: AO12/19/148–51; 13/56/628; Pybus, *Epic Journeys*, 27–8, 79; Graham Russell Hodges, *Root & Branch: African Americans in New York and New Jersey, 1613–1863* (Chapel Hill and London, 1999), 148.

9. Rick Ashton, "The Loyalist Experience: New York, 1763–1789" (PhD diss., Northwestern University, 1973), 121–37, quoting Morris to AH, May 1777, at 127. Adams: JA to Cushing, Dec. 15, 1780, in *RDC*,

iv: 195. For Morris, see James J. Kirschke, *Gouverneur Morris: Author, Statesman, and Man of the World* (New York, 2005), 30–31; William Howard Adams, *Gouverneur Morris: An Independent Life* (New Haven, CT, 2003), 42–6, 67–8; Richard Brookhiser, *Gentleman Revolutionary: Gouverneur Morris, the Rake Who Wrote the Constitution* (New York, 2003), 23.

10. For the limited survival of records, see Breen, *American Insurgents*, 186; see also 215–16 for the powerful impact of naming and shaming. Committee proceedings: Wellenreuther, *Von Chaos und Krieg*, 35 n. 85. "a species of infamy": quoted in Schlesinger, *Prelude*, 210, from an article appearing in Pennsylvania, Virginia, Rhode Island, and Massachusetts in Nov. and Dec. 1774.

11. Leora H. McEachern and Isabel M. Williams, eds., *Wilmington–New Hanover Safety Committee Minutes, 1774–1776* (Wilmington, DE, 1974), 14–15, 19, 23–4; Breen, *American Insurgents*, 190–93. For other localities, see also Wellenreuther, *Von Chaos und Krieg*, 29; *Am. Arch.*, 4th ser., II: 690, 897, 1551–2. For a probing reexamination of Associational logic, see now Thompson, "Social Death and Slavery," who sees "grounds for questioning whether the disciplinary logic of the Association was understood to be premised on the reintegration of white dissidents sidelined and subordinated within their communities" (156).

12. Hast, *Loyalism*, 21; Phillips, *1775*, 260, 270; Larry Bowman, "The Virginia County Committees of Safety, 1774–1776," *Virginia Magazine of History and Biography*, 79:3 (1971), 330–32; *Am. Arch.*, 4th ser., I: 1047. Peggy Stewart: Robert M. Calhoon, *Loyalists in Revolutionary America, 1760–1781* (New York, 1973), 145; *New Hampshire Gazette*, Jan. 20, 1775. For similar cases of tarring and feathering, see *Proceedings of the Committees of Safety of Caroline and Southampton Counties* (Richmond, VA, 1929), 129.

13. Tea: Claude Halstead Van Tyne, *The Loyalists in the American Revolution* (New York, 1970), 16–17 ("pestilential herb," also "white coffee"). See also William Duane, ed., *Passages from the Diary of Christopher Marshall*, vol. I, *1774–1777* (Philadelphia, 1839), entry for Mar. 1, 1775 ("baneful and detested weed"); *Am. Arch.*, 4th ser., I: 839 ("baneful vehicle"). For the political symbolism of tea, see Breen, *Marketplace*, 305, 327. For pastimes compromising republican values, see Ann Fairfax Withington, *Toward a More Perfect Union: Virtue and the Formation of American Republics* (New York, 1991), xv, 13–16, 245; Breen, *American Insurgents*, 202–3; Irvin, *Clothed in Robes*, 23–4, 30, 34, 48–50, 118–19, 121–3; *Virginia Gazette*, July 12, 1775; Bowman, "Virginia County Committees of Safety," 332; *Proceedings of the Committees of Safety of Caroline and Southampton Counties*, 151, 156; McEachern and Williams, eds., *Wilmington–New Hanover Safety Committee Minutes*, 3–4,

13–14, 20; "Minutes of Shrewsbury Township Committee, Monmouth County," in *New Jersey in the American Revolution*, ed. Gerlach, 149–50; *Am. Arch.*, 4th ser., I: 1178. The poem is quoted in Gould, *Writing the Rebellion*, 71. For the language of oppression, terror, and inquisition, see Henry Hulton to [Robert Nicholson], Boston, Feb. 21, 1775, quoted in Crary, *Price of Loyalty*, 29–31, at 30; Potter-MacKinnon, *Liberty We Seek*, 29; Samuel Seabury, "The Congress canvassed, or, an examination into the conduct of delegates at their grand convention," in *Letters of a Westchester Farmer, 1774–1775*, ed. Clarence H. Vance (White Plains, NY, 1930), 84–5; Suffolk, "Address to the Americans, Feb. 4, 1775," *Am. Arch.*, 4th ser., IV: 1211–13; see also *Am. Arch.*, 4th ser., I: 1094–6, 1230; II: 238, 252. *Rivington's Gazetteer*, Mar. 30, 1775; Gage to Barrington, June 26, 1774, in John W. Shy, "Confronting Rebellion: Private Correspondence of Lord Barrington with General Gage, 1765–1775," in *Sources of American Independence: Selected Manuscripts from the Collections of the William L. Clements Library*, ed. Howard Henry Peckham (Chicago, 1978), i: 115.

14. "Not thinking": DLAR 24/36/157 n.d. Tice: Intercepted letters of the Tice family, C. to Gilbert Tice, Johnstown, Oct. 28, 1775, Schuyler Papers, Box 50, NYPL. For word crimes, see *Minutes of the Committee of Safety of Bucks County, Pennsylvania, 1774–1776* (Harrisburg, 1890), 352–3, 361, 364–5, 369; DLAR 24, reel 36/168–71; Agnes Hunt, *The Provincial Committees of Safety of the American Revolution* (New York, 1968), 106–7; G. A. Gilbert, "The Connecticut Loyalists," *AHR* 4:2 (1899), 288–9 n. 1; Ferling, *Independence*, 256. Loyalist pamphletists such as Thomas Bradbury Chandler denounced the rebels' "tyranny, not only over the actions, but over the words, thoughts, and wills" of Americans. See Chandler, *What think ye of the Congress now? or, An enquiry how far the Americans are bound to abide by and execute the decisions of the late Congress?* (New York, 1775), 81. See also Bruce E. Steiner, *Samuel Seabury, 1729–1796: A Study in the High Church Tradition* (Athens, OH, 1972); Everett Emerson, ed., *American Literature, 1764–1789: The Revolutionary Years* (Madison, 1977), 63; Vance, ed., *Letters of a Westchester Farmer*, 8, 19, 60–61, 85–7; Alexander Clarence Flick, *Loyalism in New York during the American Revolution* (New York, 1970), 27–8. For an example of private correspondence that ended up in the public domain and cost the author his place in the local community, along with his livelihood, see Richard Barksdale Harwell, ed., *Proceedings of the County Committees, 1774–1776, the Committees of Safety of Westmoreland and Fincastle* (Richmond, VA, 1956), 32–6; Bowman, "Virginia County Committees of Safety," 328–9; Breen, *American Insurgents*, 229–31; Thompson, "Social Death and Slavery," 155–6.

15. For pre-Revolutionary violence and mobs, see Wayne E. Lee, *Crowds and Soldiers in Revolutionary North Carolina: The Culture of Violence in Riot and War* (Gainesville, FL, 2001), esp. part I; David Henry Villers, "Loyalism in Connecticut, 1763–1783" (PhD diss., University of Connecticut, 1976), 160–61; Ferling, *Independence*, 16, 20, 26–7; Pauline Maier, "Popular Uprisings and Civil Authority in Eighteenth-Century America," *WMQ* 27:1 (1970); Arthur Meier Schlesinger, "Political Mobs and the American Revolution, 1765–1776," *Proceedings of the American Philosophical Society* 99:4 (1955): 246. My reading of colonial mobs also draws on Gordon S. Wood, "A Note on Mobs in the American Revolution," *WMQ* 23:4 (1966); Marion Breunig, *Die Amerikanische Revolution als Bürgerkrieg* (Münster, 1998), 51–61; Gilje, *Road to Mobocracy*. *Connecticut Journal*, Aug. 30, 1775; *Norwich Packet*, Apr. 27, 1775. "people's sentinels": *Connecticut Journal*, Aug. 30, 1775.

16. "repugnant": Robert M. Calhoon, "The Reintegration of the Loyalists and the Disaffected," in *The American Revolution: Its Character and Limits*, ed. Jack P. Greene (New York, 1987), 350, with reference to a circular, Feb. 9, 1775. Cambridge: Ranlet, *New York Loyalists*, 157–8 (quotation 157).

17. In early modern England, a *V* as a brand mark stood for vagabond, an *S* for someone involved in sedition, and so forth. Burning the royal cypher on an outcast's head reversed the symbolism of the old political order. Villers, "Loyalism in Connecticut," 168; Hunt, *Provincial Committees*; Crary, *Price of Loyalty*, 57, with further references. "all these cattle": Colonel Woodford to VA Convention, *Am. Arch.*, 4th ser., IV: 244–5 (quotation 244), 346. Van Tyne, *Loyalists*, 61, 79; Chopra, *Unnatural Rebellion*, 32.

18. Wellenreuther, *Von Chaos und Krieg*, 35 n. 84; *Connecticut Courant*, Sept. 12, 1774. "thirst for": Daniel Oliver to Colonel Ruggles, Hardwick, Aug. 19, 1774, Bancroft 92/17. For the violent experiences of mandamus councillors and their evasive measures, see also Lorenzo Sabine, *Biographical sketches of loyalists of the American revolution, with an historical essay* (Boston, 1864), ii: 708; Calhoon, *Loyalists*, 277–8; *Am. Arch.*, 4th ser., I: 762, 1260–63; Anon. to [Thomas and John Fleet], Dec. 19, 1774, Schoff Collection, WLCL; Extract of Gage to Dartmouth, Boston, Sept. 2, 1774, Shelburne Papers 66/369–72, WLCL. John Trumbull, *McFingal: a modern epic poem* (1776), Canto III, 493–4. Dunbar: Justin Winsor, *History of the town of Duxbury, Massachusetts, with genealogical registers* (Boston, 1849), 140; *Gazetteer* [London], June 8, 1775; Thomas B. Allen, *Tories: Fighting for the King in America's First Civil War* (New York, 2010), 25–6.

19. For Bebee [or Beiby], see Adair and Schutz, eds., *Peter Oliver's Origin*, 157. See also *Am. Arch.*, 4th ser., I: 787; Neil Longley York, *Henry Hul-*

ton and the American Revolution: An Outsider's Inside View (Boston, 2010), 179. For a Virginia case, see Irvin, "Tar, Feathers," 234. For attacking houses as "an expressive form of planned symbolic violence," see Robert Blair St. George, *Conversing by Signs: Poetics of Implication in Colonial New England* (Chapel Hill, NC, 1998), ch. 3 (quotation 293). Withington, *Toward a More Perfect Union*, 229–34 (quotation 229).

20. My dissenting reading of the role of coercion and violence notwithstanding, it will be apparent that I have relied heavily on Breen's important *American Insurgents* (quotation here 186); see also 164, 185–6, 207, 212–14. At 208, Breen refers to "unpleasant exceptions" that should not "obscure the major accomplishments of these revolutionary bodies." See also Withington, *Toward a More Perfect Union*, 222–5, 244, for the "limited extent of the civilian violence" (244). To Don Higginbotham, *The War of American Independence: Military Attitudes, Politics, and Practice, 1763–1789* (New York, 1971), 278, the "remarkable fact about the treatment of the loyalists was its relative mildness, not its severity." Bowman, "Virginia County Committees of Safety, 1774–1776," 337, stresses the committees' "effective prevention of violence." Beeman, *Our Lives*, which almost completely ignores the Loyalists, opines: "There would be occasions on which local committees would show excessive zeal in carrying out their enforcement obligations" (174); see also 190. For my reading, see now also the excellent Thompson, "Social Death and Slavery," with a nuanced critique of Breen et al. at 149–50; Rhys Isaac, "Dramatizing the Ideology of Revolution: Popular Mobilization in Virginia, 1774 to 1776," *WMQ* 33:3 (1976): 372.

21. "orangotangs": *Pennsylvania Evening Post*, Sept. 7, 1776. "reptiles": TNA, CO5/122/118–19.

22. A committee in New Milford, CT, described two Loyalists as "despicable animals"; see Villers, "Loyalism in Connecticut," 207. "thing whose head": *New-York Journal*, Feb. 9, 1775. "vultures": *Newport Mercury*, May 27, 1776. Washington referred to Loyalists as "those execrable Parricides, whose Counsels and Aid have deluged this Country with Blood." He went further: "One or two have done, what a great number ought to have done long ago—committed Suicide." GW to John Augustine Washington, Mar. 31, 1776. Washington wanted "to root out or secure such abominable pests of Society," as quoted in Mark V. Kwasny, *Washington's Partisan War, 1775–1783* (Kent, OH, 1996), 47. Governor William Livingston defined a Tory as an "incorrigible Animal" that needed to be killed. Quoted in Kwasny, *Washington's Partisan War*, 183. Less highly placed Patriots used similar language: *Am. Arch.*, 4th ser., III: 823–4; Stokes, *Iconography of Manhattan*, iv: 874; Committee, Monmouth Co., NJ, to Boston Committee of Correspondence, [c. May] 1774, Boston Committee of Correspondence, Box 3, NYPL.

Definition of Patriots quoted in Robert Munro Brown, "Revolutionary New Hampshire and the Loyalist Experience: 'surely We Have Deserved a Better Fate'" (PhD diss., University of New Hampshire, 1983), 107.

23. Samuel Curwen, *Journal and letters of the late Samuel Curwen, judge of Admiralty* (New York, 1842), 25–6, 29–30, 58–9. For the global experiences of Loyalist exiles, see Jasanoff, *Liberty's Exiles*.

24. New York: Wetherhead's 1783 memorial is quoted in Crary, *Price of Loyalty*, 44–7, at 45–6. See also Edward F. De Lancey, ed., *History of New York during the Revolutionary War . . . by Thomas Jones* (Cranbury, NJ, 2006), i: 40; Stokes, *Iconography of Manhattan*, iv: 882. Lieutenant Governor Cadwallader Colden to Dartmouth, May 3, 1775, in *NYCD*, viii: 571; Richard Yates to John Sargent, New York, May 1, 1775 [extract], Dartmouth MSS, II/1240. For Patriot concerns over the Loyalists' "hellish schemes" and "horrid Plot," see Villers, "Loyalism in Connecticut," 141, 147, 373; Ellen D. Larned, *Historic gleanings in Windham County, Connecticut* (Providence, RI, 1899), 116–18. Virginia: *Am. Arch.*, 4th ser., III: 823.

25. David A. Copeland, *Debating the Issues in Colonial Newspapers: Primary Documents on Events of the Period* (Westport, CT, 2000), 227, 233–4. "knocking out": *Rivington's New-York Gazetteer*, Dec. 22, 1774. *Am. Arch.*, 4th ser., II: 132, 12. "Englishman": Sabine, *Biographical sketches*, ii: 217. Boycott orders: *Am. Arch.*, 4th ser., I: 1051, 1240; II: 1106; Schlesinger, *Prelude*, 225; see more generally, ibid., 222–6; "a most wretched" and further verbal abuse quoted at 225. Threats and beatings: Eric Burns, *Infamous Scribblers: The Founding Fathers and the Rowdy Beginnings of American Journalism* (New York, 2006), 180. For this account, see also Breen, *American Insurgents*, 233–4.

26. Schlesinger, *Prelude*, 219–20; Potter-MacKinnon, *Liberty We Seek*, 30; Gerlach, ed., *New Jersey in the American Revolution*, 98; Irvin, *Clothed in Robes*, 69; Ferling, *Independence*, 256.

27. Rivington's petition to Congress, May 20, 1775, in *Am. Arch.*, 4th ser., II: 836–7. Rivington would later return with new presses as the King's Printer to publish *Rivington's New York Loyal Gazette* (subsequently relabeled *The Royal Gazette*) in British-occupied New York. For the destruction of William Goddard's press in 1777, see W. Goddard, *Memorial to the Committee of Grievances, Maryland House of Delegates, Mar. 28, 1777*, Misc. Collections, U.S. States and Territories, Box 7, Maryland, NYPL. See Harry M. Ward, *The War for Independence and the Transformation of American Society* (London, 1999), 59–65, for restrictions of the freedom of press, and violence against the press.

28. For clerical networks, see, e.g., Rev. Henry Caner, Letterbook, to Bishop of London, Aug. 16, 1775, quoted in Crary, *Price of Loyalty*, 93. For as-

sociation and nonsigners, see *Am. Arch.*, 4th ser., III: 141–2. Dibblee: Crary, *Price of Loyalty*, 107–8. Mansfield: Mansfield to Rev. Samuel Peters, Jan. 12, 1776, quoted in Crary, *Price of Loyalty*, 103; Gilbert, "Connecticut Loyalists," 277. Beach: Gilbert, "Connecticut Loyalists," 279 (quotation); Crary, *Price of Loyalty*, 106–7. For cases beyond Connecticut, see "Introduction," in *Loyalists and Community in North America*, ed. Robert M. Calhoon, Timothy M. Barnes, and George A. Rawlyk (Westport, CT, 1994), 3; Villers, "Loyalism in Connecticut," 165–6; William Stoodley Bartlet, ed., *The Frontier Missionary: A Memoir of the Life of the Rev. Jacob Bailey, A.M.* (Boston, 1853), 105; Julia Martha Ross, "Jacob Bailey, Loyalist, Anglican Clergyman in New England and Nova Scotia" (PhD diss., University of New Brunswick, 1975); Jacob Bailey to "Dear Sir," Mar. 1, 1775, Jacob Bailey Papers, LOC; Jasanoff, *Liberty's Exiles*, 6–7; AO12/6/47–53, 42/1–6; 13/71A/248–55.

29. "mop filled": Samuel Peters, *General History of Connecticut* (London, 1781), quoted in Crary, *Price of Loyalty*, 91. Roberts: Irvin, "Tar, Feathers," 237. Several other priests subsequently died as a result of abuse or the harsh conditions of their imprisonment: Luke Babcock of Philipse Manor; Ebenezer Kneeland of Stratford, CT (both 1777); Thomas Barton, York County, PA (1780). See also Ranlet, *New York Loyalists*, 159; Crary, *Price of Loyalty*, 88, 187; *Gazetteer and Daily Advertiser*, Dec. 30, 1776; E. LeRoy Pond, *The Tories of Chippeney Hill, Connecticut* (New York, 1909), 19.

30. Oaths: John McKesson, Secretary to New York Provincial Congress, corr. 1775–9, DLAR, Force Papers 7E, [reel 17] item 74; *Minutes of the Committee of Safety of Bucks County*, 361; Calhoon, "Reintegration," 58–9; Breen, *American Insurgents*, 237–9; Van Tyne, *Loyalists*, 219; Edward Alfred Jones, *The Loyalists of New Jersey: Their Memorials, Petitions, Claims, etc., from English Records* (Newark, NJ, 1927), 54–5; Christopher Moore, *The Loyalists: Revolution, Exile, Settlement* (Toronto, 1994), 77; AO12/10/131. Capt. Bowater to Earl of Denbigh, June 5 and 11, 1777, in Marion Balderston and David Syrett, eds., *The Lost War: Letters from British Officers during the American Revolution* (New York, 1975), 131. Militias: McEachern and Williams, eds., *Wilmington–New Hanover Safety Committee Minutes*, 40, 31–2; Charles Neimeyer, "'Town Born, Turn Out': Town Militias, Tories, and the Struggle for Control of the Massachusetts Backcountry," in *War and Society in the American Revolution: Mobilization and Home Fronts*, ed. John Resch and Walter Sargent (DeKalb, IL, 2007); Breen, *American Insurgents*, 239; Breunig, *Amerikanische Revolution*, 71–6.

31. Kim, "Limits of Politicization," 873–5. "the Neighbourhood": quoted in Hoerder, *Crowd Action*, 303.

32. For Brown, see Jim Piecuch, *Three Peoples, One King: Loyalists, Indians, and Slaves in the Revolutionary South, 1775–1782* (Columbia, SC, 2008), 46, 57–9; Jasanoff, *Liberty's Exiles*, 23–5; Edward J. Cashin, *The King's Ranger: Thomas Brown and the American Revolution on the Southern Frontier* (New York, 1999), 27–9. "like a calf": Robert S. Davis Jr., "A Georgia Loyalist's Perspective on the American Revolution: The Letters of Dr. Thomas Taylor," *Georgia Historical Quarterly* 81:1 (1997), 126. For Loyalist associations in Connecticut in 1775, see, e.g., AO12/1/172–3, 214–15; *Am. Arch.*, 4th ser., I: 1202, 1210, 1258–60. Villers, "Loyalism in Connecticut," 207; David Henry Villers, " 'King Mob' and the Rule of Law: Revolutionary Justice and the Suppression of Loyalism in Connecticut, 1774–1783," in *Loyalists and Community*, ed. Calhoon, Barnes, and Rawlyk, 19; Yale University MS, MS 674, American Revolutionary Collection. For similar pledges in other colonies, see Loyalist Association, Maryland, Dec. 8, 1775, BHQP 88; Jonathan Grout, *Proceedings of the town of Petersham, in town-meeting, January 2, 1775* (Evans 49293); Carol Berkin, *Jonathan Sewall; Odyssey of an American Loyalist* (New York, 1974), 107; *Am. Arch.*, 4th ser., I: 1164; "A Jersey Farmer Proposes a Loyalist Association, January 26, 1775," in *New Jersey in the American Revolution*, ed. Gerlach, 114–15.

33. For the regional, ethnic, and socioeconomic demographics of Loyalism, see Ward, *War for Independence*, 36–7; William H. Nelson, "The Loyalist View of the American Revolution" (PhD diss., Columbia University, 1958), 131; Robert Middlekauff, *The Glorious Cause: The American Revolution 1763–1789*, rev. and expanded ed. (Oxford, 2007), 564–5.

34. Schaw is quoted in Crary, *Price of Loyalty*, 61; see also Breen, *American Insurgents*, 187–8, 193–7.

35. For women's roles and political status, see Linda K. Kerber, *Women of the Republic: Intellect and Ideology in Revolutionary America* (Chapel Hill, NC, 1980); eadem, " 'May all our Citizens Be Soldiers and all our Soldiers Citizens': The Ambiguities of Female Citizenship in the New Nation," in *Women, Militarism, and War*, ed. Jean Bethke Elshtain and Sheila Tobias (Savage, MD, 1990); Berkin, *Revolutionary Mothers*; Joan R. Gundersen, *To Be Useful to the World: Women in Revolutionary America, 1740–1790* (Chapel Hill, NC, 2006); Douglas Bradburn, *The Citizenship Revolution: Politics and the Creation of the American Union, 1774–1804* (Charlottesville, VA, 2009), 58; Jones, *Loyalists of New Jersey*, 238–9; Crary, *Price of Loyalty*, 78–80. For examples of women expelled from their homes, see AO12/38/403–5, 40/222, referenced in Gregory T. Knouff, "Masculinity and the Memory of the American Revolution," in *Gender, War and Politics: Transatlantic Perspectives, 1775–1830*, ed. Karen Hagemann, Gisela Mettele, and Jane Rendall

(Basingstoke, 2010), 335. See also AO12/24/118, 76/145, 89/16, 90/3, 101/114, 109/268; 13/9/183–end, 70B/363–6, 83/427–30, 94/338–45.

36. "to Make us": MS Journal of an unidentified North Carolina High-lander Loyalist officer who participated in battle of Moore's Creek Bridge, prisoner of war [Feb. 1776], Clinton Papers 14/32. Crary, *Price of Loyalty*, 208; Janice Potter-Mackinnon, *While the Women Only Wept: Loyalist Refugee Women* (Montreal, 1993), 38; Brown, "Revolutionary New Hampshire," 107–8; William Thomas Johnson, "Alan Cameron, a Scotch Loyalist in the American Revolution," *Pennsylvania History* 8:1 (1941). For the section title, see Thomas Anburey, *Travels through the Interior Parts of America* (New York, 1969), repr. of 1789 ed., ii: 303.

37. Quoted in Crary, *Price of Loyalty*, 202–3. For John Champneys's imprisonment in Charleston and subsequent banishment, see Piecuch, *Three Peoples*, 57.

38. Willard: *Connecticut Journal*, Sept. 9, 1774; York, *Henry Hulton*, 178. A critical bystander was tarred and feathered on that occasion. For other instances of the threat of imprisonment in the mines, see *Gazetteer and New Daily Advertiser*, June 8, 1775; *Am. Arch.*, 4th ser., I: 1262. British press ("the loyalists are"): *English Chronicle*, July 27–30, 1782; *London Chronicle*, July 27–30, 1782. English visitor: Edward Augustus Kendall, *Travels through the northern parts of the United States, in the years 1807 and 1808* (New York, 1809), i: 210.

39. *New-York Mirror*, i: 33 (Mar. 13, 1824): 257–8. Just before the war, the Connecticut assembly had purchased the mine for use as a makeshift colonial prison; it was soon dubbed the Newgate of Connecticut, evoking the infamous prison in the British capital. *New-York Journal*, Jan. 1, 1773; *Providence Gazette*, Jan. 15, 1774.

40. Physical description largely from "Account of the escape of Ebenezer Hathaway and Thomas Smith," *Rivington Royal Gazette*, June 9, 1781; Crary, *Price of Loyalty*, 218. See also Denis R. Caron, *A Century in Captivity: The Life and Travels of Prince Mortimer, a Connecticut Slave* (Durham, NH, 2006), 72–3. For British references, see *London Chronicle*, July 17–19, 1781; *Morning Chronicle*, July 20, 1781.

41. *Boston Post-Boy*, Nov. 21, 1774; *Connecticut Journal*, Aug. 30, 1775.

42. Criminal sentences: *Connecticut Journal*, Nov. 3, 1774; *Norwich Packet*, Mar. 31 to Apr. 7, 1774; *Massachusetts Gazette*, Apr. 15, 1774; *Essex Gazette*, Apr. 19, 1774; *Boston Post-Boy*, Nov. 21, 1774; *Am. Arch.*, 5th ser., I: 43. See also *Connecticut Courant*, Sept. 6, 1790; *Rhode-Island American*, Apr. 10, 1822. For Washington, see GW to Committee of Symsbury, Dec. 11, 1775; *Am. Arch.*, 4th ser., IV: 235–6, 376. Sheldon S. Cohen, ed., "The Connecticut Captivity of Major Christopher French," *Connecticut Historical Society Bulletin* 55:3–4 (1990): 150.

43. Crary, *Price of Loyalty*, 216; N. H. Egleston, "The Newgate of Connecticut: The Old Simsbury Copper Mines," *Magazine of American History* 15:4 (1886), 325; *Kansas City Star*, June 17, 1906 (quotation).

44. "vapour": Kendall, *Travels*, i: 212. Cf. *Connecticut Mirror*, Aug. 6, 1831; Egleston, "Newgate of Connecticut," 322.

45. "imparting": Caron, *Century in Captivity*, 73. Peters, *General History of Connecticut*, 175–6.

46. Caron, *Century in Captivity*, 73; Peters, *General History of Connecticut*, 175–6. "utter isolation": Egleston, "Newgate of Connecticut," 325.

47. Escape attempts: *Connecticut Courant*, Apr. 12–19 and Apr. 26–May 3, 1774, Dec. 18, 1775; *Connecticut Journal*, Feb. 12, 1774; Egleston, "Newgate of Connecticut," 330; Richard Harvey Phelps, *The Newgate of Connecticut* (Hartford, CT, 1876), 33–9. Newspapers alerted the public to prison escapes and bounties for recapture: *Connecticut Gazette*, Jan. 21, 1774; *Essex Gazette*, Jan. 25–Feb. 1, 1774; *Connecticut Courant*, May 3–10, 1774, Sept. 4, 1775, Dec. 2 and 9, 1776, Feb. 24, 1777.

48. "Prisoners in this gaol" and "ferocious disposition": Kendall, *Travels*, i: 215. Deaths: *Kansas City Star*, June 17, 1906; Caron, *Century in Captivity*, 75.

49. Lord Campbell to Dartmouth, Charleston, July 19, 1775 [extracts], BHQP 19; Larkin, "Loyalism," 291; Keith Mason, "The American Loyalist Problem of Identity in the Revolutionary Atlantic World," in *Loyal Atlantic*, ed. Bannister and Riordan, 45–8.

Chapter Two

1. *London Evening Post*, Dec. 1–3, 1774; *Public Advertiser*, Dec. 5, 1774. For Malcom's petition to the king and George III's response, see Hersey, "Tar and Feathers," 461–4 (quotations 463).

2. *General Evening Post*, Mar. 10–12, 1774. See also *Morning Chronicle*, Mar. 9, 1774; *London Evening Post*, Mar. 24–26, 1774. Cf. Mary A. Favret, *War at a Distance: Romanticism and the Making of Modern Wartime* (Princeton, 2010), on the mediation of distant violence.

3. Transatlantic symbols of liberty connect the American Patriot movement with domestic British radicalism: the figure 45 references issue no. 45 of the British radical John Wilkes's anti-government *The North Briton*.

4. *Report of the Lords committees, appointed by the House of Lords to enquire into the several proceedings in the colony of Massachusetts's Bay* (London, 1774), 33–4, and passim, at http://lincoln.lib.niu.edu/cgi-bin/amarch/getdoc.pl?/var/lib/philologic/databases/amarch/.11 North is cited in Bunker, *Empire on the Edge*, 261; see ibid., 327, 350, for intelligence on Americans arming.

5. By the King, *A Proclamation, For suppressing Rebellion and Sedition*

(Aug. 23, 1775). "Torrent of Violence": *His Majesty's most gracious speech to both Houses of Parliament, on Friday, October 27, 1775.* British officials in America, too, asserted the government's duty to protect the Loyalists: Gage, Proclamation, Boston, June 1775, Mackenzie Papers, Box 3.

6. Government overestimating Loyalists: Spring, *With Zeal*, 17–18; Julie M. Flavell, "Government Interception of Letters from America and the Quest for Colonial Opinion in 1775," *WMQ* 58:2 (2001): 404. Reports of violence: Gov. Franklin to Lord Dartmouth, Perth Amboy, Dec. 6, 1774, Bancroft 92/26; Alex Innes to Lord Dartmouth, Charleston, May 1, 1775, Bancroft 94/17; Governor Josiah Martin of North Carolina, quoted in Bessie Lewis Whitaker, *The Provincial Council and Committees of Safety in North Carolina* (Chapel Hill, NC, 1908), 10; Ferling, *Independence*, 95.

7. "many worthy": William Strahan to Benjamin Franklin, London, Oct. 4, 1775 [copy], Dartmouth MSS, II/1552. For Mary Murray [MM], see MM to [Edward Hutchinson Robbins], Jan. 8 (quotation); MM to "Betsy," July 20, 1775; memorial by Dorothy Forbes, Dec. 12, 1775; MM to aunt, Feb. 4 and 25, 1776, James Murray Robins, Box 1, MHS.

8. For Loyalist literature, see Gould, "American Independence and Britain's Counter-Revolution," *Past & Present* 154 (1997): 114–15. "unheard-of-cruelties": quoted in Alfred Grant, *Our American Brethren: A History of Letters in the British Press during the American Revolution, 1775–1781* (Jefferson, NC, 1995), 171. See also *London Chronicle*, Sept. 11, 1775. "extorting": *Gazetteer*, Feb. 11, 1775. Some pieces exaggerated the regularity of killings: *Gazetteer*, Feb. 21, 1775. For references to various modes of torture, see *Middlesex Journal*, Dec. 3, 1774; *Morning Chronicle*, Dec. 7, 1774, Oct. 12, 1775; *Public Advertiser*, Jan. 8, 1776; *Daily Advertiser*, Feb. 26, 1776. Live burial: York, *Henry Hulton*, 178.

9. For the role of pressure and threats, see AO12/13/80–119, 36/59–60; *Georgia Gazette*, Oct. 4, 1775; Charles A. Risher, "Propaganda, Dissension, and Defeat: Loyalist Sentiment in Georgia, 1763–1783" (PhD diss., Mississippi State University, 1976), 107–8; Jasanoff, *Liberty's Exiles*, 24; Ruma Chopra, *Choosing Sides: Loyalists in Revolutionary America* (Lanham, MD, 2013), 3, 13; Arthur M. Schlesinger, *Prelude to Independence: The Newspaper War on Britain, 1764–1776* (New York, 1958), 213.

10. *Gazetteer*, Feb. 11, 1775. See also *Morning Chronicle*, Aug. 15, 1776.

11. Deposition sworn before Gov. W. Tryon by Christopher Benson, June 16, 1776, Mackenzie Papers, Box 1, folder 2; Stokes, *Iconography of Manhattan*, iv, 923, 1001; [Great Britain, Loyalist Commission], *American Loyalists. Transcript of the Manuscript Books and Papers of the Commission of Enquiry into the Losses and Services of the American Loyalists held under Acts of Parliament of 23, 25, 26, 28 and 29 of GEORGE III*

Preserved Amongst the Audit Office Records in the Public Record Office of England, 1783–1790 (London, 1960), xii: 193; *Connecticut Courant*, Feb. 20, 1775. Villers, "Loyalism in Connecticut," 207; AO12/1/288–9, 291, 293; 57/43; 109/110; 13/70B/212; 76/191–200; 83/78–80.

12. The interception scheme was probably initiated by Lord Dartmouth. The letters used here—the less-well-known earlier portion—were selected mostly from the New York packet, which carried letters from New York, Boston, Philadelphia, Quebec. Once the colonies were proclaimed to be in open rebellion against the Crown in August 1775, London had outgoing correspondence opened, too. For the papers, the context of their interception, and the better-known stash held in TNA, see Flavell, "Government Interception." Precautionary measures: [?] London, to Thomas Quin, New York, Oct. 4, 1775, Dartmouth MSS, II/1556. "P.S.": J. G. to Thomas Charles Williams c/o Messrs Williams, Teb & Williams, Aug. 6, 1775 [extract], II/1431. See also J. Ingersoll to Jared Ingersoll, Aug. 5, 1775 [copy], II/1423; II/1483, 1490. "the Caution": Flavell, "Government Interception," 421, with reference to Anthony Todd in n. 58. John Penn to William Baker, Esq., June 5, 1775 [copy], II/1292; James Tilghman to William Baker, July 30, 1775 [copy], II/1399; Cadwallader Colden Jr. to Revd. Dr. Myles Cooper, Coldingham, July 15, 1775 [extract], 1372. "The poor proscribed Tories": to Revd. Doctor Myles Cooper or to Isaac Wilkins, Sept. 4, 1775, II/1483. See also John Cruger to Edmund Burke, May 4, 1775 [extract], II/1257. A London correspondent told Peyton Randolph, president of the Continental Congress, that, in his perspective, the Americans showed a "savage ferocity" in "the cruel Persecution of even Neutrals." Edward Montagu to Randolph, Oct. 2, 1775, II/1543. For self-censorship, see also Samuel Quincy Diary, Feb. 26, 1775, MHS. *London Chronicle*, Sept. 11, 1775; *Chester Chronicle*, Feb. 29, 1776.

13. Michael Eliot Howard, "*Temperamenta Belli*: Can War Be Controlled?," in *Restraints on War: Studies in the Limitation of Armed Conflict*, ed. idem (Oxford, 1979), 1 (quotations), 4; see also Geoffrey Best, *Humanity in Warfare* (New York, 1980); Stephen C. Neff, *War and the Law of Nations: A General History* (New York, 2005), 15–25. In the early modern period, theorists and practitioners of war shifted their attention to the just conduct of war, or *ius in bello*. For my understanding of the codes of war, I am indebted to the important work of B. Donagan on the seventeenth century, esp. "Atrocity, War Crime, and Treason in the English Civil War," *AHR* 99:4 (1994), and Wayne E. Lee on the eighteenth century, as referenced throughout this book. Lee, *Barbarians and Brothers*, fruitfully considers the relationship between restraint and excessive violence or frightfulness in terms of capacity, control, calcula-

tion, and culture. Cf. David Bell, *The First Total War: Napoleon's Europe and the Birth of Warfare as We Know It* (Boston, 2007), 49, on codes of war against "civilized" and "noncivilized" opponents. The term "civilian" was not yet used in the modern sense, but there was a clear understanding of the distinctions between soldiers and non-soldiers created by occupation, location, social status, and gender: Erica Charters, Eve Rosenhaft, and Hannah Smith, "Introduction," in *Civilians and War in Europe, 1618–1815*, ed. eaedem (Liverpool, 2012), 11, 17.

14. For the identity of the British-Americans, and the nature of their relations with metropolitan Britons, see Linda Colley, *Captives: Britain, Empire and the World, 1600–1850* (London, 2002), 207; Stephen Conway, "From Fellow-Nationals to Foreigners: British Perceptions of the Americans, circa 1739–1783," *WMQ* 59:1 (2002); Dror Wahrman, "The English Problem of Identity in the American Revolution," *AHR* 106:4 (2001), with the quotation "of the same language" at n. 13; Gould, *Persistence of Empire*; idem, *Writing the Rebellion*; Griffin, *America's Revolution*, 44; Smith-Rosenberg, *This Violent Empire*, 4–5; Breen, *Marketplace*. For Atlantic world and imperial integration and evidence of the simultaneous Americanization of the colonies, see Rhoden, "The American Revolution."

15. "though H.M.'s subjects": quoted in Wood, *Revolutionary Characters*, 22. Conway, "From Fellow-Nationals to Foreigners," 69–71, 82 (quotation); Irvin, *Clothed in Robes*, 65; Colley, *Captives*, 207; T. H. Breen, "Ideology and Nationalism on the Eve of the American Revolution: Revisions *Once More* in Need of Revising," *JAH* 84:1 (1997). See Armitage, "Civil War and Revolution," 21, for the Revolution as an imperial civil war.

16. This paragraph is based on James E. Bradley, "The British Public and the American Revolution: Ideology, Interest and Opinion," in *Britain and the American Revolution*, ed. H. T. Dickinson (London, 1998), and Conway, *British Isles*, 131–46. See also Jerome R. Reich, *British Friends of the American Revolution* (London, 1998). Samuel Quincy's London Diary for 1774/75 (MHS) shows him moving in pro-American circles, gaining the impression that "multitudes of fervent friends to America reside in this Island" (204).

17. Based on Ira D. Gruber, "For King and Country: The Limits of Loyalty of British Officers in the War for American Independence," in *Limits of Loyalty*, ed. Edgar Denton III (Waterloo, Ont., 1980). See also Richard Fitzpatrick Papers, LOC.

18. Effingham's resignation letter, with this paragraph's first two quotations, was printed widely: *London Magazine* (Sept. 1775), 456; *St James's Chronicle*, Sept. 2–5, 1775; *Morning Chronicle*, Sept. 5, 1775;

Public Advertiser, Oct. 19, 1775. For the corporations of London, Dublin, Newcastle, and others expressing their thanks to Effingham see, e.g., *Am. Arch.,* 4th ser., II: 1070–71, 1672. See also *Craftsman,* Oct. 21, 1775; *General Evening Post,* Oct. 17–19, 1775; *Morning Chronicle,* Oct. 20 and Nov. 25, 1775. "imbrue his hands": *Gazetteer and New Daily Advertiser,* Sept. 2, 1775; *Gazetteer and New Daily Advertiser,* Sept. 26, 1775; *Public Advertiser;* Sept. 14, 1775; *St. James's Chronicle,* Sept. 28–30, Oct. 17–19, Oct. 31–Nov. 2, 1775; *Chester Chronicle,* Nov. 13, 1775. *Am. Arch.,* 4th ser., II: 1635; III: 505. Effingham to Barrington, Apr. 12, 1775, extract from *Cape Fear Mercury,* Aug. 7, 1775.

19. The key article on hard-liners versus conciliators in the British Army remains Stephen Conway, "To Subdue America: British Army Officers and the Conduct of the Revolutionary War," *WMQ* 43:3 (1986). See also idem, "'The Great Mischief Complain'd of': Reflections on the Misconduct of British Soldiers in the Revolutionary War," *WMQ* 47:3 (1990); Balderston and Syrett, eds., *Lost War,* 27, 78. For this chapter, and especially the sections on individual leaders, I am indebted well beyond specific annotations to Andrew Jackson O'Shaughnessy's authoritative *Men Who Lost America: British Leadership, the American Revolution, and the Fate of Empire* (New Haven, CT, 2013), which fills a long-standing lacuna regarding British perspectives on the war. See also Troyer Steele Anderson, *The Command of the Howe Brothers during the American Revolution* (Cranbury, NJ, 2005), 10–13.

20. O'Shaughnessy, *Men Who Lost America,* 28–9; Dartmouth to [unknown], Whitehall, July 12, 1775, Add MS 21697/99–101; *By The King, A Proclamation, for Suppressing Rebellion and Sedition.* For the argument regarding moderation, see the work of Eliga H. Gould, "Zones of Law, Zones of Violence: The Legal Geography of the British Atlantic, circa 1772," *WMQ* 60:3 (2003); idem, "American Independence."

21. On the king's character, see Jeremy Black, *George III: America's Last King* (New Haven, CT, 2006), ch. 7; Stella Tillyard, *A Royal Affair: George III and His Scandalous Siblings* (London, 2006); John Brooke, *King George III* (London, 1972); Stanley Ayling, *George the Third* (London, 1972). For the king's toughening stance, see O'Shaughnessy, *Men Who Lost America,* 22 with n. 13; George III to North, Feb. 4, May 6, Sept. 11, 1774, in J. W. Fortescue, ed., *The Correspondence of King George III from 1760 to December 1783* (London, 1927–8), iii: 59, 104, 131; Black, *George III,* 84, 221; Andrew Jackson O'Shaughnessy, "'If Others Will Not Be Active, I Must Drive': George III and the American Revolution," *Early American Studies* 2:1 (2004): 5; Richard L. Bushman, *King and People in Provincial Massachusetts* (Chapel Hill, NC, 1985), 219.

22. The notion of a quarrel or family dispute was considered by early Anglophile historians of the Loyalists, such as Moses Coit Tyler, *Glimpses*

of England: Social, Political, Literary (New York, 1898), 279; see also Winston Churchill, *A History of English Speaking Peoples* (London, 1956), iii, book 8, ch. 12. William D. Liddle, " 'A Patriot King, or None': Lord Bolingbroke and the American Renunciation of George III," *JAH* 65:4 (1979), argues that most Americans delayed renouncing George III until 1775. For the anti-patriarchal critique of the king and competing 18th-century notions of parent-child relations, see Jay Fliegelman, *Prodigals and Pilgrims: The American Revolution against Patriarchal Authority, 1750–1800* (Cambridge, 1982), esp. 89–119; Sarah Knott, *Sensibility and the American Revolution* (Chapel Hill, NC, 2009), 62–3; Black, *George III*, 220–21. For the cult of the monarchy in late colonial America, see Brendan McConville, *The King's Three Faces: The Rise and Fall of Royal America, 1688–1776* (Chapel Hill, NC, 2006). For a more skeptical view of the emotional ties between colonials and the king by the early 1770s, see James Corbett David, *Dunmore's New World: The Extraordinary Life of a Royal Governor in Revolutionary America* (Charlottesville, VA, 2013), 54.

23. Tillyard, *Royal Affair*, 314–17 (quotations 315). George III to North, Feb. 15, 1775, in W. Bodham Donne, ed., *The Correspondence of King George the Third with Lord North from 1768 to 1783* (London, 1867), i: 229.

24. For North, see Alan Valentine, *Lord North* (Norman, OK, 1967); O'Shaughnessy, *Men Who Lost America*, ch. 2; Ferling, *Independence*, 43–6, 103. Bunker, *Empire on the Edge*, 88, has the speech count.

25. On North's conciliatory efforts, see O'Shaughnessy, *Men Who Lost America*, 56; "The dye is now cast": George III to North, Sept. 11, 1774, in Donne, ed., *Correspondence*, i: 202. See also George III to North, Nov. 18, 1774, in Fortescue, ed., *Correspondence*, iii: 153; George III to North, Feb. 15, 1775, in Donne, ed., *Correspondence*, i: 229. For the chronology of intelligence reaching London, new orders for Gage, and the legal verdict of treason, see Bunker, *Empire on the Edge*, 350–65. For Gage, see John Shy, "Gage, Thomas (1719/20–1787)," *Oxford Dictionary of National Biography*, Oxford University Press, 2004, online edition, Jan. 2008, at http://www.oxforddnb.com.pitt.idm.oclc.org/view/article/10275 (accessed Aug., 21, 2016); Bunker, *Empire on the Edge*, 289–90, and passim.

26. My portrait of the Howes is based on O'Shaughnessy, *Men Who Lost America*, 83–96; Ira D. Gruber, *The Howe Brothers and the American Revolution* (New York, 1972); idem, "Lord Howe and Lord George Germain, British Politics and the Winning of American Independence," *WMQ* 22:2 (1965); idem, "George III Chooses a Commander in Chief," in *Arms and Independence: The Military Character of the American Revolution*, ed. Ronald Hoffman and Peter J. Albert (Charlottesville,

VA, 1984); Phillips, *Cousins' War,* 298–9; David Hackett Fischer, *Washington's Crossing* (New York, 2004), 67–78 (quotation 68).

27. For George Augustus Howe, see Hoock, *Empires of the Imagination,* 44; Michael Kammen, *Digging Up the Dead: A History of Notable American Reburials* (Chicago, 2010), 71–3. Fischer, *Washington's Crossing,* 70. Entry for "Howe, Hon. William," in Lewis B. Namier and John Brooke, *The History of Parliament: The House of Commons, 1754–90* (London, 1964), ii: 649–50.

28. "a child": O'Shaughnessy, *Men Who Lost America,* 132. Cf. Piers Mackesy, *The War for America: 1775–1783* (London, 1964), 46; George Athan Billias, "John Burgoyne: Ambitious General," in *George Washington's Generals and Opponents: Their Exploits and Leadership,* ed. idem, vol. 2 (New York, 1994).

29. John Burgoyne, "Speech of a General Officer (Feb. 27, 1775)," in *Proceedings and Debates of the British Parliaments Respecting North America 1754–1783,* ed. R. C. Simmons and P. D. G. Thomas (Millwood, NY, 1982), v: 475–6. "a genius": quoted in O'Shaughnessy, *Men Who Lost America,* 86 with n. 9.

30. Margaret Stead, "Contemporary Responses in Print to the American Campaigns of the Howe Brothers," in *Britain and America Go to War: The Impact of War and Warfare, 1754–1815,* ed. Julie Flavell and Stephen Conway (Gainesville, FL, 2004), 119–20, with the quotation "The most plausible" at 119. Anon. author "Nottingham": *London Evening Post,* Feb. 27, 1776. Cf. Mercy Otis Warren to Catherine Macaulay, Feb. 1, 1777, Mercy Otis Warren Papers, MHS.

31. "first time": Troy Bickham, *Making Headlines: The American Revolution as Seen through the British Press* (DeKalb, IL, 2009), 7, with reference to Conway, *British Isles,* 315. For the language of "unnatural" civil war, see Chopra, *Unnatural Rebellion.*

32. The classic account of the aftermath of Lexington is Arthur Bernon Tourtellot, *Lexington and Concord: The Beginning of the War of the American Revolution* (New York, 1963). For specific references, see subsequent notes.

33. Address from the Massachusetts Congress to the inhabitants of Great Britain, April 26: *London Evening Post,* May 30–June 1, 1775; *General Evening Post,* May 30–June 1, 1775; *Public Advertiser,* May 30, 1775; *Gazetteer,* May 31, 1775; *Craftsman,* June 3, 1775; *Chester Chronicle,* June 5, 1775. Official rebel account from *Essex Gazette,* Salem, Apr. 25, 1775: *London Evening Post Extraordinary,* May 29, 1775; *Public Advertiser,* May 30, 1775. Survivors' depositions: *General Evening Post,* May 30–June 1, 1775; *Middlesex Journal,* May 30–June 1, 1775; *Daily Advertiser,* May 31, 1775. See also Massachusetts Provincial Congress,

A narrative of the excursions and ravages (1775); DLAR 382/12/80/39 (Amherst Papers); Daniel Fuller Appleton, ed., *The Diary of the Rev.:d Daniel Fuller* (New York, 1894). Defensive response by British officials in private: Dartmouth to Gage, June 1, 1775, Gage Papers, English Series 29, WLCL. See also [?]Pownall to W. Knox, June 2, 1775, William Knox Papers, Box 2, WLCL. The *General Evening Post* (June 9, 1775) cautioned that accounts by the "rebel Vermin" were "stuffed with many Falsities." British allegations of "massacre": *Stamford Mercury*, June 1, 1775. Charity: *Public Advertiser*, June 9, 1775; *Gazetteer*, June 9, 1775; *General Evening Post*, June 8, 1775; *St James's Chronicle*, June 8–10, 1775. Libel case: "Proceedings against John Horne," in T. B. Howell, ed., *A Complete Collection of State Trials and Proceedings for High Treason and Other Crimes and Misdemeanors*, xx (London, 1816); *An Interesting Address to the independent part of the People of England* (1777); Grant, *Our American Brethren*, 34–7. For a rival charity, with Loyalists in London exile raising several thousand pounds for "such occasional Acts of Benevolence as may be useful to Soldiers" serving in America, and for their widows and orphans, see Stanley Weintraub, *Iron Tears: America's Battle for Freedom, Britain's Quagmire: 1775–1783* (New York, 2005), 16. For British allegations of rebel atrocities, including a scalping, see James Abercrombie to Cadwallader Colden, May 2, 1775, in Cadwallader Colden Papers, LOC.

34. Gruber, "Lord Howe and Lord George Germain," 231–2. Admiralty to Graves, July 6, 1775, *NDAR*, ii: 1316. See also Graves to Mowat, Oct. 6, ibid., 324–6; Dartmouth to Dunmore, July 5, 1775, Bancroft 94/235.

35. Valentine, Lord North, i: 372–3; Jon E. Lewis, ed., *The Mammoth Book of War Diaries and Letters: Life on the Battlefield in the Words of the Ordinary Soldier, 1775–1991* (New York, 1999), 2; O'Shaughnessy, *Men Who Lost America*, 86; Sylvia R. Frey, *The British Soldier in America: A Social History of Military Life in the Revolutionary Period* (Austin, 1981), 46–7. Clinton is quoted in Michael Glover, *General Burgoyne in Canada and America: Scapegoat for a System* (London, 1976), 86. "The Rubicon": quoted in Balderston and Syrett, eds., *Lost War*, 31.

36. Quotations from *Morning Chronicle*, Sept. 21, 1775; see also *London Evening Post*, Sept. 23–6, 1775; *Middlesex Journal*, Sept. 21–3, 1775; *Craftsman*, Sept. 23, 1775; *Chester Chronicle*, Sept. 25, 1775. See further, *Daily Advertiser*, Oct. 11, 1775; *Morning Chronicle*, Oct. 19, 1775.

37. "unmanly and infamous kind of War": Edward Howland Tatum, ed., *The American Journal of Ambrose Serle* (San Marino, CA, 1940), 36. See also C. Stedman, *The history of the origin, progress, and termination of the American war* (London, 1794), i: 118; Roger Lamb, *An Original and*

Authentic Journal of Occurrences during the Late American War (New York, 1968), 27; "Diary of Lt. John Barker," *JSAHR* 7 (1928), entry for Apr. 19, 1775. "Military Europe": terminology and analysis after Stephen Conway, "The British Army, 'Military Europe,' and the American War of Independence," *WMQ* 67:1 (2010). For tensions rooted in the previous war, see Fred Anderson, *A People's Army: Massachusetts Soldiers and Society in the Seven Years' War* (Chapel Hill, NC, 1984); Douglas Edward Leach, *Roots of Conflict: British Armed Forces and Colonial Americans, 1677–1763* (Chapel Hill, NC, 1986), chs. 5–6; Alan Rogers, *Empire and Liberty: American Resistance to British Authority, 1755–1763* (Berkeley, CA, 1974). "King George's": *Constitutional Gazette*, Mar. 23, 1776; cf. *Pennsylvania Journal*, Aug. 28, 1776.

38. "Sea of Blood": Peter Benaudet to Ingham Foster, June 8, 1775 [extract], Dartmouth MSS, II/1303. See also II/1359. "to breathe Vengeance": [brother] to Ingham Foster, July 29, 1775 [copy], II/1395. On unanimity, see II/1240, 1252, 1253, 1257, 1266, 1273, 1292, 1294, 1348 ("Voice from one Extreme"), 1395. See also Anth. Van. Dam. to William [N/H]eate, May 3, 1775 [copy], II/1255; II/1292. Will Strahan to Dr. Franklin, Oct. 4, 1775 [copy], II/1552.

39. Lord Dartmouth to General Gage, Aug. 2, 1775, Guy Johnson Papers MSS 494, Ser. 1, Folder 19, Beinecke Library, Yale University.

40. "Hang, draw": *Middlesex Journal*, Jan. 27, 1774. *By The King, A Proclamation, for Suppressing Rebellion and Sedition.*

41. Both Olive Branch Petition and address to inhabitants at http://avalon .law.yale.edu/18th_century/contcong_07-08-75.asp. See also *Pennsylvania Journal*, July 12, 1775.

42. "destined to": quoted in Burrows, *Forgotten Patriots*, 37. According to some legal authorities, a very substantial body of rebels had to be treated *as if* they were legitimate combatants. See, e.g., Emer de Vattel, Bela Kapossy, and Richard Whatmore, *The law of nations, or, Principles of the law of nature, applied to the conduct and affairs of nations and sovereigns, with three early essays on the origin and nature of natural law and on luxury* (Indianapolis, 2008), book iii, ch. xviii, pp. 644–6, paras. 292–4. For the applicability of the codes of war, see Neff, *War and the Law of Nations*, part ii; Ian K. Steele, "Surrendering Rites: Prisoners on Colonial North American Frontiers," in *Hanoverian Britain and Empire: Essays in Memory of Philip Lawson*, ed. Stephen Taylor, Richard Connors, and Clyve Jones (Woodbridge, Suffolk, 1998), 148–9, 156–7.

43. On the relationship between the conflated classification of Jacobites as both rebels and savages and violent responses, see Geoffrey Gilbert Plank, *Rebellion and Savagery: The Jacobite Rising of 1745 and*

the British Empire (Philadelphia, 2006). See also Colin G. Calloway, *White People, Indians, and Highlanders: Tribal Peoples and Colonial Encounters in Scotland and America* (New York, 2008), 30, 99; Jonathan Hawkins, "Imperial '45: The Jacobite Rebellion in Transatlantic Context," *Journal of Imperial and Commonwealth History* 24:1 (1996): 114–17; Witt, *Lincoln's Code*, 42; Bruce Lenman, *The Jacobite Risings in Britain, 1689–1746* (London, 1980), 231–59.

44. "false humanity": G. D. Scull, ed., *Memoir and Letters of Captain W. Glanville Evelyn* (New York, 1971), 65. North: Simmons and Thomas, eds., *Proceedings and Debates*, vi: 411 [Feb. 29, 1776]. On Scotland (and Ireland) in officers' background, see Burrows, *Forgotten Patriots*, 34–5.

45. Through subsidies treaties, the British Crown hired entire regiments of trained and uniformed German (and sometimes other Continental European) troops for a certain period of time. Under international law, such auxiliary forces were acceptable in support of a just war; auxiliaries were not mercenaries, who were instead individual soldiers hiring out their services. Rodney Atwood, *The Hessians: Mercenaries from Hessen-Kassel in the American Revolution* (Cambridge, 1980), 22–3, 29, and passim. *His Majesty's most gracious speech to both Houses of Parliament, on Friday, October 27, 1775* (1776). Fischer, *Washington's Crossing*, 51, was probably the first historian of America to reference the early secret Anglo-German negotiations; Charles W. Ingrao, *The Hessian Mercenary State: Ideas, Institutions, and Reform under Frederick II, 1760–1785* (Cambridge, 1987), 136, had already done so based on European sources. For British troop numbers, see Conway, *British Isles*, 15, 27.

46. "tenderness": *His Majesty's most gracious speech to both Houses of Parliament, on Friday, October 27, 1775* (1776). See also O'Shaughnessy, " 'If Others Will Not Be Active,' " 14. Cobbett and Hansard, eds., *Parliamentary History*, xviii: 726 ("as Englishmen"), 733, 761; Simmons and Thomas, eds., *Proceedings and Debates*, vi: 95–6, 105.

47. Gruber, *Howe Brothers*, 37; O'Shaughnessy, *Men Who Lost America*, 210; George III to North, Nov. 7, 1775, in Donne, ed., *Correspondence*, i: 286. "Roman severity": a January 1775 statement quoted in Weintraub, *Iron Tears*, 35.

48. My assessment of Germain is based on O'Shaughnessy, *Men Who Lost America*, 167–87 (with a good evaluation of the court-martial); Alan Valentine, *Lord George Germain* (Oxford, 1962); George H. Guttridge, "Lord George Germain in Office, 1775–1782," *AHR* 33:1 (1927); Gruber, "Lord Howe and Lord George Germain"; Mackesy, *War for America*, 51 (admirer); entry in History of Parliament, at http://www .historyofparliamentonline.org/volume/1754-1790/member/sackville

-lord-george-1716-85. When Lady Elizabeth Germain died in 1769 without natural heirs and left her estates to him, Sackville adopted her name and was now styled Lord George Germain. For ease of reading, I am referring throughout to Germain.

49. Mackesy, *War for America*, 49; Valentine, *Lord George Germain*, 71. "sentimental manner": GG to William Knox, Dec. 31, 1776, quoted in O'Shaughnessy, *Men Who Lost America*, 176. For the extensive degree to which Germain directed the war, see Valentine, *Lord George Germain*, 107, 127–8, and passim; Guttridge, "Lord George Germain in Office," 33.

Chapter Three

1. For the orders, see Lords Commissioners to Graves, July 6, 1775, *NDAR*, i: 1316–17; Dartmouth to [unknown], July 12, 1775, Add MS 21697/99–100; Gov. Wentworth to Adm. Graves, Nov. 24, 1775, ADM1/484/385–6. See also Graves to Lords of the Admiralty, Apr. 11, 1775, CO5/121/123–4.

2. "the King's people": Graves to Gage, Boston, Sept. 1, 1775, *DAR*, xi: 98. Cf. Add MS 14039/102.

3. For the Falmouth scene I have drawn on James L. Nelson, "Burning Falmouth," *MHQ: The Quarterly Journal of Military History* 22:1 (2009); Donald A. Yerxa, *The Burning of Falmouth, 1775: A Case Study in British Imperial Pacification* (Portland, ME, 1975), 126, for Falmouth's political history. Mowat to People of Falmouth, Canceaux, Falmouth, Oct. 16, 1775, Maine Historical Society, Coll. 1157, pp. 6–7. Papers printed Mowat's ultimatum [all dates in 1775]: *New England Chronicle*, Oct. 26; *Providence Gazette*, Nov. 4; *Connecticut Courant*, Nov. 6; *Rivington's New York Gazette*, Nov. 9; *Virginia Gazette* (Dixon and Hunters), Nov. 18; *Massachusetts Spy*, Nov. 10; *Morning Chronicle*, Dec. 19, 1775. "execute" and "frightful consternation" (Rev. Jacob Bailey) quoted in Nathan Miller, *Sea of Glory: A Naval History of the American Revolution* (Annapolis, MD, 1992), 47.

4. "Never was": quoted in William Pendleton Chipman, ed., *A Tory's Revenge: Being Ben. Mathew's Account of the Burning of Falmouth in 1775* (New York, 1905), 244. "terrified": Jacob Bailey, Falmouth, Oct. 18, 1775, *NDAR*, ii: 500. Landing parties: *NDAR*, ii: 513–16. Barton: William Goold, *The burning of Falmouth (now Portland, Maine), by Capt. Mowatt in 1775* (Boston, 1873), 15.

5. Graves to Philip Stephens, Secretary to the Admiralty, Oct. 9, 1775, Maine Historical Society, Coll. 1157, pp. 6–7; see also ibid., Coll. 422, i: 54.

6. Projectiles: Chipman, ed., *Tory's Revenge*, 242–4. Destruction: Yerxa,

Falmouth, 137–42; *NDAR*, ii: 513–16, for Mowat's account to Graves, Oct. 19, 1775. *Canceaux* log: *NDAR*, ii: 516.

7. Franklin: Ferling, *Independence*, 191. *New England Chronicle*, Oct. 19, 1775. *NDAR*, ii: 536, 549, 569, 601, 603. "*British barbarians*": Joseph Greenleaf to JA, Apr. 30, 1776, at http://founders.archives.gov /documents/Adams/06-04-02-0062.

8. Fred Anderson and Andrew Cayton, *The Dominion of War: Empire and Conflict in America, 1500–2000* (London, 2005), 104–59; John E. Ferling, *The First of Men: A Life of George Washington* (New York, 2010), with the quotation from Adams at 265; Rush to Thomas Ruston, Oct. 29, 1775, in Lyman Henry Butterfield, ed., *Letters of Benjamin Rush, 1761–1792* (Princeton, 1951), i: 92; Joseph J. Ellis, *His Excellency: George Washington* (New York, 2004); Paul K. Longmore, *The Invention of George Washington* (Berkeley, 1988). On Charles Willson Peale's Revolutionary career as artist, soldier, and political activist, see Hoock, *Empires of the Imagination*, 104–9.

9. "regulate": *JCC*, ii: 96. Washington: GW to Hancock, Oct. 24, 1775 ("Outrage exceeding") and GW to William Ramsay, Nov. 12, 1775. See also *NDAR*, ii: 590; GW to Falmouth Committee of Safety, Oct. 24, 1775; GW to Philip Schuyler, Oct. 26, 1775. "the unheard of": quoted in Nelson, "Burning Falmouth," 69. See also *NDAR*, ii: 607; Robert Morris to Robert Herries, Feb. 15, 1776, *LDC*, iii: 258–9; BF to Anthony Todd, Mar. 29, 1776, *PBF*, xxii: 392–4.

10. Paul Langford and William B. Todd, eds., *Writings and Speeches of Edmund Burke* (Oxford, 1981), iii: 102–69, "Speech on Conciliation with America" (Mar. 22, 1775). For Burke's prescient political sociology, see Rakove, *Revolutionaries*, 67–9. "the *predatory*, or war by distress": Langford and Todd, eds., *Writings and Speeches of Edmund Burke*, iii: 183–220, "Second Speech on Conciliation," Nov. 16, 1775, published speech as per *The Parliamentary Register*, 185–201, at 185–6. See also Sheffield MSS 212–14, quoted in Langford and Todd, eds., *Writings and Speeches of Edmund Burke*, iii: 212–13.

11. British press, including letters between Continental officers, as well as reports about further threats and assaults on cities from New York to Newport and Plymouth: *London Evening Post*, Dec. 16–19, 1775; *Lloyd's Evening Post*, Dec. 18–20, 1775; *London Chronicle*, Dec. 19–21, 1775; *Middlesex Journal*, Dec. 19–21, 1775; *Morning Chronicle*, Dec. 20, 1775; *Morning Post*, Dec. 20, 1775; *Craftsman*, Dec. 23, 1775; *Chester Chronicle*, Dec. 25, 1775. Quotations from *St James's Chronicle*, Dec. 21, 1775 ("coercive and sanguinary Measures") and "Nauticus": *Public Advertiser*, Feb. 8, 1776. By spring 1776, some newspapers vented frank criticism of Britain's brutality towards American fellow subjects: Grant,

Our American Brethren, 174; *London Chronicle*, Feb. 20, 1776. "absurd": quoted in Nelson, "Burning Falmouth," 69.

12. "farther Violences": Graves to Capt. Wallace, Nov. 4, 1775, Add MS 14039/102. Bannister and Riordan, "Loyalism and the British Atlantic, 1660–1840," 17, 19; Gruber, *Howe Bothers*, 30.

13. Unless otherwise referenced, the Norfolk scene is largely based on Hast, *Loyalism*, esp. 9–31, 45–59; John E. Selby, *The Revolution in Virginia, 1775–1783* (Williamsburg, VA, 1988), 83–4; Michael A. McDonnell, *The Politics of War: Race, Class, and Conflict in Revolutionary Virginia* (Chapel Hill, NC, 2007), 166–73; H. S. Parsons, "Contemporary English Accounts of the Destruction of Norfolk in 1776," *WMQ* 13:4 (1933); Benjamin Quarles, "Lord Dunmore as Liberator," *WMQ* 15:4 (1958).

14. Other former Jacobites, too, would later fight for the Hanoverian king in America, although some fought for the rebels. Hugh Mercer, for example, who had witnessed Culloden as a teenager, died as a Continental brigadier general from wounds received at the Battle of Princeton (see also ch. 5 below). See Calloway, *White People*, 38–9. For Dunmore's portrait, see David Mannings and Martin Postle, *Sir Joshua Reynolds: A Complete Catalogue of His Paintings* (New Haven, 2000), i: 347.

15. [?Thomas Wharton] to Sam:l Wharton Esq., Dartmouth MSS, II/1321 [copy], June 15, 1775. On the suspicious timing of the removal of the gunpowder, see Woody Holton, *Forced Founders: Indians, Debtors, Slaves, and the Making of the American Revolution in Virginia* (Chapel Hill, NC, 1999), 144–9. See also David, *Dunmore's New World*, esp. chs. 1, 4.

16. TJ to John Page, Oct. 31, 1775, at http://founders.archives.gov/documents/Jefferson/01-01-02-0130.

17. Lord Suffolk to GG, June 15, 1775, Germain Papers, vol. 4. "the bravest": Sir John Dalrymple, Project for strengthening General Howe's Operations, Germain Papers, vol. 4. "Young King": quoted in William J. Harris, *The Hanging of Thomas Jeremiah: A Free Black Man's Encounter with Liberty* (New Haven, 2009), 117. "a set of barbarians": quoted in Alan Gilbert, *Black Patriots and Loyalists: Fighting for Emancipation in the War for Independence* (Chicago, 2012), 43, with a fuller account of the case at 39–44. See also Piecuch, *Three Peoples*, 40.

18. Brooke, *George III*, 178; Douglas R. Egerton, *Death or Liberty: African Americans and Revolutionary America* (New York, 2009), 61, 70; Pybus, *Epic Journeys*, 21, 8 ("followed by"); Piecuch, *Three Peoples*, 39–43; Sylvia R. Frey, *Water from the Rock: Black Resistance in a Revolutionary Age* (Princeton, 1991), 67–8, 77 ("horrid and wicked": 67). For fears and allegations of British-instigated or -led slave insurrections in early Revolutionary America, see Gov. J. Wright to Dartmouth, May 26, 1775, Bancroft 94/61; Robert Parkinson, "Enemies of the People: The

Revolutionary War and Race in the New American Nation" (PhD diss., University of Virginia, 2005), ch. 2.

19. On rumors of, and blacks believing in, an emancipatory purpose to a future British invasion, see Holton, *Forced Founders*, 153–4. Gage to Barrington, Boston, June 12, 1775, in Clarence E. Carter, ed., *The Correspondence of General Thomas Gage with the Secretaries of State, 1763–1775*, repr. (Hamden, CT, 1969), ii: 684; Gage to Dartmouth, June 12, 1775, ibid., i: 403–4. For cabinet hawks in London sharing Gage's sense of urgency about raising troops from multiple sources, see Earl of Suffolk to GG, June 15, 1775, Germain Papers, vol. 3.

20. Dunmore's Proclamation, Nov. 7, 1775.

21. The most recent interpretation is David, *Dunmore's New World*, 6, 103–7, with the emphasis on intimidation at 106. Holton, *Forced Founders*, 158–9, has ample documentation on the proclamation's unifying effect, for which see also Alan Taylor, *The Internal Enemy: Slavery and War in Virginia, 1772–1832* (New York, 2013), 23–4. "Hell itself": quoted in Patrick Rael, *Eighty-Eight Years: The Long Death of Slavery in the United States, 1777–1865* (Athens, GA, 2015), 53. "Dunmore's proclamation": Hodges, *Root & Branch*, 140.

22. "flock to" and "boatloads": quoted in Gilbert, *Black Patriots*, 23, with individual stories of blacks running away to Dunmore at 23–4; William Campbell's proposal for blacks and indentured servants manning guerrilla units, and the mustering of a "Company of Negroes" by the Crown's officers in New England and Philadelphia, at 28–30. Greene and Pole, eds., *Companion to the American Revolution*, 241, estimate that "probably ten times" as many slaves were ready to respond to Dunmore's call, but were "prevented or dissuaded by patriot surveillance from responding to it." See also Schama, *Rough Crossings*, 77–83; Pybus, *Epic Journeys*, 14. Taylor, *Internal Enemy*, 26, suggests (with reference to Pybus, *Epic Journeys*, 30–31) that in the face of threats to their families few of Virginia's young male slaves ran away solo. For the quotations on Dunmore, see Elizabeth A. Fenn, *Pox Americana: The Great Smallpox Epidemic of 1775–82* (New York, 2001), 56. On the Ethiopian Regiment, see Joyce Lee Malcolm, *Peter's War: A New England Slave Boy and the American Revolution* (New Haven, 2009), 112–21.

23. *London Chronicle*, Mar. 8, 1776. The injury report in Woodford to Pendleton, Dec. 10, 1775, "Woodford, Howe, and Lee Letters," *Richmond College Historical Papers* 1 (1915–17): 118. For the sale of captured slaves, see Malcolm, *Peter's War*, 112.

24. For the demographics and conditions aboard the floating town, see David, *Dunmore's New World*, 114–21.

25. Hast, *Loyalism*, 30. *Am. Arch.*, 4th ser., IV: 103. "A Gentleman, Ship *William*, off Norfolk, Dec. 25, 1776," quoted in *NDAR*, iii: 243–4.

26. *Virginia Gazette*, Jan. 18, 1776; *NDAR*, iii: 119, 140. The officer is quoted in Malcolm, *Peter's War*, 113.

27. Howe's report in *NDAR*, iii: 579–80. See also Colonel W. Woodford to Colonel T. Elliott, Norfolk, Jan. 4, 1776, ibid. 617. Analysis of destruction: Selby, *Revolution in Virginia*, 83. "The wind": quoted in McDonnell, *Politics of War*, 170.

28. Dunmore's report in *Virginia Gazette*, Jan. 18, 1776, under the date Jan. 15 and also in *Am. Arch.*, 4th ser., IV: 540–41 (quotation 541); the account was reprinted in London's *Daily Advertiser*, Apr. 16, 1776. *Virginia Gazette*, Jan. 26 and Feb. 9, 1776. See also Dunmore to Dartmouth, Jan. 4, 1776, *DAR*, xii: 62.

29. Quoted in McDonnell, *Politics of War*, 172.

30. "full of Dead Bodies": quoted in Gilbert, *Black Patriots*, 25. Fenn, *Pox Americana*, 55–62, for the smallpox epidemic among Dunmore's black shipboard population in 1775/76; ibid., 46–70, for smallpox early in the war generally, including at the sieges of Boston and Quebec, and 91 for rumors of germ warfare in Virginia. For the smallpox epidemic among Dunmore's men, see also David, *Dunmore's New World*, 121–4.

31. Quotation and computations from "Report of the Committee to investigate the burning of Norfolk, 1776," in [Virginia,] *Journal of the House of Delegates of the Commonwealth of Virginia… 1835–36* (Richmond, VA, 1835), Document 43.

32. Adams: Samuel Adams to James Warren, Jan. 7, 1776, cited in Michael Kranish, *Flight from Monticello: Thomas Jefferson at War* (New York, 2010), 85. See also Samuel Adams to Samuel Cooper, Apr. 30, 1776, *LDC*, iii: 600–602; Robert Morris to Robert Herries, Feb. 15, 1776, *LDC*, iii: 258–9. Hancock: John Hancock to GW, Jan. 6[–21], 1776. "unite the whole": GW to Lieutenant Colonel Joseph Reed, Jan. 31, 1776.

33. "strike such a terror": London, Mar. 8, 1776, *NDAR*, iii: 954. Duke of Richmond, "attended" and "in a manner": Simmons and Thomas, eds., *Proceedings and Debates*, vi: 432 (House of Lords, Mar. 5, 1776). By March, reports circulating in London papers echoed Dunmore's version but seemed to gain limited traction. See *Morning Post*, Mar. 4, 1776; *Daily Advertiser*, Mar. 8, 1776; *Morning Chronicle*, Mar. 15, 1776.

34. On rebel propaganda around the actual and planned destruction of American cities, see also Carp, *Rebels Rising*, 215.

35. For Hessians in British service, see H. M. Scott, *British Foreign Policy in the Age of the American Revolution* (New York, 1990), 216–20, 228–30; Ingrao, *Hessian Mercenary State*, 136–44; Horst Dippel, *Germany and the American Revolution, 1770–1800: A Sociohistorical Investigation of Late Eighteenth-Century Political Thinking*, trans. Bernhard A. Uhlendorf (Chapel Hill, NC, 1977), 118–27; Atwood, *Hessians*, 14–19;

Dietmar Kügler, *Die deutschen Truppen im amerikanischen Unabhängigkeitskrieg, 1775–1783* (Stuttgart, 1980); Inge Auerbach, *Die Hessen in Amerika, 1776–1783* (Darmstadt, 1996). For perceptions, see Melodie Andrews, "Myrmidons from Abroad: The Role of the German Mercenary in the Coming of American Independence" (PhD diss., University of Houston, 1986), ch. 1, and pp. 200–202; Christof Mauch, "Images of America—Political Myths—Historiography: 'Hessians' in the War of Independence," *Amerikastudien/American Studies* 48:3 (2003); H. D. Schmidt, "The Hessian Mercenaries: The Career of a Political Cliche," *History* 43:149 (1958). "Foreigners were": *St James's Chronicle*, Mar. 28, 1776. See also Alderman Bull in Hansard, *Parliamentary History of England*, xviii: 1185; 1224 for Lord Camden; and *Parliamentary Register*, iii: 263 (Apr. 25, 1776) for T. Townshend, MP. Some British officers considered the Hessians unreliable since they were "uninterested in the Event of the War." Haldimand to GG, Sept. 4, 1778, Add MS 21714/54–7.

36. Congress obtained copies of the treaties and ordered them to be published. The use of the "Hessians" featured among the grievances in almost all local declarations of independence, and instructions for the delegates to the Second Continental Congress. See *Am. Arch.*, 4th ser., VI: 650, 699–700; *Boston Gazette*, May 20, June 24, 1776; Auerbach, *Hessen in Amerika*, 115; Andrews, "Myrmidons from Abroad," 168–9, 211–19; Lyman H. Butterfield, "Psychological Warfare in 1776: The Jefferson-Franklin Plan to Cause Hessian Desertions," *Proceedings of the American Philosophical Society* 94:3 (1950): 233–4. For newspaper reports, see, e.g., *Pennsylvania Packet*, May 6, 1776; *Boston Gazette*, May 20, 1776. Hancock is quoted in Pauline Maier, *American Scripture: Making the Declaration of Independence* (New York, 1997), 39. Bartlett: *Am. Arch.*, 4th ser., VI: 1022. Cf. Livingston's satire on 500 Indian elephants, 4,000 Laplanders, 3,500 Korozan archers, and 12,000 Japanese troops offered to George III: *PWL*, i: 226–9.

37. Committee of Inspection and Observation, Lancaster County, Nov. 1775, DLAR 25/6; McEachern and Williams, eds., *Wilmington–New Hanover Safety Committee Minutes*, 9–12, 30, 64–5; *Proceedings of the Committees of Safety of Caroline and Southampton Counties*, 130–31, 143; *Minutes of the Committee of Safety of Bucks County*, 354–5, 357–9; Henry Read McIlwaine, ed., *Proceedings of the Committees of Safety of Cumberland and Isle of Wight Counties* (Richmond, VA, 1919), 14, 16, 17, 21; Sally E. Hadden, *Slave Patrols: Law and Violence in Virginia and the Carolinas* (Cambridge, MA, 2001), 154–60; Neimeyer, "Town Born, Turn Out," 25; Higginbotham, *War of American Independence*, 277.

38. For the section on the Declaration of Independence I have drawn

especially on Maier, *American Scripture*; Charles D. Deshler, "How the Declaration Was Received in the Old Thirteen," *Harper's New Monthly Magazine* 85 (July 1892), with the quotations at 168; David Armitage, *The Declaration of Independence: A Global History* (Cambridge, MA, 2007); Carl L. Becker, *The Declaration of Independence: A Study in the History of Political Ideas* (New York, 1942); Garry Wills, *Inventing America: Jefferson's Declaration of Independence* (Garden City, NJ, 1978); Robert Ginsberg, ed., *A Casebook on the Declaration of Independence* (New York, 1967), esp. essays by Tyler, Fisher, Becker, Ginsberg.

39. Maier, *American Scripture*, 156–7.

40. For a reading of this section, including the connotations of "facts," see Stephen E. Lucas, "The Stylistic Artistry of the Declaration of Independence," *Prologue: Quarterly of the National Archives* 22 (1990). Numerous local documents had previously justified independence with reference to the king's political crimes, a critical rhetorical maneuver, since the dominant colonial theory of empire acknowledged the king as the only legitimate authority over the colonies. For the earlier documents, see Maier, *American Scripture*, 47–96. See also William L. Hedges, "Telling Off the King: Jefferson's 'Summary View' as American Fantasy," *Early American Literature* 22:2 (1987); Stella F. Duff, "The Case against the King: The Virginia Gazettes Indict George III," *WMQ* 6:3 (1949). For earlier writings of Jefferson's, see Maier, *American Scripture*, 108–21. See Eric Nelson, *The Royalist Revolution: Monarchy and the American Founding* (Cambridge, MA, 2014) for the royalist theory of representation and colonial disappointment with George III's failure to reassert the royal prerogative of his Stuart predecessors. For the need to break with the monarch to complete the transfer of political legitimacy, see Marston, *King and Congress*.

41. For this reading of the grievances, see Maier, *American Scripture*, 147, including "domestic insurrections." Armitage, *Declaration*, 54–6 ("effectively placed" at 56); Ginsberg, "The Declaration as Rhetoric," in *Casebook*, ed. Ginsberg, 236. For the association between the British monarch and Native American warriors and warfare in the run-up to independence, see Robert Parkinson, "Enemies of the People: The Revolutionary War and Race in the New American Nation" (PhD diss., University of Virginia, 2005), ch. 1.

42. Copies reached London by mid-August, Scotland and Ireland between Aug. 20 and 24, and Madrid, Leiden, Vienna, and Gothenburg by the end of that month. By early September, the document had spread as far as Copenhagen and Warsaw; soon there were French and German translations. For the international audience and the law of nations as a context of the Declaration, see Armitage, *Declaration*, 17–18, 21, 70, 72; idem, "The Declaration of Independence and International Law,"

WMQ, 59:1 (2002); Eliga H. Gould, *Among the Powers of the Earth: The American Revolution and the Making of a New World Empire* (Cambridge, MA, 2012); Dippel, *Germany and the American Revolution*, 100–101. For the sentimental reading of the Declaration of Independence, see Knott, *Sensibility*, 66.

43. For American print dissemination, see Maier, *American Scripture*, 131, 159. Cf. Caesar Rodney to Capt. Thomas Rodney at Dover, Philadelphia, July 4, 1776, Caesar Rodney Correspondence, NYPL. For British commanders in America receiving copies, see Philip Schuyler Papers, Box 18, fols. 260, 262, NYPL; Bancroft 97/65–7.

44. Dover: Deshler, "How the Declaration Was Received," 170. Huntington: David Waldstreicher, *In the Midst of Perpetual Fetes: The Making of American Nationalism, 1776–1820* (Chapel Hill, NC, 1997), 31; and for Baltimore, 31 n. 21. See also for Savannah: *Connecticut Gazette*, Oct. 8, 1776; *Pennsylvania Evening Post*, Oct. 8, 1776. Boston: Winthrop D. Jordan, "Familial Politics: Thomas Paine and the Killing of the King, 1776," *JAH* 60:2 (1973): 306–8; *New York Gazette*, Aug. 12, 1776; *Connecticut Gazette*, Oct. 25, 1776. New York City: *New York Gazette*, June 4, 1770; "drove": Capt. John Montressor, quoted in Isaac Newton Phelps Stokes, *The Iconography of Manhattan Island, 1498–1909* (New York, 1967), v: 992; Arthur S. Marks, "The Statue of King George III in New York and the Iconology of Regicide," *American Art Journal* 13:3 (1981). For a more detailed account of the struggle over the statue between Patriots and Loyalists, see my *Empires of the Imagination*, 49–57. For other examples of removal and destruction, see Deshler, "How the Declaration Was Received," 166–7, 172; Bushman, *King and People*, 225; *Pennsylvania Journal*, Aug. 28, 1776, quoted in Gerlach, ed., *New Jersey in the American Revolution*, 225; *Massachusetts Spy*, July 24; Dunlap's *Pennsylvania Packet*, Aug. 5, 1776. For surviving royal symbols, see Edmund Farwell Slafter, "Royal Arms and Other Regal Emblems and Memorials in Use in the Colonies before the American Revolution," *Massachusetts Historical Society* 4 (1887–9): 254–60.

45. Strategic value: Barnet Schecter, *The Battle for New York: The City at the Heart of the American Revolution* (New York, 2002), 2. Population figures: Conway, *British Isles*, 67.

46. "wood of pine trees": quoted in Papas, *That Ever Loyal Island*, 64.

47. For this section I have drawn heavily on O'Shaughnessy, *Men Who Lost America*, esp. 192–220; Joseph J. Ellis, *Revolutionary Summer: The Birth of American Independence* (New York, 2013), 118–20; Gruber, "Lord Howe and Lord George Germain"; Frederick Wyatt and William B. Willcox, "Sir Henry Clinton: A Psychological Exploration in History," *WMQ* 16:1 (1959); William B. Willcox, ed., *The American Rebellion: Sir Henry Clinton's Narrative of His Campaigns, 1775–1782*

(New Haven, CT, 1954), xiii–xxiii. For Fischer, see *Washington's Crossing*, 77–8. For the Rhode Island expedition, see Paul David Nelson, *Francis Rawdon-Hastings, Marquess of Hastings: Soldier, Peer of the Realm, Governor-General of India* (Madison, NJ, 2005), ch. 3. For one royal official's optimistic assessment of Britain's ability soon to end the rebellion across various Northern colonies, see Gov. Hutcheson to [General Haldiman], July 10, 1776, Add MS 21680/121–6.

48. Gruber, "Lord Howe and Lord George Germain," 230–31.
49. *Lloyd's Evening Post*, Aug. 14, 1776.
50. "beautiful forests": William L. Stone, ed., *Letters of Brunswick and Hessian Officers during the American Revolution* (New York, 1970), 194.
51. Quoted in David McCullough, *1776* (New York, 2005), 145.
52. My portrait of Clinton is largely based on William Bradford Willcox, *Portrait of a General: Sir Henry Clinton in the War of Independence* (New York, 1964); Wyatt and Willcox, "Sir Henry Clinton"; O'Shaughnessy, *Men Who Lost America*, 207–19 (quotation 214). For Clinton's broad military reading, see Ira D. Gruber, *Books and the British Army in the Age of the American Revolution* (Chapel Hill, NC, 2010), 44–5.
53. Memo of conversation, Feb. 7, 1776, Clinton Papers, vol. 13. O'Shaughnessy, *Men Who Lost America*, 218.
54. Insignia: Stone, ed., *Letters of Brunswick and Hessian Officers*, 50. For later references, see Spring, *With Zeal*, 172. Storm: McCullough, *1776*, 155–6, and 119 for Long Island. For men killed by lightning, see Capt. Isaac Wood Diary, 1775–77, entry for Aug. 21, 1776, Stillman Harkness MS Collection, NYPL. John J. Gallagher, *The Battle of Brooklyn 1776* (Edison, NJ, 2002), 81.
55. S. Sydney Bradford, ed., "A British Officer's Revolutionary War Journal, 1776–1778," *Maryland Historical Magazine* 56 (1961): 157; Edwin G. Burrows, "Kings County," in *The Other New York: The American Revolution beyond New York City, 1763–1787*, ed. Joseph S. Tiedemann and Eugene R. Fingerhut (Albany, NY, 2005), 28. Graham is quoted in John C. Dann, ed., *The Revolution Remembered: Eyewitness Accounts of the War for Independence* (Chicago, 1983), 50. See also Bruce E. Burgoyne, ed., *Enemy Views: The American Revolutionary War as Recorded by the Hessian Participants* (Bowie, MD, 1996), 71.
56. For this section, see especially Andrews, "Myrmidons from Abroad," 208–9, 254, 258–63; Butterfield, "Psychological Warfare," 240; McCullough, *1776*, 181; Charles Patrick Neimeyer, *America Goes to War: A Social History of the Continental Army* (New York, 1996), 90 (on the proposal for Patriots painted as Indians). "behaved with great": quoted in Andrews, "Myrmidons from Abroad," 262. For the allegation of spitting men to trees, see Burrows, *Forgotten Patriots*, 5.

57. For sham surrenders, see Gallagher, *Battle*, 121. "Many high ranking": quoted in Burgoyne, ed., *Enemy Views*, 71. See Mark Urban, *Fusiliers: Eight Years with the Redcoats in America* (London, 2007), 85, for a Hessian admitting to beating enemy soldiers.

58. Quotations in Gallagher, *Battle*, 119, 121. For British encouragement of Hessians not to grant quarter, see also "Schreiben eines hessischen Officiers," Long Island, Sept. 1, 1776, Bancroft 40, Hessian 4/6/13, NYPL. For an example of how the narrative of Hessian cruelty was already firmly locked in place, see Samuel Miles Diary (Nov. 1776), LOC.

59. Percy: Charles Knowles Bolton, ed., *Letters of Hugh, Earl Percy, from Boston and New York, 1774–1776* (Boston, 1902), 69. Hodges, *Root & Branch*, 144.

60. The British officer is quoted in Mackesy, *War for America*, 88. The Loyalist is cited in Edwin G. Burrows and Mike Wallace, *Gotham: A History of New York City to 1898* (New York, 1999), 254. Charles Stuart to Lord Bute, Feb. 4, 1777, quoted from Violet Hunter Guthrie Montagu, ed., *A Prime Minister and His Son, from the Correspondence of the 3rd Earl of Bute and of Lt.-General the Hon. Sir Charles Stuart, K.B.* (London, 1925), 99. Conway, "The Great Mischief," 385. For Howe's political reasoning, see entries for June 29, Nov. 21, 1776, Sept. 15, 1777, in Great Britain Orderly Book, WLCL; Gruber, *Howe Brothers*, 145–6; Stephen Kemble et al., *The Kemble Papers* (New York, 1884), i: 473.

61. Ellis, *Revolutionary Summer*, 119; O'Shaughnessy, *Men Who Lost America*, 218; Wyatt and Willcox, "Sir Henry Clinton," 78; Schecter, *Battle for New York*, 166–7; Willcox, ed., *Clinton's Narrative*, 44.

62. Gallagher, *Battle*, 148–54; Burrows, "Kings County," 29. Quotations in Ellis, *Revolutionary Summer*, 119.

63. Ellis, *Revolutionary Summer*, 119–20 (quotation 119) with n. 24: WH to GG, Sept. 3, 1776, *DAR*, xii: 218; Conway, *Short History*, 76; O'Shaughnessy, *Men Who Lost America*, 96–8. See also Johann Ewald, *Diary of the American War: A Hessian Journal* (New Haven, CT, 1979), 18, 19, 25.

64. Valentine, *Lord George Germain*, 145; Mackesy, *War for America*, 88; O'Shaughnessy, *Men Who Lost America*, 100; Stephen Brumwell, *George Washington, Gentleman Warrior* (New York, 2012), 236.

65. Jay, as a member of the Committee Detecting Conspiracies, Feb. 22, 1777, at http://www.columbia.edu/cu/libraries/inside/working/jay/archive/columbia.jay.04038.html. On Robinson's committee interrogation, see also Crary, *Price of Loyalty*, 148–9. Together with his four sons, Robinson organized the Loyal American Regiment and later played a key role in negotiations with Benedict Arnold over the treasonous hand-over of West Point. Sabine, *Biographical sketches*, ii: 221–4;

Breunig, *Amerikanische Revolution*, 146–8; Jasanoff, *Liberty's Exiles*, 34–6, and passim. On volitional allegiance, see James H. Kettner, *The Development of American Citizenship, 1608–1870* (Chapel Hill, NC, 1978).

66. "an ignorant": JA to Abigail Adams, July 11, 1776, quoted in Papas, *That Ever Loyal Island*, 69. "make whigs": JA to J. D. Sergant, July 21, 1776, *WJA*, ix: 425. Executions: Villers, "King Mob," 22; Amandus Johnson, *The Journal and Biography of Nicholas Collins, 1746–1831* (Philadelphia, 1936), 250–51.

67. In Massachusetts, Rhode Island, Pennsylvania, Delaware, Maryland, Virginia, and South Carolina, the test laws demanded an oath of allegiance from all free male adults 16, 18, or 21 years and older. In New Jersey, all civil servants and those individuals who had sworn an oath during the British occupation were required to swear allegiance. After the British defeat at Saratoga (1777), half a dozen states strengthened their test laws further. An overview of the test laws in Van Tyne, *Loyalists*, Appendix B. New York: [New York,] *Journals of the Provincial Congress, Provincial Convention, Committee of Safety and Council of Safety of the State of New-York, 1775–1777* (Albany, NY, 1842), i: 669, 684, 827, 855–6 [henceforth: *JPC*]. *Am. Arch.*, 5th ser., III: 238, 251, 257; Flick, *Loyalism in New York*, 116–34.

68. New Jersey issued fines and threatened non-jurors with confiscation. New York confiscated the property of non-signers and exiled them to the British lines. Pennsylvania non-signers were threatened with the loss of civil rights as well as with fines, punitive taxes, and professional bans in the case of lawyers, apothecaries, doctors, and merchants, as was also the case in Maryland. Rhode Island and Connecticut deprived non-jurors of their rights to vote and to sue in a court of law. Delaware and Virginia banned them from public office and the latter also from voting, purchasing land, and claiming debts, as well as levying a double and treble tax. North Carolina confiscated non-jurors' property and stripped them of their civil rights; they were to leave the state within thirty days. South Carolina gave Loyalists a chance to sell property before banning them, a threat that Georgia later also dangled over non-jurors. See Calhoon, *Loyalists*, 309–10; Breunig, *Amerikanische Revolution*, 67. On confiscation versus death for traitors, see Aaron N. Coleman, "Loyalists in War, Americans in Peace: The Reintegration of Loyalists, 1775–1800" (PhD diss., University of Kentucky, 2008), 201, 203, 230–232.

69. For the Bates episode, see W. O. Raymond, ed., *Kingston and the Loyalists of the "Spring Fleet" of A.D. 1783* (Kingston, New Brunswick, 1889), with quotations at 8. Other committees gave men they felt to be "Inimi-

cal to our Common Cause" the chance to prove their loyalty to America by serving in the militia, "to wipe off the present Evil Suspicions" or, otherwise, be imprisoned: Northumberland Committee of Safety, HSP Am. 277, entries for Dec. 14 and 17, 1776.

70. Elisabeth O'Kane-Lipartito, " 'The Misfortunes and Calamities of War': Civilians and Society in the American Revolution and After 1775–1830" (PhD, University of Houston, 1993), 128–37 (quotation 136). See also Linda K. Kerber, " 'May all our Citizens be Soldiers, and all our Soldiers Citizens': The Ambiguities of Female Citizenship in the New Nation," in *Women, Militarism, and War,* ed. Jean Bethke Elshtain and Sheila Tobias (Totowa, NJ, 1990), 14; Crary, *Price of Loyalty,* 82–3; Kerber, *Women of the Republic,* 123–36. For the hardship consequent to dispossession on all sides, see also Ward, *War for Independence,* 39–40; Potter-Mackinnon, *While the Women Only Wept,* 57. Trial of girls suspected of Loyalism: William James to Elisha James, Aug. 19, 1777, Elisha James MS N–1486, MHS.

71. Holmes is quoted in Mary Beth Norton, "Eighteenth-Century American Women in Peace and War: The Case of the Loyalists," *WMQ* 33:3 (1976): 398, and Linda Grant DePauw, *Founding Mothers: Women of America in the Revolutionary Era* (New York, 1994), 137–8, with reference to AO13/65/529–30. Similar tales in AO12/49/56–8, 102/80; 13/45/530, 67/192, 68/125, 96/263, 102/1107. For continued popular violence against "tender women," see Council of Safety to Committee of Inspection and Observation, Berks Co., Oct. 5, 1776, Society Miscellaneous Collection (Collection 425), Box 15 B, HSP.

72. Ward, *American Revolution,* 263–4 (quotations 263). Michael Fellman, *In the Name of God and Country: Reconsidering Terrorism in American History* (New Haven, 2010), 10, draws a comparison with the water cure in the American-Philippine war and U.S. waterboarding in twenty-first-century Iraq.

73. For New York's demographics, see Burrows and Wallace, *Gotham,* 245–6; Conway, *British Isles,* 67. The *Newport Gazette,* May 17, 1777, a Loyalist paper during the British occupation of that town, recounted the execution of John Hart of New York after a "sham Trial." For executions and reprieves, see Ward, *American Revolution,* 265; Brown, *King's Friends,* 79, 65, 47, 34, 115, 134, 158, 169, 183, 198, 215; Moody, *Narrative*; Crary, *Price of Loyalty,* 224–39; Bradburn, *Citizenship Revolution,* 57–8. Fear of retaliation: Ward, *War for Independence,* 39. See also Stokes, *Iconography of Manhattan,* iv: 910 [1776]. "We are cast": [?]Williams to John Hancock, Jan. 2, 1777, DLAR 53.

74. John E. Ferling, *Almost a Miracle: The American Victory in the War of Independence* (Oxford, 2007), 165, for New Jersey statistics. GG to

Knox, Dec. 3, 1776, quoted in Valentine, *Lord George Germain*, 309–10; see also *DAR*, xii: 274.

Chapter Four

1. General Orders, Sept. 6, 1776.

2. In thinking about this chapter, I have benefited from John W. Shy's writings as well as Fischer, *Washington's Crossing*; Lepore, *Name of War*; Stuart D. Brandes, *Warhogs: A History of War Profits in America* (Lexington, KY, 1997); and Conway's analysis of the moral economy of plundering in "The Great Mischief" and "Moral Economy, Contract, and Negotiated Authority in American, British, and German Militaries, 1740–1783," *Journal of Modern History* 88 (2016).

3. Washington's confirmation of the verdict in General Orders, Sept. 11, 1776. See Witt, *Lincoln's Code*, 20, with reference to General Orders, Aug. 9, 1775, and GW to John Hancock, Sept. 21, 1775, for soldiers signing the Articles of War. For the military flogging scene in the following pages, see Neimeyer, *America Goes to War*, 139–40; Harry M. Ward, *George Washington's Enforcers: Policing the Continental Army* (Carbondale, IL, 2006), 162–5, 177; Charles Royster, *A Revolutionary People at War: The Continental Army and American Character, 1775–1783* (Chapel Hill, NC, 1979), 78. For whipping in early modern culture and in military culture more generally, see Sarah Covington, "Cutting, Branding, Whipping, Burning: The Performance of Judicial Wounding in Early Modern England," in *Staging Pain, 1580–1800: Violence and Trauma in British Theater*, ed. James Robert Allard and Mathew R. Martin (Burlington, VT, 2009); Matthew Pate and Laurie A. Gould, *Corporal Punishment around the World* (Santa Barbara, CA, 2012), 31. For military and naval cats, see George Ryley Scott, *History of Torture* (London, 1971), 199; Rediker, *Slave Ship*, 205. The former British drummer quoted is John Shipp, *Flogging and its substitute: A voice from the ranks* (London, 1831), 20 ("practice of stripping"), 21 ("as though the talons"). The soldier describing his own flogging was Alexander Somerville, *The Autobiography of a working man* (London, 1848), 277–91 (quotation 288). A similar description is quoted in Myra C. Glenn, *Campaigns against Corporal Punishment: Prisoners, Sailors, Women, and Children in Antebellum America* (Albany, NY, 1984), 91–2, from Jacob Hazen, *Five years before the mast*. "resembles roasted meat": Samuel Leech, *Thirty years from home; or A voice from the main deck* (Boston, 1844), 50. I used the Library of America edition (1983) of Herman Melville, *White-Jacket, or the World in a Man-of-War*, the quotations at 489 ("either from constitutional"), 492 ("stripped like a slave"), 496 ("while his back bleeds"). See Caroline Cox, *A Proper Sense of Honor: Serivce and*

Sacrifice in George Washington's Army (Chapel Hill, NC, 2004), ch. 3, on punishment in the Continental Army. On witnessing violence and the politics of empathy and complicity, see Elizabeth Barnes, *Love's Whipping Boy: Violence & Sentimentality in the American Imagination* (Chapel Hill, NC, 2011), 17, 71, and passim. For the public spectacle and shame of excessive violence, see Michel Foucault, *Discipline and Punish: The Birth of the Prison* (New York, 1979), 34.

4. A British officer denounced the Hessians as an army of locusts; an American officer used the same simile for the black women following Cornwallis's army: Tatum, ed., *American Journal*, 120; Frey, *Water*, 169. "chief of plunderers": Thomas Paine, *American Crisis*, IV, in *Virginia Gazette*, Sept. 26, 1777. American historians tend to endorse contemporary views of the Hessians as the worst of plunderers, e.g., Frey, *British Soldier*, 75; Steven R. Taaffe, *The Philadelphia Campaign, 1777–1778* (Lawrence, KS, 2003), 195. Atwood, *Hessians*, 173–6, has attempted to explain Hessian practices with reference to specific military rationales.

5. Natural disasters: "Plundering by the British Army during the American Revolution," 114 (tornado); *Virginia Gazette*, Jan. 31, 1777 (plague, earthquake). Shreve: Jason R. Wickersty, "A Shocking Havoc: The Plundering of Westfield, New Jersey, June 26, 1777," *Journal of the American Revolution* (July 21, 2015), at http://allthingsliberty.com/2015/07/a -shocking-havoc-the-plundering-of-westfield-new-jersey-june-26-1777/, quoting Shreve to Dr. Bodo Otto, June 29, 1777.

6. *New-York Gazette*, Feb. 3 and Apr. 14, 1777, quoted in Leonard Lundin, *Cockpit of the Revolution: The War for Independence in New Jersey* (New York, 1972), 247. Carl Leopold Baurmeister, *Revolution in America: Confidential Letters and Journals, 1776–1784, of Adjutant General Major Baurmeister of the Hessian Forces*, trans. Bernhard A. Uhlendorf (New Brunswick, NJ, 1957), 338–9.

7. This paragraph is indebted to Jürgen Luh, *Kriegskunst in Europa, 1650–1800* (Cologne, 2004), ch. 1, on transport, magazines, distribution; the reference to Frederick II, from *Friedrich der Große: Betrachtungen über die Feldzugspläne* (1775), is quoted at 18. See also John A. Lynn, *Women, Armies, and Warfare in Early Modern Europe* (Cambridge, 2008), 32, 294; Fritz Redlich, *De praeda militari: Looting and Booty, 1500–1815* (Wiesbaden, 1956), 72, and passim; John W. Wright, "Military Contributions during the Eighteenth Century," *Journal of the American Military Institute* 3:1 (1939). On the "thin line," see also E. Wayne Carp, *To Starve the Army at Pleasure: Continental Army Administration and American Political Culture, 1775–1783* (Chapel Hill, NC, 1984), 83; Fischer, *Washington's Crossing*, 174; Wayne E. Lee, "The American Revolution," in *Daily Lives of Civilians in Wartime Early America: From the Colonial Era to the Civil War*, ed. David S.

Heidler and Jeanne T. Heidler (Westport, CT, 2007), 45 ("fine line"); see 43–9 for foraging and plundering by regular and irregular forces and banditti.

8. For this and the previous paragraphs, see Fischer, *Washington's Crossing*, 175. DLAR 437, New Jersey, Revolutionary War: Damages by the British and Americans in New Jersey, reel 2, vol. 1. See also Society Miscellaneous Collection (Collection 425), Box 15 B, HSP.

9. On the ordinariness of wartime plundering, see Barbara Donagan, "War, Property, and the Bonds of Society: England's 'Unnatural' Civil Wars," in *Civilians and War in Europe*, ed. Charters, Rosenhaft, and Smith, 61. Frazer scene after Lee, "American Revolution," 32, with reference to Persifor Frazer, *General Persifor Frazer: A Memoir Compiled Principally from His Own Papers by His Great-Grandson* (Philadelphia, 1907), 157–60 (quotation 159).

10. For Miller, see Lee, "American Revolution," 45–6, with reference to Harry M. Ward, *Between the Lines: Banditti of the American Revolution* (Westport, CT, 2002), 39. Cf. the violence against male and female civilians documented in Pennsylvania, Division of Archives and Manuscripts. Records of Pennsylvania's Revolutionary Governments, 1775–1790, Executive Correspondence of the Council of Safety, Pennsylvania, July 1776–March 1777, depositions against Capt. Jerrad Irwin (Jan. 25, 1777), DLAR 24. The examples throughout this chapter also draw on my reading of well over one hundred orderly books in manuscript (esp. LOC, LCP, MHS, HSP) and print, as well as other accounts. For specific references, see, e.g., George F. Scheer, ed., *Private Yankee-Doodle; being a narrative of some of the adventures, dangers, and sufferings of a Revolutionary soldier* (Boston, 1962), 52, 96–7, 100, 104–5, 139–40, 203; Lundin, *Cockpit*, 246; entry for Aug. 2, 1781 in Major John Singer Dexter Orderly Books, vol. i, LOC; *PNG*, i: 215, 268; HEH, HM Orderly Book of General Lacey, Jan. 1778 to Sept. 1780, Aug. 1780; Bonnie Sue Shelton Stadelman, "The Amusements of the American Soldiers during the Revolution" (PhD diss., Tulane University, 1969), 52, 96–7, 100, 104–5, 139–40, 203. On war, property, and Englishness, see Lepore, *Name of War*. For the impact of plundering on civilians, see also Lee, "American Revolution," 43–7.

11. Neimeyer, *America Goes to War*, 139–45, esp. 140. On forms of corporal punishment, see Anne-Marie Cusac, *Cruel and Unusual: The Culture of Punishment in America* (New Haven, CT, 2009), 81; Maurer Maurer, "Military Justice under General Washington," in *Military Analysis of the Revolutionary War: An Anthology by the Editors of Military Affairs* (Millwood, NY, 1977); Cox, *Proper Sense of Honor*, 87–8. On the rationale and defense of flogging, see Richard Holmes, *Redcoat: The British Soldier in the Age of Horse and Musket* (London, 2001), 320; Cusac, *Cruel*

and Unusual, 42; Arthur N. Gilbert "Military and Civilian Justice in Eighteenth-Century England: An Assessment," *Journal of British Studies* 17:2 (1978): 64; Steven Pierce, "Punishment and the Political Body: Flogging and Colonialism in Northern Nigeria," in *Discipline and the Other Body: Correction, Corporeality, Colonialism*, ed. Steven Pierce and Anupama Rao (Durham, NC, 2006), 197.

12. In Britain, corporal punishment was the milder alternative to the death penalty in a criminal justice system that by 1776 knew some 160 capital offenses, mostly concerning property crimes. See Douglas Hay et al., *Albion's Fatal Tree: Crime and Society in Eighteenth-Century England* (New York, 1975); Douglas Hay, "Crime and Justice in Eighteenth- and Nineteenth-Century England," in *Crime and Justice: An Annual Review of Research*, ed. Norval Morris and Michael Tonry (Chicago, 1980). Early British critics of military flogging are quoted in J. R. Dinwiddy, "The Early Nineteenth-Century Campaign against Flogging in the Army," *EHR* 97:383 (1982); Peter Burroughs, "Crime and Punishment in the British Army, 1815–1870," *EHR* 100:396 (1985); Cox, *Proper Sense of Honor*, 88–9, which references criticism of brutal military punishment in late-eighteenth-century officer manuals. On flogging and the slave regime, see Cusac, *Cruel and Unusual*, 75; Rediker, *Slave Ship*; Barnes, *Love's Whipping Boy*, 17, 71, 73; http://www.mountvernon.org/digital-encyclopedia/article/slave-control; Fritz Hirschfeld, *George Washington and Slavery: A Documentary Portrayal* (Columbia, MO, 1997), 37, 50; Cleves, *Reign of Terror*, 30; Marcus Wood, *Blind Memory: Visual Representations of Slavery in England and America 1780–1865* (Manchester, 2000), 260–61. For the slave's lacerated body and abolitionism, see, e.g., Henrice Altink, "'An Outrage on All Decency': Abolitionist Reactions to Flogging Jamaica Slave Women, 1780–1834," *Slavery & Abolition* 23:2 (2002).

13. Anderson and Cayton, *Dominion of War*, 129–31. Early anti-plundering orders, among many: GW to Robert Spotswood, Oct. 31, 1755. Humphrey Bland is quoted from his *Treatise of Military Discipline* (London, 1743), 237; various London editions were published in 1727–62. On Washington's relations with British officers, and their sharing martial knowledge, see also Ferling, *First of Men*, 33.

14. "seems never": Ward, *George Washington's Enforcers*, 165. "without Order": General Orders, HQ, Cambridge, Jan. 1, 1776. See also GW to Israel Putnam, Aug. 25, 1776. "stamping order": Richard Norton Smith, *Patriarch: George Washington and the New American Nation* (Boston, 1993), 4. "I have a Gallows": quoted in Ellis, *His Excellency*, 27.

15. For Washington assessing the provincials at Cambridge, see Ferling, *First of Men*, 126–7; James Thomas Flexner, *George Washington in the American Revolution, 1775–1783* (Boston, 1968), 30. "an exceeding

dirty": quoted in Glenn A. Phelps, "The Republican General," in *George Washington Reconsidered*, ed. Don Higginbotham (Charlottesville, VA, 2001), 169. Recommendation of Bland: GW to Colonel William Woodford, Nov. 10, 1775. For military reading more widely, see Sandra L. Powers, "Studying the Art of War: Military Books Known to American Officers and Their French Counterparts during the Second Half of the Eighteenth Century," *Journal of Military History* 70:3 (2006); JA to William Tudor, Oct. 12, 1775, at http://founders.archives.gov/documents/Adams/06-03-02-0099; Conway, "British Army." Cox, *Proper Sense of Honor*, 44, doubts "military texts were reaching more than a small minority of officers." For examples of GW overruling courts-martial by replacing corporal punishment with confinement on bread and water in spring 1776, see Alexander McDougall's First New York Regiment orderly books, 1776, entries for Feb. 21 and Mar. 4, 1776, NYHS.

16. I draw here on Anderson and Cayton, *Dominion of War*, 166–7: The army "embodied the Revolution itself" and "represented an American union" when no other institution yet did. Tudor is quoted in Ward, *George Washington's Enforcers*, 34. The American Articles of War were based on the Massachusetts Articles of War, which were in turn largely derived from British regulations, although containing fewer capital offenses and lower lash limits. Articles in *JCC*, ii: 111–22, the revisions in iii: 331–4. Robert Harry Berlin, "The Administration of Military Justice in the Continental Army during the American Revolution, 1775–1783" (PhD diss., University of California, Santa Barbara, 1976). For soldiers' temporary loss of liberty, see also Cox, *Proper Sense of Honor*, 76.

17. On McCowan, see Benjamin Franklin Stevens, ed., *General Sir William Howe's Orderly Book at Charlestown, Boston and Halifax, June 17, 1775 to 1776, 26 May* (Port Washington, NY, 1970), 96–7 (quotation 97). For similar cases, see ibid., 187; WO55/677, Capt. Farrington, Orderly Book, HQ Boston, Jan. 3, 1776; Frederick Bernays Wiener, *Civilians under Military Justice: The British Practice since 1680, Especially in North America* (Chicago, 1967), 150; A. R. Newsome, "A British Orderly Book, 1780–1781," *North Carolina Historical Review* 9:1–4 (1932), esp. entries for Mar. 1 and 2, 1781. For the uncovering of female victims of flogging, see Pierce, "Punishment and the Political Body," 199–200. For British sentences of 400 to 1,000 lashes, see, e.g., "Diary of Lt. John Barker," *JSAHR* 7 (1928), entry for Aug. 14, 1775; Stevens, ed., *Howe's Orderly Book*, 101–2, 105–6, 109; Kemble et al., *Kemble Papers*, i: 437, 499, 510–11; WO71/92/336–9; WO55/677, Capt. Farrington, Orderly Book, entry for Jan. 3, 1776. For death sentences for British plunderers, see Kemble et al., *Kemble Papers*, i: 399, 428, 480, 491; Orderly Book,

unid. unit, 1778–79, Sept. 23, 1778, HSP 633; Orderly book kept during the occupation of Philadelphia, Apr. 24–June 27, 1778, fol. 81, HSP, Am. 625; British orderly book, Oct.–Dec. 1777, DLAR 9, roll 1 (cow theft). For British military justice and the gentlemanly priorities it enshrined, see G. A. Steppler, "British Military Law, Discipline, and the Conduct of Regimental Courts Martial in the Later Eighteenth Century," *EHR* 102:405 (1987); Arthur N. Gilbert, "The Regimental Courts Martial in the Eighteenth-Century British Army," *Albion* 8:1 (1976); idem, "Changing Face of British Military Justice, 1757–1783," *Military Affairs* 49:2(1985); idem, "Military and Civilian Justice."

18. Barber is quoted in Neimeyer, *America Goes to War*, 135. Waldo: Albigence Waldo, "Valley Forge 1777–8, Diary of Surgeon Albigence Waldo, of the Connecticut Line," *PMHB* 21:3 (1897): 310. For the moral economy of plundering in the rival armies, see Neimeyer, *America Goes to War*, 136; Conway, "The Great Mischief"; idem, "Moral Economy."

19. Higginbotham, *War of American Independence*, 304; Dorothy Denneen Volo and James M. Volo, *Daily Life during the American Revolution* (Westport, CT, 2003), 178; Lee, "American Revolution," 43–6. "With respect": GW to Continental Congress Committee to Inquire into the State of the Army, July 19, 1777. For troops complaining about shortages of provisions, see Scheer, ed., *Private Yankee-Doodle*, 50–52. See more generally, James A. Huston, *Logistics of Liberty: American Services of Supply in the Revolutionary War and After* (Newark, DE, 1991), 128–9; Carp, *Starve the Army*, 172–3, 181, 186, 201–11; Wellenreuther, *Von Chaos und Krieg*, 183–6; Dann, ed., *Revolution Remembered*, 23, 63, 126. Prices: Conway, *Short History*, 129.

20. After Lee, "American Revolution," 44–5.

21. Wellenreuther, *Von Chaos und Krieg*, 166. See Brandes, *Warhogs*, 38, on fraud, and Carp, *Starve the Army*, 19, 67–8, on shortage cycles when blankets and tents were made into clothing and flour bags, and tents into blankets. John W. Shy, "Logistical Crisis and the American Revolution: A Hypothesis," in *Feeding Mars: Logistics in Western Warfare from the Middle Ages to the Present*, ed. John A. Lynn (Boulder, CO, 1993), 161–79; Phelps, "Republican General," 184–5; Higginbotham, *War of American Independence*, 304–5; [?Alexander McDougall] to GW, Pecks Kill [NY], May 21, 1777; Conway, *Short History*, 129. Washington and many of his officers tended to prefer voluntary sales and civil impressment to military coercion: Royster, *Revolutionary People*, 73–4; Neimeyer, *America Goes to War*, 135; James C. Neagles, *Summer Soldiers: A Survey & Index of Revolutionary War Courts-Martial* (Salt Lake City, 1986), 24; GW, Instructions to Colonel Benedict Arnold, for Canada campaign, Sept. 14, 1775; Lee, "American Revolution," 44–5; Carp, *Starve the Army*, esp. 77–98.

22. This section after Arthur R. Bowler, *Logistics and the Failure of the British Army in America, 1775–1783* (Princeton, 1975), 8–9, 94–5, 109, 158, and passim; Edward E. Curtis, *The Organization of the British Army in the American Revolution* (New Haven, CT, 1926), 100–104; Taaffe, *Philadelphia Campaign*, 54; "The Siege of Charleston; Journal of Captain Peter Russell, December 25, 1779, to May 2, 1780," *AHR* 4:3 (1899), 481. For Britain's fundamental supply problem, see TNA, T64/118, Daniel Chamier to Robinson, Mar. 31, 1777, quoted in Curtis, *Organization*, 82. For connections between strategic decisions and logistical thinking, see Bowler, *Logistics*, 241, 62–3, 67. The underlying supply problem of the British Army in America was that it hardly ever controlled sufficient territory to meet its food requirements. The division of responsibility among poorly coordinated government departments and inadequate information flow exacerbated Britain's logistical challenges. The ration of a soldier was calculated at one pound of beef or nine ounces of pork per day, plus weekly issues of oatmeal, butter, cheese, and peas, and the occasional issue of rice at the rate of one ounce per day; six men were daily given a quart of rum. Norman Baker, *Government and Contractors: The British Treasury and War Supplies, 1775–1783* (London, 1971), 4; PRO30/55/3/238 (1); Curtis, *Organization*, 89, 172; Mackesy, *War for America*, 65–8, 222–4.

23. Bowler, *Logistics*, 53–4, 98–108; Baker, *Government and Contractors*, 3; Curtis, *Organization*, 94–7, quotation 94 ("mouldy bread"). "our army": quoted in Fischer, *Washington's Crossing*, 172. The horses consumed 14,000 tons of hay and 6,000 tons of oats annually.

24. For this paragraph, see Bowler, *Logistics*, 41–91, esp. 44–5, 48. For Murray, see Eric Robson, ed., *Letters from America, 1773 to 1780; Being the Letters of a Scots Officer, Sir James Murray* (Manchester, 1951), 29, letter to Betsy, June 17, 1776; minimal provisions: 40–41.

25. "fighting for": Robson, ed., *Letters from America*, 40, letter dated Feb. 25, 1777, quoted in Martin Joseph Clancy, "Rules of Land Warfare Observed by the American Army during the American Revolution," *World Polity* 2 (1960), 231. See also "Bamford's Diary: The Revolutionary Diary of a British Officer," *Maryland Historical Magazine* 27 (1932): 245; O'Shaughnessy, *Men Who Lost America*, 103. For the British Army seeking to disrupt Continental foraging expeditions, see, e.g., GW to NG, Feb. 12, 1778; see also six letters, Feb. 15–20, 1778, for which see also *PNG*, ii: 285–7; GW to NG, Feb. 16 and 18, 1778; correspondence between GW and Lee, Feb. 16–25, 1778; Frank H. Stewart, *Foraging for Valley Forge by General Anthony Wayne in Salem and Gloucester Counties* (Woodbury, NJ, 1929); Captain Henry Lee Jr. to GW, Feb. 19, 1778.

26. Robert Kirkwood, *The Journal and Order Book of Captain Robert Kirkwood of the Delaware Regiment of the Continental Line* (Wilmington,

DE, 1910), "Book of Gen. Orders, 1777," 98, 104; Colonel James Chambers, 1st Pennsylvania Regiment, 1778–1780, Sept. 22, 1778, HSP 973; Abraham Scranton Orderly Book, 1778, HQ Providence, Sept. 14, 1778, MCC 1262, LOC. Houses and barns: Head-Quarters, White-Plains, Nov. 2, 1776. Gardens, orchards, and mowing grounds: Colonel Ward's Order Book, Mar. 11, 1776, Force 7E, reel 55, item 155, LOC. "Orderly Books and Journals kept by Connecticut Men while taking part in the American Revolution, 1775–1778," *Collections of the Connecticut Historical Society*, vii (1899). Firewood: Ebenezer Adams Orderly Book, July to Oct. 1776, entry for Oct. 7, 1776, LOC; Kirkwood, *Journal*, 104, 125–6; Colonel James Chambers, 1st Pennsylvania Regiment, 1778–1780, entry for Sept. 25, 1778, HSP 973; Christian Myers Orderly Book, July to Sept. 1779, entry for Aug. 5, 1779, MCC 1259, LOC; "Orderly Book of the Fourth New York Regiment, 1778–80," in *Orderly Books of the Fourth New York Regiment, 1778–1780. The Second New York Regiment, 1780–1783,* ed. Almon W. Lauber (Albany, NY, 1932), 94; Charles Webb, Orderly Book, Nov. 11, 1775–July 26, 1776, entry for May 5, 1776, Connecticut Historical Society, American Revolution Collection, 1765–1844, reel 3; Collection of American Orderly Books: General William Smallwood, Smallwood's Brigade, 1778–1779, entry for Dec. 20, 1778, HSP 973; Ebenezer Huntington Orderly Book, entries for June 5 and 13, 1779, Force 7E, reel 16, item 63, LOC. Published notices: *New-York Journal*, Apr. 11, 1776, and May 2, 1776. For the section title: "Punishments being intended to deter by the terror of example," in John Williamson, *The elements of military arrangement: and of the discipline of war, adapted to the practice of the British infantry* (London, 1791), ii: 153.

27. General Orders, Sept. 19, 1776.

28. GW, camp near Kingsbridge, Sept. 22, 1776. See also the lobbying of William Tudor, the Judge Advocate General, for an increased lash maximum of one or two hundred. Tudor to JA, July 7 and Sept. 23, 1776, *PJA*, iv: 367; v: 36–7. Cf. Cox, *Proper Sense of Honor,* 95, with reference to Colonel Joseph Reed, a lawyer on GW's staff, to Hancock. GW to Hancock, Sept. 25, 1776. For a later example, see NG to GW, Aug. 26, 1780, *PNG*, vi: 233–4.

29. For this and the previous paragraph, see GW to Hancock, Sept. 25, 1776. Cf. *Am. Arch.*, 5th ser., II: 498–500.

30. Adams, *Diary,* iii: 409–10, at http://64.61.44.187/publications/apde /portia.php?mode=p&id=DJA03p409. See also Brumwell, *George Washington,* 247–8. Committee on Spies commissioned June 14; Congress discussed report Aug. 7, 19, Sept. 19, 20. Articles in *JCC*, v: 788–807, see esp. sec. XIII, art. 13, 21; sec. XVIII, art. 3. For the British Army, see Sylvia R. Frey, "Courts and Cats: British Military Justice in the Eighteenth Century," *Military Affairs* 43:1 (1979): 8; idem, *British*

Soldier, 90; Steppler, "British Military Law," 884, with reference to the 44th Foot punishment records revealing a scale from an average of 267 (actually inflicted: 200) lashes in 7 cases of abusing civilians, and 390 lashes (320) in 28 cases of theft from civilians, to 533 (494) in 7 cases of insolence to commissioned officers.

31. GW to President of Congress, Feb. 3, 1781, *PGW/EA.* For examples of much higher American lash counts than the congressional limit, see Cox, *Proper Sense of Honor,* 106–7; Ward, *George Washington's Enforcers,* 162; Royster, *Revolutionary People,* 77–80; Neimeyer, *America Goes to War,* 143–5, 210; James Thacher, *A military journal during the American revolutionary war* (Boston, 1827), entry for Jan. 1, 1780; Stuart L. Bernath, "George Washington and the Genesis of American Military Discipline," *Mid-America* 49:2 (1967): 97. One hundred lashes or more: GW to Committee of Congress, Jan. 28, 1778; General William Smallwood, Smallwood's Brigade, Orderly Book 1778–1779, entry for Apr. 27, 1778, HSP 973; Caleb Boynton, Orderly Book, White Plains, July to Aug. 1778, entry for July 16, 1778, LOC; Court Martial at Fishkill, July 1778, John Fisher Papers, Box 1, NYHS; Samuel McNeil Orderly Book, entry for Aug. 27, 1779 (threat of five hundred lashes for plunders), NYHS. Increasingly desperate orders threatened summary punishment on the spot. Kirkwood, *Journal,* 89, 98, 104, 123–6, 150, 181; see also Neimeyer, *America Goes to War,* 145. Estimates of military executions range from between 40 and 75 for all offenses and for those parts of the army for which the records are reasonably reliable, suggesting, conservatively, no more than perhaps 100 executions overall. This compares to some 142 capital convictions in the British Army, including 40 to 50 for non-military crimes such as murder, rape, robbery, plunder: Gilbert, "Military and Civilian Justice," 58–9.

32. After Fischer, *Washington's Crossing,* 117–21, 137; Ferling, *Almost a Miracle,* 164.

33. Stedman, *History,* i: 242–3. "we went on": Charles Stuart to Lord Bute, Feb. 4, 1777, quoted in Stuart-Wortley, *Prime Minister and His Son,* 99. See also Richard Fitzpatrick to brother, July 5, 1777, Richard Fitzpatrick Papers, LOC. For Patriots singing similar tunes, see Document signed W. Whipple, Baltimore, Jan. 15, 1777, John Langdon Papers, i, HSP 353; Alexander M'Whorter, Letter to unidentified correspondent, Newark, Mar. 12, 1777, printed, e.g., in *Pennsylvania Evening Post,* Apr. 26, 1777. For Loyalist claims testifying to British plundering regardless of victims' allegiance, see AO13/1/106–11; 1/442–56; 9/256–83; 1 part i, 111a; 11/C1, 14/47; 8/170–242; AO12/22/137. But other British commanders exempted the foraging of "Rebel Cattle" from general bans on plundering: see Archibald Campbell, *Journal of an expedition against the rebels of Georgia in North America under the*

orders of Archibald Campbell (Darien, GA, 1981), 14–16 (quotation 15), 20; Curtis, *Organization*, 114–15. For officers taking decisive disciplinary action against plunderers, see also Milton M. Klein and Ronald W. Howard, eds., *The Twilight of British Rule in Revolutionary America: The New York Letter Book of General James Robertson, 1780–1783* (Cooperstown, NY, 1983), 32, 37, 120–21, and passim.

34. "unfortunately": "Proposed Reformation for the American Army," n.d., Germain Papers, vol. 17/41. See Fischer, *Washington's Crossing*, 172–8, for an excellent discussion of how British compulsory foraging and plundering undermined the policy of pacification. For further materials on the politics of plunder, see also Letter to unid. correspondent, Newark, Mar. 12, 1777, printed, e.g., in *Pennsylvania Evening Post*, Apr. 26, 1777; HSP 353, John Langdon Papers, i, Jan. 15, 1777.

35. Fischer, *Washington's Crossing*, 129–32 (quotation 129), 155–6. "the ground": quoted in Schecter, *Battle for New York*, 268.

36. GW, Instructions to Colonel Benedict Arnold, for Canada campaign, Sept. 14, 1775. See also Marquis de Malmedy to NG, Mar. 10, 1781, *PNG*, vii: 424–5; Stedman, *History*, i: 242–3. "into a mere plundering scheme": GW, Circular to Pulaski and Colonels of Horse, Oct. 25, 1777. For American orders to treat particular local populations with indulgence because most were Patriots, see NG to Wayne, Dec. 19, 1778, *PNG*, iii: 120. Not just Continentals but Patriot militias, too, were regularly plundering Loyalist properties. When, conversely, Loyalist corps plundered Patriots, their victims demanded a compensatory tax be levied on them. See GW to WL, Jan. 24, 1777; Michael S. Adelberg, *The American Revolution in Monmouth County: The Theatre of Spoil and Desctruction* (Charleston, SC, 2010); Adrian C. Leiby, *The Revolutionary War in the Hackensack Valley: The Jersey Dutch and the Neutral Ground, 1775–1783*, rev. ed. (New Brunswick, NJ, 1992), 84–90; Oliver DeLancey, *Orderly Book of the Three Battalions of Loyalists Commanded by Brigadier General Oliver DeLancey, 1776–1778* (New York, 1917), 9, 21, 28, 23, 58, 66, 95; Burgoyne, *Hessian Diary*, 45–6.

37. For Washington and other commanders exhorting troops to honor the ideals of their cause throughout the war, see, e.g., General Orders, Sept. 4, 1777; Ward, *George Washington's Enforcers*, 65–6; Elijah Fisher, *Elijah Fisher's journal while in the war for independence and continued two years after he came to Maine* (August, ME, 1880), entries for Oct. 6–28, 1778; Neagles, *Summer Soldiers*, 90; DLAR 458, Gen. Wm. Heath Order Book, Aug. 14, 1777; HSP Am. 626, vol. 1, Jan. 13, 1778; Orderly Book of the New Jersey Brigade, July–Oct. 1780, entries for Aug. 9, 16, 23, Sept. 12, 1780, NYPL. Lee, *Barbarians and Brothers*, 193, 199, is optimistic about the comparative restraint of Continental foraging, concluding: "The Continentals were never perfect, but one cannot

doubt that Washington's disciplinary efforts greatly reduced the damage they inflicted on the countryside" (199).

38. Fischer, *Washington's Crossing*, 133–5. "full power": quoted in Ferling, *Almost a Miracle*, 168.

Chapter Five

1. Count Carl von Donop, Journal of the Hessian Corps in America under General von Heister, 1776–June 1777, 90–91, Morristown National Historical Park, NJ. For the Martin episode, see also Thomas J. McGuire, *The Philadelphia Campaign* (Philadelphia, 2006), i: 29–31.

2. AH to John Jay, Middle Brook Camp [NJ], June 2, 1777, *PAH*, i: 261–3 (quotation 263). Newspapers: *Pennsylvania Gazette*, June 6, 1777; *Pennsylvania Journal*, June 11, 1777; *Pennsylvania Evening Post*, June 12, 1777. Henry Melchior Muhlenberg, *The Journals of Henry Melchior Muhlenberg*, trans. Theodore G. Tappert and John W. Doberstein (Philadelphia, 1982), iii: 51. See also Israel Putnam to Godfrey Marlbon, June 24, 1777, DLAR 444/72445, for twenty-two bayonet stabbings of a British officer, most likely Martin.

3. GW to Cornwallis, June 2, 1777. "that *he was no coroner*": Alexander Graydon, *Memoirs of his own time: with reminiscences of the men and events of the revolution*, ed. John Stockton Littell (Philadelphia, 1846), 266. Cornwallis to GW, June 2, 1777. Earlier that year, General Howe had described the ambush and murder of a British captain in New Jersey "with a degree of Barbarity that Savages could not exceed." CO236/37 (Jan. 5, 1777).

4. This synthesis is based on Theodore P. Savas and J. David Dameron, *A Guide to the Battles of the American Revolution* (New York, 2006), 87–94; Fischer, *Washington's Crossing*; William S. Stryker, *The Battles of Trenton and Princeton* (Boston, 1898), 361–4, with the quotations from a Continental officer, on the weather and shoeless soldiers, at 362; Richard M. Ketchum, *The Winter Soldiers: The Battles for Trenton and Princeton* (New York, 1999), 224–319, with the quote from Hessian diarist at 236. "Soldiers keep": William S. Powell, "A Connecticut Soldier under Washington: Elisha Bostwick's Memoirs of the First Tears of the Revolution," *WMQ* 6:1 (1949), 102. See also Capt. Isaac Wood Diary, entry for Dec. 26, 1776, Stillman Harkness MS Collection, NYPL.

5. "all the blood": "The Battle of Princeton. By Sergeant R——," *PMHB* 20:4 (1896), 518. Losses: Ferling, *Almost a Miracle*, 185–6.

6. Ferling, *Almost a Miracle*, 188–91 (quotation 188).

7. "fought on": Mark Edward Lender, "The 'Cockpit' Reconsidered: Revolutionary New Jersey as a Military Theater," in *New Jersey in*

the American Revolution, ed. Barbara J. Mitnick (New Brunswick, NJ, 2005), 50–51 (quotation 51). Creswell is quoted in Fischer, *Washington's Crossing*, 259–60; see ibid. 293 on Donop. On Patriot recruiting after Trenton, see also Hutcheson to Haldimand, Feb. 10, 1777, Add MS 21680/173–4.

8. See Fischer, *Washington's Crossing*, 293 on Donop. Definitions of atrocity: Sascha Möbius, "Kriegsgreuel in den Schlachten des Siebenjährigen Krieges in Europe," in *Kriegsgreuel: Die Entgrenzung der Gewalt in kriegerischen Konflikten vom Mittelalter bis ins 20. Jahrhundert*, ed. Sönke Neitzel and Daniel Hohrath (Paderborn, 2008); idem, "'Von Jast und Hitze': Überlegungen zur Wahrnehmung von Gewalt durch preussische Soldaten im Siebenjährigen Krieg," *Forschungen zur Brandenburgischen und Preußischen Geschichte* 12 (2002): 18. Committee appointed: *JCC*, vii: 42–3 (Jan. 16, 1777).

9. Varnum Lansing Collins, *President Witherspoon: A Biography* (Princeton, 1925), i: 21.

10. "a deserted village": Butterfield, ed., *Letters of Benjamin Rush*, i: 125–6. "a shambles": Ketchum, *Winter Soldiers*, 230. Young: Sergeant Young, 1776–77, entry for Jan. 17, 1777, HSP, Am. 619.

11. Quotations from *The correspondence, journals, committee reports, and records of the Continental Congress (1774–1789)*, 53: "Papers and Affidavits Relating to the Plunderings, Burnings, and Ravages Committed by the British, 1775–84," fol. 51 [henceforth: "Papers and Affidavits"], NARA M247. All dates 1777: *Pennsylvania Evening Post*, Apr. 24; *Connecticut Journal*, May 14; *Independent Chronicle*, May 22; *Connecticut Gazette*, May 23; *Norwich Packet*, May 19–26; *Boston Gazette*, May 26; *Freeman's Journal*, June 21.

12. Order book cited in Appendix to "Papers and Affidavits," fol. 45; *Pennsylvania Evening Post*, May 10, 1777; also referred to as "two Cruel Bloody Orders of Howe," in Varnum Lansing Collins, *A Brief Narrative of the Ravages of the British and Hessians at Princeton in 1776–77: A Contemporary Account of the Battles of Trenton and Princeton* (Princeton, 1906), 21, see also 21–22 with note at 22. Paine, *Crisis*, II (Jan. 13, 1777), in Thomas Paine, *Collected Writings* (New York, 1995), 108.

13. Samuel Chase to GW, Jan. 23, 1777; GW to Chase, Feb. 5, 1777.

14. Affidavit Rev. George Duffield, Apr. 25, 1777, "Papers and Affidavits," Appendix, reprinted in, e.g., *Pennsylvania Evening Post*, Apr. 29, 1777. William D. Dwyer, *The Day Is Ours! An Inside View of the Battles of Trenton and Princeton, November 1776–January 1777* (New Brunswick, NJ, 1998), 208–10, and quotation at 322 ("this may").

15. Affidavit Rev. George Duffield, Apr. 25, 1777, "Papers and Affidavits," Appendix. Cf. John Witherspoon to David Witherspoon, Baltimore,

Feb. 12, 1777, *LDC*, vi: 269–70; Stryker, *Battles*, 266–7; Dwyer, *The Day Is Ours!*, 208–10, 322–3, 379–80; Fischer, *Washington's Crossing*, 300.

16. Yates: GW to WH, HQ at Morristown, Jan. 13, 1777. Affidavit: PRO30/55. See also WL to GW, Feb. 15, 1777, *PWL*, i: 224–6; GW to Samuel Chase, Feb. 5, 1777; "Papers and Affidavits," fol. 47. A slightly edited version was included in the congressional report's appendix, and printed as such in the press: *Pennsylvania Evening Post*, May 10, 1777. A similar version in *Purdie's* and *Dixon and Hunter's Virginia Gazette*, Jan. 31, 1777, reprinted in *Connecticut Courant*, Mar. 3, 1777. Medical experts: Deposition taken by New Jersey JP, Henry Freeman, Feb. 17, 1777, "Papers and Affidavits"; GW to Samuel Chase, Feb. 5, 1777; GW to John Hancock, Feb. 5, 1777; unidentified American officer at Chatham, NJ, Feb. 3, 1777, quoted in GW to WL, Feb. 3, 1777, n. 2; New Jersey Historical Society, *New Jersey Archives: Documents Relating to the Revolutionary History of the State of New Jersey, orig. publ. 1901–17* (New York, 1977), i: 366; Fischer, *Washington's Crossing*, 377–8. For the empirical turn in common law and science, and the medicolegal trend to provide empirical evidence in criminal trials, see Barbara J. Shapiro, *A Culture of Fact: England, 1550–1720* (Ithaca, NY, 2000); Julia Rudolph, *Common Law and Enlightenment in England, 1689–1750* (Woodbridge, Suffolk, 2013), ch. 3; Mary Poovey, *A History of the Modern Fact: Problems of Knowledge in the Sciences of Wealth and Society* (Chicago, 1998); Steven Shapin and Simon Schaffer, *Leviathan and the Air-Pump: Hobbes, Boyle, and the Experimental Life* (Princeton, 2011); Stephan Landsman, "One Hundred Years of Rectitude: Medical Witnesses at the Old Bailey, 1717–1817," *Law and History Review* 16:3 (1998): 449, 482; Tal Golan, *Laws of Men and Laws of Nature: The History of Scientific Expert Testimony in England and America* (Cambridge, MA, 2004); "butchered": GW to WL, Feb. 14, 1777. See WH to GW, Jan. 23, 1777, for Howe's answer when confronted with the case. American interpretations: Collins, *Brief Narrative*, 41–4; Butterfield, ed., *Letters of Benjamin Rush*, i: 127–8.

17. The quotation from Spring, *With Zeal*, 233.

18. "It was the Nation": William B. Reed, *Oration delivered on the occasion of the reinternment of the remains of General Hugh Mercer before the St. Andrew's and Thistle societies* (Philadelphia, 1840), 38. For the Mercer story, see also *Pennsylvania Evening Post*, Jan. 18, 1777; *Pennsylvania Journal*, Feb. 5, 1777; Collins, *Brief Narrative*, 42–4; Samuel Chase to GW, Jan. 23, 1777; "Papers and Affidavits," fols. 49–52; Fischer, *Washington's Crossing*, 332–3 with further references.

19. The report also covered rape (see the second part of this chapter), prisoner abuse, and plundering. For American circulation, see, e.g., *Penn-*

sylvania Evening Post, Apr. 24, 26, 29, May 10, 1777; *New England Chronicle*, May 29, June 5, 12, 1777; *Connecticut Courant*, June 2–9, 1777; *Norwich Packet*, June 9, 1777; *Providence Gazette*, July 12, 1777. Congress: *JCC*, vii: 42–3, 277–9; 8: 565. "furnish": Council of Safety, NY, committee of John Jay, Livingston, G. Morris, Letter to New York delegates in Congress, May 28, 1777: [New York] *Journals of the Provincial Congress*, i: 947. "the barbarities" and "odious and revolting": Duke of Richmond, *Parliamentary History of England... 1778* (Dec. 7, 1778). *Leyden Gazette*: Oct. 7, 1777, "Supplement," Oct. 5–6, 14, 1777, "Supplement," 5–6. For the *Gazette*, see Simon Burrows, "The Cosmopolitan Press, 1760–1815," in *Press, Politics and the Public Sphere in Europe and North America, 1760–1820*, ed. Hannah Barker and Simon Burrows (Cambridge, 2002), 26–7; Jack Censer, "France, 1750–89," ibid., 170; Jeremy D. Popkin, *News and Politics in the Age of Revolution: Jean Luzac's Gazette de Leyde* (Ithaca, NY, 1989).

20. For this and the following paragraph, see Frank Luther Mott, *American Journalism: A History, 1690–1960* (New York, 1962), 99–100; Trish Loughran, *The Republic in Print: Print Culture in the Age of U.S. Nation Building, 1770–1870* (New York, 2007), 3–9; Burns, *Infamous Scribblers*, 192–4, 219–20; Michael Humphrey, *The Politics of Atrocity and Reconciliation: From Terror to Trauma* (New York, 2002), 132. On Paine, see John Keane, *Tom Paine: A Political Life* (Boston, 1995), 138–41. For an analogous argument concerning the press as instrumental in constituting the new nation, its citizens a community of readers, see Smith-Rosenberg, *This Violent Empire*, 23–9, and passim. My argument is not necessarily incompatible with Loughran's in *Republic in Print* that the absence of a highly developed national infrastructure enabled a nation to be imagined across diverse American regional cultures and interests.

21. "united the colonies": Burns, *Infamous Scribblers*, 219.

22. Even though the Board of War recommended to Congress that Washington be provided with a portable printing press, a printer, and journeymen, the proposal was apparently never approved. See GW to Committee of Congress, July 19, 1777; Rollo G. Silver, "Aprons Instead of Uniforms: The Practice of Printing, 1776–1787," *Proceedings of the American Antiquarian Society* 87 (1977): 117. For the closest early modern parallel, see the depositions taken in the wake of Irish Catholic atrocities against Protestants in 1641 at http://1641.tcd.ie/. See Holger Hoock, "Mangled Bodies: Atrocity in the American Revolutionary War," *Past & Present* 230 (Feb. 2016), for a systematic investigation of witnessing and atrocity narrative.

23. "The progress": Broadside, dated Bucks. Co., Dec. 14, 1776, for which see also *Virginia Gazette*, Dec. 27, 1776; *Connecticut Journal*, Jan. 1,

1777; *Independent Chronicle*, Jan. 2, 1777; *Essex Journal*, Jan. 9, 1777; *Freeman's Journal*, Jan. 7, 1777; *Massachusetts's Spy*, Jan. 2, 1777; *Connecticut Courant*, Apr. 21, 1777. A widely excerpted "letter from an officer of distinction in the American army," which was also published in British and European papers, referenced the rape of girls, teenagers, and women by British troops under Cornwallis near Pennytown, New Jersey. Published by order of the Pennsylvania Council of Safety, in *Pennsylvania Packet*, Dec. 27, 1776; *Pennsylvania Evening Post*, Dec. 28, 1776; also in *London Evening Post*, Mar. 25–27, 1777. NG to Gov. Nicholas Cooke, *PNG*, ii: 4–5.

24. "to secure": Council of Safety of Pennsylvania, Dec. 23, 1776, in *Pennsylvania Packet*, Dec. 27, 1776; *Pennsylvania Evening Post*, Dec. 28, 1776. British reference: *Gazetteer*, Mar. 31, 1777.

25. Girls and teenagers: Sharon Block, "Rape in the American Revolution: Process, Reaction, and Public Re-Creation," in *Sexual Violence in Conflict Zones: From the Ancient World to the Era of Human Rights*, ed. Elizabeth D. Heineman (Philadelphia, 2011), 36, 38. For an emphasis on the notion of the theft of female sexual property, see Elizabeth Robertson and Christine M. Rose, "Introduction: Representing Rape in Medieval and Early Modern Literature," in *Representing Rape in Medieval and Early Modern Literature*, ed. eadem (New York, 2001), 7; Deborah G. Burks, " 'I'll Want My Will Else': 'The Changeling' and Women's Complicity with Their Rapists," *English Literary History* 62:4 (1995); Barbara J. Baines, "Effacing Rape in Early Modern Representation," *English Literary History* 65:1 (1998); Georges Vigarello, *A History of Rape: Sexual Violence in France from the 16th to the 20th Century* (Malden, MA, 2001), 2, 24, 30–31; Amy Greenstadt, *Rape and the Rise of the Author: Gendering Intention in Early Modern England* (Farnham, 2009), 12–13, 22; Laura Gowing, "Women, Status and the Popular Culture of Dishonour," *Transactions of the Royal Historical Society* 6 (1996). For references to rape in front of relatives and friends, see Colonel Measam to Colonel Wayne, Jan. 11, 1777, Bancroft 378/185–9; *Pennsylvania Evening Post*, Dec. 28, 1778; *Independent Chronicle*, July 15, 1779; *Virginia Gazette*, 7 Aug. 1779; HL to William McCulloch, Mar. 9, 1782, *PHL*, xv: 470–73. As Sharon Block has shown, rape as a political metaphor "combined the image of unrestrained, illegitimate power with images of innocent, helpless, female victims who needed to be saved by righteous American men." For Block's work on how sexual violence was implicated in the establishment of systems of power dependent upon racial, gender, and social categories, see her *Rape and Sexual Power in Early America* (Chapel Hill, NC, 2006), esp. 212–18, 230–34 (quotation 234); "Rape without Women: Print Culture and

the Politicization of Rape, 1765–1815," *JAH* 89:3 (2002); "Rape in the American Revolution."

26. Reports and rumors: Alexander MacWhorter, the pastor of the New-ark Presbyterian Church, who accompanied Washington's army across New Jersey in 1776/77, Letter to unid. Correspondent, Newark Mar. 12, 1777, printed in *Independent Chronicle*, Apr. 10, 1777; *Pennsylvania Eve-ning Post*, Apr. 26, 1777; *Boston Gazette*, June 2, 1777; *Norwich Packet*, May 26, 1777. Adam Stephen to TJ, c. Dec. 20, 1776, *PTJ*, i: 659. *Virginia Gazette*, Jan. 31, 1777. In late colonial America, castration was reserved as a punishment by Southern courts for African-American men con-victed of rape: Block, *Rape*, 190–96, 203. For rape and racial discourse in late colonial and early national America, see also Sharon Block, "Violence or Sex? Constructions of Rape and Race in Early America," in *New World Orders: Violence, Sanction, and Authority in the Colonial Americas*, ed. John Smolenski and Thomas J. Humphrey (Philadelphia, 2005); Kirsten Fischer, *Suspect Relations: Sex, Race, and Resistance in Colonial North Carolina* (Ithaca, NY, 2002), 185–7; Catherine Adams and Elizabeth H. Pleck, *Love of Freedom: Black Women in Colonial and Revolutionary New England* (New York, 2010), 44–5; Cornelia Hughes Dayton, *Women before the Bar: Gender, Law, and Society in Connecticut, 1639–1789* (Chapel Hill, NC, 1995), 184–231, 248, 270–73, 283.

27. Reissued later, e.g., as the title page of a *New England Almanac* in 1776. For rape as a political issue during the occupation of Boston in 1768–69, see O. M. Dickerson, comp., *Boston under Military Rule*, [*Essex Ga-zette*,] June 27 and July 11, 1769; Alfred F. Young, *Masquerade: The Life and Times of Deborah Sampson, Continental Soldier* (New York, 2004), 49; Susan Brownmiller, *Against Our Will: Men, Women, and Rape* (New York, 1975), 115.

28. Bell, *First Total War*; Anna Clark, *Women's Silence, Men's Violence: Sex-ual Assault in England, 1770–1845* (London, 1987), 5–6, 34; Vigarello, *History of Rape*, 25, 43. "an acceptable": Stevi Jackson, "The Social Context of Rape: Sexual Scripts and Motivation," in *Rape and Society: Readings on the Problems of Sexual Assault*, ed. Patricia Searles and Ronald J. Berger (Boulder, CO, 1995), 19. Joshua S. Goldstein, *War and Gender: How Gender Shapes the War System and Vice Versa* (Cambridge, 2001), 333. Randolph Trumbach, *Sex and the Gender Revolution: Vol-ume One* (Chicago, 1998), 277, 301–5; James Kelly, " 'A Most Inhuman and Barbarous Piece of Villainy': An Exploration of the Crime of Rape in Eighteenth-Century Ireland," *Eighteenth-Century Ireland—Iris an dá chultúr* 10 (1995): 95, 107; Nazife Bashar, "Rape in England between 1550 and 1700," in *The Sexual Dynamics of History*, ed. London Femi-nist History Group (London, 1982), 36; Thomas Lacqueur, *Making Sex:*

Body and Gender from the Greeks to Freud (Cambridge, MA, 1990), 161; Gregory Durston, *Victims and Viragos: Metropolitan Women, Crime and the Eighteenth-Century Justice System* (Bury St. Edmunds, 2007), 165, 167; Else L. Hambleton, "The Regulation of Sex in Seventeenth-Century Massachusetts," in *Sex and Sexuality in Early America*, ed. Merril D. Smith (New York, 1998), 96.

29. The historiography of rape in early modern European warfare remains slim: Holger Hoock, "Rape, *ius in bello*, and the British Army in the American Revolutionary War," *Journal of Military Ethics* 14:1 (2015), 75 with detailed references. Sexual coercion of Native American women, and the relative scarcity of rape by Native American men, has attracted somewhat greater attention: Alice Nash, " 'None of the Women Were Abused': Indigenous Contexts for the Treatment of Women Captives in the Northeast," in *Sex without Consent: Rape and Sexual Coercion in America*, ed. Merril D. Smith (New York, 2001); Thomas S. Abler, "Scalping, Torture, Cannibalism and Rape: An Ethnohistorical Analysis of Conflicting Cultural Values in War," *Anthropologica* 34:1 (1992); James Axtell, *The European and the Indian: Essays in the Ethnohistory of Colonial North America* (New York, 1981), 181 2; Lee, *Barbarians and Brothers*, 148, 160, 162; Richard Godbeer, "Eroticizing the Middle Ground: Anglo-Indian Sexual Relations along the Eighteenth-Century Frontier," in *Sex, Love, Race: Crossing Boundaries in North American History*, ed. Martha Elizabeth Hodes (New York, 1999); Sally Smith Booth, *The Women of '76* (New York, 1973), 196. Most histories of the American Revolutionary War have given little if any consideration to the subject of sexual violence, even though it is generally recognized that women in war zones were vulnerable. See Gundersen, *To Be Useful*, 179; Lee, "American Revolution"; Caroline Gilman, ed., *Letters of Eliza Wilkinson* (New York, 1969), 28–31, 46; Sidney Barclay, ed., *Personal Recollections of the American Revolution; A Private Journal* (Port Washington, NY, [1970]), 34, 76, 153–9, 165; "Historical Notes: A Woman's Letters in 1779 and 1782," *South Carolina Historical and Genealogical Magazine* 10:2 (1909); Stevens, ed., *Howe's Orderly Book*, 186–8; Berkin, *Revolutionary Mothers*, 38; Dann, ed., *Revolution Remembered*, 130–31, 141, 187; Elizabeth Evans, *Weathering the Storm: Women of the American Revolution* (New York, 1989), 29. The few scholars who consider the topic of rape in war emphasize the dearth of rape proceedings, or observe that only where British troops were stationed over a period of time did they have an opportunity to exploit civilian women in a systematic way: Lee, "Civilian Experience," 55; Mary Beth Norton, *Liberty's Daughters: The Revolutionary Experience of American Women, 1750–1800* (Boston, 1980), 202–5. Contemporary concerns about these very instances, however, are dismissed by other scholars, who consider

the raping of civilians an "extreme rarity" and largely a product of the "American propaganda mill." Ward, *War for Independence*, 84; see also Frey, *British Soldier*, 78–9. Rape is not discussed in such classics as Higginbotham, *War of American Independence*; Mackesy, *War for America*; Royster, *Revolutionary People*; Middlekauff, *Glorious Cause*; Neimeyer, *America Goes to War*. There is a perfunctory reference in Jerome J. Nadelhaft, *The Disorders of War: The Revolution in South Carolina* (Orono, ME, 1981), 68: "There was so much horror, so much death and brutality, there might well have been a corresponding amount of rape." Fischer, *Washington's Crossing*, 178–9, reliably covers the New Jersey rape cases discussed below.

30. Legal definition of rape in Sir William Blackstone, *Commentaries on the Laws of England: In Four Books* (Oxford, 1770), iv: 210. For the history of rape law, see Antony Simpson, "Vulnerability and the Age of Female Consent: Legal Innovation and Its Effect on Prosecutions for Rape in Eighteenth-Century London," in *Sexual Underworlds of the Enlightenment*, ed. G. S. Rousseau and Roy Porter (Manchester, 1987), 182–5. Vattel, Kapossy, and Whatmore, *Law of nations*, book iii, ch. viii, pp. 543–9, paras. 140–45. For early modern codes of war and rape, see also Diane Wolfthal, *Images of Rape: The "Heroic" Tradition and Its Alternatives* (Cambridge, 1999), 65, 97; Karin Jansson, "Soldaten und Vergewaltigung im Schweden des 17. Jahrhunderts," in *Zwischen Alltag und Katastrophe: Der Dreissigjährige Krieg aus der Nähe*, ed. Beninga von Krusenstjern and Hans Medick (Goettingen, 1999), 197; Vigarello, *History of Rape*, 15, 39. Peter Way, "Venus and Mars: Women and the British Army in America during the Seven Years' War," in *Britain and America Go to War*, ed. Flavell and Conway; Gundersen, *To Be Useful*, 143–4.

31. "more difficult": WL to Caesar Rodney, Feb. 24, 1777, *PWL*, i: 251; see also GW to WL, Feb. 14, Mar. 3, 1777; Collins, *Brief Narrative*, 14–15. "A man": Ira D. Gruber, ed., *John Peebles' American War: The Diary of a Scottish Grenadier, 1776–1782* (Mechanicsburg, PA, 1998), 74 (Dec. 24, 1776). See also WO71/86/201–2 (1778). Frey, *British Soldier*, 78. Vigarello, *History of Rape*, 40, for a sensitive discussion of silencing circumstances. See also Garthine Walker, "Rereading Rape and Sexual Violence in Early Modern England," *Gender & History* 10:1 (1998) with reference to Miranda Chaytor, "Husband(ry): Narratives of Rape in the Seventeenth Century," *Gender & History* 7:3 (1995): 382–3, 394–5, 399–400; Lynn A. Higgins and Brenda R. Silver, "Editors' Introduction," in *Rape and Representation*, ed. eadem (New York, 1991), esp. 4–6.

32. General Orders, Jan. 1, 1777. GW to WL, Mar. 3, 1777. See also GW to WL, Feb. 14, 1777.

33. "Papers and Affidavits," fols. 29, 31, 33, 35.

34. On rape as sexualized violence, see Jackson, "Social Context of Rape," 16; Merril D. Smith, "Introduction: Studying Rape in American History," in *Sex without Consent*, ed. eadem, 7. Catherine A. MacKinnon, "Sex and Violence: A Persepctive (1981)," in *Feminism Unmodified: Discourses on Life and Law*, ed. eadem (Cambridge, MA, 1987), insists on the convergence of male sexuality and violence. Block, "Rape in the American Revolution," 29, agrees that there were "more violent versions of sexual attacks" in wartime than "were normally seen in peacetime." A substantial minority of rapes in colonial America, and a majority of cases in eighteenth-century England where the relationship between attacker and attacked is known, were committed by the masters of servants or the master's relatives, by women's fellow workers or lodgers, and by relatives and intimates. Rape by (armed) enemy soldiers represents an extreme case of stranger rape by disruptive outsiders to a local community. See Clark, *Women's Silence*, 38, 40; Block, *Rape*, 55–80; Jansson, "Soldaten und Vergewaltigung," 207, 223; Thomas A. Foster, *Sex and the Eighteenth-Century Man: Massachusetts and the History of Sexuality in America* (Boston, 2006), 59–61; Durston, *Victims*, 147; Kelly, " 'A Most Inhuman and Barbarous Piece of Villainy,' " 81–93.

35. Only in a few British courts-martial concerning child rape did physicians testify to a girl's infection with venereal disease or to particularly brutal genital injuries. Block, *Rape*, 110–11; WO71/149/bundle 8/7–19; 71/94/253–60.

36. Maggie Craig, *Damn'd Rebel Bitches: The Women of the '45* (Edinburgh, 1997), 107; John Prebble, *Culloden* (London, 1961), 209–10; Robert Forbes and Henry Paton, *The Lyon in mourning: or, A collection of speeches, letters, journals, etc. relative to the affairs of Prince Charles Edward Stuart* (Edinburgh, 1895), iii: 107; TNA, SP 54/35/50. Elements of the army that had defeated the Jacobites later fought in the Seven Years' War in North America. General James Wolfe, who had condoned that earlier rape of Scottish Highland women, threatened that female Quebec French prisoners might be "given up to the delicate embraces of the English tars." Plank, *Rebellion and Savagery*, 54, 172 (quotation).

37. Trumbach, *Sex*, 328–30; Stephen Conway, "Locality, Metropolis and Nation: The Impact of the Military Camps in England during the American War," *History* 82:268 (1997): 550–51. Most reported cases of rape by British soldiers during the American Revolutionary War were of female army followers, especially of girls under the age of ten. Frey, *British Soldier*, 59–63; Berkin, *Revolutionary Mothers*, 52, and ch. 4; Holly A. Mayer, *Belonging to the Army: Camp Followers and Community during the American Revolution* (Columbia, SC, 1996); eadem, "Wives,

Concubines, and Community: Following the Army," in *War and Society*, ed. Resch and Sargent; Gerard J. De Groot and C. M. Peniston-Bird, eds., *A Soldier and a Woman: Sexual Integration in the Military* (New York, 2000), esp. essays by Hendrix, Crim. For army wives, see Paul Kopperman, "British High Command and Soldiers' Wives in America, 1755–1783," *JSAHR* 60 (1982), with references to venereal disease and sexual harassment at 17–18 with n. 12. For camp women motivating "British boys" against the "d——d rebels," see John Greenwood Manuscript, 1775–83, fol. 22, WLCL. Rape of girls as young as four, in the Seven Years' and the Revolutionary Wars: HEH, Loudon Memorandum Book, V, Jan. 26, 1758; Orderly Book of John Thomas's Regiment of Mass. Provincials, Feb. 12, 1760, John Thomas Papers, MHS. General Orders by Major General Howe in Kemble et al., *Kemble Papers*, i: 556, 560; WO71/80/421–2, 441–51; 71/85/290–301; 71/90/85–8; 71/149/ bundle 8/7–19; CO5/236/214.

38. Quoted in Booth, *Women of '76*, 105–6. No positive evidence documenting rape in the early Southern campaign has been found thus far, but see *Virginia Gazette*, July 27, 1776, for a report on British soldiers treating Charleston women with "great barbarity," including shooting and stabbing them.

39. *Morning Chronicle*, Apr. 2, 1777, in response to rape allegations in the Patriot press.

40. Block, "Rape in the American Revolution," 31–3, 37–8. Hoock, "Rape, *ius in bello*, and the British Army."

41. WO71/82/412–25 (Sept. 3–7, 1776).

42. Christopher: "Papers and Affidavits," fol. 39. For other references to rapes in New Jersey, 1776–77, see Joseph Galloway, *Letters to a nobleman, on the conduct of the war in the middle colonies* (London, 1779), 25 7; Edward Field, ed., *Diary of Col. Israel Angell, commanding the Second Rhode Island continental regiment during the American revolution* (Providence, RI, 1899), 26–7. For this argument, see also Block, "Rape without Women," 859.

43. There is some evidence that Continental soldiers and Patriot militia treated women rudely and indecently. Two women later testified that they had suffered miscarriages after scuffles with American troops; one woman asserted she had been raped by a rebel soldier. See *Loyalists Transcripts*, iii: 352, xiv: 209; E. Alfred Jones, *The Loyalists of Massachusetts, Their Memorials, Petitions and Claims* (London, 1930), 124, 139; Hulton, *Letters of a Loyalist Lady*, 85–6; Robert M. Dunkerly, *Women of the Revolution: Bravery and Sacrifice on the Southern Fields* (Charleston, SC, 2007), 40–42; Christopher Moore, *The Loyalists: Revolution, Exile, Settlement* (Toronto, 1994), 80; Ruairidh H. MacLeod, *Flora MacDonald: The Jacobite Heroine in Scotland and North America*

(London, 1995), 193; Capt. Pendleton's Orderly Book, 1781, entry for July 25, 1781, LOC; "Journal book of Bayze Wells of Farmington, in Canada expedition," in *Collections of the Connecticut Historical Society*, vii: 293–4; Norton, "Eighteenth–Century American Women," 399; AO12/49/56–8, 102/80; 13/45/530, 64/76–7, 65/529–30, 67/192, 68/125, 81/59, 96/263, 102/1107; Thomas Goldswaith to daughter Catherine, Aug. 20, 1779, J. M. Robbins Papers, MHS. No systematic courts-martial records survive for the Continental Army. Orderly books recording courts-martial show very limited evidence of sexual abuse proceedings. See Neagles, *Summer Soldiers*; Gundersen, *To be Useful*, 144; Kerber, *Women of the Republic*, 46; Linda Grant De Pauw and New Jersey Historical Commission, *Fortunes of War: New Jersey Women and the American Revolution* (Trenton, NJ, 1975), 18–19. Robert Howe Orderly Book, entry for Mar. 10, 1778, WLCL. For modern data, see Robert M. Hayden, "Rape and Rape Avoidance in Ethno-National Conflicts: Sexual Violence in Liminalized States," *American Anthropologist* 102:1 (2000).

44. For soldiers in Loyalist regiments sentenced to death for rape, see William Kelby, ed., *Orderly book of the three battalions of loyalists commanded by Brigadier-General Oliver De Lancey 1776–1778* (Baltimore, 1972), 86, 93–4; WO71/86/200–206; Orderly Book of General Sir A. Campbell, HQ Staten Island, Apr.–Sept. 1778, June 1, 1778, HM 617, HEH. John Graves Simcoe, *Simcoe's Military Journal* (New York, 1844), 212; Simcoe to Cornwallis, June 2, 1781, Cornwallis Papers. Greene: NG to Catherine Greene, Dec. 16, 1776, *PNG*, i: 368–9. On rape, imperial conflict, and conquest generally, see Goldstein, *War and Gender*, 365, 369; Jenny Sharpe, *Allegories of Empire: The Figure of Woman in the Colonial Text* (Minneapolis, MN, 1993); Wolfgang Reinhard, *Lebensformen Europas: Eine Historische Kulturanthropologie* (Munich, 2004), 368–9; Jansson, "Soldaten und Vergewaltigung," 201–5; Foster, *Sex*, 55; the quotation from the *Independent Chronicle* in the following paragraph is at 64.

45. Galloway, *Letters to a Nobleman*, 42–3. On Galloway, see also Wiener, *Civilians*, 145–6; Ferling, *The Loyalist Mind*.

Chapter Six

1. The Jan. 1777 acrostic, spelling "Washington," is quoted in Fischer, *Washington's Crossing*, 362. Although defeated early modern armies regularly lost an estimated 20 percent of their strength as prisoners (compared to 30 percent killed), the role of prisoners in early modern warfare remains under-researched. Peter H. Wilson, "Prisoners in Early Modern European Warfare," in *Prisoners in War*, ed. Sibylle

Scheipers (New York, 2010); Daniel Hohrath, " 'In Cartellen wird der Werth eines Gefangenen bestimmt.' Kriegsgefangenschaft als Teil der Kriegspraxis des Ancien Régime," in *In der Hand des Feindes: Kriegs-gefangenschaft von der Antike bis zum Zweiten Weltkrieg*, ed. Rüdiger Overmans (Cologne, 1999); Barbara Donagan, "Prisoners in the English Civil War," *History Today* 41:3 (1991): 31. Assessing the treatment of American captives is complicated by the lack of specific comparisons with other populations such as soldiers or captors. In certain cases it is possible to compare private notes with published versions of prisoners' testimony. The very repetitiveness of specific claims across a wide range of sources lends them a degree of plausibility. That does not mean that prisoners necessarily offered the correct explanations for the horrific conditions they suffered, or fully understood their captors' motivations. But as with narratives of raped women and mangled soldiers, the stories that prisoners and observers told about captivity mattered.

2. The best brief discussion of the contradictory reports on the Jumon ville incident and perhaps the most plausible reading is Fred Anderson, *Crucible of War: The Seven Years' War and the Fate of Empire in British North America, 1754–1766* (New York, 2000), 50–65.

3. Longmore, *Invention of George Washington*, 19, refers to the revival of the charges. On the "policy of humanity," see Fischer, *Washington's Crossing*, 375–9. On Washington's high standards for prisoner treatment, see ibid., 276; see also Witt, *Lincoln's Code*, 15, 22–3. "sacred Cause": GW to Gage, Aug. 19, 1775. For appeals to the codes of war, see also GW to WH, Jan. 13, 1777; WL to Benjamin Lincoln, Dec. 24, 1781, *PWL*, iv: 354–5. For the Lancaster county committee using similar language, see Ken Miller, *Dangerous Guests: Enemy Captives and Revolutionary Communities during the War for Independence* (Ithaca, NY, 2014), 73. For an early congressional recommendation of "Humane kind Treatment" of naval prisoners, see Marine Committee to commander of sloop *Providence*, Aug. 6, 1776, DLAR 295/1/31.

4. For the history of the law concerning prisoners of war since antiquity, see Overmans, ed., *In der Hand des Feindes*; Robert F. Grady, *The Evolution of Ethical and Legal Concern for the Prisoner of War* (Washington, D.C., 1971); Daniel Krebs, *A Generous and Merciful Enemy: Life for German Prisoners of War during the American Revolution* (Norman, OK), 80–91.

5. Unlike in other conflicts in this era, the British, at least at the beginning, and the Americans from early 1778 onward, appear to have been expected to feed the captives they held in return for monetary compensation, whether prompt or deferred. Until early 1778, British agents indirectly supplied captives in American hands with food. The system eventually ceased to work, and their American captors provisioned

Anglo-German prisoners directly for the remainder of the war, as they had been doing with respect to the Convention Army. Major General William Heath to GW, Oct. 25, 1777; WH to GW, Feb. 21, 1778.

6. Erica Charters, "The Administration of War and French Prisoners of War in Britain, 1756–1763," in *Civilians and War in Europe*, ed. Charters, Rosenhaft, and Smith, 91; Krebs, *Generous and Merciful Enemy*, 91; Betsy Knight, "Prisoner Exchange and Parole in the American Revolution," *WMQ* 48:2 (1991); *JCC*, ix: 1036–7, 1069; J. J. Boudinot, ed., *The Life, Public Services, Addresses, and Letters of Elias Boudinot* (Boston, 1896), i: 76; *LDC*, ix: 243–9; HL to GW, Mar. 15, 1778; AH to George Clinton, Mar. 12, 1778, *PAH*, i: 439–42; Burrows, *Forgotten Patriots*, 79, 153–4. It will be evident throughout this chapter and the next that I have relied much on Burrows, the most thoroughly researched and balanced treatment of American prisoners in the war to date.

7. Mackenzie: Allen French, ed., *Diary of Frederick Mackenzie, giving a daily narrative of his military service as an officer of the regiment of Royal Welch fusiliers during the years 1775–1781 in Massachusetts, Rhode Island and New York* (Cambridge, MA, 1930), i: 39, 111, entries for Sept. 5 and Nov. 17, 1776; see also De Lancey, ed., *History of New York*, ii: 27. It was only in March 1782, with the war effectively over, and four months before George III officially recognized America's independence, that Parliament classified captured Americans as prisoners of war and underwrote general cartels. Cox, *Proper Sense of Honor*, 213–14; GG to WH, Feb. 1, 1776, *Am. Arch.*, 4th ser., IV: 902–3. 22 Geo. 3, c. 10 (Mar. 25, 1782). Some Americans who had been captured at Quebec and transported to England were indeed imprisoned as traitors at Pendennis Castle, Falmouth. Hard-liners in the British cabinet, above all Germain and Sandwich, were keen to see them executed, but in the end they were not put on trial, one suspects because of fear of reprisals against British prisoners and, perhaps, the potential of domestic repercussions. Cox, *Proper Sense of Honor*, 212; John Chester Miller, *Triumph of Freedom, 1775–1783* (Westport, CT, 1979), 166, n. 3; Burrows, *Forgotten Patriots*, 40.

8. GW to Gage, Aug. 11, 1775.

9. Gage to GW, Aug. 13, 1775.

10. GW to Gage, Aug. 19, 1775. Troy Bickham, "Sympathizing with Sedition? George Washington, the British Press, and British Attitudes during the American War of Independence," *WMQ* 59:1 (2002).

11. WH to GW, July 16, 1776; Memorandum of interview with Lieutenant Colonel James Paterson, July 20, 1776; WH to GW, Aug. 19, 1776, at https://memory.loc.gov/cgi-bin/ampage?collId=mgw4&fileName =gwpage037.db&recNum=1026; GW to WH, Sept. 23, 1776; GW to WH, Nov. 9, 1776; WH to GW, Nov. 11, 1776. "render the situation": GW

to WH, Nov. 28, 1777, in Royal Commission on Historical Manuscripts, *Report on American Manuscripts in the Royal Institution of Great Britain* (London, 1904–9), i: 137. See also GW, Orders to Lieutenant Colonel Samuel Blachley Webb, Jan. 8, 1777.

12. "Half he sent": *Freeman's Journal*, Jan. 19, 1777. Cf. *Connecticut Journal*, Jan. 30, 1777. A version of this was published in *London Evening Post*, Apr. 10, 1777. General Israel Putnam saw emaciated captives released from New York that same spring: "once lads of spirit," they had "become babes and skilletons." Putnam to Godfrey Marlbon, June 24, 1777, DLAR 444/72445. See also Cox, *Proper Sense of Honor*, 200. "cool reflection": "Miserecors," *Connecticut Journal*, Jan. 30, 1777; see also *Connecticut Gazette*, Feb. 28, 1777; *Boston Gazette*, Mar. 17, 1777; *New Hampshire Gazette*, Mar. 22, 1777; *Freeman's Journal*, Mar. 22, 1777. David John Mays, ed., *The Letters and Papers of Edmund Pendleton, 1734–1803* (Charlottesville, VA, 1967), i: 249.

13. Kemble et al., *Kemble Papers*, i: 100; Larry G. Bowman, *Captive Americans: Prisoners during the American Revolution* (Athens, OH, 1976), 16; *Connecticut Journal*, Jan. 30, 1777; John Adlum Papers, Memoirs, ii: 86, WLCL; W. H. W. Sabine, ed., *The New-York Diary of Lieutenant Jabez Fitch of the 17th (Connecticut) Regiment from August 22, 1776 to December 15, 1777* (New York, 1954), 63.

14. "the prisoners": Bruce E. Burgoyne, trans., *Eighteenth-Century America: A Hessian Report on the People, the Land, the War as Noted in the Diary of Chaplain Philipp Waldeck, 1776–1780* (Bowie, MD, 1995), 23–4, entry for Nov. 16, 1776. Inge Auerbach, "Die hessischen Soldaten und ihr Bild von Amerika, 1776–1783," *Hessisches Jahrbuch für Landesgeschichte* 35 (1985): 145; Atwood, *Hessians*, 158; Burrows, *Forgotten Patriots*, 6–7.

15. Young: *Am. Arch.*, 4th ser., III: 1234. A Hessian soldier captured at Trenton made a similar comparison with animal feeding time. Lt. Wiederhold, Tagebuch eines Kurhessischen Officiers, 1776–80 [d. 1803], entry for Dec. 28, 1776, Bancroft 41, Hessian 12, NYPL.

16. Bowman, *Captive Americans*, 8. The Connecticut soldier is quoted from RWPA: W8256 (widow's pension application) in Burrows, *Forgotten Patriots*, 46. John Adlum Papers, Memoirs, ii: 90–91, WLCL. See also Ten Officers to "Gentlemen," Aug. 1, 1776, Boudinot Papers, LOC.

17. Abraham Leggett, *The Narrative of Abraham Leggett* (New York, 1971), the quotations at 20. Deposition of George Ballerman, Boston, Dec. 19, 1780, NARA M246/53/66/145–7.

18. Ebenezer Fletcher, *A narrative of the captivity and sufferings of Mr. Ebenezer Fletcher* (Amherst, MA, 1798), 6. "all moderate Men": quoted in Ranlet, *New York Loyalists*, 91, from Carleton to GG, Aug. 10, 1776, CO42/35/122–3, PAC. For examples of good treatment, see Cox, *Proper*

Sense of Honor, 202; Colonel Josiah Parker to David Jameson, Nov. 19, 1781, quoted in Philip Ranlet, "The British, Their Virginian Prisoners, and Prison Ships of the American Revolution," *American Neptune* 60:3 (200): 261; Carleton to WH, Aug. 8, 1776, Add MS 21599.

19. For this and the next paragraph, see Burrows, *Forgotten Patriots,* 19, and Appendix A for the calorific calculations; 24 for Catlin; see also 58. Sabine, ed., *New-York Diary,* 61; John Adlum Papers, Memoirs, ii: 91–2, WLCL; William R. Lindsey, "Treatment of American Prisoners of War during the Revolution," *Emporia State Research Studies* 22:1 (1973): 11; Alexander Coffin, *The destructive operation of foul air, tainted provisions, bad water, and personal filthiness, upon human constitutions; exemplified in the unparallelled Cruelty of the British to the American captives at New-York during the Revolutionary War, on Board their Prison and Hospital Ships* (New York, 1865), 120.

20. Leggett, *Narrative,* 20–21; Bowman, *Captive Americans,* 19; Lindsey, "Treatment," 11.

21. "overrun with lice": Capt. Edward Boylston, whom Loyalists had delivered from his New Jersey house to a New York sugarhouse, quoted in Burrows, *Forgotten Patriots,* 57. "upon the excrements": Coffin, *Destructive operation,* 120. For a doctor's statement regarding his limited access to prisoners, see McHenry to GW, June 21, 1777; Bernhard Christian Steiner, *The Life and Correspondence of James McHenry, Secretary at War under Washington and Adams* (Cleveland, 1907), 14. For medical care, see also Bowman, *Captive Americans,* 21. Hospitals: Cox, *Proper Sense of Honor,* 22–9. "would not go": quoted in Henry R. Stiles, ed., *Letters from the prisons and prison-ships of the revolution* (New York, 1865), 26.

22. Burrows, *Forgotten Patriots,* 18–21. The treatment of American prisoners elsewhere was fairly similar to conditions in New York. For Philadelphia, see Burrows, *Forgotten Patriots,* 118–21; Lewis, ed., *Mammoth Book,* 11; Joseph Lloyd's deposition, Nov. 16, 1777, BHQP 748; John W. Jackson, *With the British Army in Philadelphia, 1777–1778* (San Rafael, CA, 1979), 117–24; Ezekiel Williams, *Letters and Documents of Ezekiel Williams of Wethersfield, Connecticut* (Hartford, CT, 1976), 33–4; Frazer, *General Persifor Frazer,* 239–43; *New-York Gazette,* Jan. 24, 1780; *Connecticut Gazette,* June 30, 1780; *Norwich Packet,* July 6, 1780.

23. "a little Damaged": Leggett, *Narrative,* 21. Fell: Henry Onderdonk, *Revolutionary incidents of Suffolk and Kings Counties: with an account of the Battle of Long Island and the British prisons and prison-ships at New York* (New York, 1849), 219–27.

24. "he never forgot": John Pintard quoted in Ranlet, *New York Loyalists,* 109. See also deposition by John Barrett, NARA M246/53/66/159–62.

25. Ellis Franklin, *History of Northampton County, Pennsylvania* (Philadelphia, 1877), 240. The quotations in *Pennsylvania Evening Post*, May 3, 1777.

26. *Affidavits and documents relating to the burial, in the northerly part of Trinity Church yard* (New York, 1855); Burrows, *Forgotten Patriots*, 96–8; Ranlet, *New York Loyalists*, 109; Jeremiah B. Fells Diary, MssCol 906, NYPL.

27. Sherburne is quoted in Robert H. Patton, *Patriot Pirates: The Privateer War for Freedom and Fortune in the American Revolution* (New York, 2008), 241. For the various rumors, see Burrows, *Forgotten Patriots*, 74–5; Ranlet, "The British, Their Virginian Prisoners," 258–60; Danske Dandridge, *American Prisoners of the Revolution* (Baltimore, MD, 1967), 189–90; Robert C. Bray and Paul E. Bushnell, eds., *Diary of a Common Soldier in the American Revolution, 1775–1783* (DeKalb, IL, 1978), 26. For germ warfare allegations around smallpox, see Fenn, *Pox Americana*, 88–95, with the quotation from GW at 90. For rumors and history writing, see Jean-Noël Kapferer, *Rumors: Uses, Interpretations, and Images* (New Brunswick, NJ, 1990); Anjan Ghosh, "Role of Rumour in History Writing," *History Compass* 6:5 (2008); Tamotsu Shibutani, *Improvised News: A Sociological Study of Rumor* (Indianapolis, 1966), 6; Hans-Joachim Neubauer, *The Rumour: A Cultural History*, trans. Christian Braun (London, 1999).

28. "all Crouded": Connecticut captives on the *Whitby* to Gov. Trumbull, quoted in Burrows, *Forgotten Patriots*, 56. "Indians, Mullattoes": *Pennsylvania Gazette*, Apr. 29, 1777; *Connecticut Gazette*, May 30, 1777. Barrett: Deposition of Lt. John Barrett, Aug. 4, 1777, *NDAR*, ix: 705–6, and NARA M246/53/66/159–62. For the Philadelphia allegations, see Burrows, *Forgotten Patriots*, 119.

29. "was never": *Journals of the American Congress* (Washington, D.C., 1823), ii: 98. "a poor Woman": Boudinot to GW, Mar. 2, 1778. "the commonest": quoted in Burrows, *Forgotten Patriots*, 59. Bowman, *Captive Americans*, 46–7; *Connecticut Gazette*, May 30, 1777. Thomas Jefferson Wertenbaker, *Father Knickerbocker Rebels: New York City during the Revolution* (New York, 1969), 170.

30. For the rules of and disputes over parole, see Clancy, "Rules of Land Warfare," 310–14. For officers paroled in Manhattan and Long Island, see Van Buskirk, *Generous Enemies*, 77–85. Leggett, *Narrative*.

31. "in the Lap": American prisoners to HC, Nov. 30, 1777, Clinton Papers, 27/44. "Was sorry": Elias Boudinot, quoted in Burrows, *Forgotten Patriots*, 124.

32. On paroled officers in New York City, see Van Buskirk, *Generous Enemies*, ch. 3. Fitch: Sabine, ed., *New-York Diary*, 64, 75 (quotation), 180.

On the diary's credibility, see Burrows, *Forgotten Patriots*, 267 n. 12. Allen: Charles A. Jellison, *Ethan Allen: Frontier Rebel* (Syracuse, NY, 1969), 171–2, quoted in Lindsey, "Treatment," 21–2.

33. "Twenty": *Am. Arch.*, 5th ser., III: 1429–30, letter by released prisoner, quoted in Lindsey, "Treatment," 10–11. "I have seen": quoted in Dandridge, *American Prisoners*, 61. See also Thacher, *Military Journal*, 75–6. "thrown into wagons": quoted in Lindsey, "Treatment," 10. See also Cox, *Proper Sense of Honor*, 231. "Expos'd to": Fitch, unpublished "Narrative," quoted in Burrows, *Forgotten Patriots*, 58; George Taylor, *Martyrs to the revolution in the British prison-ships in the Wallabout Bay* (New York, 1855), 30–31. Live burial: Hulton, *Letters*, 86.

34. In prison narratives, the Loyalists were usually characterized as the most villainous, followed by the British (and Scots especially), then the Hessians. Albert G. Greene, *Recollections of the Jersey Prison-Ship; taken and prepared for publication from the original manuscript of the late Captain Thomas Dring* (Providence, RI, 1829), 67, 98, 104. Dring recorded his recollections just before his death, in seventy-nine closely written pages. They were edited for publication in 1829 by Albert G. Greene, whose version keeps Dring's narrative, attitudes, and sentiments intact, while rearranging a repetitive manuscript. For the publication history, see David Swain, ed., *Recollections of Life on the Prison Ship Jersey in 1782. Thomas Dring, A Revolutionary War-Era Manuscript* (Yardley, PA, 2010), xvi–xvii. Allen in Dandridge, *American Prisoners*, 60; Lt. Robert Troup in Onderdonk, *Revolutionary Incidents*, 211. For the Washington-Howe exchange, see GW to WH, Apr. 9, 1777; WH to GW, Apr. 21, 1777. For a detailed refutation of Howe's claims, see also James McHenry to GW, June 21, 1777. The quotations from Washington in GW to WH, June 10, 1777.

35. Formal responsibility for prisoner administration was shared by General Washington as commander in chief, the Congress, the Board of War and Ordnance, and individual states. Congress periodically allocated funds for the supply and relief of prisoners and sent foodstuffs and clothing. Virginia and Maryland sent food, tobacco, clothing, bedding, and medicine to their citizen-soldiers held in New York and Charleston: *JPC*, ii: 41–12; Pennsylvania Council of Safety to GW, Jan. 15, 1777; *NDAR*, vii: 997, 1003; GW to J. Trumbull Sr., Mar. 31, 1778. Address from Council to [?British commander], Mar. 4, 1783, Misc. Collections, Box 7, Maryland, NYPL. "unnecessarily rigorous" and "culpably lax": Richard Peters to Elias Boudinot, Apr. 29, 1777, Boudinot Papers, LOC. "boisterous": Boudinot to Mrs. Boudinot, July 22, 1777, in Boudinot, ed., *Life, Public Services*, 55. Joseph Lee Boyle, ed., *"Their distress is almost intolerable": The Elias Boudinot Letterbook, 1777–1778* (Bowie, MD, 2002), 16–19; Anna Catherine Pabst, ed., *American Revolutionary War*

Manuscript Records: Elias Boudinot and General Haldimand Papers (Delaware, OH, 1969), 4; George Adams Boyd, *Elias Boudinot, Patriot and Statesman, 1740–1821* (Princeton, 1952); Richard Peters, Secretary Board of War, to Elias Boudinot, Apr. 29, 1777, Boudinot Papers, LOC; Larry G. Bowman, "Lewis Pintard: Agent to American Prisoners, 1777–1780," *Journal of the Great Lakes History Conference* 1 (1976).

36. Martha Williamson Dixon, "Divided Authority: The American Management of Prisoners in the Revolutionary War, 1775–1783" (PhD diss., University of Utah, 1977), 29–30, 46–7, 91–4, 250–54, and passim; Boyd, *Boudinot*, 40–41; GW to Jonathan Trumbull Sr., July 2–4, 1777; GW to Major General Joseph Spencer, Sept. 2, 1777; Hugh Hastings and J. A. Holden, eds., *Public Papers of George Clinton, First Governor of New York, 1777–1795, 1801–1804* (New York, 1899–1914), iv: 837, 844–5; v: 129–30, 387–8; vii: 319–20.

37. David L. Sterling, "American Prisoners of War in New York: A Report by Elias Boudinot," *WMQ* 13:3 (1956) with Appendix B on clothing; Boyd, *Boudinot*.

38. Draft report Boudinot to GW, Mar. 2, 1778. The allegation of killing by jail key in Boudinot to [?], Apr. 20, 1778, in *PMHB* 43 (1919), 285. For Boudinot's February 1778 visit to New York, see also Helen Jordan, "Colonel Elias Boudinot in New York City, February, 1778," *PMHB* 24:4 (1900); Sterling, "American Prisoners of War," 380–81. See also Boudinot to GW, Mar. 2, 1778; Loring to WH, Feb. 7, 1778, BHQP 930; Burrows, *Forgotten Patriots*, 122–3; Boyle, ed., *Distress*, 111. In July 1779, a prisoner at the Provost described his "Confinement, as Close as Locks, Barrs and Boalts can make it"; his wife ought not to visit as that would expose her to "Contimptable Insults." Daniel Hendrickson to Mrs. Hendrickson, July 21, 1779, NYHS.

39. Boudinot's undated estimate of expenditures in the papers of the Continental Congress, most likely collated in spring 1778, cited £22,583 spent by Pintard for provisions for New York prisoners. See also Jordan, "Colonel Elias Boudinot"; Sterling, "American Prisoners of War," 385. Burrows, *Forgotten Patriots*, 130–32, with the quotation "worrying myself" at 130; Dixon, "Divided Authority," 100. Boudinot was succeeded by the Pennsylvania physician and former prisoner John Beattie, who also sent flour, beef, pork, firewood, and clothing and was in turn succeeded in 1780 by Abraham Skinner.

40. Even less is known about the British and German prisoners of war in American hands during this conflict than about American prisoners. We do not have the total numbers of British soldiers and sailors taken captive, let alone of those who escaped, enlisted with the enemy, or died in captivity. However, a few surviving prisoner narratives and the extant official papers afford us glimpses of what being a prisoner of

Revolutionary America entailed. For British captives, see Colley, *Captives*, 210–24. Partial exceptions are studies of the Convention Army, for which see n. 46 below. Knight, "Prisoner Exchange," is a rare comparative approach. Hessian prisoners have recently been served better by a thorough study by Krebs, *Generous and Merciful Enemy*; see also Miller, *Dangerous Guests*. "for we wish": War Office to Thomas Bradford, Nov. 13, 1779, Bradford Papers, Box 11/75, HSP; see ibid., Box 10/9.

41. See, e.g., Prisoners of War at Carlisle, Aug. 1, 1776, Boudinot Papers, LOC. See also Helga Doblin and Mary C. Lynn, eds., *An Eyewitness Account of American Revolution and New England Life: The Journal of J.F. Wasmus, German Company Surgeon, 1776–1783* (New York, 1990), 72; Philip Schuyler to Committee of Kingston, Apr. 5, 1776, Philip Schuyler Papers, Box 18, NYPL; John Smythe to Congress, Feb. 22, 1776, Boudinot Papers, LOC; Allen Cameron to Congress, Feb. 27, 1776. See also complaints cited in Burrows, *Forgotten Patriots*, 187. GG to WH, Mar. 5, 1777, Clinton Papers 18/369. Thomas Wileman, 17th Dragoons, deposition, Feb. 18, 1778, enclosed with WH to GW, Feb. 21, 1778, BHQP 948; Gerald O. Haffner, "A British Prisoner of War in the American Revolution: The Experiences of Jacob Schieffelin from Vincennes to Williamsburg, 1779–1780," *Virginia Magazine of History and Biography*, 86:1 (Jan. 1978); Clinton Papers 14/10 and 159/30; Tagebuch des hessischen Lieutenants Piel von 1776 bis 1783, entries for Dec. 26, Jan. 9, 1777, Bancroft 40, Hessian 4, NYPL. Krebs, *Generous and Merciful Enemy*, 78. Lt. Wiederhold, Tagebuch eines Kurhessischen Officiers, 1776–80 [d. 1803], entry for Dec. 28, 1776, Bancroft 41, Hessian 12, NYPL.

42. WH to GW, Jan. 19, 1778, CO5/95/145–6. From 1779 onward, as the Congress and the states were increasingly less well resourced to meet the demands of growing prisoner populations, British and German captives suffered from more serious shortages of provisions and clothing; several detention sites lacked adequate accommodation; after Yorktown, insufficient state capacity to meet the demands of thousands of prisoners scattered in towns in five states worsened the situation. Dixon, "Divided Authority," 52–3, 60–61, 182–3, 187.

43. Congress rubber-stamped the prisoner-labor practice retrospectively in May 1776. The best study so far is in Krebs, *Generous and Merciful Enemy*; see also Ray Waldron Pettengill, *Letters from America, 1776–1779; Being Letters of Brunswick, Hessian, and Waldeck Officers with the British Armies during the Revolution* (Port Washington, NY, 1964), 132–5; Thomas Bradford Papers, Box 21, p. 92; Box 22, vol. 2, p. 114; Box 23, vol. 3, p. 21, HSP. For Lancaster as a central detention site, see Miller, *Dangerous Guests*, with further details on prisoner-laborers at 113–16 and on Frederick at 153.

44. See Krebs, *Generous and Merciful Enemy*, 149–58, for an apparently exceptional case of abuse at 158. In addition to German captives, some British prisoners of war were also employed as laborers, e.g., in Virginia, Connecticut, and New Jersey, although they were considered a greater flight risk. See George G. Lewis and John Mewha, *History of Prisoner of War Utilization by the United States Army, 1776–1945* (Washington, D.C., 1955), 15.

45. O'Shaughnessy, *Men Who Lost America*, 111–14, 148–58; Mackesy, *War for America*, 113–18, 130–44; Richard M. Ketchum, *Saratoga: Turning Point of America's Revolutionary War* (New York, 1997); Gerald Saxon Brown, *The American Secretary: The Colonial Policy of Lord George Germain, 1775–1778* (Ann Arbor, MI, 1963), 81–137; Conway, *Short History*, 84–6.

46. My discussion of the Convention Army draws on Richard Sampson, *Escape in America: The British Convention Prisoners, 1777–1783* (Chippenham, 1995); George W. Knepper, "The Convention Army, 1777–1783" (PhD diss., University of Michigan, 1954); Krebs, *Generous and Merciful Enemy*, ch. 9.

47. Winthrop is quoted in Sampson, *Escape in America*, 55. Towns along the marching route provisioned the Convention Army as it passed through, expecting to be compensated later by the British: Brigadier General John Glover to GW, May 15, 1778.

48. Heerwagen: Manfred von Gall, ed., *Hanauer Journale und Briefe aus dem Amerikanischen Unabhängigkeitskrieg, 1776–1783* (Hanau, 2005), 95, 111. The suspension rested on weak legal grounds, such as that descriptive lists of men and some colors had not been surrendered at Saratoga as promised; surrendered muskets had allegedly been damaged. *New Jersey Gazette*, Feb. 25, 1778.

49. "one night": J. A. Houlding and G. Kenneth Yates, "Corporal Fox's Memoir of Service, 1766–1783: Quebec, Saratoga, and the Convention Army," *JSAHR* 68:275 (1990): 163. "so secreted": William Phillips to Horatio Gates, Cambridge, Dec. 12, 1778, Clinton Papers 48/12.

50. Houlding and Yates, "Corporal Fox's Memoir," 163–4; William M. Dabney, ed., *After Saratoga: The Story of the Convention Army* (Albuquerque, NM, 1955), 56–8; Anburey, *Travels*, ii: 315–20, 438–9, 453. Max von Eelking, trans., *Memoirs, Letters and Journals of Major General Riedesel during His Residence in America* (New York, 1969), i: 282; ii: 31–2; Kranish, *Flight from Monticello*, 109–12; O'Shaughnessy, *Men Who Lost America*, 159; Witt, *Lincoln's Code*, 28.

51. On the march to Virginia, some 300 British and 280 German prisoners, and from the Charlottesville camp in 1779 an additional 222 plus 86, disappeared. Houlding and Yates, "Corporal Fox's Memoir," 164; Frey, *British Soldier*, 72; O'Shaughnessy, *Men Who Lost America*, 159.

52. For the "want of space, as our territories were very contracted," as a limitation on British treatment of American prisoners, see Richard Fitzpatrick to brother, Mar. 3, 1777, Richard Fitzpatrick Papers, LOC. Cf. Witt, *Lincoln's Code*, 22.

53. Stacy Schiff, *A Great Improvisation: Franklin, France, and the Birth of America* (New York, 2005), 10–12, 68–9, 111, and passim. For the diplomatic history of the Franco-American alliance, see Jonathan R. Dull, *A Diplomatic History of the American Revolution* (New Haven, CT, 1985), 75–103; Ronald Hoffman and Peter J. Albert, eds., *Diplomacy and Revolution: The Franco-American Alliance of 1778* (Charlottesville, VA, 1981). For the general context, see also Middlekauff, *Glorious Cause*, ch. 17.

54. *JCC*, xii, 1080–82, Congressional Manifesto (Oct. 30, 1778).

Chapter Seven

1. "Miserecors": first published in *Connecticut Journal*, Jan. 30, 1777.

2. "Humanitas": *London Gazette*, Aug. 6, 1776. Throughout the war, in public and in private, Americans evoked imagery of prisoners being smothered and suffocated in stifling, hot, putrid air, especially on prison ships anchored offshore, to paint the inhumanity of their imperial captors. See, e.g., HL to John Burnet, Jul. 24, 1778, *PHL*, xiv: 65–7; J. Bartlett Reminiscences, MS S–27b, MHS.

3. "others grew mad": John Cooke, who believed Siraj did not intend a "massacre," in *Reports from Committees of the House of Commons, 1715–1801*, vol. 3, *First report from the committee appointed to enquire into the nature, state, and condition of the East India Company* (London, 1772), 144.

4. Recent historians have pointed out that the event only became part of the founding myth of British India in Victorian times. For the layered meanings of the Black Hole, see Kate Teltscher, " 'The Fearful Name of the Black Hole': Fashioning an Imperial Myth," in *Writing India, 1757–1990*, ed. Bart Moore-Gilbert (Manchester, 1996); Colley, *Captives*, 255–6. Partha Chatterjee, *The Black Hole of Empire: History of a Global Practice of Power* (Princeton, 2012), argues that the focus of the early published narratives was not so much on Indian cruelty as on the European captives' disconcerting "descent . . . into mindless disorder" (21). For the American Revolutionary period, a search on Eighteenth-Century Collections Online shows dozens of references in a wide range of genres. Exemplary of very numerous references in newspapers and magazines: *Freeman's Magazine* (1774), 113; *London Review of English and Foreign Literature*, Dec. 1778, 369; *Weekly Miscellany*, Nov. 16, 1778, 154–6; *General Evening Post*, Dec. 3–5, 1771; *Public Ad-*

vertiser, Apr. 26, 1773, May 6, 1774, May 18, 1776; *London Evening Post,* Apr. 5–8, 1777, Sept. 10–12, 1778; *Morning Post,* Oct. 1, 1777; *Morning Chronicle,* June 5, 1781; *Morning Herald,* Apr. 4, 1785; cf. *Pennsylvania Magazine,* Oct. 1775, 476–8.

5. "shifting 'black holes' ": *Pennsylvania Journal,* Jan. 18, 1783. "very idea": Ebenezer Fox, *The Adventures of Ebenezer Fox* (Boston, 1847), 94.

6. "a strong current," "dismal sounds," "continual noises," and "being passed": Greene, *Recollections,* 12, 14, 42, 63. Van Dyke is quoted in Dandridge, *American Prisoners,* 201. Perry: Burrows, *Forgotten Patriots,* 55–6. Cf. Lt. Jonathan Gillet(t), quoted ibid., 59: "Their natures are brook and gone," some virtually losing their voices or hearing, it becoming "shocking to human nature to behold them." Thomas Andros, *The old Jersey captive: or, A narrative of the captivity of Thomas Andros... on board the old Jersey prison ship at New York, 1781* (Boston, 1833), 13.

7. Emma Christopher, *A Merciless Place: The Fate of Britain's Convicts after the American Revolution* (New York, 2011), 31, 33, 66.

8. For this paragraph, see Swain, ed., *Recollections,* 28; Greene, *Recollections,* 23–4, 27, 29–35 ("Among the": 30); Clive L. Lloyd, *A History of Napoleonic and American Prisoners of War, 1756–1816: Hulk, Depot, and Parole* (Woodbridge, Suffolk, 2007), 127. Coffin, *Destructive operation,* 120, referred to "walking skeletons." Fox is quoted in Dandridge, *American Prisoners,* 234. Cf. Karen Zeinert, ed., *The Memoirs of Andrew Sherburne: Patriot and Privateer of the American Revolution* (Hamden, CT, 1993), 85.

9. Lindsey, "Treatment," 17; Burrows, *Forgotten Patriots,* 163–4. In August 1781, the *Boston Gazette* printed portions of a letter from an anonymous prisoner on the *Jersey,* who outlined death or enlistment as the only choices; daily there were 6 to 11 corpses and 200 men falling sick with "yellow fever, small pox." Philip Freneau, *The British Prison-Ship: A Poem in Four Cantos* (Philadelphia, 1781), 8, 9, 12; Greene, *Recollections,* 6. Swain, ed., *Recollections,* 109 with note 71, dates the period of Dring's confinement to c. May 19 to c. July 20, 1782. Dring later recounted his horrors to have lasted five months.

10. Freneau, *British Prison-Ship,* 13. For the ship's anatomy, see Swain, ed., *Recollections,* 8–15, 27–8, 44–5; Burrows, *Forgotten Patriots,* 164; Lloyd, *History,* 124–7; Coffin, *Destructive operation,* 124. For the disputed subject matter of the image in this section, see http://www.library .fordham.edu/trumbull/trumbulldetail.asp?imageID=29.

11. Greene, *Recollections,* 9–10; Burrows, *Forgotten Patriots,* 148–52; AO12/42/345–54; James Lenox Banks, *David Sproat and Naval Prisoners in the War of the Revolution* (New York, 1909); Lloyd, *History,* 130; Andros, *Old Jersey Captive.*

12. WO1/12/537. For the links between overcrowding and epidemic disease in eighteenth-century medical theory, see Friedrich Prinzing and Harald Westergaard, *Epidemics Resulting from Wars* (London, 1916), chs. 4–5.

13. For this and the following paragraphs, see Erica Charters, *Disease, War, and the Imperial State: The Welfare of the British Armed Forces during the Seven Years' War* (Chicago, 2014), 42–51 (quotations 43); Fenn, *Pox Americana*, 28, 31–2, and passim; Peter Razzell, *The Conquest of Smallpox: The Impact of Inoculation on Smallpox Mortality in Eighteenth Century Britain* (Firle, Sussex, 1977).

14. Fenn, *Pox Americana*, 32 (quotation), and 33–5 for Adams's experience. Swain, ed., *Recollections*, 25–6; Cox, *Proper Sense of Honor*, 228.

15. Greene, *Recollections*, 47–8, 50–56; Lloyd, *History*, 134–5; Bowman, *Captive Americans*, 44–5, 48–9; Cox, *Proper Sense of Honor*, 227–30. Charleston: Peter Fayssoux to David Ramsay, Mar. 26, 1785, in Robert W. Gibbes, ed., *Documentary History of the American Revolution* (New York, 1853–7), ii: 119; Charles I. Bushnell, *A Narrative of the Life and Adventures of Levi Hanford* (New York, 1863), 13–15. Burrows, *Forgotten Patriots*, 56. For Ballerman, see NARA M246/53/66/145–7, deposition, Boston, Dec. 19, 1780. Zeinert, ed., *Memoirs of Andrew Sherburne*, 86, references lifelong health issues.

16. "the prisoners": Greene, *Recollections*, 67. Slade: quoted in Burrows, *Forgotten Patriots*, 56–7. Much less well-known and researched than the *Jersey* and her sister ships, Americans also held British captives on their own prison ships. Connecticut, New York, Virginia, and Massachusetts operated prison ships for reasons of security and cost, but also to retaliate for the appalling treatment of American captives on British prison ships. Conditions on American vessels appear mostly not to have been quite as bad as on British ones, although there is evidence here, too, of overcrowding, poor provisions, illness, and corrupt guards. See Dixon, "Divided Authority," 152–7; Burrows, *Forgotten Patriots*, 189–90; *JCC*, xiv: 837; Thomas Hughes, *A Journal by Thos. Hughes, for His Amusement* (Port Washington, NY, 1970), 22–3.

17. GW to WH, Jan. 13, 1777; Congress, Dec. 19, 1777. Deposition of George Ballerman, Boston, Dec. 19, 1780, in NARA M246/53/66/145–7. On forced enlistment through starvation, see *Connecticut Journal*, Jan. 30, 1777.

18. For reports of successful escapes from prison ships, see Fox, *Adventures*, 147; Andros, *Old Jersey Captive*, 14. For Hawkins and Forten, see Emmy E. Werner, *In Pursuit of Liberty: Coming of Age in the American Revolution* (Westport, CT, 2006), 100–103.

19. J. Bartlett Reminiscences, MS S–27b, MHS.

20. Swain, ed., *Recollections*, 106 n. 68; Lindsey, "Treatment," 13. For the

devastating impact of such mortality rates on local communities, and for examples of local memory and family legend, see Burrows, *Forgotten Patriots*, 64–5. For comparative statistics, see http://www1.va.gov /vetdata/docs/specialreports/powcy054-12-06jsmwrfinal2.doc.

21. Newspaper reports in 1782 estimated that between 4,000 and 8,000 captives had died on the New York prison hulks. However, in one of the most widely circulated news items of the war, on Apr. 17, 1783, the *Continental Journal* put the number of deaths on the "filthy and malignant" *Jersey* at 11,644. The number, which tallied with references to a register David Sproat had allegedly kept, presumably referred to the total number of dead in Wallabout Bay. At seven to eight deaths per day over just under four years, this would be within the range of contemporary reports of daily deaths. We do not know the total number of prisoners on the ships. Assuming a mortality rate of 50 percent, there would have had to be 22,000 captives in total, which seems too high in light of the anecdotal evidence available; the mortality rate may therefore well have been substantially higher than 50 percent. Assuming a similar mortality rate among the 9,000 to 10,000 prisoners in the city prisons, an additional 4,500 to 7,000 captives died there, and perhaps another 1,000 men in the makeshift prisons and on prison hulks in the Southern colonies and elsewhere. For these estimates, and the underlying sources and methods, see Burrows, *Forgotten Patriots*, 197–201, 57, 278 n. 25, and passim. For the most skeptical review of Burrows's calculations, see John Fabian Witt, "Ye Olde Gitmo: When Americans Were Unlawful Combatants," *Slate* (Dec. 9, 2008).

22. "The atmosphere": quoted in Lloyd, *History*, 140.

23. A British doctor at the site was concerned with prisoners' health, the spread of infectious diseases on prison ships, and the risk to the British troops guarding the prisoners: WO11/659–61; 12/533, 537–48. Charles Herbert, *A relic of the Revolution: containing a full and particular account of the sufferings and privations of all the American prisoners* (Boston, 1847), with the quotation ("almost suffocated") at 18; Francis D. Cogliano, *American Maritime Prisoners in the Revolutionary War: The Captivity of William Russell* (Annapolis, MD, 2001), 39, with reference to *Pennsylvania Gazette*, July 2, 1777, and Viscount Barrington to GG, Nov. 5, 1778 ("Herrings"). For other early captivity experiences on cable tiers and in holds, sometimes in chains, see ibid., 35–6. Other transitional holding areas included Quebec, Newfoundland, Rhode Island, Jamaica, and Gibraltar, as well as ports in Ireland, Wales, and Scotland. In addition to Cogliano's work, the key literature on American prisoners in Britain includes Sheldon S. Cohen, *Yankee Sailors in British Gaols: Prisoners of War at Forton and Mill, 1777–1783* (Newark, DE, 1995), and a series of older articles: Olive Anderson, "The Treatment of Prisoners

of War in Britain during the American War of Independence," *Bulletin of the Institute of Historical Research* 28: 77 (1955); John K. Alexander, "Forton Prison during the American Revolution: A Case Study of British Prisoner of War Policy and the American Prisoner Response to that Policy," *Essex Institute Historical Collections* 103:4 (1967); Lindsey, "Treatment"; Catherine M. Prelinger, "Benjamin Franklin and the American Prisoners of War in England during the American Revolution," *WMQ* 32:2 (1975); Jesse Lemisch, "Listening to the Inarticulate: William Widger's Dream and the Loyalties of American Revolutionary Seamen in British Prisons," *Journal of Social History* 3:1 (1969), and, as an important corrective, Paul A. Gilje, "Loyalty and Liberty: The Ambiguous Patriotism of Jack Tar in the American Revolution," *Pennsylvania History* 67:2 (2000).

24. The quotation from Lt. Joshua Barney, about his passage from New York to Plymouth, in Cogliano, *American Maritime Prisoners*, 41. Cf. Alexander, "Forton Prison," 367–8.

25. For this and the following paragraph, see Herbert, *Relic of the Revolution*, 17–26, 31–43; John Blatchford, *The narrative of John Blatchford, detailing his sufferings in the revolutionary war, while a prisoner with the British* (New York, 1865), 22; Colley, *Captives*, 217–18; Krebs, *Generous and Merciful Enemy*, 121–7; Forton Prison Journal of Thomas McKinney, Gov. Trumbull Papers, LOC. Compare Israel Potter's experience on arriving as a captive in England: Israel Potter, *Life and remarkable adventures of Israel R. Potter* (Providence, RI, 1824), 19–20, and locals' responses to Americans they had understood to be "of much less refinement than the ancient Britains, and possessing little more humanity than the Buccaniers" (22).

26. "an independent State": GW to CC, May 11, 1776, *Am. Arch.*, 4th ser., vi: 423–5.

27. The outstanding, revisionist treatment of *habeas corpus* is Paul D. Halliday, *Habeas Corpus: From England to Empire* (Cambridge, MA, 2010); see esp. 251–3. See also Paul D. Halliday and G. Edward White, "The Suspension Clause: English Text, Imperial Contexts, and American Implications," *Virginia Law Review* 94:3 (2008): 644–51. The law, 17 Geo III, c. 9, was renewed each year to Jan. 1, 1783.

28. "shocking": Lord Abingdon quoted in Burrows, *Forgotten Patriots*, 80. For the debate, see *Parl. Hist.*, xix: 4–53; Dunning: col. 7; Fox: col. 11.

29. Edmund Burke, *A Letter from Edmund Burke* (London, 1777), 4, 8, 15. For American press, see, e.g., *New-England Chronicle*, Oct. 2, 1777; *Pennsylvania Packet*, Dec. 3, 1777; *New Jersey Gazette*, Jan. 21, 1778.

30. "spirit of the Nation": Duncan Drummond to HC, Feb. 15, 1777, Clinton Papers 20/30. "arbitrary imprisonment": *Gentleman's Magazine* 47 (1778): 457. "execrable act": Archibald Cary for the Virginia General

Assembly to HL, Jan. 12, 1778, *The correspondence, journals, committee reports, and records of the Continental Congress (1774–1789)*, 78, NARA M247. See also *Virginia Gazette*, Nov. 27, 1778. Badge of honor: Halliday and White, "Suspension Clause," 253.

31. Herbert, *Relic of the Revolution*, 28, 31–44, quotations 28, 43. Cf. Nathan Perl-Rosenthal, *Citizen Sailors: Becoming American in the Age of Revolution* (Cambridge, MA, 2015), ch. 2.

32. The Sick and Hurt Board had been responsible for some 20,000 enemy prisoners stationed throughout the British Isles at the height of the Seven Years' War. Prelinger, "Benjamin Franklin," 264; Anderson, "Treatment of Prisoners," 63–7. For prisoners of war in the Seven Years' War, see Charters, "The Administration of War." For total numbers at Forton and Mill, see John Howard, *The state of the prisons in England and Wales, with preliminary observations and an account of some foreign prisons and hospitals* (London, 1792), 185, 187. The *Pennsylvania Evening Post* reported as early as July 12, 1777, on the choice of Forton and Mill under North's Act.

33. At these smaller sites and at temporary prisons, captives in need of medical attention had to make do with the services of a local apothecary. Sheldon S. Cohen, *British Supporters of the American Revolution, 1775–1783: The Role of the 'Middling-Level' Activists* (Woodbridge, Suffolk, 2004), 59, 111; Lloyd, *History*, 232. ADM3/82/1; ADM98/11/96, 140; Cogliano, *American Maritime Prisoners*, 88. Maritime prisoners were split between those who were sent to Britain and those kept on prison ships in America, Quebec, Halifax, St. John's, and Jamaica, or under forced labor in coal pits in Cape Breton.

34. "shocking place" and "coming out of hell": quoted in Cohen, *Yankee Sailors*, 55. It was only in spring 1782 that the bread ration for American prisoners was adjusted. ADM/M/405, June 23, 1781, Apr. 23, 1782.

35. Cogliano, *American Maritime Prisoners*, 57–61; ADM97/127/1. Corrupt guards: Eunice H. Turner, "American Prisoners of War in Great Britain, 1777–83," *Mariner's Mirror* 45:3 (1959), 201; ADM/M/404, Mar. 13 and Apr. 19–26, 1777, NMM. William Hammond Bowden, ed., "Diary of William Widger of Marblehead, kept at Mill Prison, England, 1781," *Essex Institute Historical Collections* 73 (1937): 335; George Thompson, "Diary of George Thompson of Newburyport, kept at Forton Prison, England, 1777–1781," *Essex Institute Historical Collections* 76 (1940): 227; William Richard Cutter, "A Yankee Privateersman in Prison in England, 1777–1779," *New-England Historical and Genealogical Register* 32 (1878): 165. Cohen, *British Supporters*, 31; Cohen, *Yankee Sailors*, 65–7, with the quotation from Cutler at 66. The outcome of an investigation into Cowdry's alleged abuses is not known: ADM/M/404, Aug. 29, Sept. 3, 1777, NMM. Food: Herbert, *Relic of the Revolution*,

59–60, 75, 97, 83, 85, 140–41, 143, 165, 210, 212; Bowden, ed.,"Diary of William Widger," 73:316, 320; Rev. Samuel Cutler, ed., "Prison Ships, and the 'Old Mill Prison,' Plymouth, England, 1777: Journal," *New-England Historical and Genealogical Register* 32 (1878): 396; "Humanitas" to Admiralty, Aug. 29, 1777, enclosed in ADM to CSHS, Sept. 3, 1777, ADM/M/404, NMM; William Richard Cutter, "A Yankee Privateersman in Prison in England, 1777–1779," *New-England Historical and Genealogical Register* 30 (1876): 352; Zeinert, ed., *Memoirs of Andrew Sherburne*, 73. During the latter half of the war, there were apparently no acute food shortages, at least not for those who could afford to buy supplementary provisions at the gates.

36. "In general": Herbert, *Relic of the Revolution*, 93; see also 103. "powerful antispectic": ADM97/127/1. William Hammond Bowden, ed., "Diary of William Widger of Marblehead, kept at Mill Prison, England, 1781," *Essex Institute Historical Collections* 74 (1938): 143. ADM/M/404, July 12, Dec. 6, 1777, NMM; ADM98/11/118, NMM; Cogliano, *American Maritime Prisoners*, 65–9. When Andrew Sherburne was ill at the Mill in 1781, a physician attended him: Zeinert, ed., *Memoirs of Andrew Sherburne*, 77. For a failed inoculation attempt, see Bowden, ed., "Diary of William Widger," 73:315. For death rates at Mill and Forton, see Howard, *State of the prisons*, 22–3, 101–2. One American is known to have been killed by a guard, and that was apparently as a result of a personal altercation with a militia corporal. Anderson, "Treatment of Prisoners," 73, 75, 83; Cogliano, *American Maritime Prisoners*, 81, 90–92, 149–50; Lloyd, *History*, 232–3; CSHS to Admiralty, July 23, 1779, Feb. 11, 1783, ADM98/12/106–7, 14/301; *General Advertiser*, Apr. 2, 1779.

37. Herbert, *Relic of the Revolution*, 50, 106, 125; Bowden, ed., "Diary of William Widger," 73:319, 345. Lawyer: ADM98/11/150–51, Dec. 30, 1777, Jan. 2, 1778. Cogliano, *American Maritime Prisoners*, 53, refers to a "small chamber under the prison building."

38. Francis D. Cogliano, " 'We All Hoisted the American Flag': National Identity among American Prisoners in Britain during the American Revolution," *Journal of American Studies* 32:1 (1998): 25; Herbert, *Relic of the Revolution*, 119; Jonathan Haskins and Marion S. Coan, "A Revolutionary Prison Diary: The Journal of Dr. Jonathan Haskins," *NEQ* 17:2 (1944): 297, 299–300, 307; Cutter, "A Yankee Privateersman," (1878): 165.

39. See Herbert, *Relic of the Revolution*, 202, for the Mill pledge by over a hundred prisoners as cited; for a similar pledge at Forton, see Thompson, "Diary of George Thompson," 225. For the ambiguity of motives to enlist or not, see Gilje, "Loyalty and Liberty." American Commissioners to Lord North, Dec. 12, 1777, *PBF*, xxv: 275; also printed in *Lon-*

don *Evening Post*, Jan. 24–27, 1778. Prelinger, "Benjamin Franklin," 275, 281; "their Corpse": Prisoners at Forton to BF, Feb. 7, 1780, Franklin Papers, HSP, accessed Mar. 1, 2014, at http://founders.archives .gov/documents/Franklin/01-31-02-0313. For enlistment statistics, see Cohen, *British Supporters*, 69; Howard Applegate, "American Privateersmen in the Mill Prison during 1777–82," *Essex Institute Historical Collections* 97 (1961): 319; Anderson, "Treatment of Prisoners," 72. See ADM/M/404–5, NMM, for data on some 325 American recruits from Forton and Mill for 1778 to 1782, with a low in 1779 (32) and a high in 1781 (156). Cogliano, "We All Hoisted the American Flag," 33. See ADM/M/405, Feb. 21, 1781, NMM, for permission to Capt. Shaw, Royal American Regiment, to recruit Americans at the prison sites, but not French or Spanish subjects. Ibid., Jan. 29, 1782, for permission to release Forton prisoners in return for service in the East India Company.

40. For this section, see "Humanitas" to Lord Mayor of London, Aug. 5, 1776, *NDAR*, vi: 529; Anderson, "Treatment of Prisoners"; Alexander, "Forton Prison," 368–9; Herbert, *Relic of the Revolution*, 85–9. Petition of two hundred prisoners to the House of Lords, June 1781, ADM/M/405; ADM/M/404, Admiralty to CSHS, Dec. 11, 1777; Cutler, ed., "Prison Ships," 187; *Annual Register for 1778* (London, 1779): 78–9; Cohen, *British Supporters*, xi, 22–49 for Hodgson, 51–82 for Wren, and 115 for Heath; Cogliano, *American Maritime Prisoners*, 62–3 [donations]; William Gordon, *The history of the rise, progress, and establishment of the independence of the United States of America* (London, 1788), ii: 99. For the subscription, see ADM99/49, Jan. 12, Apr. 3 and 8, 1777; *Parl. Hist.* xxii: 615; "Journal of Samuel Curwen," Feb. 20, 1777, *NDAR*, viii: 599. "gentlemen in England": *General Advertiser*, Jan. 26, 1778; also *Morning Chronicle*, Jan. 26, 1778. For local and other charitable initiatives, see also ADM/M/404, Dec. 11, 1777, NMM; ADM 98/11/146, NMM; Thompson, "Diary of George Thompson," 234.

41. Arrogance: SP78/302, Stormont reporting to Lord Weymouth, Apr. 3, 1777. *Public Advertiser*, Dec. 26, 1777. Cohen, *Yankee Sailors*, 84; John Sainsbury, *Disaffected Patriots: London Supporters of Revolutionary America, 1769–1782* (Kingston, Canada, 1987), 142. American Patriot press acknowledging British charity: *Boston Gazette*, May 28, 1781; *Norwich Packet*, May 31, 1781; *Pennsylvania Packet*, June 23, 1781; *Boston Evening Post*, Dec. 21, 1782. Sample donors: *Gazetteer and New Daily Advertizer*, Jan. 12, 1778. *London Courant*, Nov. 24, 1780. For the precedent of British charity for French prisoners of war during the Seven Years' War, see Charters, "Administration of War." From summer 1779 until 1781 or 1782, a less-well-endowed fund yielded decreasing sums, as the prospect of exchange grew and enthusiasm for the cause waned.

For the self-help aspect of the prison economy at English sites, whereby prisoners such as Charles Herbert made and sold charity boxes, ladles, chairs, and miniature ship models to pay for a modicum of extra food, clothing, and small luxuries, see Herbert, *Relic of the Revolution*, 29, 45, 47, 112.

42. This section mostly after the well-documented Prelinger, "Benjamin Franklin." For exchanges, see also Commissioners to the American Prisoners in Great Britain, Sept. 19, 1778, *PJA* vii: 54–5. See also Richard B. Morris, ed., *John Jay: The Winning of the Peace, Unpublished Papers, 1780–84* (New York, 1980), 82–4; John Porter to BF, June 6, 1777, *NDAR*, ix: 381; Commissioners: Wickes and Samuel Nicholson to American Commissioners, Sept. 6, 1777, *PBF*, lx: 26.

43. Hartley: BF to Hartley, Oct. 14, 1777, with PS of Dec. 11, 1777 (1st quotation), and Hartley to BF, Dec. 25, 1777 (2nd quotation), *PBF*, xxv: 64–8 (quotation 66–7), 349–52 (quotations 350). American commissioners to Major John Thornton, [Dec. 11, 1777], in Albert Henry Smyth, ed., *The Writings of Benjamin Franklin* (New York, 1905–7), vii: 75; BF to Sir Grey Cooper, Dec. 11, 1777; G. H. Guttridge, *David Hartley, M.P., An Advocate of Conciliation, 1774–1783* (Berkeley, CA, 1926). Thornton: Thornton Memorandum, to American Commissioners, Jan. 5–7, 1778, Arthur Lee Papers, iv: 11, Harvard University Library. *General Advertiser,* June 10, 1778. On clothing as an intermittently serious issue, see also Alexander, "Forton Prison," 377. On Rev. Thomas Wren and other priests, see Prelinger, "Benjamin Franklin," 270, 288–9. In the summer of 1781, prisoners reported having their back allowances distributed among them; for the winter of 1781–82, Franklin sent Hodgson another £400.

44. Cogliano, *American Maritime Prisoners*, 122–7; Lloyd, *History,* 230–31; Cohen, *British Supporters*, 73–5; Francis Abell, *Prisoners of War in Britain 1756 to 1815; A Record of Their Lives, Their Romance and Their Sufferings* (London, 1914), 224; Prelinger, "Benjamin Franklin," 282–5. Moses Young's Account of Himself, Osborn c625, Beinecke Library, Yale University.

45. British records suggest that between June 1777 and April 1, 1782, 536 men ran away from Forton, and from June 1777 to March 1779, 102 escaped from the much-higher-security Mill prison. Security concerns and escapes loom large in official records throughout ADM/M/404–6, NMM. See, e.g., ADM/M/404, June 25, July 10, 1777; Feb. 26, Aug. 1, Sept. 11, 29, 30, Nov. 3, 1778; Jan. 5, 12, 22, 28, Feb. 1, 10, 1779. ADM/M/405, Feb. 16, 1782. For the inegalitarian nature of escape, see Gilje, "Loyalty and Liberty," 177–8. For this paragraph, see also ADM/M/404, NMM; ADM1/5117/11; ADM98/11–14; Bowden, ed.,

"Diary of William Widger," 73:338, 343; Caleb Foot, "Reminiscences of the Revolution: Prison Letters and Sea Journal of Caleb Foot," *Essex Institute Historical Collections* 26 (1889): 11 (entry for Aug. 21, 1780); Cogliano, *American Maritime Prisoners*, 103. Herbert, *Relic of the Revolution*, 128, 215–16; the quotation at 136. *London Evening Post*, Aug. 9–12, 1777; *London Evening Post*, Dec. 11, 1777, July 25, 1778; *General Evening Post*, Jan. 1–3, 1778; *St James's Chronicle*, Aug. 1, Sept. 8, 1778; *General Advertiser*, Dec. 22, 1778; *Morning Post*, Nov. 12, 1779. *Massachussetts Spy*, Jan. 7, 1779; *Morning Herald*, July 2, 1781; *Boston Evening Post*, Nov. 3, 1781, Apr. 13, 1782; *Pennsylvania Packet*, Nov. 24, 1778, Nov. 8, 1781; *Providence Gazette*, Apr. 18, 1778.

46. Herbert, *Relic of the Revolution*, 203–10, 227–42. *Dolphin* episode: Cogliano, *American Maritime Prisoners*, 105–6 with n. 53.

47. American commissioners to Lord North, Dec. 12, 1777, in *London Evening Post*, Jan. 24–27, 1778; Arthur Lee to Committee of Secret Correspondence, Nantes, Feb. 14, 1777, *RDC*, i: 400–401; Dandridge, *American Prisoners*, 82–3. BL, IOR/E/4/623/148, 148; IOR/E/44/867/76–8, 349. *JCC*, xi: 477. Black, *George III*, 229, for George III's proposal to send American prisoners to British India.

48. Blatchford, *Narrative of John Blatchford*, iv ("most barbarous treatment"), v (physical description and "as a record"), 46 on credibility, and passim.

49. American Commissioners to Lord Stormont, Apr. 2, 1777, TNA, SP 78/302/13. Commissioners to Lord North, Dec. 12, 1777, *PBF*, xxv: 275; also in *London Evening Post*, Jan. 24–27, 1778. Proposed letter to Lord North, June 1778, *PBF*, vii: 165.

50. John Paul Jones to BF, May 2, 1779, with enclosure, from "Well Wis[h]-ers," Papers of Benjamin Franklin, American Philosophical Society. (Box xiv: 79). BF to Sartine, May 8, 1779, in *RDC*, iii: 158. Also in May 1779, Franklin included a scene of "Americans put on board Ships in Irons to be carried to the East Indies, & Senegal, where they died with Misery & the unwholesomeness of the Climate" in a list of 26 prints for an illustrated American schoolbook detailing British atrocities: "Franklin and Lafayette's List of Prints Illustrating British Cruelties," *PBF*, xxix: 590–93. That spring, Franklin and Jones had been corresponding about America's humanitarian obligations towards prisoners: e.g., DLAR 295/580; see ibid., 801, 836, 840, for Jones's humanitarian concerns.

51. Christopher, *Merciless Place*, 89–92, quotations at 89 (George III) and 92 ("used as a threat"). For Senegambia's role in the slave and gum trades, see Joseph E. Inikori, "Gentlemanly Capitalism and Imperialism in West Africa: Great Britain and Senegambia in the Eighteenth

Century," in *Africa, Empire and Globalization: Essays in Honor of A. G. Hopkins*, ed. Toyin Falola and Emily Brownell (Durham, NC, 2011).

Chapter Eight

1. For the race of the ships, see Nathan R. Einhorn, "The Reception of the British Peace Offer of 1778," *Pennsylvania History* 16:3 (1949): 192; Kirschke, *Gouverneur Morris*, 81–2. *Morning Chronicle*, Mar. 31, 1778.

2. GW to President of Congress, Apr. 18, 1778. Congressional committee reporting on Washington's letter and the draft bill: *JCC*, ii: 521–4 (Apr. 22, 1778).

3. "express": *JCC*, xi: 417. Congressional consideration, ratification, and address, May 2–6, 1778: ibid., 468, and at http://avalon.law.yale.edu /18th_century/fr1778r.asp. Valley Forge: Philip Van Cortlandt to father, May 10, 1778, Van Wyck Papers, Box 1, folder 1, NYPL.

4. Address: *JCC*, xi: 474–81 (quotations 476). Printed *inter alia* in *Scots Magazine* 40 (Aug. 1778): 421–4.

5. For the peace commission, see Charles R. Ritcheson, *British Politics and the American Revolution* (Norman, OK, 1954), 258–86; Weldon A. Brown, *Empire or Independence: A Study in the Failure of Reconciliation, 1774–1783* (Port Washington, NY, 1966), 244–82; Reginald E. Rabb, "The Role of William Eden in the British Peace Commission of 1778," *Historian* 20:2 (1958); Leonard J. Sadosky, "Reimagining the British Empire and America in an Age of Revolution: The Case of William Eden," in *Old World, New World: America and Europe in the Age of Jefferson*, ed. Leonard J. Sadosky et al. (Charlottesville, VA, 2010); HMC, MSS of the Earl of Carlisle, 323, 377, and passim; Carl Van Doren, *Secret History of the American Revolution* (New York, 1941), chs. 3–4; Max M. Mintz, *Gouverneur Morris and the American Revolution* (Norman, OK, 1970), 104–5; Add MS 46491/1, 21–2; Bancroft 104/219–20, 105/101–3. Entries for the commissioners in the *ODNB*. For the commissioners' instructions and work in America, see also Add MS 34415/199–230, 358–88, and passim; Add MS 34416/33. CO5/180–81. "the honor of": *RDC*, vi: 35.

6. A draft of George III's instructions in Add MS 34415/358–88. Leonard J. Sadosky, *Revolutionary Negotiations: Indians, Empires, and Diplomats in the Founding of America* (Charlottesville, VA, 2009), 109–13; Eugene Heath, ed., *Adam Ferguson: Selected Philosophical Writings* (Exeter, 2007), 77.

7. For Britain's global war, see Stephen Conway, *Short History*; idem, *The War of American Independence, 1775–1783* (London, 1995); Mackesy, *War for America*; O'Shaughnessy, *Empire Divided*. "Great Britain has

its choice": Lee to GW, May 6, 1778, in James Curtis Ballagh, ed., *The Letters of Richard Henry Lee* (New York, 1911–14), i: 399.

8. Mintz, *Gouverneur Morris*, 110. "a deep sense": Colonel Stuart to Lord Bute, Sept. 16, 1778, in Stuart-Wortley, *Prime Minister and His Son*, 130–33 (quotation 132). See also Carlisle to Eden, Sept. 9, [1778], Add MS 34416/33–4; Carlisle, Eden, and HC to GG, Sept. 21, 1778, *DAR*, xv: 204. Manifesto and Proclamation, Oct. 3, 1778: Yasuo Amoh, D. Lingley, and H. Aoki, eds., *Proceedings of the British Commissioners at Philadelphia, 1778–1779, Partly in Ferguson's Hand* (Kyoto, 2007). Manifesto also printed in *Scots Magazine* 40 (Nov. 1778): 607–10. Distribution to each colony: Bancroft 105/145–91. Only *after* they had published the manifesto did Clinton and his co-authors justify their actions in a letter to the British government. For the broader strategic debate among British officers, see Conway, "To Subdue America."

9. I have chosen to employ a detailed narrative to evoke the events as they transpired from the perspectives of perpetrators, victims, and witnesses. The extant sources include the records of a congressional inquiry conducted in the weeks following the event; official correspondence of army officers on both sides; the private journals and correspondence of a few American and British participants; American Patriot, Loyalist, and British newspapers; and archaeological evidence brought to light in the late twentieth century. All of the material postdates the violent action, although almost all the responses I draw on were recorded within hours, days, and weeks. In considering this reconstruction, readers should bear in mind that all descriptions concerning specific actions carried out by, and specific utterances attributed to, both victims *and* perpetrators during the assault itself, are quoted from the victims' depositions. To improve readability, unless otherwise noted, quotations in this section are from the congressional inquiry documented in *The correspondence, journals, committee reports, and records of the Continental Congress (1774–1789)*, 53: "Papers and Affidavits Relating to the Plunderings, Burnings, and Ravages Committed by the British, 1775–84," NARA M247. For Grey, see Rory T. Cornish, "Grey, Charles, first Earl Grey (1729–1807)," *Oxford Dictionary of National Biography*, Oxford University Press, 2004; online ed., Jan. 2015, at http://www.oxforddnb .com.pitt.idm.oclc.org/view/article/11525 (accessed Aug. 21, 2016). Paul David Nelson, *Sir Charles Grey, First Earl Grey: Royal Soldier, Family Patriarch* (Madison, NJ, 1996). For the challenge of writing an anthropography of violence without becoming guilty of offering a pornography of violence, see E. Valentine Daniel, *Charred Lullabies: Chapters in an Anthropography of Violence* (Princeton, 1996), 4, and passim.

10. For Paoli, see Nelson, *Sir Charles Grey*, 43–5; Anthony Wayne et al., "The Massacre of Paoli," *PMHB* 1:3 (1877): 311; Richard St. George, "The Actions at Brandywine and Paoli, Described by a British Officer," *PMHB* 29:3 (1905): 368–9; Thomas J. McGuire, *Battle of Paoli* (Mechanicsburg, PA, 2000); Armstrong Starkey, "Paoli to Stony Point: Military Ethics and Weaponry during the American Revolution," *Journal of Military History* 58:1 (1994); Donald Grey Brownlow, *A Documentary History of the Paoli "Massacre"* (West Chester, PA, 1952); Baurmeister, *Revolution in America*, 115. Casualty figures: *Pennsylvania Ledger*, Dec. 3, 1777; *Morning Post*, Dec. 29, 1777. Casualty figures are not precise, but the ratio of the numbers of killed to captured on the defeated side broadly indicates whether the normal restraints were or were not likely applied. Lee, *Barbarians and Brothers*, 182–3, collates rough figures for thirty combat incidents in 1777 in which British regulars in the Northern theater defeated or drew equal with American forces. This gives a ratio of killed to captured of 1:1.9. Removing the most extreme incidents (Paoli, Brandywine, Germantown) yields a ratio of 1:3.4. For Paoli, modern historians cite 112 to 200 killed, 40 to 100 wounded, 71 captured. Assuming either 110 to 150 or 150 to 200 killed to 71 captured, the ratio would have been between 1.5:1 and 2:1 or 2:1 and 3:1. Based on figures in Brownlow, *Documentary History*, 23; Hugh F. Rankin, "Anthony Wayne: Military Romanticist," in *George Washington's Generals*, ed. Billias, 266; Lee, *Barbarians and Brothers*, 183; Peckham, *Toll*, 41; Paul David Nelson, *Anthony Wayne, Soldier of the Early Republic* (Bloomington, IN, 1985), 57; Nelson, *Sir Charles Grey*, 45; Tagebuch des Hauptmanns v. Dincklage beim Leibregiment, 1776–1784, Bancroft 42, Hessian 26/137. For the codes at nighttime, see Starkey, "Paoli to Stony Point," 9; S. Paul Teamer and Franklin L. Burns, "One Hundred Sixtieth Anniversary of the Paoli Massacre Copies of Itinerary, Maps, and Address," *Tredyffrin Easttown History Society Quarterly* 1:1 (1937); Glenn Tucker, *Mad Anthony Wayne and the New Nation: The Story of Washington's Front-Line General* (Harrisburg, PA, 1973), ch. 7, n. 11; William Heath, *Memoirs of Major General Heath: containing anecdotes, details of skirmishes, battles and other military events during the American war* (Boston, 1798), 179–80. For Paoli's terrifying effect on the Patriot militia and Continental Army, see Richard Barksdale Harwell, ed., *Washington: An Abridgement in One Volume by Richard Hardwell of the Seven-Volume George Washington by Douglas Southall Freeman* (New York, 1992), 354; Flexner, *George Washington*, 229. For a mildly skeptical British voice, see Loftus Cliffe to Jack Cliffe, Oct. 24, 1777, Loftus Cliffe Papers, WLCL.

11. On bayonets, see Erik Goldstein, *The Socket Bayonet in the British Army, 1687–1783* (Lincoln, RI, 2000). "in the hands": Thomas Mante,

The history of the late war in North-America (London, 1772), 215. J. A. Houlding, *Fit for Service: The Training of the British Army* (Oxford, 1981), 261 n. 10, points out that bayonet drill was "curiously, rather neglected" until later in the century, and only first discussed in depth in Anthony Gordon, *Treatise on the science of defense: For the sword, bayonet, and pike in close action* (London, 1805).

12. See Conway, " 'The Great Mischief,' " for rank-and-file prejudice towards American soldiers. "respectable body": Dr. John Berkenhout's "Journal of an Excursion from New York to Philadelphia in the Year 1778," Aug. 24, 1778, Germain Papers, vol. 8. But see Germain's earlier warning to WH that "that very pusillanimity which prevents them from facing you in the open Fields, may occasionally operate like Courage itself, and instigate them to seek opportunities of attacking by Surprize." GG to WH, Mar. 3, 1777, CO5/94, part I, fols. 105–6.

13. For contemporary comparisons between the bayonet and the tomahawk and scalping knife, see *Parliamentary Register* (1778), 80, 99.

14. The detail on Banta after Ward, *Between the Lines*, 77.

15. *Royal Gazette*, Oct. 3, 1778. "Then we": *New-York Gazette*, Oct. 5, 1778.

16. Pension application of William Bassett, W9739 (Dec. 29, 1833).

17. "spitted": a Hessian colonel quoted in Fischer, *Washington's Crossing*, 97.

18. The time of violence, explains the sociologist Wolfgang Sofsky, *Traktat über die Gewalt*, 2nd ed. (Frankfurt a.M., 1996), 37, 179, is fast, short, intense. But the time of massacre is diverse, as assailants attack, let go, recapture, even play—and then kill.

19. Pension application of William Bassett, W9739. For the theory of traumatic memories and the use of such historical evidence, see Caroline Cox, "Public Memories, Private Lives," in *Remembering the Revolution*, ed. McDonnell et al., 113–14.

20. John Robert Shaw, *A Narrative of the Life & Travels of John Robert Shaw* (Lexington, KY, 1807), 20–21. De Lancey, ed., *History of New York*, i: 286. The word "massacre" has a complicated, somewhat uncertain etymology, with various derivations from post-classical Latin and Old French words for butcher, butcher's shop, slaughterhouse, and a butcher's implements, such as the chopping block. In early modern English, the word "massacre" referred to "the indiscriminate and brutal slaughter of people," "carnage, butchery, slaughter in numbers." To distinguish "massacre" analytically from "atrocity," scholars generally deem massacres to involve the killing, and often the especially cruel and wanton killing, and often the mutilation, of several or many unresisting or defenseless human beings by, typically, an overwhelming force, in an action that is specific to a particular place as well as limited in time. Mark Levene, "Introduction," in *The Massacre in History*,

ed. Mark Levene and Penny Roberts (New York, 1999); in the same collection, Mark Greengrass, "Hidden Transcripts: Secret Histories and Personal Testimonies of Religious Violence in the French Wars of Religion," esp. 69; Philip G. Dwyer and Lyndall Ryan, eds., *Theatres of Violence: Massacre, Mass Killing and Atrocity throughout History* (New York, 2012); Christine Vogel, ed., *Bilder des Schreckens: Die mediale Inszenierung von Massakern seit dem 16 Jahrhundert* (Frankfurt a.M., 2006), 7–14, esp. 10; Karl Heinz Metz, *Geschichte der Gewalt: Krieg–Revolution–Terror* (Darmstadt, 2010), 64–5; Humphrey, *Politics of Atrocity.* "massacre, n.," OED Online, at http://www.oed.com; Möbius, "Kriegsgreuel"; idem, " 'Von Jast und Hitze wie vertaumelt': Überlegungen zur Wahrnehmung von Gewalt durch preußische Soldaten im Siebenjährigen Krieg," *Forschungen zur Brandenburgischen und Preußischen Geschichte* 12 (2002).

21. Stewart to GW, Sept. 28, 1778; Williams to GW, Sept. 28, 1778; Putnam to GW, Sept. 28, 1778.

22. "horrible murders," "give no quarter," and "a considerable": *New-Jersey Gazette*, Oct. 7, 1778; also in: *Connecticut Journal*, Oct. 21, 1778, under Trenton, Oct. 7; *Massachusetts Spy*, Oct. 22, 1778 ("By the Hartford Post"). "in the most": *Continental Journal*, Oct. 8, 1778 (extract of a letter from HQ, Sept. 29, 1778). Cf. Pettit to NG, Oct. 1, 1778, *PNG*, ii: 531–6.

23. Baylor to GW, Oct. 19, 1778; GW to HL, Sept. 29, 1778; GW to Charles Scott, Sept. 29, 1778; GW to Horatio Gates, Sept. 30, 1778; GW to HL, Oct. 3, 1778 (read in Congress on Oct. 7, *JCC*, xii: 987). *Connecticut Journal*, Oct. 28, 1778: Extract of a letter GW to Congress, Oct. 3, 1778. Baylor declared dead: *Royal Gazette*, Oct. 3, 1778; *New-York Gazette*, Oct. 5, 1778, the same issue praising the British achievement in terms of enemy soldiers bayoneted, but also some receiving quarter.

24. *Virginia Gazette*, Oct. 13, 1778. "disagreeable suspense": Mr. Pendleton, Caroline County, VA, to General Woodford, Oct. 17, 1778, quoted in C. F. William Maurer, *Dragoon Diary: The History of the Third Continental Light Dragoons* (Bloomington, IN, 2005), 162.

25. *JCC*, xii: 987. HL to WL, Oct. 6 [1778], *LDC*, xi: 34–5. WL to Stirling, Oct. 11, 1778. Stirling to GW, Sept. 30, 1778; WL to GW, Oct. 13, 1778; Stirling to GW, Oct. 14 and 16, 1778. Stirling to Griffith, Oct. 15, 1778, quoted in Thomas Demarest, "The Baylor Massacre—Some Assorted Notes and Information," *Bergen County History* (1971): 39. For Griffiths, see also Maurer, *Dragoon Diary*, 143–7.

26. Maurer, *Dragoon Diary*, 141, 152. See Clancy, "Rules of Land Warfare," 223–6, for Anglo-American belligerents working out how codes of war could function between them, e.g., with regard to the evacuation

of noncombatants during sieges; safe conduct passes; the care of the wounded and recovery of the dead after battles; and so forth.

27. Livingston to Congress, Oct. 22, *The correspondence, journals, committee reports, and records of the Continental Congress (1774–1789)*, 68/413, NARA M247. Stirling to HL, Oct. 21 (read in Congress on Oct. 26, *JCC*, xii: 1062), in *PHL*, xiv: 435–6; printed in extracts in, e.g., *Pennsylvania Packet*, Oct. 29, 1778.

28. Stirling's report to Congress, with Griffith's letter and the affidavits collected by him and Livingston, was published between late Oct. and mid-Dec. in, e.g., *Pennsylvania Packet*; *Pennsylvania Evening Post*; *Boston Gazette*; *Norwich Packet*; *New-Hampshire Gazette*; *Independent Chronicle*; *Massachusetts Spy*; *South-Carolina and American General Gazette*. For the *Virginia Gazette*, see the issue of Oct. 23, 1778. "burnt alive": quoted in Conway, *War of American Independence*, 107–8. Congress also considered retaliatory action. Immediately after commissioning the inquiry from Livingston on Oct. 6, Congress voided recent agreements for prisoner exchanges with the British. See HL to John Beatty, Oct. 9, 1778, *PHL*, xi: 41–2.

29. "awareness": Nelson, *Sir Charles Grey*, 69. Grey's superiors: HC to GG, Oct. 8, 1778, and to Cornwallis, [Oct. 8, 1778], Clinton Papers 43/3–4. *General Evening Post*, Dec. 3, 1778, prints copy of Cornwallis to HC [?], Sept. 28, 1778; also in *London Chronicle*, Dec. 1–3, 1778; *Morning Chronicle*, Dec. 2, 1778.

30. *London Chronicle*, Nov. 26–28, 1778 (under date New York, Sept. 29); also in *Daily Advertiser*, Nov. 28, 1778; *St James's Chronicle*, Nov. 26–28, 1778; *Westminster Journal*, Dec. 5, 1778.

31. Stuart to Lord Bute, Oct. 7, 1778, in Stuart-Wortley, *Prime Minister and His Son*, 136–7. For Kemble, see the *Journal* entry for Sept. 22–27, 1778. For the archaeological evidence discussed in the caption to the photograph of the skeletons, see Demarest, "Baylor Massacre," 70–76, with further references. For the site in the twenty-first century, see http://www.co.bergen.nj.us/Facilities/Facility/Details/Baylor-Massacre-Burial-Site-6.

32. Ferguson to HC, Oct. 15, 1778: *Royal Gazette*, Oct. 24, 1778; *Pennsylvania Packet*, Nov. 5, 1778; *Independent Ledger*, Dec. 28, 1778; *Adams Weekly Courant*, Dec. 8, 1778; *Gazetteer and New Daily Advertiser*, Dec. 2, 1778; *Public Advertiser*, Dec. 2, 1778. Stedman, *History*, ii: 46–50. See also William S. Stryker, *The Affair at Egg Harbor, New Jersey, October 15, 1778* (Trenton, NJ, 1894), 3–5, 11, 15, 23, 30–31, 34.

33. *Virginia Gazette*, Oct. 23, 1778.

34. *JCC*, x: 81–2; xi: 613–15, 621; xii: 1080–82 (Oct. 30, 1778, the text of the manifesto). For Morris, see Mintz, *Gouverneur Morris*, 105, 111;

J. Jackson Barlow, ed., *To Secure the Blessings of Liberty: Selected Writings of Gouverneur Morris* (Indianapolis, 2012), 25. Gouverneur Morris, *Observations on the American Revolution* (Philadelphia, 1779); *JCC*, xii: 1063, xiii: 421; Sadosky, *Revolutionary Negotiations*, 90–118.

35. Commons: *Parl. Hist.*, xix: 1389–1401, with the quotations at 1400. Lords: *Parl. Hist.*, xx: 1–13, with the quotation at 13.

36. Government: *Parl. Hist.*, xx: 8–9, 15. Shelburne: *Parl. Hist.*, xx: 30–33.

37. *Parl. Hist.*, xix: 1397–8.

38. *Parl. Hist.*, xx: 23.

39. *Parl. Hist.*, xx: 43–6.

40. "Burn the sea coast": John Adams to James Lovell, Dec. 19, 1778, *PJA*, vii: 290. "entirely changed": JA's draft of the commissioners [BF, Lee, Adams] to the Comte de Vergennes, 294–305, and actual letter as sent, Passy, ante Jan. 9, 1779, *PJA*, vii: 305–11 (quotations 305, 306). See also A. Lee to Schulenberg, Paris, Dec. 25, 1778, *RDC*, ii: 867–9. Donna T. Andrew, *London Debating Societies, 1776–1799* (London, 1994), entry 248.

Chapter Nine

1. For this chapter, in addition to the journals and other documentary evidence cited in the notes, I have drawn especially on Barbara Alice Mann, *George Washington's War on Native America* (Lincoln, NE, 2008); Lee, *Barbarians and Brothers*, esp. 130–41 and ch. 8; Colin G. Calloway, *The American Revolution in Indian Country: Crisis and Diversity in Native American Communities* (Cambridge, 1995); Albert Hazen Wright, *The Sullivan Expedition of 1779: Contemporary Newspaper Comments and Letters* (Ithaca, NY, 1943). Physical description of Sullivan: Max M. Mintz, *Seeds of Empire: The American Revolutionary Conquest of the Iroquois* (New York, 1999), 87–8. For the July 5, 1779, dinner and toasts, see Frederick Cook, ed., *Journals of the Military Expedition of Major General John Sullivan against the Six Nations of Indians in 1779* (Auburn, NY, 1887), 39, 64, 182; Lloyd A. Brown, Howard Henry Peckham, and Hermon Dunlap Smith, eds., *Revolutionary War Journals of Henry Dearborn, 1775–1783* (Freeport, NY, 1969), 159.

2. John W. Jordan, "Adam Hubley, Jr., Lt. Colo. Commandant 11th Penna. Regt. His Journal, Commencing at Wyoming, July 30th, 1779," *PMHB* 33:2 (1909), 133–4.

3. Bones: Cook, ed., *Journals*. "[s]calped and inhumanly" and "Golgotha": 225 (Major J. Norris). "shockingly gashed" and "that the poor creatures": 250 (Rev. W. Rogers). "Here and there": Nathan Davis, "History of the Expedition against the Five Nations, Commanded by General Sullivan, in 1779," *Historical Magazine* 3:4 (1868): 199. All other quota-

tions from Rogers in Cook, ed., *Journals*, at 251. See also Mintz, *Seeds of Empire*, 97–8.

4. On Wyoming, I follow Lee's balanced appraisal in *Barbarians and Brothers*, 217–18. Only fairly recently have historians drawn attention to the fact that Native Americans were not just agents of terror but routinely also victims of white violence: Mann, *George Washington's War*, 15–16.

5. Mann, *George Washington's War*, 19–20, 56; Mintz, *Seeds of Empire*, 97, 102. See n. 1 for references to the dinner and toast.

6. "Most of": Calloway, *American Revolution in Indian Country*, 24. The simplified overview in this section is based on Calloway's study of the Revolution's impact on Indian communities, with a discussion of the complex allegiances of many Indian nations at 32–46, and the quotation "to excel them" from George R. Clark at 48; John Grenier, *The First Way of War: American War Making on the Frontier, 1607–1814* (Cambridge, 2005), on the context of Indian, European, and American ways of war; Peter Rhoads Silver's erudite, eloquent exploration of the pathology and rhetoric of the anti-Indian sublime in *Our Savage Neighbors: How Indian War Transformed Early America* (New York, 2008); Lee's innovative insights in the cultures of violence and restraint, especially in "Peace Chiefs and Blood Revenge," *Journal of Military History* 71:3 (2007), and in *Barbarians and Brothers*, 119–41. See also Patrick Griffin, *American Leviathan: Empire, Nation, and Revolutionary Frontier* (New York, 2007), for the American Revolution as a frontier war; Richard White, *The Middle Ground: Indians, Empires, and Republics in the Great Lakes Region, 1650–1815* (Cambridge, 1991), for a more broadly contextual history of European–Native American interactions, and accommodation in the Great Lakes region, for which see also the forum in *WMQ* 63:1 (2006), and Lepore, *Name of War*. The classic formulation of the frontier myth of regeneration through violence, and the taming of the wilderness linked with notions of American exceptionalism, is Slotkin, *Regeneration through Violence*; see also Tirman, *Deaths of Others*, 13–23.

7. Lee, "Peace Chiefs and Blood Revenge," and *Barbarians and Brothers*, esp. 119–41. For "mourning war," see Daniel Richter, "War and Culture: The Iroquois Experience," *WMQ* 40:4 (1983); Lepore, *Name of War*, 117. On scalping, see also Abler, "Scalping, Torture."

8. For the Cherokee War of 1776, see Anderson and Cayton, *Dominion of War*, 170. Smith-Rosenberg, *This Violent Empire*, 218.

9. Bickham, *Making Headlines*, 210–18; idem, *Savages within the Empire: Representations of American Indians in Eighteenth-Century Britain* (New York, 2005), ch. 7; Harold E. Selesky, "Colonial America," in *The Laws of War: Constraints on Warfare in the Western World*, ed. Michael

Howard, George J. Andreopoulos, and Mark R. Shulman (New Haven, CT, 1994), 80.

10. On Cherry Valley, see Lee, *Barbarians and Brothers*, 219. DLAR 60, Draper MSS Collection, Brant MSS, 20F, contains correspondence and petitions, in English and German, mostly addressed to General Edward Hand, who would serve under Sullivan in 1779, that vividly evoke the fear in the surrounding regions in the wake of the Cherry Valley attack. GG to Haldimand, Aug. 3, 1779, Add MS 21703/177–80.

11. For the conflation of black, red, and Britain as a foreign enemy, see Parkinson, "Enemies of the People." For Franklin and Lafayette's print project, see Franklin and Lafayette, "List of British Cruelties, [May 1779]," LOC; *PBF*, xxix: 521–2, 590–93. The Revolutionaries were handed a propaganda gift when Native Americans in British pay captured, killed, and scalped Jane McCrea, a young, beautiful woman from a largely Loyalist family, who was engaged to be married to a Loyalist lieutenant. In newspaper articles, broadsides, poems, engravings, novels, and plays, the Patriots presented the incident as cold-blooded murder and incontrovertible proof of Britain's indiscriminate savagery. See Silver, *Our Savage Neighbors*, 245–8; Horatio Gates to Burgoyne, Sept. 2, 1777, and Burgoyne to Gates, Sept. 6, 1777, Horatio Gates Papers, DLAR 23.

12. *JCC*, xiii: 252.

13. For the planning of Sullivan's campaign, see Mann, *George Washington's War*, 55–67; Barbara Graymont, *The Iroquois in the American Revolution* (Syracuse, NY, 1972), 193; Thomas S. Abler, *Cornplanter: Chief Warrior of the Allegheny Senecas* (Syracuse, NY, 2007), 49; Glenn F. Williams, *Year of the Hangman: George Washington's Campaign against the Iroquois* (Yardley, PA, 2005), chs. 10–11.

14. Orders: GW to Sullivan, May 31, 1779. For Washington's awareness of deprivation hitting Indians, see GW to Sullivan, Aug. 1, 1779. "to extirpate": Alexander C. Flick, ed., "New Sources on the Sullivan-Clinton Campaign in 1779," *Quarterly Journal of the New York State Historical Association* 10:4 (1929): 310. Fogg: Cook, ed., *Journals*, 98. See also Sullivan to Oneida, Sept. 1, Oct. 1, 1779, in *Letters and Papers of Major General John Sullivan, Continental Army*, ed. Otis Grant Hammond (Concord, 1939), iii: 114–5, 137. On the equation of Native Americans and wolves as species marked for extinction, see Peter Coates, " 'Unusually Cunning, Vicious and Treacherous': The Extermination of the Wolf in United States History," in *The Massacre in History*, ed. Levene and Roberts, 168; Mann, *George Washington's War*, 48. The genocidal nature of the campaign is discussed in ibid., 52, 75, and passim. On the "feed fight," see also Lee, *Barbarians and Brothers*, 221–2; Calloway, *American Revolution in Indian Country*, 47. One of the definitions of

the UN Convention on the Prevention and Punishment of the Crime of Genocide (1948) is deliberately inflicting on a (national, ethnic, racial, or religious) target group those "conditions of life calculated to bring about its physical destruction in whole or in part." The text of the 1951 CPPCG is at http://www1.umn.edu/humanrts/instree/x1cppcg.htm.

15. "no light": Charles P. Whittemore, "John Sullivan: Luckless Irishman," in *George Washington's Generals*, ed. Billias, 157. "rush on": GW to Sullivan, May 31, 1779.

16. Diary of Barnardus Swartwout, Jr., 1777–83, entry for Aug. 26, 1779, Barnardus Swartwout Papers, NYHS; Lee, *Barbarians and Brothers*, 209; Cook, ed., *Journals*, 6, 20.

17. R. W. G. Vail, ed., "Diary of Lieut. Obadiah Gore, Jr. in the Sullivan-Clinton Campaign of 1779," *Bulletin of the New York Public Library* 33 (Oct. 1929): 735. For the symbolic and vengeful qualities of the destruction of things, see Zara Anishanslin, "'This Is the Skin of a Whit[e] Man': Material Memories of Violence in Sullivan's Campaign," unpubl. paper. Thanks to the author for sharing a copy of her suggestive paper.

18. For details of the spring campaigns, see Calloway, *American Revolution in Indian Country*, 49; Mann, *George Washington's War*, 27–50.

19. Capt. John Weidman, notes, entries for July 11 (quotation), Oct. 18, 1779, HSP. See also Samuel McNeil Orderly Book, entry for Aug. 27, 1779, NYHS.

20. Vail, ed., "Diary," 732; Robert W. Venables, "'Faithful Allies of the King': The Crown's Haudenosaunee Allies in the Revolutionary Struggle for New York," in *Other Loyalists*, ed. Tiedemann, Fingerhut, and Venables, 135; Davis, "History of the Expedition," 203. Diary of Barnardus Swartwout, Jr., 1777–83, entry for Sept. 6, 1779, Barnardus Swartwout Papers, NYHS, for an example of a detachment destroying smaller settlements.

21. For the connections between Iroquois narratives of origins, corn, and blood sacrifice, see William Engelbrecht, *Iroquoia: The Development of a Native World* (Syracuse, NY, 2003), 22, 37–8. For an overview and detailed examples of destruction, see Mann, *George Washington's War*, 67–74, with the quotation from Hubley at 74. R. W. G. Vail, ed., "The Western Campaign of 1779: The Diary of Quartermaster Sergeant Moses Sproule of the Third New Jersey Regiment in the Sullivan Expedition of the Revolutionary War, May 17–October 17, 1779," *New-York Historical Association Quarterly* 41 (1957): 63. For Brodhead's extensive corn burning, see Wright, *Sullivan Expedition*, ii: 15, quoting *Maryland Journal*, Oct. 26, 1779. Van Campen: John N. Hubbard, *Sketches of border adventures, in the life and times of Major Moses Van Campen, a surviving soldier of the revolution* (Bath, NY, 1842), 177. "there was not": quoted in Calloway, *American Revolution in Indian Country*, 51.

22. Vattel, Kapossy, and Whatmore, *Law of nations*, book iii, ch. ix, pp. 570–71, para. 166–7. "degradation" and "Indians shall": Gordon, *History of the rise*, iii: 311. See also Lee, *Barbarians and Brothers*, 228. General William Stone (1838) is quoted in Mann, *George Washington's War*, 76. Sullivan reported to Congress on the 1,500 trees in a single orchard: Wright, *Sullivan Expedition, iii:* 19. Joshia Bartlett to Colonel Langdon, July 17, 1778, HSP, Langdon Papers, critiques British destruction of fruit trees during the occupation of Philadelphia.

23. Beatty: Cook, ed., *Journals*, 30–35 (quotation 32); Hubley: ibid. 162–3. For other descriptions, see ibid., 11, 60, 99, 142, 281–2; Vail, ed., "Western Campaign," 62; idem, ed., "Diary," 736–7. Lee, *Barbarians and Brothers*, 225.

24. For Bucktooth, see Mintz, *Seeds of Empire*, 144–5. On beheading, skinning, and displaying body parts, see Lepore, *Name of War*, 81–2, 179–80 (quotation 180). The toast in Cook, ed., *Journals*, 165.

25. For earlier Pennsylvania bounties for Indian scalps, which especially endangered unsuspecting friendly Indians, see Neimeyer, *America Goes to War*, 100–103. See also Witt, *Lincoln's Code*, 36. Skinning of legs to produce leggings: Barton in Cook, ed., *Journals*, 8; see also Lee, *Barbarians and Brothers*, 213, with further details. Burning of woman and boy: ibid. 225–6. For a frequently retold story of an ancient Indian woman protected under Sullivan's orders, and the murder of her young female companion, possibly in the context of attempted rape or rape, see Mann, *George Washington's War*, 91–2.

26. The story of the Onondaga chief is referenced in Add MS 21779/109–10. Clinton is quoted in Venables, " 'Faithful Allies of the King,' " 148. For anthropological views, see Abler, "Scalping, Torture," 13–15.

27. "found a good": Graymont, *Iroquois*, 204. See also Mintz, *Seeds of Empire*, 106; Mann, *George Washington's War*, 86–7; Calloway, *American Revolution in Indian Country*, 53; Barbara Alice Mann, *Native Americans, Archaeologists, & the Mounds* (New York, 2003), ch. 1; Jordan, "Adam Hubley," entry for Sept. 5, 1779. For Iroquois spirituality and grave goods, see also Engelbrecht, *Iroquoia*, ch. 3. For the connection between the British military and archaeology across the late-eighteenth- and early-nineteenth-century empire, see Hoock, *Empires of the Imagination*. For destroying things and hurting bodies as a proxy for assaulting people, see Anishanslin, " 'This Is the Skin of a Whit[e] Man.' "

28. "with considerable": Diary of Barnardus Swartwout, Jr., 1777–83, entry for Sept. 15, 1779, Barnardus Swartwout Papers, NYHS. Mann, *George Washington's War*, 107–8; Venables, " 'Faithful Allies of the King,' " 149–50. For a detailed discussion of the "politics of hunger" at Fort Niagara, see Calloway, *American Revolution in Indian Country*, ch. 5.

29. Sullivan Report to Congress, Sept. 30, 1779, published by Congress, reprinted in Wright, *Sullivan Expedition, iii:* 13–21; cf. Capt. John Weidman, Sept. 14, 1779, Misc. MSS, HSP. Congress and *Virginia Gazette* quoted in Mann, *George Washington's War,* 107. Sullivan's report and the congressional response were noted in orderly books on the campaign; see, e.g., Henry Dearborn Diary, entries for Sept. 14, 1779, Oct. 17, 1779, NYPL.

30. "His description": quoted in Wright, *Sullivan Expedition,* 21. "The whole country": e.g., in *General Evening Post,* Dec. 23–25. British press, on the beginnings of the campaign: *Public Advertiser,* Oct. 3; *London Chronicle,* Oct. 5; *Gazetteer,* Oct. 7; *St James's Chronicle,* Oct. 7. Inflated casualty reports of several hundred Indians killed: *General Evening Post,* Oct. 16–19; *London Evening Post,* Nov. 20–23. Progress reports: *London Evening Post,* Oct. 16–19; end of campaign: *General Evening Post,* Nov. 27–30.

31. Smith is quoted in Gary B. Nash, *The Unknown American Revolution: The Unruly Birth of Democracy and the Struggle to Create America* (New York, 2005), 347. Indian raids in 1780: ibid., 348; Joseph R. Fischer, *A Well-Executed Failure: The Sullivan Campaign against the Iroquois, July–September 1779* (Columbia, SC, 1997), 193; Mann, *George Washington's War,* 110; Higginbotham, *War of American Independence,* 329; Lee, *Barbarians and Brothers,* 214. "The nests are": Cook, ed., *Journals,* 101 (Fogg).

32. Davis, "History of the Expedition," 203.

33. "I really feel": quoted in Mintz, *Seeds of Empire,* 186. Mann, *George Washington's War,* 109–10 (quotation "land-grabbing agenda" 109). Topographical and aesthetic appreciation: Samuel McNeil Orderly Book, entry for Aug. 3, 1779, NYHS. Israel Evans, *A discourse, delivered at Easton, on the 17th of October, 1779, to the officers and soldiers of the Western Army* (Philadelphia, 1779), 22; see also Venables, " 'Faithful Allies of the King,' " 133.

34. For GW's 1783 tour, see Anderson and Cayton, *Dominion of War,* 176; GW to Governor Clinton, Nov. 25, 1784, *WGW* xxvi: 501. Smith-Rosenberg, *This Violent Empire,* 5, 17 (quotation). For an Indian perspective on early America, see Daniel Richter, *Facing East from Indian Country: A Native History of Early America* (Cambridge, MA, 2001). In Griffin, *American Leviathan,* Native Americans are at the center of the Revolutionary narrative. "Town-destroyer": Seneca Chiefs to GW, Dec. 1, 1790.

35. P. du Simitière, *American Museum* (Philadelphia, 1782); Mairin Odle, "Buried in Plain Sight: Indian 'Curiosities' in Du Simitière's American Museum," *PMHB* 136:4 (2012); Ellen Fernandez-Sacco, "Framing 'The Indian': The Visual Culture of Conquest in the Museums of Pierre

Eugene Du Simitière and Charles Willson Peale, 1779–96," *Social Identities* 8:4 (2002); Paul Ginsburg Sifton, "Pierre Eugene du Simitière (1734–1784): Collector in Revolutionary America" (PhD diss., University of Pennsylvania, 1960). See also Anishanslin, " 'This Is the Skin of a Whit[e] Man.' " For this paragraph and the caption to the illustration on page 294, see also Library Company of Philadelphia, *Pierre Eugene Du Simitiere: His American Museum 200 Years After* (Philadelphia, 1985).

36. Quotation in William John Potts, "Du Simitière, Artist, Antiquary, and Naturalist, Projector of the First American Museum, with Some Extracts from His Note-Book," *PMHB* 13:3 (1889): 366.

37. Fernandez-Sacco, "Framing 'The Indian,' " 591.

38. Cf., ibid., 582.

Chapter Ten

1. For David George in this and the following paragraphs, see David George, "An Account of the Life of Mr. David George, from Sierra Leone in Africa; given by himself in a Conversation with Brother Rippon of London, and Brother [Samuel] Pierce of Birmingham," in *Unchained Voices: An Anthology of Black Authors in the English-Speaking World of the Eighteenth Century. Expanded Edition*, ed. Vincent Carretta (Lexington, KY, 2004), 333–41 (quotations 333, 336); Jasanoff, *Liberty's Exiles*, 46–7; Pybus, *Epic Journeys*, 38–40, 210; Schama, *Rough Crossings*, 98–102.

2. For this and the following paragraph, see Robert Olwell, *Masters, Slaves & Subjects: The Culture of Power in the South Carolina Low Country, 1740–1790* (Ithaca, NY, 1998), 246; Higginbotham, *War of American Independence*, 354–7; Ricardo A. Herrera, "The King's Friends: Loyalists in British Strategy," in *Strategy in the American War of Independence: A Global Approach*, ed. Donald Stoker, Kenneth J. Hagan, and Michael T. McMaster (London, 2010), 101–19; O'Shaughnessy, *Men Who Lost America*, 262–3, 271–2; McDonnell, *Politics of War*, 367; Christopher Leslie Brown, *Moral Capital: Foundations of British Abolitionism* (Chapel Hill, NC, 2006), 310–12; Nash, *Unknown American Revolution*, 329–31; Lee, "American Revolution," 58. Philipsburg Proclamation, labeled after Clinton's HQ at Philipsburg Manor, NY: PRO30/55/17.

3. Pybus, *Epic Journeys*, 37–8 (Prevost cited at 38), 209, 211–12; Gilbert, *Black Patriots*, 170; Piecuch, *Three Peoples*, 169–70. In this chapter, I focus on the civil war between white Patriots and Loyalists, and the role of blacks. See Piecuch, *Three Peoples*, for the interplay of white Loyalists, African-Americans, and Native Americans in the Southern war.

4. See references in n. 1 above. The pass is quoted in Pybus, *Epic Journeys*, 40.

5. On the global strategic contexts in this chapter, I follow Conway, *Short History*, ch. 3; for this and the following paragraphs, see esp. 87–101. For the Anglo-Spanish war over Central and Spanish America, see O'Shaughnessy, *Men Who Lost America*, 178–85. In summer 1781, Germain sought to reassure Clinton in the face of changed global troop allocations: GG to HC, July 17, 1781, Shelburne Papers 68/59, WCLC.

6. Lord Germain had also ordered Clinton as early as the spring of 1778 to prioritize the naval war fought from the bases in New York and Nova Scotia. In preparation for the pivot south, British troops withdrew from Philadelphia in June 1778, with 3,000 Loyalists in tow.

7. Wayne E. Lee, "Restraint and Retaliation: The North Carolina Militias and the Backcountry War of 1780–82," in *War and Society*, ed. Resch and Sargent, quotation at 171. On the South's violent history, see Griffin, *America's Revolution*, 176–7, and passim; Walter B. Edgar, *Partisans and Redcoats: The Southern Conflict That Turned the Tide of the American Revolution* (New York, 2001), 122; Lambert, *South Carolina Loyalists*.

8. For blacks using the war for their advantage, in both the North and the South, see Egerton, *Death or Liberty*, 88–9 (quotation 88).

9. For the regional and socioeconomic demographics of Loyalism, see Ward's succinct summary in *War for Independence*, 36–7. Boost: Conway, *Short History*, 87. "bloody Rebellion" and "bound by": Brigadier General Montfort Brown to [My Lord], Jan. 20, 1778, CO23/24/3–8 at 4.

10. Selesky, "Colonial America," 81.

11. On Clinton's unwillingness to wage "a full campaign of terrorism," see John Shy, "Armed Loyalism: The Case of the Lower Hudson Valley," in idem, *People Numerous and Armed*, 185–92, at 192. On the shift from a moderate to an aggressive majority, see Conway, "Subdue America."

12. Pybus, *Epic Journeys*, 41; Mackesy, *War for America*, 252–6; Robert Middlekauf, *Washington's Revolution: The Making of America's First Leader* (New York, 2015), 222. "risked their": Carl P. Borick, *A Gallant Defense: The Siege of Charleston, 1780* (Columbia, SC, 2003), 43.

13. Pybus, *Epic Journeys*, 40, 210, 217–18; Egerton, *Death and Liberty*, 86–7.

14. For King, see Pybus, *Epic Journeys*, 43, 213; Schama, *Rough Crossings*, 109. The quotation from "Memoirs of the Life of BOSTON KING, a Black preacher, Written by Himself, during his Residence at Kingswood-School," in *Unchained Voices*, ed. Carretta, 353. For the spread of smallpox in the South in 1778–80, see Fenn, *Pox Americana*, 110–28.

15. On the numbers of slaves running away, see, for an overview, Jasanoff, *Liberty's Exiles*, 351–2; Frey, *Water*, 211, for the high maximum; Cassandra Pybus, "Jefferson's Faulty Math: The Question of Slave Defections in the American Revolution," *WMQ* 62:2 (2005), for the conservative

figures based on a thorough examination of the extant documentary evidence. For this paragraph, see also Frey, *Water*, 113–16; Olwell, *Masters*, 248–51 (quotation 248), with reference to John Lewis Gervais to HL, Apr. 30, 1782; see 253 for army patrols suppressing slave unrest on plantations. Nash, *Unknown American Revolution*, 331. Slaves escaping from South Carolina in 1782: Egerton, *Death or Liberty*, 151. Slave trade: Piecuch, *Three Peoples*, 219; Frey, *Water*, 159.

16. Gilman, ed., *Letters*, quotations at 27–31, 46; see also Frey, *Water*, 116.

17. Ewald is quoted in Nash, "The African Americans' Revolution," in *Oxford Handbook of the American Revolution*, ed. Gray and Kamensky, 260–61. "A stronger": Jeffrey J. Crow, "Slave Rebelliousness and Social Conflict in North Carolina, 1775 to 1802," *WMQ* 37:1 (1980): 88. For the inversion of racial hierarchy and the questioning of the plantation society order, see also Olwell, *Masters*, 258, with the quotation from Bull.

18. On the congressional proposals and state rejection: Schama, *Rough Crossings*, 104–6; Egerton, *Death or Liberty*, 82–4; Nadelhaft, *Disorders*, 62–3. "the Blessings": William Whipple to Josiah Bartlett, Philadelphia, Mar. 28, 1779, DLAR 37. Patriots seizing slaves and evidence of British arming them in defense: Nash, *Unknown American Revolution*, 329–30; Piecuch, *Three Peoples*, 226; Olwell, *Masters*, 266 7. Black recruitment to Patriot forces: Nash, "African Americans' Revolution," 254–6.

19. This paragraph in part after O'Shaughnessy, *Men Who Lost America*, 249–55 (quotation 254). For French reinforcements, and allied plans to attack New York City, see Middlekauf, *Washington's Revolution*, 224–7.

20. For the domestic context, see the brief summaries in Conway, *Short History*, 101–2; idem, *British Isles*, 218–24, 233–8. American South: Ward, *Between the Lines*, 221, 230–34, and passim; Edgar, *Partisans & Redcoats*, 137.

21. For Tarleton, see Stephen Conway, "Tarleton, Sir Banastre, baronet (1754–1833)," *Oxford Dictionary of National Biography*, Oxford University Press, 2004, online ed., Jan. 2012, at http://www.oxforddnb.com .pitt.idm.oclc.org/view/article/26970 (accessed Aug. 21, 2016); Robert D. Bass, *The Green Dragoon: The Lives of Banastre Tarleton and Mary Robinson* (New York, 1973), 12–17. Legion: Anthony J. Scotti, *Brutal Virtue: The Myth and Reality of Banastre Tarleton* (Bowie, MD, 2002), 33. "I proposed": Tarleton to HC, July 2, 1779, quoted in *Scots Magazine* 41 (1779), 492.

22. "Upon the": Banastre Tarleton, *A history of the campaigns of 1780 and 1781, in the southern provinces of North America* (London, 1787), 89–90. For the iconography and politics of Tarleton's 1782 portraits, see John Bonehill, "Reynolds' *Portrait of Lieutenant-Colonel Banastre Tarleton*

and the Fashion for War," *British Journal for Eighteenth-Century Studies* 24 (2001). Cruden: Sketch by John Cruden to Lord Dunmore, Jan. 5, 1782 [endorsed in Lord Dunmore to HC, Feb. 2, 1782], Bancroft 118/ 49–52 (quotations 50–51); Frey, *Water*, 140; Crow, "Slave Rebelliousness," 87–8. Gibson: Piecuch, *Three Peoples*, 225. Knight (McIntosh): National Society Daughters of the American Revolution, *African American and American Indiun Patriots of the Revolutionary War* ([Washington, D.C.], 2001), 169–70.

23. "the blood": Tarleton to Buford, May 29, 1780, Thomas Addis Emmet Collection, NYPL. "rage of the British": first printed in the Patriot Alexander Garden's *Anecdotes of the American Revolution* (Charleston, SC, 1828), 135–8 (quotation 138). "for fifteen minutes": Dr. Brownfield, quoted in David K. Wilson, *The Southern Strategy: Britain's Conquest of South Carolina and Georgia, 1775–1780* (Columbia, SC, 2005), 257.

24. Tarleton to Cornwallis, Aug. 5, 1780, Cornwallis Papers, PRO30/11/ 63/19–21; Tarleton, *History*, 100; Stedman, *History*, ii: 193. For detailed source criticism, see Jim Piecuch, *The Blood Be Upon Your Head: Tarleton and the Myth of Buford's Massacre* (Charleston, SC, 2010), 23–40.

25. Rape at plantation: Clinton Papers 92/47; Tarleton to John Andre, [Apr. 1780], cited in Borick, *Gallant Defense*, 152–3; Stedman, *History*, ii: 183, quoted in Wilson, *Southern Strategy*, 248; see also 247; Lyman Copeland Draper, ed., *Diary of Lieut. Anthony Allaire* (New York, 1968), 12, entry for Apr. 14, 1780; p. 8, entry for Mar. 22, 1780. For other cases of rape in the South, see Simcoe, *Military Journal*, 212; PRO30/11/6/156–7. "the terror of": Cornwallis to HC, Dec. 3, 1780, in Charles Ross, ed., *Correspondence of Charles, First Marquis Cornwallis* (London, 1859), i: 71. Richardson: Jane G. Landers, *Atlantic Creoles in the Age of Revolutions* (Cambridge, MA, 2011), 28–9; Nadelhaft, *Disorders*, 57; Edward McCrady, *The History of South Carolina in the Revolution, 1775–1780* (New York, 1969), 816–17; Edgar, *Partisans & Redcoats*, 133–4. For Anglo-American criticism of Tarleton, see also Greene to Cornwallis, Dec. 17, 1780, *PNG*, vi: 591–2; Cornwallis to Rawdon, July 26, 1780, PRO30/11/78/48–9. "exercised more acts": quoted in Scotti, *Brutal Virtue*, 93. For Tarleton's reputation, see also James Parton, *Life of Andrew Jackson* (New York, 1860), i: 82–5; Bass, *Green Dragoon*, 83; Hugh F. Rankin, "Cowpens: Prelude to Yorktown," *The North Carolina Historical Review* 31:3 (1954); Calhoon, *Loyalists*, 491–2, 494–5; Christopher Ward, *The War of the Revolution*, ed. John Richard Alden (New York, 1952), ii: 701.

26. Frey, *Water*, 112; Cornwallis to Lieutenant Colonel Cruger, Sept. 24, 1780, PRO30/11/80/5–6; O'Shaughnessy, *Men Who Lost America*, 258; Conway, *Short History*, 104–5; John Buchanan, *The Road to Guilford*

Courthouse: The American Revolution in the Carolinas (New York, 1997), 170, for the difficulty of estimating American losses at Camden.

27. Conway, "To Subdue America," 405–6; Nadelhaft, *Disorders*, 57; Edgar, *Partisans & Redcoats*, 134; Conway, *Short History*, 104. For Wemyss advising a stricter treatment of rebels professing a newfound loyalty to the Crown, see Wemyss to Cornwallis, July 11, 1780, PRO30/11/269–70. For the counterproductive effect of such conduct, see Conway, *Short History*, 104.

28. After Lee, "Restraint and Retaliation," and idem, *Crowds*, ch. 7.

29. On Ferguson, see Rankin, "An Officer out of his Time"; Buchanan, *Road to Guilford Courthouse*, 195–8; O'Shaughnessy, *Men Who Lost America*, 263. For the difficulty of assessing true loyalties, and a cautious approach to building up the militias, see PRO30/11/2/347–8 [March 1780].

30. Proclamation: Melissa Walker, *The Battles of Kings Mountain and Cowpens: The American Revolution in the Southern Backcountry* (New York, 2013), 77. "pissed upon": Hank Messick, *King's Mountain: The Epic of the Blue Ridge "Mountain Men" in the American Revolution* (Boston, MA, 1976), 89. "butchering": Piecuch, *Three Peoples*, 199. See also *PNG*, viii: 501; ix: 30; Robert M. Dunkerly, *The Battle of Kings Mountain: Eyewitness Accounts* (Charleston, SC, 2007), 38–40; O'Shaughnessy, *Men Who Lost America*, 264–5; John S. Pancake, *This Destructive War: The British Campaign in the Carolinas, 1780–1782* (Tuscaloosa, AL, 1985), 117.

31. Dunkerly, *Battle of Kings Mountain*, 60, 83, 92–3, 126, 146; David J. Dameron, *King's Mountain: The Defeat of the Loyalists, October 7, 1780* (Cambridge, MA, 2003), 45–6 and maps at 54, 56, 62, 68. Collins's *Autobiography* is quoted in Ed Southern, ed., *Voices of the American Revolution in the Carolinas* (Winston-Salem, NC, 2009), 163–4.

32. "but as": Alexander Chesney's Diary, quoted in Dunkerly, *Battle of Kings Mountain*, 132. See also Joseph Hughes's Federal Pension Application S31764, 52–3; Leonard Hice's Federal Pension Application, S8713, 49–50; Peter Starns's pension application, quoted in Dunkerly, *Battle of Kings Mountain*, 88. "who had": quoted in Southern, ed., *Voices*, 159–60; statement of Silas McBee, 64–5 (quotation 64), in Roy McBee Smith, *Vardry McBee: Man of Reason in an Age of Extremes* (Spartanburg, SC, 1997), 37–40. In Lee's balanced assessment, the "need to excuse the crime says more about the underlying value system, and the demand for virtuous war, than it does about the merits of the defense." Lee, *Crowds*, 186–7 (quotation 187), with nn. 48, 51. Official Patriot version without references to irregularities: *Pennsylvania Evening Post*, Nov. 18, 1780; *Connecticut Journal*, Nov. 30, 1780; *Massachusetts Spy*, Nov. 30, 1780. I have also consulted *JCC*, xviii: 1048–9; *LDC*, xvi: 458–9; *New-Jersey*

Gazette, Oct. 25, 1780; *Connecticut Journal*, Nov. 2, 1780; *Providence Gazette*, Nov. 8, 1780; *Pennsylvania Packet*, Dec. 30, 1780.

33. Caroline Cox, "Public Memories, Private Lives," in *Remembering the Revolution*, ed. McDonnell et al., 121. Bobby Gilmer Moss, *Roster of the Loyalists in the Battle of Kings Mountain* (Blacksburg, SC, 1998), 34. "The groans": quoted in Dunkerly, *Battle of Kings Mountain*, 84. See also ibid., 132, for Alexander Chesney's Diary. Injured Loyalist: Buchanan, *Road to Guilford Courthouse*, 235. See also Joseph Johnson, *Traditions and Reminiscences Chiefly of the American Revolution in the South* (Charleston, SC, 1851), 101–2, 583; Ward, *Between the Lines*, 225; Lambert, *South Carolina Loyalists*, 200–203. Collins quoted in Southern, ed., *Voices*, 165 ("husbands, fathers").

34. Collins, *Autobiography*, quoted in Southern, ed., *Voices*, 164; Robert W. Blythe, Maureen A. Carroll, and Steven H. Moffson, *Kings Mountain National Military Park: Historic Resource Study* (Atlanta, GA, 1995), 43. Dogs and hogs: quotations from Collins in Dunkerly, *Kings Mountain*, 35.

35. "to restrain": William Campbell's General Orders, Oct. 11, 1780, quoted in Dunkerly, *Battle of Kings Mountain*, 28. Loyalist reporting orders: Walker, *Battles of Kings Mountain*, 85. Charges made against prisoners: statement of Silas McBee, 64–5, in McBee Smith, *Vardry McBee*, 37–40; Ensign Robert Campbell's Account, in Dunkerly, *Battle of Kings Mountain*, 22; Buchanan, *Road to Guilford Courthouse*, 239–40. Mills's wife: Bobby Gilmer Moss, ed., *Uzal Johnson, Loyalist Surgeon: A Revolutionary War Diary* (Blacksburg, SC, 2000), 77. Lee, "Restraint and Retaliation," 169, stresses the attempt to give an "air of legality" to the proceedings by referencing North Carolina law authorizing magistrates to summon a jury; hanging "lent a judicial aspect to the killing, but also emphasized the supposed criminality of the victims."

36. Cornwallis's remonstrations: Cornwallis to Smallwood, Nov. 10, 1780, PRO30/11/91/9–10; cf. ibid., fols. 13–14 for Cornwallis to Major General Gates, Dec. 1, 1780 (referring to "inhumanity scarcely credible" in the treatment of captives); PRO30/11/3/261–2; PRO30/11/91/9–11, 13–14, 21–4. HC to GW, Oct. 9, 1780, PRO30/11/98/3–4; GW to HC, Oct. 16, 1780, PRO30/11/98/7–8; NG to Cornwallis, Dec. 6, 1780, PRO30/11/91/21–4.

37. O'Shaughnessy, *Men Who Lost America*, 265; North Callahan, *Royal Raiders: The Tories of the American Revolution* (Indianapolis, 1963), 222. "put an end": Klein et al., eds., *Twilight of British Rule*, 192; Mackesy, *War for America*, 345.

38. Theodore Thayer, "Nathanael Greene: Revolutionary War Strategist," in *George Washington's Generals*, ed. Billias, 109–36. "nothing but": NG

to AH, Jan. 10, 1781, *PNG*, vii: 88. "pursue[d] each other": NG to President of Congress, Dec. 28, 1780, ibid., 9. "those private massacres" and "this Country": NG to Colonel William Davies, May 23, 1781, *PNG*, viii: 298. "My dear": NG to Catherine Greene, June 23, 1781, ibid., 443.

39. Ward, *Between the Lines*, 225; Buchanan, *Road to Guilford Courthouse*, 215–16 ("on a log" 215). See also, for General Henry Lee, Witt, *Lincoln's Code*, 38–9; Ward, *Between the Lines*, 205, 225; for Levi Smith's experiences: Piecuch, *Three Peoples*, 252–3. Lee, *Crowds*, 189, emphasizes that "Loyalists taken in arms were in danger of summary execution by shooting, but in general they were usually held for a more or less formal court-martial . . . superimposing appearances of legality on what were often acts of revenge." See also idem, "Restraint and Retaliation," 190; Ferguson to Cornwallis, Oct. 1, 1780, PRO30/11/160–61, LOC.

40. Piecuch, *Three Peoples*, 201; Ward, *Between the Lines*, 225–7; Cashin, *King's Ranger,* 120. "found his": Griffin, *America's Revolution*, 176.

41. For modern assessments of Pyle's Massacre, see George Troxler, *Pyle's Massacre: February 23, 1781* (Burlington, NC, 1973); Lee, *Barbarians and Brothers*, 207.

42. For Hall in the previous and this paragraph, see Dann, ed., *Revolution Remembered*, 202–3. Cf. ibid., 185–9, and Lee, *Crowds*, 189, for William Gipson's recollections of his mother's abuse by Loyalists and his satisfaction at the later cruel treatment of those Loyalists.

43. Higginbotham, *War of American Independence*, 375. "most cruel": General D. Morgan to NG, Jan. 19, 1781, *PNG*, vii: 152–3 (quotation 153). "fear or intimidation": Lord Rawdon to Cornwallis, Mar. 7, 1781, PRO30/11/69/7–11, at 8. War of attrition: O'Shaughnessy, *Men Who Lost America*, 265; Thayer, "Nathanael Greene," 134. Cowpens: Lawrence E. Babits, *A Devil of a Whipping: The Battle of Cowpens* (Chapel Hill, NC, 1998); Piecuch, *Three Peoples*, 240–41; O'Shaughnessy, *Men Who Lost America*, 266–7.

44. On British cause for optimism, see O'Shaughnessy, *Men Who Lost America*, 247 ("widespread"). "more passive": Cornwallis to HC, Apr. 18, 1781, CO5/239. "to occupy": O'Shaughnessy, *Men Who Lost America*, 273.

45. After Frey, *Water,* 150–59; Gilbert, *Black Patriots*, 168; Pybus, *Epic Journeys*, 79–80, on Furman, quoting from AO13/29/658; Sylvia R. Frey, "Between Slavery and Freedom: Virginia Blacks in the American Revolution," *Journal of Southern History* 49:3 (1983): 379–82.

46. Ewald is quoted in Frey, *Water,* 154. See Pybus, *Epic Journeys*, 46–9, for Washington's and Jefferson's defecting slaves. Savage: N. L. Savage Account Book, MssCol 3575, NYPL. See also Francis D. Cogliano, *Emperor of Liberty: Thomas Jefferson's Foreign Policy* (New Haven, CT, 2014), 15–25.

47. "I have marched": quoted in Fenn, *Pox Americana*, 129.

48. Ibid., 382; Nash, *Unknown American Revolution*, 331 (quotation), 344. McDonnell, *Politics of War*, 367–477, details significant levels of disaffection in various parts of Virginia during the invasion.

49. Witt, *Lincoln's Code*, 39–40, with reference to *JCC*, xxi: 977–8 ("to ashes" 978), 1017–18 ("immediately consigned" 1018), 1029–30. For proposals of retaliation against British cities in 1779, see *LDC*, xiii: 228, 236–7, 261–3; *JCC*, xiv: 851–3; 914–15. On retaliation, see also Burrows, *Forgotten Patriots*, 192–3; *LDC*, xvii: 88, 481; Samuel Huntington to TJ, Jan. 9, 1781, DLAR 43. For Yorktown in strategic context, see O'Shaughnessy, *Men Who Lost America*, 279–81.

50. Fenn, *Pox Americana*, 130–32.

51. "numbers": quoted in Taylor, *Internal Enemy*, 27. Robert Donkin, *Military Collections and Remarks* (New York, 1777), 190; "valiant soldiers": iii. Fenn, *Pox Americana*, 132 with n. 48, Leslie to Cornwallis, July 13, 1781, PRO30/11/6/280–81.

52. Fenn, *Pox Americana*, 132 with n. 48, Leslie to Cornwallis, July 13, 1781, PRO30/11/6/280–81.

53. See Frey, *Water*, 164–71, with the quotation from Tucker at 171. The estimates in Pybus, *Epic Journeys*, 53. Free blacks in the North: O'Shaughnessy, *Men Who Lost America*, 277. Armistead: Nash, "African Americans' Revolution," 256.

54. Pybus, *Epic Journeys*, 41–2, 52, 55, 212–13. Brown, *Moral Capital*, 311.

55. Numbers: Jasanoff, *Liberty's Exiles*, 352, 358; Pybus, "Jefferson's Faulty Math." For the mini-biographies, see Pybus, *Epic Journeys*, 209–18, and on George, Jasanoff, *Liberty's Exiles*, 172–5, 276–82, 299–309, 349. Loyalists selling or freeing slaves: George Smith McCowen Jr., *The British Occupation of Charleston, 1780–82* (Columbia, SC, 1972), 106. Sierra Leone: Pybus, *Epic Journeys*, chs. 9, 11; Schama, *Rough Crossings*; Walker, *Black Loyalists*; O'Shaughnessy, *Men Who Lost America*, 277, on street names.

56. O'Shaughnessy, *Men Who Lost America*, 281, who also references congressmen demanding that Cornwallis be executed for war crimes. The quotation in Armstrong Starkey, *War in the Age of Enlightenment, 1700–1789* (Westport, CT, 2003), 97.

57. Conway, *Short History*, 113–19; Prisoners: "Return of prisoners taken at the Surrender of York & Gloucester, 19th Oct. 1781," Revolutionary War, Box I: British and Hessian Army, NYHS. News of Yorktown reached London in late November: Hillsborough to [Eden], Nov. 26, 1781, Add MS 34418/188. Britain's post-Yorktown holdings and troop strength after O'Shaughnessy, *Men Who Lost America*, 360.

58. On Admiral Sir George Rodney's role in the American Revolutionary War, see O'Shaughnessy, *Men Who Lost America*, ch. 8.

59. Leslie in the South: Schama, *Rough Crossings*, 125; Olwell, *Masters*, 258–9; Gilbert, *Black Patriots*, 157–9; Piecuch, *Three Peoples*, 316–18; Walter Finney and Joseph Lee Boyle, "The Revolutionary War Diaries of Captain Walter Finney," *South Carolina Historical Magazine* 98:2 (1997): 137. "abhorrence": Lt.-Gov. Bull to GG, Mar. 25, 1782, Bancroft 118/267–79.

60. Gilbert, *Black Patriots*, 157; AO13/4/321, Jonathan McKinnon, deputy quartermaster general, certificate on the beheading of the slave Harry.

61. John Childs, "The Laws of War in Seventeenth-Century Europe and Their Application during the Jacobite War in Ireland, 1688–91," in *Age of Atrocity*, ed. Edwards et al., 300.

62. O'Shaughnessy, *Men Who Lost America*, 271; Frey, *Water*, 114.

Chapter Eleven

1. The placard is in George Washington Papers, microfilm, reel 84, n.d., LOC. For the tailor, see Skemp, *William Franklin*, 256–7. "mixed Company": *Independent Gazette*, Apr. 20, 1782.

2. For this chapter I have drawn especially on L. Kinvin Wroth, "Vengeance: The Court-Martial of Captain Richard Lippincott, 1782," in *Sources of American Independence*, ed. Peckham, vol. 2; Ward, *Between the Lines*, 63–8; A. S. Bolton, "Asgill, Sir Charles, second baronet (1762–1823)," rev. S. Kinross, *Oxford Dictionary of National Biography*, Oxford University Press, 2004, online ed., May 2006, at http://www.oxforddnb .com.pitt.idm.oclc.org/view/article/733 (accessed Aug. 21, 2016). See also Larry Bowman, "The Court-Martial of Captain Richard Lippincott," *New Jersey History* 89:1 (1971).

3. On the *lex talionis*, see Lee, *Crowds*, ch. 7; Barbara Donagan, "Codes and Conduct in the English Civil War," *Past & Present* 118 (1988).

4. Shy, *People Numerous and Armed*, 189. My section on armed Loyalism and the internecine war draws heavily on the amply documented Edward H. Tebbenhoff, "The Associated Loyalists: An Aspect of Militant Loyalism," *New York Historical Society Quarterly* 63:2 (1979); Fowler, "'Loyalty Is Now Bleeding in New Jersey'"; Michael S. Adelberg, "'A Combination to Trample All Law Underfoot': The Association for Retaliation and the American Revolution in Monmouth County," *New Jersey History* 115:3–4 (1997). For Tye I have relied on Hodges, *Slavery and Freedom*, ch. 3, the quotation at 92. See also Schama, *Rough Crossings*, 116–17; Ward, *Between the Lines*, 61–4; Egerton, *Death or Liberty*, ch. 3.

5. The vigilante organization eventually had 463 signatories. "An eye for": N. Scudder to HL, July 17, 1780, quoted in Fowler, "'Loyalty Is

Now Bleeding in New Jersey,'" 60. See also Graham Russell Hodges, *Slavery and Freedom in the Rural North: African Americans in Monmouth County, New Jersey, 1665–1865* (Madison, WI, 1997), 103–4.

6. For Franklin's plans and negotiations with British leadership, see Skemp, *William Franklin*, 234–46, the character sketch at xi. For the British debate over the role of armed Loyalists, see also Shy, *People Numerous and Armed*, 181–92.

7. Largely after Chopra, *Unnatural Rebellion*, 194–5. "in no better": CO5/175/231v. See also Clinton Papers 200/57; Bancroft 117/171–4. For Cornwallis, see O'Shaughnessy, *Men Who Lost America*, 282.

8. For this and the next paragraph, see Deposition John North before David Forman, Apr. 15, 1782, Bancroft 119/145–7. For versions of White's death, see Ward, *Between the Lines*, 65. John Covenhoven to GW, Apr. 14, 1782, *PGW/EA*.

9. GW to John Hanson, Apr. 20, 1782, with enclosures including affidavits and a copy of the placard. The quotations from GW to HC, Apr. 21, 1782, *PGW/EA*.

10. HC to GW, Apr. 25, 1782, *PGW/EA*.

11. Ibid.

12. Board of Inquiry to HC, Apr. 26, 1782, BHQP 4476. Larry G. Bowman, "The Court-Martial of Captain Richard Lippincott," *New Jersey History* 89:1 (1971): 30, references street fights between Loyalists and British soldiers in New York City in early May. For the jurisdictional wrangles and Carleton's review, see Wroth, "Vengeance," 507–13, and Wiener, *Civilians*, 116–20. For American press, all in 1782: earliest references mid-April, e.g, *Freeman's Journal*, Apr. 17, 24. Text of the placard reproduced in *Freeman's Journal*, May 1; *Pennsylvania Packet*, May 2; *Independence Gazetteer*, May 4; *Independent Chronicle*, May 9; *Norwich Packet*, May 9; *Salem Gazette*, May 9; *Boston Gazette*, May 13; *Connecticut Gazette*, May 17; see also *Gazette of Saint Jago de la Vega (Jamaica)*, Aug. 29, 1782. GW to HC, Apr. 21, in *Pennsylvania Packet*, May 4, 1782; *Freeman's Journal*, May 8, 1782; *Pennsylvania Journal*, May 1, 1782; *New Jersey Gazette*, May 15, 1782. The late April exchange between GW and HC also in [George Washington,] *Epistles domestic, confidential, and official from George Washington* (New York, 1796), 106–9.

13. GW to WL, May 6, 1782, at http://founders.archives.gov/documents/Washington/99-01-02-08344. Carleton to WL, May 7, 1782, *PWL*, iv: 405.

14. Wroth, "Vengeance," has a transcript of WO71/95/321–408, City Hall, NY, May 3 to June 22, 1782, with an excellent introduction on which my summary of proceedings draws; the quotation, "a Prisoner," at

536–7. American leaders were aware of Clinton risking the anger of British Army officers and Loyalists, respectively. See Robert Livingston to William Carmichael, May 1, 1782, *RDC*, ix: 120.

15. Wroth, "Vengeance," 515, 560.

16. "label that was": Affidavit Capt. William Cunningham, May 10, [1782], CO5/105/225, *DAR*, xxi: 68–9 (quotation 69).

17. "several of my": Wroth, "Vengeance," 582.

18. GW to Moses Hazen, May 3, 1782, *WGW*, xxiv: 217–18. Hazen to Benjamin Lincoln, May 27, 1782, Gilder Lehrman Collection, #GLC01147. Asgill to GW, May 30, 1782, *PGW/EA*. The boy is referenced in Clinton Papers 194/25, 26.

19. "has distressed me exceedingly": GW to Lincoln, June 5, 1782, Lincoln Papers, MHS, at http://www.masshist.org/database/viewer.php?item _id=1706&img_step=1&pid=3&ft=Object%20of%20the%20Month &nodesc=1&mode=transcript#page1. The other quotations are from GW to Elias Dayton, June 4, 1782, *PGW/EA*. See also Flexner, *George Washington*, 479–82.

20. Paine, "A Supernumerary Crisis. To Sir Guy Carleton, Philadelphia, May 31, 1782," *Pennsylvania Packet*, June 1, 1782 and *Pennsylvania Gazette*, June 5, 1782. Paine also advised Washington to use the captive to put moral pressure on Britain: Paine to GW, Sept. 7, 1782, *PGW/EA*.

21. British military legal authorities at the time did not allow the distinction between murder and manslaughter: Wroth, "Vengeance," 525. Franklin to HC, Apr. 27, 1782, BHQP 4485 [abstract in Bancroft 119/209]; unknown to GW, May 1, 1782, at http://founders.archives.gov/documents /Washington/99-01-02-08308.

22. Franklin to Carleton, Aug. 12, 1782, BHQP 5274, with enclosures at BHQP 5173, 5233. See also Bancroft 121/17–33.

23. With all dates in 1782, the quotations from *Public Advertiser*, June 17. *General Evening Post*, July 11; *General Advertiser*, July 15; *Morning Herald*, July 15, 30; *English Chronicle*, July 27; *London Chronicle*, July 11–13, 27–30, July 30–Aug. 1; *Morning Chronicle*, July 15, 29; *Public Advertiser*, July 30; *Felix Farley's Bristol Journal*, July 20, Aug. 3; *General Evening Post*, July 11. See Clinton Papers 195/24, Peter Russell to Henry HC, July 25, 1782 [from London]: sent copies of Clinton's, Robertson's, and Carleton's correspondence with Washington to the editor of the *Morning Chronicle*, who promised to publish the materials.

24. *St James's Chronicle*, July 23, 1782; *Whitehall Evening Post*, July 23–25, 1782, for James Robertson to GW, May 1, 1782. "tenderness": GW to James Robertson, May 4, 1782, *PGW/EA*. "impolitic": *London Chronicle*, July 27–30, 1782; *Public Advertiser*, July 30, 1782. Grotius: *Gazetteer*, Aug. 7, 1782.

25. Shelburne to Carleton, July 8, 1782, Bancroft 120/197–9.
26. Paine: *General Advertiser*, Aug. 7, 1782; *Morning Post*, Aug. 7, 1782; *Morning Herald*, Aug. 8, 1782. Lippincott to be handed over to Americans: *Morning Herald*, Aug. 23, 1782; *Craftsman*, Aug. 24, 1782; *Whitehall Evening Post*, Aug. 31–Sept. 3, 1782; *Morning Chronicle*, Sept. 2, 1782; *General Advertiser*, Sept. 2; *Public Advertiser*, Sept. 4, 1782; *London Chronicle*, Sept. 19–21; Loyalists "in ferment": *St James's Chronicle*, Aug. 31; *Morning Chronicle*, Sept. 4, 1782. Guilty verdict: *London Chronicle*, Sept. 14–17, 1782. Verdict pending: *London Chronicle*, Sept. 24–26; *London Packet*, Sept. 23–25, 1782. Lippincott's suspected acquittal: *Morning Chronicle*, Sept. 10, 1782; *Morning Herald*, Sept. 10, 1782. Washington's "humane heart": *London Chronicle*, July 13–16, 1782; *General Advertiser*, July 15, 1782. "detestation of all mankind": *Gazetteer*, Aug. 7, 1782. "the first question": cited in Thacher, *Military Journal*, footnote on p. 308. Livingston's letter, May 29, 1782: *London Evening Post*, Sept. 19–21, 1782; *Morning Chronicle*, Sept. 20, 1782; *Public Advertiser*, Sept. 21, 1782.
27. Carleton to GW, August 13, 1782, CO5/106/241, *DAR*, xxi: 106–8. For the transfer of powers regarding prisoners, see BHQP 5128–9.
28. GW to President of Congress, Aug. 19, 1782, *PGW/EA*.
29. *LDC*, xix: 248–51, 331–2, 356–8, 367–9. James Madison's notes on Congress, Nov. 7, 1782, at http://founders.archives.gov/documents/Madison/01–05–02–0108. Boyd, *Boudinot*, 104–5. *JCC*, xxiii: 716–20.
30. James Duane to GW, Oct. 12, 1782, *LDC*, xix: 248–50.
31. "an electrical shock": William Wallace Atterbury, *Elias Boudinot: Reminiscences of the American Revolution* ([New York,] 1894), 34–5. "The President": Elias Boudinot, *Journal or Historical Recollections of American Events during the Revolutionary War* (Philadelphia, 1894), 63. The following paragraphs are based on Lady Asgill to Vergennes, July 18, 1782, and Vergennes to GW, July 29, 1782 [trans.], both enclosed with GW to President of Congress, Oct. 25, 1782, PGW/EA (whence also the quotation, "a very pathetic"). For independent corroboration of the Asgill family's situation, see Sir James Jay to GW, July 19, 1782, in Morris, ed., *John Jay*, 264–5. Lady Asgill's and Vergennes's letters were widely reprinted in newspapers in France and in the American Loyalist and Patriot press, e.g., all in 1782, *Massachusetts Spy*, Dec. 19; *Boston Evening Post*, Dec. 21; *Pennsylvania Packet*, Dec. 24; *Freeman's Journal*, Dec. 25; *Royal Gazette*, Dec. 25; *Connecticut Journal*, Dec. 26; *Independence Chronicle*, Dec. 26; *Salem Gazette*, Dec. 26; *Connecticut Gazette*, Dec. 27; *Newport Mercury*, Dec. 28; *Pennsylvania Evening Post*, Dec. 28; *New-York Gazette*, Dec. 30; *New-York Gazetteer*, Dec. 30; *Connecticut Courant*, Dec. 31; and in 1783: *New Jersey Gazette*, Jan. 1; *Connecticut*

Journal, Jan. 2; *New Hampshire Gazette*, Jan. 4. British papers carried Lady Asgill's letter in 1783: *London Chronicle*, Feb. 8–11; *Whitehall Evening Post*, Feb. 8–11; *Morning Herald*, Feb. 12. George III's order is quoted in Jayne E. Smith, "Vicarious Atonement: Revolutionary Justice and the Asgill Case" (MA diss., New Mexico State University, 2007), 79. See also Townshend to Carleton, Aug. 14, 1782, Bancroft 121/37 and 41. Cornwallis to Carleton, Aug. 4, 1782, BHQP 5205.

32. "with its emphasis": Simon Schama, *Citizens: A Chronicle of the French Revolution* (New York, 1989), 29. For introductions to sentiment and sensibility, see John Brewer, "Sentiment and Sensibility," in *The Cambridge History of English Romantic Literature*, ed. James Chandler (Cambridge, 2009); G. J. Barker-Benfield, "Sensibility," in *An Oxford Companion to the Romantic Age: British Culture, 1776–1832*, ed. Iain McCalman (Oxford, 1999); Knott, *Sensibility*, 185, distinguishes between Anglophone and French cults of sensibility.

33. "enough to move": quoted in Boyd, *Boudinot*, 105. See also Knott, *Sensibility*, 186. *JCC*, xxiii: 691, 695 n., 715. James Madison's notes on congressional deliberations, Nov. 7, 1782, at http://founders.archives.gov/documents/Madison/01-05-02-0108. JA to Robert Livingston, Jan. 23, 1783, *RDC*, vi: 228. GW to Carleton, Nov. 20, *PGW/EA*; Adye to Maurice Morgann, Nov. 30, 1782, BHQP 6286. Carleton to GW, Dec. 11, 1782, *PGW/EA*. *JCC*, xxiii: 829 n. 1.

34. GW to Asgill, Nov. 13, 1782, *PGW/EA*. For Loyalist and Patriot papers carrying the letter, in 1782, see *Royal Gazette*, Nov. 23, *New-York Gazette*, Nov. 25; *Pennsylvania Journal*, Nov. 27; *Pennsylvania Evening Post*, Nov. 29; *Providence Gazette*, Dec. 7; *New-York Gazetteer*, Dec. 9; *Salem Gazette*, Dec. 12.

35. *Pennsylvania Packet*, Dec. 31, 1782.

36. "An American": first in *Pennsylvania Packet*, Dec. 28, 1782, from where also in 1783 in *Massachusetts Spy*, Jan. 23, *Independent Ledger*, Jan. 27; *New Hampshire Gazette*, Feb. 1; see also *Boston Evening Post*, Jan. 25; *Connecticut Gazette*, Feb. 14. See Knott, *Sensibility*, 190: "Casting patriots as a community of sensibility apart from the British elaborated the wounded protests so fleetingly made in the Declaration of Independence." Cf. petition from South Carolina Loyalists to the Crown, via Lord Germain, Apr. 19, 1782, in CO5/82. "melting arguments" and "national honor": quoted in Charles H. Browning, ed., *The American Historical Register* (1895), 460. The committee considering Asgill's fate was also looking into complaints concerning, among others, Hayne. For the Hayne affair, see Carl P. Borick, *Relieve Us of This Burthen: American Prisoners of War in the Revolutionary South, 1780–1782* (Columbia, SC, 2012), 102–5.

37. *Morning Chronicle*, Dec. 27, 1782; see also *Felix Farley's Bristol Journal*, Dec. 28, 1782. The *Annual Register for 1783* (London, 1784), 243–4, printed the congressional resolution freeing Asgill, Nov. 7, 1782, and Washington's letter to the captive, Nov. 13, 1782.

38. Quotations from GW to James Tilghman, June 5, 1786. See also De Lancey, ed., *History of New York*, ii: 232–3, and n. xxx at 484. The papers were published first in the *Columbian Magazine* for Jan. and Feb. 1787; they appeared in book form in David Humphreys, *The Conduct of General Washington: respecting the confinement of Capt. Asgill* (New York, 1859), complete also with Lady Asgill's and Vergennes's letters. For Clinton's self-justification, see Willcox, ed., *Clinton's Narrative*, 359–61.

39. Robert Tombs and Isabelle Tombs, *That Sweet Enemy: The French and British from the Sun King to the Present* (London, 2006), 174. On French literary resonances, see Schama, *Citizens*, 30. GW to Barbier, Sept. 25, 1785. J.-L. Le Barbier le jeune, *Asgill: drame, en cinq actes, en prose; dédié a Madame Asgill* (Paris, 1785). Between 1793 and 1815, at least three more plays about Asgill were performed on the Parisian stage.

40. AH to William Knox, June 7, 1782, *PAH*, iii: 91–3.

Chapter Twelve

1. To explore fully the aftermath of America's foundational civil war, and the experiences of individuals and communities, requires a book of its own. For the vast majority of Loyalists, it is difficult to track the precise ways, speed, and extent of their political, economic, and social reintegration. For the limited historiography, see Roberta Tansman Jacobs, "The Treaty and the Tories: The Ideological Reaction to the Return of the Loyalists, 1783–1787" (PhD diss., Cornell University, 1974); David Edward Maas, *The Return of the Massachusetts Loyalists* (New York, 1989); Oscar Zeichner, "The Rehabilitation of Loyalists in Connecticut," *NEQ* 11:2 (1938). For Loyalist exiles, see Jasanoff, *Liberty's Exiles*; Mary Beth Norton, *The British-Americans: The Loyalist Exiles in England, 1774–1789* (London, 1972). For Chipman, see Phillip Buckner, "Chipman, Ward (1754–1824)," in *Dictionary of Canadian Biography*, vol. 6, University of Toronto/Université Laval, 2003–, at http://www.biographi.ca/en/bio/chipman_ward_1754_1824_6E.html.

2. Morris, ed., *John Jay*; Ronald Hoffman and Peter J. Albert, eds., *Peace and the Peacemakers: The Treaty of 1783* (Charlottesville, VA, 1986); Jasanoff, *Liberty's Exiles*, 78–80; Dull, *Diplomatic History*, 137–60. For Franklin, see BF to Richard Oswald, Nov. 26, 1782, at http://franklinpapers.org/franklin/framedVolumes.jsp?vol=38&page=311;

Richard B. Morris, *The Peacemakers: The Great Powers and American Independence* (Boston, 1983), 375; Jay is quoted ibid., 369. See also Richard Oswald to Shelburne, July 10, 1782, Shelburne Papers 70/40–48, WLCL; Richard Oswald to [?], Paris, Nov. 16, 1782, Richard Oswald Collection, WLCL.

3. For the preliminary articles of peace, see http://avalon.law.yale.edu /18th_century/prel1782.asp.

4. Charles R. Ritcheson, " 'Loyalist Influence' on British Policy towards the United States after the American Revolution," *Eighteenth-Century Studies* 7:1 (1973); Jasanoff, *Liberty's Exiles*, 119. For Bootle, see *Morning Chronicle*, Feb. 24, 1783.

5. Abigail Adams to JA, Apr. 28–29, 1783, at http://www.masshist.org /digitaladams/archive/doc?id=L17830428aa. Zabdiel Adams is quoted in Sarah J. Purcell, *Sealed with Blood: War, Sacrifice, and Memory in Revolutionary America* (Philadelphia, 2002), 68.

6. For the Coffins, see Conrad Edick Wright, *Revolutionary Generation: Harvard Men and the Consequences of Independence* (Amherst, MA, 2005), esp. 98–101, 107.

7. On Russell, see Cogliano, *American Maritime Prisoners*. For the final prisoners in New York, see Burrows, *Forgotten Patriots*, 195. The preliminary treaty stipulated the release of all prisoners of war; GW and Lincoln ordered POWs freed in mid-April 1783. See Miller, *Dangerous Guests*, 181.

8. "declared Traitors": Boston, Town Meeting, April 10, 1783 [Evans 44350]. See also Maas, *Return*, 445–6. The committees quoted after Boston Committee of Correspondence, Box 3, correspondence with town committees, May and June 1783, NYPL. "villains": [Chandler] to [Samuel Thorne], Sept. 2, 1783, Misc. collections, MssCol 3754/1, NYPL.

9. "with a handspike": *Boston Gazette*, May 5, 1783. See also Maas, *Return*, 445–6, 453–4.

10. Jouet: Jones, *Loyalists of New Jersey*, 108–17 (quotation 112); AO 12/ 13/161–79, 100/158. For collusion between an anti-Loyalist populace and officers of the law, see also BHQP 9138.

11. For the violent experiences of ex–Queens Rangers attempting to return to their former communities, see, e.g., BHQP 8036, 8089, 9584, 7940, 8100. For Thomas Crowell Jr., captain of a Loyalist regiment, and Elias Barron, who had supplied the British Army, see Jacobs, "Treaty," 66. For Oliver, see Peter Orlando Hutchinson, ed., *The Diary and Letters of Thomas Hutchinson* (London, 1886), ii: 412. For the "Association of the inhabitants for united action opposing the return of Tories to the State," see Misc. Collections, U.S. States and Territories, Box 21, Monmouth Co. folder, NYPL.

12. Prosper Brown to Carleton, June 4, 1783, BHQP 7878.
13. British officials reporting on the spirit of anti-Loyalist resentment, persecution, and violence throughout 1783 continued to hear civilian Loyalists testify to beatings, whippings, imprisonment followed by banishment, and threats of various forms of physical abuse, even to women. See BHQP 7489, 9047–8, 9132, 9584. Evidence in self-defense: Van Buskirk, *Generous Enemies*, 184–5 (widows and Bayley); *Independent Gazette*, Dec. 20, 1783.
14. "much affected": quoted in Jasanoff, *Liberty's Exiles*, 86. "Almost all" and "violent . . . associations": Carleton to Townshend, May 27, 1783, BHQP 7783. "unless there is": Chipman to Hodgson & Co., May 31, 1783, in W. O. Raymond, ed., *Winslow Papers A.D. 1776–1826* (St. John, N.B., 1901), 86. See also *Connecticut Journal*, Sept. 24, 1783; John Williams to [?Francis Bailey], Apr. 20, 1783, American Loyalist Box, NYPL.
15. For manifestations of anti-Loyalist sentiment, see Jacobs, "Treaty," 79; *Pennsylvania Journal*, June 4, 1783; *Maryland Journal*, June 20, July 8, 1783; *South Carolina Gazette*, July 8 and 26; *Political Intelligencer*, Aug. 10, 1784, Sept. 28, 1785. Henry Addison Papers, WLCL, Box 1, folders 1–6, esp. HA to J. Boucher, Apr. 14, July 12, Sept. 14, Oct. 29, 1783.
16. For Chipman and Coffin's journey, and quotations in this section unless otherwise referenced, see Joseph B. Berry, "Ward Chipman Diary: A Loyalist's Return to New England," *Essex Institute Historical Collections* 87 (1951). DeLancey: BHQP 7727, deposition Oliver DeLancey, May 20, 1783. Cf. ibid., 8517, Carleton to Gov. George Clinton, NY, July 25, 1783. Foshay: BHQP 7623. For related cases, see ibid., 7727, 7735. For further instances of intimidation and physical violence, see ibid., 7489, 7738 (with reference to the beating of a woman), 8523. For physical violence towards Loyalists in New York see also Bancroft 122/285, 289; 123/141–9, 191–7. For militant grassroots anti-Loyalism elsewhere, see, e.g., Miscellaneous Collections: U.S. States and Territories, Box 21, folder Monmouth Co., Association of the inhabitants for united action opposing the return of Tories to the State [1783] , NYPL.
17. Quoted from contemporary newspapers in Jacobs, "Treaty," 72.
18. For further cases, see, e.g., BHQP 9506; Maas, *Return*, 455. "a bitter": *Independent Gazette*, Dec. 13, 1783.
19. Maas, *Return*, 470–71, 476; Jacobs, "Treaty," 104–5. New York's alien bill prevented Loyalists from establishing citizenship; the assembly denied or tabled the citizenship petitions of over 20 Loyalists. A 1784 North Carolina law excluded from state citizenship non-jurors and those who had actively aided the British; see ibid., 94–5.
20. Lambert, *South Carolina Loyalists*, 293, 300–301. Len Travers, *Celebrating the Fourth: Independence Day and the Rites of Nationalism in*

the Early Republic (Amherst, MA, 1997), 40–41. "Who can brook": *Gazette of the State of South-Carolina*, Jan. 8, 1784, quoted in Purcell, *Sealed with Blood*, 68–9. In North Carolina, Loyalists who had joined the British, fled behind British lines, or been fined for refusing a loyalty oath were permanently banned from public office. Georgia's executive council mandated that no Loyalists proscribed in any state could be admitted until the definitive treaty had been signed. Exclusionist legislative activity continued beyond 1784. See Jacobs, "Treaty," 103–10; Lambert, *South Carolina Loyalists*, 289–91; Robert M. Weir, " 'The Violent Spirit,' the Reestablishment of Order, and the Continuity of Leadership in Post-Revolutionary South Carolina," in *An Uncivil War: The Southern Backcountry during the American Revolution*, ed. Ronald Hoffman, Thad W. Tate, and Peter J. Albert (Charlottesville, VA, 1985).

21. Lambert, *South Carolina Loyalists*, 296–8.

22. Leslie F. S. Upton, ed., *Revolutionary versus Loyalist: The First American Civil War 1774–1784* (Waltham, Toronto, London, 1968), 134–6 (quotation 136).

23. For the section on Hamilton I have drawn epecially on Ron Chernow, *Alexander Hamilton* (New York, 2004), 187–99; see also Richard Brookhiser, *Alexander Hamilton, American* (New York, 1999), 56–60; Lawrence S. Kaplan, *Alexander Hamilton: Ambivalent Anglophile* (Wilmington, DE, 2002), 57–62. For resentment and reconciliation in postwar New York, see also Van Buskirk, *Generous Enemies*, 186–93. George Washington considered it "of the utmost importance to stamp favorable impressions upon" America's national character, "let justice then be one of its characteristics." GW to Theodorick Bland, Apr. 4, 1783, *PGW/EA*. Evans's *Discourse, delivered in New-York*, of 1783, published in 1784, is quoted in Purcell, *Sealed with Blood*, 70.

24. Stokes, *Iconography of Manhattan*, iv: 886; Michael P. Federici, *The Political Philosophy of Alexander Hamilton* (Baltimore, 2012), 12–14; Kaplan, *Alexander Hamilton*, 19–20. "the passions": AH to John Jay, Nov. 26, 1775, at http://founders.archives.gov/documents/Hamilton/01-01-02-0060.

25. For this and the next paragraph, see Alexander Hamilton, *A letter from Phocion to the considerate citizens of New-York: on the politics of the day* (New York, 1784), 4, 16; idem, *A Second Letter from Phocion to the Considerate Citizens of New-York. Containing Remarks on Mentor's Reply* (New York, 1784), PAH, iii: 557. "Our state will feel": AH to Robert Livingston, Aug. 13, 1783, at http://founders.archives.gov/documents/Hamilton/01-03-02-0277. Other voices, too, from ordinary citizens to congressional delegates and state governors, urged tolerance in the name of Revolutionary values and America's treaty-worthiness: Jacobs, "Treaty," 143; *South Carolina Gazette*, July 15, 1783.

26. On postwar encounters generally, see Van Buskirk, *Generous Enemies*, 170–71. Livingston to AH, Aug. 30, 1783, cited in Julius Goebel Jr. and Joseph Henry Smith, eds., *Law Practice of Alexander Hamilton; Documents and Commentary* (New York, 1964–81), i: 216; AH to Morris, Feb. 21, 1784, cited ibid., 220.

27. For *Rutgers v. Waddington*, see Goebel and Smith, eds., *Law Practice*, i: 282–419. For related arguments, see Deposition Solomon Ferris, Oct. 11, 1783, BHQP 9338.

28. Jacob E. Cooke, *Tench Coxe and the Early Republic* (Chapel Hill, NC, 1978).

29. For the raids, see "Papers and Affidavits," fols. 223–6; Thomas J. Farnham, " 'The Day the Enemy Was in Town': The British Raids on Connecticut, July, 1779," *Journal of the New Haven Colony Historical Society* 24:2 (1976); Townshend, *British Invasion*; Paul David Nelson, *William Tryon and the Course of Empire: A Life in British Imperial Service* (Chapel Hill, NC, 1990), 168–72; Villers, "Loyalism in Connecticut," 341–3; Franklin B. Dexter, ed., *The Literary Diary of Ezra Stiles* (New York, 1901), ii: 351–61; Kemble et. al., eds., Kemble Papers, "Kemble's Journal," i: 180. *Connecticut Journal*, July 15, 1779. For sexual assault and the killing of unarmed men, see "Papers and Affidavits," fols. 221–3, 226–38; *Connecticut Journal*, July 7, 1779; *New-York Journal*, July 19, 1779; Block, *Rape*, 234, 236–7. Goodrich, Hillhouse: Farnham, " 'The Day the Enemy Was in Town,' " 31–2. John Anthony Scott, ed., *The Diary of the American Revolution. Compiled by Frank Moore* (New York, 1968), 376.

30. Damage estimates: ibid., 38, 50–51; *Connecticut Journal*, July 7, 1779; Clinton Papers 63/10; Papers and Affidavits, fols. 165–219. The lost property advertisements are quoted in Farnham, " 'The Day the Enemy Was in Town,' " 39.

31. New Haven Colony Historical Society, "New Haven Town Records, 1769–1807," unpubl. typescript, i: 95–9; 547–52, "Record of Militia Service, July 1779." See also Franklin Bowditch Dexter, "Notes on Some of the New Haven Loyalists, Including Those Graduated at Yale," *Papers of the New Haven Colony Historical Society* 9 (1918): 41.

32. "Miscreants": quoted in Charles H. Levermore, *The Republic of New Haven: A History of Municipal Evolution* (Baltimore, 1886), 222. Yale students debated amnesty in 1783 and 1784: Betsy McCaughey Ross, *From Loyalist to Founding Father: The Political Odyssey of William Samuel Johnson* (New York, 1980), 194. "Flexibles" and "an Endeavor": Dexter, ed., *Literary Diary of Ezra Stiles*, iii: 111–12.

33. For this and the next paragraph, see "New Haven Town Records, 1769–1807," i: 144–6.

34. Stiles is quoted in Levermore, *Republic of New Haven*, 226. That same

winter, the town applied again to the state for assistance to citizens who had suffered as a result of the 1779 British-Loyalist invasion; by 1791, New Haven claimants received some 34,000 acres of the so-called Firelands in the Western Reserve of Ohio. Farnham, " 'The Day the Enemy Was in Town,' " 60–61.

35. David Daggett, *An oration, pronounced in … New-Haven* (New Haven, CT, 1787), 17–18. See also Benjamin Trumbull, *God is to be praised for the glory, Dec. 11, 1783* (New Haven, CT, 1784).

36. Jacobs, "Treaty," 146; Zeichner, "Rehabilitation of Loyalists in Connecticut"; Rebecca Starr, " 'Little Bermuda': Loyalism on Daufuskie Island, South Carolina, 1775–1783," in *Loyalists and Community*, ed. Calhoon, Barnes, and Rawlyk, 55–65; Gerlach, ed., *New Jersey in the American Revolution*, 266–7. Stearns: Mass, *Return*, 497; John C. L. Clark, " 'The Famous Doctor Stearns': A Biographical Sketch of Dr. Samuel Stearns with a Bibliography," *Papers of the American Antiquarian Society* 45 (1935).

37. See also Benjamin Rush's argument for the restoration of Pennsylvania citizenship rights, i.e., that non-jurors were responsible for paying two-thirds of tax revenues since 1779: Benjamin Rush, *Considerations upon the present test-law of Pennsylvania: addressed to the legislature and freemen of the state* (Philadelphia, 1784), 13–15. For William Franklin in exile, where he helped other Loyalists prepare their petitions to the claims commission, and the enduring split with his father, see Skemp, *William Franklin*, 266–73 (quotation 273).

38. Kettner, *Development of American Citizenship*, 185; Chernow, *Alexander Hamilton*, 199; Oscar Zeichner, "The Loyalist Problem in New York after the Revolution," *New York History*, 21:3 (1940): 292, 302.

39. Robie: Maas, *Return*, 493. For merchants reintegrating in postwar New York City, see Zeichner, "Loyalist Problem," 301. For Joseph Shoemaker, a Philadelphia Loyalist who by 1794 helped represent West Indian trading interests to the secretary of state, and his ardently Loyalist brother Samuel being successfully reintegrated, see Sabine, *Biographical sketches*, ii: 301–2.

40. Clark, "The Problem of Allegiance in Revolutionary Poughkeepsie," 308–9. "prevent": Fred. Weissenfels to Colonel Lamb, May 23, 1783, John Lamb Papers, NYHS.

41. Kenneth Shefsiek, "A Suspected Loyalist in the Rural Hudson Valley: The Revolutionary War Experience of Roeloff Josiah Eltinge," in *America's First River: The History and Culture of the Hudson River Valley*, ed. Thomas S. Wermuth, James M. Johnson, and Christopher Pryslopski (Poughkeepsie, 2009).

42. For this and the following paragraph, see Richard C. Haskett, "Prosecuting the Revolution," *AHR* 59:3 (1954); J. Lawrence Boggs, "The

Cornellia (Bell) Paterson Letters," *NJHSP* 15 (1930): 508–17; 16 (1931): 56–67, 186–201, the quotations from the entries for April 7, May 2, and July 29 at 193, 195, 198. On miniature portraiture, representation, and absence, in the context of Loyalist displacement, see Katherine Rieder, " 'The Remainder of Our Effects We Must Leave Behind': American Loyalists and the Meaning of Things, 1765–1800" (PhD diss., Harvard, 2009), 112–14, and, on the genre more generally, Marcia Pointon, " 'Surrounded with Brilliants': Miniature Portraits in Eighteenth-Century England," *Art Bulletin* 83:1 (Mar. 2001).

43. Henry C. Van Schaack, *The Life of Peter van Schaack* (New York, 1842); William Jay, *The Life of John Jay* (New York, 1833), i: 161; see also John Jay to Peter Van Schaack, June 16, 1783, in Morris, ed., *John Jay*, 542. Ronald W. Howard. "Van Schaack, Peter," at http://www.anb.org.pitt .idm.oclc.org/articles/11/11-00872.html (accessed Aug. 21, 2016); *American National Biography Online*, Feb. 2000. For ex-Loyalists assuming legal and political offices at state level, see also Zeichner, "Loyalist Problem," 294, 296; Bradburn, *Citizenship Revolution*, 59; Calhoon, "Reintegration of the Loyalists."

Epilogue

1. Berry, "Ward Chipman Diary," 218 ("must have"), 237, 239–40; see also BHQP 8089. For the remains of prison ship captives, and commemorative efforts throughout the long nineteenth century, see Burrows, *Forgotten Patriots*, 205–40 (quotation 205). For British and German troops wreaking havoc in collections of books and scientific instruments in New York, New Haven, and Princeton, see Charles Hervey Townshend, *The British Invasion of New Haven, Connecticut* (New Haven, CT, 1879), 51–2; Jones, *History of New York* (1879), i, 136–40; Thacher, *Military Journal* (1827), 71, 77; Collins, *Brief Narrative*, 50; McGuire, *Philadelphia Campaign*, 324.

2. *The Papers of George Washington, Diaries*, ed. Donald Jackson et al. (Charlottesville, VA, 1976–79), vi: 138. Native American lands: Alan Taylor, *William Cooper's Town: Power and Persuasion on the Frontier of the Early American Republic* (New York, 1995), 62–3; idem, *Divided Ground*, 180; Hubbard, *Sketches*, 159. "trees, their limbs" and "unburied bones": Winslow C. Watson, ed., *Men and times of the revolution; or, Memoirs of Elkanah Watson, including journals of travels in Europe and America, from 1777 to 1842, with his correspondence with public men and reminiscences and incidents of the revolution* (New York, 1856), 254, 259. Boyd: Anishanslin, " 'This Is the Skin of a Whit[e] Man," 25, quoting *Notices of Sullivan's Campaign* (1842), 102.

3. "blood still": quoted in Frederick English, *General Hugh Mercer,*

Forgotten Hero of the American Revolution (New York, 1975), 103. "some of": quoted at "Baylor Massacre," Bergen County Historical Society, at http://www.bergencountyhistory.org/Pages/baylormassacre.html. Baylor's death on Barbados: Pension application of Lucy Burwell, Baylor's widow, Mar. 21, 1837, W5966.

4. Boudinot is cited in the still-critical Charles Royster, "Founding a Nation in Blood: Military Conflict and American Nationality," in *Arms and Independence*, ed. Hoffman and Albert, 34 with n. 20.

5. Troy Bickham, *The Weight of Vengeance: The United States, the British Empire, and the War of 1812* (New York, 2012), 19 ("sovereignty"), 276, 279, 13 ("a people," "served him"). "civil war": Alan Taylor, *The Civil War of 1812: American Citizens, British Subjects, Irish Rebels, & Indian Allies* (New York, 2010), 12. Baylor site: Democratic Press, Aug. 7, 1813. "our internal," regarding Loyalist violence at Crooked Billet: Gregory T. Knouff, *The Soldiers' Revolution: Pennsylvanians in Arms and the Forging of Early American Identity* (University Park, PA, 2004), 233–5; Collection of the Mercer Museum Library, MSC 39, Folder 1, Doylestown, PA.

6. "untarnished": Benjamin Gleason, *An oration, pronounced before the republican citizens of Charlestown: on the thirty-seventh anniversary of our national independence: Monday, July 5, 1813* (Boston, 1813), 7, quoted in Royster, "Founding a Nation in Blood," 47 with n. 55. "Other revolutions": Samuel Berrian, *Oration before the Tammany Society* (New York, 1815), quoted ibid., 48 with n. 57.

7. John P. Resch, *Suffering Soldiers: Revolutionary War Veterans, Moral Sentiment, and Political Culture in the Early Republic* (Amherst, MA, 1999); idem, "Politics and Public Culture: The Revolutionary War Pension Act of 1818," *Journal of the Early Republic* 8:2 (1988). R. E. Cray, "Major John Andre and the Three Captors: Class Dynamics and Revolutionary Memory Wars in the Early Republic, 1780–1831," *Journal of the Early Republic* 17:3 (1997); Thomas A. Chambers, *Memories of War: Visiting Battlegrounds and Bonefields in the Early American Republic* (Ithaca, NY, 2012), 91, 96, and passim; Sarah Purcell, "Martyred Blood and Avenging Spirits: Revolutionary Martyrs and Heroes as Inspiration for the U.S. Civil War," in *Remembering the Revolution*, ed. McDonnell et al. Pension Applications: Noel Battles S12960 [1832]; Philip Lauman S40072 [1818]; William Whaley S37532 [1818]; Joseph Graham S6937; Reuben Plunkett S25752 [1824]; Samuel Johnson (widow Mary's claim) W5012.

8. Chambers, *Memories of War,* 90, points out the three monuments' associations with victimhood. See ibid., 76, for the Marquis de Lafayette meeting battle-scarred veterans at the Bunker Hill memorial site in 1825. Fort Griswold: *Middlesex Gazette,* Aug. 30, 1826; *Norwich Cou-*

rier, Sept. 13, 1826 ("the small"); *Connecticut Courant*, Sept. 20, 1825 ("perforated," "numerous scars"), and Sept. 4, 1826; *Sentinel and Witness*, Sept. 13, 1826; *New Hampshire Patriot*, Sept. 18, 1826; *Sun* [Mass.], Sept. 21, 1826. See Hoock, "Mangled Bodies," 135–6, for the history of atrocity allegations regarding Fort Griswold.

9. Chambers, *Memories of War*, 59, with reference to *Army and Navy Chronicle*, Aug. 10, 1837.

10. Eileen Ka-May Cheng, "American Historical Writers and the Loyalists, 1788–1856: Dissent, Consensus, and American Nationality," *Journal of the Early Republic* 23:4 (2003); Billias, "The First Un-Americans"; Purcell, *Sealed with Blood*, 69–71; Cleves, *Reign of Terror*, 53–4. Jasanoff, *Liberty's Exiles*, 345, on Arcadians, Jacobites, and post–Civil War Southerners.

11. For more detail, with full references, on Wragg's story and monument, and a discussion of private versus official Loyalist monuments, see Hoock, *Empires of the Imagination*, 76–8.

12. "for the uncommon" and "he appears": quoted in Hersey, "Tar and Feathers," 469. On wartime pension payments of up to £70,000 in some years, see Jasanoff, *Liberty's Exiles*, 120.

13. For a reading of the claims commission in terms of paternalism, not rights, see Jasanoff, *Liberty's Exiles*, 120–23, 131 with n. 64 on the numbers of claims submitted. Bevins: AO13/26/45–7. Palmer: AO12/36/59–60. Smith: AO12/47/236–41. See also AO12/1/50, 310–11; 29/148–9, 321–3; AO13/14/235–52; 25/57–60; 30/581–8; 31/81–96, 358–401. Known or reputed Tory hunters were excluded from relief efforts. See, e.g., Abraham Cuyler to Capt. Mathews, n.d., Add MS 21825/50. Wartime fiscal statistics: Conway, *British Isles*, 54, 63–4, 76–7. British historians have argued that, at the same time as the British state thus looked after loyal subjects from overseas, the loss of the thirteen American colonies was a catalyst for British national identity to become more cohesive and geographically commensurate with the British Isles: Bickham, *Making Headlines*, 252; Colley, *Britons*, 143–5; Conway, *British Isles*, 315–25.

14. Jasanoff, *Liberty's Exiles*, 89–90; Brown, *Moral Capital*, 311–12 (quotations 312).

15. For compensation claimed for slaves, see AO12/6/47–53; 13/279–82; 19/201v–208v; 47/226–34, 236–41; AO13/1, part 1, 40–42; 28/237–43. Handley: Norton, "Fate of Some Black Loyalists," 404 n. 6. Anderson: Schama, *Rough Crossings*, 179–80. Furman: Jasanoff, *Liberty's Exiles*, 127–8, 138; AO13/59/658–9.

16. This and the following paragraph largely after Calloway, *American Revolution in Indian Country*, 293–5, and the quotation at 290; Taylor, *Divided Ground*, 111–15, 119–28; Jasanoff, *Liberty's Exiles*, 190–96, 320;

Alan Taylor, *American Colonies: The Settling of North America* (New York, 2001), 443; Gregory H. Nobles, "Historians Extend the Reach of the American Revolution," in *Whose American Revolution Was It? Historians Interpret the Founding*, ed. Alfred F. Young and Gregory H. Nobles (New York, 2011), 185–92.

17. Knox is quoted in David C. Hendrickson, "Escaping Insecurity: The American Founding and the Control of Violence," in *Between Sovereignty and Anarchy*, ed. Griffin, 225. Wallace is quoted in Engelbrecht, *Iroquoia*, 170. See also Taylor, *American Colonies*, 443; Stephen Aaron, *American Confluence: The Missouri Frontier from Borderland to Border State* (Bloomington, IN, 2006), 69–70, 75; Michael A. McDonnell, *Masters of Empire: Great Lakes Indians and the Making of America* (New York, 2015), 311–15.

18. Conway, *British Isles*, 128, 345. Brown, *Moral Capital*, explores the American Revolution's impact on the timing, scope, and drive of antislavery in Britain; see 311–12 on Britain partially fulfilling its moral obligations towards black Loyalists. Jasanoff, *Liberty's Exiles*, esp. 139–42, builds on Brown's notion of moral capital in discussing the reform impulses catalyzed by the "spirit of 1783." See also her "Revolutionary Exiles," 53; P. J. Marshall, *Remaking the British Atlantic: The United States and the British Empire after American Independence* (Oxford, 2012), 130; Wahrman, "English Problem"; Seymour Drescher, "The Shocking Birth of British Abolitionism," *Slavery & Abolition* 33:4 (2012). For Britain's post–American Revolution empire, see Chris Bayly, *Imperial Meridian*; P. J. Marshall, "Britain without America—a Second Empire?," in idem, ed., *The Oxford History of the British Empire*, ii. *The Eighteenth Century* (Oxford, 1998).

19. O'Shaughnessy, *Men Who Lost America*, 283 ("imperial troubleshooter"), 284. Antiwar sentiment and 1790s pacifism: Conway, *British Isles*, 315–25; Langford, *Polite and Commercial People*, 626–7; J. E. Cookson, *The Friends of Peace* (Cambridge, 1982).

20. For the expansion of the total black population in the U.S. from 1790 to 1800, with nearly steady proportions of blacks who were slaves in the Upper (more than 90 percent) and Lower South (more than 95 percent), but a dramatic drop in that proportion in New England (from about 23 to 7 percent) and the mid-Atlantic (72 to 54 percent), see U.S. census figures cited in Egerton, *Death or Liberty*, 173. On the historiography of slavery and the Revolution, see Nobles, "Historians Extend," 145–55. Cynthia A. Kierner, *Southern Women in Revolution, 1776–1800: Personal and Political Narratives* (Columbia, SC, 1998), 102, 101. On the Constitution and slavery, see David Waldstreicher, *Slavery's Constitution: From Revolution to Ratification* (New York, 2009).

21. The text of the U.S.-Prussian treaty at "A Treaty of Amity and Com-

merce between His Majesty the King of Prussia, and the United States of America," at http://avalon.law.yale.edu/18th_century/prus1785.asp. See also "Draft of a Model Treaty," *PTJ*, vii: 486–7, Article 24, and the quotation from Jefferson at 491. JA to De Thulemeier, Auteuil, 13 Feb. 1785, Founders Online, at http://founders.archives.gov/documents /Jefferson/01-07-02-0356-0001. For discussion of the treaty, see also Witt, *Lincoln's Code*, 47; Krebs, *Generous and Merciful Enemy*, 268–73; Peter Onuf and Nicholas Onuf, *Federal Union, Modern World: The Law of Nations in an Age of Revolutions, 1776–1814* (Madison, WI, 1993), 112. U.S. diplomats wrote similar clauses into subsequent treaties both with Prussia and other states, including Mexico in 1848.

22. Jeffrey L. Pasley, "Whiskey Chaser: Democracy and Violence in the Debate over the Democratic-Republican Societies and the Whiskey Rebellion," in *Between Sovereignty and Anarchy*, ed. Griffin et al., 192–5; Burrows, *Forgotten Patriots*, 210; Sam W. Haynes, *Unfinished Revolution: The Early American Republic in a British World* (Charlottesville, VA, 2010).

23. Michael A. McDonnell, "Introduction," in *Remembering the Revolution*, ed. McDonnell et al., esp. 6–7, 10; Purcell, "Martyred Blood," in ibid., esp. 282–5, 290–91; Chambers, *Memories of War*, 167–9. Jacob Belville, *Address at the inauguration of the Hatborough Monument* (Doylestown, PA, 1862). For a deep history of the Lieber Code and its international impact, see Witt, *Lincoln's Code*.

24. On Tyler, see the excellent essay in Michael Kammen, *Selvages & Biases: The Fabric of History in American Culture* (Ithaca, NY, 1987), 222–51, with the quotation ("to interpret") at 225; Moses Coit Tyler, *Literary History of the American Revolution, 1763–1783* (New York, 1897); see also Bailyn, *Ordeal*, 402–3. Cf. George Macaulay Trevelyan, *Sir George Otto Trevelyan: A Memoir* (London, 1932), 139, 141, and passim; Burrows, *Forgotten Patriots*, 242–3.

25. For cultural rapprochement, see Erik Goldstein, "Origins of the Anglo-American Special Relationship 1880–1914," in *Peacemaking, Peacemakers and Diplomacy, 1880–1939*, ed. Gaynor Johnson (Newcastle, 2010), with a discussion of the 1914 plans at 12–13. On the Special Relationship, see also Keith Robbins, "The Special Relationship: An Overview," *Revue Francaise de Civilization Britannique* 12:1 (2002); Kathleen Burk, "Great Britain in the United States, 1917–1918: The Turning Point," *International History Review* 1:2 (1979).

26. For the Goldstein case, see Anthony Slide, ed., *Robert Goldstein and "The Spirit of '76"* (Metuchen, NJ, 1993), with key materials, including press cuttings and court rulings. The quotations are from *United States v. Motion Picture Film "The Spirit of '76,"* District Court S.D. California, Nov. 30, 1917, 252, *Federal Reporter* 946, at 209–11, reprinted also

in David Holbrook Culbert and Richard E. Wood, eds., *Film and Propaganda in America: A Documentary History* (New York, 1990–91), i: 287–303. See also Burrows, *Forgotten Patriots*, 244.

27. *Times*, Apr. 20, 1918. Churchill is quoted in Simon P. Newman, "Losing the Faith: British Historians and the Last Best Hope," *Comparative American Studies* 6:2 (June 2008): 166.

28. For the 1920s war over textbooks that some U.S. patriotic societies and historians criticized as unpatriotically favorable towards Britain, and the Anglophiles' response, see Burrows, *Forgotten Patriots*, 246–7; George T. Blakey, *Historians on the Homefront: American Propagandists for the Great War* (Lexington, KY, 1970); Charles Altschul, *The American Revolution in Our School Text-Books; An Attempt to Trace the Influence of Early School Education on the Feeling towards England in the United States* (New York, 1917); Joseph Moreau, *Schoolbook Nation: Conflicts over American History Textbooks from the Civil War to the Present* (Ann Arbor, MI, 2003), ch. 5; Claude Halstead Van Tyne, "The Struggle for Truth about the American Revolution," in idem, *England & America: Rivals in the American Revolution* (New York, 1927). For the persistence of Anglophobe currents in U.S. political discourse, see John E. Moser, *Twisting the Lion's Tail: American Anglophobia between the World Wars* (New York, 1999).

29. Kings Mountain Celebration Committee, *Official Progamme of Sesqui-Centennial Celebration of the Battle of Kings Mountain* (S.I., 1930), n.p., 11, 24, 26–7. Hoover's speech: http://www.presidency.ucsb.edu/ws/?pid=22379. Ferguson monument: Kings Mountain Celebration Committee, *Official Progamme*, 10–11; "The Colonel Patrick Ferguson Memorial," the Historical Marker Database: http://www.hmdb.org/marker.asp?marker=17655. See, similarly, House Report No. 2565, 70th Congress, 2nd Session, Report of the Committee on Military Affairs, to accompany H.R. 14449, Feb. 16, 1929; House Report No. 1671, 71st Congress, 2nd Session, Report of the Committee on Military Affairs, to accompany H.R. 6128, May 27, 1930.

30. For historical fiction in the 1930s and '40s, see Michael Kammen, *A Season of Youth: The American Revolution and the Historical Imagination* (New York, 1978), 173–4. "In a fearful": quoted in Michael Heale, "The British Discovery of American History: War, Liberalism and the Atlantic Connection," *JAS* 39:3 (2005): 363. See also Newman, "Losing the Faith," 169–70.

31. For counterprogressive historians, see Young and Nobles, eds., *Whose American Revolution Was It?*, 47–56; Novick, *That Noble Dream*, 333–6 (quotation 336).

32. This and the previous two paragraphs after Lepore, *Whites of Their Eyes*, 23–4 (the quotation from King 23), 64–83 ("so agitated" 64, "offer

an answer" 69), 133–5; for the PBC, see also Edward Tabor Linenthal, *Sacred Ground: Americans and Their Battlefields* (Urbana-Champaign, IL, 1991), 40–43; Louis P. Masur, *The Soiling of Old Glory: The Story of a Photograph That Shocked America* (New York, 2008). See Burrows, *Forgotten Patriots*, 247–8, for a "modest revival of interest" in Revolutionary-era prisoners but widespread dismissal of alleged British abuse.

33. Cf. Richard Middleton, "British Historians and the American Revolution," *Journal of American Studies*, 5 (1971): 55.

34. U.S. Congress, Congressional Record, V. 152, Pt. 15, Sept. 26, 2006, to Sept. 28, 2006, 20295, printing into the record Robert F. Kennedy Jr., "America's Anti-Torture Tradition," *Los Angeles Times*, Dec. 17, 2005, at http://articles.latimes.com/2005/dec/17/opinion/oe-kennedy17. Scott Horton, "George Washington: No Torture on My Watch," Dec. 24, 2007, at http://antiwar.com/blog/2007/12/24/george-washington-no-torture-on-my-watch/. See Newman, "Losing the Faith," 171–5; Simon P. Newman, "British Historians and the Changing Significance of the American Revolution," in *Europe's American Revolution*, ed. idem (Houndsmill, 2006), 83, on American imperialism changing international perceptions of the American Revolution's legacies.

35. Cf. Anderson and Cayton, *Dominion of War*, 424.

MAP AND ILLUSTRATION CREDITS

PAGE 2: Sir Thomas Hyde Page, *A Plan of the Town of Boston with the Intrenchments &ca. of His Majesty's forces in 1775, from the Observations of Lieut. Page of His Majesty's Corps of Engineers, and from those of other Gentlemen* (London, 1777). Pen-and-ink and watercolor. 45 x 32 cm. Library of Congress.

PAGE 9: Paul Revere, *The Bloody Massacre perpetrated in King Street Boston on March 5th 1770 by a party of the 29th Regt.* (Boston, 1770). Engraving with watercolor on laid paper, 25.8 x 33.4 cm. Library of Congress.

PAGE 22: Samuel Dunn and Robert Sayer, *A Map of the British Empire in North America* (London, 1774). Hand-colored, 48 x 31 cm. Library of Congress.

PAGE 25: François Godefroy, *John Malcom* (Paris, [1784]). In Nicolas Ponce, *Recueil d'estampes représentant les différens événemens de la Guerre qui a procuré l'indépendance aux Etats Unis de l'Amérique* (Paris, [1784]), plate 2. Library of Congress.

PAGE 27: National Archives at Kansas City, Record Group 21, Records of the District Courts of the U.S. U.S. District Court for the Second (Mankato) Division of the District of Minnesota. Law Case Files. National Archives Identifier 283633 and 283634. *John Meints v. O.R. Huntington et al.*, 1917–1918.

PAGE 43: *Hancock's Warehouse for Taring & Feathering* (London, [1778]). Etching, 15 x 10.2 cm. Courtesy of the John Carter Brown Library at Brown University.

PAGE 46: *A View of the Guard-House and Simsbury-Mines, now called Newgate—A Prison for the Confinement of Loyalists in Connecticut* (London, 1781). Etching, 15.2 x 12.1 cm. *The political magazine and parliamentary, naval, military, and literary journal* (London, Oct. 1781), 596–7. Library of Congress.

PAGE 54: *An accurate Map of England, Scotland, and Ireland, with all the adjacent Islands, etc.* [London, 1761]. BL Maps 1080 (13). © The British Library Board.

PAGE 56: Philip Dawe, attr., *The Bostonians Paying the Excise-Man, or Tarring & Feathering* (London, Oct. 1774). Mezzotint, 35.6 x 24.1 cm. Library of Congress.

PAGE 57: Carington Bowles, *A New Method of Macarony Making, as practised at Boston* (London, Oct. 1774). Mezzotint, 24.1 x 32.4 cm. Library of Congress.

PAGE 60: Philip Dawe, *The Patriotick Barber of New York, or the Captain in the Suds* (London, Feb. 1775). Mezzotint, 35.3 x 25 cm. Library of Congress.

PAGE 60: Philip Dawe, *The Alternative of Williams-Burg* (London, Feb. 1775). Mezzotint, 25.4 x 32.4 cm. Library of Congress.

PAGE 67: Benjamin West, *George III* (1779). Oil on canvas, 255.3 x 182.9 cm. Royal Collection Trust © Her Majesty Queen Elizabeth II 2016.

PAGE 70: *The Hon. Sir Willm. Howe Kt. of the Bath, Commander in Chief of all his Majesty's Forces in America*, illustration in *An impartial history of the war in America, between Great Britain and her colonies, from its commencement to the end of the year 1779* (London & Carlisle, [1780]), i: 204. Engraving, 19 x 11.2 cm. Library of Congress.

PAGE 72: Sir Joshua Reynolds, *General John Burgoyne* (circa 1766). Oil on canvas. 127 x 101.3 cm. Copyright The Frick Collection.

PAGE 81: Johann Jacobé (after George Romney), *Lord George Germain, one of his Majesty's Principal Secretaries of State* (London, [1780]). Mezzotint, after George Romney. The Colonial Williamsburg Foundation. Gift of Mr. James Lewis.

PAGE 84: Robert Sayer and John Bennett, *The Theatre of War in North America, with the Roads and Tables, of the Superficial Contents, Distances, &ca. By an American* (London, 1776). Copper Engraving, 42 x 50 cm. Map Reproduction Courtesy of the Norman B. Leventhal Map Center at the Boston Public Library.

PAGE 87: John Norman, *The Town of Falmouth, Burnt by Captain Moet, Octbr. 18th 1775* (Boston, 1782). Engraving, 13.3 x 28.6 cm. Library of Congress.

PAGE 89: Charles Willson Peale, *George Washington* (1776). Oil on canvas, 111.7 x 97.3 cm. Brooklyn Museum, Dick S. Ramsay Fund, 34.1178.

PAGE 93: Sir Joshua Reynolds, *John Murray, 4th Earl of Dunmore* (1765). Oil on canvas, 238.1 x 146.2 cm (framed: 269 x 176.3 cm). Scottish National Portrait Gallery, Edinburgh.

PAGE 104: Hamilton, *The Manner in which the American Colonies Declared themselves Independant [sic] of the King of England, throughout the different Provinces, on July 4, 1776* [1783]. Mixed-method engraving. Edward Barnard, *The new, comprehensive and complete history of England* (London, [1783]), 689, Library of Congress.

PAGE 111: *General Clinton*, illustration in Rev. James Murray, *An impartial history of the war in America; from its first commencement, to the present time* (Newcastle upon Tyne, 1782), ii, opp. p. 186. Engraving. Library of Congress.

PAGE 112: *The Seat of Action between the British and American Forces; or An Authentic Plan of the Western Part of Long Island, with the Engagement of the 27th August, 1776, between the King's Forces and the Americans: also containing Staten Island, and the environs of Amboy and New York, with the course of Hudson River, from Courtland the Great Magazine of the American Army, to Sandy Hook* (London, 1776). Hand-colored, 45 x 39 cm. The New York Public Library.

PAGE 126: Thomas Pownall and Samuel Holland, *The Provinces of New York and New Jersey; with part of Pensilvania, and the Province of Quebec* (London, 1776). Hand-colored, 134 x 51 cm. Library of Congress.

PAGE 150: William Faden, Bernard Ratzer, and Gerard Bancker, *The Province of New Jersey, Divided into East and West, commonly called the Jerseys* ([London], 1777). Hand-colored, 78 x 57 cm. Library of Congress.

PAGE 153: William Faden, *Plan of the Operations of General Washington against the Kings Troops in New Jersey from the 26th of December 1776 to the 3rd of January 1777* (London, 1777). Colored, 29 x 39 cm. Library of Congress.

PAGE 154: Andreas Wiederholdt, *Sketch of the engagement at Trenton, given on the 26th of December 1776 betwixt the American troops under command of General Washington, and three Hessian regiments under command of Colonell Rall, in which the latter a part surrendert themselves prisoner of war* [1776]. Manuscript, pen-and-ink and watercolor, 23 x 28 cm. Library of Congress.

PAGE 161: Jonathan Trumbull, *The Death of General Hugh Mercer* (1786). Ink washes on paper, 10.2 x 15 cm (sheet). Princeton University Library.

PAGE 165: *The able Doctor, or, America Swallowing the Bitter Draught* (London, May 1774). Mixed method, 9.5 x 14.9 cm. Library of Congress.

PAGE 180: Bernard Ratzer, *Plan of the city of New York, in North America: Surveyed in the Years 1766 & 1767* (London, 1776). 105 x 91 cm. The New York Public Library, The Miriam and Ira D. Wallach Division of Art, Prints and Photographs: Print Collection.

PAGE 191: The Provost, from Benson John Lossing, ed. *Harper's Encyclopedia of United States History (vol. 7)* (New York, 1912), retrieved from http://etc.usf.edu/clipart/57800/57891/57891_provost_jail.htm.

PAGE 194: Van Cortlandt's Sugar House, from Benson John Lossing, ed. *Harper's Encyclopedia of United States History (vol. 7)* (New York, 1912), retrieved from http://etc.usf.edu/clipart/57800/57889/57889_sugar_house .htm.

PAGE 210: Carington Bowles, *Bowles's New and Accurate Map of the World, or Terrestrial Globe* (London, [1780]). Hand-colored. Two hemispheres each 59 cm in diameter, on sheet 106 x 130 cm. Library of Congress.

PAGE 216: *Jersey,* prison ship moored in Wallabout Bay, New York, fig. 1 in *Recollections of the Jersey prison-ship; taken and prepared for publication from the original manuscripts of the late Captain Thomas Dring, of Providence, RI, one of the prisoners,* by Albert G. Greene (Providence, 1829). Public domain, via Wikimedia Commons, ⊖.

PAGE 220: *Unidentified Subject (formerly titled* [Jonathan Trumbull,] *American Prisoners on Board a British Prison Ship)* (c. 1782–?1831). India ink wash, 12.7 x 15.9 cm. Fordham University Library, Bronx, NY, Charles Allen Munn Collection.

PAGE 223: Robert Smirke, *Cruelty Presiding over the Prison Ship (Cruelty holding the Register of Death),* illustration for Joel Barlow's epic poem *The Columbiad* (1807). The Miriam and Ira D. Wallach Division of Art, Prints and Photographs, New York Public Library.

PAGE 242: Louis Denis, *Carte du theatre de la guerre presente en Amerique* (Paris, 1779). Hand-colored, 67 x 51 cm. Library of Congress.

PAGE 245: Daniel Berger, *1. General Washington. 2. General Gates. 3. Dr. Franklin. 4. Präsid Laurens. 5. Paul Jones.* (1784). Etching. Illustration in Matthias Christian Sprengel, *Allgemeines historisches Taschenbuch* (Berlin, 1784). Library of Congress.

PAGE 246: *[Britannia toe] Amer[eye]ca* (London, May 1778). Etching, hand-colored. Library of Congress.

PAGE 247: *[America toe] her [miss]taken [moth]er* (London, May 1778). Etching, hand-colored. Library of Congress.

PAGE 265: Photograph from an 1967 excavation near Tappan. Author's collection.

PAGE 274: John Lodge, *A New and Correct Map of North America: in which the Places of the Principal Engagements during the Present War are accurately inserted* (London, 1780). 27 x 38 cm. *Political magazine*, 1 (Apr. 1780). The New York Public Library.

PAGE 280: John Almon (publ.), *The Allies—Par nobile Fratrum* (London, 1780). Etching, 23.2 x 36.3 cm (sheet, trimmed). Library of Congress.

PAGE 282: Anonymous, *Map of General Sullivan's March from Easton to the Senaca & Cayuga Countries* [1779]. Colored, on sheet 76 x 75 cm. Library of Congress.

PAGE 294: Pierre Eugène du Simitièrc, "Various Indian Hieroglyphicks drawn on trees, found on the march of the western Army." Undated ink sketch copied from originals of 1779. Courtesy of Library Company of Philadelphia.

PAGE 298: William Faden, *The Marches of Lord Cornwallis in the Southern Provinces, now States of North America; Comprehending the Two Carolinas, with Virginia and Maryland, and the Delaware Counties* (London, 1787). From Banastre Tarleton's *A history of the campaigns of 1780 and 1781, in the Southern Provinces of North America* (London, 1787), facing p. 1. Colored, 66 x 50 cm. Library of Congress.

PAGE 311: *Lt. Col. Tarleton*, engraving in the *Westminster Magazine* (March 1782). The New York Public Library.

PAGE 326: Robert Donkin, *Military Collections and Remarks* (New York, 1777), pp. 189–90. Rare Book Collection. New York Public Library. Astor, Lenox, Tilden Foundations.

PAGE 334: *A New and accurate Map of New Jersey, from the best Authorities*, from *The universal magazine of knowledge and pleasure* [London, June 1780]. 32 x 72 cm. Library of Congress.

PAGE 338: Benjamin Morgan and Anthony Dennis, *A Map of Monmouth County, Reduced from the Original Survey by John Hills, Asst. Engineer* [1781]. Pen-and-ink and watercolor, 73 x 134 cm. Library of Congress.

PAGE 345: John Fielding (publ.), *Captain Asgill* (London, 1786). Engraving, from John Andrews, *History of the war with America, France, Spain, and*

Holland: commencing in 1775 and ending in 1783, 4 vols. (London, 1785–6), iv: 416. Library of Congress.

PAGE 360: Thomas Kitchin, *Map of the United States in North America with the British, French and Spanish dominions adjoining, according to the Treaty of 1783* (London, 1783). Copper engraving, 40 x 51 cm. Lawrence H. Slaughter Collection, The Lionel Pincus and Princess Firyal Map Division, The New York Public Library, Astor, Lenox and Tilden Foundations.

PAGE 363: *Shelb—ns sacrifice / invented by Cruelty; engraved by Dishonor: Or the recommended Loyalists, a faithful representation of a Tragedy shortly to be performed on the Continent of America* (London, Feb. 1783). Engraving. Library of Congress.

PAGE 364: *The Savages Let Loose, or The Cruel Fate of the Loyalists* (London, Mar. 1783). Etching, 28 x 38.8 cm (sheet). Library of Congress.

INDEX

ABOUT THE AUTHOR

H OLGER HOOCK WAS EDUCATED AT FREIBURG, CAM-
bridge, and Oxford. He currently serves as the J. Carroll
Amundson Professor of British History and Associate
Dean for Graduate Studies and Research in the Dietrich School
of Arts and Sciences at the University of Pittsburgh, as well as
as editor of the *Journal of British Studies*. He previously taught at
the Universities of Cambridge and Liverpool, where he was also
founding director of the Eighteenth-Century Worlds Research
Center. Hoock is the author of *Empires of the Imagination: Politics,
War, and the Arts in the British World, 1750–1850* (London, 2010),
and *The King's Artists: The Royal Academy of Arts and the Politics of British Culture, 1760–1840* (Oxford, 2003), runner-up for the
Royal Historical Society's Whitfield Prize. He has recently held
fellowships at the Library of Congress, New York Public Library,
Corpus Christi College, Oxford, and the Konstanz Institute for Advanced Study. He served as research curator for *Nelson & Napoleon* at London's National Maritime Museum in 2005 and received
the U.K.'s Philip Leverhulme Prize for internationally recognized
young historians in 2006. An elected fellow of the Royal Historical Society, he lectures widely across North America and Europe.
Hoock and his family divide their time between Pittsburgh, Pennsylvania, and the U.K.